The Coriolis Group, LLC • 14455 North Hayden Road, Suite 220 • S...

A Note from Coriolis

Coriolis Technology Press was founded to create a very elite group of books: the ones you keep closest to your machine. In the real world, you have to choose the books you rely on every day *very* carefully, and we understand that.

To win a place for our books on that coveted shelf beside your PC, we guarantee several important qualities in every book we publish. These qualities are:

- *Technical accuracy*—It's no good if it doesn't work. Every Coriolis Technology Press book is reviewed by technical experts in the topic field, and is sent through several editing and proofreading passes in order to create the piece of work you now hold in your hands.

- *Innovative editorial design*—We've put years of research and refinement into the ways we present information in our books. Our books' editorial approach is uniquely designed to reflect the way people learn new technologies and search for solutions to technology problems.

- *Practical focus*—We put only pertinent information into our books and avoid any fluff. Every fact included between these two covers must serve the mission of the book as a whole.

- *Accessibility*—The information in a book is worthless unless you can find it quickly when you need it. We put a lot of effort into our indexes, and heavily cross-reference our chapters, to make it easy for you to move right to the information you need.

Here at The Coriolis Group we have been publishing and packaging books, technical journals, and training materials since 1989. We have put a lot of thought into our books; please write to us at **ctp@coriolis.com** and let us know what you think. We hope that you're happy with the book in your hands, and that in the future, when you reach for software development and networking information, you'll turn to one of our books first.

Coriolis Technology Press
The Coriolis Group
14455 N. Hayden Road, Suite 220
Scottsdale, Arizona
85260

Email: ctp@coriolis.com
Phone: (480) 483-0192
Toll free: (800) 410-0192

Look for these related books from The Coriolis Group:

A+ Exam Cram, 2nd Edition
by James Jones and Craig Landes

A+ Exam Prep, Third Edition
by Scott and Kalinda Reeves, Stephen Weese,
and Christopher Geyer

Network+ Exam Cram, 2nd Edition
by Brad Grandorff

Server+ Exam Cram
by Deborah Haralson and Jeff Haralson

i-Net+ Exam Cram
by Martin Weiss and Emmett Dulaney

Also published by Coriolis Technology Press:

Microsoft Project 2000 Black Book
by Tracey J. Rosenblath

Java 2 Black Book
by Steven Holzner

Windows 2000 Registry Little Black Book, 2nd Edition
by Nathan Wallace and Anthony Sequeira

Windows 2000 Server Architecture and Planning, 2nd Edition
by Morten Strunge Nielsen

*To all of the hardworking PC technicians who are underpaid,
underappreciated, and overworked.*

*To my loving, supportive wife and family, Diane, Jeana, Rob, Kirstie,
and Mimi—thanks for everything.*

And to Margot—you've earned it.

 è

About the Author

Ron Gilster (Walla Walla, WA) has been involved with computing for over 32 years, including 20 years working with and repairing personal computers. Although now working full-time as a writer, Ron's experience includes stints as a trainer, teacher, developer, consultant, merchant, manager, executive, and end user. Ron holds a variety of hardware and software certifications including A+ (1998, 2001), I-Net+, Network+, Server+, CCSE, and CCNA. He also holds a masters degree in business administration (MBA). Ron is a prolific writer of computer hardware and software books with over 14 in print and well-over 200,000 copies sold. Ron is married with four children and when he is not sitting at his computer keyboard, he and his wife breed and show Havenese dogs.

Acknowledgments

I'd like to thank Charlotte Carpentier, acquisitions editor at Coriolis, who shares my vision for technical books and has the patience of Job, for continuing to believe in me over the long haul.

Special thanks to Stephanie Palenque, the project editor for this book. Her guiding hand is responsible for putting this book together and seeing it through to completion. Something I'm not sure I could have done alone.

And thanks to the others who worked behind the scene to produce this book, especially Carla Schuder, the production coordinator; Tracy Rooney, the marketing specialist; Laura Wellander, the cover designer; and April Nielsen, the layout designer.

I'd also like to acknowledge the following fine companies for their information and art for this book: Advanced Micro Devices, Inc., Amptron USA, Inc., AOpen America, Inc., A-Top Technology, Belkin Components, Enlight Corporation, Epson Corporation, Hewlett Packard Corporation, Intel Corporation, InTouch Systems, Inc., In Win Development, Inc., Iwill USA, Inc., Lexmark International, Niagara Technology, Nidec America, Inc., Oki Data Americas, Inc., PC Power and Cooling, Inc., Rainier Company, Silicon Integrated Systems Corporation, Supermicro, Inc., VIA Technologies, Inc., and several others I'm sure I've overlooked.
—*Ron Gilster*

Contents at a Glance

Table of Contents

Immediate Solutions

Part II   Storage and Access Devices

Chapter 11
Video Cards **283**

Part III   Power

Part IV   Peripherals

Chapter 15
Monitors and Displays 407

Part V   Preventive Care

Part VI   General Troubleshooting and Repair

Introduction

Thanks for buying the *PC Technician Black Book*.

If you are a working PC technician or a PC hobbyist, this book is a must-have for your bench top library. This book provides you with a ready-reference for all of the major components of a personal computer. For each of the PC's technology areas, you are provided with both in-depth background and reference information as well as step-by-step instructions for dealing with many common PC problems.

The objectives of this book are to provide an easy-to-read, informative book on the major technologies that make up a personal computer as well as easy-to-find and easy-to-follow guidelines on troubleshooting, diagnosing, isolating, and resolving PC hardware problems.

Adding this book to your technical library, puts at your fingertips everything you need to know, and perhaps even then some, about the components of a PC.

Is This Book for You?

PC Technician Black Book was written with the intermediate or advanced user in mind. Among the topics covered, are:

- In-depth information and background on the history, development, and technology of each major component of a personal computer.
- Step-by-step guidelines on troubleshooting and diagnosing common PC hardware problems.
- Tips on hardware upgrades and repairs for each of the major PC components.
- The tools and diagnostic aids to use to troubleshoot each hardware type.

How to Use This Book

Each chapter of this book is divided into two parts: "In Depth" and "Immediate Solutions." The "In Depth" section of each chapter provides you with a thorough review of the evolution and development of each technology and a comprehensive look at current technologies and how they are employed. The "Immediate

Solutions" section details the processes used to identify, isolate, and resolve common hardware problems as well as how many of the major components of the PC are installed and configured.

This book is written to be a reference that you use to understand a certain technology in more detail and to resolve a particular problem you are experiencing. At the beginning of each chapter is a list of the common problems addressed in the chapter and where you will find the help you need to solve the immediate problem.

Reading the "In Depth" sections of every chapter is also an excellent way to improve your overall knowledge of PC hardware and how it works. The "Immediate Solutions" part of each chapter is a little more difficult to read for information, but nonetheless, it is full of information and tips on fixing problems on a PC.

The *Black Book* Philosophy

Written by experienced professionals, Coriolis *Black Books* provide immediate solutions to global programming and administrative challenges, helping you complete specific tasks, especially critical ones that are not well documented in other books. The *Black Book*'s unique two-part chapter format—thorough technical overviews followed by practical immediate solutions—is structured to help you use your knowledge, solve problems, and quickly master complex technical issues to become an expert. By breaking down complex topics into easily manageable components, this format helps you quickly find what you need to solve PC hardware problems.

I welcome your feedback on this book. You can either email The Coriolis Group at **ctp@coriolis.com** or email me directly at **rgilster@gohighspeed.com**. Errata, updates, and more are available at **www.coriolis.com**.

Part I

On the Motherboard

Chapter 1

Motherboards

In Depth

Features and Function

The motherboard can easily be called the most important part of the computer. Although there are many components a PC cannot function without, the motherboard ties them all together and allows them to become a personal computer.

The *motherboard* is a large printed circuit board that is home to many of the most essential parts of the computer:

- Microprocessor (see Chapter 2)
- Chipset (see Chapter 3)
- Memory sockets and RAM (random access memory) modules (see Chapter 5)
- Cache memory (see Chapter 6)
- IDE (integrated drive electronics), EIDE (Enhanced IDE, or SCSI (small computer system interface) controllers (see Chapter 8)
- Expansion bus (see Chapter 10)
- Parallel and serial ports (see Chapter 12)
- Mouse and keyboard connectors (see Chapter 17)

As this list shows, nearly one-third of this book covers those devices that are found on or plug into the circuitry of the motherboard. The motherboard, a.k.a. the *mainboard* or *system board*, of the computer is the glue that binds all of the PC's components together. Even those devices that are covered in this book but not listed above, such as printers, hard disks, CD-ROMs, and so on, either connect to or are controlled by the devices or controllers in this list.

Motherboard manufacturers attempt to differentiate their products and increase their value by integrating various devices and controllers into their boards. The upside of this is that a motherboard may be able to fit a wider range of systems and provide a deeper list of features. The downside is that if you aren't careful in the selection of your board, you may get stuck with lower quality peripherals than if you had bought them separately.

Motherboard Designs

There are two design approaches for mainboards in a PC: the true motherboard design and the backplane design.

Motherboards

A *motherboard*, which is also known as a system board or a planar, contains all of the computer's primary system components on one circuit board. A motherboard contains most of the circuitry of a PC and is the conduit through which all operations flow. On a typical motherboard (see Figure 1.1) you will find the microprocessor, the ROM BIOS (read-only memory basic input/output system), the chipset, RAM, expansion cards, perhaps some serial and parallel ports, disk controllers, and connectors for the mouse and the keyboard, among other components. It is safe to say that, if your computer is designed around a motherboard, without it, your PC will not function.

Figure 1.1 identifies each of the following major parts of the motherboard:

1. Ports

2. Expansion slots

3. AGP (accelerated graphics port) slot

4. CPU (central processing unit) slot and socket

5. Chipset

6. Power connector

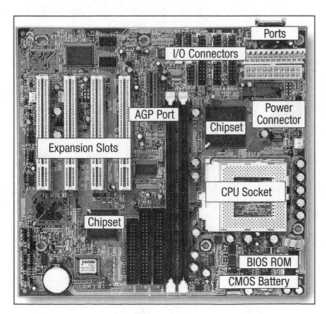

Figure 1.1   A motherboard and its components.

7. Memory sockets

8. I/O connectors

9. CMOS (complementary metal oxide semiconductor) battery

10. ROM BIOS

Backplanes

There are actually two types of *backplane* mainboards: passive and active. A *passive backplane* mainboard is only a receiver card with open slots into which a processor card, which contains a CPU and its support chips, and I/O (input/output) cards, which provide bus and device interfaces, are plugged. These add-in cards are referred to as *daughterboards*. The backplane interconnects the system components through a bus and provides some basic data buffering services. The backplane design is popular with server type computers and is quickly upgraded or repaired. This design type provides the advantage of getting a server back online with only the replacement of a single slotted card, instead of replacing the whole mainboard.

An *active backplane* design, also called an intelligent backplane design, adds some CPU or controller-driven circuitry to the backplane board that can speed along the processing. The CPU itself is still on its own card, which provides for easy replacement.

The utility of the backplane design is being challenged by newer mother-boards that incorporate the Slot 1 and Slot 2 styles of processor connectors for Pentium II and Pentium III Xeon processors. The advantage of the active backplane is that the processor can easily be accessed and replaced, and the Slot 1 and 2 motherboards offer this same advantage.

For the discussions in this chapter, as well as the rest of the book, I refer to the motherboard design when referring to a PC's mainboard. I will specifically reference the backplane design when the information directly relates to it.

Motherboard Form Factors

When the original IBM PC was introduced in 1981, it had a simple motherboard designed to hold an 8-bit processor (the Intel 8088), 5 expansion cards, a keyboard connector, 64 to 256K RAM (from individual memory chips mounted on the motherboard), a chipset, BIOS ROM, and a cassette tape I/O adapter for permanent storage. The PC was designed to be a desktop computer and its system case layout dictated the first of what are now called motherboard form factors. Simply, a *form factor* defines a motherboard's size, shape, and how it is mounted to the case. However, form factors have been extended over time to include the system case, the placement and size of the power supply, the power requirements of the system,

Table 1.1 Motherboard form factors.

Style	Width (Inches)	Length (Inches)	Introduced	Location of Adapter Slots	Case Type
IBM PC	8.5	13	1981	Onboard	IBM PC
IBM PC XT	8.5	13	1982	Onboard	IBM PC XT
AT	12	11 - 13	1984	Onboard	AT Desktop or Tower
Baby AT	8.5	10 - 13	1983	Onboard	Baby AT Desktop or Tower
LPX	9	11 - 13	1987	Riser	Low profile
Micro-AT	8.5	8.5	Early '90s	Onboard	Baby AT Desktop or Tower
ATX	12	9.6	1996	Onboard	ATX Desktop or Tower
Mini-ATX	11.2	8.2	1996	Onboard	Smaller ATX Desktops
Mini-LPX	8 - 9	10 - 11	199x	Riser	Low profile
Micro-ATX	9.6	9.6	1997	Onboard	Low profile
NLX	8 - 9	10 - 13.6	1997	Riser	Low profile
Flex-ATX	9	7.5	1999	Onboard	Flexible design

external connector placements and specifications, and case airflow and cooling guidelines. Table 1.1 lists the common form factors that have been and are being used in PCs.

AT and Baby AT

The IBM PC XT had a motherboard that measured 8.5 inches wide by 13 inches deep, which was the same size as the earlier IBM PC motherboard. However, the XT increased the number of adapter card slots from 5 to 8, and the cassette tape interface port was replaced by the 5.25-inch floppy drive that would become the standard for storing and transferring information between computers.

When IBM released its first 16-bit computer, the PC AT, the additional circuitry expanded its size of the motherboard and case to 12 inches wide by 13 inches deep. At the same time, many clone manufacturers began releasing XT-compatible motherboards that included keyboard connectors, expansion slots, and mounting holes to fit AT style cases. This set the AT size, shape, and mounting placements as the first motherboard standard.

By the time that clone manufacturers began releasing their own 16-bit PCs, higher integration in the supporting chipsets allowed them to be mounted on a smaller motherboard. This smaller form became known as the Baby AT, shown in Figure 1.2, because it would mount in AT cases. The Baby AT became very popular because of its flexibility and joined the AT motherboard as a *de facto* standard.

Figure 1.2   The Baby AT Motherboard.

Most of the system cases manufactured between 1984 and 1996 were made to the Baby AT form factor. However, with further integration and miniaturization of the processor chipset and other support components, an even smaller version of the AT motherboard emerged. The Micro-AT motherboard (see Figure 1.3), which still fit the AT and Baby AT mounting hardware, was nearly half the size of the Baby AT main board.

LPX and Mini-LPX

Originally created by Western Digital as a way to build slim line cases, the LPX and Mini-LPX form factors have been copied by many other companies resulting in many variations on the originals. Actually, the LPX and Mini-LPX

Figure 1.3   Micro-AT System Board.

specifications are more of a general motherboard category than a specific form factor, and there is no standard definition.

One quick note on the meaning of form factor names: There aren't any. If the form factor names ever had meanings, they are lost to time.

Manufacturers like Packard Bell and Compaq used their own proprietary configurations of these boards in their PCs. Unfortunately, this guaranteed that their customers could not upgrade their computers without swapping the motherboard. The LPX style is characterized by a daughterboard that plugs into a slot in the middle of the motherboard that includes two or three peripheral expansion slot sockets. The number of sockets available depends on the size of the daughterboard and whether it has slots on both sides. This arrangement allows the expansion cards to be mounted sideways on the daughterboard, which allows for a much slimmer case design.

The LPX-style also features the inclusion of integrated device controllers on the motherboard, including IDE video, and sound. Integrating these controllers into the motherboard reduces the number of expansion slots required by the system. External connections, illustrated in Figure 1.4, are mounted in a row on the motherboard, which allows for easy access to keyboard and mouse connectors, serial ports, parallel ports, and video and audio connectors. Some LPX versions also feature one or more USB (universal serial bus) connectors in place of a serial port or an onboard NIC (network interface card).

Although some of the design features of the LPX motherboards were ahead of their time, the lack of a standard form factor makes this format a virtual dead end for users. However, many of the best innovations from the LPX cards have been incorporated into the ATX and NLX boards discussed in the following sections.

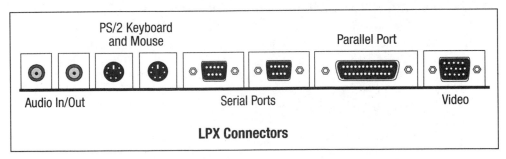

Figure 1.4   LPX Rear Connections.

ATX and Mini-ATX Form Factors

The ATX form factor was developed and released by Intel in 1995 with the goal of "improving the end-user experience," as well as that of the manufacturer's. The ATX form is an improvement over the form factors that preceded it because it is a published and continuously maintained standard. This guarantees compatibility among all ATX system cases, system boards, and power supplies.

The ATX form factor is based on the Baby AT board size, but it involves more than just a compatible board size and mounting specification. Intel started over with ATX, rotating the board 90 degrees and incorporating new mounting locations and power supply connections. All I/O connections are located on the back of the board (see Figure 1.5) in a two-row block that is able to fit many different configurations with bezels.

Figure 1.5 shows the standard placement for external connectors on an ATX form factor motherboard. The top row of the figure shows a Mini-DIN PS/2-type keyboard or mouse connector, a parallel port, and a blank slot that could support a second parallel port. The bottom row shows a second Mini-DIN PS/2-type keyboard or mouse connector, two serial ports, and a series of blank ports that might be used for sound card connectors. The Intel specification for the size of the connector area shown in Figure 1.4 is defined as 6.25 inches wide by 1.75 inches tall. This design helps eliminate the internal clutter of the motherboard and adapter card cables that connect to the rear panel typical of the Baby AT form factor.

The ATX form factor specification incorporates the experience and problems associated with the Baby AT motherboards and those of the LPX forms. As illustrated in Figure 1.6, the ATX form places the CPU and RAM slots out of the way of expansion cards and near the power supply fan, which improves the airflow over the CPU and RAM chips. The original specification for the ATX form changed the direction of the airflow, directing it inward through the power supply, over the CPU, and out through the case vents. The idea supposedly was to eliminate the need for separate CPU fans. The downside was that dust and other airborne particles entered the case and settled inside, which required more preventive

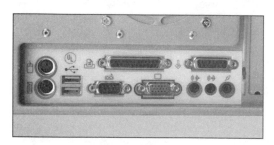

Figure 1.5   ATX Back Panel.

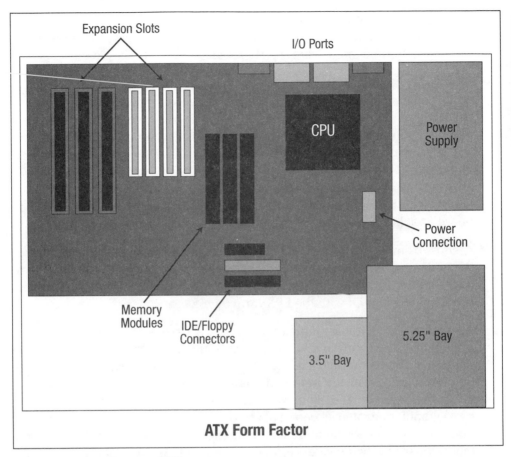

ATX Form Factor

Figure 1.6   The standard ATX layout.

maintenance. The lesson learned is that air inflow is less efficient than air out-flow and instead of eliminating fans, may actually require additional fans to cool the CPU properly. Recent ATX versions have reversed the airflow once again so that the power supply fan is now venting the case. The ATX case design allows for mounting additional case fans. It is highly recommended that PCs with 3D video accelerators, other high-heat producing cards, or multiple hard disk drives should consider adding an additional case fan or two.

The ATX form uses a power supply that is not compatible in Baby AT cases. It allows for *soft switching*, that is, of controlling the power on and off functions under motherboard control. The ATX power supply uses a one-piece connector that is keyed to fit in only one way, which prevents the possibility of frying the motherboard, and possibly injuring yourself. The power supply also eliminates the need for a motherboard voltage regulator by providing what is called *split voltage*, which is a range of voltages, usually 12v, 5v, and 3.3v, to the motherboard.

The ATX specification also defines the mini-ATX subspecification, which has a board size of 11.2 inches by 8.2 inches. Other subspecifications of the ATX form factor you may encounter are the Micro-ATX and the Flex-ATX.

NLX Form Factor

NLX is a new, standardized, low-profile motherboard form factor. It is designed to support a number of current and emerging microprocessor technologies along with many newer developments, including support for AGP video adapters, and tall memory modules and DIMMs. The NLX form provides more flexibility for the system-level design and for easy removal and replacement of the motherboard, allegedly without tools. The NLX motherboard measures about 8 inches by 13.6 inches and uses a plug-in riser board for its expansion bus support. The riser board attaches to the edge of the mainboard, as shown in Figure 1.7.

A consortium of computer and component manufacturers combined to create the NLX specification and has published the standard for all to use. It is hoped that sharing the information and standardizing the form factor can prevent the problems associated with the LPX form factor.

There were three primary influences behind the development of the NLX standard: processor and system cooling requirements, the number of connectors needed by multimedia hardware, and a further reduction of interior cable clutter. The size and thermal characteristics of newer microprocessors, especially those configured into multiple processor sets, along with the addition of high-performance (and high-heat) graphics adapters, forced a new look at the airflow in slimline cases. As multimedia systems became more common, the need for more connectors from the motherboard to the outside world also increased. As more internal adapters and controllers were added to the motherboard, the interior of the system case was cluttered with cabling, which impeded repair or upgrade activities.

Figure 1.7   NLX form factor as illustrated in its published specification.

Immediate Solutions

Tools and Diagnostics

The following is a list of the tools that you should have in your toolkit when working on motherboards:

- *A good set of screwdrivers (including a Torx)*—In your collection of screwdrivers, be sure you include at least one each of a standard and a Phillips mini-screwdriver and a full-size Phillips with a magnetic tip. Yes, magnetic screwdrivers are potentially dangerous if you use them incorrectly, such as gouging the motherboard or stabbing yourself. However, they are excellent for those jobs where you can't catch the screw when it falls or for starting a screw in an inaccessible place.

- *An antistatic mat with a grounding wrist strap*—If you do not have access to an antistatic mat (see Figure 1.8) on which you can set any static-sensitive parts you remove, then by all means wear a wrist strap (see Figure 1.9) and use antistatic bags. Never stack cards or parts on top of one another, and ground yourself to the metallic cross-members of the system case as often as possible.

- *Software system testing utilities*—As long as you are able to boot into some operating system, a set of diagnostic utilities, like Norton Utilities, can be among the best tools in your kit. Use these software aids to diagnose a number of suspected motherboard or system performance problems, such as system slowdowns and inexplicable crashes.

- *A digital multimeter*—If the motherboard is running strangely, one of the first places to look is its power connections. A multimeter or a digital

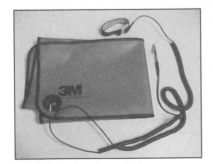

Figure 1.8   An antistatic mat and grounding strap.

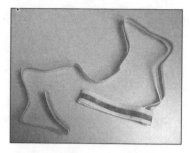

Figure 1.9   A grounding wrist strap.

Figure 1.10   A digital multimeter.

voltmeter, (see Figure 1.10) is a good tool to have for testing continuity of power cables and the power supply output. Check out Chapter 14 for details on how to use a multimeter to check out a power supply.

- *Penlights or mini flex-type flashlights*—Having some light, like that shown in Figure 1.11, to help you see small identifying marks on the motherboard, its chips, and expansion cards can prevent a serious error and save the time removing and reinserting the wrong parts. You may want to consider spare batteries as well.

- *Dental mirror*—This tool, shown in Figure 1.12, can be purchased from a tool supplier rather than a dentist. It is perfect for seeing around corners in an assembled system. If you need to see a detail that is being blocked by the drive cage, the dental mirror is your tool. They're also great for seeing the back of a PC when you're trying to attach a connector.

• *Your eyes, ears, and nose*—You are among your best tools. As corny as that may sound, your senses are probably the most often used in a quick trouble-shooting script.

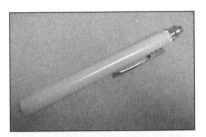

Figure 1.11   A small flashlight is a must-have in your toolkit.

Figure 1.12   A dental mirror is used to see in tight places and around corners.

Troubleshooting Guide for the Motherboard

Before you do anything else, you must remove enough of the case cover so that you can see the CPU and the BIOS ROM. Then, get out your penlight and your notebook and pen or pencil. As you move through the next few steps, write down every bit of information you identify.

1. *Identify the processor's class and model*—What kind of processor is in use? For example, is it an Intel 8088, 286/16, Intel Pentium III 600, Slot 1, AMD Athlon, or another processor?

2. *Identify BIOS manufacturer and its revision level*—For example, Phoenix BIOS I4HS10 rev 4.05.10. This information can be obtained during the boot sequence, if you're fast, or from a label on the BIOS ROM chip itself. If the motherboard doesn't have a model number printed on it, you can get this information another way. Motherboard manufacturers commonly have custom BIOS versions for each chipset and motherboard combination, so a motherboard's model number can often be derived from the BIOS serial number. Check the BIOS manufacturer's Web site for details. Some sites even offer search tools specifically for this sort of lookup.

3. *Identify motherboard manufacturer and model*—Near an edge of the motherboard, you will find a block of printed information that identifies the manufacturer, the model number, and possibly a revision level.

4. Identify the bus type—Which expansion buses are supported on the motherboard or any riser boards in use? PX XT, ISA, MCA, EISA, VLB, PCI, etc. (see Chapter 10 for more information on PC expansion bus types).

Identifying the Problem

There are three general types of failures directly related to the motherboard. These are best characterized by a POST (power-on self-test) beep code and the action immediately following it. I've named these three failure modes as: *no beep, no boot; beep, no boot;* and *beep, boot, and bam.*

To begin the identification process, power on the PC, listen and look and then go to the section below that most approximates what you heard and saw.

No Beep, No Boot

The PC's power is on, you can see lights on the front panel, but as near as you can tell the POST process did not run.

1. Check both ends of the main power cord, especially where it connects to the back of the PC, to make sure that it is fully pushed into the connector or receptacle. Inspect the power cord for cuts or crimps that may have damaged the inner wires. Inspect the plug head and the female connector of the cord for corrosion or metal damage. Take a look at the connector on the back of the PC to make sure that the prongs aren't bent and not connecting properly.

2. Check the power source outlet or proper voltage with a multimeter or DVM (digital voltage meter). If may be easier just to try plugging the PC into a different outlet (not on the same set). If it works on a different outlet, then the problem was the source. If the PC is plugged into a power strip, its varistor may have been blown out by an electrical surge. Some plug strips have a fuse or circuit breaker that can be reset.

3. Check the power supply's fan to see if it is turning. If it's not turning, the problem may be in the power supply, and you need to troubleshoot it. See Chapter 14 for information on troubleshooting the power supply.

4. If the power supply fan is spinning, but nothing else is happening, the power to the motherboard may be faulty. For example, you may have a +12v source, but no +5v or +3.3v supplies. It may also be that the power-good line from the power supply is not coming on for some reason. These conditions are also covered in troubleshooting the power supply, described in Chapter 14.

5. Verify that the power connectors from the power supply are firmly seated and in the correct position. Check to make sure the power supplies power connector on the motherboard is firmly seated. The type of connectors and

how they connect is dependent on the form factor of the motherboard. AT and Baby AT power supplies have two 6-wire connectors that must be connected just so, and the ATX and later usually have a single 20-wire connector that can't be connected incorrectly without force.

6. The power connectors on a Baby AT motherboard, which are usually labeled as P8 and P9, attach to the motherboard side-by-side. The trick to making sure you have them in the right positions is to see if all four of the black wires, or ground wires (two on each plug), are together in the middle. If so, the connectors are in the right orientation. However, be very cautious about plugging these connectors—any in the wrong orientation will likely damage the motherboard.

7. The power connection on ATX or later form factors is keyed with a prong, lip, or finger that prevents it from being connected incorrectly.

8. Confirm that the motherboard's voltage setting jumpers are correctly positioned for the PC's motherboard and CPU combination. See the motherboard's documentation for the proper settings of these jumpers.

9. If the PC is in a public area, such as a laboratory, student lab, library, or another open and unsecured location, there could be a missing processor, memory, or expansion card. Unfortunately, theft is common on PCs to which there is public access.

10. Look for smoke and smell for burnt wire. There is a running joke among PC technicians that the smoke is the magic that makes all electronic and electrical parts work. (If the smoke gets out, then the part stops working.) Examine the board, chips, and pathways for burn marks and bubbling that may be associated with excessive heat damage that may have let the smoke out. You may want to use a small magnifying glass to examine the motherboard and its components for heat damage.

11. Try reseating all of the expansion cards, memory modules, and if the PC is older, the ROM BIOS chip. You may want to check on any socket-mounted chips on the motherboard. All chips are subject to *chip creep*, which is the very slight movement of a device out of its socket that is caused by thermal shifts, such as powering the computer on and off. If you discover any chips that need to be reseated, you may want to remove them and check for corrosion on the connector edges.

12. Look for anything that may be shorting the motherboard, drives, peripheral cards, or power supply. Screws that fall into the case may become lodged underneath the system board or the board retainer tray and could ground the motherboard to the case. If a foreign object has been causing a problem, just removing it may not solve all of the problems. There could be lingering

damage to the motherboard. Don't just assume there was no damage: Use a chipset/memory/CPU test and diagnostic program, such as SiSoft's Sandra, TweakBIOS, or CTCHIPZ (visit **http://sysopt.earthweb.com/** for more information on these tools) to verify the function of the motherboard.

13. If your motherboard is mounted on brass standoffs that hold it off the case tray, check that paper washers are inserted between the standoff and the motherboard to isolate the metal from the board. If you don't have little paper washers, then use a small piece of electrical tape over the end of the standoff where it contacts the motherboard. If the standoff is contacting the motherboard directly, it can cause a short in some instances.

14. Remove the motherboard from the case and place it on an antistatic/anti-conductive surface or material. Reconnect the motherboard to its power and device connectors and attempt to boot. If this works, something in the case or a part of the mounting of the board is causing it to short while it is in the case.

15. Disconnect all external connectors—the ones to serial, parallel, USB, keyboard, mouse, etc. Reboot the system. If the system boots, begin a cycle of replacing the connectors one at a time and cold-booting the PC each time, until the problem reoccurs. If the system fails after a certain device is attached, troubleshoot the connector or the device. See Chapter 12 and the chapters in Part III for information on troubleshooting connectors or a specific device.

Beep, No Boot

If the PC powers on, but the POST process appears to halt after sounding one or more beeps, then follow this troubleshooting procedure:

1. Make sure the PC's monitor is on and operating properly. Don't laugh.

2. Look up the pattern used on the BIOS in your PC. Each BIOS manufacturer uses a different and unique pattern of beep tones to signal errors. Once you know what you are listening for, attempt to write down the pattern of the beep tones. Remember that tones are short or long with varying length pauses inserted between beep series. Once you are sure of the beep signal pattern (you may need to reboot several times before you are sure), consult your motherboard's documentation or visit the BIOS manufacturer's Web site for its meaning and a suggested procedure to correct the problem. Understand that every manufacturer has a different meaning for a certain signal pattern and it can even differ for different revisions of a BIOS of one manufacturer.

3. Check to make sure that the CMOS battery jumper is in the correct position. Surprisingly, many new PCs and motherboards are shipped with the CMOS battery jumper in the wrong setting. Check the motherboard's documentation for the correct settings.

4. Inspect the CMOS battery for leaks, corrosion, or burns. On older motherboards, the CMOS battery is often a little blue "barrel" (see Figure 1.13) and something like a big watch battery (a flat silver disk like that shown in Figure 1.14). In either case, it is located on the motherboard near the CMOS chip. You should also check the battery with a multimeter. It could just be time for a new battery. These batteries can go bad and leak their chemicals on the motherboard, which can short or melt circuit traces. On that note, look for broken circuit traces on the motherboard or solder blobs accidentally connecting two circuit trace paths.

5. If the beep codes are for something very generic, check the video card by removing and reinstalling it. If that doesn't work, try swapping it out for another video card of the same type, if available.

Figure 1.13   Old style "blue barrel" CMOS battery.

Figure 1.14   Newer systems have a flat battery.

6. Depending on when the error is detected by the POST, you may get some text message or a part of the BIOS information. If so, study the information displayed; it can usually provide clues to where the problem is occurring. If you are familiar with the PC, you should know what would come next in the POST process and that is likely the point of failure. If you are unsure, check with the BIOS or motherboard manufacturer for information on its boot sequence.

7. Remove the RAM chips or modules and try booting with different combinations of memory modules in different slots on the board. It is a common occurrence that a pair of SIMMS (single inline memory modules) will work great in one set of slots, but hang the system in another set of slots. If the PC includes Level 2 (L2) cache boards, try booting the PC without it.

8. Verify that the RAM chips or modules in use are compatible with the motherboard, chipset, and processor. Also be sure that the modules are installed in the proper sets. Some PCs allow single modules, some require module pairs, and still others require four of the same module type be installed to work. Remember that you can't mix and match memory module types in sets. See Chapter 5 for more information on memory modules.

9. Reseat the expansion cards (see Step 8 in the "No Beep, No Boot" procedure). If you have a spare IDE controller, replace the installed card with it.

10. Confirm that the motherboard's voltage setting and motherboard speed (multiplier) jumpers are correctly positioned for the PC's motherboard and CPU combination. See the motherboard's documentation for the proper settings of these jumpers (see Figure 1.15).

11. If you can access the BIOS' setup program by pressing the access key (usually **DEL** or a function key), use its reset function to reset the CMOS settings to their defaults values and reboot.

12. Remove all of the expansion boards, except the video adapter, and try to reboot. If the system reboots, the problem is likely one of the boards or the expansion bus on one of the expansion slots. Begin replacing the boards one at a time, rebooting after each card is installed. If the system fails on a particular card, put it in a different slot and reboot to isolate whether it is the card or the slot that has the problem.

13. Disconnect the system speaker. It could be shorting to the board.

14. Disconnect each of the case-to-motherboard wires, such as the connections to the front panel LED (light-emitting diode) lights and switches. Do these one at a time and reboot after removing each one.

15. Check keyboard and mouse connections and check to see if their receptacles are securely connected to the motherboard. Check to see if the

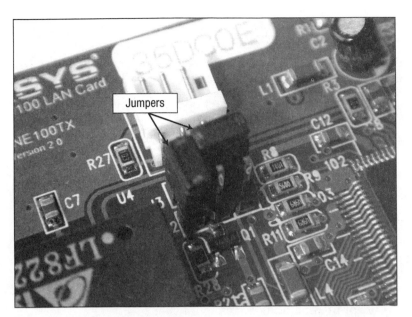

Figure 1.15   Motherboard jumpers.

keyboard fuse is blown. This fuse can blow if a serial mouse is connected to a PS/2 connector through an adapter or if there is an electrical short somewhere in the keyboard. And, if all else has failed, try a different keyboard.

Beep, Boot, Bam
In this situation, the PC is powered on, the POST completes and singles an all clear, but the PC fails at the beginning or the boot sequence or right after the boot completes.

1. Study the BIOS information displayed on the monitor and verify that the boot drive sequence is set correctly. If the correct drive is set as the first boot drive, check its power and data connections. If the PC's BIOS supports it, set the boot drive to Autodetect.

2. Check the hard disk drives to ensure that you have only one Master disk and one Slave disk on each IDE cable. If you wish to boot from a hard disk drive (the most common choice), be sure that it is the Master disk on the primary IDE channel. See Chapter 8 for more information on IDE disk drives.

3. If your primary disk drive is a SCSI interface drive, be sure that the end device has terminated the line. Verify that the SCSI BIOS and the motherboard's BIOS are set to allow a SCSI disk drive to be the boot disk. Verify that the SCSI device ID assigned to the disk drive matches that in the BIOS and make sure the SCSI controller is connected to the SCSI drive. Check all SCSI connectors to ensure they are pushed all of the way on.

4. If the boot still fails, change the boot sequence and attempt to boot off an alternate media (floppy, CDROM).

5. If you can boot with an MS-DOS floppy disk, try using the **FDISK /MBR** command to rebuild the master boot record.

6. Try replacing the controller card of the boot disk and reboot. Alternately, put the device you think may be causing the problem into a PC you know is working and test if that PC can boot off the device.

7. If the disk drives are not the problem, check the processor fan or heat sink. If they are not properly installed, or if thermal grease has not been applied, the CPU may be overheating and shutting down.

8. Check your RAM as described in Steps 7 and 8 in the "Beep, No Boot" section earlier in the chapter.

9. Confirm that the CPU and chipset are compatible with the operating system you are attempting to load. You should be able to get this information from either the CPU manufacturer (who may or may not be the chipset manufacturer) or the operating system publisher.

10. Review your motherboard manufacturer's Web site for bulletins of known problems or incompatibilities. I had a problem with a VIA chipset motherboard and the AGP video adapters that I would have never been able to figure out, had I not visited the manufacturers' Web sites.

TIP: *Find out which chipsets the motherboard manufacturer is using for video, audio, and SCSI, if it is an option. Always go with well-known companies, such as ATI, Creative Labs, and Adaptec, if you have a choice. Generally, information about any known flaws in peripheral controller chipsets is readily available on the Internet or in technical hardware-related magazines. Study up on the components on the motherboard. This will save you from disabling parts of the motherboard in the BIOS or through a jumper or waste an expansion slot with a redundant replacement card.*

Removing the Motherboard

There is nothing on the PC that holds as much potential for disaster as removing and replacing the motherboard. However, if you proceed methodically and carefully, there is really nothing to fear and usually much to gain. The game plan is to proceed cautiously, write everything down, draw pictures, label parts, protect everything from ESD (electrostatic discharge), and use the right tools correctly. Follow this plan and you should have very few problems.

Here is a step-by-step procedure for removing a motherboard from a tower case.

Opening the Case

The right case makes removal and reinstallation of a motherboard a snap. In fact, there are system cases where almost every component is removable and almost without the use of tools. While this is great for the PC technician, it may not be so good in environments where a PC's RAM or processor can magically disappear if it isn't locked down. Manufacturers are always looking for ways to reduce the number of hard connectors (such as screws and clips) that hold cases and components together as a means to simplify production and lower costs. The result, good or bad, is that the insides of the PC are more accessible.

1. First, remove all cables from the connectors on the back or side of the PC, including the monitor, speakers, printers, and external drives. It is recommended that you both label the cables as to which connector they were attached to and create a diagram illustrating the connections and cables. A sample diagram in shown in Figure 1.16.

2. Every PC case is a little unique, even between models of the same manufacturer. Usually the case is secured with screws around the edge of the rear panel of the PC. However, there are new breeds of PCs on which the motherboard, CPU, and memory modules are exposed by simply lifting off the front or side panel, usually without tools. If your PC is one of these, the front or side panel is held in place by spring catches and friction retainers. A strong and steady pull should release the panel. Watch for protruding floppy disk and CD-ROM drives or interior cables that may catch on the panel and be dislodged or damaged in the process. If the panel will not pull off without significant effort or possible damage, stop and look for screws securing it to the case.

3. Most newer computers have separated the sides of the case to allow only one side to be removed. This exposes the motherboard and its components which is usually enough for normal maintenance. On others, the entire case slips off the rear of the PC, exposing the motherboard on all sides.

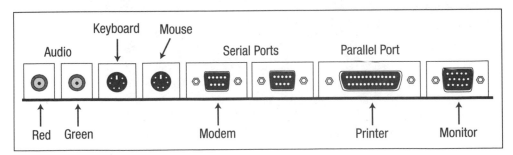

Figure 1.16   Sample diagram of PC connectors and cables.

Regardless, since complete access is needed to remove the motherboard, remove all of the case to expose both sides of the motherboard, if possible.

4. Remove the retaining screws in the expansion cards. Also remove the cables connecting the cards to the computer, such as the drive cables from IDE or SCSI cards and the CD-ROM audio cables on sound cards. Label each cable with a piece of masking tape or with a fine-point marker as to what it is and its orientation. The disk drive data cables should have a red or blue edge to indicate their Pin 1 location. Draw a diagram that shows which expansion card went into which expansion slot. It is a good idea to mark each slot with a number and then label each card with a piece of tape on which is written the slot number from which it was removed. Include the connecting cables and the device to which each was attached in the diagram.

5. Mark or label the cables that connect directly into the connectors integrated into the motherboard, including the power supply, floppy disk controller, IDE controller, and possibly the sound controller. Indicate the device, which is usually printed on the motherboard surface next to each socket, as shown in Figure 1.17. Create a diagram for these cables that indicates the source, destination, orientation, and any special markings on the cable that will be important at reassembly time.

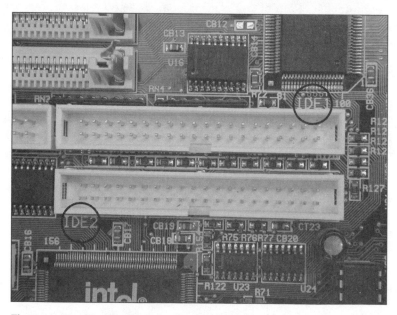

Figure 1.17   The device type is printed on the motherboard for integrated controllers.

6. From the back or underside of the PC, remove the motherboard mounting screws and lift out the motherboard. On some PCs there may be a mounting plate from which the screws must be removed to swing the motherboard out of its mounting. Place the board on an antistatic mat or on an antistatic shipping bag and document any other connectors or mountings that you have not previously noted.

7. If the motherboard is mounted on brass standoffs that are used to lock into the case, remove the screws attaching the board into the brass standoffs and slide it to unlock the standoffs. Lift the board out of the standoff keys and place it on an antistatic surface.

8. To re-install the motherboard, use your diagrams and notes and reverse the order of operations.

1. Motherboards

Chapter 2

Processors

In Depth

Digital Logic and Binary Numbers

Computers are electronic devices, and they internally represent binary numbers as two voltage levels. These two voltage levels are also referred to as the *high* and *low logic* levels. In turn, the logic levels represent the binary values 1 and 0.

The voltage of a logic level must remain constant so that it can be properly registered by the circuitry. This is the reason that microprocessors and their associated support chips require a direct current (DC) power source.

Digital Elements of the Computer

Here are some of the key digital elements involved with the digital logic of the computer:

- A *bit* (binary digit) is a single binary number that can be either 1 (on) or 0 (off).

- A *binary word* is a number made up of more than 1 bit. Generally, the word length of a computer ranges from 4 to 64 bits.

- A *byte* (the simple 8-bit word), illustrated in Figure 2.1, is by far the most commonly referenced binary word size. Even the newer 64-bit machines rate their RAM in megabytes and their hard drives in gigabytes (or even terabytes). A single byte can represent a binary value that is equivalent to a decimal number in the range of 0 to 255; in other words, it can hold two hexadecimal digits (see "The Hexadecimal System" later in this chapter).

- A *nybble* (also *nibble*), depicted in Figure 2.2, is a 4-bit word used to simplify hexadecimal number conversion. A nybble can hold the binary representation

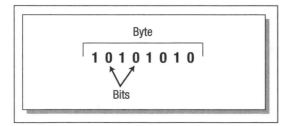

Figure 2.1   A byte consists of 8 bits.

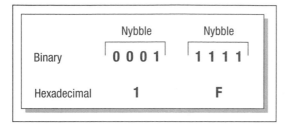

Figure 2.2   A nybble holds a 4-bit hexadecimal value.

of the decimal equivalent of 0 to 15, which also equates to the hexadecimal values 0 to F. An 8-bit binary number that is broken into nybbles can be easily substituted for hexadecimal numbers.

- A *machine word* is the largest binary number (expressed as a number of bits) that a single CPU's data register can hold at one time. The machine word is commonly used to refer to the bit size of the processor (for example, 16-bit processor, 32-bit processor, and 64-bit processor).

Just a Bit of Fun

There have been a number of attempts to create other names for other sizes of bit blocks over the years. It is almost a case of the good names being taken. The attempts range from the unusual to the witty to the downright silly. For example, a 2-bit block has been labeled a "crumb" or a "tayste." A 5-bit block has been designated as (what else?) a "nickel," but the 10-bit block is not a dime; instead, it is a "deckle." Here are a few more: 16-bits, a "playte" or, on 32-bit computers, a "chawmp"; 32-bits, "dynner"; and 48-bits, a "gawble."

Binary (Logical) Arithmetic Operations

There are three main types of CPU binary computation functions: arithmetic, logical, and data shift operations. Each CPU function has a corresponding binary operator: the **AND**, **OR**, and exclusive **OR** (**XOR**), respectively. Each binary operator requires two binary numbers (usually taken from CPU registers). These two numbers are combined to derive a third number that is based on the interaction of the original two numbers.

ANDing Operations

In an **AND**ing operation, the answer can be true (represented by the value 1) only if both of the operands are true.

Figure 2.3 illustrates how this works. First, the binary numbers are aligned position-by-position, right to left. Then each pair of bits (one from each number) is combined. In the leftmost column of Figure 2.3, the two 1's result in a 1, and all

Binary Value 1	1	1	0	0
Binary Value 2	1	0	1	0
Result of AND Operation	1	0	0	0

Figure 2.3   A logical **AND** operation.

the other number pairs result in a 0. This is because only two trues (1's) will result in a true (1) value. Anything else results in a false (0) condition.

When **AND** operations are applied to a bit word, each column is treated as an individual equation and there is no carryover to adjoining columns. Here is another example:

```
10010110
AND        11001101
        10000100
```

Only those bit pairs that are both 1 values (true) result in a 1 (true). All other combinations of 1's and 0's (including two 0's) result in a zero (false). The basic logic behind the **AND** operation is that in order for two bits to result in a true, the first **AND** the second **AND** must both be true.

A common use for the logical **AND** operator is to "mask" a binary number. This involves arbitrarily masking out (reducing to 0) a certain portion of the target binary number by applying a second number (the mask) that has 0's in the positions to be discarded and 1's in the positions of the bits to be kept. The **AND** operator can also be used to force 0's into certain binary positions while leaving the other bits unchanged.

The Logical OR

In an **OR** operation, which also combines two binary number values to achieve a logical result, the result will be true (1) if either of the bits in each column pair is a 1 (true). Figure 2.4 illustrates how the logical **OR** works.

In Figure 2.4, only those columns that have at least one true (1) result in a true. An **OR** operation is the reverse of the **AND** operation. The **OR** function places 1's in any nonduplicated positions. You can also force 1's into specified bit positions without disturbing the surrounding digits. The following is an example of **OR**ing two bytes together:

Binary Value 1	1	1	0	0
Binary Value 2	1	0	1	0
Result of **OR** Operation	1	1	1	0

Figure 2.4   The logical **OR** operation.

```
       10010110
OR     11001101
       11011101
```

Any column that has at least one true (or 1) value results in a true value. Only true values matter; two falses are always false. The logic of the **OR** function is that any one bit **OR** the other can be true, resulting in a true for the pair.

The Exclusive OR Operation

An exclusive **OR** (**XOR**) operation requires one, and only one, of the two bit operands to be true exclusive of the other bit's value. So in the **XOR** logical operation, if only one bit is true (1), then the pair results in a true. If both or neither of the bits is true, the result is false (0). Figure 2.5 illustrates this operation of the **XOR** function.

Because the two bits in the leftmost column of Figure 2.5 are both 1's, the **XOR** operation results in a false. However, in the center two columns, where only one bit is true, the results are both true. Again, false is false and only truth matters.

XOR can be used in column style to combine two binary digits to form a third. Here is another example:

Binary Value 1	1	1	0	0
Binary Value 2	1	0	1	0
Result of **XOR** Operation	0	1	1	0

Figure 2.5   The **XOR** (exclusive **OR**) operation.

```
10010110
XOR       11001101
     01010011
```

Only in the columns where only one of the bits is a 1 is the result also a 1. The logic is that one bit, exclusive of the other bit, can be true to result in a true condition. **XOR** is often used to find the complement of a bit string. Exclusive **OR**ing any byte with a byte of all 1's will produce its complement, as shown in this example:

```
     10010110
XOR       11111111
     01101001
```

The Binary Number System

The primary storage device inside a computer is a *transistor*, which holds exactly one bit. The transistor stores binary values in the form of electrical voltage levels that are either positive or nonpositive. The *binary number system* matches the capabilities of the transistor perfectly because they both have only two states or values. The computer stores a single binary numeral (either a 1 or a 0) in a single transistor.

The binary number system represents values as exponential values of 2. Binary is a base 2 number system just as decimal is a base 10 number system. Decimal numbers, such as 101, are a combination of various powers of the base 10. The decimal number 101 represents 1 plus no 10s plus one 100, which is the same as 1 times 10 to the zero power plus 0 times 10 to the first power plus 1 times 10 to the second power:

$(1*10^2) + (0*10^1) + (1*10^0) = 101$

Similarly, the number 221 represents

$(2*10^2) + (2*10^1) + (1*10^0) = 221$

Decimal values have 10 numerals (0 to 9) to express how many of a particular power of 10 are included in a number. The binary number system works like the decimal system, with two exceptions: Each position in a binary number represents a power of 2, and the binary system uses only two numerals (0 and 1) to express whether a particular power of 2 value is included in a number.

Earlier I proved why the number 101 represents "one hundred one." Now let's look at why the binary number 101 represents the decimal value 5:

$$(1*2^2) + (0*2^1) + (1*2^0) = 5$$

In this example, 1 times 2 to the second power plus 1 times 2 to the zero power adds up to the decimal number 5. So the binary number 101 is the equivalent of 5. Figure 2.6 shows the binary numbers equivalent to the decimal numbers from 0 to 20. Notice the progression of numbers. What would be the next binary number?

Each position in a binary number represents an increasingly larger power of 2 (starting from 0) as you move from right to left. Each position can hold only a 1 or a 0. A binary number cannot hold other values, such as a decimal 4,321. To store this number as a binary number, you must substitute the binary values represented in this decimal number into the binary number. Table 2.1 lists the first eight powers of 2.

To learn more about converting decimal numbers to binary, see "Converting Decimal to Binary" in the Immediate Solutions section.

Binary	Decimal
00000000	0
00000001	1
00000010	2
00000011	3
00000100	4
00000101	5
00000110	6
00000111	7
00001000	8
00001001	9
00001010	10
00001011	11
00001100	12
00001101	13
00001110	14
00001111	15
00010000	16
00010001	17
00010010	18
00010011	19
00010100	20

Figure 2.6   Binary numbers in an 8-bit byte.

Table 2.1   Powers of 2.

Power of 2	Calculation	Decimal Equivalent
2^0	2 * 0	1
2^1	2 * 1	2
2^2	2 * 2	4
2^3	2 * 2 * 2	8
2^4	2 * 2 * 2 * 2	16
2^5	2 * 2 * 2 * 2 * 2	32
2^6	2 * 2 * 2 * 2 * 2 * 2	64
2^7	2 * 2 * 2 * 2 * 2 * 2 * 2	128

The Hexadecimal System

Many of the addresses and configuration values on a PC are expressed as hexadecimal numbers. *Hexadecimal* means "six and ten," or a base-16 number system. *Hex*, as it is commonly called, uses a combination of 16 values: the decimal numbers 0 through 9 for the first 10 values, and the six letters A through F to represent the decimal values of 11 through 15 (see Figure 2.7).

Hexadecimal numbers use 4 bits, or a nybble, to store each digit. The nybble represents the binary values ranging from 2^0 in the rightmost position to 2^3 in the leftmost position. This arrangement allows the nybble to store the equivalent of a

Hexadecimal Values

Binary	Hexadecimal
0001	1
0010	2
0011	3
0100	4
0101	5
0110	6
0111	7
1000	8
1001	9
1010	A
1011	B
1100	C
1101	D
1110	E
1111	F

Figure 2.7   The values of the hexadecimal number system.

decimal 15, or the hexadecimal value F. Because of its larger base (base 16), hexadecimal can store values such as 11 or 15 as a single character.

Our friendly number 101, which represents "one hundred one" in decimal and 5 in binary, now represents the decimal value 257 when stored in hexadecimal. This is an excellent illustration of how hexadecimal can store much larger values. Another example is that the hexadecimal value ABCDEF represents 11,259,375 in decimal.

Semiconductors

The world of microprocessors is the world of the *semiconductor*, a material that is neither a conductor nor an insulator. A semiconductor can be made to perform electronically encoded instructions in microscopic environments.

Physical Characteristics of Semiconductors

A *conductor* is a material that allows electrical current to pass through it because it has many free electrons to act as a transfer medium. Free electrons are electrons that have become dislodged from the outer shell of an atom. If a material cannot support the flow of electrical current, it is called an *insulator*. Insulators are materials that contain relatively few free electrons.

Some materials may or may not pass electricity, depending on their purity. These materials are called *semiconductors*. Silicon is an example of a material that exhibits the properties of a semiconductor. Silicon by itself holds on to its electrons quite strongly and is naturally neutral: neither a conductor nor an insulator. Silicon with phosphorus impurities, known as N-type silicon, has a negative charge because of its free electrons. Phosphorus has more electrons than does the silicon atom; phosphorus has donor electrons that do not find a place to bind and therefore become free electrons. Silicon containing boron impurities, known as P-type silicon, lacks electrons, and that results in a positive charge. Boron has fewer bound electrons than silicon and leaves holes in the silicon's electron structure. The holes behave like a positively charged particle. So when silicon is mixed with phosphorus or boron, the silicon can be made into either an insulator or a conductor. This property makes it an ideal material for transistors and other electronic components.

Manufacturing Semiconductors

The creation of a microprocessor starts with a seed crystal slowly dipped into a molten silicon bath. As the seed crystal is slowly extracted, it grows into an ingot of pure silicon. After it is removed, it is ground into a perfect cylinder and the ends are cut off. A very thin wafer is sliced from the cylinder and polished. By exposure of the wafer to extreme heat and gases, a contaminant-free layer of silicon dioxide is grown to approximately 3 percent of the wafer's original thickness. Next, the wafer is coated with a photoresistant chemical (which is resistant to ultraviolet light) and allowed to dry.

For each circuit layer of the microprocessor, a mask with the circuit patterns is placed over the wafer, and exposed to ultraviolet light. This process is repeated until each layer of the circuit pattern is added. The microprocessor then undergoes a series of steps that expose the silicon in some places and protect it in others. Next, the microprocessor is exposed to gases and temperatures that change the semiconductor properties of the chip into conductors and insulators, thereby creating the transistors and other electronic functions of the microprocessor. The last step in this part of the process adds conduits to the components on the processor, and the conduits are connected with aluminum "wires."

In the final stage of manufacturing, the processor package is placed in its mounting. Each of its pins is connected to a corresponding pin on the package frame using either a thin gold wire or an aluminum wire. Finally, the whole package is sealed into a molded plastic compound or in another form of sealed packaging.

Power and Voltage

The amount of power used by the microprocessor is not very large. From the 8086 to about halfway through the life cycle of the 486, Intel processors ran on 5 volts DC. Remember that the microprocessor stores data in bits by switching between high and low voltage states that represent binary 1's and 0's. Switching between these two voltage values, a range of 10 volts total, does take a certain amount of time.

If the voltage range required to change from one value to the other is smaller, it takes less time, and the microprocessor can do more. By decreasing the voltage of the microprocessor from the original 5 volts to as low as 2.2 volts, Intel and the other chip manufacturers were able to increase the speed of the microprocessors. Starting with the 486 processors, Intel lowered its chip voltages to 3 volts. Examples of other manufacturers' processor voltages include 3.3 volts, 2.5 volts, and 2.2 volts. Another benefit of reducing the voltage is that it also reduces the amount of electricity needed (important in portables) and reduces the amount of heat generated by all those transistors.

Cooling

Before the Intel 486, processors were cooled largely by the case fan and what is called *radiant cooling*. Beginning with the 486, processors were cooled with a heat sink or fan (or both) that was attached to the surface of the processor package. This system was designed to draw the heat up and out of the

Figure 2.8   Microprocessor with heat sink and fan.

processor and carry it away on the tines of the heat sink and airflow from the fan (see Figure 2.8).

The Pentium processor is designed to operate at around 185 degrees Fahrenheit (85 degrees Celsius), and the cooling system must keep it at or near this temperature. On the 486, Pentium, and Pentium Pro processors, heat sinks and fans are either clipped to the processor or attached with a dielectric gel, also called thermal grease, or both. Later Pentium models, including the Slot 1 Celeron, the Pentium II, and the Pentium III, use a SECC (single edge contact cartridge) type of packaging that includes mounting points for fans and heat sinks as part of the design.

Often, the processor is not the only high-heat device inside the computer case. Other high-performance devices, such as accelerated video cards and high-speed hard drives, can also cause the inside of a computer case to become an inferno. Computer case designs should provide for enough ventilation to allow cool air to be drawn in and hot air to be expelled. Otherwise, the life of the system, including each of its parts, will be dramatically shortened.

Packaging

What users usually see as the microprocessor is actually its *packaging*. The outer covering of the processor protects its core, and it both connects and distributes the processor's pin grid array (PGA) to the mounting socket (or the slot edge connectors). Older processor packaging was often made of ceramic, which has excellent heat resistance and dissipation properties. However, most of today's processors are now mounted in plastic-encased SECC cards that feature built-in heat sink and fan mounts, are easily upgraded, and allow the motherboard high-speed access to the CPU (see Figure 2.9).

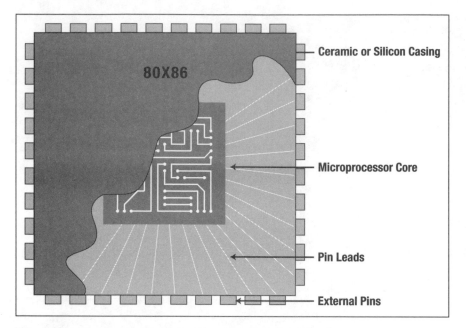

Figure 2.9   A cross-section of a microprocessor's packaging.

Sockets and Slots

Motherboards have two types of receptacles into which modern microprocessors can be inserted: sockets and slots. Which one is used by the processor manufacturer is largely a matter of preference. The functional differences are minimal. Both socket types ease upgrades (a popular feature with manufacturers because it increases sales of newer processors) and eliminate the stress in the delicate circuitry caused by heat-soldering during manufacturing.

Socket Types

Here are the most commonly used socket types:

- *Socket 0*—A 168-pin inline-layout processor connector for 5v 486DX processors.

- *Socket 1*—A 169-pin inline-layout processor connector for 5v 486DX and 486SX processors (see Figure 2.10).

- *Socket 2*—A 238-pin inline-layout processor connector for 5v 486DX, 486SX, and 486DX2 processors (see Figure 2.11).

- *Socket 3*—A 237-pin inline-layout processor connector supporting 3v and 5v 486DX, 486SX, 486DX2, and 486DX4 processors (see Figure 2.12).

Figure 2.10   Socket 1 processor connector.

Figure 2.11   Socket 2 processor connector.

- *Socket 4*—A 273-pin inline-layout processor connector supporting 5v Pentium 60 and Pentium 66 processors.
- *Socket 5*—A 320-pin staggered-layout connector supporting early 3v Pentium processors.
- *Socket 6*—A 235-pin inline-layout processor connector for 3v 486DX4 processors (see Figure 2.13).
- *Socket 7*—A 321-pin staggered-format socket created to support later Pentium processors. It uses a common interface between the L2-cache bus and the main system bus. This common interface typically limits the bus's clock speed. AMD K6, Cyrix 6x86, and IDT processors also use this socket format. This design also provides for a voltage regulator module to allow different voltage levels to be implemented by the socket.
- *Super 7 Sockets*—An extension of the Socket 7 design to support 100MHz bus speeds on AMD K6-2 and K6-3 processors, allowing them to see an almost 50 percent increase in bandwidth and get around the limitations of the Socket 7.
- *Socket 8*—A 386-pin staggered ZIF (zero insertion force) socket format for the Pentium Pro processor.

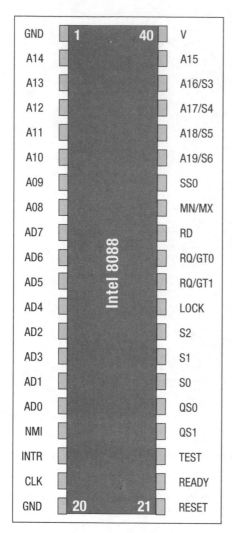

Figure 2.12   Socket 3 processor connector.

- *Socket 370*—The original Celeron main board connection. This supports the early Celerons in the plastic pin grid assembly (PPGA) format.

Slot Types

Here is a list of the slot types used to mount processors to motherboards:

- *Slot 1 (SC-242 connector)*—A proprietary Intel connector supporting Celeron SEPP, Pentium II SECC, Pentium II SECC2, and Pentium III processors. It has a 242-pin edge interface and allows higher bandwidth than the original socket designs.

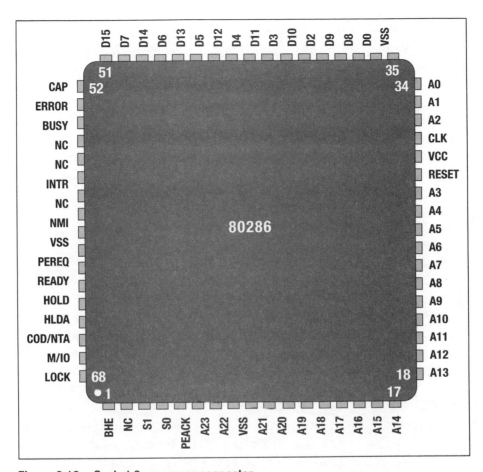

Figure 2.13   Socket 6 processor connector.

- *Slot 2 (SC-330 connector)*—Another Intel processor bus connector style for the high-performance Pentium II Xeon and Pentium III Xeon chips. These processors are designed for symmetric multiprocessing (multiple processors working together), and this slot style enhances this interaction.

- *Slot A*—Used by the AMD Athlon processors. It is physically the same as a Slot 1 connector but has incompatible pin outs.

- *Slot M*—Connectors are planned for the upcoming 64-bit Intel Itanium processor.

CPU Operations

There are three types of CPU operations:

- Data transfer
- Arithmetic logic
- Control

Data Transfer Operations

This type of CPU operation consists of instructions that direct the CPU to move data from one location to another. The CPU can move data in a variety of lengths, including bytes, words, *dwords* (double, or 32-bit, words), or *blocks* (larger groups of bits). The data is moved from *registers* (CPU data-holding spaces) to memory, from memory to registers, from registers to registers, and from memory to memory. However, in many systems, memory-to-memory commands are executed from DMA (direct memory access) chips to unload this type of action from the CPU. The way that its internal registers are laid out is one of the defining characteristics of an individual CPU line.

Arithmetic Logic Unit

The brain of a microprocessor is its *arithmetic logic unit (ALU)*. This is where data is used to develop a value or a comparative result. Operands are loaded into specific registers, and then an instruction is executed that places a result in another register, which is often referred to as an *accumulator*. This is one of the most complex portions of the microprocessor. The ALU's logic gates, which consist of small networks of transistors, perform all data transformations and combinations requested by an executing instruction. More-recent processors include integrated integer and floating point math coprocessors in their ALUs.

Control Unit

If the ALU is the CPU's brain, the *control unit* is its heart. It is in this portion of the processor that commands—such as tracking program counters, organizing return locations for subroutine calls, and performing logic jumps—are executed. The control unit also dynamically maps the virtual memory system to control program segments moving in or out of memory or the hard disk. This part of the CPU is where most of the speed increases are being made through smarter pre-execution and caching of potentially needed instructions. The control unit is also where power management functions and processor mode changes are performed.

Microprocessors

Intel is by far the leading manufacturer of the microprocessors used in PCs. Although it has competition, from companies such as AMD, VIA Cyrix, and a few others, Intel has consistently set the standard by which all processors are measured.

Intel 8086 and 8088

The Intel 8086, which was introduced in June 1978, had a clock speed of 5MHz. It was capable of running 0.33 MIPS (million instructions per second) and had 29,000 transistors. The 8086 was a 16-bit processor (meaning its data bus was 16-bits wide) with an address bus of 20 bits. It could also address 1MB of memory, which was a huge amount at the time. Although the 8086 was not used in very many PCs, it established the basis for all Intel 8086 processors that followed.

A year later, Intel released the 8088, which was an 8086 with its data bus reduced to 8 bits and its 20-bit address bus left intact. Lowering the data bus's size reduced the system's cost, and that allowed the 8088 to support more generally available chipsets. Most of the other features of the 8086 remained, including the transistor count and the CPU's clock speed, still at 0.33 MIPS. The 8088 was the micropro-cessor IBM chose to use for its first personal computer, the IBM PC-XT.

As illustrated in Figure 2.14, the 8088 (and 8086) was packaged in a 40-pin dual inline package (DIP) integrated circuit.

The original IBM PC-XT used six chips (chipset) to support the 8088 processor. These chips performed clock pulse generation, bus control, programmable inter-rupt control, parallel peripheral interfacing, direct memory access, programmable interval timing, and intelligent keyboard control. A second version of the 8088 was later released that allowed the processor to run at two clock rates: the regu-lar 4.77MHz and a new Turbo mode that ran 8MHz.

Processor Modes

Before I get any deeper into microprocessors, I'd like to discuss processor modes. All Intel (and Intel-compatible) processors up to the Pentium III were based on the architecture of the 8086 processor. This arrangement has many benefits, the primary one being backward compatibility (to a point) for systems running on this processor family. To maintain this compatibility, each of the new chips must run special modes to emulate an 8086 and all its children.

- *Real mode*—The processor mode that allows the CPU to operate in the limited environment of the 8086.

Figure 2.14   The Intel 8088 microprocessor.

- *Protected mode*—This first appeared in the 80286 and provides a one-way mode switch to gain the new features included on that processor. Later processors included an easier way to switch between modes.

- *Virtual real (or virtual 86) mode*—This first appeared in the 80386 as a way to run multiple coexisting programs, each in its own simulated 8086 environment.

Intel 80286

Although there was an Intel microprocessor generation between the PC-XT and the IBM PC-AT (the Intel 80186), the Intel 80286 (shown in Figure 2.15) was chosen for the PC-AT. The 80286, commonly shortened to 286, was released in February 1982. It had 6MHz clock speed, included 134,000 transistors, and, at 0.9 MIPS, was three times more powerful than the 8086. The address bus was expanded from 20 to 24 bits—which meant that it was able to access 16MB of memory—and the data bus was restored to 16 bits. Later versions of the 80286 operated at 10MHz and 12MHz.

The IBM PC-AT was released with a four-piece chipset, which included and expanded on the features of the original XT chipset. This chipset featured the appearance of two linked (cascaded) interrupt controllers that provided for 15 interrupts compared with the PC-XT's 8 interrupts.

The 80286 came in three 68-pin package styles: the ceramic leadless chip carrier (CLCC), shown in Figure 2.15; the plastic leaded chip carrier (PLCC); and the PGA. Although the overall shape and size of these chips was different, their pin outs and functions remained the same.

Intel 80386, 80386DX, and 80386SX

In 1985, Intel released the 16MHz 80386—commonly called the 386—microprocessor, which was a full 32-bit processor packaged in a 132-pin PGA package.

Figure 2.15   The Intel 80286 microprocessor.

The 386 had 275,000 transistors and supported between 5 and 6 MIPS. It used a 32-bit mode to communicate with memory but supported a 16-bit I/O channel so that it would remain backward compatible with 286 systems. The 386 was able to move data in bytes, 16-bit words, or 32-bit double words (dwords).

The 80386 provided improved virtual memory capabilities that allowed large amounts of memory to be temporarily stored on the hard disk. It also featured instruction pipelining, wherein the instructions that follow the one currently being executed are pre-evaluated in the microprocessor, resulting in faster processing speeds. The Intel 386 had clock speeds ranging from 16MHz to 33MHz, but other manufacturers, specifically AMD and Cyrix, offered fully functional versions with speeds up to 40MHz. During its life cycle, the 386 was released in 20MHz, 25MHz, and 33MHz configurations.

The 386DX

The 386DX chip was the first of the 386 processors introduced by Intel. It is a full 32-bit processor with 32-bit internal registers and both a 32-bit internal data bus and a 32-bit external data bus. The 386 processor contains 275,000 transistors in what is called a VLSI (very large scale integration) circuit. It is also power–efficient, using only 400 milliamps (less than the 8086 used) because it is made of CMOS (complementary metal-oxide semiconductor) materials.

The 386DX can address 4 gigabits of physical memory. Its built-in virtual memory manager enables software designed to take advantage of enormous amounts of memory to act as though a system has 64 terabytes of memory (a *terabyte* is actually 1,099,511,627,776 bytes of memory).

The 386SX

In 1988, Intel released the 386SX, which was a low-cost version of the 386DX chip. The SX is a 16/32-bit hybrid processor that is packaged in a surface-mount 100-pin plastic quad flat pack (QFP). The primary difference between the 386SX and the 386DX is that the SX model has only a 16-bit external data bus and a 24-bit address bus, something that makes it compatible with the 286 processor. Essentially, the 386SX performs like the 386DX but costs only a bit more than a 286.

The 386SL

In 1990, Intel released the 386SL, a 20MHz processor. The 386SL is similar in design to the 386SX but is specifically designed for use in portable computers with additional power management functions.

Intel 80486DX And SX

In early 1989, Intel released the 25MHz 486DX microprocessor, which broke and surpassed the one million-transistor barrier by more than 20 percent and was able to generate 20 MIPS. A number of innovations were included in this processor, 8K of processor cache (L1 cache), the introduction of burst mode memory access, and an integrated math coprocessor. Until this point, processors required a separate math processor if the user wished to accelerate arithmetic functions. The 486 was packaged in a 168-pin ceramic pin grid assembly (CPGA) package and required an external fan to cool the large amounts of heat it generated.

In 1991, an SX model of the 486 was released to provide a lower-cost processor. The SX model had all the features of the DX model except that it had no math coprocessor. Many 486SX motherboards remedied this deficiency by including a slot where an 80487SX math coprocessor could be added.

Intel 80486DX2

In 1992, Intel introduced the 80486DX2. The "2" referred to a new technology that doubled the processor's clock speed while the bus speed remained the same, resulting in a processor that ran twice as fast as previous 486 models. The DX2 was released in a 50MHz model (having twice the 25MHz bus speed), available in either a 3v or a 5v configuration, and a 66MHz model (33MHz bus times 2), which was available in only a 5v configuration. The technology that runs a processor faster than its bus speeds is called *overclocking*.

Intel 80486DX4

Overclocking technology was also applied to the 486DX4 processors to triple the internal CPU speed. The DX4 processor was available with 75MHz (25MHz times 3) and 100MHz (approximately 33MHz times 3) clock speeds and included a 16-kilobit Level 1 cache.

AMD 5x86

Advanced Micro Devices (AMD), an Intel competitor, released the 75MHz 5x86 microprocessor. It was compatible with 486 motherboards and was competitive with the early Pentium processors.

Cyrix 5x86

Also known as the M1SE, the Cyrix 5x86 is comparable to and socket-compatible with the Intel 80486. Like the AMD 5x86, the Cyrix 5x86 was intended to compete with early Pentium processors.

The Pentium

By 1992, Intel had discovered that it could not trademark a model number, so it chose to use a trademark name for its next processor. Instead of the 80586, the newest Intel processor became the Pentium (the prefix *penta-* meaning five).

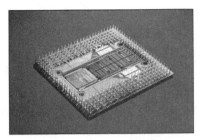

Figure 2.16   A Pentium microprocessor.

The Pentium processor, shown in Figure 2.16, had many new features, including two 8-bit caches (one for data and one for instructions) and a floating point unit (FPU) that operated as much as five times faster than that of the 486. The Pentium used a data bus of 64 bits but kept the 486's 32-bit address bus. It also featured a new superscalar architecture that could execute multiple instructions simultaneously. *Pipelining*, which attempts to sequence the multiple parts of an instruction for faster execution, had been introduced with the 386, but the Pentium took it one step further with dual pipelining. This new technology could execute all the parts of an instruction in a single cycle. Pentium processor speeds ranged from the original Pentium 60MHz to the Pentium 200MHz.

MMX Technology

The Pentium microprocessor with MMX (Multimedia Extensions), shown in Figure 2.17, had clock speeds that ranged from 166MHz to 233MHz. MMX represents the instruction set that allows the FPU to perform the same operation on several pieces of data simultaneously using what is called SIMD (single instruction multiple data). The MMX instructions, which use matrix math (another meaning for MMX), provide added support for compression and decompression algorithms (such as JPEG, GIF, and MPEG) and 3D graphics rendering.

Figure 2.17   A Pentium processor with MMX.

Cyrix 6x86 Processors

Cyrix (now VIA Cyrix) produced a line of Pentium workalikes that ranged from its original 6x86-P120 to the 6x86-P200. Because the 6x86-P series had reported heat problems and some alleged incompatibility issues, Cyrix also produced a low-power version called the 6x86L that also operated at a lower temperature. The assumption is that the *L* stood for "low-temperature," but many observers contend it stood for "later."

Cyrix also produced a Socket 7-style processor that required a special motherboard. This processor, called the MediaGX, included an onboard sound processor and graphics adapter. The MediaGX was designed for low-end computers, but its poor graphics quality was largely responsible for its short life.

Other Pentium Clones

The K5 line of processors was AMD's attempt to compete directly with the Pentium. The K5 suffered from a lack of speed caused by its complexity. The K5 processors were available in versions with 75MHz to 166MHz.

The Integrated Device Technology (IDT) Centaur WinChip C6 (also known as the Evergreen Technologies 200 MxPro) includes MMX extensions, has a large L1 cache, and is less expensive than the Intel 200MHz Pentium MMX. The WinChip C6, which was more popular outside the United States, was available in 180MHz to 240MHz versions. Of the MMX clones, the WinChip C6 delivers almost identical performance to that of the Intel Pentium with MMX.

Intel Pentium Pro

The Pentium Pro, shown in Figure 2.18, was developed primarily to be the processor in a network server. It was designed to be used in configurations of one, two, or four processors on specially designed motherboards. The Pentium Pro featured 1 megabit of advanced second-level (Level 2) cache that ran at the processor's core clock speed. The 200MHz Pentium Pro was also designed to support 32-bit operating systems, such as Windows NT and Windows 95.

Figure 2.18   The Intel Pentium Pro microprocessor.

The Pentium II

The Pentium II, shown in Figure 2.19, is the Pentium Pro with the MMX instruction set added. When it was released, there was a great to-do over a floating point math bug in the chip, which Intel fixed promptly. The PII is available in versions with clock speeds of 233MHz, 266MHz, and 300MHz. It is especially well suited for multimedia reproduction that includes full-motion video and 3D images. Although it has twice the L1 cache of the Pentium Pro at 32K, it has only half of its predecessor's L2 cache at 512K.

Celeron

Intel's Celeron microprocessor, shown in Figure 2.20, is intended to be the low-cost version of the Pentium II models for use in desktop and mobile computers. It uses two mounting styles: the Pentium II's Slot 1 and a socket style named after the number of pins in use. Socket 370 is shown in Figure 2.18. The Celeron has been released in versions with clock speeds in the range of 333MHz to 500MHz. The newer Celerons, those with clock speeds of 566MHz or faster, will be built on the Pentium III core.

Figure 2.19   The Intel Pentium II microprocessor in the Slot 1 package.

Figure 2.20   The Intel Celeron microprocessor in the Socket 370 configuration.

Xeon

Intel's Xeon processor, shown in Figure 2.21, began as a regular Pentium II, the successor to the Pentium Pro, as a server microprocessor. The Xeon has a range of L2 cache size choices, including 512K, 1MB, and 2MB, all of which run at the processor's core clock speed. The Xeon cache is Intel's proprietary 512K CSRAM (custom static RAM) chips, which are used like building blocks to build up the cache size. The Xeon can address and cache as much as 64GB of memory using a 36-bit memory address bus. The PII Xeon can support four or even eight CPUs in one server.

AMD K6

The AMD K6, developed to compete with the Pentium MMX, was actually able to outperform it in speed and price. It was available in 166MHz, 200MHz, 233MHz, and 266MHz versions, as well as a 300MHz model that used the Super 7 socket style to achieve 100MHz bus speeds.

Cyrix 6x86MX

Also known as the MII, the Cyrix 6x86MX processor contained the MMX instruction set. To make its processors comparable to Intel's, Cyrix (and later AMD) began using a PR (processor rating) designation for equivalent clock speeds. A PR-166 rating indicated that a processor had a speed equivalent to 166MHz. The Cyrix 6x86 processors had PR speeds ranging from PR-166 (on a Socket 7 mounting) to PR-366 (on a Super 7 motherboard). Cyrix, which is now owned by VIA Technologies, now offers the 6x86 in a PR-433 version.

VIA Cyrix III

The VIA Cyrix III microprocessor, shown in Figure 2.22, runs at clock speeds of 433, 466, 500, and 533MHz. It has enhanced performance features, such as a 100/133MHz

Figure 2.21   The Intel Pentium II Xeon processor.

Figure 2.22   The VIA Cyrix III microprocessor.

front side bus and 128K full-speed L1 cache. It also supports two versions of multimedia extensions: Intel's MMX and AMD's 3DNow. This processor competes with the Intel Pentium II Celeron processors.

AMD K6-2 and K6-III Processors

The AMD K6-2 processor, shown in Figure 2.23, has an added set of 3D graphics instructions called 3DNow, which extends the MMX instructions already included in the K6 design. The K6-2 processors are built primarily for the 100MHz Super 7 socket. K6-2 models are available with clock speeds from 266MHz to 550MHz.

A newer model, the K6-2+, has added 128K of L2 cache as well as new power control features. The K6-III Super 7 processor features 256K of L2 cache and clock speeds from 400MHz to 600MHz. A newer model, K6-III+, includes 1MB of cache and runs at the same clock speeds as the K6-III.

Intel Pentium III

The Pentium III processor has 9.5 million transistors and a 32K L1 cache, and it supports 512K of L2 cache. The Pentium III is available in versions with clock speeds from 450MHz to 1GHz. The Pentium III is packaged in a second-generation single

Figure 2.23   The AMD K6 Processor.

Figure 2.24   The Pentium III processor in the Slot 1 SECC2 package.

edge connector package called SECC2, shown in Figure 2.24, which conducts and removes heat better and fits into the Slot 1 bus.

Most Pentium II motherboards can be upgraded for Pentium IIIs with only a flash BIOS upgrade (see Chapter 4). A newer version of the PIII (see Figure 2.25) will sport 256K L1 cache and a 133MHz bus speed. It will also be packaged in the less expensive Slot 370-like FC-PGA (flip chip pin graphics assembly).

AMD Athlon

The new powerhouse on the block is the 1GHz AMD Athlon, shown in Figure 2.26. This chip boasts 22 million transistors, support for Intel's MMX, an enhanced version of AMD's own 3DNow, and improved FPU functions. It can also simultaneously decode more instructions than the Pentium III. Although it plugs into a Slot 1 connector, AMD's Slot A specification is based on the Alpha EV-6 bus, which runs at speeds of 200MHz to 400MHz. The Athlon processor also features the first

Figure 2.25   The Pentium III in the FC-PGA socket package.

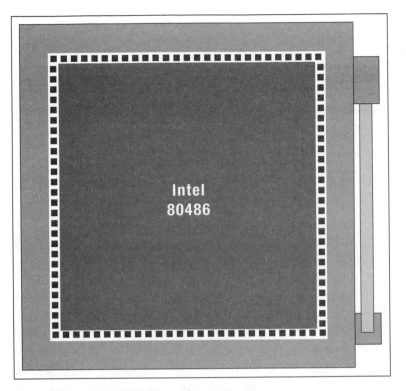

Figure 2.26   The AMD Athlon microprocessor.

fully pipelined, superscalar FPU for x86 platforms as well as 256KB of L2 cache and 128KB of L1 cache on the chip.

AMD Duron

The AMD Duron processor is a derivative of the AMD Athlon processor. It is designed for business and home-user desktop and mobile computing. The Duron processor is available at clock speeds of 600MHz, 650MHz, and 700MHz.

Tools and Diagnostic Processes

Processors go through many revisions *(steppings)* in their lifetimes, usually in response to very small and unpublicized bugs. Recently, Intel has been good about revealing this information (possibly in response to criticism over the original handling of the Pentium FDIV bug), and its Web sites are a tremendous resource for identification of processor stepping and possible bugs. To their credit, some of Intel's competitors have also put together good Web sites in support of their processors and include similar data.

Here are some Web sites you can use for information on microprocessors:

- Intel processors: **www.intel.com**
- AMD processors: **www.amd.com**
- VIA Cyrix processors: **www.cyrix.com**
- Legacy Cyrix processors (supported by National Semiconductor): email to **support@nsc.com**
- General information on processors: **www.geek.com**

Upgrading Processors

The most valuable first step to upgrading a computer's microprocessor is to find the motherboard's documentation to see whether it lists the processors it supports. Many computer manufacturers, such as Gateway (**www.gateway.com**), use off-the-shelf motherboards from major manufacturers and usually offer upgrade information on its Web sites. Before you go online, write down anything on the motherboard that looks like a model number. Additional information can be found at the motherboard manufacturer's site.

Socket Information

Here is a very good Web site for information on sockets and the processors that fit into them: **http://users.pandora.be/romain.wenmaekers/SOCKE.HTM**.

Known Processor Bugs

In this section, I include lists of some things that have been discovered on a few of the more popular processors. Many of them have fixes and have been fixed, but you never know when you might encounter a PC with a legacy processor to which no updates have been applied.

Cyrix Bugs

The Cyrix processors have had a couple of problems in their life cycles. Here are three of the most significant problems they've experienced.

5x86

Problem: The 5x86 processor blacks out or functions erratically after running for longer than 20 minutes.

Solution: This processor experiences serious problems with heat generation and must be well-cooled. Upgraded cooling systems are available to help solve this problem.

6x86

Problem: The 6x86 processor is slow when running Windows NT 4.

Solution: Windows NT 4 includes instructions that switch off part of the system cache to prevent system crashes on the 6x86 (version 2.7). This results in about one-third less processor speed. If you are experiencing this problem, Cyrix has a software patch that turns the cache back on.

Problem: The processor and the system crash for no apparent reason.

Solution: Although nearly every user thinks his or her system has this bug, on the Cyrix 6x86 it is usually a result of the problem relating to system cache discussed in the preceding entry. Switch off the system cache, and then repeat the conditions that caused the system to crash. If that doesn't solve the problem, you'll need to expand your troubleshooting.

Pentium Bugs

The Pentium may have other small bugs, but none received the attention of what was designated as the Pentium FDIV bug (which stands for floating point division).

Problem: If a PC has one of the 60MHz, 66MHz, 75MHz, 90MHz, or 100MHz Pentium processors, it is possible that your processor contains a floating point flaw that affects its ability to accurately calculate some numbers. The best way to check to see whether the computer has this flaw is to use Intel's Processor Frequency IV utility. Any Intel Pentium processor with 120MHz or greater does not have the FDIV flaw.

You can access the Processor Frequency IV utility at **http://support.intel.com/support/processors/tools/frequencyid/**.

Solution: If your PC has this problem, Intel will replace it under its FDIV Pentium Replacement Program. For more information on this program, visit Intel's Web site for details at **http://support.intel.com/support/processors/pentium/fdiv**.

Pentium III Bugs

Problem: In some Pentium III processors, there is a bug that requires a computer to be powered on twice before the system will start.

Solution: This bug shows up on only around 2 percent of the PIII processors. If you have or suspect that you have one of the processors with this error, Intel has issued a recall for them. Details on the recall program are available at **ftp://download.intel.com/design/pentiumiii/specupdt/24445309.pdf**.

Immediate Solutions

Converting Decimal to Binary

To convert the decimal number 222 to binary, you must determine which power-of-2 values can be subtracted from the decimal number, and then place a 1 into the power-of-2 position for that value. Here is how it is done:

1. The largest power of 2 that is not greater than 222 is 128 (the next power-of-2 value is 2^8, or 256). The binary number at this point is 10000000, which now includes a 1 to indicate the inclusion of the value of 2^7, or the decimal value 128.

2. Subtract the value placed into the binary number (128) from the beginning number to find the number remaining to be converted: $222 - 128 = 94$.

3. The largest power of 2 that is not greater than 94 is 64 (see Table 2.1). The binary number now includes a 1 to indicate the inclusion of the 2^6 position (11000000). If you stopped now, your binary number would represent the decimal value of 192. Find the remaining value: $94 - 64 = 30$.

4. The largest binary value not greater than 30 is 16, or 2^4. The binary number is now 11010000, or the equivalent of a decimal 208. This particular number conversion does not use the 2^5 (32) position. Find the remaining value: $30 - 16 = 14$.

5. The largest binary value that is less than or equal to 14 is 8, or 2^3. The binary number at this point is 11011000, which represents the decimal value of 216 ($128 + 64 + 16 + 8$). The remaining value is $14 - 8 = 6$.

6. The largest binary value less than or equal 6 is 4 (2^2). Placing a 1 in the third position of the binary number makes it now 11010100, or the equivalent of 220. The remaining value is 2.

7. To complete the conversion, turn on the binary value for 2 (2^1), which results in the binary number 11011110, which represents the decimal value of 222 ($128 + 64 + 16 + 8 + 4 + 2$).

To store the number 222 in the computer, 8 bits would be used to store the binary number 11011110. Remember that the computer can store only the binary values of 1 and 0. It can't store, work with, manipulate, add, or use any value not expressed as a binary number. There isn't any way to store, for example, a 2, a 4, or a 9 in a single bit.

Upgrading a Pre-Pentium Computer to a Pentium (Style) Processor

If you have a 486-style processor in a PGA, the first step is to determine the type of socket used on your motherboard. Most likely the socket will be a Socket 1 or a Socket 2 or 3. However, before you take any other action, carefully examine the processor and its mounting to be absolutely sure what you have. If there is an unoccupied row of pins around your processor (and the processor is in an upgrade or Overdrive socket, if one exists on your motherboard), then you have a 237- or 238-pin socket (Socket 2 or 3).

At one time Intel produced a Pentium Overdrive processor that was used to upgrade pre-Pentium 25MHz and 50MHz processors to 63MHz, and 33MHz and 66MHz machines to 83MHz. Unfortunately, it has been discontinued. Unless you can find someone who still stocks it (item number BOXPODP5V83), you must use a clone upgrade processor, such as one produced by Evergreen Technologies (**www.evertech.com**).

For a reasonable price you can buy a kit that packages a processor, instructions, processor removal tools, fans, BIOS upgrade utilities, and performance monitoring software. If you are new to processor upgrades, I recommend that you either visit your local computer supply store or contact one online and use an upgrade kit—at least for the first few times you do a processor upgrade.

Using a Kit to Upgrade a 486 (or Older) Processor

To upgrade a processor with an upgrade kit, follow these steps:

1. The kit should include software to check the speed of the processor on a floppy disk or CD-ROM. Run this software to check the speed of the existing processor, and write it down in your notes. It is an especially good idea for you to take notes throughout this process. When in doubt, write it down.

2. If the kit includes a BIOS update, it doesn't necessarily mean you have to apply it. Check the BIOS or motherboard manufacturer's Web site for compatibility information of the new processor with this motherboard and BIOS. If an upgrade is required, verify that the one in the upgrade kit is the correct version. If it is not correct, download the correct version and install it. I hope you have been writing all this down.

3. Upgrade the BIOS if necessary. See Chapter 4 for instructions on how to go about flashing your ROM BIOS. For later reference, write down any ID numbers you see during the POST.

4. Before proceeding, put on an ESD (electrostatic discharge) wrist strap or take other ESD preventive measures. See Chapter 14 for more information on ESD and how to avoid it.

5. Open the system case. Even with a wrist strap on, use caution inside the system unit.

6. If your processor mounting socket is a zero insertion force (ZIF) socket, such as that illustrated in Figure 2.28, unlock the lever and move it up and around to unbind the processor's pins. Grasp the lever next to the socket, and lift it up and back until it is vertical. You may need to pull the lever away from the socket very slightly before lifting it up. This causes the top of the socket to shift and open the socket. On older motherboards, the lever may stick, perhaps requiring a bit more pressure before opening. Never yank or jerk the ZIF lever. If you break it off, you'll most likely need a new motherboard.

   If the mounting is not a ZIF socket, locate the processor removal tool (also called a spoon or a fork), an L-shaped tool that looks something like a small pry bar. Using the processor removal tool, gently pry one side of the processor up about one-quarter inch. Repeat this operation on each of the three other sides until you are able to grasp the edges of the processor with your fingers and lift it out of the socket.

7. Holding the new processor lightly by its edges with your fingertips, align the processor over the socket. Because both the processor and the socket are square, you must orient the processor so that its pins are lined up to fit into the correct holes. The processor will have some distinguishing characteristic to let you know where Pin 1 is (usually the lower-left corner of the processor). Look for one of the following marks on the processor: a dot in one corner, a notch in one corner, or a bit of gold running diagonally from the underside of the chip, or, on the underside of the processor, look for one of the corner pins to be inside a gold square. Typically, the marking you will find is the numeral 1 or a notch in one corner. As illustrated in Figure 2.28, some 486 motherboards have sockets with four rows of pins. These are intended for use by a Pentium Overdrive processor (ODP). A 486 processor has only three rows of pins, so you must use caution when inserting an ODP into a socket that has four rows of holes. Some processors also have specially shaped pins that cannot be inserted into the wrong hole without damaging them.

8. Gently and with even force, press the processor's pins into place. When you first start, recheck to be sure the pins are aligned.

If the socket is a ZIF, you should not need to force the processor into the socket. Remember, ZIF means "zero insertion force," which means that little or no force is needed to seat it in the socket. After it is pressed into place, lock the lever.

If the socket is not a ZIF, you must push the processor into place carefully to avoid damaging the processor. First, set the pins just on the socket's holes. Then apply light pressure with your fingers, moving around the processor's surface and applying firm, even pressure. Don't rush, and don't press too hard. Apply even pressure.

9. Check the motherboard documentation to see whether any voltage or clock speed settings need to be changed. If changes are needed, most likely they are effected through jumpers on the motherboard. Make these adjustments, if any, before the system is powered up.

10. Before closing the system case, boot the system. If the system does not boot, check the POST error codes and make any needed adjustments. It is not uncommon for wires, cables, or connectors to be dislodged during the installation of the processor. If the system boots, so far so good.

11. If the system has booted, test it using the CPU performance software that came with the kit. If the performance is less than you reasonably should expect, check the clock multiplier jumpers on your motherboard (see the motherboard's documentation for their location). Recheck to see whether you should have upgraded the BIOS for the new processor.

12. If all is well, close the system unit. Now is also an excellent time to perform any needed preventive maintenance inside the system unit (see Chapter 20 for information on preventive care of the computer).

Upgrading a Pentium Processor

As with the pre-Pentium upgrades, I recommend using a kit for these upgrades. There are a number of Overdrive Pentium upgrades available for Intel processors. Table 2.2 lists the upgrades you are likely to need.

Table 2.2   Intel Overdrive upgrades.

Original Pentium Speed	Overdrive Pentium Speed
75	150
90, 120, 150	180
100, 133	166 or 200 (Socket 7 only)
166	200

As before (see "Using a Kit to Upgrade a 486 (or Older) Processor" earlier in this chapter), read the motherboard's documentation before proceeding to determine whether jumper or BIOS changes are required before the processor will function.

Upgrading a Pentium Pro Processor to Pentium II

Moving up from the Pentium Pro to the Pentium II is a simple matter of a drop-in upgrade. Because both processors use a ZIF socket, it is as easy as removing the Pentium Pro and installing the Pentium II. There should be no other changes necessary. For more information, visit Intel's Web site (**www.intel.com**) or visit your local computer hardware vendor.

Fixing the PC If It Locks Up After POST

If the PC locks up immediately after completing the POST, try these solutions:

- The processor is likely overheating. The fan attached to the processor may not be operating properly, or the heat sink is not properly attached. Remove and reattach either or both, applying thermal compound (thermal glue) as appropriate.

- If you encounter this problem immediately after a processor upgrade, it could be the result of incorrect voltage settings on the motherboard. Refer to the motherboard's documentation, and correct the voltage settings accordingly.

- The problem could also be the result of an incorrect processor clock multiplier. This should happen only right after the processor has been upgraded. Check the motherboard and processor documentation to determine what the proper setting should be, and adjust it.

Erratically Functioning System

The system functions erratically with several intermittent problems. The assumption is that the processor may be overheating. Try performing the following steps:

1. To verify your suspicions, run the PC for an hour and then open the system case (using ESD protection). Carefully place your fingertip on the processor or its heat sink near where it attaches to the processor. If you cannot

comfortably leave your finger there for more than one or two seconds, the processor is too hot and adjustments are definitely needed.

2. The number-one cause of processor problems is cooling, or the lack thereof. If you suspect that the PC's problems result from insufficient cooling, the first thing you should check is the processor's documentation or the manufacturer's Web site for cooling requirements and information. To operate properly, the newer Pentiums and clones require a constant operating temperature. Be sure you have the correct cooling devices (fans, heat sink, thermal lubricant, etc.) installed for the specific processor installed.

3. Another source of overheating is improper speed and configuration settings. After verifying that the processor is supported by the motherboard, check your motherboard documentation and verify all the jumper settings that affect the processor.

4. Too much voltage can cause the processor to overheat. Check the voltage requirements for the processor, and adjust the system's settings appropriately.

5. Make sure that the processor fan is not blocked by cables or other hardware when the system case is closed. Also look for an object lodged in the processor fan blades. The processor fan could also be worn out and need replacing, or the processor may need a bigger fan. If the machine doesn't have a processor fan, it may be time to install one.

6. Verify that the PC's cooling system, on which the processor's cooling system is indirectly dependent, is doing its job.

Device Lights Come On but PC Does Not Boot

The device lights come on and the fan operates when the power is turned on, but the PC does not boot and no beep codes are sounded. Try the following:

- If this happens immediately after a processor upgrade, it is very likely that the processor is not completely seated in its socket. Using ESD protection, open the system case and verify the installation of the processor.

- If the processor is installed properly, the problem may lie in the processor itself. If you have a spare CPU (of the same type), swap it out and reboot the system. If the system boots, then it is the processor. If it still fails, then the socket may be damaged or the motherboard itself was damaged during the upgrade.

2. Processors

Processor Being Incorrectly Identified During the Boot Process

If the processor is incorrectly identified during the boot process, it may cause a problem. It could be one of the following:

- There may not be a problem at all. Some processors, especially early Pentium and late 486 clones, were identified by some BIOSes as Pentiums.

- It could be that the processor is a clone (AMD, Cyrix, or IDT) that was released after the BIOS version on the PC. See Chapter 4 for information on how to upgrade the BIOS.

Processor Speed Being Listed Incorrectly During Booting

Another problem can occur if the processor speed listed during booting is incorrect. Try the following options:

- The reported speed of the processor is reported from the BIOS or motherboard settings and not from the processor itself. Check the documentation of the motherboard to determine how to properly indicate the processor speed, or upgrade the BIOS.

- If the number you are referring to is the LC readout on the front of a pre-Pentium computer, it too is displaying the speed indicated in the BIOS or set by the clock rate jumper on the motherboard. Check the documentation and adjust accordingly.

ZIF Socket Not Opening

If the ZIF socket does not open, or it does not release the processor's pins so that the processor can be removed, try the following

- This may sound like a no-brainer, but check to see whether anything is blocking the lever or holding it in place.

- Many ZIF sockets require you to pull the socket lever out away from the socket slightly before it can be lifted up to release the processor's pins.

- Never force the lever to the point that you can feel it beginning to bend or break. The lever may just be stuck. Use a gentle rocking motion, applying steadily increasing pressure to release the lever. Don't, at any cost, break off the lever or damage the socket. If you do, you will need a new motherboard and most likely another processor as well.

Chapter 3

Chipsets and Controllers

In Depth

An Introduction to Chipsets

Arguably, the motherboard is by far the most important component in a PC, and what helps to make the motherboard so important is the chipset with its associated controllers. The chipset is a group of devices that provides the PC with much of its functionality, including its ability to take data in, display it, and move it about internally. The *chipset* controls the system buses and facilitates the movement of data and instructions among the central processing unit (CPU), cache memory, and internal and external peripheral devices. The system's chipset also fixes the features of the PC and plays a major role in its speed.

This chapter on chipsets is meant to provide some information and background on this essential component. Except in extremely rare cases, the chipset is not a component that can be removed, replaced, or upgraded without changing the motherboard. However, its functions and services are very important to the efficient operation of the PC. This chapter does not provide much in the way of troubleshooting because, in most cases, the problem lies with an incompatibility of a device driver or perhaps the device itself with the chipset, microprocessor, or motherboard. In case of a problem, the choices are few: Change the device driver, the device, or the motherboard.

A chipset, such as the one shown in Figure 3.1, is a group of functions that may or may not be on separate chips. It provides the software and protocols necessary for the microprocessor and other components of the PC to communicate with and control all of the devices plugged into the motherboard. The instructions on the chipset are not very sophisticated; in fact, they are only at the most rudimentary level. Most of the functions that occur between the chipset and any device are actually performed by the software driver of the device as it reacts to the commands of the chipset.

The chipset controls the flow of bits (data, instructions, and control signals) over the motherboard's buses between the CPU and system memory. This includes data transfers among the CPU, memory, and peripheral devices. The chipset also provides support for the expansion bus, where expansion and adapter cards are placed, and any power management features of the system.

Image courtesy of Intel Corporation.

Figure 3.1   The Intel 820E chipset.

Historically, a chipset consisted of several small, single-purpose controller chips. Each separate controller, which could be made up of one or more chips, managed a single function, such as controlling the cache memory, handling interrupts, or managing the data bus. Present-day chipsets combine the controller functions into one or two larger, multifunction chips, as illustrated in Figure 3.1.

Chipset chips are also referred to as *Application-Specific Integration Circuits*, or *ASICs* (pronounced as "a-six"). However, not all ASICs are chipsets. Some are timers, memory controllers, bus controllers, digital sound processors, and other devices. The term "chipset" is also used by manufacturers of video graphics cards to indicate the function set on a video card, but don't confuse the two—one cannot be substituted for the other (see Chapter 11 for more information on video cards and their "chipsets").

Much of the discussion about chipsets surrounds their support for device controllers and bus and interface structures, but another important characteristic of a chipset is that it dictates the maximum amount of random access memory (RAM), or system memory, a motherboard supports. For modern systems, this can be as low as 64MB or as high as 4GB and higher. There are many different styles and sizes of system memory, and many different technologies in use today. The chipset dictates many of the allowable characteristics of the memory used on a motherboard.

Chipset Groupings

Chipsets are grouped by a number of distinguishing characteristics, such as the socket type of the processor, the generation of the processor, the controllers required, and the number and type of chips in the set. A chipset may actually belong to many of these groupings, based on its characteristics and features. The chipset that is compatible for any given PC fits the characteristics of that system. The following sections describe the major characteristics used to group chipsets.

Socket Types

One characteristic that is commonly used to group chipsets is the socket type that mounts the CPU on the motherboard. For example, Socket 7 chipsets are in one grouping, Socket 8 chipsets in a second grouping, Socket 1 and 370 chipsets in a third, and Slot A chipsets in yet another. Chipsets for Intel processors fit nicely into this grouping scheme, but chipsets from other manufacturers often do not fit this grouping scheme. For example, AMD's K-7 chipsets are typically considered to form their own separate groupings, regardless of their mountings. Chapter 2 has more information on the various processor mountings.

North Bridge and South Bridge

The number of chips in the chipset is another characteristic used to group chipsets. Chipsets can have one, two, or more chips in their sets. The most common grouping is chipsets with two chips. The two-chip chipset contains what is called a *North Bridge* and a *South Bridge*. However, manufacturers such as SiS and VIA produce mostly single chipsets today. Chipsets are known to contain as many as six chips.

The North Bridge chip contains the major bus circuits that provide support and control for main memory, cache memory, and the PCI bus. The North Bridge is typically a single chip (usually the larger of a two or more chipset), but it can also consist of more than one chip. In a chipset, the North Bridge supplies the chipset with its alpha designation and distinction in a family of chipsets. For example, the chip *FW82439HX* is the North Bridge chip of the Intel *430HX* chipset and supplies the "HX" to the chipset name.

The South Bridge includes controllers for peripheral devices and those controllers that are not a part of the PC's basic functions, such as the *enhanced integrated device electronics (EIDE)* controller and the serial port controllers. A chipset family shares the South Bridge among all of its variations and often between manufacturers as well.

Figure 3.2 illustrates the relationship of the North Bridge and the South Bridge chips on a PC.

Processor Generations

A grouping scheme that is no longer used groups chipsets by the processor's generation. The evolution of the PC processor has been tracked by the generation of its technology. The 8088 processor marked the first generation, the 386 is a third-generation processor, the 486 is a fourth-generation processor, and the Pentium is a fifth-generation processor. As long as Intel was the dominant processor manufacturer and the company that decided when a new generation occurred, it was easy to track processor generations. However, AMD and VIA Cyrix processors now have gained a place in the market, and the generation of processors is a bit more fuzzy.

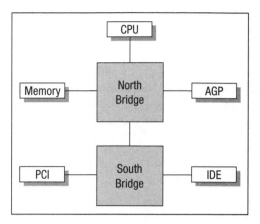

Figure 3.2   The relationship of a chipset's North Bridge and South Bridge.

There are no first- through third-generation chipsets because they didn't show up until the processor's fourth generation. Some legacy chipsets are still grouped by the generation of the processor they support.

Controller Chips

Controller chips control the transfer of data to and from peripheral devices, which interact with the processor and the rest of the PC through the device controllers. Device controllers are typically single chips mounted directly on the motherboard or on adapter cards that are inserted into an expansion slot on the motherboard.

Most motherboard designs include two or more controller chips outside of the chipset. In most cases, the keyboard controller and an input/output (I/O) controller (which is also known as the *Super I/O* controller chip) are mounted directly on the motherboard and supplement the controller set of the chipset. In addition, some video adapters, sound cards, network interface cards (NICs), and small computer system interface (SCSI, pronounced "skuzzy") adapters have their own built-in device controller chips.

Bus Architectures

Because they control the flow of data to and from peripheral devices, device controllers must be matched to the bus architecture of the PC. The PC's bus architecture is made up of wires, connectors, and devices over which data and instructions travel around the PC (see Chapter 10 for more information on the various PC bus architectures). The bus structure, which gets its name from the fact that it resembles the lines on a city bus map, connects device controllers on or connected to the motherboard to the CPU, memory, and I/O ports. Each of the bus architectures supported on a PC has its own bus controller chip function either incorporated into the chipset or mounted separately on the motherboard. Most of the newest motherboard designs include expansion slots for a variety of bus and interface structures, including peripheral component interconnect (PCI), the AT bus, and possibly SCSI.

Although not technically a bus structure, the *accelerated graphics port (AGP)* is listed on most newer motherboard and chipset designs. The AGP interface is a 66MHz interface structure that is typically combined with a 32-bit, 33MHz PCI bus to provide advanced video support and faster data transfers from system memory to video and graphics adapters.

The following sections present overviews of many of the bus and interface structures supported by most of the popular chipsets.

AT Bus

The AT bus is included on most chipsets primarily to provide support for expansion cards, such as network adapters, from older systems. The AT bus runs at 8MHz and uses a 16-bit data path. It is commonly referred to as *Industry Standard Architecture (ISA)*.

The *Extended ISA (EISA)* bus is another AT bus structure supported by many chipsets. EISA bus expansion slots have been included on some motherboards since the time of the 386 processor. EISA is a 32-bit bus, but is also backward compatible to the AT and ISA buses.

Local Bus

Because AT and ISA bus structures cannot keep up with the speeds required for high-resolution graphics and faster processors, many manufacturers now use *local bus* architectures. A local bus device, which provides for very fast data transfers, is local to the processor through its dedicated controller, which bypasses the standard bus controller. PCI, and VESA (Video Electronics Standards Association) local bus, or *VL-bus*, are the most common of the local bus structures. Because Intel promotes PCI, it has become the de facto standard local bus structure for virtually all Pentium class computers.

SCSI Bus

The SCSI bus attaches peripheral devices to a PC through a dedicated controller card that is able to support a chain of devices over a dedicated interface structure that features very fast data transfers. Very few PCs, outside of the Apple Macintosh and some higher-end server-type computers, feature a SCSI interface as a standard. A SCSI host adapter is added to the PC through an expansion slot, typically a PCI slot.

USB and IEEE 1394

The *universal serial bus (USB)* and the IEEE 1394 interfaces (such as Apple's FireWire and Texas Instrument's Lynx) are emerging standards for device connectors and interfaces. USB and 1394 are plug-and-play (PnP) architectures, which allow users to add a wide range of peripheral devices to the PC without the need of an adapter board. These devices have their controllers built in, as do many SCSI devices. USB supports low-speed devices, such as keyboards, mice, scanners, and printers; newer standards also support many higher-speed devices. The 1394 interface is also known as the high-performance serial bus and provides support for devices requiring isochronous (real-time) support.

IrDA and Infrared

The Infrared Data Association (IrDA) has established standards for the use and interaction of infrared light beams as an interface for peripheral devices to a PC. Infrared, or IrDA, connectors are little red plastic windows on a PC or notebook that can be used to connect a keyboard, mouse, and other specially equipped devices.

Keyboard Controller

The keyboard controller controls the transfer of data from the keyboard to the PC. The keyboard controller interacts with the controller located inside the keyboard over a serial link built into the connecting cable and connector. When data comes to the keyboard controller from the keyboard, the keyboard controller checks the parity of the data, places the data in a buffer, and then notifies the processor that keyboard data is in the buffer. A separate keyboard controller is common on most older PCs. On newer PCs, this function is either included in the chipset or in the Super I/O chip, which is discussed in the next section.

The functions performed by the keyboard controller, or its equivalent, are:

- *Keyboard control and translation*—When a key is pressed on the keyboard, a scan code is sent from the controller inside the keyboard to the PC's keyboard controller, which then signals the processor through IRQ1 (interrupt request 1). The keyboard controller then translates the scan code into the character it represents and places it on the bus to move it to the appropriate location in memory.

- *Support for the PS/2 mouse*—On those systems that have an integrated PS/2 connector on the motherboard, the keyboard controller supports its functions. This port is most commonly used to connect a PS/2-style mouse.

- *Access to the HMA*—Although the support for the high memory area (HMA) of system memory (RAM) is now incorporated into the system chipset on most newer PCs, access to this part of memory is controlled through the keyboard controller. See Chapter 7 for more information on the high memory area.

Super I/O Controller

The Super I/O controller chip incorporates many of the controller functions previously performed by many separate chips. Combining these functions onto a single super chip not only provides an economy of scale for similar activities, but also minimizes the space required on the motherboard, which is very valuable real estate, as well as the cost of the chips used to support these activities.

The Super I/O chip is "super" because it combines many controller chips into a superset that controls the standard input/output peripheral devices and ports found on virtually every system. These controller functions can be combined because they control very mature, standardized devices that are virtually the same on every PC. Combining them allows the motherboard and the system chipset to concentrate on other high-priority and unique functions.

The Super I/O chip combines many of the functions that were provided on older PCs through adapter cards for example, for serial ports, parallel ports, and the hard disk drive. Putting these functions on a single chip frees up at least one expansion slot as well.

The major functions of the Super I/O controller chip are:

- *Serial ports*—The *universal asynchronous receiver/transmitter (UART)* is used to drive the serial ports, and the control functions of data transfer are included in the Super I/O chip.

- *Parallel ports*—The functions that drive the parallel ports, including the various parallel port standards, such as the enhanced parallel port (EPP) and enhanced capabilities port (ECP), are included in the Super I/O controller.

- *Floppy disk drives*—Support for the floppy disk drive and floppy-disk-type tape drives are included on the Super I/O chip.

- *Miscellaneous functions*—Newer versions of the Super I/O controller may also incorporate the keyboard controller's functions, the real-time clock (RTC), and perhaps the integrated drive electronics (IDE) hard disk controller, although this is more commonly found in the system chipset.

Other Device Controllers

Every device on the PC that needs to interact with the data bus or the processor must have a device controller. Peripheral devices generally have their controller chips either on an adapter card (expansion card) or built into their electronics. On older, pre-Pentium PCs, each device had its own adapter or shared a controller card. For example, the floppy disk and hard disk drives commonly shared an I/O controller card.

Each device controller must be matched to the bus interface with which it is to interact. An IDE disk drive requires an IDE (ATA) controller, and a SCSI controller is needed to connect a device with a SCSI interface.

The peripheral devices that are installed inside the system case are interfaced to an IDE controller on the motherboard that is supported by either the PC's main chipset or the Super I/O controller. It is very common for the *floppy disk controller (FDC)* and the *hard disk controller (HDC)* to be on the motherboard and, provided they are not SCSI devices, any tape drives, CD-ROM (compact disk-read only memory), or DVD (digital versatile disk) devices added to the system will share these controllers.

Chipsets and Their Functions

The microprocessor is always faster than the PC's peripheral devices with which it must communicate. Because of this fact, designers have been forced to develop interfaces to serve as buffers between peripheral devices and the faster CPU. These buffers match up the speeds of the peripherals to the CPU and smooth out the timing of the PC's operations.

The very first PCs had an individual chip to control each of the various operations, including:

- *Math coprocessor interface*—Controls the flow of data between the processor and math coprocessor.

- *Clock generator*—Controls the timing of the PC's operations.

- *Bus controller chip*—Controls the flow of data on the motherboard's buses.

- *Direct memory access (DMA) controller*—Controls the processes that allowed peripheral devices to interact with memory without involving the processor.

- *Programmable peripheral interface (PPI)*—Supervises some of the simpler peripheral devices.

- *Floppy disk controller*—Controls the PC's diskette and tape drives.

- *CRT (cathode ray tube) controller*—Facilitates the PC's display.

- *UART*—Sends and receives synchronous serial data.

These functions are explained more fully in the section, "Built-in Controllers."

Any component that attaches to a PC's motherboard depends on the system chipset to interact with the other components of the PC. The chipset is designed specifically to support a particular CPU and, in some cases, a specific motherboard design. The chipset's design and function are tied closely to the design of the CPU, motherboard, basic input/output system (BIOS), memory, and the devices it supports. A PC's memory, CPU, and hard disk can all be upgraded with not much trouble, but changing the chipset requires a motherboard change. The chipset is integral to the functions of the motherboard.

The chipset dictates many of a PC's characteristics, including its memory type, L2 cache type and size, CPU, data bus speed, and whether the PC can support two or more processors. The interfaces supported on a PC, such as IDE, AGP, USB, or IrDA, their features, and configurations are determined by the motherboard's chipset.

In terms of the sheer number of chipsets it produces and that are in use, Intel is the largest chipset manufacturer. The original Intel chipset was developed to promote the PCI bus on Pentium motherboards. There are other chipset manufacturers, but Intel, because it makes the Pentium-brand microprocessor, is typically the chipset used by motherboard manufacturers of Pentium-compatible motherboards.

Chipset Characteristics

Chipsets are created from the combination of a number of *very large scale integration (VLSI)* chips that could each easily be standalone chips. By integrating these chips into a single chip, the controllers and devices in the chipset can share common actions and commands, reduce the physical space required on the motherboard, and reduce the overall cost of the system.

The characteristics of a chipset can be grouped into six categories: host, memory, interfaces, arbitration, South Bridge support, and power management. These characteristics define and differentiate one chipset from another, and are included in the specifications for most chipsets. The characteristics defined in each of these categories are:

- *Host*—Defines the host processor to which the chipset is matched along with its bus voltage, usually *GTL+ (Gunning Transceiver Logic Plus)* or *AGTL+ (Advanced Gunning Transceiver Logic Plus)*, and the number of processors the chipset will support.

- *Memory*—Defines the characteristics of the dynamic RAM (DRAM) support included in the chipset, including the DRAM refresh technique supported; the amount of memory supported (usually in megabits); the type of memory supported; and whether memory interleave, error correcting code (ECC), or parity is supported.

- *Interfaces*—Defines the type of PCI interface implemented and whether the chipset is AGP-compliant, supports integrated graphics, pipelining, or side band addressing (SBA).

- *Arbitration*—Defines the method used by the chipset to arbitrate between different bus speeds and interfaces. The two most common arbitration methods are *multitransaction timer (MTT)* and *dynamic intelligent arbiter (DIA)*.

- *South Bridge support*—All Intel chipsets and most of the chipsets for all other manufacturers are two-processor sets. In these sets, the North Bridge is the main chip and handles CPU and memory interfaces, among other tasks, whereas the South Bridge (or the second chip) handles such things as the USB and IDE interfaces, real-time clock, and support for serial and parallel ports.

- *Power management*—All Intel chipsets support both the *system management mode (SMM)* and *Advanced Configuration and Power Interface (ACPI)* power management standards.

To view the information that is included for a given chipset, visit Intel's chipset website at **www.intel.com/design/chipsets/index.htm** for several examples.

Built-In Controllers

The devices and controllers supported on a chipset are those common to the type of processor, motherboard, and PC that the chipset is designed to support. A few of the controllers and devices typically included in a chipset are:

- *Memory controller*—This is a logic circuit that controls the reading and writing of data to and from system memory (RAM). Other devices on the PC that need to access memory must interface with the memory controller. This feature usually also includes error handling to provide for parity checking and ECC for every memory word.

- *EIDE controller*—Nearly all mid- to upper-range motherboards now include at least one EIDE connector for hard disks, floppy disks, CD-ROMs, DVDs, or other types of internal storage drives. The EIDE controller typically supports devices with ISA, ATA, and perhaps an ATA-33 or ultra-DMA (UDMA) interface.

3. Chipsets and Controllers

- *PCI bridge*—Like a network bridge that connects two dissimilar networks, this device logically connects the PCI expansion bus on the motherboard to the processor and other non-PCI devices.

- *Real-time clock*—The RTC holds the date and time on the PC, which is displayed on the monitor and is used to date stamp file activities. This should not be confused with the system clock, which provides the timing signal for the processor and other devices.

- *DMA controllers*—This controller manages the seven DMA channels available for use by ISA/ATA devices on most PCs. DMA channels are used by certain devices, such as floppy disk drives, sound cards, SCSI adapters, and some network adapters, to move data into memory without the assistance of the CPU.

- *IrDA controller*—The IrDA is the international organization that has created the standards for short-range line-of-sight, point-to-point infrared devices, such as a keyboard, mouse, and network adapters. The IrDA port is the small red window on the front or side of notebooks and some desktop computers.

- *Keyboard controller*—This controller is the interface between the keyboard and the processor. A chipset may include the keyboard controller; many of the newer ones do. See the section "Keyboard Controller" for more information on this device.

- *PS/2 mouse controller*—When IBM introduced the PS/2 system, the controller for the mouse was included in the keyboard controller. This design has persisted, and usually wherever the keyboard controller is, so is the PS/2 mouse controller. This device provides the interface between the PS/2 mouse and the processor.

- *Secondary (L2) cache controller*—Located on the motherboard, a daughterboard, or, as on the Pentium Pro, in the processor package, this controller caches the primary memory (RAM), the hard disk, and the CD-ROM drives. The secondary cache controller controls the movement of data to and from the L2 cache and the processor.

- *CMOS (complementary metal-oxide semiconductor) static RAM (SRAM)*—The PC's configuration settings are stored in what is called the CMOS memory. The chipset contains the controller used to access and modify this special SRAM area.

A Look at Intel Chipsets

Intel invented the chipset and has dominated the market since the days of the 486 processor. About the only time a competitor gains ground in the chipset market is when Intel decides to abandon a particular product. The reason Intel dominates the market is simple—chipsets support processors and motherboards, and Intel dominates the processor market. Intel intimately knows its processors, so it is very easy for Intel to design chipsets that support its processors.

The following is a review of the major chipsets and chipset families that Intel has produced over the years.

486 Chipsets

There were several styles of 486 systems. As a result, there were many different 486 chipsets. The two most common 486 chipsets (fourth-generation chipsets) were:

- *420EX (Aries)*—Supported motherboards that combined the PCI and VL (VESA Local) buses.

- *420TX (Saturn)*—80486 chipset family that supported systems through the 486 DX4 and most of the 486 overdrive processors adding power management support. The 420TX chipset was released in three revision levels, numbered 1, 2, and 4, which was known as the Saturn II chipset.

Chipsets for the Pentium and Beyond

Pentium (fifth-generation) chipsets were more closely in tune with the design of the processor than were the 486 chipsets. Along with the Pentium processor, Intel developed the PCI bus and a chipset to support it. This chipset, which was exactly matched to the Pentium processor, became known as a *PCIset*.

The Intel chipsets are designated in numbered family series: the 420 for 486 chipsets, the 430 for Pentium chipsets, the 440 series for Pentium II chipsets, and the 450 series for Pentium Pro chipsets (along with the 440FX). The newer 460 and 800 series chipsets just being announced are designed to support the IA-64 (Intel Architecture–64 bits) processors, such as the Itanium, now emerging.

Some of the more common Intel Pentium and later chipsets are:

- *430LX (Mercury)*—The first Pentium chipset developed to support the 60MHz and 66MHz, 5V (volt) processors. This chipset supported the PCI bus and up to 128MB of RAM.

- *430NX (Neptune)*—Chipset developed to support Intel's second generation of Pentium chips. It supported Pentium processors running at 90MHz to 133MHz, and offered dual processors, 512MB of RAM and 512KB of L2 cache.

- *430FX (Triton I)*—The first of the Triton chipsets. It featured support for extended data out (EDO) RAM, pipelined burst and synchronous cache, plug–and-play, and PCI level 2.0. However, it supported only 128MB of RAM and did not support dual processors.

- *430MX (Mobile Triton)*—A special chipset version designed for laptop, notebook, and other portable PCs.

- *430HX (Triton II)*—Chipset designed for business- and enterprise-level servers, supported 512MB of EDO RAM and concurrent PCI buses.

- *430VX (Triton III)*—The last of the Tritons, developed for the home PC market. It featured support for USB, synchronous dynamic RAM (SDRAM), and PCI interfaces.

- *430TX*—Chipset that was adaptable for both desktop and mobile use and provided PCI, USB, DMA, and other interfaces.

- *440LX*—AGPset that features support for AGP interfaces. Was designed for the Pentium II. Supports the LS-120 "superdisk," Ultra DMA, AGP, USB, SDRAM, ECC RAM, and the PC97 power management specification. Figure 3.3 shows Intel's marketing image for this chipset.

- *440LXR*—A low-end version of the 440LX chipset.

- *440BX*—Another Pentium II chipset that supports 100MHz bus, dual processors, IEEE 1394, and up to 1GB of RAM.

- *440GX*—AGPset designed for midrange workstations. Supports dual CPUs and up to 2GB of SDRAM, along with dual AGP interfaces. The 440GX AGPset is shown in Figure 3.4.

Figure 3.3   The Intel 440LX AGPset and the Pentium II processor.

Image courtesy of Intel Corporation.

Figure 3.4   The Intel 440GX AGPset.

- *440FX (Natoma)*—Supports the Pentium II and the Pentium Pro processors with USB, EDO RAM, ECC memory, dual processors, and PCI.

- *450GX (Orion server)*—The 450GX chipset and the 450KX share the same basic design, with the GX version designed for use with the Pentium Pro processor with support for up to four processors, 8GB of RAM, but only fast page mode (FPM) memory.

- *450KX (Orion workstation)*—The KX version of the 450 chipset, designed to support workstations with dual processors and 1GB of RAM.

- *450NX*—Designed to provide high-powered support for Xeon workstations and servers with up to four CPUs, 2MB of L2 cache, 8GB of EDO memory, and two 32-bit or one 64-bit PCI interface. Figure 3.5 shows the chips that make up this chipset.

- *460GX (Merced)*—Designed for very high-end servers and workstations. Supports up to four CPUs and other high-performance features. Is projected for use with the new high-powered Itanium processor.

Image courtesy of Intel Corporation.

Figure 3.5   The Intel 450NX chipset.

- *810*—Designed for value-priced PCs. Includes support for integrated AGP 3D graphics, MPEG-2, 100MHz system bus, 2 USB ports, and 266Mbps (megabyte per second) data bus speed between system memory and peripheral devices.

- *810e*—Based on the 440BX chipset. Is an extended version of the 810 chipset (thus, 810*e*). Intended for home market and office PCs. Includes support for the same features as the 810 chipset, with added support for 133MHz system bus and the ATA-66 interface. Figure 3.6 shows the 810e chipset.

- *820*—Another extension of the 810 chipset. Designed to support high-end desktops and workstations.

Non-Intel Chipsets

Besides Intel, Acer Labs (ALI), VIA Technologies, and Silicon Integrated Systems (SiS) manufacture Pentium-class chipsets. The chipsets of each of these manufacturers are covered in the sections that follow.

Acer Laboratories, Inc.

ALI manufactures chipsets for its Acer Open motherboards. The Aladdin III and Aladdin IV chipsets are comparable to the Intel 430VX and 430TX chipsets. The Aladdin V, which is also known as the M1541 chipset, provides support for up to 100MHz CPU bus speeds, and includes a high-performance RAM controller, a 64-bit ECC/parity memory bus interface, an AGP interface, and device controllers for IDE, USB, and PS/2, as well as a Super I/O controller.

Silicon Integrated Systems

SiS manufactures a single-chip chipset that combines the North Bridge and South Bridge into a single chip. SiS chipsets are available for nearly all processor mountings since the Socket 7 and feature a shared memory architecture and a Unified Memory Architecture (UMA) type of video adapter.

Figure 3.6   The Intel 810e chipset.

Figure 3.7   The SiS 730S single-chip chipset.

Popular SiS chipsets are:

- *730S*—Single-chip chipset designed to support the AMD Athlon Slot A/Socket A processor. The SiS 730S is shown in Figure 3.7.

- *630/630E/630S*—Single-chip chipsets designed for Slot 1 and Socket 370 processors. They feature an advanced 2D/3D GUI engine and a Super-South Bridge package.

- *600/620*—Two-chip chipset that integrates a high-performance host bus interface, a DRAM controller, an IDE controller, a PCI interface, a 2D/3D graphics accelerator, and a video playback accelerator for Slot 1 and Socket 370 processor-based systems.

- *540*—Single-chip chipset designed for the AMD K6 processor mounted in a Super Socket 7 socket. It features support for highly integrated PCI devices.

VIA Technologies, Inc.

VIA Technologies is the third-largest chipset manufacturer, after Intel and SiS. VIA produces chipsets to support processors with Slot 1, Socket 7, and Socket 370 legacy systems. However, their more recent chipsets concentrate on the Cyrix and AMD processors. VIA also manufactures the Cyrix processor.

VIA chipsets include (among others):

- *Apollo KX133/KT133*—Single-chip chipsets designed to provide support to the AMD Duron, Thunderbird, and Athlon processors. They feature an AGP4X graphics bus, up to 2GB of RAM, a 200MHz processor bus, and an ATA-66 IDE hard disk interface. The KX133 is shown in Figure 3.8.

Figure 3.8   The VIA Apollo KX133 chipset.

- *Apollo PM601*—Single-chip chipset that supports the Intel Pentium III processor and the Cyrix III processor. It features advanced graphics, a scalable processor bus, a full set of integrated controllers, and several other advanced features. The PM601 chipset is shown in Figure 3.9.

- *Apollo MVP3*—A Super Socket 7 chipset that supports the AMD K-6 and Cyrix MII processors. It has speeds up to 533MHz and a flexible processor bus that scales from 66 to 100MHz, advanced AGP graphics, power management, and other integrated features. The MVP3 is a high-performance, energy-efficient chipset that supports AGP, PCI, and ISA buses on desktop and notebook PCs. It features support for EIDE, USB, and Keyboard/PS2-Mouse interfaces, a 64-bit CPU and system memory bus, 32-bit PCI and AGP interfaces, and both 3.3V and sub-3.3V power.

- *Apollo MVP4*—Another Super Socket 7 chipset that combines the Apollo MVP3 chipset with a high-end Trident Blade3D graphics engine for value PCs, Internet appliances, and notebook PCs. The MVP4 is shown in Figure 3.10.

- *Pro Savage PM133*—A two-chip chipset that supports Intel Pentium III and Celeron processors as well as the VIA Cyrix processor. Features high-performance graphics support, an integrated 10/100 Ethernet adapter, audio support, a built-in modem, Super I/O controller, flat panel monitor support, advanced power management, and support for 4 USB ports.

Figure 3.9   The VIA Apollo PM601 chipset.

Image courtesy of VIA Technologies, Inc.

Figure 3.10   The VIA Apollo MVP4 chipset.

New Developments

It is very daring to even attempt to include here what are considered to be new developments, but there are some things on the horizon that will be embedded into the technology in the not-too-distant future.

Intel has developed a new bus architecture, which it calls *Intel Hub Architecture (IHA)*, that improves the interface between the elements of the chipset. Before this, chipsets used the PCI bus as the interface between the North Bridge (host, memory, and AGP) and the South Bridge (PCI and IDE controllers). IHA attempts to solve the problems caused by the South Bridge being both a PCI device and the PCI controller, which results in loss of efficiency (and one PCI slot). IHA dedicates a high-speed data bus between the North Bridge and South Bridge, which is redesignated as the memory controller hub (MCH) and the I/O controller hub (ICH), which is not a PCI device, freeing up a PCI slot. The dedicated link allows the two hubs to transfer data much faster. VIA has developed a similar improvement that it calls V-Link, which is an interface bus to replace the PCI link between the North Bridge and South Bridge of its chipsets.

Acer Labs and VIA have announced chipset designs that support both double data rate (DDR) DRAM and single data rate (SDR) memory architectures. These two memory technologies have not been supported together in the past. In spite of the fact that DDR has a relatively small market share at present, experts expect DDR to grow to about half of the motherboard market in the next five years. In fact, VIA has committed to using only DDR in its new chipsets.

Tools and Diagnostics

Because it is matched to the motherboard and processors, a chipset is very difficult to diagnose as the source of a performance problem. Instead, another chip, adapter card, device, or function will have a conflict with the chipset and create a functional problem. Chipset manufacturers publish the software diagnostics tools that do exist primarily for software developers working at the chipset level.

However, some good diagnostic packages are available that test the functions of the motherboard, including its buses, controllers, and interfaces, all of which are controlled by the chipset. A chipset issue may be the cause of a faulty or badly functioning PCI bus.

Among the software tools available to isolate problems are:

- *PC-Check*—Performs an extensive array of advanced diagnostics that allow pinpointing the source of both fixed and intermittent faults in all major hardware components. From EuroSoft-USA (**www.eurosoft-usa.com**).

- *PC Clinic*—A family of menu-driven programs that combine systems information, diagnostics, utilities, and benchmark tests. From Data Depot (**www.datadepo.com/clinic.htm**).

- *Micro-Scope, Version 8*—Package used by many technical schools to teach diagnostics on the motherboard. Features tests for virtually all buses, interfaces, and processors. From Micro 2000 (**www.micro2000.com**).

- *Check-It Utilities*—Package that performs a fast and thorough evaluation of a PC's configuration and performance. From Smith Micro Software (**www.smithmicro.com**).

- *PC Doctor*—A set of diagnostic and system information tools with over 250 test functions that provide a specific diagnostic for each part of the system's core technologies. From Watergate Software (**www.pc-doctor.com**).

- *PC Pitstop*—Web site that features a series of diagnostics and tests that can be used to check out a PC's configuration or to track down a particular problem. The Web site is **www.pcpitstop.com**.

Immediate Solutions

Identifying a PC's Chipset (without Opening the System Case)

To identify the chipset on a particular PC, assuming it is a Windows PC, use the following steps:

1. Access the Windows Control Panel and double-click the System icon. The System Properties window, as shown in Figure 3.11, will open.

2. Choose the Device Manager tab.

3. Expand the System Devices selection. The display in the window should be as shown in Figure 3.12. Scan down the list. If your PC has an Intel processor, then there will be at least two entries beginning with "Intel 82xxx" or the like, as shown in Figure 3.13. These chips should be the Processor to PCI and PCI to ISA bridge controllers, and are the chips in your chipset.

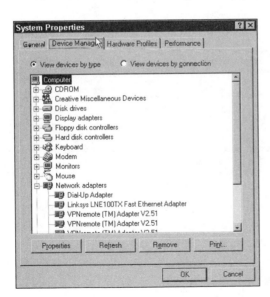

Figure 3.11   The System Properties window for a Windows system showing the Device Manager information.

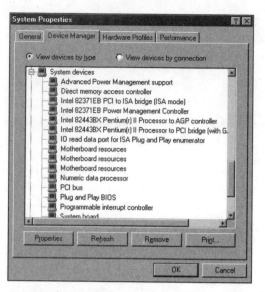

Figure 3.12   The System Properties window showing the System Devices information.

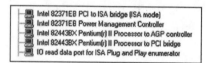

Figure 3.13   The chipset entries in the System Properties window.

Related solution:	Found on page:
Troubleshooting Guide for the Motherboard	15

Identifying a PC's Chipset (by Opening the System Case)

Another way to find out the chipset in use on a PC is to open the system case and locate the large square chips, which are larger than everything else on the motherboard, except the processor, of course. Remember that a chipset can have as few as one chip or as many as four separate chips.

Limiting Memory as a Workaround for Cache Limitation Problems

The 430TX (Triton III) and the 430VX are common chipsets in Pentium-class PCs. Like just about every chipset, these two had their problems. The TX and VX chipsets come from the time when 64MB was considered a lot of RAM. These chipsets are designed to cache only the first 64MB of RAM in L2 cache. More RAM can be added above 64MB, but it will not be cached and may cut the PC's performance in half. So, unless you really need the additional RAM, you may be better off not to add it. It may be time to upgrade the PC or the motherboard and processor.

Other Intel Pentium-class chipsets also have memory caching limits. The Triton I FX chipset is also limited to caching the first 64MB of RAM. The Mercury LX chipset is a little better in that it will cache 128MB of memory.

Unfortunately, the chipset is part of the system board and cannot be replaced. Performance problems may be the result of more than 64MB on the PC. Windows 98 and Windows 2000 ME provide the ability to limit the amount of RAM the system sees. Follow these steps:

1. Open the Run box from the Start menu and enter "MSCONFIG". The System Configuration Utility window, shown in Figure 3.14, will open.

2. Click on the Advanced button in the lower-right corner to display the window shown in Figure 3.15.

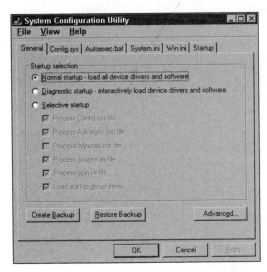

Figure 3.14   The System Configuration Utility (MSCONFIG).

Figure 3.15   The Advanced Troubleshooting Settings of the System Configuration Utility.

3. Find the entry for "Limit memory to" and set the scroll box value to 64MB.

4. The MSCONFIG utility is not available on Windows versions before Windows 98, but the entry "MaxPhysPage=04000" can be inserted in the SYSTEM.INI file of a Windows 95 system after the "[386enh]" (386 enhanced) title.

Identifying Potential Problems with a Chipset

Once you have identified the chipset on a PC, the very best way to learn about problems with a chipset is to visit the manufacturer's Web site. Finding if there are known problems with a chipset may save a lot of diagnostic trouble.

The Web sites of the major chipset manufacturers are:

- Intel Corporation—**www.intel.com**
- Silicon Integrated Systems Corp (SiS)—**www.sis.com.tw**
- VIA Technologies—**www.via.com.tw**

For a complete list of chipset manufacturers, not all of whom manufacture PC chipsets, visit **www.matrix-bios.nl/cmanad.html**.

Chapter 4

BIOS and Boot Operations

In Depth

Background on BIOS

Way back before computers got their first operating systems, programmers had to write their own routines to get input in and output out. Each programmer had to include a routine in each program to read the input data source (usually punched cards) and to control the creation of output media (usually the printer). Eventually, some ingenious person put two and two together—given that almost every program wants to handle some kind of input to and output from the peripheral devices attached to the computer, wouldn't it be an excellent idea to standardize these functions and include them in the system software? In that way, efficient and error-free input and output functions would be available to every program, eliminating at least one area of programming problems.

In the present-day computer, this concept has advanced to the point that the computer has a built-in specialized set of instructions to tell it exactly which internal and peripheral devices are attached to it so that it can look for the input and output device drivers it needs to perform I/O (input/output) tasks. These special instructions form what is known as the computer's basic input/output system or, as it is more commonly known, its BIOS.

BIOS Backgrounder

The BIOS performs three primary functions, all of them vital to the usefulness and function of the computer:

- Boots the computer.
- Verifies the information provided to it about which internal and peripheral devices are supposed to be connected to the computer.
- Serves as the interface between the hardware (attached devices) and the software (operating system, drivers, and applications).

Part of the BIOS is the set of instructions that are used to start the computer and get its operating system loaded into memory and running. The process of starting the computer is called *booting,* or the *boot sequence. Boot* refers to the phrase "pulling yourself up by your own bootstraps," or being able to start by itself. When the computer boots up, the BIOS is behind the scenes taking care of all the details of the boot sequence.

Although it may seem obvious, no computer can do anything at all without software. The computer's hardware is incapable of independent actions and must be given instructions before it will do anything at all. As I'm sure you are aware, what we call "software" is really only a block of instructions that guide the hardware to perform a specific activity.

The BIOS supplies your hardware with its first set of instructions when it is powered up. It is the instructions provided by the BIOS that your computer executes during its power-on or boot-up sequence until the computer is able to fetch and execute instructions on its own.

BIOS Chips

The programs and information that form the BIOS are permanently loaded to an integrated circuit (IC), or chip, during manufacturing. This prevents tampering or changing of the BIOS data and routines. The following sections give an overview of the various types of chips used to store the BIOS on a computer.

Read-Only Memory (ROM)

As its name implies, a ROM chip is a type of memory chip that cannot be altered; it can only be read. ROM is nonvolatile, which means that its contents are safely held even after a power source is removed. This makes it the ideal place to store system startup instructions. Typically, the BIOS is stored on a ROM chip, and that is why you often hear the BIOS referred to as the ROM BIOS. Figure 4.1 shows a ROM BIOS chip.

Programmable Read-Only Memory (PROM)

A PROM is essentially a blank ROM chip that must be programmed with the data you want it to store. Using a ROM *burner*, or ROM programmer, you can load the chip with any data you desire. The ROM burner programs the PROM by inducing a high voltage (12 volts as compared with the 5 volts used for normal PROM operation). The higher voltage burns the memory location, turning the preexisting binary 1 into a 0. This process is irreversible, so what you burn is what you get (WYBIWYG). You can't turn a 0 back into a 1. For this reason, you may hear PROM memory referred to as OTP memory, or one-time programmable memory.

Figure 4.1   A ROM chip on a computer motherboard.

Erasable Programmable Read-Only Memory (EPROM)

An EPROM (pronounced "e-prom") is a variation of the original PROM with an added feature: the data can be erased, and the chip can be reprogrammed. This means that the chip can be reused instead of being discarded when its contents are no longer valid. The EPROM chip looks identical to the PROM chip with the exception of a quartz crystal window on the top of the chip. The window allows ultraviolet rays to access the chip's circuitry. The UV light causes a chemical reaction that erases the EPROM by turning the 0's back into 1's again. To prevent accidental erasure of the EPROM chip, a label tape is usually placed over the quartz crystal window. Figure 4.2 shows the quartz window on an EPROM chip.

Electronically Erasable Programmable Read-Only Memory (EEPROM)

An EEPROM (pronounced "e-e-prom") chip is a popular type of BIOS chip on newer systems. Like an EPROM chip, an EEPROM chip can be reprogrammed. But unlike the EPROM, it does not need to be removed from the motherboard. You can update an EEPROM chip using specialized software usually supplied by the BIOS or chip manufacturer from its Web site. This process is known as *flashing*, and that's why this chip is also commonly called *flash ROM*. Because they are easy to upgrade, EEPROM chips are also used in a variety of other applications, such as cars, modems, cameras, and telephones.

With flashing, you can apply bug fixes or easily add new features that may not have been available at the time your system was manufactured—features such as booting to a CD-ROM drive. Improving the BIOS can also add new routines that improve your system's boot or overall performance.

Complementary Metal-Oxide Semiconductor (CMOS)

CMOS ("see-moss"), which is also known as NVRAM (nonvolatile RAM), is used to store system configuration data. Although CMOS is technically a technology from which memory and IC chips are manufactured, it has become synonymous with the system configuration data.

The CMOS stores the system setup as well as any changes made to the system concerning its hard drive parameters, peripheral settings, or any other BIOS

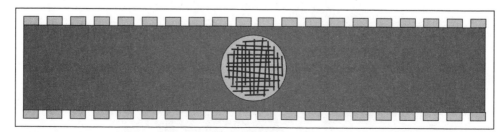

Figure 4.2   An EPROM chip showing its erasing window.

settings. CMOS is also used to store the system clock or RTC (real-time clock) settings. Because it runs on about one-millionth of an amp of electrical current, the CMOS can store configuration data for many years powered only by low-voltage dry cell or lithium batteries.

ROM BIOS

When a PC is powered up, the processor is ready to function, but because its memory is empty, the processor has no instructions to perform. The first instructions needed by the processor are those that direct the computer's startup activities, the BIOS program. Because these instructions must be available to the processor each time it starts, they are stored on a ROM chip located on the motherboard.

From its ROM chip, the BIOS program is loaded into a special reserved area in memory. Normally, this is the upper 64K of the first megabyte of system memory (memory addresses F000h to FFFFh), although some BIOS programs use more than this 64K area. This special reserved area has been established as a uniform standard by processor and BIOS manufacturers, so the processor will always look in the same place in memory to find the start of the BIOS program. The processor gets its first instructions from this location, and the BIOS program begins executing. The BIOS program then begins the system boot sequence.

A PC has several BIOS programs. In addition to the main BIOS program, there are BIOSes to control the peripheral devices added to the computer. Most video cards have their own BIOSes, which contain instructions for displaying video information. Hard disks and many SCSI adapters also have their own BIOS instructions.

In older 16-bit computers, a technique called ROM shadowing is used to speed up the boot process because ROM chips have a very slow access speed (150 nanoseconds). *ROM shadowing* copies the ROM data into RAM (random access memory) and assigns to the RAM the address originally assigned to the ROM. This allows the computer to ignore the ROM and work directly with the much faster RAM. RAM is discussed in detail in Chapter 5.

Newer 32-bit or higher PC systems use 32-bit drivers that are loaded into RAM at startup, bypassing the 16-bit ROM code during system startup, referred to as *"Shadow Ram."*

Hardware Intermediary

The BIOS relieves the computer's operating system and applications from the need to know the exact details about any attached hardware devices. Without the BIOS, each piece of software running on the computer would need to be updated concerning the location of the hardware and drivers on each computer. This information also would need to be updated each time it changed. Because the BIOS manages this information for the computer, only the BIOS data must be updated when new devices are attached. As illustrated in Figure 4.3, the BIOS serves the needs of the processor and the hardware devices as well as those of the software on the computer.

The information on the computer's hardware is stored in the computer's CMOS memory. Originally, CMOS technology was used only for storing the system setup information. Although most circuits on the computer are now made using this technology, the name CMOS usually refers to the storage of the computer's hardware configuration data. When the computer is started, the CMOS data is read and used as a checklist to verify that the devices indicated are in fact present and operating. After the hardware check is completed, the BIOS loads the operating system and passes control of the computer to it. From that point on, the BIOS is available to accept requests from device drivers and application programs for hardware assistance.

BIOS Setup

Virtually all PCs are shipped from the factory with all their peripheral devices already installed and the system configuration and setup information already completed, but it is possible to view and alter this information should it be necessary. BIOS setup and configuration data is accessed through a startup program that is available only for a very short time each time the computer is booted. Typically, you access the system setup program by pressing the Delete or the F1 key immediately after the BIOS program begins its processes.

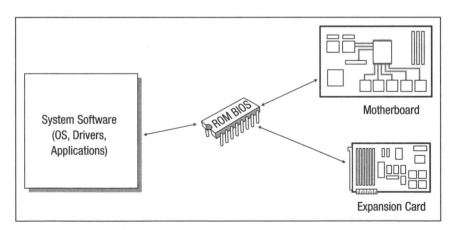

Figure 4.3   The BIOS acts as an intermediary between the parts of the computer.

The BIOS Programs

The BIOS is a collection of software utilities and programs that can be invoked by the operating system or application software to perform a variety of hardware-related tasks. For the sake of improved performance, many operating systems now contain their own device-oriented programs. But the BIOS contains a program for almost every activity associated with accessing hardware, including the basics such as reading and writing to the hard disk and moving data between devices.

BIOS Manufacturers

Three of the larger BIOS manufacturers are Award, AMI (American Megatrends, Inc.), and Phoenix. These manufacturers license their BIOS ROM to motherboard manufacturers, which assume responsibility to support the BIOS. At one time, AMI was the sole provider of BIOS ROM chips to Intel, the market leader in motherboards. However, more than 80 percent of the motherboards on the market are Intel boards with a Phoenix BIOS. Award was bought by Phoenix in 1998, and Phoenix now markets the Award BIOS brand with the Phoenix name.

BIOS Activities

The most important activities performed by the BIOS are to start or boot the computer and to perform the POST (power-on self-test). The next two sections describe the actions that take place during each of these activities.

System Boot Sequence

The steps that are performed by the BIOS in its boot sequence vary slightly from manufacturer to manufacturer, but generally they look like this:

1. When the computer is powered up, the internal power supply initializes. As I discuss in Chapter 14, the PC's power supply does not immediately provide power to the rest of the computer. However, as soon as it determines that it can supply reliable power, it sends out a Power Good signal, which causes the chipset to issue a system reset signal to the processor.

2. The reset signal stimulates the processor to look for the jump address of the BIOS boot program at a hard-wired preset address. The jump address (normally address FFFF0h or the end of the system memory) contains the actual address of the BIOS boot program on the ROM BIOS chip.

3. The BIOS performs the POST process. Should any fatal errors be encountered, the appropriate beep codes are sounded, perhaps an error message is displayed, and the boot process stops.

4. If all is well with the POST (see "The POST Process" later in this section), the startup process continues. The system BIOS looks for the BIOS of the video card and starts it. While this part of the process is happening, you'll see information about the video card displayed on the screen. This typically precedes information about the system BIOS itself.

5. The BIOS routines for any other hardware devices, such as storage devices, are started. Any device BIOS routines found are executed.

6. Information on the system BIOS is displayed. This display usually includes information on the BIOS manufacturer and version.

7. The BIOS begins a series of tests on the system, including the runup of the amount of memory detected on the system. Because the monitor is now available, any errors found at this point are indicated by error messages displayed on the screen, rather than only the earlier beep codes.

8. At this point, the system checks whether all the devices contained in the CMOS configuration data are present and functioning, including determining device speeds, access modes, and other parameters. The serial and parallel ports are also assigned their identities (COM1, COM2, LPT1, and so on). A message is displayed on the screen for each device found, configured, and tested.

9. If the BIOS program supports plug and play (PnP), any PnP devices detected are configured. Although typically the display scrolls by much too fast to read, the BIOS displays a message for each device it finds and configures.

10. If all is well, most BIOS programs display a summary data screen that details the computer as the BIOS sees it. At this point, the system is verified and ready for use. Only one thing is missing.

11. The BIOS looks in the CMOS data to determine which disk drive it should look to first for the operating system. This data is contained in the boot sequence setting of the CMOS data. If the boot device is the hard disk, the BIOS looks for the master boot record; if the boot device is a floppy disk, the BIOS looks at the first sector of the disk for the OS boot program. If the boot program is not found on the first device listed, then the next device is searched, and so on, until the boot program is found. If no boot device is found, the boot sequence stops and an error message ("Operating System Not Found") is displayed.

Cold Boots Vs. Warm Boots

The boot sequence that is used after the computer is powered on from a powered-off state is called a *cold boot* because the computer is being started from a cold (or off) status. In a *warm boot,* the computer is already powered on and is being reset using the **Ctrl+Alt+Del** key combination or something similar. The primary difference is that the POST process is not performed on a warm boot.

The POST Process

After the BIOS is loaded to memory, it immediately begins the POST, which performs a check to see that all the system components and hardware listed in the system setup (CMOS) data are present and functioning properly. The POST is performed before the BIOS begins the startup procedure for the computer.

The POST process is very fast and goes largely unnoticed unless there is a problem. In that case, the POST has no means of notifying you except through the system speaker (which is technically a part of the motherboard) with beep tones. While the POST is running, none of the hardware I/O functions are loaded, so the display or printer is not available to let you know what is going wrong. Depending on the type of error, the POST routine uses a prescribed beep tone pattern to tell you exactly what type of problem it encountered—somewhat like a POST Morse code. The pattern in use (the number of beeps and the length of each beep) depends on the manufacturer of the BIOS. Most POST problems are fatal because the POST is verifying the essential system components.

BIOS Beep Codes

Almost all BIOS programs sound a single beep just before displaying the BIOS startup screen. If the boot sequence continues successfully, the single beep means that there weren't any problems. If the boot sequence stops, you can use the beep code to troubleshoot the hardware problems that caused the boot process to fail. You may need to cold-boot the computer again to decipher the beep code, because often it will catch you by surprise the first time it sounds.

Each BIOS manufacturer has its own collection of POST error beep codes. Four main sets of beep codes are used: IBM standard, AMI, Award, and Phoenix. Each BIOS beep code set uses a different sound pattern to indicate different problems. They involve short beeps, long beeps, and a varying number of beeps in a three- or four-beep series. These beep codes are listed in Tables 4.1 to 4.4.

4. BIOS and Boot Operations

Table 4.1   Standard IBM beep codes.

Beeps	Meaning
No beep	Power supply or system board failure
1 Short	POST is OK
2 Short	POST error with error code display on screen
Repeating short beeps	Power supply or system board failure
1 Long, 1 Short	System board error
1 Long, 2 Short	Video display adapter failure
1 Long, 3 Short	Video display adapter error
3 Long	Keyboard error

Table 4.2   AMI BIOS beep codes.

Beeps	Meaning
1 Short	POST is OK
2 Short	Memory failure
3 Short	Memory/Parity failure
4 Short	System timer failure
5 Short	Motherboard failure
6 Short	Keyboard controller failure
7 Short	CPU failure
8 Short	Video adapter failure
9 Short	ROM BIOS checksum error
10 Short	CMOS read/write error
11 Short	Cache memory error
1 Long, 3 Short	Memory failure
1 Long, 8 Short	Video adapter failure

Table 4.3   Award BIOS beep codes.

Beeps	Meaning
1 Long	Memory error
1 Long, 2 Short	Video error
1 Long, 3 Short	Video failure
Continuous Beeps	Memory or video failure

Table 4.4 Phoenix BIOS beep codes.

Beeps	Meaning
1-1-3	CMOS memory is corrupt
1-1-4	BIOS failure
1-2-1	System timer error
1-2-2	Motherboard error
1-2-3	Motherboard error
1-3-1	Motherboard error
1-4-1	Motherboard error
1-4-2	Memory error
2-x-x	Memory failure (two beeps with any combination of beeps)
3-1-x	Chipset error (three beeps followed by one beep with any combination of beeps)
3-2-4	Keyboard controller error
3-3-4	Video adapter failure
4-2-4	Expansion card failure
4-3-4	Time of day clock failure
4-4-1	Serial port error
4-4-2	Parallel port error
4-4-3	Math coprocessor error

Actually, the codes listed in Table 4.3 are only examples of the Award BIOS codes. Award relies on the motherboard manufacturers to generate the beep codes used with its BIOS and for that reason shares its code with them. To get a list of the beep codes, you must check with the manufacturer of a particular motherboard using Award BIOS.

The Phoenix BIOS POST error beep codes are more complex than the others. When an error happens, three (or four) sets of beeps are sounded, with a slight pause between each set. For example, the beep code that indicates the BIOS is corrupt is 1-1-4, which would sound something like beep, pause, beep, pause, beep, beep, beep, beep.

BIOS Startup Screen

Immediately after the BIOS loads the video BIOS, it displays its startup screen. Although this display varies by manufacturer, it generally contains the following information:

- The name of the BIOS manufacturer and the version number of the BIOS.

- The release date or version date of the BIOS. This is important because it is the key to the features included in the BIOS version.

- The keyboard key used to access the BIOS setup program. Typically, this is the **Del** or a function (**F1** or **F2**) key, but it could also be a key combination, such as **Ctrl+Esc**.

- A logo from one or more of the following: the BIOS manufacturer, the PC manufacturer, or the motherboard manufacturer.

- If the BIOS supports the Energy Star standard, also known as the Green standard, an Energy Star logo is displayed. Virtually all newer computers display this logo. For pre-Pentiums, only those with an upgraded BIOS display it.

- At the end of the display—and, in some cases, at the bottom of the screen— the serial number of the BIOS is displayed. The serial number is specialized to indicate which motherboard, chipset, and BIOS version are in use. It also indicates which combinations of these components are compatible with the BIOS version. The BIOS manufacturer should have information on its Web site on the meaning of the serial number. Some of them—for example, AMI— have downloadable utility software to help you decode the serial number. An excellent site to visit for BIOS version and serial number information is *Wim Bervoets's BIOS site* (**www.ping.be/bios/**).

System Configuration Summary

After the BIOS completes its work and just before it starts loading the operating system into memory, it displays a summary of the system configuration. As with everything else, what is displayed depends on the manufacturer and version of the BIOS. Typically, the following information is displayed:

- *Processor*—The type of microprocessor, such as Pentium, Pentium Pro, and so on. Most of the newer BIOSes recognize all Intel processors as well as those from Cyrix and AMD. Some of the older BIOS versions may erroneously indicate processors from other manufacturers as a Pentium, but this is not an operational problem. Those processors that incorporate the SMM power management standard may be indicated as a Pentium-S.

- *Coprocessor*—If a math coprocessor or floating point unit (FPU) is installed on the system, it will be indicated as "Installed." Virtually every processor since the 386DX (except SX models of the 386 and 486 processors) has had an FPU integrated into it and will be indicated as "Integrated."

- *Clock speed*—The clock speed of the processor (in MHz) is displayed. Sometimes this is displayed on the same line as the processor type.

- *Floppy disk drives*—If detected, the size and capacity of each floppy disk are displayed.

- *Hard disk and CD-ROM drives*—If the system includes IDE/ATA disk drives or ATAPI CD-ROM drives, the BIOS displays each of the drive types it detected, including the primary master and slave drives and any secondary slaves and masters. The manufacturer, capacity, and access modes are displayed for each drive detected. At this point in the startup process, the disk drives are designated physically as C: and D: regardless of the logical drive configuration of the disk drive.

- *Memory size*—The amount of memory in base, extended, and cache memory is displayed. The base memory (conventional memory) size will always be 640K. The amount of extended memory on the system minus the amount set aside for the BIOS is displayed. The BIOS does not report the amount of memory reserved for the UMB (upper memory block) that contains the BIOS itself. The cache size is displayed separately.

- *Memory type*—The type and configuration of the physical memory are displayed. This includes the number of memory banks or modules installed and the memory technology in use. For example, the display may indicate that "EDO DRAM at Bank 1" or "FP: 0" was detected.

- *Video type*—Unless your computer is more than 10 years old, the display type will be indicated as "VGA/EGA," which tells you only that the video adapter was detected.

- *Serial ports*—The system resource address of any serial or COM ports detected is displayed. These addresses are usually 3F8h and 2F8h, which are the default I/O port addresses for COM1/COM3 and COM2/COM4, but there may be others.

- *Parallel ports*—The system resource address of any parallel port detected is displayed. There is usually only one parallel port, and its I/O port address is normally 378h, the default address for the LPT1 port, but it may also be 278h or 3BCh.

- *Plug-and-play devices*—If any plug-and-play adapter cards are detected by the BIOS, it may display a description of each.

BIOS Updates and Flash BIOS

It's hard to draw the line between the old BIOS and the new BIOS, but with most older systems, upgrading the BIOS required a physical replacement. You had to physically remove the BIOS ROM chip and replace it with a new ROM chip that contained the newer BIOS version. This process had the potential for introducing new problems into your system, including ESD (electrostatic discharge), bent pins, damage to the motherboard, and more. To avoid this anxiety and any possible problems, most people simply upgraded to a new computer.

4. BIOS and Boot Operations

When the EEPROM began replacing the PROM and EPROM as the BIOS vessel, with it came flash BIOS. Although some motherboard models still require a physical replacement of the BIOS PROM, most of them now support flash BIOS, which can be upgraded using special software.

Dangers of Flashing

When you begin flashing the BIOS ROM, you must complete the process. Otherwise, you will likely end up with a corrupted and unusable BIOS. If for any reason the flashing process is interrupted—for example, if somebody trips over the power cord or there is a power failure—depending on where you are in the flashing process, the probability of a corrupted BIOS chip is high.

Another way to corrupt your flash BIOS is to load the wrong BIOS version onto the chip. The software provided to flash your BIOS may not include any security features to prevent this mistake. The flashing utilities from the larger BIOS companies, such as Award and AMI, do include features that check the version of the flash file against the model of motherboard and alert you to any mismatch.

Should your BIOS become so corrupted that it will not boot, you may be stuck. To flash your BIOS ROM you need to boot the PC, and you can't do that until you repair the BIOS. In spite of the dangers, the whole process of flashing the BIOS usually takes only a few seconds and the risks of catastrophe are very low. But you should take no chances. Avoid flashing your BIOS in an electrical storm, and be sure to use a UPS (uninterruptible power supply) to protect your computer against power surges or brownouts. And don't forget to check twice that you are flashing your BIOS with the current version.

Flashing Security

With the convenience of flash BIOS comes the danger of accidental flashing. There is no harm done if the BIOS is replaced with the same complete version. However, if the flashing operation is interrupted or for some reason an older or incompatible version is inadvertently (or maliciously) loaded, the effect may be the same as no BIOS at all—a system unable to start.

To prevent this, most motherboards include a jumper block that can be set to disallow flash updates. To flash the BIOS ROM, you would need to open the case and reset the flashing security jumper. If you use this feature (and don't then set it open and forget it), there is no way for an accidental flashing to occur. Another excellent reason to use the flashing security jumper is to prevent access from computer viruses that attempt to change flash BIOS code.

The Boot Block

Because there is a risk of corrupting the BIOS in a flashing operation, many newer systems now have a boot block feature. This is similar to the switch in newer cars that will start the car when the battery is dead. The *boot block* is a 4K program that is included as part of the BIOS. This small program allows the system to recover from an incorrect or corrupted BIOS by restoring the BIOS from a special floppy disk or CD-ROM. If the motherboard supports it, you may need to enable this feature through a jumper.

System Configuration Data

The hardware configuration of the computer is stored in the computer's CMOS memory. You manage this data using the BIOS setup program. This section discusses how to access the setup program and explains each of the menu types it displays.

Setup Program

To gain access to the BIOS setup program, you press a designated key, usually displayed during the initial boot process, as shown in Figure 4.4. Table 4.5 shows the keystrokes used to access the setup program for most of the popular BIOSes.

The hardware configuration of a computer is stored in the CMOS memory. Exactly which data is stored depends on the type of computer and the BIOS in use. If you want to see or modify the system setup data—that is, the BIOS or CMOS configuration—you press the key indicated immediately after the POST process has completed (usually **Del** or a function key such as **F1** or **F2**). After you press the indicated key, the BIOS setup program displays its configuration menu.

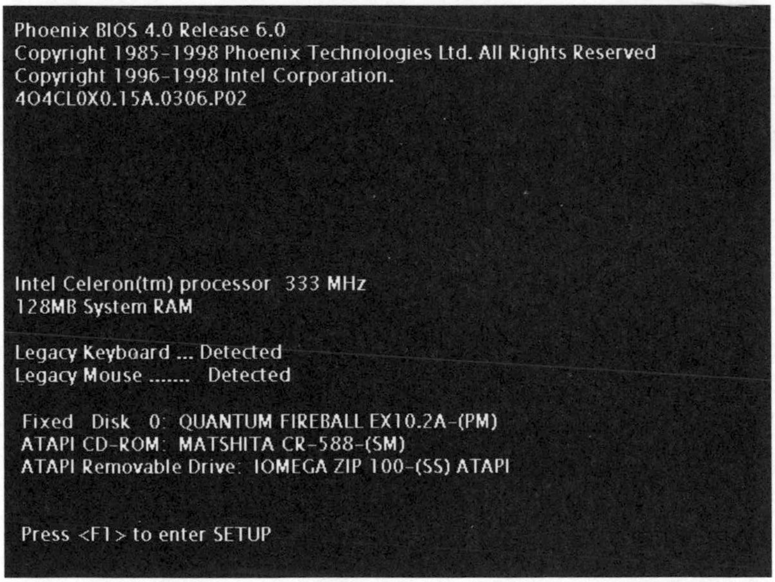

```
Phoenix BIOS 4.0 Release 6.0
Copyright 1985-1998 Phoenix Technologies Ltd. All Rights Reserved
Copyright 1996-1998 Intel Corporation.
4O4CLOX0.15A.0306.P02




Intel Celeron(tm) processor  333 MHz
128MB System RAM

Legacy Keyboard ... Detected
Legacy Mouse .......  Detected

 Fixed  Disk  0:  QUANTUM FIREBALL EX10.2A-(PM)
 ATAPI CD-ROM:  MATSHITA CR-588-(SM)
 ATAPI Removable Drive:  IOMEGA ZIP 100-(SS) ATAPI


 Press <F1> to enter SETUP
```

Figure 4.4   The BIOS diagnostic screen, displaying the key used to access the
startup program.

Table 4.5   BIOS Setup program access keys.

BIOS	Keystroke
AMI BIOS	Delete
Award BIOS	Delete or Ctrl+Alt+Esc
IBM Aptiva	F1
Compaq	F10
Phoenix BIOS	F2

Standard Settings

Most newer computers have two levels of configuration data: the standard configuration and advanced features. The initial menu of a typical BIOS has standard information, including the system clock, hard disk drives, the floppy drive, and the video adapter. The standard menu also lists other computer configuration information, such as the processor type, memory type and speed, and the amount and type of memory.

Advanced Features

The advanced features—which are specific to the motherboard, processor, and chipset—are also accessible through the BIOS setup program. A typical advanced settings menu has the following common options:

- *System BIOS Cacheable*—The system BIOS is cached to memory address F0000–FFFFFh, resulting in faster performance.

- *Video BIOS Cacheable*—The video BIOS is cached to memory address C0000–7FFFh.

- *Video RAM Cacheable*—When this option is enabled, the caching of video RAM to memory address A0000–AFFFFh is allowed.

- *Auto Configuration*—When this option is enabled, the default values of all chipset options are used.

- *DRAM (Dynamic Random Access Memory) Integrity Mode*—If your computer has error correcting code memory, choose ECC. Otherwise, set this option to No.

- *EDO DRAM Speed Selection*—If the system is using EDO DRAM, this option is used to set its access speed. The speed selected must match the actual speed of the system's EDO DRAM.

- *SDRAM CAS (Column Access Strobe) Latency Time*—If the system is using SDRAM (synchronous DRAM), this option sets the number of cycles that elapse between the time that the SDRAM command sample is read and the time that the controller reads sample data from the SDRAM.

- *SDRAM RAS (Row Access Strobe) Precharge Time*—This option sets the number of cycles to be allowed for a charge to accumulate in the RAS before the DRAM refreshes. If this time is too short, it will not allow the DRAM to fully refresh and perhaps it will be unable to store data.

- *SDRAM RAS-to-CAS Delay*—This option is used to control the number of cycles between a Row Activate command and a read/write command.

- *SDRAM Precharge Control*—When this option is enabled, all CPU cycles sent to SDRAM signal an All Banks Precharge command.

- *Memory Hole at 15M-16M*—If this option is enabled, a 1MB block of empty RAM is created between the 15th and 16th MB of system RAM. This is used to allow some older software programs to run on systems that have more than 16MB of RAM.

- *Passive Release*—Allows CPU-to-PCI access.

- *Delayed Transaction*—Enables support for PCI 2.1.

- *AGP Aperture Size*—Sets the size of the AGP aperture port, which is used for graphics memory.

- *CPU Warning Temperature*—Sets the high and low temperatures at which the environmental monitoring system should trigger CPU temperature warnings.

- *Current CPU Temperature*—If the computer has an environmental monitoring system, this option displays the CPU's temperature.

- *Shutdown Temperature*—If enabled, this setting causes the CPU to be shut down when either of the high or low CPU Warning Temperatures is reached.

- *CPU FAN Turn On Speed*—If the computer has an environmental monitoring system, this option displays the speed of as many as three internal fans.

- *IN0-IN6 (V)*—If the computer has an environmental monitoring system, this feature displays the current voltage of as many as seven lines (IN0 through IN7).

Plug and Play

Most new motherboards have options for PnP and PCI, and there may be a special menu for these options in the system setup program. If the BIOS supports plug and play—which depends on the chipset in use—the features and options for it are also found in the advanced settings. In addition, you may need to set the Plug and Play option in the advanced settings to off (No) or on (Yes) to match the capabilities of the operating system. Some operating systems, such as Windows NT and 2000, are not themselves directly compatible with PnP, and this means that the BIOS must deal with any plug-and-play device configurations. Setting the

4. BIOS and Boot Operations

Plug and Play option to Yes causes the system to skip any BIOS-related PnP. This means that the operating system must perform it, and that speeds the boot process. This menu and its options vary according to the motherboard chipset. A few of the more common options on this menu are the following:

- *Used Memory Length*—Defines the size of the memory to be used as high memory.

- *Used Memory Base Address*—Sets a base memory address for use by any peripheral that requires high memory.

- *Assign IRQ for USB*—This option should be disabled if a USB controller is not in use. Otherwise, it should be enabled.

- *PCI IRQ Activated by*—Some devices require that this option be changed to allow for edge-triggered interrupts.

Extended System Configuration Data

If the BIOS supports plug and play, the CMOS is also used to store the *extended system configuration data (ESCD)*, which stores the system resource assignments of plug-and-play devices. ESCD also serves as a communications link between the BIOS and the operating system.

Power Management

The Power Management menu contains the options used to control when the system will automatically power down using power conservation settings. The Advanced Configuration and Power Interface (ACPI), in use since 1998, is the power conservation standard applied to most PCs. The power management settings are configured in the Power Management Settings menu in most modern BIOS setup programs.

Integrated Peripherals

The peripherals controlled through the settings on this menu are integrated into the motherboard. The more common settings on this menu are the following:

- *Base I/O Address*—Sets the system resource I/O address for the serial and parallel ports.

- *Interrupt*—Designates the system resource interrupt for each serial and parallel port.

- *Mode*—Sets the mode for the serial, parallel, and infrared ports on the motherboard.

- *Serial Port A and B*—A setting of Select Auto allows the system to assign the first available COM port. The value Enable sets the COM port designation and I/O address manually. This feature can also be used to disable the port for testing.

- *Parallel Port*—This option works like the serial port setting. The option Select Auto lets the system assign the available LPT port; the option Enable forces you to set the port address manually. The port can also be disabled.

- *Audio*—Enables or disables the audio system built into the motherboard.

- *Legacy USB Support*—Allows you to activate USB devices, such as keyboards or mice, without loading the device drivers.

IDE Device Setup and Auto-Detection

The IDE Configuration menu provides access to the IDE device configuration, including configuration for hard disk drives, CD-ROM drives, tape drives, and so on. Here are many of the features found on this menu:

- *Auto detect*—If you enable this feature, which is not available on all BIOSes, any IDE devices (primary master, primary slave, etc.) on the system will be automatically configured by the BIOS each time the PC is booted.

- *IDE Controller*—Designates which of the IDE controllers are enabled: the primary, the secondary, or both (the default for multiple IDE devices).

- *Hard Disk Predelay*—Normally, this option is disabled, but the user can set disk predelays from 3 to 30 seconds.

IDE Configuration Submenus

The IDE Configuration menu contains submenus for configuring the primary and slave IDE drives. The options found on these submenus are as follows:

- *Type*—This option configures the type of IDE device installed on the system. The choices are Auto (default), ATAPI Removable, Other ATAPI, IDE Removable, CD-ROM, None, and User (user-defined).

- *Maximum Capacity*—The capacity of the hard disk.

- *Multisector Transfers*—Sets the number of sectors per block in data transfers from the hard drive to memory.

- *LBA (Logical Block Addressing) Mode Control*—Enables or disables the use of logical block addressing for hard disk drives larger than 528MB.

- *Transfer Mode*—Specifies the method to be used for moving data from one disk to the next. The choices are Standard, Fast PIO1, PIO2, PIO3, PIO4, FPIO 2/DMA1, and FPIO 4/DMA2.

Security and Passwords

In the Security menu you will find options for both a user password and a supervisor password. With the user password set, the computer will not be allowed to boot until the proper password is entered. The supervisor password is to protect the BIOS settings. Without the supervisor password, a user can't access the BIOS settings, but the system will boot.

4. BIOS and Boot Operations

If you set either or both of these passwords, you must remember the password. If you forget the user password but remember the supervisor password, you can enter the BIOS setup and clear the password by pressing the Enter key when prompted. If you forget both passwords, you will be unable to boot your system without the user password, or get access to the BIOS without the supervisor password. Your only recourse is to open the computer and use the password-clear jumper (see Figure 4.5) located on the motherboard. On most motherboards this password-clear jumper is near either the lithium battery or the BIOS ROM chip. You can also clear the CMOS settings—including all advanced settings you may have changed and the passwords—by removing the CMOS battery (see Figure 4.6). This is one reason that you should keep a written copy of the system setup in a safe place.

Related solution:	Found on page:
Troubleshooting Guide for the Motherboard	15

Figure 4.5   The password-clear jumper on a PC motherboard.

Figure 4.6   The BIOS ROM battery on a PC motherboard.

Tools and Diagnostics

A variety of tools are available for repair and maintenance of computer systems and peripherals. Here is a list of what I think are the electronics tools you need to work on BIOS-related problems:

- *Multimeter and ohmmeter*—A multimeter measures resistance, current, and voltage. An ohmmeter measures electrical resistance. These are essential tools for PC technicians and computer repairpersons. There are a wide variety of inexpensive multimeters, such as the one shown in Figure 4.7, that are useful for in-depth testing and general electronic measurements. An ohmmeter is handy for checking for short circuits or open circuits.

- *BIOS POST cards*—No, these aren't picture cards you mail to a friend saying, "Wish you were here." Recall that in the POST process, the BIOS sounds beep codes and displays error codes. The POST sends these codes as well as an error code stream to a special memory location, usually address 80h. The BIOS POST card (see Figure 4.8) captures and displays the codes sent to this

Figure 4.7   A digital multimeter.

Photo courtesy of Earthweb, Inc.

Figure 4.8   A BIOS POST card displays POST error codes.

address so that you can locate exactly where the system is having problems. This information can be extremely helpful in debugging stubborn systems. The POST card is installed in an ISA slot. When the computer is turned on, the POST card uses the two alphanumeric/hex-type displays to display information concerning POST error codes and the four power supply status indicators. The card is designed to withstand reasonable electrostatic abuse. It is protected against reversal in an ISA bus slot, and it is fused against defective motherboards that could damage it.

- *Test bed*—It is a good idea to have an older system—but not too old a system—to use as a test bed for components. You can use the test bed to test an unknown device with other components that are known to work, something that cuts down on guesswork and saves time. The cost of a simple computer to use for this purpose is minimal when you consider the time you can save.

Hard Tools You Should Have

Here are some hard tools I recommend you definitely have in your toolkit:

- *An ESD wrist strap*—This is more a safety device than a tool. It protects you and the systems and components you're working with from ESD (see Figure 4.9).

- *Needle-nose pliers*—Very useful for grasping small items or removing and replacing jumpers on circuit boards.

- *A small flashlight*—The inside of a computer is dark and has many hiding places for dropped screws and small things you need to see or read, such as "pin 1" on a connector. A flashlight makes it possible to work inside the box.

- *Tweezers*—Tweezers are handy for picking up small items like a lost jumper. An alternative is a part retriever, which looks like a tiny set of retractable claws with a spring-loaded handle.

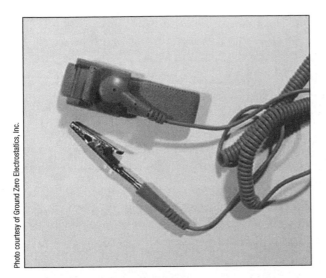

Photo courtesy of Ground Zero Electrostatics, Inc.

Figure 4.9   An ESD wrist strap.

Soft Tools You Should Have

The use of diagnostic software tools can save you a great deal of time. Although they don't necessarily identify what is causing a problem, software tools often provide hints or other information about which components are working and which are not. Some software programs are free, others are included with the operating system, and still others—commercial products—can be very expensive.

Here are a few commonly used software diagnostic tools you may want to consider including in your troubleshooting kit:

- *Power-on self-test (POST)*—In addition to what you've learned about the POST in this chapter, it can also provide you with good information about a PC when you are first starting your diagnostic procedure. Pay close attention to its audio and video messages.

- *Boot disk*—You should always have a boot disk—either a floppy disk or CD-ROM—that you can use to boot the computer in the event of a disk failure. I recommend that you include the MS-DOS commands **FDISK**, **FORMAT**, and **MEM** on this disk along with the operating system.

- *Microsoft Diagnostics*—This software utility, which has been around for a while, is also known as MSD.EXE. It is an MS-DOS utility that takes an inventory of the contents of a PC and displays them in a text-based format. It is a very useful tool for viewing a system's current configuration and system resource assignments. MSD.EXE even displays the BIOS in use and the UART chips the serial ports are using. MSD.EXE is included with later versions of MS-DOS and can be downloaded from the Web.

- *MEM.EXE*—This utility is built into nearly all versions of MS-DOS and Windows. It displays details on the memory configuration and the current contents of memory. A common command line is **MEM /C /P**.

- *The Windows 9x Device Manager*—When you're working with Windows 9x or 2000 systems, this is probably the most useful tool available for identifying system configuration and resource usage information. The Device Manager, shown in Figure 4.10, is accessed through a Windows 9x Control Panel's System icon and the Device Manager tab. On a Windows 2000 system, it is opened from the Control Panel's System icon and the Hardware tab, where you'll find the Device Manager button.

- *Norton System Information*—This program, which is a part of Symantec's Norton Utilities bundle, is very similar to MSD.EXE, but it provides more-detailed information about the components of the PC. It is really only an information utility and not a true diagnostic utility.

- *Norton Diagnostics*—Another utility in the Norton Utilities suite, Norton Diagnostics performs tests on the microprocessor, the motherboard, resource allocations, and RAM to identify any existing problems or conflicts.

- *Microsoft Scandisk and Norton Disk Doctor*—These programs—one an MS-DOS utility and the other a Norton Utilities member—check for hard disk drive problems such as file system corruption and hard disk read errors.

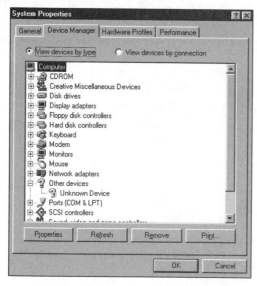

Figure 4.10   The Windows Device Manager.

Immediate Solutions

System Booting from Hard Drive Instead of Floppy Disk

The system should have booted from the floppy disk, but instead it booted from the hard disk drive. The following are some possible solutions:

- Run the BIOS setup program, and check the CMOS settings for the boot drive sequence. If the floppy disk is not shown first on the list, correct the settings and reboot.

- If the boot sequence settings are correct, check to see whether the floppy disk drive is installed in the system configuration data. If it is not in the data, enter its data and reboot.

- If the BIOS data is correct, the floppy disk drive data connector or its power cable may be unplugged or improperly installed. Open the case to check the cables, verifying that the data cable is properly installed with Pin 1 aligned correctly.

"Invalid System Disk" Message

The BIOS diagnostic screen displays the message "invalid system disk" during the boot process. The following are some possible solutions:

- Remove any data or nonboot floppy disks from the floppy disk drive.

- Access the BIOS IDE configuration data, and check whether all hard disks are set to Auto detect or that they have been manually set up and properly installed.

4. BIOS and Boot Operations

111

BIOS Not Detecting the Hard Disk During the POST

The BIOS IDE configuration is set to Auto detect and should automatically be detected when the system boots. The boot process stops at the point at which the disk should be found or displays an error that indicates no disk drive was detected. The following are some possible solutions:

- Make sure that the jumpers on the hard disk drives are set to master (primary) or slave (secondary) appropriately. Figure 4.11 shows where the jumpers are on an IDE disk drive.

- The BIOS settings that enable auto-detection during the boot process may be incorrect. Recheck the IDE Configuration setting to ensure it is set for Auto detect.

- If the IDE Configuration settings are OK, the problem is likely in the hard disk itself, its power connection, or its connection to the hard disk controller card, or the problem may originate in the motherboard. One way to test whether the hard disk controller can detect the hard disk itself is to use the BIOS Auto detect feature. If the disk cannot be auto-detected, troubleshoot the controllers (see Chapter 8).

- The hard disk drive may not be ready at the time the boot process is seeking it. If the disk isn't ready at the instant the BIOS is looking for it, it will appear not to exist to the system. Check the hard disk predelay in the IDE Configuration menu.

- If all else fails, connect a working hard disk drive into the controller to verify that the controller is good.

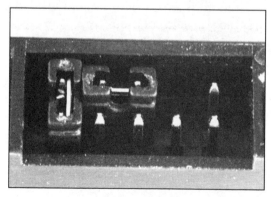

Figure 4.11   The master/slave jumpers on a hard disk drive.

Blank Monitor with Beep Code

A beep code (other than a single short beep) is sounding, and the monitor is blank. The following are some possible solutions:

- As listed in Tables 4.1 through 4.4 earlier in this chapter, beep codes indicate that there is a system problem that is causing the POST process to stop before the video BIOS is available. Beep codes generally indicate that there is a problem with a system component that is required for the POST to continue—a component such as the motherboard, video adapter, chipset, memory, and so on. The display is not functioning, so the only signaling device available is the set of audible tones (beeps) played through the system speaker.

- Check the video adapter card to be sure it is seated in its expansion slot completely and properly.

USB Device Not Functioning

When you plug a USB device into the USB port, the device does not function and cannot be accessed. The following is a possible solution:

- Check the Legacy USB feature in the Peripheral Configurations menu of the BIOS to see whether it is set to Enable. If this feature is set to Disable, USB ports will not function and USB mice and keyboards will not function.

Neither Supervisor nor User Password Allowing PC to Boot

Neither the supervisor nor the user password works to allow the PC to boot or access the BIOS configuration data. The following are possible solutions:

- Reference the documentation for the PC's motherboard to determine the location of the password-clear jumper (see Figure 4.5 earlier in the chapter). After removing the computer case, remove the jumper to clear all the BIOS CMOS settings, including the supervisor and user passwords. Reboot the PC. Then replace the jumper and the computer case.

- Remove the CMOS battery (see Figure 4.6 earlier in the chapter), and replace it after a few seconds. This action resets the BIOS CMOS settings to their default values. Remember that it also resets any values that may have been modified in the BIOS configuration settings. For this reason, it is a good idea to keep a written record of the BIOS settings.

Determining When to Flash the BIOS

How do you know when to flash the BIOS? This is a tough question. Let's look at a step-by-step approach to analyzing your situation. The following are some possible solutions:

Determining If the BIOS Should Be Updated

To find out whether your BIOS should be updated, perform the following steps:

1. Find the version level of the BIOS loaded to BIOS EEPROM.

    The BIOS version is usually displayed during the boot sequence. When it appears on the screen, use the Pause key to stop the boot sequence (this doesn't work on some systems). Record the version information from the screen. To resume the boot, press any key.

    For example, on an ASUS motherboard, here is how the version level is determined: While the memory count is running up, watch for the line #401A0-XXXX (where the XXXX is the BIOS version). This is usually on the third line from the top of the screen. A display of #401A0-0614, for example, would mean that you have a BIOS version level of 0614.

2. When you have the BIOS version, note the model of your motherboard, the computer model number, and the CPU type. Use this information to contact the motherboard manufacturer or visit its Web site to see whether a newer version of the BIOS is available. If several versions are available since your version, you need only update to the latest version. It will incorporate all previous updates.

BIOS upgrades generally contain some or all of the following:

- New BIOS features
- Fixes for bugs and compatibility problems
- Support for additional CPUs

If your PC is working without problems, then don't flash your BIOS! "Fixing" a working system may result in a broken system.

Preparing to Update the BIOS

To prepare for updating your BIOS, perform the following steps:

1. Write down the existing BIOS settings so that you can reenter them after upgrading the BIOS. Any settings that have been altered will be lost as a result of the upgrade.

2. Be absolutely sure that you get the upgrade file from the motherboard manufacturer and not the ROM manufacturer. This shouldn't be a problem because the ROM manufacturer probably won't have BIOS upgrades for you to download anyway. You must contact the motherboard manufacturer to get the update files or download the correct EEPROM BIOS files from its Web site. Usually, these files also include the software used to install the upgrade.

3. Follow the manufacturer's installation instructions specifically. Not every BIOS upgrade is the same, but most of them follow the same general procedures.

Determining Whether You Can Flash the BIOS

Next, you must determine whether or not you can flash the BIOS on your motherboard. To do that, you must determine three things about your system:

- Does your motherboard have a flash BIOS? Most newer motherboards have an EEPROM that can be flashed. The rule of thumb is that if the motherboard has one or more PCI slots, it most likely also has a flash BIOS.

- Does your motherboard version support the new BIOS version? The version of the motherboard is printed close to the motherboard's model number, which is located somewhere near the CPU or the center of the motherboard.

- Does your BIOS EEPROM chip support the new BIOS version? Your motherboard manufacturer should list which chips are compatible with each BIOS version. Also check to see whether the new BIOS version supports plug and play. Otherwise, plug and play will not work.

Getting the Computer to Boot After Flashing the BIOS

After you've flashed the BIOS, the computer will not boot. Now what? First, remain calm. All is not lost. In the download files, some manufacturers include restore utilities and recovering routines. If this is not the case, you can call the vendor or visit its Web site to get instructions on how to obtain a fresh working BIOS. You'll have to pay a charge, plus shipping (more for rush orders). But, after all, this rescue BIOS is a lifesaver.

Chapter 5

Memory

In Depth

Computer Memory

Memory refers to the electronic components of the PC that store data and instructions either temporarily or in various degrees of permanently. Technically, memory is any storage device on the computer, including the hard disk, floppy disks, ROM, RAM, and cache. However, in its more common usage, and in this book, memory is the part of the computer's hardware used to hold data and instructions before and after they are passed to the CPU (central processing unit or microprocessor) for analysis and execution. The scope of the discussion in this chapter focuses on RAM (random access memory) and the various RAM technologies. Another form of memory, ROM (read-only memory) is covered in Chapter 4. Also included in this chapter is a discussion on how the DOS/Windows operating systems allocate and manage memory.

Random Access Memory (RAM)

The term *RAM (random access memory)* has become synonymous with the primary working storage of the PC, which is also known as main memory and primary storage. Virtually every piece of data and every instruction processed or executed by the CPU is stored in RAM at one time or another.

RAM is "random access" because each memory location is individually addressed and can be accessed randomly and directly. The origination of the random access name came from the early mainframe computers to distinguish internal core memories from external memory units, such as a tape drive or another sequentially accessed device, which had to be accessed sequentially start to finish. RAM is organized to support access requests for the contents of randomly placed locations.

RAM Characteristics

The most distinguishing characteristic of RAM is that it is *volatile*, which means that it must have an active power source in order to hold its contents. When the power source is interrupted, all data and instructions stored in RAM are lost.

Units of Measure

RAM is measured in bytes. In what is being called the Communications Age, where speeds and capacities are measured in bits, the capacity of a PC's RAM is stated in bytes—actually megabytes or perhaps gigabytes. Table 5.1 lists the measurement units commonly used with RAM.

To put the units in Table 5.1 into perspective, 1 byte holds a single alphabetic character (for example, "A" or "a"), one KB holds approximately one page of double-spaced text, a megabyte will hold a short novel (without illustrations), and a gigabyte should hold about 1,000 of the short novels (without illustrations), and so on.

Calculating RAM Size

The early PCs, such as the IBM PC XT and PC AT, supported 640KB to 1MB of RAM. It is very common today, that a multimedia computer has a gigabyte of RAM. How much RAM a computer needs has always been a guessing game, with a "more is better" philosophy. How much RAM is right for a particular PC depends on a number of factors, not least of which is how the PC is to be used and what software will be running on it. Kingston Technology, a leading manufacturer of memory, has an online RAM calculator that you can use to determine how much RAM a PC should have at **www.ec.kingston.com/ecom/assessor/ index.htm**.

Access Speed

Memory access time, or *memory speed*, is very important to its ability to operate with the other components on the PC. In the past, RAM speeds were in the range of 80 to 120 ns, but on today's PCs, most memories are 60 ns or faster. RAM speeds must be matched to the speed of the motherboard's bus. Typically, a motherboard's documentation contains information on the RAM speed it requires and supports. Most RAM manufacturer's have guides (some online) to help you match RAM

5. Memory

Table 5.1   RAM units of measure.

Unit	Size	Description
Bit	One binary digit	Binary 0 or 1
Byte	8 bits	One character
Word	16 to 64 bits	Use to store numeric values, including addresses
Kilobyte (KB)	1,024 bytes	Common memory size unit on pre-Pentium PCs
Megabyte (MB)	1,048,576 bytes	Memory size unit on all newer PCs
Gigabyte (GB)	1,073,741,824 bytes	Memory size unit on servers and high-end PCs
Terabyte (TB)	1,099,511,627,776 bytes	Memory size on larger network or content servers
Petabyte (PB)	1,125,899,906,842,624 bytes	The next level of memory sizing to come

Table 5.2   RAM/Bus Speeds.

RAM Speed	Bus Speed
50 ns	20MHz
40 ns	25MHz
30 ns	33MHz
20 ns	50MHz
15 ns	66MHz
10 ns	100MHz
6 ns	133MHz

speeds to bus speeds. Table 5.2 contains a sampling of which RAM speeds match up to clock speeds.

The speed of a system's existing memory may limit its ability to take faster memory. Avoid mixing memory speeds in the same computer, but if you must, follow these precautions:

- *Use identical memory in a bank*—You should only use the same type, speed, and technology of memory in a memory bank.

- *Put the slowest memory in the first bank*—Some BIOS systems have an auto-detection feature that determines the speed of the memory installed in bank 0. For example if 50ns memory is installed in bank 0 and 70ns memory is installed in bank 1, the system will set the memory speed at 50 ns. This will definitely cause problems for the slower memory. Solution: Install the slower memory in bank 0.

Memory Latency and Burst Mode Access

Memory is arranged something like a spreadsheet in rows and columns. When a process requires something to be read from memory, first the row's identity is used, then the starting column ID, and finally, the specific cells to be transferred. The time it takes to find the row, the column, and then the starting cell takes longer for the first cell than the next one, two, or three cells. This additional amount of time is called *memory latency*.

Memory accesses are generally done in sets (bursts) of four data segments, read in series from a starting cell location. The size of the data segment is determined by the width of the memory (see "SIMMs and DIMMs," later in the chapter). This type of memory access is called *burst mode access*. The time it takes to access the first block of memory, which included finding it, is not repeated saving several clock cycles. Burst mode access is generally used in conjunction with Level 2 caching, which is sized to receive as many of these bursts as it can. If the data width of the memory is 32-bits, a 256-bit L2 cache could receive and buffer as many as 2 burst sets from memory.

Burst mode operations are usually stated with a notation (1-2-3-4) that indicates the number of clock cycles used in each of its four data transfers. This notation represents the number of clock cycles required for the first data transfer and each of its three subsequent transfers. For example, 4-1-1-1 indicates that 4 clock cycles are required to transfer the first data segment, but only 1 clock cycle is needed for each of the following three accesses. The whole transfer requires 7 clock cycles. Without burst mode operations, each access would require 4 clock cycles for a total of 16 for the four segments.

RAM Types

There are actually many different RAM types and technologies of RAM in use in PCs. Table 5.3 lists the more common RAM types. These RAM technologies are discussed in the following sections.

DRAM

The most common form of RAM is a technology called *dynamic RAM* or *DRAM* (pronounced as "dee-ram"). DRAM is inexpensive and can store a large number of bits on a single very small chip. Each DRAM storage cell contains a capacitor, which holds one bit of data. A *capacitor* is an electronic component that stores an electric charge. In the DRAM cell, the capacitor holds either a positive or negative voltage value to indicate a 1 or 0 binary value.

DRAM is not without its faults. It must be refreshed every two milliseconds. Whether it needs it or not, the contents of every DRAM cell are read and then rewritten by a special refresh logic circuit, whether the cell is in use or not. DRAM is the slowest type of memory, with clock speeds of around 50 nanoseconds (ns) or higher (remember that higher means slower).

DIP Packaging

DRAM chips are mounted on a PC motherboard as an individual memory chip in a bank of DRAM chips or as a part of an integrated memory module that mounts in a single slot. A single memory chip is packaged in a DIP (dual inline packaging) package, shown in Figure 5.1. Memory chips in this packaging were mounted into

Table 5.3 RAM types.

Type	Description	Usage
DRAM	Dynamic RAM	Desktop PCs
PRAM	Parameter RAM	Stores internal configuration data
PSRAM	Pseudo-Static RAM	Portable PCs
SRAM	Static (flash) RAM	PC Cards (PCMCIA)
VRAM	Video RAM	Video and color graphics support

5. Memory

Figure 5.1   A DIP (dual inline packaging) chip has two inline rows of pins.

individual sockets directly on the motherboard in banks of 4 or more chips. This type of memory is hard to come by these days should you have an older PC and wish to add or replace its memory. Be careful to match up any new or additional chips you add to the chips already in place or replace all of the memory with the newer type. Fill up one bank (socket set) before moving on to the next.

SIMMs and DIMMs

More common on computers starting about the time of the 386DX, RAM has been mounted to PC motherboards in a single-edge packaging that incorporates several DIP style memory chips onto an integrated module. A single inline memory module (SIMM) module consists of DRAM chips in special packaging (small outline J-lead (SOJ) or thin, small outline package (TSOP)) soldered on a small circuit board with either a 30- or 72-pin edge connector. The capacity of a SIMM can range from 1 to 128MB with chips mounted on either one or both sides of the board.

As illustrated in Figure 5.2, a SIMM is installed on the motherboard in a special socket designed to maximize the amount of memory that can be installed in a

Figure 5.2   A SIMM memory module mounted on a PC motherboard.

minimal space. SIMMs must be installed in pairs and each SIMM memory bank has two slots, which must both be filled before the next bank is populated.

An adaptation of the SIMM is the 168-pin dual inline memory module (DIMM), which has emerged as the memory standard for newer, larger 64-bit PCs. Matching a DIMM (see Figure 5.3) to a PC is slightly more complicated because there they are available in different voltages (3.3v and 5.0v) and either buffered or unbuffered. A smaller DIMM version is the small outline DIMM (SODIMM), which is used primarily in portable computers.

A memory chip, regardless of its packaging, has to be matched to the bus capacity of the motherboard over which data from memory to the CPU or peripheral devices flows. The bus capacity is stated in bits and represents how much data can flow in one clock cycle. The memory circuits on a motherboard are arranged to take advantage of the data bus' width and use the full data bus to transfer data.

On the motherboard, each arrangement of memory that matches the data bus width is called a *memory bank*. The PC will work only with completed banks that match up to the data bus width. If a memory bank is not filled, the PC ignores it. In fact, if the first memory bank (usually numbered as 0) is not completely filled, the PC will not boot because it cannot detect any memory. The majority of motherboards (see Chapter 1) include one or more memory banks, which are numbered from 0 or 1. Regardless of which number is used for the first bank, be sure you fill the lowest numbered bank first and then proceed in sequence to the other banks.

Each memory module is marked with its bit width, which indicates the number of bits it can transfer simultaneously to the data bus. For example, a 30-pin SIMM has an 8-bit width; a 72-pin SIMM has a 32-bit width; and a 168-pin DIMM has a width of 64-bits. So, on a system with a 32-bit data bus, the memory banks could hold either four 8-bit SIMMs (30-pin) or one 32-bit SIMM (72-pin), but it could not handle even one of the 64-bit DIMMs. If the memory module includes parity or ECC (see "Parity and ECC" later in the chapter), the memory bus is expanded by

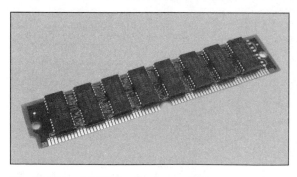

Figure 5.3   A DIMM memory module.

one bit. Parity and ECC technologies add 1 bit for each 8-bits in the bus width. An 8-bit SIMM that uses parity has a data width of 9 bits and a 32-bit SIMM with parity has a data width of 36 bits. Parity bits are not transferred over the data bus, so they do not affect the match to the data bus. Table 5.4 lists the combinations of SIMMs and DIMMs that could be used for different data bus widths.

Newer, Pentium and after, motherboards do not support the 30-pin SIMM because it would take 8 of them to fill a memory bank, which would take up way too much space on the motherboard.

You should be able to find the bus width and data capacities marked on a memory circuit, and definitely in its technical specifications. The memory size of a SIMM or DIMM is usually included in its specification as a *DWS (depth, width, and speed)* notation. This should look like "16×64-60" to indicate that the module, in this case a DIMM, has 16 million bits available for each of its 64-bits of width with a speed of 60 ns. The small "×" in the notation indicates that this example is 16 megabits *by* 64 bits in size.

The depth of the module is usually in millions, ranging from 1 to 32. Some older and smaller SIMMs use 256 and 512, but this is the exception and represents kilobits, not megabits. The width of the module is always in bits and is usually 8 or 9 (parity) for 30-pin SIMMs (or 32 for 256 or 512 kilobit SIMMs), 32 or 36 for 72-pin SIMMs, and 64 or 72 for 168-pin DIMMs.

The depth times the width yields the number of bits on the memory module. For example, a DIMM with a 16×64 notation has just over 1 billion bits (1,024,000,000). To compute the number of bytes of memory this represents, divide this number by 8 (8-bits to a byte). So, a 16×64-60 DIMM has 128,000,000 (128MB) of storage capacity. Table 5.5 lists the capacities for the more popular SIMM and DIMM modules.

Table 5.4   Matching data bus widths to memory modules.

Bus Width	30-pin SIMM	72-pin SIMM	168-pin DIMM
8-bits	1	-	-
16-bits	2	-	-
32-bits	4	1	-
64-bits	-	2	1

Table 5.5   Storage capacities for common SIMM and DIMM modules.

Module	Depth x Width (MBits)	Capacity (MB)
30-Pin SIMM (no parity)	1 × 2	1
	1 × 8	1
	2 × 8	2
	4 × 8	4
	16 × 8	16
30-Pin SIMM (parity)	1 × 3	1
	1 × 9	1
	2 × 9	2
	4 × 9	4
	16 × 9	16
72-Pin SIMM (no parity)	1 × 32	4
	2 × 32	8
	4 × 32	16
	8 × 32	32
	16 × 32	64
72-Pin SIMM (parity)	256(K) × 36	1
	512(K) × 36	2
	1 × 36	4
	2 × 36	8
	4 × 36	16
	8 × 36	32
	16 × 36	64
168-Pin DIMM (no parity)	8 × 32	32
	4 × 64	32
	16 × 32	64
	8 × 64	64
	16 × 64	128
168-Pin DIMM (parity)	4 × 72	32
	8 × 72	64
	16 × 72	128

5. Memory

SIMMs in Gold and Tin

There are two metals used for the pins and sockets of SIMMs and DIMMs: gold and tin. You'll find that SIMM modules are available in either gold or tin, because older motherboards have gold SIMM sockets and newer boards have tin sockets. DIMMs only use gold for both their edge connectors and sockets.

Only memory modules with gold contacts should be installed in sockets with gold contacts, and a SIMM with tin contacts should only be placed in a tin socket. If you mix the two metals, it can produce a chemical reaction that can cause tin oxide to build up on the gold and create an unreliable electrical connection.

SODIMM

A special type of DIMM that is manufactured primarily for use in portable devices is the *small outline dual inline memory module (SODIMM)*. This module is thinner and smaller overall than a standard DIMM and has only 144 pins.

SIMM Converter

In case you want to re-use some older 30-pin SIMMs on a motherboard that has only the newer 72-pin SIMM sockets, there is an adapter board, called a SIMM converter. This board plugs into the 72-pin socket and features two or more 30-pin sockets to receive your older SIMMs. You still have to get enough on the board to match the data bus width.

Non-Parity Memory

Because parity and ECC memories (see the next section) are more expensive than non-parity memory, non-parity memory is much more common. Non-parity memory is what you most likely think of as regular memory, with parity and ECC memories being the exception. Non-parity systems include about what their name implies for memory testing—nothing.

If your system has non-parity memory, you can't mix in parity or ECC memory. If you do, expect a memory parity error as soon as the system boots.

Parity and ECC

DRAM memory includes one of two mechanisms to verify and maintain the integrity of the data stored in memory. The two methods used are parity and error correcting code (ECC).

Memory parity has been in use about as long as PCs have been around. Memory that implements parity adds an additional bit for every 8-bits of data. The extra "parity" bit provides the system to verify the data using one of two parity protocols: odd-parity and even-parity. Odd-parity validates that the number of 1 bits in the byte is an odd-number and even-parity validates that the number of 1 bits is an even number. The extra bit is used by the system to apply an additional 1 bit to make the number of 1 bits in a byte into either an odd or even number. Parity is achieved if the number of 1 bits in a byte adds up to an odd or even number, depending on the protocol in use. Table 5.6 shows the impact of the parity bit on SIMM and DIMM modules.

A *parity error* results when a byte does not have the appropriate number of bits. Parity errors in memory can be the indication of a one-time anomaly to a faulty memory module. In fact, repeated memory parity errors are a good indication of a faulty memory module.

That it can only detect an error is the major shortcoming of the parity method. Parity mechanisms do not have a means of identifying specifically where the error is, only that an error was detected. Specifically, all it knows is that the even or odd bit count was wrong.

Parity memory will work in a non-parity system with the extra bit being ignored. You can turn off parity checking on some systems in the BIOS setup.

TIP: *There are systems available that use what is called fake parity, which makes every bit count come out correctly, even or odd. Fake parity has the effect of turning off the parity checking.*

Error correcting code (ECC) is able to both detect up to 4-bit errors and correct 1-bit errors in memory. The discrepancy isn't as bad as it may sound. Four-bit errors in memory (half of a byte is bad) are very rare. One-bit errors are much more common and ECC corrects these without reporting a parity error. However, multiple-bit errors (2, 3, or 4-bits) are reported as a memory parity error.

DRAM Technologies

There are an increasing number of technologies used for DRAM that have been developed over the years to address the need for faster and faster memory. In effect, each new DRAM technology is based at least in part on a preceding technology. The differences lie in their organization and access methods.

Table 5.6 Memory module non-parity and parity bit widths.

Module Type	Size	Memory Module	Non-Parity Bit Width	Parity Bit Width
SIMM	30-pin	8 bits	9 bits	
SIMM	72-pin	32 bits	36 bits	
DIMM	168-pin	64-bits	72-bits	

Here are the more common of the memory technologies used in DRAM:

- *Fast page mode (FPM)*—FPM DRAM, also known as non-EDO DRAM, is generally compatible with virtually all motherboards, except those with a bus speed over 66MHz.

- *Extended data out (EDO)*—This is the most common type of DRAM. It is slightly faster than FPM memory and is common in most Pentium and later PCs, except those with bus speeds over 75MHz.

- *Synchronous DRAM (SDRAM)*—SDRAM is synchronized to the system clock and reads or writes memory in burst mode. SDRAM is becoming more common for higher bus speeds.

- *Burst extended data out (BEDO) DRAM*—This is EDO memory with pipelining technology that lets it transfer data from memory access while accepting the next request. It bursts data over successive clock cycles. It is found on PCs with clock speeds up to 66MHz.

Here are a few additional DRAM technologies you may encounter:

- *Enhanced DRAM (EDRAM)*—A combination of SRAM (static RAM, see next section) and DRAM used for a Level 2 cache. The faster (15 ns) SRAM ("ess-ram") is packaged with slower (35 ns) DRAM.

- *PC100 SDRAM*—This is a special type of SDRAM designed to work with Intel's i440BX chipset over a 100MHz bus speed, using a 4-1-1-1 access cycle.

- *Double data rate (DDR) SDRAM*—This SDRAM type is designed to operate on bus speeds of at least 200MHz.

- *Enhanced SDRAM (ESDRAM)*—ESDRAM is SDRAM with a small SRAM cache that lowers memory latency times and supports bus speeds up to 200MHz.

- *Direct Rambus DRAM (DRDRAM)*—This is a proprietary DRAM technology developed by Rambus, Inc. (**www.rambus.com**) and Intel, that along with another similar approach, SLDRAM (SyncLink DRAM), features RAM speeds up to 800MHz.

- *FRAM (ferroelectric RAM)*—This RAM technology has the features of both DRAM and SRAM, which gives it the ability to save stored data when its power source is removed.

Video RAM

When most PC monitors were monochrome, the system could easily allocate 2K of memory space to generate the display. The color monitor of today requires a considerably much larger memory area to generate its display. In order to provide the video system the RAM it needs, memory has been put on the video adapter. This memory is called *video memory* or *video RAM (VRAM)*.

The first type of video memory was standard DRAM, which didn't work out because it had to be continually refreshed, couldn't be accessed during the refresh process, and couldn't support the extremely fast clock speeds of video systems. These problems lead to memory technologies specifically developed for video systems.

VRAM requires a feature called *dual-porting*, in which data is being written to VRAM by the system CPU at the same time that data is being simultaneously read from RAM by the video controller, for example to refresh the display image.

Here are a few of the video memory systems in use:

- *Video RAM (VRAM)*—This is DRAM that has been dual-ported, which means it can be written to and read from simultaneously, and needs refreshing less often than ordinary DRAM.

- *Windows RAM (WRAM)*—This video memory type is also dual-ported like VRAM, but because its contents can be accessed in blocks, it is faster than VRAM.

- *Synchronous graphics RAM (SGRAM)*—A single-ported DRAM technology that runs as much as four times faster than conventional DRAM memories.

VRAM

Video RAM is any RAM that stores imaging data for the PC's monitor and video adapter. However, the most common type of video RAM is *VRAM*, which also stands for *video RAM*. VRAM (pronounced as "vee-ram"), which is the general type of video RAM, is a special type of DRAM that acts as a buffer (it is also called the *frame buffer*) between the CPU and the video display. When an image is to be displayed on the monitor, the image data is transferred from the system RAM to video RAM. From there, it is converted by a *RAM digital-to-analog converter (RAMDAC)* into analog signals, which are used by the monitor's display device, such as a CRT (cathode ray tube), into the image desired. You'll find more details on the RAMDAC and other elements of the video system in Chapter 11.

VRAM, which comes in 1 or 2MB packages, is usually located on the video adapter or graphics card that is inserted into an expansion slot on the motherboard. Typically, the refresh cycles of the display and its rate of image generation are much faster than the bus speeds of the motherboard and CPU, and VRAM is definitely faster than DRAM. Because it is dual-ported, it can be receiving new image data from DRAM at the same time it is providing the display processor with new image data or the information needed to refresh the display.

Window RAM

Window RAM (WRAM), which has absolutely nothing to do with Microsoft Windows, is a high-performance VRAM type that is dual-ported and about 25 percent more throughput than standard VRAM. Its higher-performance features provide better support than VRAM for filling in large color blocks and text and high-resolution (1600×1200 pixels) images in true color.

Synchronous Graphics RAM

Synchronous graphics RAM (SGRAM) is a single-ported clock-synchronized video RAM. SGRAM (which is pronounced as "ess-gee-ram"), uses a number of specialized instructions, such as its masked write and block write commands to combine what would be a series of instructions for other forms of VRAM to allow data to be handled more efficiently.

Static RAM

The primary difference between DRAM and *SRAM (static RAM)* is that SRAM (pronounced as "ess-ram") is more expensive, SRAM requires more physical board space to store the same amount of data as DRAM, and SRAM does not need to be refreshed. Because SRAM eliminates the overhead and access conflicts associated with DRAM, it provides for faster access times over DRAM, although DRAM is getting faster. The primary use for SRAM is for Level-1 and -2 caching, often as on-board caching built into the microprocessor or motherboard.

Parameter RAM

Parameter RAM (PRAM) is to a Macintosh computer what CMOS is to a non-Macintosh computer. PRAM is used to store the internal configuration information, the date and time, and other system-wide parameters that need to be saved between system restarts. There is a process on a Macintosh called "zapping the pram" that is very much akin to resetting the CMOS jumper or removing the CMOS battery on a PC to reset the system configuration parameters to their default values. See Chapter 4 for more information on PC CMOS and system parameters.

What Is Virtual Memory?

Virtual memory is not memory at all. In fact, it is usually space on a hard disk drive. Virtual memory is a software-managed facility in a PC that allows you to address a portion of your hard disk as if it were an extension of system RAM. This is a very handy feature to have available, should your PC suddenly run out of RAM space. Virtual memory is included in this chapter only to acknowledge the word memory in its name. Virtual memory is covered in more detail in Chapter 8.

Logical Memory Layout

If you work with older PCs that run MS-DOS, PCDOS, or any of the other DOS versions or if you work on PCs that run Windows versions before Windows 2000, it is a good idea to know how DOS and Windows logically divide up its memory.

Table 5.7 DOS/Windows Logical Memory Layout.

Memory Division	Description
Conventional memory	The first 640K of system memory. Used by standard DOS programs, device drivers, TSRs (terminate-and-stay-resident), and anything that runs on standard DOS.
Upper memory area	The remaining 384K of the first megabyte of memory, located immediately above conventional memory. Reserved for system device drivers and special uses like BIOS ROM shadowing. Also called expanded memory or reserved memory.
High memory area	The first 64K (less 16 bytes) after the first megabyte of memory. Used to store the startup (boot) utilities. The 16 bytes set aside hold the boot address for the CPU.
Extended memory	All memory above 1MB and after the high memory area. Used for programs and data.

DOS/Windows defines memory into four basic divisions, as shown in Figure 5.3 and described in Table 5.7.

Conventional Memory

The first 640K of system memory (RAM) is reserved as *conventional memory*, as illustrated in Figure 5.4. The reason for the fixed 640K size is because early processors could not address more than 1MB of RAM and IBM decided to reserve the upper 384K of the 1MB for the BIOS and its utilities, defaulting to 640K for the user and operating system.

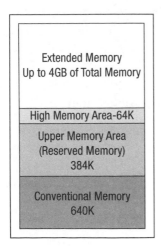

Figure 5.4 The DOS logical memory layout.

Conventional memory contains operating system files, application programs, memory-resident and terminate-and-stay-resident (TSR) routines, and system-level device drivers.

Upper Memory Area

The next 384K, after conventional memory, in the first megabyte of RAM is set aside for the upper memory area. Originally this area was allocated to such things as the system and adapter BIOS' and video RAM. However, it didn't take long before developers, tired of the 640K limitation, reassigned this space as *expanded memory*, and released special device drivers to facilitate its use, such as EMM386.EXE, which is an expanded memory services (EMS) driver. This program and the other expanded memory managers free up space in conventional memory by reallocating DOS drivers and memory-resident programs into unused spaces in the upper memory area.

EMM386.EXE is implemented by adding the following command lines to the CONFIG.SYS file in the DOS root directory:

```
DEVICE=C:\DOS\EMM386.EXE
DOS=UMB
```

UMB stands for upper memory blocks, yet another name for the upper memory area.

If you don't want to start the expanded memory manager, but you do want the ability to relocate drivers and TSRs to the upper memory area, then add the NOEMS option to the command:

```
DEVICE=C:\DOS\EMM386.EXE NOEMS
DOS=UMB
```

High Memory Area

The *high memory area (HMA)* is the first 64K of the extended memory area, see Figure 5.3. To activate the use of this area for the operating system, include this statement in the CONFIG.SYS file:

```
DOS=HIGH
```

This statement allows the operating system to load a large portion of its code to the high memory area instead of to conventional memory. This frees up around 45K of conventional memory space for other software.

Extended Memory

Extended memory is all memory after the first 1MB of RAM. However, there are limits to the amount of memory that can be in extended memory. Every PC has a maximum for how much total memory its hardware and operating system will support. The maximum ranges from 16MB on a 286 to 4GB on Pentiums and above.

Extended memory is often confused with expanded memory. Remember that expanded memory (upper memory area) expands conventional memory to fill up the first 1MB of RAM and extended memory extends RAM to its limit.

Tools and Diagnostics

There are both software and hardware diagnostic tools available to test a PC's memory. Software tools check on the functionality of the memory and the hardware tools check the reliability and structural integrity of the memory.

Software Tools

Memory errors are often intermediate and difficult to diagnose. An essential tool in memory troubleshooting is a memory diagnostic program. There are many programs made for this purpose and the most popular program is the POST (the power-on self-test program included in your PC's BIOS startup utilities).

The POST tests and counts all of the memory it detects and compares the result to previous POST results. If the latest POST memory count is different from the previous, a memory error is signaled with an audible beep or a text message alert. See Chapter 4 for detailed information on BIOS beep codes.

The testing performed by the POST is not very thorough so the use of memory diagnostic software may be necessary. These programs, such as DocMemory from SimmTester (**www.simmtester.com**), Memory+ from TFI Technology (**www.tfi-technology.com**), and Gold Memory from Goldware CZ (**www.goldmemory.cz**), are executed from a command prompt or from a boot disk. These tests can be run continuously for hours or even days, if necessary, to find the source of an intermittent memory problem.

The limitation of both the POST test and memory diagnostic software programs is that they are software programs limited to pass or fail judgments. These programs can't predict when a memory chip will fail or if a chip is about to fail. These programs are limited to writing data to each memory location and then reading it back to test the read/write and parity and ECC functionality of the memory.

For a host of software diagnostic and troubleshooting tools, visit TweakFiles.Com (**www.tweakfiles.com**).

Hardware Tools

The best way to test memory is with a SIMM/DIMM tester. This device thoroughly tests a memory module at different speeds, voltages, and timing to indicate whether the memory is good or bad, or if there are any indications that the memory may fail in the future. SIMM/DIMM testers are expensive, but if you are maintaining or repairing a group of PCs on a regular basis, this device is a must have.

Memory Errors

Memory errors occur in large part because memory is an electronic storage device. There is always the potential to incorrectly return stored information. As discussed earlier in the chapter it is expected that DRAM memory will occasionally experience memory errors. These errors are the result of the way DRAM memory stores ones and zeros in the form of electrical charges in small capacitors that require continual refreshing to ensure data will not be lost. SDRAM is more reliable because it does not require the constant refreshing.

Hard and Soft Errors

The two most common memory errors are *repeatable errors*, also known as "hard" errors, and *transient errors*, also called "soft" errors. A hard error occurs when a memory module is defective and because of its physical flaw, the memory consistently returns the same erroneous results. For example, a memory cell may become damaged because of power surges or ESD (electrostatic discharge) and be stuck in a state that reads as a 1. This could cause parity errors or simply just return the wrong data.

A hard memory error is commonly the result of a loose memory module, a system board defect, or a defective or blown memory chip. In most cases, hard errors are relatively easy to diagnose and fix because they are not intermittent. Hard errors are consistent and repeated, allowing you a better chance to isolate the source of the problem.

A transient error or soft error occurs when a bit provides the wrong data value one time or intermittently, but otherwise continues to function correctly. Because these errors are moving targets, they are much harder to diagnose. In most cases, soft memory errors are usually the result of poor quality memory, motherboards, or ESD, and not necessarily the physical memory chip itself. The system timing could be too fast for the memory or vice versa or the stray radioactivity naturally present in the materials used in computer components is affecting the electromagnetic operation of a chip. Unlike a hard error, soft errors aren't consistent, but usually, if you're patient enough, they do eventually repeat. However, how soon the error will repeat may be in minutes or even years, so it is always better to diagnose the problem as best as you can.

Using a software tool or a memory tester is the best way to detect as well as prevent memory errors. Be sure to match the tool to the task and especially to the error. Some software only detects one-bit errors, while others are able to detect multi-bit errors automatically. Still others, the really good ones, can detect and, better still, correct memory problems.

Common Memory Errors

Memory errors that show up during the boot process are usually caused by physical defects or installation problems with the RAM chips. These problems should be identified by the POST and signaled with beep codes or text messages. Memory errors that occur after the operating system has started running are identified with a range of error messages.

Some of the more common memory-related error messages are:

- *Divide by zero error*—A divide by zero error has occurred, which means that some operation on the computer either returned an erroneous value, there is a serious logic flaw in a running program, or more likely this message is the result of an operation with a value too large to fit a register.

- *General protection fault*—A program in memory has been corrupted and has provided an erroneous memory address outside of its addressable space. This could be the result of a program flaw, or a bad patch of memory. This message usually indicates the offending program has been terminated.

- *Fatal exception error*—An illegal instruction has been encountered, an invalid operation code was passed to the CPU, or data was attempted to be read from an erroneous memory location. Faulty memory may be the cause; it's worth checking.

Checking Memory

Before you begin testing memory, you must disable any write-back cache memory on the PC (see Chapter 6 for more information on cache systems). You can disable the write-back cache through the setup or advanced configuration menus of your BIOS program. How memory testing programs work is that they write data to a memory location and then immediately read it back. If cache is left on, you are likely testing the cache rather than the memory. Disabling the write-back cache assures you that the test will be performed on the system memory and the results will reflect the read/write performance of your PC's SIMMs or DIMMs.

After disabling the write-back cache, you can begin to troubleshoot the system memory. Follow these troubleshooting steps:

1. First, restart the system. If a memory error is detected during the POST, a memory chip or module may be defective or improperly installed.

2. If the POST does not detect a memory error, check the BIOS setup for the memory's speed in the timing parameters. If the BIOS setup does provide a memory timing parameter, reset the memory speed to the BIOS or setup default values, which are usually the slowest of the available options. If you make any changes to the BIOS settings, save the changes and reboot the system. If the system successfully reboots, the source of the problem was an incorrect BIOS setting.

3. If the POST still beeps or displays a memory error message, it is likely you have a bad SIMM or DIMM. Other possibilities are that a memory module is not installed or seated properly or the SIMM modules may not be installed in matching pairs.

   Remove all but the first bank of memory modules and reboot the system. If you have a memory error at this point, you know it is in the first bank of RAM; replace the memory in the first bank and reboot. If the system boots, continue adding the rest of the untested memory until you either run out of replaced memory or experience another failure. You may even want to reinstall the seemingly bad modules into another bank, to see if they have been miraculously healed during the testing.

4. If after moving or replacing the memory modules the system will still not boot, it is possible that the motherboard itself is bad. Unfortunately, the best way to verify if the motherboard is faulty is to replace it and retest (see Chapter 1 for more information on testing the motherboard).

Memory Testing

If the memory errors show up after the operating system is running, you will need to access the BIOS to disable the write-back cache and then reboot the system from a floppy disk that contains the memory testing application. Follow the instructions of the software to complete its tests.

If the test software finds an error, perform the memory checking steps described in the previous section. However, if the test software does not find a problem, but you are still getting memory errors when you reboot, you may want to check with the motherboard or memory module manufacturer for updated software drivers, BIOS revisions, patches, or updates. If there are none, then either whip out your handy SIMM or DIMM module tester, or take your memory modules to a professional PC repair shop.

If you are still getting memory problems, test your power supply or the immediate physical environment of the PC for excess static, RFI (radio frequency interference), EMI (electromagnetic interference), or any other environmental factors that may be interfering with the operation of the PC.

Enable the Write-Back Cache

After testing your system and fixing your memory problems, be sure that you enable the write-back cache. This will avoid a slow running system that may have you chasing after wild geese.

Immediate Solutions

Installing Memory Modules

Before beginning to install any new memory modules in your PC, especially if you plan to mix different types, sizes, or speeds of memory, there are precautions you should take:

- Back up the hard disk drive.

- Work in a well-lighted and anti-static environment.

- Always wear a static strap.

- Keep memory modules in their protective packaging until you are ready to install them.

- Handle memory modules by their edges only and avoid touching a module's connectors.

Installing a SIMM

When inserting a memory module, be sure to line up the notched end of the module with the matching end of the socket. A SIMM module is placed into the module slot on the motherboard using about a 45 degree angle sloping away from the back of the slot. When inserting a SIMM, line up its edge-connector pins with the connectors of the socket. With the module seated in place, lift the module gently until it clicks into place. The module should stand vertically in the socket.

Installing a DIMM

DIMMs are installed by aligning the notches on the module and pressing it straight down into the socket on the motherboard. The DIMM should snap into the socket's locking tabs.

If you encounter a socket that is keyed differently than the DIMM module you are trying to install, it may be that the new DIMM is not of the correct voltage (3.3v or 5v are the choices) or it may be buffered on a non-buffered system. Unlike a SIMM, DIMMs must be compatible to the motherboard. Never force a DIMM into the socket. Double-check the motherboard's specifications and make sure you have the correct DIMMs. If the key of the socket doesn't match the DIMM, it is likely you have the wrong voltage or buffer type and must exchange it. While

Figure 5.5   A DIMM module installed on a motherboard.

DIMMs come in either 3.3 volts or 5 volts and buffered or unbuffered, the standard DIMM is 3.3 volts and unbuffered. Figure 5.5 shows a DIMM module installed on a motherboard.

Installing Memory—Part II

After adding memory to a PC, you may need to make changes to the BIOS configuration before the computer will recognize the new memory. You may even need to adjust jumpers or dip switches on the motherboard to configure the system for the memory on some older systems. Newer systems automatically recognize the memory and make any necessary adjustments by themselves.

Removing Memory Modules

To remove a DIMM, release the locking tabs on the socket and pull the module straight up and out of the socket. Remember that SIMMs install at an angle. So, a SIMM module is removed at an angle after the locking tabs are released. Once the SIMM is at an angle in the socket, lift it up and out of the socket.

Chapter 6

Cache Memory

In Depth

Defining Cache

The basic definition of a PC's *cache*, also referred to as *cache memory*, is fast computer memory that is used to store frequently used data or instructions. As you will see in this chapter, there is much more to it than that.

Actually, the term *cache* refers to any buffer storage that is used to improve computer performance by reducing its access times. A cache holds instructions and data that are likely to be needed for the CPU's next operation. Caching copies frequently accessed data and instructions from either primary memory or disk (secondary) storage. You will hear caching referred to in two contexts:

- *Cache memory*—Smaller, faster storage placed between primary memory (RAM) and the CPU. Cache copies and stores instructions and data from the primary memory for high-speed access by the CPU.

- *Disk cache*—A portion of primary memory or memory located on the disk controller card that is used to hold large blocks of frequently accessed data that is copied from a disk drive to improve disk access speed.

What Is Cache Memory?

Cache memory is special type of high-speed dynamic random access memory (static random access memory, or SRAM; see Chapter 5) that is used to supply the instructions and data most frequently requested by the CPU. SRAM ("ess-ram"), which is made up of transistors, is used for cache memory because it doesn't require the frequent refreshing of DRAM, which is made up of capacitors. Cache memory allows the CPU to work more efficiently because the data and instructions it needs are served from high-speed cache memory, something that allows the whole computer to run faster than if cache were not used at all.

Because SRAM—with access speeds as fast as 15 ns—is faster than DRAM, cache memory works at speeds closer to those of the CPU. Data and instructions stored in cache memory are transferred many times faster than those stored in the PC's main memory (RAM). It seems logical that if SRAM is so much faster than DRAM, it would be used for primary memory, eliminating the need for cache memory. The problem is that SRAM can cost as much as six times more than DRAM and can take up much more space on the motherboard to store the same amount of data.

6. Cache Memory

How Caching Works

In the PC, the processor is faster than the memory, which in turn is faster than the hard disk. As depicted in Figure 6.1, caching solves some of the speed issues by providing an intermediary buffer between a faster device (the processor or RAM) and a slower device (RAM or the hard disk).

Caching operates on the principle of *locality of reference*, which presumes that the next data to be processed or the next instruction to be fetched by the CPU is the one immediately after the data or instruction just passed to the CPU. The effectiveness of cache memory is expressed as a *hit ratio*, which is calculated according to the number of times that cache memory is successful in anticipating the data or instructions that the processor will want next. Each time the caching system is correct, it is tallied as a *cache hit*.

Although caching may seem to be a gamble, it is actually highly efficient and accurate. On average, cache memory systems correctly identify the next data or instruction the CPU wants about 90 to 95 percent of the time. When the CPU must access data or instructions from the PC's main memory, it requires several wait states. During these wait states, the data is located and transferred from RAM (assuming it is in RAM). The efficiency of the cache memory system eliminates these wait cycles for the CPU, and that makes the CPU and the entire PC more efficient.

How does a PC work if it doesn't have cache memory? Here's a comparison. Suppose that each time you wanted to drink a cold beverage you had to drive to the local supermarket and buy a single can or bottle. It's as if the CPU (you) had to

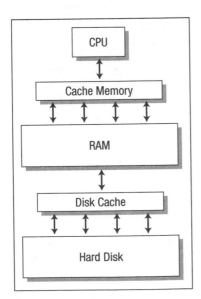

Figure 6.1   Caching provides an intermediary buffer between a faster device and a slower device.

access primary memory (drive to the store) each time it needed to fetch data (the can of pop). And because of the time it took to locate and transfer the memory, the PC's memory may as well be clear across town. The solution is to install a refrigerator at your elbow, and that's the effect you get when you add cache memory to the system. No longer does the CPU need to access data directly from the cross-town memory, because what it needs is right at hand. Cache even goes this one better. Instead of storing only the next drink, it keeps the equivalent of a case of your favorite beverage on hand and cool, just waiting for your request, guessing that you'll want the same drink next time. Similarly, when the cache controller retrieves a piece of data or an instruction from main memory, it also gets a few chunks of data as well as several subsequent instructions.

When you open a document in a word processor or an electronic spreadsheet, it is common for the document's image to extend beyond the display. Suppose each time you scrolled up or down or left or right, the data to be displayed had to be located in RAM and transferred to the display. Your system would likely be slow to respond. Each movement of the screen would require that the data—and the instructions used to format or calculate it—be passed from RAM to the CPU to your application, where the image would then be passed to the video RAM. Cache memory eliminates the inherent delays in this process by storing the data most likely to be needed in a much faster memory source that exists solely to serve the data and instruction needs of the CPU.

Internal and External Cache

There are two general locations for cache memory on a PC:

- *Internal cache*—This is also called *primary cache* or *Level 1 (L1) cache*. It is typically placed inside the CPU chip and ranges from 1K to 32K.

- *External cache*—This is also called *secondary cache* or *Level 2 (L2) cache*. It is normally placed on the motherboard but can instead be located in the CPU. External cache ranges from 64K to 1MB, but 256K and 512K are common cache sizes.

Although it may seem obvious, another distinction between the two placements for cache memory is that only external cache can be upgraded. L2 cache modules are plugged into special cache module mounts or cache memory expansion sockets, both of which are located on the motherboard. To increase the amount of L1, or internal, cache on a PC would require that the CPU be replaced.

On older PCs, notably those with 286 or 386 processors, the processor does not include internal cache. This means that any cache memory located on the motherboard is likely to be the primary cache. This cache, if it's present at all, likely has a fairly low capacity limit. If you are uncertain about adding cache to one of these systems, check with the motherboard manufacturer.

Sizing Cache

As with most things on the PC, more is better when it comes to cache memory, but there are limits. The amount of cache on your PC can increase the overall speed of the system, but it can decrease it, too. There is a point at which keeping the cache filled begins to erode the performance gains of the cache memory.

As described earlier in this chapter, if one refrigerator provides a caching buffer that eliminates trips to the store for drinks, it seems logical that two refrigerators should save twice as much time. Yes—but only if you could carry two refrigerators' worth of drinks in one trip. If you must make a second trip to the store to fill the second refrigerator, your time savings are significantly reduced. On some systems, adding too much L2 cache can have the same effect on performance. The first 256K of cache may improve the performance of a PC, but adding an additional 256K may not improve performance nearly as much and may even reduce it.

Too Much RAM

Another important consideration in cache sizing is the amount of RAM that your PC can cache. Nearly all Pentium and later PCs include caching for 64MB of RAM, but some cannot cache any additional RAM. In fact, many of Intel's most popular chipsets—including the 430FX, 430VX, and 430TX—cannot cache more than 64MB of RAM. This is an issue only if you plan to add more primary memory to your PC than it can cache, something that would likely result in reduced system performance. What happens is that all the memory in excess of the cache size limit is *uncached*. Serving requests for data stored in the uncached memory takes longer, in part because of the overhead time required to first determine that the memory is in fact uncached.

Tag RAM

Level 2 cache memory is divided into two parts:

- *Data store*—This is the area in L2 cache where the actual data is stored. The size of the data store determines the amount of data the cache can actually hold.

- *Tag RAM*—The value stored in tag RAM is used to determine whether a cache search will result in a hit or a miss.

PCs typically have 256K of L2 cache (data store) and 8 bits of tag RAM. This combination can cache 64MB of primary memory. To cache more memory, you must increase the size of the tag RAM. Having more bits of tag RAM lets a system address larger memory addresses. You can add additional tag RAM chips to some motherboards, but this feature is still fairly rare. Most systems include the tag RAM in their chipset, and some—such as the Pentium Pro—include additional tag RAM that can allow the system to cache as much as 4GB of RAM.

Cache Bursting

Level 2 cache is made up of a series of cache blocks, or *lines*, each of which has 32 bytes. Data is transferred into and out of the cache one line (32 bytes or 256 bits) at a time. Typically, the data bus widths of most cached PCs are 64 bits. This means that it requires four consecutive 64-bit transfers to move the 256-bit line.

On a 32-bit system with no cache memory installed, when the processor requests data from RAM it is usually provided with a *burst* containing the four consecutive 32-bit or 64-bit blocks. The number of clock cycles required to locate and transfer each block determines the timing of this transfer. The first block is located by its address, and the data is transferred. Each of the second, third, and fourth blocks is transferred from consecutive blocks, so no addressing or lookup is required. For example, the first block may require four cycles, and each of the other blocks, one cycle. This is shown in the notation 4-1-1-1, which indicates the burst speed of the cache.

Cache Misses

Some overhead is involved in checking to see whether the data requested is in the memory cache. If the data is not in the cache—a *cache miss*—some cycles have been expended looking for it even before it is requested from primary memory. If it normally takes 10 clock cycles to transfer a burst of data from RAM, it may actually take 12 cycles on a cache miss, slowing system performance.

A too-small L2 cache can aggravate this situation. A small cache translates into a low cache hit ratio, meaning that too much data is being served from RAM after cache misses. Increasing the cache size does not increase the overhead of checking to see whether data is in the cache. As a result, adding more L2 cache increases the chance that data is there without adding overhead to look for it.

Types of Cache Memory

Three types of cache memory are used on PC systems:

- *Asynchronous*—This type of cache memory transfers data without regard to the system clock cycles.

- *Synchronous burst*—This type of cache memory is tied to the cycles of the system clock.

- *Pipelined burst (PLB)*—This synchronous cache memory type transfers the blocks of a burst in an overlapping mode that allows them to be partially transferred at the same time.

These types of cache memory differ primarily in their timing and their level of support from chipsets. More than anything else, the type of cache memory used on a PC is dictated by its chipset and motherboard.

Asynchronous Cache

Asynchronous (also called *async*) cache memory, the oldest type, is also the slowest. It is common on 486 systems but is seldom found in later systems. When the CPU requests data, the cache responds independently of the system clock timing on the memory bus, and that is why it is comparatively slow. Asynchronous cache memory also has problems with clock speeds greater than 33MHz. In fact, at speeds of 66MHz or higher, asynchronous cache actually requires about twice as long to transfer data than at slower clock speeds. At 33MHz, asynchronous cache transfers data in a four-block burst at 2-1-1-1 (meaning that it requires two cycles to locate and transfer the first block and one cycle for each of the remaining three blocks), a speed that is actually very good. However, at 66MHz, async cache slows down to 3-2-2-2. This is the primary reason it is not used on Pentium or later PCs.

Synchronous Cache

Synchronous cache, also known as *synchronous burst cache*, transfers data to and from cache in sync with the cycles of the memory bus clock. This arrangement allows it to work at faster bus speeds, unlike asynchronous cache. To avoid caching problems, such as system crashes or lockups, synchronous cache does require that the speed of the SRAM match the system speeds. However, this type of cache had problems similar to those of asynchronous cache at very high speeds, so it was soon replaced by pipeline burst cache.

Pipelined Burst Cache

The pipelined burst cache, also called PB cache, includes special circuitry that transfers the four data blocks in a burst to be done essentially at the same time. The transfer of the second block begins before the transfer of the first block has completed. The analogy of the pipeline is that before the first gallon of water leaves the hose, the second and subsequent gallons enter the hose for transport.

Because of the overhead of setting up the "pipe," PB cache is actually slower on its first block than is synchronous cache. However, PB cache is faster for the remaining blocks, averaging bursts of 3-1-1-1 on systems as fast as 100MHz. Most Pentium-level motherboards include pipelined burst cache.

Cache Write Policies

Cache write policies allow the system to keep data in cache in sync with the data in memory. If the system updates a certain block of data that is being held in cache memory, the data stored in cache must also be updated. The approach used for this update, called its *write policy*, can affect system performance. Two policy types are used:

- *Write-back cache*—When memory locations that are mirrored in cache memory are updated, the system writes its new data only to the affected cache location. When the data is cleared from cache, the changed data is

6. Cache Memo

written back to the appropriate location in system memory. This type of cache reduces the required number of write cycles to memory, which are time- and cycle-consuming. In most cases, write-back is better than write-through.

- *Write-through cache*—Updates to data currently held in cache are written to both cache and main memory at the same time. This caching policy is simpler to implement and ensures that the cache is never out of sync with main memory. However, it does not perform as well as a write-back caching policy.

Nonblocking Cache

Many caching systems can handle only one request at a time, and that can be a problem when the data requested by the CPU is not in cache (a cache miss). When a cache miss occurs, the requested data must be transferred from memory, leaving the cache blocked while it waits for the transfer action to complete. *Nonblocking* cache—also called *transactional* cache—can set aside a request for data not in cache and work on other data requests while the missing data is transferred from main memory. Nonblocking cache is commonly used for L2 caching on higher-end Pentium processors. For example, the Pentium Pro and Pentium II microprocessors can support as many as four nonblocking requests simultaneously on the Intel DIB (dual independent bus) architecture.

The Impact of Cache on Memory

It is generally believed that adding more or faster memory to a PC will increase its performance. However, the size of a PC's cache can neutralize any benefit of the faster memory. A PC with a large L1 and L2 cache serves the majority of its requests for data and instructions from its memory cache. If the cache system is able to accurately predict the CPU's next request 90 to 95 percent of the time, only 5 to 10 percent of such requests come from RAM. This is great system performance, but it can offset the impact of faster memory. Adding memory that is 100-percent faster than the old memory would improve performance only 5 to 10 percent.

Cache Mapping

Some Pentium systems split the Level 1 cache to store data and instructions in separate cache partitions. Among the characteristics that differentiate these caches are their mapping techniques, which set a number of a cache's functional features, including its hit ratio and transfer speed.

Three mapping techniques are used with caching:

- *Direct-mapped cache*—Most motherboard-mounted caches are of this type. A single cache line is used to address several memory locations in a direct address mapping. This approach is the least complex of the mapping techniques used in cache memory.

- *Full-associative cache*—Because a memory location can be referenced from any cache line, this mapping approach is complex and applies complicated search techniques to locate a cache hit. It can be slow, but it provides the best hit ratios.

- *N-way set associative cache*—The cache is divided into sets with N cache lines each, typically 2, 4, 8, and more. This mapping technique combines the other two mapping techniques, providing better hit ratios than direct-mapped cache without the speed impact of a complicated search. Processor-based L1 caches commonly apply either a two-way or a four-way set associative cache.

Cache Mounts

Older cache systems use SRAM chips that are mounted directly on the motherboard in individual sockets, and that means that the cache can be replaced or upgraded. In most newer systems, however, cache memory is fixed—usually soldered—directly on the motherboard. If your PC mounts its cache in sockets, you may be able to add additional SRAM to increase its size. Some motherboards with soldered SRAM will also let you add cache modules, something that may require you to change a jumper setting. The size and type of SRAM chips you can add are determined by the motherboard and chipset, so check your motherboard's documentation or visit its manufacturer's Web site.

A cache module that is commonly used to add cache to a system is available in a packaging called COAST (cache on a stick). This is the silly name for a cache module that looks something like the SIMM (single inline memory module) packaging used for RAM. A COAST module is mounted on a motherboard in a special socket type called a CELP (card edge low profile). Some motherboards include only a CELP socket for mounting cache memory, whereas others let you add COAST modules to soldered cache chips.

TIP: *One word of warning about COAST—there is no standard for CELP mounted modules. Be sure to check your motherboard's documentation for compatibility before purchasing a COAST module for your system.*

6. Cache Memory

Immediate Solutions

Installing a Cache Module

1. Review the motherboard's documentation or check with the PC manufacturer or vendor to determine whether the PC permits expansion of its L2 cache. If no caching is installed and you wish to include caching, use the motherboard's specifications to select the correct SRAM chips or COAST module.

   Most newer motherboards that have cache modules installed do not have a cache slot. It is very common to find cache sockets instead of a cache module slot or CELP socket.

2. Place the motherboard on a flat, solid, clean, and static-free work surface. Place the motherboard so that it will not flex or bend when you are pressing the caching module or chips into their sockets.

   Cache (COAST) modules are usually keyed. This means that they have a guide pin or feature placed on the leading edge that matches the socket to prevent it from being inserted into its socket incorrectly.

3. Before installing the module into the socket, line it up with the socket to visually match the pins of the edge connector to the socket connectors.

4. Place the module into the socket slot and press down gently but firmly until the module seats into the slot. If the module does not seat easily, try gently pressing down on first one end of the module and then the other until it begins to seat into the slot. The module is seated when the edge connectors are most of the way into the socket and the module will not fit further into the socket under firm pressure.

Troubleshooting Problems After You Install New Cache

It's possible to have a problem right after you have installed new or additional cache memory in a PC, such as the system failing to boot or failing immediately after the POST. More than likely, the problem is that you have installed the wrong cache for your motherboard and chipset.

6. Cache Memory

In an existing system in which no changes have been made, a cache failure is extremely rare. Cache problems are generally the result of human intervention, such as removing, replacing, or adding the wrong type of cache memory modules. Other possibilities are that you have not properly configured the motherboard jumpers or you have dislodged something while installing the cache.

If your PC fails after you have installed cache memory, run through this checklist:

- Before purchasing new cache memory and definitely before installing it in your PC, check the motherboard's documentation or visit the manufacturer's Web site to verify the type and mounting of the cache the motherboard supports.

- If you have replaced the old cache modules or added new cache to the system, check the motherboard's documentation to see whether you need to change the settings of any jumpers. Newer PCs automatically adjust for new or additional cache, but some PCs configure the size or type of cache memory through jumper settings.

- If you have a spare cache module, this is probably the most foolproof trouble-shooting step: Replace the suspicious cache. If the problem goes away, you know that the original module was bad.

- Disable the cache options in the PC's BIOS configuration data. These options are accessed through the BIOS setup program. If the problem goes away, you need to continue checking to determine the source of the error.

- After the PC has been powered on for a few minutes, try holding your finger on the cache module for a few seconds. If it is too hot, the cache module itself could be bad. Replace the cache module. If the new module also gets too hot to touch, the motherboard is probably the problem. Verify that the cache is the right type for the motherboard and, if it is, test the motherboard.

- Ensure that you are using the correct cache memory type for your system. If not, immediately remove and replace it. Remember to check—and if necessary, change—the cache memory options in the BIOS settings.

- Verify that the cache is installed in its mounting correctly and that it is properly oriented and firmly seated in its socket or slot on the motherboard.

- Check all drive and power supply connectors to see whether you accidentally unseated or dislodged one when installing the cache.

- If you still cannot locate the problem, test the primary memory and check for any updated device drivers or software patches that have been recently installed. The problem could very well be coincidental.

6. Cache Memory

Analyzing Your System If Adding Cache Didn't Improve Performance

It is a common belief that adding more L2 cache will improve system performance. So, after you have added more L2 cache—assuming that the installation is correct and uses the right type of cache memory—what should you do if the PC does not seem to be performing any better?

If your PC already has 256K of L2 cache and is already caching 90 percent or more of memory requests, you should expect performance improvement to be marginal, perhaps in the range of 5 to 10 percent. At the speed of the processor and SRAM, it is unlikely that you can notice this slight improvement.

On the other hand, the lack of improvement may reflect an improperly installed cache that is not being recognized by the PC. To verify that the new cache is installed correctly, follow these steps:

1. Check the BIOS display during the boot to determine how much cache is detected and reported. If it is not the correct amount, check the cache modules to see whether they are the right type for the motherboard and are installed correctly.

2. Check the motherboard's documentation to see whether adding cache memory, especially more cache memory, requires jumpers to be changed. Check the BIOS data for settings that may need to be changed.

3. If everything looks OK and checks out, it is a good idea to use benchmark software, before and after the installation of the cache memory, and then compare the results. Even on the most efficient systems, you should see some improvement, no matter how small.

Here are some benchmark software packages you may want to try:

- *CacheChk*—This program measures the speed of L1 and L2 cache in megabytes per second. To download a copy of it, visit **www.janics.com/kirk/diagnostic/**.

- *CCT386*—This program analyzes the fit of memory and cache and the impact of the fit on performance. It displays a graphic showing the relationship of memory to cache and the efficiency of the cache. It is also available at **www.janics.com/kirk/diagnostic/**.

- *CompTest*—This benchmark program works on PCs with 486 processors. It tests the throughput of L1 cache separately from that of L2 cache.

- *Norton SysInfo (SI)*—This program is packaged in the Norton Utilities suite, which is available commercially. It tests more than 100 factors that affect a system's performance, including the transfer rate between memory and the CPU, the motherboard chipset, and both L1 and L2 cache. For more information on this product, visit **www.symantec.com**.

- *Nucache*—In addition to the L1 and L2 cache sizes, types, and speed, this program reports the CPU and external bus speeds in frequency (MHz) and microseconds. It is available for Pentium PCs only. To download a copy of this program, visit **http://optimize.bhcom1.com/english/benchmarks/ benchmarks.htm**.

Troubleshooting When the Processor Disables the Cache

This problem is caused when the BIOS system cannot properly recognize the processor installed on a PC.

First, verify that the processor is properly seated in its socket. If it is, you can usually fix this problem by upgrading the BIOS. Contact the motherboard or BIOS manufacturer to obtain a new BIOS ROM or flash BIOS upgrade file that supports the processor.

Related solution:	*Found on page:*
Troubleshooting Guide for the Motherboard	15

Determining Why Adding More Than 64MB of RAM Slows the PC

Some chipsets support the caching of more than 64MB of primary memory. However, if the chipset—such as Intel's Triton II 430HX, which supports caching of as much as 512MB of RAM—is installed on a motherboard with only 8 bits of tag RAM, then the system is limited to 64MB of caching.

To cache more primary memory, you must add more tag RAM to those systems that can support the caching of more than 64MB of RAM. If the motherboard includes a chipset that supports higher levels of caching, whether or not you can add tag RAM depends entirely on the motherboard. Check the motherboard's documentation for the location, type, and specification of the tag RAM chips that are supported.

You need to understand that even if you add tag RAM, the size of your L2 cache will still control how much actual RAM you can cache. You must balance these two elements.

To determine the problem caused by adding RAM to your system, use this checklist:

- Using the motherboard's documentation, check to see whether the motherboard supports and has the 11 bits of tag RAM needed to cache as much as 512MB of RAM. If it supports this much tag RAM but it is not installed, check with the motherboard manufacturer for the specification of the chip that will provide this capability. Be sure to match the capacity of the tag RAM to the your system's L2 cache and primary memory. You may need to add additional L2 cache.

- If your motherboard supports the additional tag RAM, it should have a chip socket into which you can install a second tag RAM chip. The motherboard's documentation or the manufacturer's Web site should list the tag RAM chips that are compatible with the chipset and cache memory as well as any jumpers that must be changed.

- Motherboards that have CELP slots for COAST modules may accept the type of cache module that incorporates an extra tag RAM chip. If your system has this type of motherboard, when you add the extra 256K of cache you also add the extra tag RAM needed to cache more than 64MB of RAM. Not all COAST modules include tag RAM, so be certain which modules are compatible with your motherboard and chipset. Remember that it is the tag RAM, and not the extra cache, that lets more memory be cached.

- If you can't add additional tag RAM, your only recourse is to either live with only 64MB of cached RAM—regardless of how much RAM is on the PC—or to replace the motherboard with one that allows you to increase the caching and thereby improve your system's performance.

- If the tag RAM needed to exceed 64MB is installed, the problem lies in mismatched components, an improper configuration, or even the wrong components. Check the RAM and then the cache memory to find the possible causes for the slowdown. If RAM and cache memory check out, the cause is likely in the motherboard, its configuration, or an incompatibility of its components.

Enabling the Internal (L1) Cache

Virtually all microprocessors sold today include some amount of internal cache memory. A system's internal cache is enabled or disabled through the BIOS setup program and the BIOS configuration data. There is no reason to disable internal cache unless you are trying to troubleshoot a caching problem.

Enter the BIOS setup area of your PC by using the key indicated by your BIOS during the boot process. Check your BIOS settings to make sure the internal cache is enabled and functioning. If for any reason you cannot enable the internal cache, there is a problem with hardware configuration (among the motherboard, chipset, and processor). If you disable the internal cache, you can expect the performance of the PC to degrade.

Enabling the External (L2) Cache

External cache is located between the processor and a PC's primary memory. If your PC has L2 cache, it should be enabled. Like the L1 (internal) cache, L2 cache is enabled through the BIOS settings. If you cannot enable the L2 cache, there is a problem with the PC's hardware configuration—either in the external cache or on the motherboard.

Understanding Caching Terms

Here is a list of terms commonly used in and around caching. They may come in handy when you are referring to the motherboard's documentation, visiting the manufacturer's Web site, or searching the Web for information or help on caching system issues.

- *Asynchronous SRAM*—This type of SRAM (static RAM) doesn't use the system clock to control its actions. It is slower but also about one-third less expensive than synchronous SRAM.

- *Cache controller*—A special circuit that controls the interface between the CPU, cache, and the main memory controller.

- *Cache hit*—The data or instruction requested by the CPU is located in cache.

- *Cache miss*—The data or instruction requested by the CPU is not located in cache.

- *CELP (card edge low profile) socket*—The socket type normally used to mount a COAST cache module on the motherboard.

- *COAST (cache on a stick)*—A silly name, but a popular design for socket-mounted cache modules. A COAST is similar to a SIMM memory module.

- *Data RAM*—The division of cache memory that stores data or instructions.

- *Direct-mapped cache*—The type of cache that assigns only one possible location to each cached data entry.

- *External cache*—Cache that is located outside the processor; it is either soldered on the motherboard or mounted in a socket or slot very near the processor.

- *Full-associative cache*—A cache policy that allows any main memory location to be mapped to any cache line.

- *Internal cache*—Cache that is located inside the microprocessor chip.

- *Level one (L1) cache*—Cache that is located closest to the CPU and commonly located inside the processor. Also known as *primary cache.*

- *Level two (L2) cache*—Cache that is next closest to the processor after Level 1 (L1) cache. It is typically located outside the processor on the system board. Also known as *secondary cache.*

- *SRAM (static random access memory)*—The type of RAM normally used for cache memory. It is faster but more expensive than DRAM.

- *Tag RAM*—The division of cache memory that stores the address of data in cache. This section is smaller than the data RAM section, which stores the actual data or instruction.

- *Write-back (or copy-back) cache*—A cache write policy that writes data back to primary memory only when its space in cache is required for other data.

- *Write-through cache*—A cache write policy that writes data into cache and primary memory at the same time.

6. Cache Memory

Chapter 7

System Resources

In Depth

Introduction to System Resources

The inner workings of a PC—meaning how the processor works with the other components of the computer—are not as magical as they may seem. What may appear to be smoke and mirrors is actually a well-coordinated series of actions and interactions using a relatively small amount of the overall system's resources. When your application program needs a file or you wish to connect to the Internet, the processor seamlessly executes the required actions and provides the application with the requested data or displays the Web site you were seeking. How the PC's processor and components communicate to facilitate these and other similar actions is a study of how, when, and why system resources are allocated and used.

Getting the CPU's Attention

The processor controls the activities of all of the devices integrated into or attached to a PC's motherboard either directly or indirectly. Actually, these activities must be controlled from a single point or there would be chaos inside the system as the devices and services all competed for control of memory and the bus. The processor carries out the role of "traffic cop" by communicating commands, requests, and data directly to each device over communication facilities assigned specifically to each device. These communications facilities allow the processor to communicate with the PC's devices and allow the devices to pass requests and information back to the processor.

To illustrate how this communication process takes place, imagine that every device installed inside the case, either connected to or mounted on the motherboard, is assigned a light bulb and an associated mailbox. Just as a student in class raises her hand to get the teacher's attention, a device must light its light bulb to indicate when it needs the processor to do something for it. In the PC, some devices can take care of their own needs, but, for the most part, peripheral devices and other hardware components need assistance from the processor for many actions, such as moving data to and from memory.

When an application program wishes data from the hard disk drive, the hard disk's device driver works with the operating system and basic input/output system (BIOS) to instruct the processor that data is needed from the hard disk. To get the attention of the hard disk, it turns on the hard disk's light and puts a request for the data in the hard disk's mailbox. When the hard disk sees the light, it reads the request and moves the data into a buffer and turns on the hard disk light (see step 1 in Figure 7.1) and puts a request in its mailbox asking the processor to move the data from its buffer into memory. When the processor can be interrupted, it turns off the light and performs the service requested. It is very likely that while this was going on, other devices have turned on their lights as well (step 2 in Figure 7.1).

Self-Sufficient Devices

Some devices have the capability to perform the services normally requested of the processor for themselves. By taking care of their own needs, the processor is freed up to serve the requests of those devices that require assistance, in addition to all the other tasks the processor must do. The majority of the tasks requested by peripheral devices of the processor involve moving data in and out of memory. Devices that are able to directly access memory on their own without bothering the processor improve the performance of the entire PC.

What Are the PC's System Resources?

A PC's system resources, described in very general terms in the preceding sections, comprise a set of three mechanisms used by the components of a PC to communicate with the processor. The three system resource mechanisms are:

- *Interrupt Request*—An interrupt request (IRQ) is a mechanism used by devices to request services from the central processing unit (CPU). An IRQ is

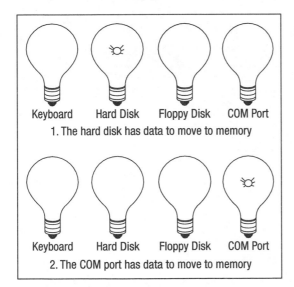

Figure 7.1   Devices signal the processor that its services are needed with a mechanism that is similar to turning on a light.

a wire in the motherboard's bus on which a device sends a signal to the processor to get its attention. All newer PCs (which means all PCs since the PC XT) have 16 IRQs. Only 10 of the IRQs are available for devices to use, and the remaining 6 are reserved for system-level purposes. Even though 10 devices may seem like a goodly number of peripherals on any PC, often there are not enough to go around, as shown in this chapter.

- *Input/Output Address*—The input/output (I/O) address is the message box used by the processor and a device to pass information, such as memory addresses, to each other. Every device attached to a PC is assigned an I/O address. This resource is also called an I/O port or an I/O base address.

- *Direct Memory Access*—A limited number of direct memory access (DMA) channels are available to devices that have the ability to access memory directly without the assistance of the CPU.

Many devices require only one of these system resources, typically an I/O address, but others may require two and perhaps all three system resources. To view the system resources on your PC, access the System Information applet from the Accessories|Systems Tools menu (see Figure 7.2).

Interrupt Requests

A peripheral device communicates with the processor through an IRQ. A device sets an IRQ to get the processor's attention whenever it needs services that only the processor can perform. When the processor notices the IRQ, it interrupts its activities to service the request (thus the term "interrupt request"). IRQs are

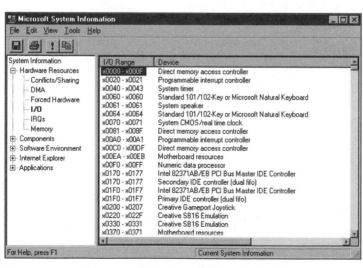

Figure 7.2   System resources on a Windows PC can be viewed through the System Information applet.

assigned to those devices that require assistance from the processor to handle data movement, data interpretation, error processing, or other tasks.

The 16 IRQs on a PC are actually two sets of 8 IRQs linked together. Of the 16 IRQs, 5 are set aside for use by internal system-level devices and 1 is used as the link between the two IRQ sets (IRQ 2 on the first set is linked to IRQ 9 on the second set), leaving only 10 available for assignments to I/O devices. Table 7.1 lists the standard default assignments of IRQs.

IRQ Connections

An interrupt request is an individual wire on the motherboard's system bus. An IRQ wire is connected to every one of the expansion ports and slots on the motherboard. Regardless of into which port, connector, or expansion slot an I/O adapter is placed, it has access to the PC's IRQs, and an expansion slot can be assigned a particular IRQ line. The particular IRQ used to support the adapter or device is determined by either the preset values of the device itself or those established in the BIOS configuration settings. Each specific hardware device can occupy only one IRQ, but an IRQ can be assigned to multiple devices. Once a device has been assigned an IRQ, the processor knows the device by its particular IRQ number. When a device sends an IRQ signal over the bus line, the number

Table 7.1   Typical IRQ assignments.

IRQ	Assignment
0	System timer
1	Standard keyboard
2	Programmable interrupt controller (PIC)
3	Serial ports 2 and 4 (COM2 and COM4)
4	Serial ports 1 and 3 (COM1 and COM3)
5	Standard sound card
6	Floppy disk controller (FDC)
7	Parallel port (LPT1)
8	CMOS and real-time clock (RTC)
9	Hardware MPEG (Moving Pictures Experts Group)
10	Modem audio
11	Video graphics array (VGA) card
12	PS/2 mouse
13	Math coprocessor/numeric data processor
14	Primary integrated drive electronics (IDE) controller
15	Secondary IDE controller

7. System Resources

of the bus line identifies the device. When the processor has completed the requested task, it sends a clearing signal over the IRQ bus line, and the device knows it may proceed.

IRQs have priorities set by the system to indicate which IRQ is to be handled first if two or more requests come in at the same time. The programmable interrupt controller (PIC) manages priorities and other IRQ control issues. PICs are discussed in a later part of this section.

Multiple Device IRQ Assignments

Because an IRQ can be assigned to multiple devices, problems can arise if this assignment is not managed properly. If two active devices share a single IRQ, the processor has no way to determine which of the two devices may have sent a request. In fact, the processor does not know if there is more than one device on an IRQ. The processor knows only that at least one device on an IRQ line has requested a service. When two active devices are contending for a single IRQ line, conflicts are inevitable. In an extreme case, both devices could send a bus signal (which is voltage on the line) simultaneously, which could short the bus, the motherboard, or the device controller.

When two devices, such as COM ports (see Table 7.1), share an IRQ, only one of the devices should be active at a time. In the early days of the mouse when most mice were serial devices, a mouse on COM3 and a modem on COM1 often shared IRQ4. When both devices were in use, there was a problem. The resolution in that case is simple: Move one of the devices to either COM2 or COM4, providing no additional conflicts arise. Today, a scanner or a Zip drive commonly shares IRQ7 with the LPT (parallel) port. The device drivers and operating systems know to compensate for some expected conflicts, but two active devices should not share an IRQ.

IRQ Assignments

Although no official standards board exists to set a standard for IRQ assignments, IRQs are assigned to a device by using common practice and working standards currently in use by the computing industry. There has never been a firm standard for IRQ assignments; processor, motherboard, chipset, and I/O adapter manufacturers have simply followed the lead of some of the larger motherboard and processor manufacturers (primarily Intel) on IRQ settings.

Table 7.2 compares the IRQ settings of the three primary bus structures that have been used in PCs. Notice that even Tables 7.1 and 7.2 differ slightly. Table 7.1 shows common IRQ settings used today, and Table 7.2 shows the default settings that were or are used on different bus structures.

Table 7.2   IRQ assignments on bus structures.

IRQ	PC XT Bus	PC AT Bus	Pentium-Class
0	System timer	System timer	System timer
1	Keyboard controller	Keyboard controller	Keyboard controller
2	8-bit available	Second IRQ controller	Second IRQ controller
3	COM2/COM4	COM2/COM4	COM2/COM4
4	COM1/COM3	COM1/COM3	COM1/COM3
5	Hard disk controller (HDC)	LPT2	Sound card
6	Floppy disk controller (FDC)	FDC	FDC
7	LPT1	LPT1	LPT1
8	Real-time clock (RTC)	RTC	RTC
9	N.A.	Available	Available
10	N.A.	Available	Available
11	N.A.	Available	Available
12	N.A.	PS/2 mouse	PS/2 mouse
13	N.A.	Math coprocessor	Math coprocessor
14	N.A.	HDC	Primary IDE controller
15	N.A.	Available	Secondary IDE controller

N.A., not applicable

Configuring IRQ Settings

A device is configured for an IRQ setting by using one of a variety of methods. Most expansion cards today use the PCI (peripheral component interconnect) interface and are plug-and-play (PnP)-compatible (more on this in a later part of this section). These cards are automatically configured to the PC, including system resource settings, by the BIOS and operating system. Legacy adapter and controller cards that use the ISA (Industry Standard Architecture), EISA (Extended ISA), and VESA (Video Electronics Standards Association) local-bus interfaces are still in use. These devices may require physical configuration to assign the system resource settings, including the IRQ. Physical configuration is usually done through jumpers or dual inline packaging (DIP) switches on the expansion card itself.

Many older adapter cards, such as video adapters and network interface cards (NICs), use jumper blocks to configure IRQ settings. The position of the jumper, as shown in Figure 7.3 on a NIC card, sets the card to use one of typically two alternative IRQ choices. Adapter cards that are configured through jumpers are usually sold preset to a preferential setting, but can be configured to one or more alternative settings through the jumper block.

Figure 7.3   A jumper is used on some adapter or controller cards to set the system resource settings.

Another means used to configure the system resources of an expansion card is the DIP switch. A DIP switch is a block of typically four or eight switches, such as that shown in Figure 7.4, that represent a binary value by moving the switches to on (open) or off (closed) positions. A card that is configured through DIP switch settings should have documentation that specifies the switch settings to use for the desired resource configuration. Like cards configured with jumpers, the DIP switches should be in their default settings from the factory, but check them anyway—it is very easy to change a switch inadvertently.

A common means of configuring the system resource settings of an expansion card is through a proprietary installation program. A card that is configured through a proprietary program will typically include a diskette or CD-ROM with the program. The disk may hold only a startup program that downloads the installation software from the manufacturer's Web site, so make sure you have Internet

Figure 7.4   A DIP switch supplies a binary value based on the positions of its switches.

access before purchasing a card that requires this type of setup. However, this approach ensures that the latest system resource setting values and device drivers are being installed. Some installation software can adjust the IRQ assignment of its device drivers to fit the existing system resource environment. However, you should always check the system resources assigned by a manufacturer's installation software to avoid resource conflicts.

BIOS Settings

If automatic resource allocation is disabled in the PCI/PnP section of the BIOS configuration data, you can specify the IRQs and DMA channels you want PnP to automatically assign to particular devices. For each IRQ or DMA channel, you can designate whether it is a PCI/PnP device, which means it is available to be assigned to PnP and PCI devices, or an ISA legacy device, which is not available for automatic assignment. PCI/PnP is the default type on all Pentium-class or later PCs.

IRQs 1, 2, 6, 8, and 13 are reserved for system use. The remaining IRQs can be designated for automatic or manual assignment. It is better to let the IRQs default to PCI/PnP unless you wish to specifically reserve one or two particular IRQs for legacy devices.

PCI and IRQs

PCI devices share a common IRQ. Each port (slot) on the PCI bus has four interrupts of its own that are mapped to the single system IRQ through a process called *IRQ steering*. The IRQ assigned to the PCI bus is typically IRQ 9, 10, 11, or 12. The four interrupts on each PCI port are designated as PIRQs (PCI interrupt requests) A through D. In most cases a PCI card uses PIRQ A.

IRQ steering prevents the system BIOS from assigning each PCI slot to a different IRQ, thus avoiding resource conflicts or a lack of resources for other devices. IRQ steering is an operating system feature of the Windows system on versions beginning with Windows 95 OSR2 (OEM). However, for IRQ steering to work correctly, the BIOS, chipset, PCI cards, and software drivers must all support it. Should IRQ conflicts occur between PCI devices, however, you should disable the PCI bus IRQ steering so you can determine exactly where the conflict is occurring.

PnP Resource Assignments

PnP is a great feature for automatically detecting and configuring system resource assignments for new PC hardware. For it to work effectively, however, it must be supported by the PC's operating system, chipset, and BIOS.

PnP is not immune to IRQ conflicts. PnP can assign only those IRQs designated in the BIOS as being available for PCI/PnP use. The way a PnP BIOS looks at the system, only PCI/PnP and legacy (ISA) devices exist. PnP will not configure a

7. System Resources

legacy device. In cases where a PnP device requires a certain IRQ or when all IRQs are in use, PnP cannot solve the problem by itself. It will add the hardware to the system, but flag it in the Device Manager with either a yellow exclamation point or a red X to indicate that a problem exists. When this happens, check the resource information on the System Information applet display for conflicts.

Note that all PCI devices are PnP devices, but not all PnP devices are PCI devices.

Programmable Interrupt Controllers

IRQs are handled by two special integrated circuits called programmable interrupt controllers. These circuits are integrated into the PC's chipset, along with many other devices (see Chapter 3 for more information on chipsets). Each PIC controls 8 IRQ lines. Figure 7.5 illustrates the general design of a PIC. The reason this controller is called programmable is that system component manufacturers can program the circuit so that each of its registers performs a particular function.

Figure 7.5 illustrates the general workings of a PIC. The IRQ lines have an interrupt mask register (IMR) and two interrupt status registers named PIC1 and PIC2. The IRQ enters the PIC through its IMR. The IMR determines if the IRQ is masked (disabled), and if it is, the request is ignored. If the IRQ is not masked (which means it is enabled), the request is recorded in the interrupt request register (IRR). The IRR holds the IRQ requests until they have been either processed or acknowledged, depending on what was requested. The priority resolver (PR) ensures that

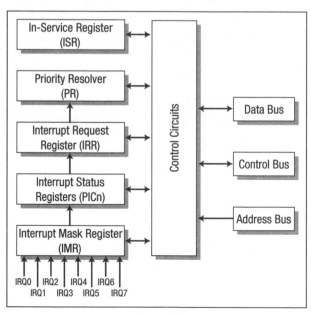

Figure 7.5   The circuitry of a PIC.

the highest priority request is handled first. Essentially, the lowest IRQs have the highest priority. When the IRQs are ready for processing, the processor is notified that requests are pending with a signal on its interrupt (INT) line. As soon as the processor completes its current task, it responds with an interrupt acknowledgment (INTA).

Once the processor has acknowledged the INT query, the active IRQ is placed in the in-service register (ISR), which always holds the IRQ currently being processed. The status of the active IRQ is updated in the IRR and the applicable ISR. The address of the IRQ is sent to the processor, and the IRQ is serviced. When the requested activity is completed, the ISR tells the PIC that the IRQ has ended, and the ISR is cleared. The highest-priority pending IRQ in the IRR is then placed in the ISR and the process repeats.

I/O Addresses

As explained in the section "Getting the CPU's Attention" at the beginning of this chapter, the processor and peripheral devices use a two-way mailbox to communicate with one another. The mailbox for each device is actually a small space in system memory, which is known by many names: the I/O address, the I/O port, and the I/O base address. The term I/O address is used most commonly—a reference to the address in memory through which a device performs its input and output operations.

For example, when the processor has data to pass to the NIC so it can be sent over the network, the data is placed at the NIC's I/O address. Likewise, when the NIC gets data from the network that the processor needs to know about, the data is placed in the NIC's I/O address. The size of the memory reserved for each device at its I/O address is large enough to hold the data it passes in and out of memory. The size of the I/O address varies; not every device is assigned the same amount of space. An NIC handles much more data than a keyboard and thus needs a bigger I/O area than does the keyboard. The amount of space assigned to a device depends mostly on the bus architecture it uses. Most devices are assigned 4, 8, or 16 bytes, but some devices use as little as 1 byte and some use as much as 64 bytes.

Literally thousands of I/O areas are available, but conflicts do occur when multiple devices attempt to use the same I/O address or when devices have overlapping areas. For example, NICs are commonly assigned the I/O address of 360h (the "h" indicates the address is expressed as a hexadecimal number). The default I/O address for LPT1 is 378h. If the NIC requires 32 bytes of I/O space, its ending address would be 37Fh, which creates an overlapping conflict with the parallel port. As long as no parallel devices are in use, there shouldn't be a problem. However, if an external device, such as a printer, is attached to the LPT1 port, the NIC will need to be assigned a different I/O address.

This approach to moving data is called *memory-mapped I/O*. Each device is mapped to a specific location in memory (hence the name). After a device has placed data in its I/O address area, it contacts the processor, typically with an IRQ, to let it know the data is ready. Because the device is mapped to its memory area, the processor knows where in memory the device's I/O buffer is located.

Common I/O Address Assignments

Even though no formal standards exist to permanently set I/O address assignments, a generally accepted list of I/O address assignments is commonly used. Table 7.3 lists the most common default I/O address assignments used on PCs.

Table 7.3   Commonly used I/O address assignments.

I/O Address	Area Size (Bytes)	Assigned To
0000–000Fh	16	Slave DMA controller chip
0010–001Fh	16	System
0060–0063h	4	Keyboard
0064–0067h	4	PS/2 port
00C0–00DEh	32	Master DMA controller
0130–014Fh	32	Small computer system interface (SCSI) host adapter
01F0–01F7h	8	Primary IDE channel
0200–0207h	8	Game port
0220–022Fh	16	Sound card
0270–0273h	4	PnP hardware
0278–027Ah	2	Parallel port (LPT2)
0280–028Fh	16	LCD Display
02E8–02EFh	8	Serial port (COM4)
02F8–02FFh	8	Serial port (COM2)
0300–031Fh	32	NICs
0320–032Fh	16	Legacy HDCs
0330–0331h	2	Musical instrument digital interface (MIDI)
0360–036Fh	16	NICs (alternate)
0378–037Ah	2	Parallel port (LPT1)
03C0–03DFh	32	VGA video display adapter
03E0–03E7h	8	PC card (PCMCIA) port controller
03E8–03EFh	8	Serial port (COM3)
03F0–03F6h	8	Floppy disk drive interface

(continued)

Table 7.3   Commonly used I/O address assignments *(continued).*

I/O Address	Area Size (Bytes)	Assigned To
03F8–03FFh	8	Serial port (COM1)
0533–0537h	4	Windows sound system
0678–067Fh	8	Enhanced parallel port (EPP)
0CF8–0CFBh	4	PCI data registers
FF00–FF07h	8	IDE bus mastering

I/O addresses are assigned in the area between addresses 0000h and FFFFh, which represents 65,536 bytes. Table 7.3 does not list every possible I/O address assignment. Several other I/O addresses are used for supplemental space for some devices and services, such as IDE bus mastering, serial ports, parallel ports, and IDE controllers.

An I/O address is intended for a single device; multiple active devices sharing an I/O port can have disastrous results. Because the system is designed to be one-on-one, no identification is involved, which means that the processor or a device cannot possibly know for which device a message is intended or even which device is sending data. Legacy situations do exist, such as on older parallel ports and ISA adapters, in which more than one device is hard-wired to a particular I/O address, but these situations are quickly disappearing. These situations occur when a legacy adapter card, which can be physically configured to only one of two I/O addresses, creates an I/O address collision with another legacy device.

I/O Addresses in Windows

Like IRQs, I/O address assignments can be viewed on a Windows PC through the Device Manager or the System Information applet. Figure 7.6 shows the Computer Properties window with the I/O address resources displayed. This list displays the I/O addresses assigned to the PC's devices. You may also see entries that are listed as "In use by an unknown device" or as "Alias to" entries for devices requiring additional space.

You can also use the Device Manager to display the system resource assignments of an individual device (see Figure 7.7), including its I/O address. If a conflict exists for a device, it will have either a black exclamation point in a yellow circle or a red X on the Device Manager's tree. Any conflict that exists can be resolved by assigning the device to a different I/O address. Because some system resources are set aside for standard devices that are not found on every PC, they can be reassigned.

7. System Resources

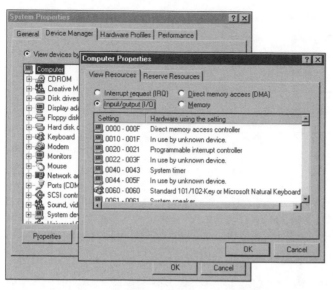

Figure 7.6   The I/O assignments on a PC displayed on the Computer Properties window.

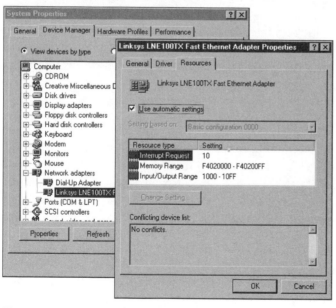

Figure 7.7   The Properties window of a specific device showing its I/O address assignments.

Direct Memory Access

DMA allows non-PCI bus adapters and devices to access memory directly without assistance from the processor. This means a DMA device can move data in and out of random access memory (RAM) on its own. The processor normally controls all activities on the bus, but on most newer systems, the DMA controller is allowed to move data in and out of RAM while the processor takes care of other tasks. The DMA controller is integrated into the motherboard. ISA cards and integrated drive electronics/advanced technology attachment (IDE/ATA) interface devices have access to a PC's DMA channels. PCI and AGP (accelerated graphics port) buses do not support DMA.

DMA Operation

Without DMA, data is transferred from a peripheral device, such as a modem, through the IRQ process. However, when a DMA device, such as the floppy disk drive, needs to transfer data, it requests assistance from the DMA controller. The DMA controller takes control of the system bus and acts as a pass-through between the DMA device and RAM, as illustrated in Figure 7.8. With the DMA controller controlling the system bus, data is transferred directly from the DMA device into memory. The DMA controller releases control of the bus when the data transfer is complete.

DMA data transfers require fewer steps than those that use the IRQ process to move data, and they eliminate the overhead of the interrupt processing. When the processor is interrupted, it must save its current state (what it was doing), process the interrupt, restore its state, and then resume what it was doing. Saving and restoring its state requires numerous processor cycles. DMA devices thus help to make the entire PC more efficient.

DMA Channels

DMA devices are assigned to DMA channels, another single-device system resource. Only in very limited instances can two DMA devices share a single DMA channel, and, like IRQs, they cannot both be active at the same time. Table 7.4 lists the eight DMA channels and the devices most commonly assigned to each. Channels 0 and 4 are reserved for use by the system, and channel 2 is typically assigned to the floppy disk drive. If the PC includes an enhanced capabilities port (ECP) parallel port, another DMA channel (either DMA channel 1 or 3) is reserved

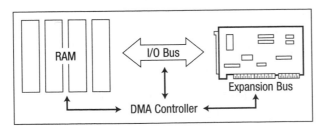

Figure 7.8   The components of a DMA channel.

Table 7.4   DMA channel assignments.

DMA Channel	Common Device	Other Uses
0	Memory refresh	None
1	Sound card	SCSI host adapter, ECP, NIC, voice modem
2	Floppy disk drive	Tape drive
3	Open	SCSI host adapter, ECP, NIC, voice modem
4	Cascade to DMA 0-3	None
5	Sound card	SCSI host adapter, NIC
6	Open	Sound card, NIC
7	Open	Sound card, NIC

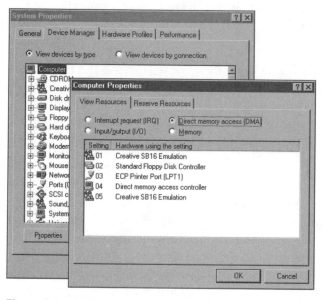

Figure 7.9   DMA channel assignments shown in the Computer Properties window of the
Windows Device Manager.

for it. A PC thus has either four or five DMA channels available to assign to ISA
devices. Figure 7.9 shows the DMA assignments on a Windows PC.

DMA Modes

Some IDE/ATA devices, such as floppy disk drives, use two sets of DMA modes
to transfer data. The modes are differentiated by the amount of data moved.
Single-word DMA modes move one word (2 bytes or 16 bits) of data in each

transfer with data transfer speeds ranging from 960 nanoseconds (ns) to as fast as 240 ns, or from 2.1 to 8.3 megabytes per second (MBps). A single-word DMA transfer must repeat the entire DMA transfer process for each two bytes of data. A multiword DMA transfer transfers data in bursts of multiple words, eliminating the overhead of transferring only two bytes at a time. Multiword DMA modes move data at speeds between 480 ns (4.2 MBps) in mode 0 and 120 ns (16.7 MBps) in mode 3. Virtually all DMA modes on current PCs are multiword.

Bus Mastering

Most ISA devices implement what is called third-party DMA or conventional DMA, in which the DMA controller, located on the motherboard, manages the data transfer between a DMA device and RAM (which are the first two parties of the transfer). Third-party DMA is an older implementation and is considered slow compared to first-party DMA.

A first-party DMA device has its own DMA controller built into the device. This allows the device itself to control the DMA data transfer directly. First-party DMA uses what is called bus mastering to control the data transfer and does not require assistance from the motherboard's DMA controller.

Bus mastering means that the DMA device takes over the bus, thus becoming the bus "master." This allows the device and memory to transfer data without either the processor or the DMA controller. For an IDE/ATA device to implement bus mastering, its adapter must be installed in a PCI bus slot. The main benefit of bus mastering DMA is that it frees the processor to work on other tasks.

Memory Addresses

Some devices also require a block of memory in the upper memory area of RAM in addition to the space at the I/O address. This block of memory is used primarily for mapping a device's BIOS into memory or as a temporary holding area. Memory address blocks are assigned during the system boot process. These memory blocks are not system resources in the sense of IRQs, I/O addresses, and DMA channels; however, Windows lists them along with the system resources on the Computer Properties window (see Figure 7.10). Like system resources, memory addresses can create problems or conflicts if two devices should overlap their memory blocks.

As illustrated in Figure 7.10, the devices that use memory address blocks are those that require their own device BIOS running in memory, such as PnP devices, SCSI host adapters, bus controllers, processor to bus bridges, NICs with wake-on-LAN technology, and other chipset and expansion card services.

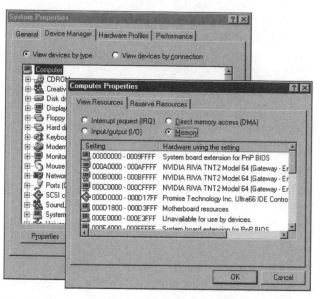

Figure 7.10   The Computer Properties window showing memory address assignments.

Immediate Solutions

Resolving Resource Conflicts

Resource conflicts do not just happen. They normally show up after you have installed a new device. If you have any of the following symptoms, you very likely have a resource conflict:

- The PC locks up frequently for no apparent reason.
- The mouse operates erratically or not at all.
- The PC boots into Windows Safe Mode.
- You cannot format a floppy disk in the floppy disk drive.
- Anything printed on the printer is gibberish.
- The monitor displays distorted or strange images.
- The sound card either doesn't work or doesn't sound just right.
- Any existing device that was working before a new device, especially a modem, was installed suddenly stops working.

TIP: You should update your antivirus software and scan the PC just to verify that a virus is not causing the problem.

The Windows Device Manager is a good place to start when you think you may have a system resource conflict. The Device Manager will indicate if any of the installed devices have an issue by displaying one of three symbols: a blue i, a yellow exclamation point, or a red X. If a device has one of these symbols, you should investigate. The blue symbol is just a flag, but the yellow and red symbols indicate trouble and need to be resolved. See the explanations of these symbols in the solution "Troubleshooting IRQs" later in this chapter.

7. System Resources

Avoiding Resource Problems When Installing New Hardware Devices

Virtually every device installed in a PC expansion slot or directly to the motherboard requires system resources. The best way to avoid resource conflicts when installing new or replacement hardware is to install one device at a time and then test the system after each one. You should not install several new devices and then try to determine which is causing a resource conflict. Troubleshooting is much easier if you add each device in a completely separate installation process.

Read the documentation that comes with a new device or component, especially the sections covering installation and troubleshooting. In the best case, the documentation presents a remedy for a problem caused by the device. If not, the telephone number of the technical support desk of the manufacturer is probably indicated in the documentation.

Troubleshooting IRQs

The most common, and just about only, problem you can experience with IRQs is that two devices have been assigned to the same IRQ. The solution is to reassign one of the devices to a new IRQ using the Device Manager, the BIOS settings, or by changing the card's jumper or DIP switch values.

A common IRQ problem involves conflicts on IRQs 2 and 9. Originally, PCs had only eight IRQs. When the second set of eight IRQs was added, the two sets were linked through IRQs 2 and 9 (on the upper group). Video cards and other devices are occasionally assigned to IRQ 2, which means that they may conflict with any device installed on IRQ 9 if they are both active at the same time.

Two devices that will not be used at the same time, such as a modem and a NIC (although this is a very strange pair of devices to share on an IRQ), installed on the same IRQ should not create a problem. However, a more common situation is to have devices installed on both COM2 (e.g., a modem) and COM4 (e.g., a serial mouse) that cannot operate at the same time. This is common with a legacy system on which a device is installed using proprietary installation software.

Checking Out IRQ Settings

Not every PC has all of the devices listed in Table 7.1. In fact, on any particular PC, the IRQs can be assigned differently. To find what the IRQ settings are on a Windows PC, use the following steps:

1. From the Windows Desktop, right-click the My Computer icon. From the shortcut menu that appears, choose Properties to display the System Properties window, as shown in Figure 7.11.

2. Select the Device Manager tab. Highlight the Computer entry and click the Properties button located at the bottom of the Device window. This displays the Computer Properties window, as shown in Figure 7.12.

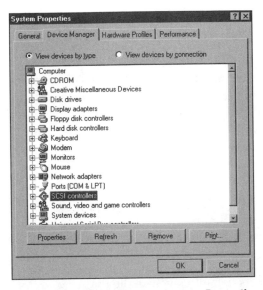

Figure 7.11   The Windows System Properties window.

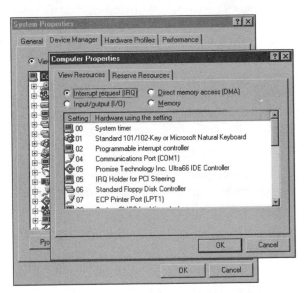

Figure 7.12   The Windows Computer Properties window.

3. Select the View Resources tab and click on the Interrupt Request (IRQ) radio button to display the IRQ assignments on your PC.

4. Compare the IRQ assignments of your PC to those in Table 7.1. They should match for the most part. Any exceptions are likely due to PnP devices or to adjustments made to avoid conflicts. If there are differences, you don't

necessarily have to change your IRQ settings. Table 7.1 lists typical or default settings, which are by no means the only settings that will work.

You should always review the current IRQ settings before installing new hardware in the PC that requires an IRQ or any system resources. You should also review the documentation of the new device to determine the IRQ (and system resources) settings it requires. If the device's default IRQ is available on the system, there should be no problem with the installation or the operation of the device. However, if that IRQ is not available, you may need to reassign the IRQ or reconfigure the new device to an available IRQ.

Setting an IRQ with the Windows Device Manager

Use the Windows Device Manager to configure IRQs after a PnP device or a proprietary installation program has created a conflict by assigning a new device to an IRQ already in use by another device.

When you open the Device Manager, its default view lists the PC's devices by type, which means the general category of each device, as was shown in Figure 7.11. Clicking on the plus sign (+) of a category expands the device category to show its devices.

If a problem exists with a device, it is indicated with one of three symbols:

- *A yellow circle with a black exclamation point*—This symbol before a device name indicates a possible resource conflict.

- *A red circle with a white X*—This symbol before a device name indicates the device has been disabled, removed, or that Windows is unable to locate it.

- *A white circle with a blue lower case i*—This symbol before a device name indicates only that automatic settings are disabled and the device was configured manually, possibly under software control. There is not necessarily a problem. This symbol is really just a reminder.

If a device conflict exists, the details of the problem are listed on the Properties window for the device itself in the Conflicting Device List box at the bottom of the window. Figure 7.13 shows a device with no device conflicts, but if this device is having problems, it is more likely a device driver issue.

If you encounter an IRQ or I/O address conflict with a device, it may be necessary to change its resource assignments. If required, follow the steps listed in the solution "Changing a Device's System Resource Settings" later in this chapter to change the resource settings for a hardware device on a Windows PC.

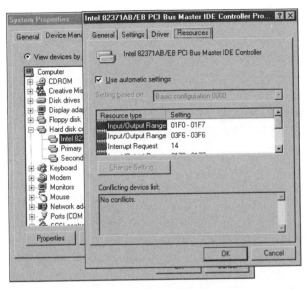

Figure 7.13   The Device Properties window showing no resource conflicts.

You may find that very few of your system resources can actually be changed, and when you attempt to change a resource, an error message box pops up telling you that you cannot change the values of a resource. The primary reasons for this condition are:

- The device is a legacy device and its resource settings are configured with jumpers or DIP switches on the adapter card.
- The device is integrated into the motherboard or chipset, or mounted to the motherboard through a riser (daughter) board and has a preset resource setting.
- The device cannot be configured to any of the available resources unless resources are freed up.

Troubleshooting DMA Channels

Troubleshooting DMA channels is fairly straightforward. A DMA device will use whatever channel is available to it, so what may look like a DMA channel problem (meaning it is not an IRQ problem) may actually be either an I/O address or memory address issue.

First, try choosing another I/O address or memory address for the device if the device lists alternatives. If that fails, try using the Windows Troubleshooting utility before calling the manufacturer's technical support.

Changing a Device's System Resource Settings

If you wish to change the IRQ settings of a device, provided the system will let you, use the following steps:

1. Open the Device Manager by right-clicking the My Computer icon and choosing Properties.

2. Highlight the device you wish to change and click the Properties button.

3. On the device's Properties window, choose the Resources tab. If there is no Resources tab, this means that the device does not use system resources or does not have any alterable resources.

4. Remove the checkmark on the Use Automatic Settings checkbox.

5. Highlight the resource you wish to choose and click the Change Settings button. Figure 7.14 shows the dialog box that should display if the resource

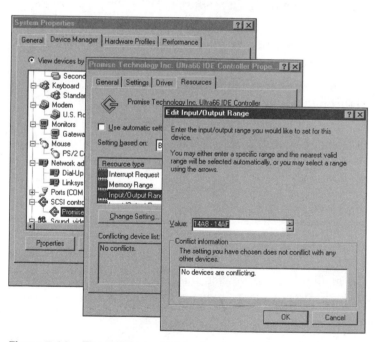

Figure 7.14   The Edit box used to change a system resource setting in the Windows Device Manager.

you have chosen can be changed. If the resource cannot be changed, a message box will display to tell you that.

6. After you change the value of the setting, verify that no conflicts show up in the Conflict Information box before you click OK to effect the change.

7. Click OK to close the open Device Manager windows and restart the system to completely verify that no problems exist.

8. If the system will not boot after the change, enter Windows Safe Mode and make any necessary adjustments to remove the resource problem. To start the PC in Windows Safe Mode, press the F8 key when you see the first Windows splash screen. The Startup menu will display. Choose Safe Mode from the menu. Windows will start but with only essential device drivers.

Running Windows Troubleshooting

If the system resource problems cannot be resolved through the Device Manager, it may be time for more serious troubleshooting. Boot the PC into Safe Mode (see preceding solution) and from the Safe Mode desktop, do the following:

1. Open the Control Panel and double-click the System icon.

2. Choose the Performance tab and choose the File System button from the Advanced Settings near the bottom of the window.

3. The File System Properties window shown in Figure 7.15 displays. Choose the Troubleshooting tab. Check every option in the Settings area and attempt to reboot the PC into normal mode. If the PC does boot into normal mode, uncheck one item and restart the PC. Keep repeating this step, unchecking another item and restarting the PC until the system fails. You should have isolated the problem device.

4. If the PC would not reboot into normal mode, reboot into Safe Mode. Use the Device Manager to disable every device (except those under System Devices) and then attempt to reboot into normal mode. If you can, more than likely the issue is a bad or out-of-date device driver. Re-enable devices by type and restart the PC. You should eventually isolate the device group that has the problem device.

5. If the PC will not boot into Safe Mode, you need to begin physically removing devices from the PC one at a time and restarting until the PC will boot and you have isolated the device causing the problem. Once you have isolated the problem device, try putting the other devices back into the PC and rebooting. More than one or a combination of devices may be causing the problem.

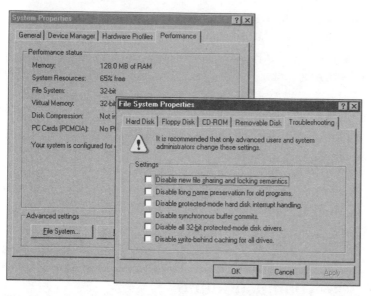

Figure 7.15   The Troubleshooting tab on the File System Properties window.

Decoding Resource Error Codes in the Windows Device Manager

If a resource conflict exists and you are unsure of the source of the problem, you should look on the General tab of a device's Properties window. Although Figure 7.16 shows a device with no problems, if a problem did exist related to the device's system resource settings, an error code and message would be included in the device Status box. Windows 98 and 2000 PCs include a Solutions button that provides suggestions on possible solutions.

Many Device Manager error codes exist (around 35 and growing), and most of them deal with device driver issues. The ones that relate to resource conflicts are:

- *Code 6*—Another device is already assigned the resources requested by a device. Change the new device's resource settings.

- *Code 9*—The BIOS is reporting the device's system resources incorrectly. It could be that you need only remove the device from the Device Manager and let the system detect and install it, or you may need to upgrade the BIOS on the PC.

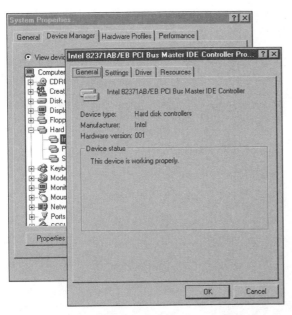

Figure 7.16   The Device Status box on the General tab of a device's Properties window.

- *Code 12*—No available resources exist of the type requested by a device. Another device must be removed, disabled, or its resources shared to install the new device.

- *Code 15*—The device is causing a resource conflict and must be reconfigured.

- *Code 16*—Windows cannot identify the resource needed by the device. You may need to fill in some missing resources on the device's Properties window. Follow the device documentation for the values you should use.

- *Code 17*—A child device has been assigned a resource not assigned to the parent. Either use automatic settings or configure the device to be compatible to its parent.

- *Code 27*—Windows is unable to specify the resources for the device as configured. Check the documentation and make any necessary adjustments.

- *Code 29*—No resources were assigned to the device by the PC's BIOS. Most likely, the device needs to be enabled in the BIOS Setup configuration data.

- *Code 30*—The requested IRQ is already in use by a device that cannot share the IRQ. Change the IRQ setting for the device or find a more compatible device with which to share.

7. System Resources

Dealing with IRQ Steering

To check to see if IRQ steering is enabled on your system, follow these steps:

1. Open the Windows Device Manager. Click on the plus sign (+) to expand the System Devices device type.

2. Highlight the selection for PCI Bus and click Properties.

3. Select the IRQ Steering tab to display the window shown in Figure 7.17.

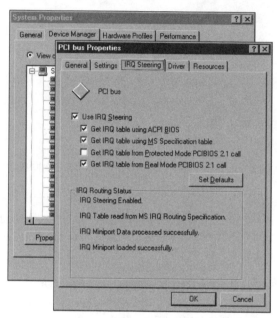

Figure 7.17   The IRQ Steering tab of the PCI Bus Properties window.

For IRQ steering to be activated, the checkbox Use IRQ Steering must be checked. The other checkboxes on this window tell IRQ steering where it should look for its IRQ routing information:

- *ACPI (Advanced Configuration and Power Interface) BIOS*—Indicates the first IRQ routing table to use to program IRQ steering. ACPI is a power management specification that provides hardware status information to the operating system.

- *MS specification table*—Indicates that the Microsoft specification table is the second IRQ routing table to be used to program IRQ steering.

- *PCI BIOS 2.1 real mode*—Is not checked by default. This mode is selected only when a PCI device is not working properly. When checked, it specifies that this is the third IRQ routing table to be used to program IRQ steering.

- *PCI BIOS 2.1 protected mode*—When checked, indicates that this routing table is to be used to program IRQ steering.

If the system BIOS cannot configure a PCI device, try a different combination of options, including selecting the PCI BIOS 2.1 real mode. If the default selections do not work, it is more likely that you need to update the BIOS. One sure way to tell that you may need a BIOS update is that IRQ steering is causing the system to lock up or display **kernal32.dll** error messages.

To unselect IRQ steering, merely click on the Use IRQ Steering checkbox to deselect it, and reboot the system.

7. System Resources

Chapter 8

Hard Disks and Floppy Disks

In Depth

PC Storage Devices

Originally, the PC did not have a hard disk drive, but it is now difficult to imagine a PC without one. Virtually every PC sold in the past five or so years has had at least one hard disk drive installed inside its case. The floppy disk, which has been virtually obsolete for at least five years, still hangs on, and can still be found in most PC systems—even new systems being sold today. Rumor persists that the floppy will die off and be replaced by Zip/Jaz disks, super disks, and other removable storage media.

The hard disk and floppy disk are secondary storage devices on a PC. The primary storage is the PC's main memory, or random access memory (RAM; see Chapter 5 for more information about memory). Thus, the primary storage is the PC's active storage, which temporarily stores data while it is in use by the system, and is referred to as temporary storage. The secondary storage, which holds data, programs, and other objects, even after the power goes off, and includes hard disks, floppy disks, Zip disks, compact disk recordable (CD-R) disks, and others, is referred to as permanent storage.

The hard disk and floppy disk drives are by far the most commonly used forms of secondary storage. The future of disk storage definitely includes the hard disk drive, but the future of the floppy disk drive is probably less secure.

Hard Disk Drives

The hard disk used in virtually all PCs is derived from mainframe fixed disks and the early Winchester drives introduced in the early 1980s. These drives became known as hard disk drives on the PC to differentiate them from floppy disk drives. The technology used to record data on a hard disk has remained essentially the same as that used on these early drives, although the size of the present drive is quite smaller, its speeds are much faster, and the capacity is very much larger than that of the earlier versions.

Data Organization

Hard disk and floppy disk drives organize their media into tracks, sectors, cylinders, and clusters. This organization, along the servo system on the disk (see the section "Servo Systems" later in this chapter), sets up the addressing system used to locate, store, and retrieve data from the disk.

The basic organization elements on hard and floppy disks are the following:

- *Tracks*—A floppy disk has around 80 tracks; a hard disk may have a thousand or more tracks. Figure 8.1 illustrates how disk tracks are concentric bands that complete one circumference of the disk. The first track on a disk, typically track 0, is on the outside edge of the disk.

- *Sectors*—Disks are divided into cross sections that cut across all tracks, as illustrated in Figure 8.1. The result is that each track is broken into a number of addressable pieces, called sectors. A sector is 512 bytes in length. A hard disk has from 100 to 300 sectors per track, and a floppy disk from 9 to 18 sectors per track. Sectoring creates addressable elements on a track, including its starting point.

- *Cylinders*—All of the tracks with the same number on all of the platters of a hard disk drive create a logical entity called a cylinder. The read/write heads of a disk move in unison and all are over the same track number on each disk platter. A hard disk with three platters, as illustrated in Figure 8.2, has six disk surfaces and six track 27s, which logically create cylinder 27. Cylinders are not a part of floppy disks.

- *Clusters*—Clusters are logical groupings of disk sectors used by operating systems to track and transfer data to and from the disk. Typically, a cluster has around 64 sectors, with the total capacity of the disk drive and the operating system determining the number of sectors in a cluster on any particular PC. Operating systems that use clusters as the basic transfer units operate in what is called *block mode*.

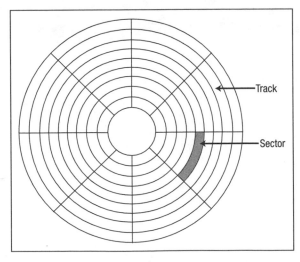

Figure 8.1   Tracks and sectors on a disk.

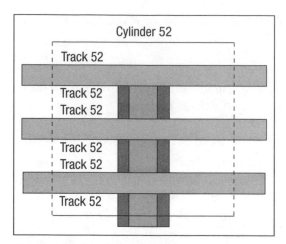

Figure 8.2   Disk cylinders are made up of the same tracks on each platter.

Disk Capacities

Disk drive capacities are stated in megabytes (millions of bytes) and gigabytes (billions of bytes), and drives with terabyte (trillions of bytes) capacity are beginning to appear. Table 8.1 lists the common data capacity measurements used with disk drives.

Most of the hard disk drives available today are in the 1GB to 40GB range and come in many different types and styles. However, they use the same basic components, are constructed essentially the same way, and operate the same. Where they differ is in their storage capacities, speeds, how they encode the data, and the interface used to communicate with the PC.

Table 8.1   Data capacity measurements.

Measurement	Abbreviation	Capacity
Kilobyte	KB	One thousand bytes
Megabyte	MB	One million bytes
Gigabyte	GB	One billion bytes
Terabyte	TB	One trillion bytes
Petabyte	PB	One quadrillion bytes
Exabyte	EB	One quintillion bytes

Hard Disk Drive Components

A typical hard disk has the following major components (see Figure 8.3):

- Disk platters
- Spindle and spindle motor
- Storage media
- Read/write heads
- Head actuators
- Air filter
- Logic and controller boards
- Connectors and jumpers
- Bezel

With the exception of the connectors and jumpers and the controller board, all of the other components on this list are inside the metal enclosure of the disk drive, which is called the head disk assembly (HDA). The HDA is a sealed unit that is never opened except at the factory.

Disk Platters

The platters are primary components of a hard disk drive. The data stored in the hard disk is recorded on the platters. Hard disk platters are made from one of two primary materials: aluminum alloy and a glass-ceramic composite. Aluminum

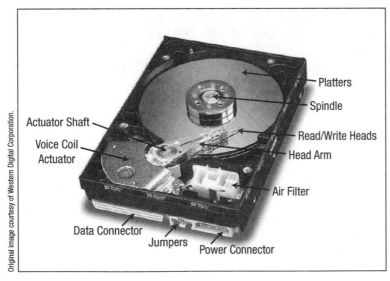

Figure 8.3   The major components of a hard disk drive.

Original image courtesy of Western Digital Corporation.

alloy has been used for hard disk platters almost from the beginning because it provides strength in a lightweight material. However, because aluminum platters expand and flex when heated, which can result in misreads and corrupted data, a glass-ceramic material is now used for most disk platters.

Glass-ceramic platters need to be only about half the thickness of an aluminum disk to have the same rigidity. Because glass disks do not expand or contract as the temperature changes, they are more reliable than those made of aluminum alloy. As the size of disk drives continues to shrink and the amount of data increases, all hard disks will likely be manufactured with glass-ceramic platters. Many of the top hard disk manufacturers, including Seagate, Toshiba, and Maxtor, are already using glass composite materials.

PC hard drives have between one and ten platters, with the majority using two platters to store data. The smaller form factor hard disks use either one or two platters. The number of platters used is controlled by the overall size of the disk drive. The form factor of the hard disk drive is derived from the diameter of its platters. However, it can also mean the size of the drive bay into which the drive can be installed.

The common hard disk form factors and their platter sizes are listed in Table 8.2.

The 3.5-inch form factor drive has been the most popular of the disks listed in Table 8.2 for some years. Prior to that, the 5.25-inch drive was used in most desktop and tower-style PCs. The 2.5-inch drive and 1.8-inch drives are popular for notebook computers because of their size and weight.

Platters are mounted to a spindle inside the HDA, as illustrated in Figure 8.4. The platters are separated with disk spacers that keep them evenly spaced and provide the space needed for the read/write heads to access the data on each side of the platter. Each surface of the platter is polished and covered with a very thin layer of magnetic material that is used to hold the electromagnetic charge representing the data stored on the disk.

Table 8.2   Common PC hard disk drive form factors.

Form Factor	Platter Size
5.25 inch	5.12 inches (130 mm)
2.5 inch	2.5 inches (63.5 mm)
3.5 inch	3.74 inches (95 mm)
1.8 inch	1.8 inches (45.7 mm)

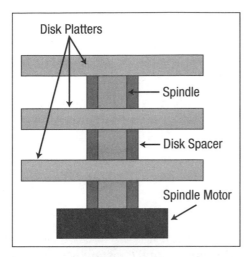

Figure 8.4   The platters of the disk drive are attached to the disk spindle.

When Is a Disk a Disc?

Many so-called experts insist that the platters inside the hard disk are "discs," and they are referred to with that spelling in different publications and Web sites. Essentially, the two spellings ("disk" versus "disc") are now interchangeable, but some diehards still insist on the "disc" spelling. The CD-ROM and DVD folks insist that "disc" is reserved for optical disks. In reality, either spelling is fine—a disk is a disc is a disk—and the "disk" spelling is used most often.

The Spindle Motor

As discussed in the preceding section and shown in Figure 8.4, the platters are mounted to the disk spindle. The spindle (including the platters mounted to it) is rotated by the spindle motor at speeds of 3,600, 4,800, 5,400, 7,200 and 7,400 revolutions per minute (rpm). Many newer hard disk drives have rotational speeds of 10,000 or 15,000 rpm. The spindle motor is a direct-drive motor mounted to the bottom on the spindle assembly.

The spindle motor, shown in Figure 8.5, is connected directly to the spindle. No belts or gears are used in this mechanism, to eliminate noise and vibration that could cause read/write problems on the platters. The two types of spindle motors used in hard disk drives are in-hub motors, which are placed inside the HDA, and bottom-mount motors, which are placed outside the HDA. The spindle disk motor, which is a brushless and sensorless direct current (DC) motor, is designed to prevent oil or dust from contaminating the sealed dust-free environment inside the HDA. Special seals are placed in the spindle drive assembly to prevent the lubricating oil, which can turn into a mist at the spindle motor's high rotation

8. Hard Disks and Floppy Disks

Photo courtesy of Samsung Electro-Mechanics of Korea.

Figure 8.5   Views of a spindle motor.

rates, from getting inside the HDA. The spindle motor is obviously a vital part of the disk drive's operation, but because of its speeds and constant use, many hard disk failures are the result of a spindle motor failure.

Read/Write Heads

The hard disk's read/write heads are constructed with a magnetic core wrapped by one or more electrical wires through which an electrical current is passed in one direction or the other to change the polarity of the magnetic field emanating from the core. As the read/write head passes over the magnetic media, the polarity of the core is changed as needed to change the value stored in a certain location on the platter's magnetic media (see the section "Storage Media" later in this chapter for more information on the magnetic media on the disk platter).

Each side of a disk platter has magnetic media to store data and at least one read/write head. Figure 8.6 illustrates a disk drive with two disk platters and four read/write heads, one for each platter surface. The read/write head for each surface is connected to an actuator mechanism that moves the read/write heads in and out together, moving between the inside edge of the platter near the spindle to the outside edge. When the read/write head over the top platter, or disk 0, is over track 29, for example, all of the other read/write heads are also over track 29 on the other platter surfaces. As the read/write heads are moved around the disk surfaces, only one head is active at a time.

Read/Write Head Technology

The four types of read/write heads that have been or currently are used in hard disk drives are the following:

- *Ferrite heads*—Ferrite heads use an iron-oxide core wrapped with an electromagnetic coil that is energized to create a magnetic field. They are the oldest, biggest, and heaviest of the magnetic-head designs. Due to their size, ferrite

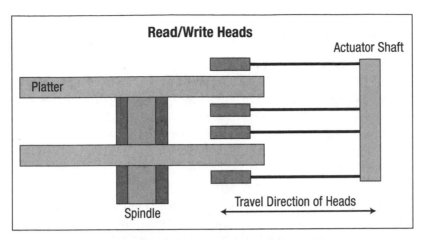

Figure 8.6   Each platter has a read/write head for each of its sides.

heads use a larger floating height, compared to other heads, to guard against contacting the disk surface.

- *Metal-in-gap (MIG) heads*—MIG read/write heads are an enhanced version of ferrite heads. Additional metal is added to the head on the leading and trailing edges of the head gap, which allows it to ignore nearby fields and focus only on the fields beneath the head.

- *Thin-film (TF) heads*—TF read/write heads are manufactured from semiconductor material (see Chapter 3) and are used in small form factor high-capacity drives. They are light and much more accurate than ferrite heads and operate much closer to the disk surface.

- *Magneto-resistive (MR) heads*—MR heads are used as the read heads in most 3.5-inch disk drives with a capacity above 1GB. Disk drives with MR heads typically also have a TF head for writing data.

Reading and Writing the Disk

As the read/write head passes over the platter in a write operation, its polarity changes the orientation of the magnetic particles of the disk's media (see the section "Storage Media" later in this chapter) to represent an electrical value, either a binary 1 or 0. As the polarity of the head is changed, the electrical value of the disk's media also changes. The polarity of the read/write head is changed by reversing the direction of the electrical flow in the wire wrapped around the head's core, which influences the storage media, and data is written to the disk. To read data from the disk, the read/write head needs only to detect the polarity of the storage media's stored electrical value.

On new, formatted, or erased disks, the particles in each magnetic field are randomly assigned, which makes the disk appear blank to the read/write heads. When the particles in a field are aligned in one direction or another, the read/write heads will recognize them as having a value representing a binary digit.

The disk's read/write heads float over a platter's surface on a cushion of air. When the disk drive is operating, the high-speed rotation of the disk platters creates air pressure that pushes the read/write heads away from the disk surfaces. Springs in the read/write head's actuator arm provide resistance that keeps the head floating above the disk's surface at a constant height of 3 to 5 microinches (millionths of an inch). This space is called the floating height or the head gap. When the disk drive is not operating and the platters are not turning, the springs force the heads onto the surface of the disk, but only after they have been retracted to a safe parking zone. Disk drives have a landing zone, located beyond the inside edge of a disk's recording area, where the head can be safely parked. Virtually all disks automatically park their heads when the power is turned off.

Recording Data on the Disk

Magnetic flux is used to record data on the disk's media. Flux refers to the process used to align the particles in a single magnetic field to a single direction. The read/write head reverses its polarity back and forth to change the particle alignment of each field on the disk—a process called flux reversal. The read/write head uses a series of flux reversals to alter the particles in a bit cell, or a cluster of magnetic particles that represents a single binary digit (bit).

As illustrated in Figure 8.7, the read/write head acts as a flux voltage detector. Each time the head detects a flux transition, it sends a voltage pulse. A flux transition is a change from a positive charge to a negative charge or from negative to positive. If no transition is detected, no pulse is sent.

A component called an encoder/decoder (endec, for short) converts the voltage pulse signals into binary data and converts binary data into flux transitions. When the read/write head is performing a write operation, the endec creates a signal pattern to be stored on the disk. During a read operation, the endec interprets the voltage pulses and converts them to binary data.

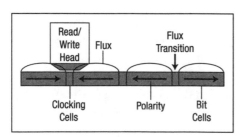

Figure 8.7   The read/write head senses the flux transition of the disk's media to store data on the disk.

Read/write operations use a clock signal to ensure that all of the electronic devices involved remain synchronized. Each data signal is preceded with a clock signal that is used by the read/write head and the endec to ensure they are working on the same clock signal. Should they get out of sync, they use the clock signals to resynchronize themselves. Clock cells are also stored on the disk media between bit cells. Because a voltage pulse is sent for a flux transition, two clock cells in a row indicate no transition was detected. The clock signals also help the endec determine the data value being stored or retrieved.

Head Actuators

A head actuator positions the hard disk's read/write heads by extending and retracting the heads over the platters. Two very different types of actuators are used on modern hard disk drives: stepper motor actuators and voice coil actuators. A stepper motor actuator is slow, sensitive to temperature changes, and less reliable than a voice coil actuator. A voice coil actuator is fast, unaffected by temperature changes, and extremely reliable. It would thus appear obvious which type you would desire, but a stepper motor actuator is also less expensive, which makes it desirable to some manufacturers. The type of actuator used in a disk drive speaks volumes about the drive's performance, reliability, and cost.

A stepper motor is an electrical motor that moves in a series of steps. The motor cannot stop between steps and must advance from one step to the next to operate. On a disk drive that uses a stepper motor actuator to move the read/write heads, the stepper motor is located outside of the HDA and connects to the head arm gang through a sealed hole in the HDA case. The stepper motor connects to the read/write heads with either a flexible steel band wrapped around the actuator motor's spindle or through a rack-and-pinion gearing arrangement. The steps of the actuator motor coincide with the tracks on the disk. To move the read/write heads 10 tracks, the stepper motor must rotate 10 steps. The biggest problem with this approach is that the head actuator arms may drift slightly off their original positions. A stepper motor actuator uses a blind location system, which means the disk heads must rely solely on the stepper motor to place them correctly over the track to be accessed.

Virtually all disk drives with capacities above 80MB, which is just about all currently manufactured disk drives, use a voice coil actuator. The technology used to create the core mechanism on the voice coil actuator is very similar to the voice coil of an audio speaker. The voice coil in a hard disk drive is an electromagnetic coil attached to the ends of the arms on which the read/write heads are located. As the voice coil is energized, it produces an electromagnetic field that, depending on the flow direction of the electricity used to energize it, either attracts or repulses a stationary magnet located opposite the voice coil actuator. As the voice coil moves away from or closer to the stationary magnet, the read/write heads are extended or retracted.

A voice coil actuator does not move in steps like the stepper motor actuator. Instead, it relies on a feedback system, called a servo, to position the heads over a particular location on the disk. The servo, which is a block of data stored on the disk, lets the actuator know exactly where its heads are on the disk. Unlike the blind location system of the stepper motor, a voice coil actuator receives feedback signals from the servo that guide it to exactly the correct location.

Virtually all voice coil systems in use today use rotary voice coil actuators. This actuator system attaches its voice coil to an actuator arm that is mounted like a pivot. As the coil moves to or from the stationary magnet, the head arm rotates in and out, moving the read/write heads over the disk. The one problem that develops with a rotary voice coil is that as the heads are moved deeper into the disk (closer to the spindle), they tilt slightly. This tilt of the heads creates what is called an azimuth problem. Azimuth measures the alignment of the heads to the disk. To deal with such azimuth issues, data is typically not stored on the center part of the disk.

Servo Systems

Servo systems have special coding stored on a formatted disk to help the read/write head actuator mechanism position the heads precisely over a specific location on the disk. This special coding is called *gray code*, and it is placed on the disk when it is manufactured (see Figure 8.8). Gray code, which identifies each track—and in some cases each sector—on the disk, cannot be overwritten, and its area is set aside and not included in the disk's total data capacity.

Data Encoding Methods

The different read/write head and storage media technologies (see the next section, "Storage Media") directly affect how densely the data cells can be placed on the disk media, which translates to the amount of data that can be stored on the disk. Data can be encoded or arranged in a bit cell using different schemes, which are called *encoding methods*. Several encoding methods can be used with hard disk drives, and each read/write head and storage media combination uses the encoding method that minimizes the number of flux transitions required to store a maximum amount of data.

The three primary encoding methods used on hard disk drives are the following:

- *Frequency modulation (FM)*—This encoding scheme simply records a binary 1 or 0 as different polarities. FM was one of the earliest encoding methods used for disk drives. Although it was very popular through the late 1970s, it is not used on new disk drives.

- *Modified frequency modulation (MFM)*—This encoding method is still used on all floppy disks and a few hard disks as well. MFM reduces the number of

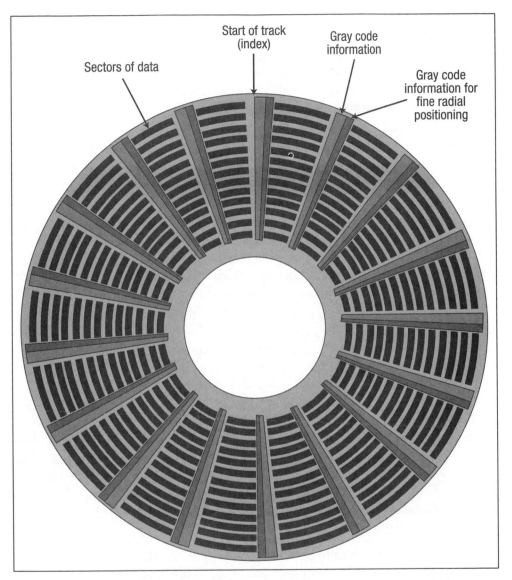

Sectors of data

Start of track
(index)

Gray code
information

Gray code
information for
fine radial
positioning

Figure 8.8 Gray code is inserted on the disk to provide feedback to the read/write
head actuators.

flux transitions required to store data, using clock cells only to separate 0 bits
(for which the read/write head does not generate a voltage pulse). MFM
stores about twice as much data with the same number of flux transitions as
the FM encoding method. MFM enables high-density floppy disk media.

• *Run length limited (RLL)*—This is the currently the most commonly used
encoding method. RLL produces higher densities by spacing 1 bits farther

apart and specially encoding bit cell groups so they can be accessed together. RLL introduced data compression techniques, and virtually all current disk drives, such as integrated drive electronics/advanced technology attachment (IDE/ATA), small computer system interface (SCSI), and so on, use some form of RLL encoding.

Storage Media

Data is stored on a hard disk (or a floppy disk) by using electromagnetic principles (see the section "Recording Data on the Disk" earlier in the chapter) to alter the particles of the disk media placed on each side of a disk platter. The quality of the storage media can directly impact the performance of the disk drive. Two types of media are used on hard disk platters:

- *Oxide media*—This is the media used on older disk drives. Oxide media are relatively soft materials that are easily damaged by a head crash (when the read/write head strikes the disk's surface). The primary ingredient in oxide media is ferrous oxide (popularly known as rust).

- *Thin-film media*—This is the media used on virtually all disk drives manufactured today. Thin-film media refers to an extremely thin layer of metals plated on disk platters by somewhat the same process as used to plate chrome on a car. Thin film media are harder, thinner, and allow stronger magnetic fields to be stored in smaller areas.

Air Filters

Two air filters, a recirculating filter and a barometric (or breather) filter, are permanently sealed inside the HDA. The HDA does not pull in outside air and circulate it. The recirculating filter traps any media particles that are knocked off the platters by the read/write heads or any particles trapped in the HDA during manufacturing.

The HDA is not airtight or watertight, so outside air can get inside and cause problems. A vent and a breather filter on the HDA allow the air pressure inside the HDA to be equalized for barometric pressure changes, such as the change between the factory in China at near sea level and an office in Denver at more than 5,000 feet above sea level. As the altitude changes, air is pulled in or vented out through the breather filter until the internal and external air pressures are equal. This is important to create the air pressure used to float the heads.

Logic, or Controller, Boards

Hard disk drives have a logic board, also called the controller board, which controls the functions of the drive's read/write mechanisms and supports the interface of the drive, typically either IDE/ATA or SCSI. The logic board contains the microprocessor that executes the firmware stored on the hard disk drive to perform the device control, data conversion, interface, and command queuing activities of the hard disk drive.

Connectors and Jumpers

Figure 8.9 shows two of the three general types of connectors found on most disk systems: the data connector and the power connector.

The data connector carries both the data and command signals to and from the controller board and central processing unit (CPU). Most current disk drives, which are primarily SCSI and IDE/ATA drives, use only a single 40-pin data cable. The IDE interface supports up to 2 disk drives on a single cable, an EIDE (enhanced IDE) interface supports up to 4 disk drives on an interface, and the SCSI interface allows up to 7 or 15 drives on the same interface cable, depending on the SCSI standard in use. Special adapters and controllers are available to extend the number of drives that can share an interface. For example, a special EIDE controller is available that allows eight EIDE devices to share an IDE controller.

Hard disk drives use a standard 5-pin power connector from a PC power supply to receive 5V (volts) and 12V of DC power. The logic board and other circuitry of the disk drive use 5V, and the spindle motor and head actuator use 12V.

Many hard disk drive units have a grounding tab that can be connected to the PC's chassis to create a positive ground. Disk drives that are mounted directly to the metal of a drive bay do not need to take this extra step, but for a hard

Original photo courtesy of Western Digital Corporation.

Data Connector

Jumpers

Power Connector

Figure 8.9   The connectors and jumpers on a standard IDE/ATA disk drive.

disk installed in a plastic or fiberglass mounting, you should connect the grounding tab to the PC's chassis. Electrical ground problems show up as read and write errors.

Hard disk drives use jumpers for a couple of different purposes. IDE/ATA disks use jumpers to configure the master/slave configuration of a disk on a shared interface. SCSI disks use jumpers to set the unique SCSI identification (ID) of the drive.

TIP: *An excellent site to lookup hard disk terms is Western Digital Corporation's Hard Disk Glossary Web site at* **www.wdc.com/company/glossary.html**.

Hard Disk Interfaces

The processor and hard disk drives communicate using one of several transfer interface standards. Hard disk drives are manufactured to work in virtually any PC system, and interface standards help ensure the hard disk will be compatible with a PC's motherboard and processor. Exactly which interface a disk drive uses is defined in its device controller and drive electronics.

ST506/412 Interface

The first widely adopted disk interface standard was the ST506/412 interface developed by Seagate Technologies in the early 1980s for its 5MB (ST506) and 10MB (ST412) disk drives. It was universally adopted because it used standard cables to connect any compatible drive to a ST506/412-compatible adapter. This interface is now obsolete, except in older systems still in use.

ESDI

The enhanced small disk interface (ESDI) standard introduced a number of innovations, such as adding the endec into the HDA. ESDI drives were used on high-end systems from brand-name manufacturers in the late 1980s, but this interface is now largely obsolete, except on a few high-end proprietary systems.

IDE/ATA Interface

The IDE/ATA interface is the most popular hard disk interface used for PC systems. IDE and ATA are interchangeable names for essentially the same technology. IDE defines a disk drive type that incorporates the disk controller functions into the hard disk drive, and ATA defines the interface used to communicate to the PC. Because most current design motherboards include at least one IDE interface connector, IDE/ATA devices can be connected directly to the motherboard, or in cases in which the motherboard does not include an on-board connector, to a pass-through IDE/ATA board. If you do need to add a separate IDE/ATA adapter card in a motherboard PCI expansion slot, the card will also include support for a floppy drive, a game port, perhaps a serial port, and more.

The standard IDE/ATA interface supports up to two devices. In addition to hard disk drives, IDE/ATA also supports CD-ROM (compact disk–read-only memory), DVD (digital versatile disk), and tape drives using the compatible ATAPI (AT Attachment Packet Interface). EIDE, which is also called ATA-2, is an upgraded version of IDE that increases the capacity of the interface to four devices; with special interface adapters, an EIDE channel can support up to eight drives.

SCSI Interface

SCSI is a system standard made up of a collection of interface standards that includes a wide range of peripheral devices, such as hard disks, tape drives, optical drives, CD-ROMs, and disk arrays. Several SCSI devices can connect to a single SCSI host controller over a common interface, which is called a SCSI bus or SCSI chain. Figure 8.10 illustrates a simple SCSI chain.

The device controller card for each SCSI device is built into each device, but each device must communicate with the SCSI host adapter. To uniquely identify each device so the host adapter can direct data traffic appropriately, a unique ID number is assigned to each device. The SCSI host controller and the device use this ID number

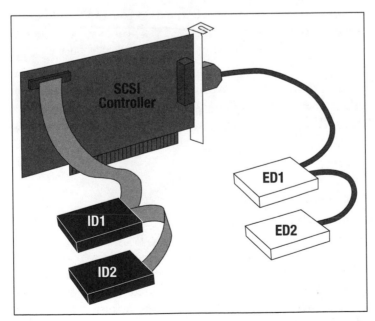

Figure 8.10   A SCSI interface supports multiple devices on a single chain.

8. Hard Disks and Floppy Disks

in all communications. To prevent messages and data blocks sent over the SCSI bus from bouncing back onto the bus, the SCSI bus must be terminated at each end.

The Fiber Channel Interface

The fiber channel-arbitrated loop (FC-AL), or fiber channel interface, is used primarily in very large network disk arrays. The FC-AL interface has built-in data recovery and fault-tolerant components. Fault-tolerant fiber channel disks are more expensive than other types of disk drives, including SCSI devices.

NOTE: *Fault-tolerant (also called high-availability) systems have built-in mechanisms and protocols to combat the effects of a device failure. Fault-tolerant systems can withstand the loss of a server, hard disk, power supply, network adapter, and other mission-critical components on a system.*

FC-AL uses fiber-optic cables to connect up to 127 devices that can be up to 10 km (kilometers) apart on a single interface channel. FC-AL devices can also be hot-swapped, which means that they can be inserted and removed without interfering with the operation of the system.

Data Transfer Protocols

The most commonly used data transfer protocols to transfer data between the hard disk drive and memory are the following:

- *Programmable input/output (PIO)*—This is the data transfer protocol used by nearly all older disk drives that relied on the PC's processor to execute the instructions needed to move data from the disk to the PC's memory.

- *Direct memory access (DMA)*—This protocol transfers data directly between the hard disk and RAM without involving the PC's CPU in the transfer. The DMA device's built-in processor completely manages the transfer between the disk and memory. All IDE/ATA hard disks support DMA transfers. DMA is also common on floppy disks, tape drives, and sound cards.

Data Addressing

Data is addressed on a hard disk using one of two methods:

- *Cylinder-head-sector (CHS)*—IDE/ATA drives use this data-addressing scheme, which locates data on a hard disk drive by its cylinder, head, and sector. The cylinder refers to the track, the head indicates the platter surface, and the sector is within the track. For example, a data file could have the addressing of cylinder 27, head 4, and sector 33, which pinpoints the data at track 27 on the top side of the third platter (the first platter is accessed by head 0) and sector 33 on the track. (See the section "Data Organization" earlier in this chapter for information on cylinders, tracks, and sectors.)

TIP: *The number of cylinders, heads, and sectors on your hard disk can be found in the basic input/output system (BIOS) setup configuration data.*

- *Logical block address (LBA)*—LBA assigns each sector on the disk a logical block number, or a logical block address. A data file is addressed by its LBA location, which is associated with a CHS-type location address. SCSI and EIDE disk drives use LBA addressing.

RAID

The redundant array of independent (or inexpensive) disks (RAID) is a high-availability technique used to create a fault-tolerant environment that protects the data stored on disk from the failure of a disk drive. RAID systems store mirrored copies of data files on separate disks or spread data over several disk drives in "stripes." RAID technology is not frequently implemented on standalone PCs or small networks; due to its cost and overhead, it is usually reserved for larger enterprise-level networks. However, many small networks have started implementing RAID 1 (see below) to provide a data backup. The cost of an additional hard drive is a small price to pay for the data integrity it provides.

The two primary data storage methods used in RAID are data striping and data mirroring. Striping writes data files across several disks in stripes, which speeds up input/output (I/O) operations (as one stripe is being written or read, the next stripe can be staged on another disk drive), and in the event of a disk failure, the lost data can be rebuilt using information on the other disks. Data mirroring involves creating a duplicate file that is stored on a separate hard drive.

Many RAID levels or implementations exist, but only four RAID levels are commonly used:

- *RAID 0 (data striping)*—Data striping does not provide any redundancy. If a disk drive fails, the data stripes written to it are lost.

- *RAID 1 (data mirroring)*—Although it doubles the amount of disk space needed to store the same data, RAID 1 is very popular because it provides complete data redundancy.

- *RAID 3 (data striping with fault tolerance)*—RAID 3 adds parity and error correction code (ECC) to RAID 0. The parity information is maintained on a separate disk and can be used to reconstruct the data should a hard disk drive fail. RAID 3 uses at least three hard disk drives—two for the data stripes and one for the parity information. The maximum number of drives supported by a RAID is typically 32.

- *RAID 5 (data striping with fault tolerance)*—RAID 5, like RAID 3, uses at least three hard disks, but stores data stripes on all disk drives along with stripes of the parity information. This adds fault tolerance to all aspects of the RAID configuration.

RAID 0+1 and 1+0 (striping and mirroring) are two other RAID variations that are gaining popularity. RAID 0+1 is also known as RAID 01, or striping plus mirroring; and RAID 1+0 is also known as RAID 10, or mirroring plus striping. These two implementations use the best of both RAID features to provide highly reliable disk arrays.

Floppy Disk Drives

The floppy disk drive continues to be included in new PC systems, even though years ago it was to have been made obsolete by newer storage devices. The floppy disk has come in a variety of sizes over its lifetime, including 8-inch, 5.25-inch, and 3.5-inch disks. The 3.5-inch disk has been the most popular size for about the past 10 years. Figure 8.11 illustrates the features of the 3.5-inch diskette.

Floppy Disk Construction

The floppy disk drive is an internal device mounted into an open drive bay of the system case. Even though it is an internal device, its bezel extends through the drive bay opening and should be visible through a removable bay cover on the case, as well.

A 3.5-inch floppy disk drive is about the same size as most newer hard disk drives. Newer cases either mount the diskette in a smaller drive bay or require an adapter kit to mount it into a full-size drive bay. If your system is old enough to have a 5.25-inch drive, it is most likely a half-height drive (about 1.75-inches in height) that fits into a full-sized drive bay.

The floppy disk drive comprises a number of components that are very similar in name and function to those of a hard disk drive. The primary components of the floppy disk drive are the following:

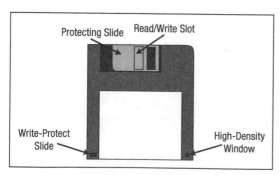

Figure 8.11   The components and features of a 3.5-inch diskette.

- *Read/write heads*—The process used by a floppy disk drive to read from or write to the disk media is very much like that used with a hard disk drive. An electromagnetic field is used to align the media particles to store electrical values that represent binary data. However, because the floppy disk media has a lower areal density, its read/write heads do not need to be as sensitive as the heads used on a hard disk. The read/write heads of a floppy disk, typically one for each side of the disk, access the media through a slot in the disk's outer jacket. The heads move in a straight line up and back over the slot to access the disk's tracks.

TIP: *Areal density measures the number of bits per square inch on a disk's media and is calculated by multiplying the number of bits per inch by the number of tracks per inch. A larger areal density indicates a disk uses more bits per inch to store data.*

- *Head actuator*—Most floppy disks have 80 tracks per side, and the head actuator, which is powered by a stepper motor, moves the read/write heads from track to track. The stepper motor has a stop for each track on the disk. Should the head develop alignment (azimuth) problems, replacing the disk drive is less expensive than realigning the heads.

- *Spindle motor*—When a floppy disk is inserted into a drive, a clamping mechanism attached to the spindle motor locks the disk into a fixed position. The spindle motor rotates the disk inside of its jacket and under the read/write heads. The speed of the spindle motor is tied to the physical size of the disk, but for the 3.5-inch disk, the spindle motor rotates the disk at 300 rpm. This very slow rotation speed adds to the latency and data transfer speeds of the disk, but it also keeps the contact heads from wearing out the disk.

- *Connectors*—A floppy disk drive uses two connecters to connect to the system: a data connector, which connects the drive to the floppy disk controller (FDC), and a power connector, which supplies DC power from the power supply. Most floppy disk data cables, such as the one in Figure 8.12, connect either one or two floppy disk drives to the FDC. On the rare system that connects two floppy disk drives, Drive A is connected to the cable above (after) the twist in the cable, and Drive B is connected below (before) the twist. Depending on the manufacturer and model, the floppy disk drive uses either a power supply connector similar to the one used for the hard disk drive or a smaller flat connector. Virtually all power supply form factors include at least one power connector for a floppy disk drive.

- *Media*—Except on PCs more than 10 years old, virtually all floppy disk drives are made to use 3.5-inch diskettes. The 3.5-inch disk was developed to overcome the fragility of the 5.25-inch disk, which preceded it, and to provide a smaller, better protected disk. The 3.5-inch diskette features a rigid outer jacket, a sturdy metal slide to protect the read/write slot, and a sliding window switch used to write-protect the disk. A floppy disk has between 70 and 150 tracks, compared to the thousands of tracks on a hard disk.

8. Hard Disks and Floppy Disks

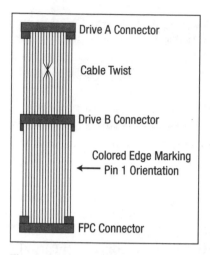

Figure 8.12   A standard two-drive floppy disk data cable.

Data is read and written to a floppy disk by the read/write heads directly contacting the media. The read/write heads should be cleaned on occasion because the head picks up bits of the recording media (which, like the hard disk, is a magnetic oxide material) and any dirt or debris that gets inside the disk. In most cases, the head is able to brush aside any large bits of debris, but dust and other fine particles can collect on the head and damage it. The head should not be cleaned too often because the cleaning process can also wear out the heads. There is a read/write head for each side of the disk.

Formatting

A floppy disk, regardless of its size or density, must be formatted before it can receive and store data. Formatting performs two tasks, in two separate steps of the same process:

- *Low-level formatting*—Creates the organization structures on the disk, including the tracks and reference points for the sectors on each track.

- *High-level formatting*—Adds the logical structures, including the file allocation table (FAT) and the root directory.

Already-formatted disks are available everywhere, including drug stores, supermarkets, discount clubs, and even computer supply stores. Preformatted diskettes may not work with every floppy disk drive, however, and may need to be reformatted before you can use them. Formatting can also be used to completely erase a diskette for future use.

---

*TIP: If you would like additional information on floppy disks, Accurite Technologies, Inc. has an excellent floppy disk reference site at **www.accurite.com/FloppyPrimer.html**.*

Immediate Solutions

Choosing a Hard Disk Drive by Using Performance Metrics

Gilster's Law on Choosing the Right Hard Disk (or any other peripheral device) is "You never can tell; and it all depends." Seriously, what may be the best hard disk for any given situation really depends on the situation. In most cases, the price and capacity of the disk are usually the most heavily weighted factors, but a number of performance metrics and indicators included in the specifications of most disk drives also can be used to choose the best disk drive to meet your requirements.

The most common performance specifications are the following:

- *Seek time*—Seek time measures the time it takes the head actuator to move the read/write heads from one track to the next in milliseconds (ms). However, seek time does not include the time required to move to a specific data location. Average seek time, which is a commonly used to compare the performance of different drives, is calculated from the drive's seek times for a number of randomly located requests. Nearly all quality disk drives have an average seek time between 8 and 14 ms.

- *Access time*—Access time measures the time required to position the read/write heads over a particular track and to find the sector containing a particular data location. Access time adds latency, or rotational delay, to the seek time to calculate the total time required for the disk to position the read/write head over a specific data location. Latency is measured in milliseconds and is generally around one-half the time required for the disk to make a single revolution. At 10,000 rpm, latency is around 3 ms. As the rotational speed of the drive increases, the latency time decreases proportionately.

- *Data transfer rate*—The data tranfer rate is the amount of data that can be moved between the disk and the PC's main memory (RAM) in one second, measured in megabytes per second (MBps). A higher data transfer rate, which means more data transferred per second, translates to less time that a user must wait for a program to load or a document to be opened. Today's hard disks support transfer rates from 5 to 70 MBps.

- *Data access time (QBench)*—QBench time combines the access time with the data transfer rate to produce an indicator that rates a disk drive's overall performance. QBench is a specification developed by Quantam Corporation (**www.quantum.com**), which also provides the QBench benchmarking tool that is widely used as a standard for drive performance measurement and comparison.

- *Disk capacity*—Disk drives typically have two capacity ratings: unformatted and formatted. Formatted disk capacity is usually the most important of the two because it states the usable disk space on the drive.

- *Areal Density*—A disk's areal density is an indicator of its storage capacity. Areal density is calculated by multiplying a disk's bits per inch (bpi) by the total number of tracks on the disk, which yields the number of bits (typically in megabits or gigabits) per square inch. An area density of around 1.5Gb per square inch is common on most newer disk drives.

Preparing a Hard Disk Drive for Use

Essentially two major steps will prepare a disk drive to receive an operating system and to store data: partitioning and formatting. The following projects detail the steps used to complete each of these steps.

Partitioning the Hard Disk

A disk drive must be physically formatted (low-level format), partitioned, and logically formatted (high-level format) before it can store data. Low-level formatting is performed at the factory on IDE/ATA and SCSI hard disks, so partitioning is the first step you perform to prepare a disk for use. Partitioning creates logical divisions on a disk that can be individually addressed and managed.

When you partition a hard disk drive, you can:

- Divide the disk into logical subdrives that are assigned different drive letters, such as C:, D:, and E:, and can be separately addressed.

- Load multiple operating systems on the same disk, such as Windows 98 and Linux, with each operating system in its own partition.

- Support multiple file systems, such as NTFS (NT file system) and FAT32, on the same disk drive.

- Separate data files from application files on different partitions to speed up data backups.

Partitioning a hard disk can improve the disk's efficiency and overcome an operating system's sizing issues. For example, Windows sizes disk clusters in proportion to the size of the partition. A bigger partition can result in bigger clusters, which translates to numerous small unused spaces on the disk. Strategically reducing the partition sizes or creating many smaller partitions reduces cluster sizes to better match the data.

A disk can have only one partition, but because some operating systems limit the partition size they can support, on some systems, larger disks must be divided into smaller partitions. DOS, Windows 3.*x*, or early releases of Windows 95 do not support partition sizes larger than 2GB. This means that to use the entire disk drive, a disk larger than 2GB must be divided into two or more partitions. Windows 98 and Windows 2000 allow you to create partitions that range from 2GB to 4TB, depending on the file system in use.

A hard disk can be divided into two types of partitions:

- *Primary partitions*—A primary partition is created to hold an operating system and is typically the partition used to boot the PC. A hard disk can be divided into as many as four primary partitions, but only one primary partition (set as the boot partition) can be active at a time.

- *Extended partitions*—An extended partition can be divided into as many as 23 logical subpartitions. Each logical partition can be assigned its own drive identity, such as D:, E:, F:, and used for any purpose.

Using **FDISK** to Partition a Hard Disk

The DOS command **FDISK** is the most commonly used utility for partitioning a hard disk drive. It is typically included on a DOS boot disk that also includes the DOS **FORMAT** command, and is used to partition and format the hard disk during system setup.

To use the **FDISK** command, perform these steps:

1. At a DOS command line prompt, enter the command **FDISK**.

2. A PC with a hard disk drive larger than 512 MB will display a dialog box message (see Figure 8.13). This box contains a message advising you that you can enable large disk support and warning you of the consequences of doing so. Press the Enter key to accept the default value of yes (Y), which accepts large disk support, or enter an N and press the Enter key. The **FDISK** menu displays (see Figure 8.14).

3. Use menu choice 1 to create partitions on the disk, one at a time. Another menu will appear with three options: 1, to create a primary DOS partition (meaning a boot partition); 2, to create an extended partition; or 3, to create logical partitions within an extended partition. If you are partitioning a new drive, choose option 1 (see Figure 8.15).

8. Hard Disks and Floppy Disks

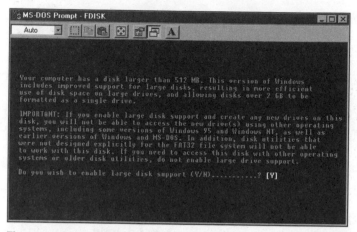

Figure 8.13   The large disk support message is displayed by **FDISK** on PCs with large hard disk drives.

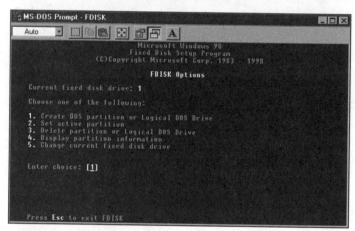

Figure 8.14   The **FDISK** menu.

4. You can create one large partition for the entire disk, which is commonly done. Alternatively, if you have a plan for how the disk is to be divided (by using percentages to divide the disk into primary and extended partitions), you would use options 1, 2, or 3, accordingly. If you do create more than one primary partition, you will need to activate the one you wish to use as a boot partition.

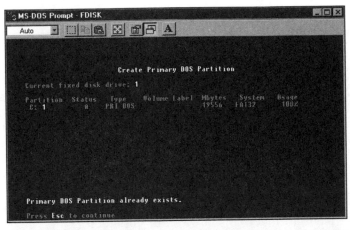

Figure 8.15 Creating a single primary partition on a hard disk with **FDISK**.

Formatting a Hard Disk Drive

Before the partition or partitions on a hard disk drive can receive the operating system or be used to store data, they must be high-level formatted. Although the majority of new PCs now come from the factory with the operating system installed, when a new hard disk drive is installed or when the operating system is upgraded, or for many other reasons, a hard disk may be repartitioned and formatted.

Two formatting levels are performed on a hard disk drive, whether it is an IDE/ATA or SCSI: low-level formatting and high-level formatting.

- *Low-level formatting*—A low-level format is a destructive scan of the disk intended to find any defects in the recording media. The location of any defect found is recorded as unusable to avoid data problems.

TIP: *A low-level format should not be done on an IDE/ATA or SCSI hard disk outside of the factory, except in extreme situations, such as a boot sector virus. Should a drive ever need low-level formatting, contact the manufacturer to obtain the necessary software.*

- *High-level formatting*—High-level formatting is used to prepare disk partitions to receive the operating system and to store data files. The high-level format prepares the disk's partitions by creating a root directory and the FAT. The FAT is used to record the location and relationships of files and directories on the disk. When you format a hard disk that contains data files, the FAT is reconstructed, removing all references of the existing files.

8. Hard Disks and Floppy Disks

The two choices to format a hard disk drive on most PCs are the following:

- Use the **DOS FORMAT** command from a DOS command line prompt. The command used should be:

```
FORMAT X:
```

In this command, X: is replaced by the drive letter of the partition you wish to format. The active primary partition is usually the C: drive.

- Use the Windows Explorer to format an existing partition for reuse by the following steps:

  - Right-click the drive letter in the left pane of the Windows Explorer window of the drive you wish to format to display a short-cut menu (see Figure 8.16).

  - Choose Format from the short-cut menu. The formatting dialog box will display (see Figure 8.17). Windows will not allow you to format the C: drive from the Windows Explorer.

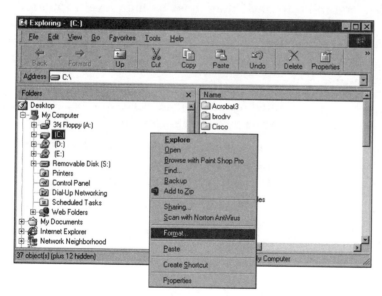

Figure 8.16   The Windows Explorer drive short-cut menu includes the option used to format a disk.

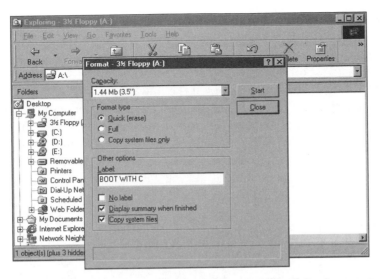

Figure 8.17   The Windows Explorer Format option dialog box.

Installing a New Hard Drive

Follow these steps to install a new hard disk in a PC system case:

1. If you are upgrading to a new and larger hard disk drive or adding a second (or higher) disk drive, create a full backup of the disk drive being replaced.

2. Enter the BIOS Setup program and document the settings that impact the disk drives. It is never a bad idea to have a complete written record of the Startup program's configuration data.

3. Create a bootable floppy disk. Use the following command on a DOS command line prompt to create a floppy boot disk:

```
FORMAT A: /S
```

If you have a blank formatted disk, you can also execute the following command from a DOS command line prompt or in the Open box of the Start|Run option:

```
SYS A:
```

Or you can use the Windows Explorer to format a disk and select the Copy System Files option on the Format disk dialog box (see Figure 8.17).

4. If the new hard disk drive is in addition to an existing disk drive, decide which drive is to be configured as the master and which is to be the slave. Check the drive's documentation for the correct jumper settings and make the necessary changes on the new disk drive. Most disk drives are preconfigured at the factory as masters. If the new drive is to be a slave, set the jumper accordingly. If the disk drives are SCSI drives, you will need to set the device ID jumpers; SCSI devices do not use a master/slave configuration. Also, check the SCSI bus and the position of the new disk on the bus to verify that the disk drive does not have to provide termination.

5. Shut down the PC, turn off the power switch, and unplug the PC's power cord from its AC power source. Put on an electrostatic discharge (ESD) strap.

6. Remove the system case cover; watch out for snagged data cables and power connectors.

7. Create a diagram of the placement of the hard disk's cables. Study the orientation of the hard disk drive's data (ribbon) cable and power cable. Remove the cables from the old drive (even if you are not replacing it). Do not jerk on any of the cables. Use steady, firm pressure to pull the cable connectors apart. If necessary, use a rocking motion (side-to-side) to remove it. Never flex the connectors up and down.

8. If you are replacing the existing hard disk drive, remove its mounting screws and save them (a paper cup or an egg carton is good for this) because you will need them for the new drive. If you are adding the new drive in addition to the existing drive, make sure you have mounting screws available. If you need to remove any expansion cards to get to the hard disk, draw a diagram of their placement and their cable orientations, if any, before you remove any card anchor screws.

9. If you are replacing the existing drive, remove it from the drive bay. Unless the drive is damaged and not usable in the future, protect it in antistatic material.

10. If you are adding a drive to the PC, remove the existing drive and verify that its device configuration jumpers are appropriately set to the configuration you wish to use.

11. Install the new disk drive in a drive bay and anchor it to the drive bay's walls with mounting screws. You may need to attach the data and power connection before anchoring the drive in place.

12. Reinstall the cables on the existing drive, if needed. Make sure you align the red or blue edge of the data cable to pin 1 on the disk drive's connector, and the connector on the adapter card or motherboard.

13. Replace the cover, connect the PC to its power source, and boot the PC using the floppy boot disk.

14. Prepare the disks by partitioning and formatting as needed (see the preceding solution, "Preparing a Hard Disk Drive for Use"). Verify the BIOS is correct for the new disk (if it is in addition to an existing disk) and that its interface is enabled.

Troubleshooting a Hard Disk Drive

A variety of problems may arise with your hard disk drive. The following scenarios are just two examples you may run into.

The PC Will Not Boot

If the PC will not boot, check the following:

1. If there is only one disk drive, make sure it is configured as a master. This is not a problem on most systems with only one disk drive, but on some, a single drive must be configured as a master.

2. If two drives are on a single IDE/ATA channel, check the jumpers on the drives to verify that one is a master and one is a slave. If the drives are from different manufacturers, check the manufactuers' Web sites for possible compatibility alcrts.

3. Check the power connection on each disk drive to be sure the connectors are snuggly fitting and that there are no bent or broken pins. Try using a different power connector from the power supply if you suspect that the power connector is the problem.

4. Verify that the red or blue edge of the data cable is aligned to pin 1. Typically, this connector is keyed (which means a locking or guiding feature is built into the connector and port). Also verify that the connector is not off by one row of pins up or across.

5. You may need to partition and format the hard disk. If you are getting a drive C: boot failure even after formatting the C: drive and copying the system files to it, you may have a corrupted boot sector. Boot with the floppy boot disk and copy the system file to the C: drive (**SYS C:**). If the drive continues to have problems, try a different hard disk drive to see if the device interface may be the problem. If so, acquire a new adapter card. If the new drive works, the problem is the original disk drive itself.

6. Use the Windows Device Manager to verify that the hard disk drives of the primary and secondary device controllers do not have system resource conflicts.

8. Hard Disks and Floppy Disks

The System Boots but Has Problems

If the system does boot, but you are having problems, check out the following:

1. If a large disk drive (more than 500MB) is recognized by the BIOS as only a 500MB drive, you need to update your BIOS.

2. If you are getting a disk read/write error when running applications, run the Windows utility SCANDISK to check for disk media problems. You may also want to take this opportunity to run the Defragmenter utility as well. If you continue to have problems reading or writing the disk, repartition and reformat it or simply replace it.

3. Just about any operational problem with a hard disk drive will be the result of one of three things: bad configuration, improper installation, and improper maintenance. Problems caused by any one of these areas can show up immediately or later. Should you begin to develop disk read and write errors, recheck the physical installation, especially that the connectors are properly fitted, and check the complementary metal-oxide semiconductor (CMOS) setup data. Check the configuration jumpers on IDE/ATA devices and the device ID and termination jumpers on SCSI devices. Regularly scan the disk for viruses, use SCANDISK at least once a week, and run the Defragmenter at least once a month.

Related Solution:	Found on page:
BIOS Not Detecting the Hard Disk During the POST	112
Resolving Resource Conflicts	175
Troubleshooting a Serial Port	334
Checking and Troubleshooting a Power Supply	396

Removing the Spindle Ground Strap on a Hard Disk Drive

Many hard disk drives have a spindle ground strap, which is a small angled copper arm that has a piece of carbon or graphite (some older drives have a Teflon pad) that contacts the bottom of the disk spindle outside the HDA. The ground strap is a safety precaution against any static electricity created by the rotation of the spindle being discharged inside the HDA and damaging the disk drive or corrupting data. Typically, you never encounter this component, but on occasion, the strap's pad wears out and the metal rubs on the spindle rod, creating a high-pitched whining sound. If the spindle ground strap begins to shriek, carefully remove the strap, which is typically glued in place.

Troubleshooting a Floppy Disk Drive

Whether the floppy disk is a newly installed device or an existing drive, problems with the floppy disk drive are usually caused by one of the following conditions, listed with troubleshooting directions.

1. A newly installed floppy disk drive is not properly connected to the FDC or the power supply. Verify that the A: drive is above (after) the cable twist and the B: drive, if installed, is below (before) the cable twist. The A: drive cannot connect to the B: position.

2. The floppy disk drive is not enabled or setup correctly in the Setup program configuration data (CMOS). Make sure the device settings are appropriate for the drive, which is normally a 1.44MB, 3.5-inch drive.

3. The system resource assignments of the floppy disk drive are conflicting with another device. If you have recently installed a new device, such as a tape drive or another floppy disk, remove it to see if the problem is resolved. If so, reinstall the device so that it does not conflict with the floppy, or remove the floppy disk drive.

4. The wrong version of the floppy disk drive device driver is in use. Install the correct version.

5. The diskette in the drive is bad, unformatted, or write-protected. This is the most common cause of floppy disk problems. Replace the diskette, format it, or change the write-protect slide.

6. The floppy disk drive (most likely its read/write heads) has gone bad. Replace the drive.

Related Solution:	Found on page:
BIOS Not Detecting the Hard Disk During the POST	112
Resolving Resource Conflicts	175
Checking and Troubleshooting a Power Supply	396

8. Hard Disks and Floppy Disks

Chapter 9

CD-ROMs and DVDs

In Depth

Emergance of the CD-ROM

Like the cassette tape, the CD-ROM (compact disk–read-only memory) was not originally developed for use on a PC, but it has been adapted for this purpose very nicely. In fact, it has become the *de facto* standard for software product releases in a very short time. Compared to its predecessor, the floppy disk, the CD-ROM has enormous storage capacity, it is a little more durable, and—to many users— it is easier to use. The CD-ROM, originally developed as an alternative to the cassette tape for audio content, really took off for PCs when the PC CD-ROM drive became commonplace. CDs are now used to distribute music, software, multimedia, databases, books, encyclopedias, mailing lists, and more, to PC users. A CD-ROM drive is now sold as standard equipment on virtually all PCs, including notebook PCs, although many higher-end PCs feature a digital versatile disk–read-only memory (DVD-ROM) drive instead (more on DVDs later in this chapter in the section "Digital Versatile Disk")

The Technology of the CD and CD-ROM

The CD-ROM for the PC uses the same compact disk (CD) technology used for audio CDs. In fact, the physical media (see Figure 9.1) used to record data, programs, music, and multimedia on a CD-ROM for use on a PC is exactly the same as that used to record Creed, Garth, and Herbie Hancock.

CD-ROM Formats

CD technology includes a variety of formats and applications, although most are not intended for the PC. The two most common formats are the one used for music CDs and the one used for data CDs on the PC. A CD's format is the pattern and method used to record its contents. In general, a CD is recorded in a spiraling pattern, in contrast to the circular track pattern used on a floppy or hard disk or a cassette tape. On a CD, however, information is placed between the different files on the disk to identify the beginning and end, size, and content of the files to the player.

The following sections discuss each of the formats used to record a CD for different types of content.

Figure 9.1   A CD can be used to record music for audio playback or data for use on a PC.

CD-Digital Audio

The first standard CD format was developed for audio content (music and other recorded sounds). The Royal Philips Electronics Company and the Sony Corporation developed this format, called CD-digital audio (CD-DA), as the first standard for recording CDs. CD standards are defined in a series of "books" that are designated by different colors. The specification of CD-DA is defined in the Red Book, and thus CD-DA is known as "Red Book audio."

The Red Book standard defines the technical specifications for CD-DA, the number and spacing of tracks on the disk, the number of minutes of content, the data transfer (playback) rate, the error correction methods used to correct for minor sound errors, the format of the digital audio, and the physical specifications for compact disks, including the media's size. The Red Book standard, although now more than 20 years old, is still in use for audio CDs.

The Red Book standard defines the following characteristics for a CD-DA recording:

- The sample size is 16 bits.
- The sampling rate is 44.1kHz (kilohertz), or about twice as high as humans can hear.
- Sampling is in stereophonic sound.
- One second of audio stored on a CD takes up 176,400 bytes of space.
- A Red Book CD holds up to 74 minutes of digital sound.
- The data transfer rate is 150KBps (kilobytes per second), which is designated as "single-speed" or "1X" in terms of the transfer speed used by a CD-ROM drive on a PC.

Sampling

When sound is converted from an analog (natural sound) format into a digital (computer readable) format, the analog sound wave is sampled. This means that at different points along the sound wave, a snapshot (sample) is taken of the sound and a description is created using binary codes. Figure 9.2 illustrates this concept. The vertical lines in the figure represent the points at which samples of the sound are taken. A 16-bit sample size indicates that 16 bits are used to describe the sound in a digital format. The sampling rate translates to how many samples are taken per second. The CD-DA sampling rate of 44.1kHz translates to 44,100 samples per second. See Chapter 19 for more information on sound conversion, recording, and playback.

Compact Disk–Read Only Memory

The CD's large data capacity makes it attractive to software developers, database compilers, and multimedia producers. The CD-ROM, the CD designated for use with the PC, has a capacity of 650MB (megabytes) of data. The first CD-ROMs also used the 150KBps "single-speed" transfer rates used by audio CDs, which established the transfer rate as being relative to the CD-DA transfer rate. CD drives on PCs are still rated using a multiple of the CD-DA transfer rate. The CD-DA transfer rate is designated as 1X (one time). Modern CD-ROM drives are boasting 40X transfer rates, meaning that they transfer data from the CD disk 40 times faster than the single-speed (1X) CD-DA standard of 150KBps.

The CD-DA standard was developed to store music on a CD, however, and not to store data. To provide for the addressing requirements of data stored on a CD, the Red Book standard was modified. Philips and Sony developed the original Yellow Book standard, which specified how data is stored on a CD-ROM. The Yellow Book designated two content sectors and recording modes: Mode 1 is used to store computer data, such as programs and files, and Mode 2 is used to store

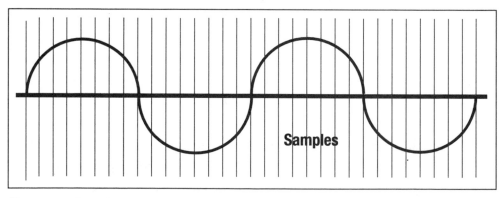

Figure 9.2   Sampling takes a snapshot of the sound wave thousands of times per second.

compressed audio, video, graphic, or multimedia data. The Yellow Book standard recognizes the need for the CD-ROM to store data more precisely than is possible on a Red Book CD.

Both Mode 1 and Mode 2 sector formats have a few bytes at the front of each sector. Table 9.1 lists the contents of a Mode 1 sector.

As indicated in Table 9.1, the first 16 bytes of a Mode 1 sector is a header that contains 12 sync bytes used as the sector separator, 3 bytes to indicate the time of the track (typically there is one track to a sector), and a byte to identify the Cross Interleaved Reed-Solomon Code (CIRC) method in use. The sync bytes are primarily used to separate one sector from another. CIRC is the standard error detection and correction method for both CD-DA and CD-ROM. For a CD-ROM Mode 1 sector, the CIRC method is the layered error detection code/error correction code (EDC/ECC). The EDC/ECC code is used to determine if a data block contains an error and, if so, to fix it. Additional space is reserved in the sector for error detection and correction: the EDC uses 4 bytes, the ECC uses 276 bytes, and between them are 8 bytes of unused space. A Mode 1 sector provides 2,048 bytes of user data, which can be divided into blocks of 512, 1,024, or 2,048 bytes each, but if multiple blocks are used, they must all be the same size and together cannot be larger than 2,048 bytes.

A CD-ROM Mode 2 sector has sync and header bytes at the beginning of the sector the same as for a Mode 1 sector. However, a Mode 2 sector does not apply EDC/ECC, which allows the remainder of the sector, all 2,336 bytes, to be used for digital data, such as programs, multimedia content, data, and more.

The total size of a sector, regardless of whether it is CD-DA (Red Book) or CD-ROM (Yellow Book) Mode 1 or Mode 2, is the same. The CD-DA format uses all 2,352 bytes of a sector for user data (music), but because of its formatting, a

Table 9.1 CD-ROM Mode 1 (audio) format.

Element	Size in Bytes
Sync separator	12
Addressing (minutes and seconds)	3
CIRC type indicator	1
Data	2,048
EDC (error detection code)	4
Reserved space	8
ECC (Error correction code)	276

9. CD-ROMs and DVDs

CD-ROM Mode 1 block has 2,048 bytes of user data and a Mode 2 block has 2,336 user bytes. Another characteristic difference between the two CD-ROM modes is their data transfer speeds. CD-ROM Mode 1 transfers data at 1.22Mbps (megabits per second), and Mode 2 transfers data at 1.4Mbps.

CD-ROM Extended Architecture

Because the original Yellow book format was somewhat restrictive for software producers, the Yellow book format was later modified to allow CD-ROM Mode 1 and Mode 2 sectors to be interleaved, or mixed, on the disk. The CD-ROM Extended Architecture (CD-ROM XA) format eliminates the EDC/ECC data in Mode 1 sectors, which opens up an additional 288 bytes in each sector. This format allows different types of data, music, programming, and graphics to be intermixed and stored on the same CD.

Accessing a CD-ROM XA disk requires a CD-ROM drive certified for the CD-ROM XA format. A CD-ROM XA drive contains a hardware compressor/decompressor (CODEC) to deal with the compressed audio and video typically found on a CD-ROM XA disk.

CD-Interactive

A CD-ROM format developed specifically to meet the needs of multimedia producers was the CD-interactive (CD-I). CD-I disks hold text, graphics, audio, and video in a single disk format. Special hardware is used to connect CD-I players to television screens for playback. CD-I, like the CD-ROM XA, is a derivative of the Yellow Book, but CD-I uses proprietary and unique formatting.

Bridge CD

Bridge CD refers to a disk format defined in the White Book. The Bridge CD format "bridges" the CD-ROM XA and the CD-I formats and is compatible to either format interchangeably. Using the White Book specification, CD-I disks will work in CD-ROM XA drives and CD-ROM XA disks will work in CD-I drives. Examples of a Bridge CD are the Kodak Photo CD and the Video CD format.

Video CD

The Video CD (VCD) format stores compressed video using a standard also defined in the White Book. VCDs use the Motion Pictures Experts Group (MPEG) compression algorithms to store 74 minutes of full-motion video in the same space used by CD-DA audio. To play a Video CD requires a Video CD–compatible CD-ROM drive or a Video CD player. The compression algorithm used for VCD does not produce a high-quality video and this format is giving way to the DVD.

Photo CD

The Photo CD standard, developed by Philips but this time with the Kodak Corporation, holds photographs in a digital form. The Photo CD standard is defined in the Orange Book, which also defines the CD-recordable (CD-R) format. A Photo CD uses CD-ROM Mode 2 formatting to store photographic images on a CD. The Photo CD is a Bridge CD that can be read by a CD-I drive or player.

CD-Recordable

The CD formats covered to this point have been read-only disks to which data cannot be stored or modified after manufacture. The Orange Book format allows users to take advantage of the large storage space on a CD and provides methods to allow data to be written to special CD media using special CD drives.

Two types of CD-R processes are used to record data to a CD:

- *Write once read many (WORM) disk*—A CD-R disk that can have data or music written to it, but only once. Data written to a CD-R WORM disk is permanently recorded and cannot be erased or modified; also, the disk itself cannot be written to a second time.

- *Magneto-optical (MO) disk*—More commonly known as a CD-RW (read/write) disk, a CD-MO disk can be written to, read, modified, and written to again.

Compact Disk Media

A CD, like other forms of data storage on a PC, stores data in digital form, which means binary data (ones and zeroes) is actually stored on the media. Hard disks, floppy disks, and memory store data in electromechanical forms, but data is recorded on a CD using a more physical recording method. A look at how a CD is made is the first step to understanding how data is recorded to it.

A CD starts out as a slice of polycarbonate substrate with a diameter of about 4.75 inches and a thickness of 1.2 millimeters (about .05 inches). A metal stamp that is actually the reverse image of a finished disk is used to master (stamp) indentations into the substrate, a process called *mastering*. After it is mastered, the disk substrate has a pattern of *pits* and *flats*, also called *lands*, on its surface.

Figure 9.3 illustrates the makeup of what is called a single-session disk. At the core of the disk is the substrate surface, which has pits and lands after it is mastered. This substrate is overlaid with a shiny, reflective silver or aluminum coating. This shiny coating has a very important role in the ability of the drive to read the data stored on the CD. A clear plastic protective cover is placed over this coating. The CD's label or silk-screening is applied to the clear plastic cover.

Reading the CD

A CD-ROM drive works somewhat like a floppy disk drive (see Chapter 8 for more information on floppy and hard disks). The difference is that in place of a read/write head to sense electromagnetic flux on the magnetic disk media, a CD

9. CD-ROMs and DVDs

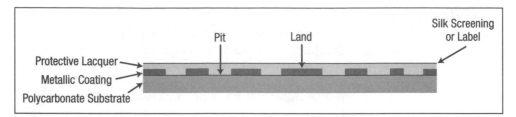

Figure 9.3   The layers of a CD.

disk spins, and a laser beam sweeps over the lands and pits. The reflection of the beam back to a sensor triggers whether the data in a certain location is a one or a zero. As the laser beam sweeps across the disk surface, if it hits a land, the beam is reflected by the shiny metal coating and detected by a sensor as a binary zero. If the beam hits a pit, the beam is deflected and therefore not detected by the sensor. All of this takes place very fast—the beam shines on thousands of pits and lands per second. Another difference between a floppy disk and a CD is that the CD is recorded on a single, long, spiraling track instead of the floppy disk's circular track. This spiral track is about three miles long on a CD-DA disk, the equivalent of about 16,000 tracks on a hard disk platter.

Data is recorded on the CD's substrate core, which is located directly beneath the CD's label. The laser is beamed from the bottom of the CD directly through the clear portions of the substrate, which are about 1 mm thick. A CD can have minor scratches and still be read just fine. As long as the scratches do not interfere with the laser striking the substrate or reflecting back to the sensors, and the substrate is intact and undamaged, the disk should be readable. However, should the scratches be deep enough (about 1 mm or more) and remove or damage the reflective coating, the disk would be unreadable.

The first sector on the CD is located at 0 minutes, 2 seconds, and no hundredths of a second (00:02:00), or 600 blocks, into the CD's spiral track. A CD uses blocks of 512 bytes. A minute of data uses 18,000 blocks and there are 300 blocks in a second of data and 600 in the first two seconds. This means that the first block in the first sector (logical block 0) is at 00:02:00 as well.

A CD-R disk is manufactured essentially the same as a CD-ROM disk, with only slight variations. In place of the substrate is a layer of organic dye, over which is placed a reflective gold-colored metallic coating. Over this is the protective lacquer layer, just as on a CD-ROM. A CD-RW (CD-MO) disk contains a layer of a special metal alloy over which is placed the reflective gold-colored metallic coating and protective lacquer layer.

Writing to a CD

Data is recorded on a CD-R WORM disk by changing the reflective properties of the organic dye. Once changed, the properties of the dye cannot be changed back. The light properties of the metal alloy used in the CD-RW also are changed to store a data bit, but these properties can be reset to their original values to re-write the disk.

The newest form of CD-RW is the CD-erasable (CD-E) disk. This disk uses a technology called phase change to record or erase data stored on the disk. A CD-E uses a layer of silver alloy and different laser energy levels and temperatures to record, read, and erase data from the disk. Data is recorded on and erased from the silver alloy substrate using a higher temperature than is used to read the disk The higher energy and temperatures crystallize the silver alloy, thus changing its reflective properties.

CD-ROM Drive Operation

A CD-ROM drive (and any other type of CD drive made to be used with a PC, including CD-R, CD-RW, and CD-E) typically fits in a PC's 5.25-inch half-height drive bay. A drive or a drive bay with a height of 1.75 inches is considered a half-height device or bay, which is standard on virtually all newer PC cases. A CD-ROM drive has a sheet metal enclosure that surrounds the drive. Screw holes are tapped into the sides of the enclosure so it can be mounted directly into a standard drive bay. On some older PCs, a CD-ROM—as well as a hard or floppy disk drive—is mounted in the PC bay with mounting rails that attach to the sides of the drive and then slides into the drive bay. Another option is an external CD-ROM drive (see Figure 9.4) that is connected via a small computer system interface (SCSI) adapter.

The Read Head Assembly

The CD-ROM's laser, which is produced by an infrared laser diode, is not aimed directly on a CD; rather, it is directed toward a reflecting mirror in the read head assembly (see Figure 9.5). The read head moves along the CD's spiral track just above the surface of the disk. The light beam from the laser reflects off the mirror

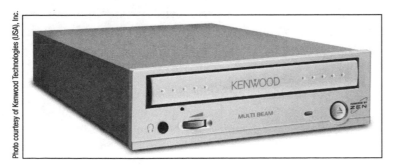

Figure 9.4　An external CD-ROM drive.

9. CD-ROMs and DVDs

Figure 9.5   The read head and head assembly of a CD-ROM drive.

to a lens that focuses the light on a specific point, where the light is reflected back from the disk's metallic layer. The reflected light, the intensity of which depends on whether it is being reflected from a land or a pit on the disk substrate, is passed through a series of collectors, mirrors, and lenses that focus the reflected light and send it to a photo detector. The photo detector converts the light into an electrical signal. The CD-ROM rarely has read errors, except when the laser is obstructed, a mirror becomes dusty, or some foreign object gets on the disk. If the CD-ROM disk and the mirrors are clean, very little can go wrong.

Because the CD-ROM disk spins, the components that read the disk do not require much movement. The read head assembly adjusts its position side to side to move along the spiraling track. The CD-ROM, unlike the DVD, is a one-sided media with all of its data recorded on the substrate. The CD-ROM drive requires only one read head and head assembly.

The read head is guided over the disk on a set of rails that position the head on the outermost edge of the disk on one end and stop it near the CD's hub ring on the other. A small motor integrated into the read head mechanism controls the positioning of the read head over the disk.

Constant Linear Velocity and Constant Angular Velocity

The CD-ROM disk rests on a spindle that is rotated by a motor that spins the disk at variable speeds. The speed of the disk depends on the part of the disk that is being read. In contrast, a hard disk drive spins at the same speed regardless of the position of the read/write heads. Devices that use a constant spin speed use what is called constant angular velocity (CAV), which means that every spin takes the same amount of time.

A hard disk or floppy disk drive's inside tracks are much shorter than its outside tracks. When the read/write heads are over the outside tracks, the disk travels a longer linear path than it does with inside tracks. This phenomenon is measured as linear velocity, which is higher for outside tracks and shorter for inside tracks, and it is never constant across an entire disk. To compensate, many newer hard disk drives now use what is called "zoned bit recording" to place more data on the outside tracks and less on inside tracks.

A CD-ROM drive adjusts the speed of the spindle motor to maintain the disk in a constant linear velocity (CLV). The spindle turns slower when the read head is near the outside edge of the CD and turns faster as the read head moves toward the hub ring. CLV ensures that the same amount of data is passing under the read head in any amount of time. Early CD-ROM drives operated at about 210 to 539 rpm (revolutions per minute) and a standard data transfer rate of 150KBps, or one times (1X) the CD-DA's rate. As the electronics in CD-ROM drives improved, the spindle motor developed faster speeds to increase transfer rates. CLV is used on CD-ROM drives with transfer speeds of 12X or slower. Newer CD-ROM drives use CAV and vary the transfer rate to the linear velocity of the disk. On CD-ROM drives with speed ratings higher than 12X, the transfer speed rating (e.g., 13X, 24X, 32X, 72X) represents the best possible data transfer rate of the drive, usually for data located nearest the outside edge. A CAV drive claiming a 50X transfer rate, for example, is not capable of transferring data at that speed over the entire CD.

The Disk Loading Mechanism

The disk loading mechanism is the physical way by which a CD is loaded into the CD-ROM drive. Three distinct ways are used to load a CD:

- *Tray-loading*—Tray-loading is the most common CD loading mechanism in use. The tray-loading method uses a plastic horizontal tray that is opened and closed with motorized gears inside the drive (see Figure 9.6). Pressing the eject button on the CD-ROM drive activates the gears and servos that extend the tray out of the drive. The CD is placed in the portion of the tray designed to hold the disk, and either with a gentle push on the tray or by pressing the eject button, the tray is pulled back into the drive. On some PC cases, the CD-ROM drive is installed vertically. These drives use tabs that extend and retract to hold or release the disk as the tray closes and opens.

- *Caddy*—A CD caddy, such as that shown in Figure 9.7, is a small plastic case that is similar to a CD jewel case. The caddy is hinged on one side and opens so a disk can be placed inside. The caddy has a metal cover on its bottom that slides out of the way when the caddy is inserted into the CD drive. With the sliding cover open, the laser can access the disk. When the CD is inserted into the caddy and placed inside the drive, the effect is very much like the action of a 3.5-inch floppy disk.

9. CD-ROMs and DVDs

Figure 9.6   A CD-ROM drive with its tray extended.

Figure 9.7   A CD caddy is used on some models of CD-ROM drives.

- *Front-loading*—Front-loading CD-ROM drives are very common on automobile CD players and Macintosh computers, but not very common on PCs.

Audio Output and Controls

Early CD-ROM drives included playback controls on the front of the drive that were used to play and listen to audio CDs. Most current CD-ROM drives have eliminated audio controls and allow audio playback software, such as the Windows CD Player, Windows Media Player, or the WinAmp Player, to control the playing of an audio CD. Figure 9.8 shows the audio playback controls of the CD Player utility included with Windows 9x. Many earlier CD-ROM drives also included an eighth-inch headphone jack, although now this is seen only on some CD-RW drives, and the headphone jack on the sound card is used to listen to an audio CD.

The audio playback controls found on some CD drives and definitely included in audio playback software are:

Figure 9.8   The audio playback controls of the Windows CD Player.

- *Volume Control dial*—This dial is present only on drives with a headphone jack.
- *Start and Stop*—Typically the only controls on the drive, these controls are used to start and stop the playback of the CD.
- *Next Track and Previous Track*—These buttons are typically found only on early CD-ROM drives with ratings of 4X and below. A drive with these controls is the equivalent of a CD player.

Amplifier

If the CD-ROM drive has audio playback controls on its front panel, it also includes an amplifier that provides just enough power to drive the headphones. The amplifier does not improve the sound quality of the CD playback, and typically better sound quality is available through the sound card and the PC's speakers.

Jumpers and Connectors

The jumpers and cable connections on a CD-ROM drive are similar to those found on a hard disk drive. CD-ROM drive manufacturers have standardized the location and use of the jumpers and connectors. The jumpers and connectors are always located at the back of the CD-ROM drive, as shown in Figure 9.9.

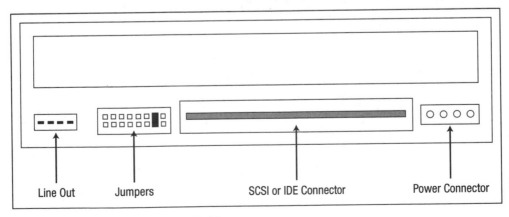

Figure 9.9   The back of a CD-ROM drive.

9. CD-ROMs and DVDs

A 4-pin Molex-style connector is used to connect to the power supply. The data and other connections or jumpers on the drive depend on the type of interface in use. The two most popular interfaces are the integrated drive electronics/AT Attachment Packet Interface (IDE/ATAPI) and the SCSI. An ATAPI drive uses a standard 40-pin data cable and connector and jumpers to set the drive as either the master or slave device on its channel. A SCSI drive, depending on whether it is an internal or external device and the SCSI mode in use, typically uses either a 50-pin or 68-pin connector. A SCSI device must have a device ID configured, which is done through jumpers on the device. If the device is the last on the SCSI bus, it must also be terminated (see Chapter 8 for more information on the SCSI interface).

ATAPI is an interface between the PC and the CD-ROM drive that adds the commands used to control a CD-ROM (or DVD or tape drive) to the standard integrated drive electronics/advanced technology attachment (IDE/ATA) interface. SCSI is an interface type that allows the PC to communicate directly with peripheral hardware, including, among others, disk drives, tape drives, and CD-ROM drives. The two interfaces, IDE/ATA and SCSI, are not compatible, however.

A CD-ROM also has a thin audio connector that is used to connect it to a sound card (see Figure 9.10). The audio connector is either a three- or four-wire cable that sends the CD's audio output directly to the sound card so it can be recorded on the PC or played back on the PC's speakers.

Single and Multiple Drives

The most common CD-ROM drives can load only a single CD at a time. However, some drives can handle two, four, or more disks at once. The primary benefit of a multi-CD drive (see Figure 9.11) is that it allows you to access multiple disks, although still only one at a time, without requiring you to physically remove and replace the disks in the drive. The disks that you use frequently can remain in the CD-ROM drive until they are needed.

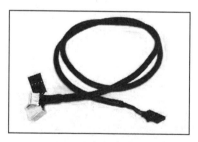

Figure 9.10   The CD audio connector cable used to connect the CD-ROM drive to a
             sound card.

Figure 9.11   A multidisk CD-ROM drive.

A single disk CD-ROM drive is mapped to the PC with a single drive letter, usually **E:** or something close to that. However, a multiple disk CD-ROM drive is mapped to the PC with a drive letter for each disk it is capable of loading. Multiple disk drives also require special software device drivers to give you access to each disk independently.

Digital Versatile Disk

Today's digital versatile disk (DVD) began life back in the early 1990s as a compromise between two proposed formats: the multimedia CD (MMCD) and the super density disk (SDD). The DVD is used now primarily to distribute motion pictures as an alternative to the VHS cassette tape. Many higher-end PCs now include a DVD drive (see Figure 9.12) as an option, but it presently has little use on the PC except to read standard CD-ROMs, to which a DVD is backward compatible.

Figure 9.12   A DVD disk and drive in a PC.

9. CD-ROMs and DVDs

DVD Technology

A DVD disk is capable of storing the equivalent of 17GB (gigabytes) of data, which is about 25 times more than a CD-ROM. Through the use of MPEG and Dolby compression technologies, a DVD can also store hours of high-quality audiovisual content, such as a full-length movie plus other supporting content. One DVD-audio disk can hold up to 400 minutes of 2-channel stereo sound, or it can hold 74 minutes of 6-channel sound.

The DVD was designed to be backward compatible with existing CD-ROM media, which means DVD drives are able to read CD formatting. The read mechanism on a DVD is very similar to that used on the CD except that the DVD uses a dual focus pick-up to read the disk. The DVD disk is the same physical size as a CD-ROM disk, but the formatting on the DVD disk is considerably different than that used on a CD. Table 9.2 compares the formatting of a DVD-audio disk to a CD-DA disk.

DVD Types

A number of DVD types are available:

- *DVD-ROM*—Type of DVD drive installed in a PC.

- *DVD-R (DVD-recordable)*—A WORM-type disk that can record up to 3.95GB. DVD-R is recorded using the same dye-layer technology as the CD-R.

- *DVD-video*—A read-only DVD disk that has the capacity to hold around 133 minutes of full-motion video. DVD-video is most commonly used for full-length movies.

- *DVD-RAM*—A rewritable form of DVD that looks more like a big diskette than a CD-ROM. A DVD-RAM has a capacity of 4.7GB per side and is available in both single-sided and double-sided versions. A DVD-RAM drive will also read virtually all DVD-video and DVD-ROM disks, as well as all types of CD media.

- *DVD-R/W (read/write)*—A competing technology for the DVD-RAM that also holds 4.7GB per side and can be rewritten more than 1,000 times.

Table 9.2   Comparison of DVD and CD formatting.

Feature	DVD–Audio	CD
Capacity	4.7GB	640MB
Recording time	200 minutes	74 minutes
Transfer rate	9.6Mbps	1.4Mbps
Maximum sampling rate	192kHz	44.1kHz

Immediate Solutions

Installing an Internal IDE/ATAPI CD-ROM Drive

Before opening the PC's case to install the drive, be sure to do the following:

1. Have available a Phillips screwdriver and possibly a slotted screwdriver as well (for cases with slotted screws).

2. Back up the PC's hard disk drive. Any time you open the case, you should back up the hard disk.

3. Have a boot disk that boots the system to a DOS command-line prompt.

4. Check the basic input/output system (BIOS) configuration information for the PC to determine the configuration assigned to all existing IDE/ATA devices, noting which are masters and which are slaves and the channel to which each is attached.

5. Wear an electrostatic discharge (ESD) wrist, heel, or ankle strap, or place the PC on an antistatic mat. Doing both is always better.

6. Have handy the documentation for the CD-ROM drive and the motherboard (or IDE/ATA adapter card, if the IDE/ATA cables are attached to one).

7. Turn off the PC with its power switch and remove the power cord from the power supply. Also power off and disconnect all peripheral devices connected to the PC.

Follow these steps to install the drive:

1. Remove the PC's case cover. If you need to slide the case to remove it, do so carefully so you don't snag or nick any interior cables. The ones you are most likely to ding are the power cables.

2. You should always take the opportunity to clean out the inside of the case any time you remove the case covers. Use a PC vacuum or a can of compressed air to clean up any dust or debris. Make sure you wear eye protection when using compressed air. (See Chapter 20 for more information on cleaning the PC.)

3. Study the case's available half-height drive bays and choose the one that is most accessible and the one that is least likely to require you to move other drives to accommodate cabling and fit. If the case has a bay cover on the bay you choose, take it off by removing the screws holding it to the case or by snapping it out.

9. CD-ROMs and DVDs

4. Examine the IDE/ATA arrangement already installed in the PC. If the PC has only one hard disk drive, it is very likely an IDE/ATA drive, which is good. The flat ribbon cable that is about 2 inches wide and connects the disk drive either to the motherboard or to an adapter card is the IDE/ATA data cable. Check to see how many IDE/ATA connectors are available on the motherboard or the adapter card. Check the documentation of the motherboard or adapter card if you are unsure of their location. On the motherboard, the connectors should look like those shown in Figure 9.13.

If there is an available IDE connector on the motherboard or adapter card, you can use it to install your CD-ROM. You may need to purchase an IDE cable to do so, because very few CD-ROM kits include an IDE/ATAPI data cable. However, if there are no empty IDE connectors, you must connect the CD-ROM drive to an existing cable. One more thing you should verify is the type of interface the CD-ROM drive uses. You must match the interface to the cable (ATA-33 or ATA-66 or something else).

WARNING! The cable used by the floppy disk drive is not an IDE/ATA cable. Don't try to use this cable for installing a CD-ROM drive, even if it does have an available connector on it. It could damage the floppy drive, the CD-ROM drive, and the motherboard.

5. If you are connecting the CD-ROM to an existing compatible cable, an available connector should be about midway between the disk drive and the adapter connection. Once you have found the connector, verify your

Figure 9.13   IDE/ATA connectors on the motherboard.

choice of location for the CD-ROM drive. You may need to swap some drives around to reach the CD-ROM drive with the connector without putting strain on the cable or the hard disk drive's connector.

6. Before installing the drive in its bay, check and set the Master/Slave jumpers. Refer to the CD-ROM drive's documentation for the proper jumper placement for the configuration you are assigning the drive. Figure 9.14 shows the jumpers of an IDE/ATA device.

   You must know the master/slave configuration of each existing IDE/ATA device installed in the PC. (See Chapter 8 for more information on configuring IDE/ATA devices.) In most cases, the PC has only one IDE device, the hard disk drive, and it should be set to Master. If so, set the jumper of the CD-ROM drive to Slave, which should be its default setting from the factory. If the hard disk drive's jumper is not set to Master, you should set it as well. If you do not have access to the hard disk's documentation, visit the manufacturer's Web site for this setting.

   Figure 9.15 illustrates the common positions for the jumpers on an IDE/ATA device. The CSEL (cable select) position is used on only some devices and eliminates the Master/Slave jumper problems. A special cable determines the master device from its position on the cable, in much the same way as floppy drives.

7. Remove the CD-ROM drive from its packaging and slide it into the drive bay you have chosen from the front of the PC. Push it in about halfway and then check to see if the power cable and data cable will reach. If so, connect

Figure 9.14   The Master/Slave jumpers of an IDE/ATA device.

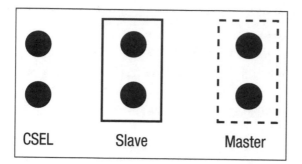

Figure 9.15   The device configuration jumpers on an IDE/ATA device.

them; if not, keep pushing the drive in a bit at a time and checking the cables for reach. As soon as the cables can be connected to the drive, connect them. It is sometimes very difficult to connect the cables on the drive after it has been pushed all the way back into position in the bay. The cables involved in this step are the ribbon data cable (pin 1 is indicated by the red or blue stripe down the edge of the cable) and the power connector from the power supply. The connectors on these two cables are keyed to fit only one way.

8. Attach the DA (digital audio) cable to the back of the CD-ROM drive and to the appropriate lead on the sound card. Refer to the CD-ROM's documentation for the correct settings and connections. (See Chapter 19 for information on configuring sound cards.)

9. Insert and tighten the screws that attached through the side of the drive bay to hold the CD-ROM drive in place. Make sure there are no loose cables or wires hanging down between the sides of the drive and the bay before tightening the screws completely.

10. Recheck the fit of all connectors and cables on the devices in the immediate area to make sure you haven't accidentally dislodged them. You may want to take this opportunity to check the connectors and chips on the motherboard for fit as well.

11. Replace the case cover and secure its screws. Reconnect the device connectors and the PC's power cord. Turn on the peripheral devices and cold start the PC, watching carefully for any power-on self-test (POST) or boot problems.

12. If the CD-ROM drive requires a special device driver, use the Add New Hardware icon on the Windows Control Panel to install it.

Related solutions:	Found on page:
Choosing a Hard Disk Drive by Using Performance Metric	209
Fixing Common Sound Card Problems	571
Cleaning and Caring for a Monitor	595

Installing a DVD Drive

Installing a DVD-ROM drive in a PC uses essentially the same process as the CD-ROM drive installation (see the preceding project). A DVD has an extra step to be performed.

A DVD drive usually comes in an installation kit that includes an ATAPI/EIDE DVD drive, an MPEG II decoder card, the cables needed to connect the drive, and usually a CD (or DVD) with some software and drivers. If the DVD drive uses software decompression, it will not have an MPEG card, but you should understand that software decompression does not perform as well as the hardware kind.

The additional step required for installing a DVD drive is that the MPEG decoder card is installed in a peripheral component interconnect (PCI) expansion slot and connected to the sound card with a DA cable, and perhaps to the video card as well. (See Chapter 19 for information on working with audio or visual devices.) The PCI decoder card is a plug-and-play device, but you will be prompted for the device drivers. Use the Have Disk option and insert the CD that came with the drive.

Related solution:	*Found on page:*
Connecting a CD-ROM or DVD to a Sound Card	572

Installing a SCSI CD-ROM Drive

A SCSI CD-ROM drive has two jumper settings that must be made to the disk drive beyond those done in an IDE/ATA drive installation:

- *Termination*—Many new SCSI devices build a termination capability right into the device itself that can be set through a jumper. If the CD-ROM drive is the last device on the SCSI bus, it needs to terminate the bus. If the CD-ROM does not include termination, then a terminator block, likely the one previously used, is placed after the new device. You should also check to make sure that the device now preceding the CD-ROM device, most likely a hard disk drive, does not need to have a termination jumper changed.

- *SCSI ID*—Each SCSI device must have a unique ID number set. This is done with a jumper on the SCSI device. You can avoid duplicating a SCSI ID number already in use on the SCSI bus in one of two ways. The first is to use a utility available from most SCSI manufacturers that reports the IDs in use and which devices are using which numbers. The EZSCSI utility from Adaptec (**www.adaptec.com**) is one example of this utility. The second way is to look at the jumpers of the other SCSI devices to see what IDs they are set to use. Some SCSI host adapters report this information during the boot process as well.

Beyond these steps, the process is very close to that used to install an IDE CD-ROM drive. Just be sure you match the SCSI standard of the host controller with that of the SCSI CD-ROM drive. Chapter 8 presents information on working with SCSI devices.

Related solution:	Found on page:
Preparing a Hard Disk Drive for Use	210

Adding CD-ROM Support to a Boot Disk

When you create a boot disk using the DOS command **FORMAT A: /S**, the startup files of the operating system and the **COMMAND.COM** command line interpreter are placed on the diskette. Any other functions you may want, such as **FORMAT**, **FDISK**, or **EDIT**, must be copied to the disk after it is formatted. The same is true if you wish to have access to the CD-ROM after you have booted a system using the boot disk.

To add CD-ROM access to a DOS boot disk, you must first create a CONFIG.SYS file on the boot disk, using the **EDIT** command or the Windows Notepad utility. The CONFIG.SYS file must have a line to start the HIMEM.SYS extended memory device driver, which is:

```
DEVICE=C:\WINDOWS\COMMAND\HIMEM.SYS
```

After this command, enter the following:

```
DEVICE =A:\<filename of device driver> /D:MSCD001
```

The device driver's file name should be something like NEC_BM.SYS. If you do not know the name of the device driver, open the Windows Device Manager from the My Computer folder and find the CD-ROM drive on the components tree. Right-click the CD-ROM entry and choose Properties to find the device driver's file name. Close and save the CONFIG.SYS file. Make sure you copy the device driver file onto the boot disk.

Now you need to create an AUTOEXEC.BAT file on the boot disk. Using EDIT or the Windows Notepad utility, create the file with the following entry:

```
C:\WINDOWS\COMMAND\ MSCDEX /X:MSCD001 /V
```

Close and save the AUTOEXEC.BAT file. Your boot disk is now ready to provide access to the CD-ROM should you need to completely restore the operating system or take any other emergency measures.

Troubleshooting an IDE/ATA/ATAPI CD-ROM Drive

Not many physical things can be checked on an IDE CD-ROM drive when it begins to perform badly or not at all. The things you should check out to troubleshoot an IDE CD-ROM drive are as follows:

1. If the drive light is on all of the time, or the tray is extended or retracted when the system starts, but the device does not respond, the problem is likely with the cabling. Remove the case cover, using proper ESD protection, and check the cables on the CD-ROM drive to make sure they are correctly oriented and snuggly connected. Commonly, the 40-pin data cable is connected either one row off or shifted one or two pins to the side, or even completely reversed. These connectors are keyed to prevent this, but it still happens. The 40-pin data cable has a red or blue stripe down the edge on which pin 1 is located.

2. If no lights are showing at all and the system does not see the device at all (it does not show up in the Device Manager list), most likely the CD-ROM drive does not have a power connection. It could be that one was not there to use and it was forgotten. If there are no available power connections, purchase a power cable "Y" splitter and share power with another device, preferably one that is not often in use at the same time as the CD-ROM drive.

3. Check the device configuration jumper to make sure that the drive is properly set to Master, Slave, or Cable Select, as is appropriate for the channel. Every IDE device must be configured to one of these settings. Cable Select is not very common and requires a special cable, so the device typically must be either a master or a slave. Each channel (most Pentium-class motherboards support two IDE/ATA channels) can have only one master and one slave device, unless it is an EIDE (enhanced IDE) channel, in which case it can have one master and three slaves. If the CD-ROM is the only device on its channel or connected to an IDE adapter card, it should be set as a secondary master; otherwise, it is either a primary or secondary slave.

4. An IDE cable longer than 18 inches can cause problems for some IDE/ATA devices. Try a shorter cable to see if that is not the problem. Devices that support the ATA-66 and ATA-100 interface standards use a special 80-wire/40-pin cable. Make sure you have the correct cable for the device and controller you are connecting.

9. CD-ROMs and DVDs

5. Check the BIOS settings to be sure that the IDE channel controller is enabled and that the drive type selector for the IDE channel is set to its auto-select choice, which is usually AUTO.

6. Open the Windows Device Manager or start the System Information applet to check for hardware conflicts or device driver problems. If a yellow exclamation point or a red x appears next to the CD-ROM entry in the Device Manager, investigate further. Or, start the System Information applet from the Accessories|System Tools menus and look in the CD-ROM or Problem Devices folders. Figure 9.16 shows the System Information window.

7. Check whether another device, such as a Zip or Jaz drive, has been assigned the same drive letter.

8. If the Device Manager and System Information tools do not show a problem, but you get the error message "Drive is not accessible or device is not ready" when you try to read from the CD, the problem is probably that the CD tray is not completely closed or the CD is not centered in the tray.

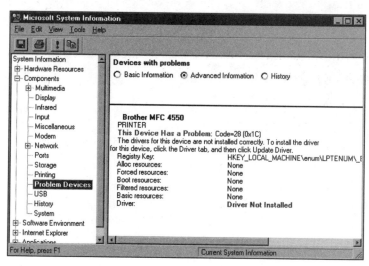

Figure 9.16   The System Information applet can be used to identify device problems.

Troubleshooting a SCSI CD-ROM Drive

The two things you should check first on a SCSI CD-ROM drive that isn't responding as it should are the same two things that were emphasized during the installation process: termination and SCSI ID. (See Chapter 8 for information on working with SCSI devices.) To troubleshoot a SCSI CD-ROM drive, use these steps:

1. Check to make sure the drive is properly terminating the SCSI bus. You may be using the wrong kind of termination for the signaling mode of the system. Some systems require active termination, but some older systems still support passive termination. Verify the type of termination that should be in use. If the device itself supplies the termination through a jumper setting, verify that the setting is correct.

2. Recheck the SCSI ID numbers assigned to the devices on the bus and eliminate any duplication.

3. Check the SCSI cable for loose connections or broken or damaged connectors.

4. Test another SCSI device on the same bus to verify that it is working. If not, the problem may be with the host adapter or perhaps too many devices are installed on the bus or the bus is too long.

Related solution:	Found on page:
Installing a New Hard Drive	215

Troubleshooting IDE CD-ROM Master and Slave Conflicts

Use the following steps to check out why a CD-ROM drive is not responding in a situation for which you are unsure that the correct master/slave configuration has been made.

1. Some CD-ROM drives will not work if they are the only device on an IDE/ATA channel set as a slave; others have no problem with being a slave as the only device on a channel. Check the CD-ROM's documentation to determine if this is the case for your drive. If this information is not in the documentation, contact the manufacturer.

2. When you add a second drive on an IDE channel, you may need to reconfigure the drive that was already on the channel. Some drives have two master-level settings: Master and Master with Slave. It could be that the device will not work with another device on the same channel unless it is configured to a sharing mode. On the same note, if you remove one of the two drives on an IDE channel, you may need to reconfigure the remaining device to work alone.

3. Some hard disk drives will not work with a CD-ROM attached to the IDE channel as a slave. Call it hardware snobbery or whatever, in these cases, you will need to move the CD-ROM drive to another channel.

9. CD-ROMs and DVDs

Improving the Performance of a CD-ROM Drive

The following suggestions can improve the performance of a CD-ROM drive in terms of speed, throughput, and avoiding minor problems.

1. DMA (direct memory access), which is supported by many newer CD-ROM drives, can be used to lighten the load of the processor. To enable DMA on a CD-ROM drive, perform these steps:

   - Right-click the My Computer icon on the Windows Desktop and choose Properties to display the System Properties window. Select the Device Manager tab.

   - Select CDROM from the Computer components list (see Figure 9.17) and click the Properties button to display the CD-ROM drive's properties.

   - Select the Settings tab on the CD-ROM drive's Properties window and check the box next to the DMA option, as shown in Figure 9.18. Click on OK to apply the change and click OK to close the other windows.

   - Restart the PC. After the system is back up, check the DMA setting to see if it is still selected. If so, the CD-ROM drive supports DMA and should speed up just a bit. If not, the drive does not support DMA, but it was worth a try anyway.

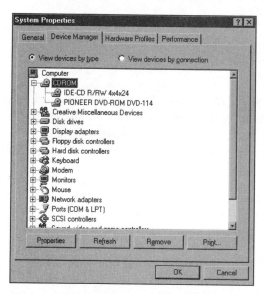

Figure 9.17   System Properties window with the CD-ROM devices selected.

2. Turning off the Auto Insert Notification option, which is on by default, stops the system from launching the support software for the CD's contents whenever a new CD is loaded. For example, each time you place a music CD in the tray and load it, the CD Player automatically starts up. If you did not wish to run this software, you must manually stop it and close it each time. To avoid this problem, you can turn off the automatic startup option. To do so, choose the System icon from the Windows Control Panel and select the Device Manager tab. Double-click the CDROM device entry to open the properties window and select the Settings tab. Unselect the box for Auto Insert Notification and click OK (see Figure 19.18). You will then need to restart the system.

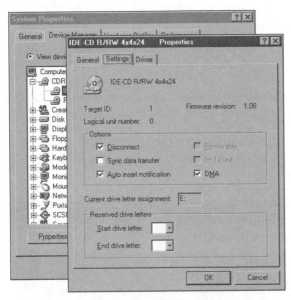

Figure 9.18   Settings option on the CD-ROM Properties window.

Troubleshooting CD-ROM Sound Problems

Obviously, when the CD is playing but you can hear no sound, you should check that the speaker is turned up. Double-click the speaker symbol in the Task Bar tray to open the Play Control window. Slide the volume button up the scale on the Play Control slide (on the left-hand side of the box). If there is still no sound, make sure that the sound is not muted on any of the other sound choices on this box (see Figure 19.19).

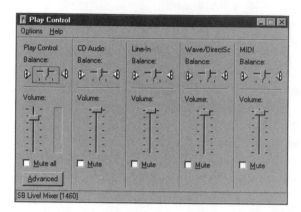

Figure 19.19   The Windows Play Control window is used to adjust the sound volume for each of the various sound players on the PC.

If the sound is turned up, but still no sound is being heard, open the PC's case and check to see that the CD-ROM drive is connected to the sound card with a DA cable. You may want to check the documentation of the sound card to ensure that no additional settings need to be made to it to enable a certain CD-ROM drive brand or model.

If you can listen to a CD using the headphone jack on the CD-ROM drive's front panel, but cannot hear its sound through the speakers attached to the sound card, the DA cable is definitely missing or misconnected.

If the sound quality produced by a CD-ROM drive is very poor, the problem usually is not the CD-ROM drive. It could be any one of a variety of problems, including not enough RAM, bad speakers, a poor speaker connection, or even a bad CD. However, you can check one setting to perhaps improve this situation. Right-click the My Computer icon on the Windows Desktop and choose Properties. Select the Performance tab and click the File System button to open the File System Properties dialog box shown in Figure 9.20. Choose the CD-ROM tab. Slide the "Supplemental cache size" arrow to Large and set the "Optimize access pattern for" option on Quad-speed or higher. This last value is valid only on CD-ROMs with transfer speeds of 4X (quad speed) or higher.

Another option you have to speed up a CD-ROM drive is to install a CD-ROM caching program, such as Symantec's Speedrive, Circuit System's CD Quick Cache, or CD Speedster from Syncronys. However, a faster drive is probably the best way to speed up CDs.

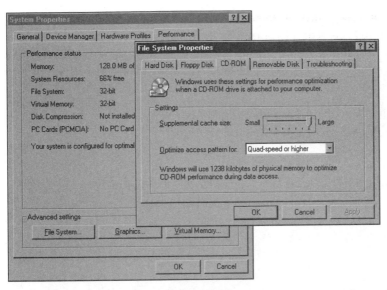

Figure 9.20   The File System Properties window is used to set the performance enhancing or limiting settings for several hardware devices on the PC.

Caring for CD-ROM and DVD Drives

Two things should be regularly cleaned on a CD-ROM or DVD: the disk tray and the CD-ROM's read/write lens. Here are some tips on cleaning the disk tray:

- The tray is cleaned with some general purpose cleaner or isopropyl alcohol by applying the solution to a soft, lint-free cloth or cotton swab.
- Gently wipe out the CD-ROM tray. Avoid pressing down on the tray. A swab is good for getting down into the creases of the disk tray without pressing down on it.
- Allow the tray to completely dry before closing it.

To clean the lens, you need to purchase a CD drive cleaning kit designed for tray-based CD players. Other versions of CD cleaning kits are available, including some for caddy drives, automobile drives, and others. The cleaning kit typically contains a CD disk that has a set of very small brushes built into it and perhaps some CD disk cleaning wipes. The brushes on the cleaning CD sweep across the lens and clean it as the disk spins in the drive. Follow the directions on the package exactly to avoid damaging your CD drive.

9. CD-ROMs and DVDs

To clean a CD-ROM disk, remember to wipe the silver side (gold side on a DVD) with a soft, lint-free cloth or a Scotch-Brite HPCC cloth. Don't use paper towels or other textured paper that may leave streaks or scratch the disk. You can also purchase disposable CD-ROM cleaning towelettes that come packaged individually.

To wipe the disk, start from the center and move outward from the inside edge to the outside edge and don't use a circular motion.

9. CD-ROMs and DVDs

Chapter 10

Expansion Cards

In Depth

Introducing Expansion Cards

Since the early days of the PC, we have been able to add to or alter the PC's capabilities by adding expansion cards inside the case. Expansion cards, which are also called expansion boards, adapters, add-in cards, and daughterboards, allow upgrading the quality of the PC's graphics and sound, connection to the outside world, or connection to a local network. Figure 10.1 shows a typical expansion card. In the context of the PC, expansion means broadening the capabilities of the system by inserting special-purpose circuit cards.

At the risk of being obvious, expansion cards are inserted into expansion slots, which are connector receptacles located on the PC's motherboard. Inside the expansion slot are metallic (typically copper) spring fingers that clamp onto the expansion card when it is inserted into the slot. Each of the fingers matches up with one segment of the card's edge connector to complete one of many different connections of the slot and card combination. Figure 10.2 shows a card being inserted into a slot.

On early PCs, expansion cards were used to add some of the basic functions of the system, including memory, hard disk and floppy disk controllers, video controllers, serial and parallel ports, modems, and even the clock and calendar function of the PC. Today's PCs still add some of these functions through expansion cards, but many of these capabilities are now built into the motherboard. On

Figure 10.1   An expansion card is added to a PC to increase its capabilities.

Figure 10.2   An expansion card and an expansion slot on a motherboard.

modern PCs, expansion cards are used to improve or add to the capabilities of the system, to add controllers and adapters for special-purpose hardware, and to connect to a network. Expansion cards now allow a PC to have video capture, sound, fax, scanner, and network capabilities.

As discussed in this chapter, the challenge of expansion cards, beyond getting the correct one, is getting the card installed, configured, and operating. A PC is configured to the set of features included when it was manufactured. Adding any other functions to the mix can create conflicts and introduce problems in areas that were perfectly fine before the card was inserted. The world of expansion cards is one of *interrupt requests (IRQs)*, dual inline packaging (DIP) switches, and jumper blocks. But, before we get to that, let us review the expansion buses and the unique expansion slot used by each.

Expansion Buses

Bus structures, which are also called *bus architectures*, define the length, width, number of contacts, and interface used to add expansion cards to the motherboard. Why one bus would be used over another can be a matter of preference, but each of the popular bus structures, illustrated in Figures 10.3 through 10.6, has a unique set of operational features that differentiates it from the others.

The PC bus structures that have been the most popular over the years are:

- *ISA (Industry Standard Architecture)*—This bus structure has been around the longest of all the buses still in use. In fact, it is now largely obsolete, but most motherboards still have at least one ISA slot to provide some backward compatibility to support older hardware. The 8MHz ISA bus is a 16-bit bus that also supports 8-bit cards. Some ISA cards (newer cards) are plug and play (PnP), and others (typically older cards) are not, which means an ISA device may need some—if not a complete—manual configuration and setup. The ISA bus is also called the AT bus, for the IBM PC AT on which it was featured. Figure 10.3 shows a drawing of an ISA card.

- *EISA (Extended ISA)*—This PC bus extends the 16-bit ISA bus to 32 bits and adds bus mastering (see the section "Bus Mastering"). EISA expansion slots are backward compatible to ISA cards and run at the same slow 8MHz speed to maintain compatibility. The PCI bus, although still available on some motherboard designs, has largely replaced EISA. Like the ISA slots, EISA slots are black and are located next to the ISA slots on those motherboards that include them.

- *VESA Local Bus (VL-Bus)*—VL-bus is a local bus architecture developed by the Video Electronics Standards Association (VESA) for use with the 486 processor. VL-bus is a 32-bit bus that supported bus mastering (see the section "Bus Mastering") and ran at speeds up to 40MHz. The PCI bus has essentially replaced the VL-bus on modern PCs. If you have a PC with a VL-bus expansion slot, there is no mistaking it. VL-bus slots are similar in appearance to ISA slots, but have an extra slot added to the end and are four inches long. Figure 10.4 is an illustration of the relative sizes of the most common expansion slots.

- *PCI (peripheral component interconnect)*—The PCI showed up with the first Intel Pentium computers and it was the *de facto* standard for add-in cards on most motherboards. PCI is commonly used on PCs, Macintoshes, and workstations. It provides a high-speed data path between the central processing

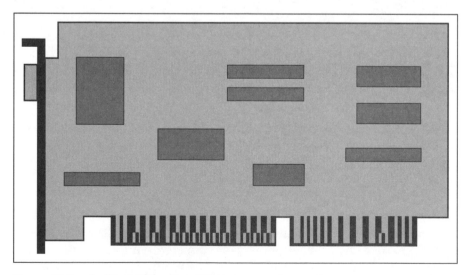

Figure 10.3   An illustration of an ISA bus expansion card.

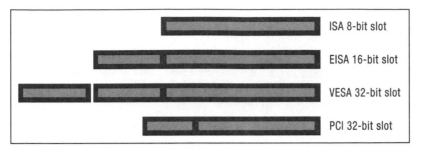

ISA 8-bit slot

EISA 16-bit slot

VESA 32-bit slot

PCI 32-bit slot

Figure 10.4   Common PC expansion slots.

unit (CPU) and the peripheral devices connected to it. The PCI bus, which is a local bus (see the section, "Bus Mastering"), usually includes some devices mounted or connected directly to the motherboard as well as in the PCI expansion slots. Most motherboards include three or four of the white PCI expansion slots.

PCI provides 32- and 64-bit interfaces that support either 33MHz or 66MHz data bus speeds. PCI also supports full PnP capability, which provides nearly foolproof installations and configurations. The shorter slot length helps in making motherboards smaller. Figure 10.5 shows a PCI expansion card.

- *AGP (accelerated graphics port)*—This expansion bus is a little different than the ISA and PCI buses in that it was invented for one purpose only—the support of video cards. Its primary purpose is to improve the performance of three-dimensional (3D) graphics on the system and to make video cards less expensive by removing the need for memory on the video card. However, PCI video cards are more popular because they are cheaper, and although the AGP interface does help, it doesn't provide the benefit it was intended to deliver. AGP does run at faster speeds than the PCI bus, with data speeds up to 133MHz. The different

Figure 10.5   PCI bus network interface card.

speed ratings for AGP video cards are 264Mbps, or 1xAGP; 528Mbps, or 2xAGP; and 1Gbps, or 4xAGP. The AGP slot is a brown slot that is just a little shorter than the white PCI slot. Figure 10.6 shows the placement of the AGP slot on an AT form-factor motherboard in relation to the ISA and PCI slots. A motherboard's form factor defines its shape, size, and compatibilities. See Chapter 1 for more information on motherboard form factors.

Bus Mastering

The PCI bus architecture features a technology called bus mastering, which allows expansion cards to directly access the PC's main memory (random access memory, or RAM) and other peripheral device controllers without the need to pass through the CPU. Bus mastering allows the PCI bus controller to transfer data from a PCI device directly to memory while the CPU is executing other instructions.

Local Bus

Bus architectures that are connected directly into the same internal bus structure that supports the CPU and that run at its data speeds are said to be "local" to the CPU. Local bus (also called system bus) structures are largely things of the past, because the system bus of most motherboards now has data speeds well above that of the peripheral devices and expansion buses.

Portable PC Interface

Portable PCs, most notably notebook computers, have a special expansion bus that allows expansion cards to be inserted while the system is running, without the need to open the computer's case. The PC Card interface, formally called the PCMCIA (Personal Computer Memory Card International Association) interface after the standards body that developed it, uses a 68-pin socket that connects

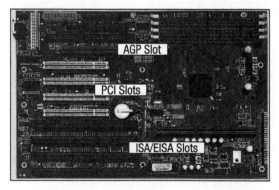

Figure 10.6   The placement of the expansion slots on a motherboard.

Figure 10.7   A PC Card is the expansion card for notebook computers.

directly to the computer's expansion bus. PC Cards are inserted into this socket to add resources or devices to the computer. Figure 10.7 shows a notebook computer with a PC Card network adapter being inserted.

PC Cards use a special socket into which credit-card-size expansion cards that can encompass entire peripheral devices are inserted. These expansion cards can contain additional memory, a hard disk drive, a modem, a network adapter, a sound card, or other devices.

The PCMCIA has established standards for three PC Card slots (and the devices that fit into them):

- *Type 1*—This slot and card is 3.3mm thick and is used to add additional RAM and flash memory. Type 1 slots are most common on very small computers, such as palmtops.

- *Type 2*—This slot is 5mm thick and its cards are typically able to perform input/output (I/O) functions, such as for modems and network adapter cards. Figure 10.8 shows a Type 2 PC Card network adapter with its dongle connector. The dongle is the cable (the white cable in Figure 10.8) that provides the interface to the network cable and its RJ-45 connector.

- *Type 3*—This slot is a whopping 10.5mm thick and used mainly for add-on hard drives and 802.11 wireless network devices.

Most PC Cards are hot-swappable, which means they can be inserted and removed while the system is running and do not require the system to be restarted to recognize the card. Not all PC Card devices totally adhere to the PCMCIA specifications, and some require a software driver before they are fully functional.

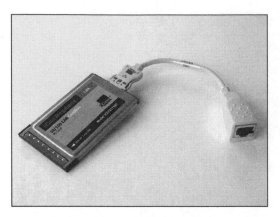

Figure 10.8   A Type 2 PC Card network adapter.

SCSI

The SCSI (small computer system interface; pronounced "skuzzy") is not actually an expansion bus structure, but it can be used to add both internal and external devices to a PC. SCSI devices are more commonly found on network servers rather than personal computers because they tend to be more expensive than ISA or PCI devices. However, SCSI adapters provide a very easy way to connect multiple devices on a single interface, both inside and outside of the system unit. SCSI, which is covered in detail in Chapter 8, has been around for some time and has a variation to fit just about every system, including both ISA- and PCI-compatible host adapter (expansion) cards.

A SCSI host adapter card can handle up to seven devices in addition to itself, including both internal and external devices. Newer versions, such as the SCSI-3 standard, now handle up to 15 devices, but these cards are almost prohibitively expensive for a home computer. A SCSI interface with multiple devices must be terminated at each end of the chain. Each device on the chain is assigned a unique identity number that is used by the host adapter to communicate with it.

Serial and Parallel Ports

From the beginning, PCs have had at least two ports: a serial port and a parallel port. On older PCs, such as PC XTs through and including most 486s, these ports were added through expansion cards, which were inserted primarily into ISA slots. See Chapter 12 for more information on these and other I/O ports and connectors.

USB and IEEE 1394 Interfaces

Two of the newer connector and interface types used to connect external peripherals to a PC are the universal serial bus (USB) and the IEEE (Institute of Electrical and Electronics Engineers) 1394 standard. The IEEE 1394 standard is more commonly known as FireWire (Apple), i.Link (Sony), or Lynx (Texas Instruments) proprietary interfaces, or by its generic name, high-performance serial bus (HPSB). These are flexible device interfaces that can support both low-speed devices such as keyboards and mice as well as high-speed, high-end devices such as video cameras, scanners, and printers. Both of these are hot-swappable and plug-and-play interfaces, which means devices can be added or removed from a PC without the need for reboot or installation procedures. Windows 98 and 2000 directly support USB and IEEE 1394.

USB devices can be connected to external USB hubs, which can be daisy-chained together to the point of 127 devices on a single USB bus. This means 127 devices are sharing not only one bus, but one set of system resources as well. Figure 10.9 shows a USB port and connector.

IEEE 1394 is a slightly faster interface than USB, and it is designed to handle the bandwidth and data transfer speeds and requirements of devices requiring an isochronous (real-time) interface. The 1394 interface supports up to 63 devices, which can have different device transfer speeds on a single bus.

Expansion Cards

For all of the different bus and interface types that you can plug an expansion card or device into on a PC, there really aren't that many types of expansion cards. Historically, any additional function you wished a PC to have beyond those included on the motherboard (which wasn't very much beyond the processor and basic input/output system, or BIOS) had to be added via an expansion card. Today, motherboards have quite a few of the functions that once required a separate adapter or controller card built into the chipset or the Super I/O chip.

Figure 10.9   A USB port and connector.

Each of the following sections gives a quick overview of one of the many common expansion card types that can be added to a PC.

Controller Cards

A controller card, also known as an adapter card, is an expansion card that contains the circuitry and components needed to control the operations of a peripheral device, such as a disk drive. Controller cards are less common on newer PCs because device controllers are typically included in either the system chipset or the Super I/O chip (see Chapter 3 for more information on chipsets).

Controller cards are fairly easy to find in the PC. They are the ones with flat ribbon cables attached to them that run to the hard disk, CD-ROM (compact disk-read only memory), DVD (digital versatile disk), and floppy disk drives. In many older PCs, the disk controller card supports both the hard disk drive and the floppy disk drives. If a CD-ROM device is installed in an older PC, it typically had its own controller card, but could also share the common (multipurpose) controller card.

The SCSI host adapter is not a controller card, although it may appear to be one. SCSI devices, such as IDE (ATA) devices, have their controllers integrated into the device itself (see Chapter 8 for more information on IDE and SCSI storage devices).

I/O Cards

I/O cards are used to add I/O ports, such as serial and parallel ports, to a PC. These cards were once a mainstay of PC configurations, but they are nearly obsolete today because the ports they support are typically included as a part of the motherboard.

Interface Cards

Interface cards are the most nondescript of the expansion cards. In fact, just about any expansion card can be and usually is classified as an interface card. But, in general use, an interface card connects a PC to any external device, network, or gadget, such as a mouse, an external CD-ROM, scanner, or camera. Interface cards are also the PC Cards that are used to connect external devices to notebook PCs.

Memory Cards

Most PC technicians do not think of memory modules as expansion cards, but in the strictest interpretation of an expansion card, the memory modules used to add memory to a PC are in fact performing an expansion function. Figure 10.10 shows a memory module being installed on a motherboard.

Figure 10.10   A memory module being installed on a motherboard.

Memory Expansion Card

Higher-end PCs, such as those in use as network servers or graphics workstations, often fill up their memory module slots and still require additional memory.
Many of these systems are able to install a special expansion card, called a *memory
expansion card (MEC)*, that can add up to 16GB of additional RAM (usually synchronous dynamic RAM, or SDRAM) to the system. This is where the amount of
RAM the CPU can address becomes important. Figure 10.11 illustrates a MEC
manufactured by Dell Computer for its workstation line of computers.

As Figure 10.11 shows, the MEC is able to mount a number of memory modules
(usually dual inline memory modules, or DIMMs). The card illustrated has eight
memory slots, and some are available to handle as many as 16 DIMMs. One drawback, although slight when weighed against the advantage of the additional

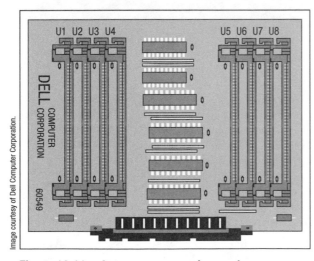

Figure 10.11   A memory expansion card.

memory, is that the MEC sits on the system bus and is therefore slower than the memory mounted in the SIMM (single inline memory module) or DIMM slots on the motherboard.

PC Card Memory

Memory can be added to a portable PC, virtually on the fly, with a Type 1 PC Card memory card. Remember that the standards organization for PC Cards is the Personal Computer Memory Card International Association, with the emphasis on memory card.

PC Card memory cards are credit-card-size memory modules that incorporate flash memory (static RAM, or SRAM). When a flash memory card, such as the one shown in Figure 10.12, is added to a portable PC, the memory added should not be used as a substitute for a disk drive, but used to extend the working storage of the PC. PC Card memories are available with 8MB to 512MB of flash memory.

Modem Cards

A modem (which is short for modulator/demodulator) allows you to connect to and communicate with other computers over the public telephone network. An internal modem is one that plugs into an expansion slot on the motherboard. External modems, which connect to the PC via a serial or USB port, have indicator lights to signal the activity of the modem. However, when using an internal modem, because it is mounted inside the system case, the user must rely on a software interface to control the modem and view the status of a communications session.

Figure 10.12   A PCMCIA flash memory card.

Internal modem cards, like most other expansion cards, are available for either the ISA or PCI expansion buses. Installation of the modem card may require some COM (serial) port assignment, but typically the modem will have an installation disk that also includes its device driver. Any problems created with the installation of the modem usually involve system resource conflicts. Serial ports are called COM ports, interchangeably. This term comes from the days of the earliest PCs on which all communications were carried through the serial ports. Eventually, the serial port became known as the communications, or COM port, and the name stuck. Today, serial ports are more commonly known as COM ports.

Almost all notebook computers and other portables have a modem built into the system. Should you wish to use an external modem, it would typically be added to the system in the form of a Type 2 PC Card. The telephone cable is attached with what is called an X-jack, a connector that pops out of the end of the card to allow the phone cable's RJ-11 connector to plug in.

Chapter 19 deals specifically with the functions and configuration of modems, both internal and external.

Sound Cards

Although sound (audio) processing is included on the motherboard of some newer PCs, it is usually a feature that is added through an expansion card. Sound cards, which are discussed in detail in Chapter 20, are fairly standard in their basic function of producing sound. However, the number of voices, or the different distinct instruments or sounds that the sound card can reproduce, continues to grow. The number in the sound card name, such as a SoundBlaster 16, Soundwave 32, or a SoundBlaster AWE 64, refers to the number of voices the sound card can reproduce. It is not the number of bits the sound card uses to decode the sound samples. A piano sound takes one voice, a trumpet another, a drum, a third, and so on. The resolution of the sound in bits describes the sound's amplitude and frequency. Nearly all sound cards use a 16-bit digital sound resolution, which is the same as used on all compact disk (CD) players and CD-ROM drives.

The components included on a PC sound card are illustrated in Figure 10.13. Chapter 20 discusses just what these components are and what they do.

Don't forget that installing the sound card is only half the battle; you will also need a set of speakers. Most sound cards have a full set of output jacks into which you can plug speakers as well as amplifiers and microphones (see Figure 10.13).

About the only problem you'll run into when installing a sound card in a PC, like most expansion cards, is system resource conflicts, especially IRQs. See the "Immediate Solutions" section of this chapter for more information on resolving resource conflicts for expansion cards.

10. Expansion Cards

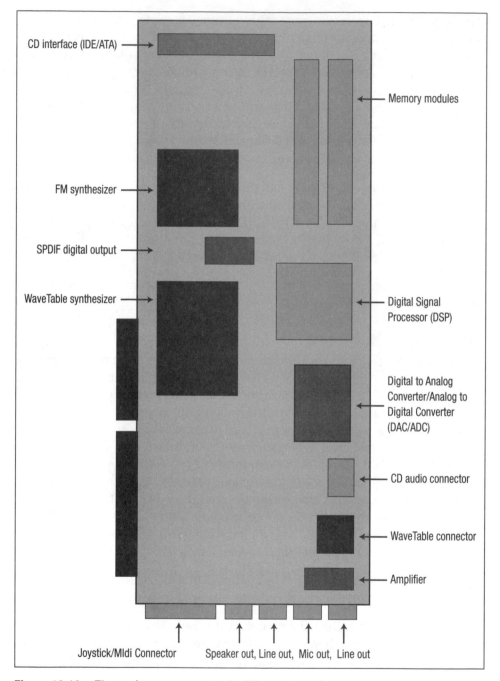

CD interface (IDE/ATA)

Memory modules

FM synthesizer

SPDIF digital output

WaveTable synthesizer

Digital Signal Processor (DSP)

Digital to Analog Converter/Analog to Digital Converter (DAC/ADC)

CD audio connector

WaveTable connector

Amplifier

Joystick/MIdi Connector   Speaker out, Line out, Mic out, Line out

Figure 10.13   The major components of a PC sound card.

Video Cards

The video card in your PC may be arguably the most important expansion card in your system, depending on how you look at it. The video card provides your PC with the ability to display a picture on the monitor. Although some newer motherboards now integrate the video processing into the chipset or on the motherboard itself, for the vast number of PCs in use, a video expansion card is used to drive the video signal.

The video card must be matched to the monitor (see Chapters 11 and 15 for more information on video cards and monitors, respectively). It will do little good to buy a screaming video card to drive a wimpy monitor. These two components must be matched in their capabilities. The video card must be able to drive the monitor, and the monitor must be able to display the output of the video card.

When choosing a video card for a PC, look at these three important features or components: its processor or chipset, its bus, and its memory.

Video Processors

Video cards all have a processor or chipset on the card. The onboard processor generates some or all of the image to be displayed on the monitor. How much of the video load the video card's processor and chipset carry depends on the age of a video card and is usually related to its cost.

Older cards use the frame buffer technology, in which the video card is tasked with displaying only one video frame at a time and the CPU (the one inside the PC) actually creates each video frame.

The next step up for video processors is graphic acceleration. In fact, some video cards are called graphic accelerators. On this type of video card, the video processor performs the routine tasks associated with generating graphic images under the guidance of the system CPU. This type of video card processing is the most common in PCs.

On newer, high-end video cards, the onboard processor and chipset have the complete responsibility for generating all displayed graphics, which leaves the CPU free to do other tasks.

Video processors are divided into two categories:

- *2D*—This is the type of graphics used by most of the standard applications, such as word processing and spreadsheets, as well as many multimedia applications, such as PowerPoint and CorelDRAW. This is the minimum level of graphics on a PC.

- *3D*—This is the graphics type used by games and 3D rendering and drawing software. Unfortunately, 3D graphics and the processor commands that are used to generate them are not standardized. As a result, some 3D programs and games may not work with every video card.

Video Bus

Over the years, video systems have improved from the monochrome video bus of the early PCs to the 3D, color, high-resolution systems of today. Most of today's PCs support video through either a PCI or accelerated graphics port (AGP) bus connector. The PCI bus is independent of the processor, which makes for fast video. The AGP bus offers a higher bandwidth, and with it, higher frame rates. It has a direct line to RAM, which allows it to better prepare 3D images and textures.

Video RAM

Video RAM (VRAM) serves two purposes on the video card: (1) it acts as a buffer between the CPU and data bus and the monitor, and (2) it is the work area used by the video processor and chipset to perform the calculations used to formulate the graphic image as an analog signal for the monitor.

Video RAM is a bit different than the RAM used as primary memory on the PC. It is usually dual-ported, which means it can be written to at the same time it is being read. This allows the CPU to write to VRAM while the monitor is reading it. A new type of VRAM that is becoming very popular on high-end graphics packages is RAMBUS memory, which operates much faster than other forms of VRAM.

Audiovisual Outputs

Beyond the standard output ports for the monitor, some video cards may come with additional output ports. These extra ports can be used to connect the video card to a television, videocasette recorder (VCR), or projector. Generally, these extra video output ports are either composite or S-Video. Composite video is the most common type of output port on video cards. It supports good image quality on most TVs and VCRs. S-Video is a high-quality display interface that provides better color and resolution than composite video.

Other Video Outputs

Other miscellaneous output ports and interfaces can be included on some video cards. A few of the most common ones are:

- *VR (virtual reality) goggles*—This type of port supports video for VR goggles or can be used to produce a display with increased depth on a standard monitor.

- *DVD*—DVD drives need special video interfaces, and many of the newer high-end video cards come with ports to support DVD drive or MPEG-2 decoder card interfaces.

- *TV tuner*—This port allows the computer to receive video streams from a TV, VCR, Laserdisc, or TV antenna.

- *SLI (scan line interleaving)*—This interface enables two 3D acceleration cards to share the load of generating the displayed image by dividing the screen between the two cards.

Expansion Card Operation

The CPU communicates with an expansion card to get data, give commands, or send data using IRQs, I/O addresses, and DMA (direct memory access) channels. As a group, these elements are called the "system resources." Chapter 7 discusses system resources in detail.

Interrupt Requests

Suppose there was a big electric light mounted to your desk that any number of people could turn on whenever they needed you to do something for them. Each time the light was on, you had to drop whatever you were doing to take care of whatever was needed. As willing as you may be, the problem is that you would not know which person had turned on the light. A solution to this problem would be to place a light on the desk of each person who could request your services. This way when a light was turned on, you would know who needed you.

This is essentially the way the CPU interfaces with the devices in the PC. In effect, each device is assigned an IRQ that it can turn on to signal the CPU that it needs some service performed. The services needed might be to move data from RAM to a device, transfer data from a device to RAM, or the like. Whatever is needed, the device requests service from the CPU by turning on its IRQ. The CPU then interrupts what it is doing to take care of the request.

One issue that is common to nearly all expansion cards is IRQ conflicts. When two devices are assigned the same IRQ, the CPU will not know which device is requesting a service. Of course, two devices can share an IRQ, but only when just one is active at a time. Chapter 7 discusses IRQs in more detail.

The normal or default assignment of IRQs on a PC are listed in Table 10.1.

The unassigned IRQs listed in Table 10.1 are available to be used by any expansion card added to the system. The reason IRQs 3 and 4 are shared among the COM (serial) ports is that all four ports are rarely installed on a PC, and if they are, they are rarely in use at the same time.

Table 10.1   Default IRQ assignments on a PC.

IRQ	Default Assignment
0	System timer
1	Keyboard
2	Video card
3	COM2, COM4
4	COM1, COM3
5	Sound card or LPT2
6	Floppy disk controller (FDC)
7	LPT1
8	CMOS clock
9	Reserved link to IRQs 0-7
10	Unassigned
11	Unassigned
12	Unassigned
13	Math coprocessor
14	Hard disk controller (HDC)
15	Unassigned

I/O Addresses

After a device requests an action from the CPU using an IRQ, the CPU must respond to the requesting device with a signal that indicates the task either is completed, could not be done, or has returned some particular data. The CPU cannot send the data to the device over the IRQ line, so a small amount of memory is set aside for each device to receive responses from the CPU.

A device's I/O address (or base memory address, I/O port, or port address, as they are also called) is represented as a hexadecimal address range in memory. Table 10.2 lists a few of the I/O addresses assigned on a PC.

Direct Memory Access

Direct memory access (DMA) allows a device to communicate directly with the system memory without the assistance or intervention of the CPU. In a normal programmable input/output (PIO) data transfer, the CPU controls the movement of the data into RAM. A DMA transfer moves data directly from its source to RAM.

Table 10.2   Default I/O address assignments on a PC.

Device	I/O Address Assignment
Primary IDE	1F0–1F7h
Games port	0200–0207h
Sound card	0220–022Fh
Plug and Play	0270–0273h
Parallel port	0278–027Ah
Network adapter	0300–031F
VGA adapter	03C0–03DF
PCMCIA port	03E0–03E7

DMA devices are assigned a DMA channel, which cannot be shared between two devices. There are eight DMA channels. The expansion card that is typically assigned a DMA channel is the sound card, which may actually get two or more channels, if they are available. The most common assignments of DMA channels are listed in Table 10.3.

Setting System Resources

System resources are assigned on expansion cards either physically on the card (either through DIP switches or with a jumper block) or with software. The software used to assign a card to a set of system resources may be a dedicated installation program or a configuration interface, such as the BIOS setup program or the Windows Device Manager.

A DIP switch block has either four or eight slide switches that can be moved between two settings (representing on and off, or 0 and 1). The documentation

Table 10.3   Default DMA channel assignments on a PC.

DMA Channel	Assignment
0	Reserved for system
1	Sound card (8-bit transfer)
2	Floppy disk controller (8-bit transfer)
3	Open (8-bit transfer)
4	Link to DMA Channels 0-3
5	Sound card (16-bit transfer)
6	Open (16-bit transfer)
7	Open (16-bit transfer)

with the expansion card should specify the settings for a card's physical configuration for a particular PC type. The same is true of jumper blocks. The jumper is set to cover two pins (on), one pin (off), or no pins (neutral). A three-pin jumper can be set to represent eight values, each of which designates a different system resource setting for the card.

If the expansion card comes with installation software, the system resources will be automatically set. However, if system resource conflicts result, you can use the Windows Device Manager (assuming a Windows system) to check on the resource settings. These settings can also be modified in the BIOS setup program.

Plug and Play

Plug and play enables expansion boards to be automatically configured, including system resource settings, by the BIOS and operating system. Windows 98 and Windows 2000 support PnP devices right out of the box, but Windows NT supported only some devices. Understand that plug and play does not mean hot-swap, such as what can be done with a PC Card.

Immediate Solutions

Installing an Expansion Card

Follow this general procedure to install an expansion card in a PC, assuming that you are following the electrostatic discharge (ESD) protection guidelines, outlined in Chapter 14:

1. Create a backup of the hard disk's contents. Typically, installing an expansion card should not have any effect on the hard disk, but it is better to take this precaution.

2. Turn off the computer's power and remove the AC power cord from the outlet.

3. Open or remove the system case, depending on the case design of the PC.

4. Identify an available slot of the appropriate expansion bus. Remember, expansion cards are manufactured to fit the slot style of a certain bus structure. If the PC and card are fairly recent, more than likely either an ISA or PCI slot is what is needed. An older 8-bit card will fit into an ISA 16-bit slot. To make room for the card, you may need to rearrange the existing cards.

5. Remove the screw holding in the metal slot cover for the slot in which you will be inserting the new expansion card. Keep the screw handy; you'll need it to secure the expansion card.

6. Before inserting the card, read its documentation to verify its configuration and settings. It is very difficult to set DIP switches and jumpers once the card is inserted into a slot and fastened down.

7. Handle the expansion card only by its edges, and avoid touching its circuit side (the one with the electronic stuff on it), the pin side (the backside), or the edge connector. That doesn't leave much, but the top and side edges do give you enough of the card to hold.

8. Insert the card by aligning it to the slot, as shown in Figure 10.14, and then with steady pressure, press the card into the slot. You may need to rock it very slightly front to rear to get it to settle into the slot. Don't force it. It should be snug, but you can damage the slot or the card, or both, by forcing the card into the slot too fast and too hard. As you work, keep the card from rubbing or touching other cards already installed. Figure 10.14 is a bit unrealistic; Figure 10.15 shows a more realistic situation.

Figure 10.14   Aligning the expansion card to the slot.

Figure 10.15   Installing an expansion card in a PC.

9. When the card is evenly and securely in the slot, fasten it with the slot screw.

10. You may want to plug the PC in and test it for a very short while the system case cover is removed. This way, if there is a problem, it is a much shorter path back to where you are. When you are sure all is well, replace the system case cover.

Troubleshooting Expansion Cards

After you have installed an expansion card, or at any later time, if you get a boot or POST (power-on self-test) beep code or error message that indicates a possible expansion card problem, or if an expansion card doesn't perform as it should, there are three possible scenarios: a bad connection, system resource conflicts, or the card is bad.

Follow this troubleshooting regime to track down which of these scenarios is causing the problem:

1. Always begin by organizing a workspace around the PC as much as possible and preparing the workspace, the PC, and yourself against ESD, as outlined in Chapter 14. This cannot be emphasized too much. Even the smallest static discharge can inflict enough damage to the expansion card to have caused the problem you are now trying to track down.

2. Turn off the PC and unplug it from its electrical outlet. Turn off any peripheral devices attached to the PC and unplug their power cords from their AC outlets as well. Just turning off the plug strip is not enough. If there are any phone cables, network cables, or any other telecommunications lines connected to the PC, disconnect them.

3. Remove enough of the PC's case to allow as much of an unobstructed access to the expansion slots on the motherboard as possible.

4. Check that each expansion card, not just the last one installed, is firmly seated in its slot. Cards can creep out of their slots over time, or you may have accidentally push a card slightly out of its slot when installing another. If any of the cards are loose or not seated completely, you may have found the problem. Without putting the case back on, power on the PC and test to see if the error condition is gone.

5. Check the connecting cables on each of the expansion cards to verify that each end of the cable is snuggly connected. Disconnect the cable connector one end at a time and reconnect it tightly. Never force a connector, and pay attention to the key on the connector that is meant to prevent you from connecting it incorrectly. You have a choice now: You can power the PC up after reconnecting each card or you can wait until you have done so for all of the cards. If the error is gone when you reboot the system, the problem was obviously a loose connector.

6. If you have gotten this far in the procedure, then the problem is not a generic one, such as loose cards or connectors. At this point, you will need to gather a few tools: a Phillips screwdriver, the documentation for your expansion cards, and possibly a probe or stylus or needle-nose pliers.

7. If you have just installed an expansion card, start with it. Verify any DIP switch or jumper settings you made to the card against the documentation. A common error here is that when you set the jumpers or switches, the card was not oriented as the documentation assumed. For example, you may have had the card upside-down. ISA cards have configuration settings for all three of the system resource settings (IRQ, DMA, and I/O address). Verify that you have set all three, if applicable, according to the recommended settings in the card's documentation. Retest the system after verifying each expansion card.

8. If the problem persists, use the operating system's device manager to verify that no system resource conflicts exist. On a Windows system, you would use the Device Manager that is accessed through either My Computer's properties or the System icon on the Control Panel. Figure 10.16 shows the Computer Properties screen. To view the system resource assignments for an individual device, display the properties for the device and click the Resources tab, as shown in Figure 10.17.

   If any conflicts are identified, which are likely to be IRQs, reconfigure the newer device or the one used less frequently to an available resource setting. Retest the system. A red X or a yellow exclamation point in front of the device or resource name indicates conflicts in the Device Manager.

9. If the problem persists, it is all or nothing time. Write down the order and slot placement of each card in the PC and label each cable. You may want to sketch the expansion slot area to show where the cards and cables are connected. You should also enter the system BIOS configuration data and record all of the BIOS settings for the PC.

   Get a supply of antistatic bags or make lots of room on a clean static-free surface. Leaving only the hard disk controller card, if one is in use, remove all of the expansion cards from the PC. Place each card in an antistatic bag or where it will be safe.

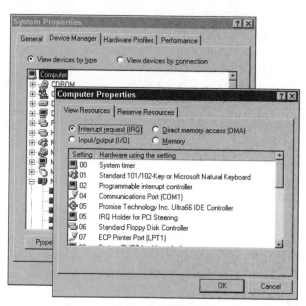

Figure 10.16   System resource values on the Computer Properties window of the Windows Device Manager.

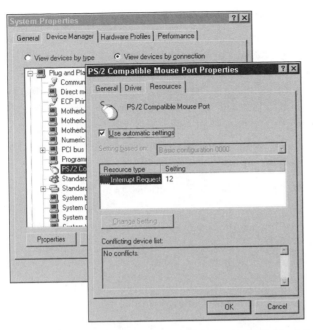

Figure 10.17   The system resources for an individual device are displayed on the
Properties window for the device.

NOTE: *Never stack expansion cards on top of each other, even if they are in antistatic bags.*

Install one expansion card at a time and test the system after each card. This procedure tries to isolate the card that is causing the problem. It is your call, but to test for the fault with this process, you really should put the case cover back after installing each card. The problem could actually be something such as the card is grounding to the case. If you find the suspect card, retest it without the case on, just to be sure.

You may need to change the system BIOS setup data to indicate that one or more of the cards have been removed, and then reconfigure the BIOS data after it is installed using the data you recorded prior to starting this procedure.

10. Should you find an expansion card that causes the original problem, and not some new problem, you may want to verify that the slot is not causing the problem. Retest the slot with a different compatible card.

11. If the problem persists, it may be related to the motherboard. See Chapter 1 for procedures to test the motherboard. It could also be time to contact technical support at the manufacturer of the PC or the motherboard.

Dealing with Choke Points

A choke point on a PC occurs when too much data is trying to get through too small of a passageway. A common choke point is using an inappropriate expansion card for a system. For example, on a Pentium PC, using an ISA video card will likely cause a choke point when the monitor display graphics tries to run over the low-speed ISA bus. If an expansion card is performing poorly or very slowly, it may be bound by a choke point of its own doing or one caused by too much traffic on a bus.

Some things you can do to prevent or eliminate a choke point for peripheral devices and expansion cards are:

1. Upgrade to a motherboard with built-in controllers for the floppy disk and hard disk and as many other ports as possible to eliminate controller and adapter cards on the expansion bus.

2. If one is not available on the motherboard, install a USB or IEEE 1394 port expansion card and use it for future peripheral devices you add to the PC, where possible.

3. Consider USB devices that provide additional serial and parallel ports, which can also save expansion bus slots.

Installing a SCSI Host Adapter

1. Follow the procedures outlined previously in "Installing an Expansion Card" to install the SCSI host adapter. Be sure you have the appropriate card for the type of expansion bus slot available on your PC.

2. Before inserting the SCSI card, verify its termination settings. Use the card's documentation to find these settings. Some cards use a switch or jumper to enable or disable termination, and others use a firmware utility that is included on the card that runs at boot-up to configure termination. Also verify any system resource settings that must be made physically on the card. Find in the documentation any resource settings that must be entered into the BIOS setup data or an installation program and make a note of them for later.

3. Before you insert the card into its slot, attach any internal SCSI device to the adapter card. It is much easier and safer for the connectors and neighboring cards to do it now than after the card is seated. External devices should be attached after the card is seated and secured.

4. Make any configuration changes to the BIOS configuration data and reboot the system. You should see a SCSI BIOS boot message immediately after the POST completes, if all is well.

See Chapter 8 for more information on the SCSI interface bus.

Installing Serial and Parallel Add-On Ports

1. Follow the procedures outlined previously in "Installing an Expansion Card" to install the SCSI host adapter. Be sure you have the appropriate card for the type of expansion bus slot available on your PC.

2. Because most serial and parallel port expansion cards are 8-bit cards, you can get by using a short ISA slot, if one is available. Little else will fit this slot anyway, so this is a good use for it, and it leaves the long (16-bit) slots available.

3. Using the card's documentation, check the card's configuration settings, which for serial and parallel cards are typically set on the card through jumpers and DIP switches. If other serial or parallel ports are installed on the system, verify which system resources are assigned to them. The IRQ and I/O addresses assigned to these ports determine to which logical port (COM1, COM2, LPT1, etc.) they will be assigned during the boot sequence.

4. After the card is installed and secured, reboot the system and install any device drivers required.

See Chapter 12 for more information on serial and parallel ports and their uses.

Installing a USB or IEEE 1394 Expansion Card

Although this procedure refers to USB ports, the same process can be used to install IEEE 1394 (FireWire) expansion cards.

1. Follow the procedures outlined previously in "Installing an Expansion Card" to install the SCSI host adapter. Be sure you have the appropriate card for the type of expansion bus slot available on your PC.

2. USB expansion cards are installed in PCI slots, so make sure one is available before getting too far along. Install the card as you would any other. These cards are plug and play, so you should not have any configuration to

perform. If you are on a Windows NT system, you may need to enter the System Devices area to add the card. When the system reboots, you will be prompted to load the device drivers. Windows 98 and 2000 will most likely have the driver you need onboard, but the card should also have a disk or CD with it that contains the driver needed.

See Chapter 12 for more information on the USB and IEEE 1394 buses.

Resolving Resource Conflicts on Windows PCs

If a PC has system resource conflicts, one of the following is likely to be happening:

- The system fails to boot, with an error beep code or error message indicating an error on the motherboard or expansion bus.
- During the boot sequence, the system freezes and will not complete the boot.
- The system halts or freezes during an I/O operation or while an application program is running, for no apparent reason.
- An I/O device performs erratically or intermittently.

The only cause for a resource conflict is a recent hardware upgrade, and if the answer to any one of the following questions is "Yes," then most likely the problem is a system resource conflict.

- Have you recently added a new internal device, expansion card, or device driver?
- Did the problem show up after a new component was added to the PC?
- Was the PC operating fine before the new component was added?

If you answered "Yes" to at least one of the above questions, you need to troubleshoot the system resources to resolve the problem. You can just about count on the problem being a system resource conflict if the device added was a sound card.

1. Write down the current resource settings and assignments, including those in the BIOS configuration data. It is also a very good idea to run a virus checker on the system before making any changes. Make sure that the PC isn't suffering from a virus, which can appear as a system resource problem.

2. Open the Device Manager and select the device (expansion card) that was recently added to the PC. If the device has a yellow exclamation mark or red X symbol in front of its name, it is conflicting with another device or its configuration cannot be resolved by the BIOS.

3. Open the Properties window and display the Resources tab information. At the bottom of the display (refer to Figure 10.17), there should be information regarding the device with which there is a conflict.

4. At this point, you will need to change the conflicting resource (probably an IRQ, and definitely an IRQ if the device is a PCI card) to another available setting. If there are no available resources of the kind you need, you may need to share with another device that would not be in use at the same time as the new device. You may need to change the settings on the expansion card by using jumpers or DIP switches, and referring to the card's documentation as your guide to the new values or positions. The system BIOS of the PC may support the reassignment of IRQs (for PCI slots) in the setup program. Most resource conflicts exist between expansion slots, and many can be resolved in the BIOS settings.

Resolving Resource Conflicts with Plug-and-Play Devices

Plug-and-play devices can cause IRQ conflicts because the PnP processes in the operating and BIOS may not detect all other devices or it may not correctly detect a new device. There are standards, but standards are open to interpretation. PnP devices are configured after all other devices are squared away during the boot cycle.

To resolve a resource conflict on a plug-and-play device:

1. Remove the new device's configuration using the Windows Device Manager and restart the PC to see if the problem was a one-time thing. You cannot just disable the device in the BIOS configuration data; it must also be removed from the Device Manager's settings as well.

2. If the device is still having problems, verify that the most current device drivers are installed. Visit the manufacturer's Web site to find the latest drivers and install them on your PC.

3. If the new device is not being detected, use the Add New Hardware Wizard from the Control Panel to install it. If the Add New Hardware Wizard is not able to install the device. You will need to configure the system resources manually.

4. Open the Device Manager, highlight the selection for the device in question, and click on the Properties button. In the Properties window, choose the Resources tab. Clear the Use Automatic Settings checkbox. Now choose

the system resources that are in conflict and use the Edit Resource function to reassign them to available or unassigned resources. The Device Manager will keep you inbounds and not let you assign values outside the assignable range. If you assign a resource already in use, you will also get a warning. When all is well, click on OK and close it out.

5. Restart the system, and the problem should be solved. If not, repeat this process until you arrive at a workable set of system resources. If the manufacturer has technical support available, call or email it.

Installing a Video Card

1. Follow the procedures outlined previously in "Installing an Expansion Card." The steps listed in this project are specific to video cards.

2. Remove the monitor connection from its plug on the old video card. Open the system case and remove the old video card. If the card doesn't pull out easily, rock it gently front to back, never side to side, until it frees up and pulls out. Some systems have video systems integrated into the motherboard. Check the motherboard's documentation on the procedure to use to disable this system before installing a new video card. Typically, a jumper plug or switch is used to disable this circuitry.

3. Insert the new video card and connect any external parts that are a part of the video card system, such as those included with some Matrox cards.

4. The system should detect the new card and ask for device drivers. Always use the drivers that came with the video card in lieu of the stock drivers included with the operating system. You may want to check the manufacturer's Web site for updated drivers once the installation is complete.

Part II

Storage and Access Devices

Chapter 11

Video Cards

In Depth

Overview

The outputs of a PC are geared to two human senses: sight and sound. (So far, technology hasn't mastered touch and taste outputs, but they can't be too far off.) This chapter provides information and background on video cards and the sights they generate for display on the PC monitor. Chapter 19 covers sound and sound cards.

In its most basic form, the video card provides a connection for the monitor to the PC. But it is much more than that. It controls how images look on the monitor, where they are placed, and how well the user can see them. All of the data destined for the monitor travels through the video card, which converts the binary data supplied by the central processing unit (CPU) into text, graphics, and images for the monitor to display.

A video card can be an expansion card, in which case it can also be a graphics or video accelerator, or it can be built into the motherboard. In either case, the video system of the PC can also be called a video controller or a video adapter.

How a Video Card Works

What is displayed on the monitor actually begins in a piece of software running on the PC. It could be the operating system, as in the case of Windows, or in an application program, such as Microsoft Word, Adobe Photoshop, or Paint Shop Pro. The software generates instructions to the PC that tell it exactly how each frame of video output should look.

The instructions generated by the operating system or application software are sent to the CPU and video card, which work together to create images by putting pixels (picture elements, discussed in Chapter 15) together to form text or two-dimensional (2D) images or tiny triangles (a great many tiny triangles, actually) for three-dimensional (3D) graphics. The images formed by the pixels, or triangles made up of pixels, are generated in two phases:

1. Transform and lighting phase
2. Setup phase

Transform and Lighting Phase

On some systems, transform and lighting data is processed by the CPU; on other systems, the video card processes the data, in which case all of the graphics-related information generated by the application software is sent to the video card.

In the transform and lighting phase, the PC figures out how to assemble the pixels and triangles to create the image desired by the application software— the transform part of the process. Then the PC adds any lighting effects included in the graphics instructions, which are applied to the tips of the triangles (vertices)—the lighting process.

Setup Phase

During the setup phase, the video card plots out exactly where the monitor should place each piece of the image. This involves another very math-intensive process. Next, the digital graphics data is passed through the hardware triangle setup, a feature of the video card, which prepares the data for display.

Dividing Up the Work

If you are playing a video game and one of the scenes shifts to the right, the game software sends out instructions on what color and how bright each pixel in the display should be. Actually, it doesn't wait for movement to send out instructions. The display information is updated not less than 30 times a second—typically around 70 times per second—to eliminate screen flicker, and as a result, the animation on the screen moves smoothly.

Newer, more robust video cards now handle both the transform and lighting and the setup phases with the CPU simply routing the graphics information from the application to the video card. This frees the CPU to perform other tasks, such as the physics or calculations related to the game's logic, which creates a more efficient overall operation. Less powerful or older video cards rely on the CPU to perform the transform and lighting phases and perform only the setup phase themselves. This puts a drain on the CPU and results in less efficient performance of the whole PC.

The processes used to generate 3D graphic images are somewhat more involved than those required to generate 2D graphics and use considerably more computing resources. This is why most 3D graphics cards handle the whole job.

To create a 2D image, essentially the information required for each pixel is the color, the brightness, and a set of x/y coordinates (the two "D's" of the image). However, a 3D image has a third D, which means the image has height, width, *and* depth. This means that the video card must not only track all pixels and triangles up and down and side to side on the monitor, but also track which ones are in front and which are behind each other. Add to that all of the technologies used to improve the quality of the image, such as antialiasing, mip mapping, alpha blending, and Gouraud shading (more on these technologies later), all of which consume considerable resources, adding to the reasons why the graphics card should handle the entire job. For your information, the term "mip" as in mip mapping, comes from the Latin phrase *multum in parvo*, which means "many things in a small place."

Pathways and Converters

Regardless of which handles the transform and lighting phase, the CPU and video card communicate over two PC bus structures: the accelerated graphics port (AGP) bus and the peripheral component interconnect (PCI) bus. We discuss these bus structures later in this chapter as well as in Chapter 10.

The video card contains a component that may well be the most important part of the entire process—the RAM digital-to-analog converter, or RAMDAC. Although, it sounds like a character in a very bad science-fiction movie, it actually has a very important function. It converts the digital data stored in the video card's RAM into the analog signal used by the monitor to create images on the screen.

Video Card Standards

In the beginning, the monochrome display adapter (MDA) displayed only text on a monochrome (one-color) monitor. The monochrome graphics adapter (MGA), which combined graphics and text on a monochrome monitor (using a technology developed by a company named Hercules Computer Technology) soon followed, and the PC graphics evolution began.

NOTE: *MGA is now used by Matrox Graphics, Inc. to mean Matrox graphics accelerator. If you see it used again in this chapter, it is far more likely that this usage is intended and not the older one.*

Next came the color graphics adapter (CGA) standard developed by IBM. CGA was the first graphics adapter standard that included a range of colors (other than shades of one color). CGA could display 16 colors, but only 2 colors at its highest resolution of 640×200. IBM also developed the next graphics standard, the enhanced graphics adapter (EGA), which increased resolution to 640×350 with 64 colors.

In 1987, IBM developed the video graphics array (VGA) standard that increased the number of colors to 256 on a resolution of 640×480. The VGA standard remains the default standard for many operating systems, including Windows.

Between the times of the CGA and the VGA standards, some PCs included the multicolor graphics array (MCGA) system, which provided graphics capabilities equal to or greater than CGA, but was not as powerful as VGA.

Figure 11.1 shows the Windows Display Properties window set for 640×480 with 256 colors. Figure 11.2 gives an example of what this same window looks like using VGA settings.

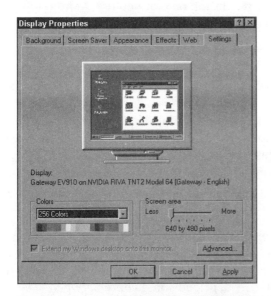

Figure 11.1   The Windows Display Properties window.

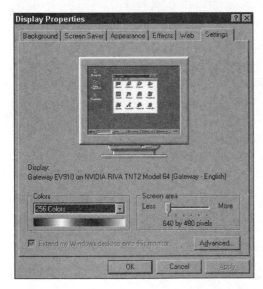

Figure 11.2   A screen capture of a 640×480 display.

Most of the video graphics standards that followed the VGA are grouped and labeled as the super video graphics array (SVGA), a standard developed by the Video Electronics Standards Association (VESA), which includes just about all video graphics standards with better resolution or more colors than VGA. VESA members are monitor and graphics card manufacturers.

In general, SVGA has a color palette with more than 16 million colors and offers several resolutions, including 800×600, 1024×768, 1280×1024, 1,600×1,200, and higher. Not all models of SVGA boards will display all 16 million colors or support all SVGA resolutions, depending on the manufacturer. Table 11.1 lists the more popular video graphic adapter standards in use today. Notice that as resolutions increase, the number of simultaneous colors that can be displayed decreases. While SVGA seems to contradict this, notice that VGA 640×480 supports only 16 colors, but the lower VGA resolution of 320×200 supports 256 colors. This effect is also evident in the XGA standard, where its highest resolution supports only 256 colors, but its lowest resolution supports over 65,000 colors.

Although the video or graphics cards on the market today are, for the most part, SVGA cards, they are tied less to video standards than they are to increasing the capabilities of the card itself to process all of the graphic information and better images. In general, most video cards are all priced somewhere between $100 and $400; they have double data rate dynamic RAM (DDR DRAM), synchronous DRAM (SDRAM), or DDR SDRAM; and probably either an Open GL or a Direct3D application program interface (API), which is used by the video card to produce 3D graphics.

One last thing that video cards all have in common is that they all use a high-density 15-pin (HD15) DB-style connector.

Table 11.1   PC video adapter standards.

Video Standard	Resolution(s)	Colors
VGA (Video Graphics Array)	640×480	16
	320×200	256
SVGA (Super VGA)	800×600	16
	1024×76	256
	1280×1024	256
	1600×1200	256
XGA (Extended Graphics Array)	640×480	65,536
	1024×768	256

11. Video Cards

What Does the DB in the DB-15 Connector Mean?

Why this connector is designated as a DB connector is a lesson in PC history. When the original PCs emerged they used the D-shaped 25-pin connector that was designated as DB-25. The D connectors available at the time were the DE9, DA15, DB25, DC37, and DD60 where the first D indicates a D-shaped connector, the second letter indicating its place in D connector evolution, and the number representing the number of pins on the connector. Because the PC used the DB-25, all D connectors eventually picked up the DB prefix.

Video Card Components

A video card is essentially a separate computer mounted inside the PC to handle video graphics reproduction on the monitor. It has its own processor, basic input/output system (BIOS), memory, chipset, and connectors, all of which are focused on processing graphic images for display.

Video Processor

On most older video cards, the PC's CPU is the video processor. For these cards, the CPU performs the geometric and mathematical calculations that are used to complete the transform and lighting phases of the graphic image generation. The CPU sends the raw screen image to the video card's frame buffer, where the video card reads it and performs the setup phase.

The video cards that include a graphics processing unit (GPU) are able to process the graphics information through the transform and lighting phase with assistance from the CPU. A GPU is able to process the graphics information as much as 10 times faster than the CPU, because that's all it does.

On newer cards, the PC's CPU passes this task to the video card's GPU over the AGP or PCI bus. The CPU extracts the drawing instructions for the stream of data generated by the application or other software producing the images. The GPU works with its video driver firmware to produce the data needed for the setup phase. The processes performed by the GPU include bitmap transfers and painting, window resizing and repositioning, line drawing, font scaling, and polygon creation. Like the data processed on the CPU, this data is written to the video card's frame buffer for use in the setup phase. Much more information goes into the frame buffer than was transmitted to the GPU by the CPU, resulting in less data on the system bus, which further reduces the workload of the CPU.

Video Memory

A certain amount of memory is needed to hold the graphics information being passed to the setup phase from the transform and lighting phase of the video graphics process. Exactly how much memory is needed is directly related to the amount of information that is being passed, the resolution of the monitor, and the number of graphic dimensions being generated. For example, a monochrome text display on an MDA monitor required less than 2 kilobytes (KB) of space, but today's 3D high-resolution displays may need as much as 64 megabytes (MB).

Along with the video memory's size, its location has also changed. The 2KB memory area that supported the MDA display was carved out of the upper memory block (UMB) in the PC's random access memory (RAM). Remember that for monochrome text graphics, the PC's CPU also did most of the processing for the display. Working out of main memory was convenient and, at the time, less expensive than putting more RAM on the video card. Video memory, or video RAM, if you prefer, is now located on the video card. As the need for video memory increased from kilobytes to megabytes and as the GPU began taking on more of the processing, it made more sense to conveniently locate video memory on the video card.

In some less-expensive home PCs, some of the video processing functions are included on the motherboard and a portion of the system RAM is used for the frame buffer. This approach to video memory is called Unified Memory Architecture (UMA), which means that the system RAM is being used to support video as well. This eliminates the need for a separate video card and its cost. However, these systems always have a lower-quality video system compared to those supported directly by a video card with its own video RAM.

The AGP technology allows the video GPU to use a small amount of the system RAM for scratchpad memory to make calculations, but has dedicated RAM for the frame buffer on the video card. The AGP approach to RAM provides flexibility without impacting the video system's performance. AGP is discussed in "Video System Interface" later in this chapter.

Resolution

The factor that impacts how much video RAM should be on the video card is the monitor's resolution. Each of the pixels on the monitor's display requires a certain amount of data to encode exactly how the pixel should appear. For example, nearly 6MB of data are needed to generate a true color image for the 1600×1200 pixels on a monitor's screen.

A monitor's resolution is the number of pixels it uses to generate its display. The size of the display (e.g., 15-inch, 17-inch) has some bearing on the number of pixels available. Obviously, the more pixels that can be used to display the image, the better the detail in the picture. A monitor with 640×480 resolution uses 307,200 pixels to create the image it displays. The same monitor set to display with a resolution of 1280×960 now uses 1,228,800 pixels in the same display space. As the pixel count increases, the size of the pixel and the amount of space around it decrease. Try using the Settings tab on the Display Properties of a Windows PC to change the display resolution. As the resolution increases, the detail in the display also increases, although its size decreases.

Aspect Ratio

Another defining measurement of the video display is its aspect ratio. This is the ratio of the number of horizontal pixels to vertical pixels used to create the display. The standard aspect ratio is 4:3 (read as "4 to 3"), which is used for 640×480, 800×600, 1280×768, and other resolutions. This helps the monitor to define shapes and graphics, such as a circle, on the screen.

Color Depth

Another important factor in determining the amount of video RAM needed on a system is the color depth of the monitor. The color depth represents the number of individual colors that each pixel on the screen could display. It is always expressed as the number of bits used to describe each color in the color set. The common color depth settings are 8-bit, 16-bit, 24-bit, and 32-bit color. Figure 11.3 shows the settings available on a Windows 98 PC and its monitor.

The number of bits in the color depth determines the number of colors that can be displayed. For example, 8-bit color uses 8-bits to number each of the colors. In binary numbers, the range of numbers is 00000000 to 11111111, or the range of 0 to 255, or 256 colors. To determine the number of colors that a particular color depth includes, it is the largest binary number than can be displayed in the number of bits of the color depth. This means that a 16-bit color depth can display

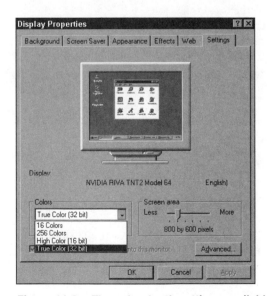

Figure 11.3   The color depth settings available on a Windows PC.

65,536 (or $2^{15}+1$) colors, 24-bit color depth has 16.7 million colors that each pixel could conceivably display, and 32-bit color supports more than 4 *billion* colors. Depending on the PC, video card, and monitor, either 24-bit or 32-bit will be designated as the true color setting.

NOTE: The human eye cannot distinguish more than 16 million colors; above that, it may have difficulty discerning the colors of two adjacent pixels.

How Much Video Memory Is Needed?

Although most video cards on the market today come with 8MB to 32MB of video RAM, high-end cards are available with as much as 64MB. Some people feel that 64MB is far more than is needed, but others, especially the 3D crowd, think that soon this may not be enough.

To figure the amount of video RAM needed for a particular system, perform the following calculation:

```
Resolution * (Color Depth / 8) = Video RAM required
```

Dividing the color depth by 8 converts the calculation of the resolution times the color depth into bytes, the common measurement for RAM.

If you plan on using 24-bit color depth on a monitor with 1024×768 resolution, the calculation for the minimum amount of video RAM you need is given by:

```
1024 * 768 = 786,432 (pixels in the resolution)
24 / 8 = 3 (bytes in the color depth)
786,432 * 3 = 2,359,296 (bytes of video RAM needed)
```

So, for 1024×768 using 24-bit color depth, the video card must have at least 2.4MB of video RAM.

For a monitor with 1600×1200 resolution on which you want to display 32-bit color depth, the graphics card needs about 8MB, calculated as:

```
1600 * 1200 = 1,920,000 (pixels of resolution)
32 / 8 = 4 (bytes of color depth)
1920000 * 4 = 7,680,000 (bytes of video RAM required)
```

These sample calculations are for the RAM requirements for 2D images. Table 11.2 shows the amounts of video RAM (VRAM) required by several common graphics settings.

Table 11.2 Common 2D video RAM requirements.

Resolution	Color Depth	VRAM Required
640x480	8-bit	307KB
1024x768	16-bit	1.57MB
1024x768	24-bit	2.36MB
1600x1200	24-bit	5.76MB
1600x1200	32-bit	7.68MB

Video cards that support 3D graphics require more video RAM than do 2D cards, even on the same resolution. This is because in addition to the two dimensions (down and across), a third dimension of depth is added. Real 3D cards use three buffers to hold the graphics data: a front buffer, a back buffer, and a Z-buffer. This is why a 2D video card with 4MB of video RAM can support a 1600×1200 16-bit display, but can support a 3D game with only an 800×600 16-bit setting. The Z-buffer consumes enough of the available RAM to require the resolution to be reduced.

The front and back buffers are set to the size required by the color depth, and the Z-buffer uses 16-bits (or 2 bytes). To calculate the amount of video RAM needed to support a 3D display, use the following calculation:

```
Resolution * ((Color Depth (in bytes) * 2) + 2) = 3D video RAM requirements
```

For a 1024×768 resolution using 16-bit color, the calculation is:

```
1024 * 768 = 786,432 (pixels of resolution)
16 / 8 = 2 (color depth in bytes)
2 * 2 + 2 = 6 (buffers required in bytes)
786,432 * 6 = 4,718,592 (video RAM required for 3D graphics)
```

The result of this calculation is that more RAM is required to support a video card with 4MB of RAM (even if it is a 3D card) using 1024×768 resolution with a 16-bit 3D display.

Video RAM Technologies

The video card's memory is also called the frame buffer, because it holds the graphic instructions about each frame to be displayed. The earliest video RAM was standard DRAM, which requires constant electrical refreshing to hold its contents. DRAM didn't work well for video RAM because it cannot be accessed while it is being refreshed, which meant video performance suffered.

A variety of memory technologies have been and are being used as video RAM on video cards. The most common RAM technologies used with video cards are:

- *Dynamic Random Access Memory (DRAM)*—DRAM is the same RAM used on early PCs. Extended data output DRAM has largely replaced DRAM on the PC, but other types of video RAM are in use.

- *Extended Data Output DRAM (EDO DRAM)*—EDO DRAM provides a higher bandwidth than standard DRAM and manages read/write cycles more efficiently.

- *Video RAM (VRAM)*—VRAM, not to be confused with the generic term "video RAM," is dual-ported, which means it can be written to and read from at the same time. VRAM, which is a special type of DRAM, doesn't need to be refreshed as often as standard DRAM.

- *Windows RAM (WRAM)*—WRAM is the video RAM used on Matrox video cards. It is dual-ported and runs a bit faster than VRAM.

- *Synchronous DRAM (SDRAM)*—SDRAM is very much like EDO DRAM, except that it is synchronized to the video card's GPU and chipset, which allows it to run faster. SDRAM is a single-ported memory technology that is very common on video cards.

- *Multibank DRAM (MDRAM)*—MDRAM is a newer memory type that is divided into 32KB banks that can be accessed independently. MDRAM also offers the advantages of interleaving, true memory sizing, and better memory performance. Interleaving allows memory accesses to overall memory banks. MDRAM can be sized exactly to the amount of video RAM needed to support a particular display type.

- *Double Data Rate SDRAM (DDR SDRAM)*—DDR SDRAM doubles the data rate of standard SDRAM to produce faster data transfers. DDR memories are becoming more commonplace on video cards, especially 3D video accelerators.

- *Synchronous Graphics RAM (SGRAM)*—SGRAM is an improvement on SDRAM that supports block writes and write-per-bit, which yield better graphics performance. It is found only on video cards with chipsets that support these features, such as many Matrox video cards. SGRAM is a single-ported memory technology.

- *Double Data Rate SGRAM (DDR SGRAM)*—DDR SGRAM is showing up on the very latest cards. It doubles the data rate of SGRAM and offers better performance.

- *Direct Rambus DRAM (RDRAM)*—A newer general-purpose memory type, RDRAM is also being used on video cards, which includes bus mastering and a dedicated channel between memory devices. RDRAM runs about 20 times faster than conventional DRAM.

See Chapter 5 for more information on memory technologies.

Bus Mastering

Bus mastering allows the video card to control the PC's system bus and transfer data into and out of system RAM directly without the assistance of the CPU. This improves the performance of certain video operations that use RAM for calculations, such as 3D acceleration.

Video Chipsets

The logic circuits that control the functions of the video card are grouped together as the video card's chipset, which is also called the graphics chip, the accelerator, or the video coprocessor. Much like the functions performed by the system chipset on the motherboard, the video chipset supports all of the functions performed by the GPU, as well as the interfaces, data transfers, and compatibility of the card.

Some video card manufacturers, such as Matrox and 3dfx, who design and build their cards from start to finish, manufacture their own video chipsets. Others use chipsets manufactured by other companies, such as Diamond Multimedia. When buying a video card, you should know the capabilities of the video chipset because it holds the key to the card's performance, capabilities, and compatibility. You need to match the video card to the needs of the system into which it will be inserted and the monitor that it will drive.

An important feature of the video chipset not covered here is the refresh rate of the video card. A higher refresh rate means less flicker on the screen, which translates to less user eyestrain. A good video chipset should provide a refresh rate of at least 75Hz. However, the refresh rate must be balanced to the resolution settings. Using a higher resolution setting will result in a lower refresh rate, and vice versa.

The Video BIOS

The video BIOS functions very much like the system BIOS. It provides an interface between video hardware and the PC, its BIOS, operating system, and application programs. The issues that impact the video card at the BIOS level are video interfaces, system resource requirements, and video drivers.

Video System Interfaces

A large amount of information has to be moved about on the video system between the video card and the PC's CPU and RAM. The pathway over which this data travels is the video system interface, which connects the GPU and video RAM to the PC. Due to the amount of data to be transferred, the video system interface requires more bandwidth than any other peripheral device on the PC.

One common mistake made by users is thinking that the number of bits used on the video card is also the number of bits required in the video system interface. Actually, a 64-bit or 128-bit video card uses this bandwidth only internally on the video card between its components. The width in bits of the interface to the CPU and memory will be either 16-bits (Industry Standard Architecture [ISA]/enhanced ISA [EISA] cards) or 32-bits (VL-Bus, PCI, or AGP).

The two most popular video system interfaces in use today are the PCI and AGP buses (see Figure 11.4).

- *Peripheral Component Interconnect (PCI)*—Support for the PCI interface bus is included in the system chipset on all Pentium-class computers. PCI is commonly used for 2D graphics cards, sound cards, network interface cards, and other expansion cards that attach directly to the motherboard. Of course, a PCI card slot is required.

- *Accelerated Graphics Port (AGP)*—The AGP interface was designed specifically for use as a video system interface. AGP, which runs twice as fast as the PCI interface, creates a high-speed link between the video card and the PC's processor. The AGP interface is also directly linked to the PC's system memory, which makes it possible for 3D images to be stored in main memory and 2D systems to use system RAM for some calculations. All AGP video cards require that the motherboard have an AGP slot.

The AGP interface is fast replacing the PCI interface as the interface of choice for video cards due to its faster transfer rates. In fact, AGP has evolved into several standard versions, each noting its multiple of the original standard. For example, AGP 1X has a data transfer rate of 266Mbps (compared to PCI's 133Mbps), AGP 2X supports 533 Mbps, and AGP 4X transfers data at 1.07Gbps.

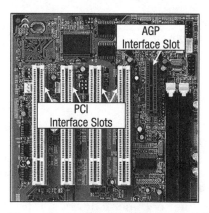

Figure 11.4   A motherboard with PCI and AGP interface slots.

Video System Resources

Unlike most internally mounted peripheral devices, video cards do not use much in the way of system resources. Not all video cards use an interrupt request (IRQ). Those video cards that do use an IRQ use one of the pair set aside for PCI devices (IRQ 11 and IRQ 12). All VGA-compatible video cards, which is virtually all of them, use the same input/output (I/O) addresses (3B0-3BBh and 3C0-3DFh). Manufacturers of other types of expansion cards avoid these addresses, which eliminates conflicts during installation.

Video Device Drivers

The device driver for the video card translates the images generated by an application program into instructions that the GPU can use. The software may consider the display as a collection of pixels, but the GPU sees it as a series of line and shape drawings, and it is the job of the graphics driver software to convert between the application's vision and that of the graphics processor.

Typically, separate graphics drivers exist for each resolution and color depth combination, which is why the video system may perform differently on different resolution and color depth settings. The same may be true of the different drivers used on different operating systems for a video card. Video drivers are frequently updated, so if optimum video performance is what you want, check the manufacturer's Web site frequently.

The RAM Digital-to-Analog Converter

The RAMDAC solves the simple problem that the PC and video card are digital and the monitor is an analog device. The information stored in the video memory is digital data that must be converted into an analog signal before it can be used by the monitor to create the display image.

The RAMDAC reads data from the video memory, converts it to an analog signal wave, and then sends it to the monitor over the cable connected to the back of the PC. The RAMDAC has a direct impact on the quality of the screen's image, how often the screen is refreshed, the color palette used, and the resolution and color depth used in the display.

Three digital-to-analog converters (DAC), one for each of the three primary colors (red, green, and blue), are used together to create the right color mix for each pixel. The speed of the RAMDAC has a lot to do with how well it is able to support the quality of the display. A fast RAMDAC has a rating between 300MHz and 350MHz; only a year ago 150MHz was considered fast.

3D Graphics

Creating the graphic images for 3D involves the same three-step process as for 2D: transform, lighting, and setup. As you watch a 3D game or animated image, the objects on the screen move, rotate, and change in scale and perspective. When an item, such as a car, a plane, the focus of a camera, or an imaginary gun, moves, it creates what is called movement or translation. Whenever your point of view on the screen changes, movement has occurred. When an object changes in size relative to other objects, the action is called scaling. If the object should turn or spin, the action is called rotation. Movement, translation, scaling, and rotation as a group are called transforms. Once an object is on the screen, it must also be lighted, which involves shadows, spotlights, and other effects. The third step is setup, where the 3D data is translated to a format so the graphics accelerator can convert the graphics to your flat (or 2D) computer screen. However, 3D graphics adds a few more steps to those used for 2D graphics. Each of these processes is discussed in the following sections.

Rendering

Rendering draws the scene after the transform, lighting, and setup phases are complete. In this phase, the 3D graphics card renders, or draws, the screen, creating the triangles and filling in those triangles with appropriate textures. How fast this happens is the card's fill rate, or how many pixels or texels, the triangles used to create texture on the screen, can be created per second.

Rendering includes a number of key actions:

- *Antialiasing*—A technique used to reduce the "noise" added to the image when all of the graphic information is not available. The information about an image should include its position, colors, size change, and more, but if this information is not available, the missing factors are filled in with what is called "noise." Antialiasing attempts to remove this noise.

- *Bilinear filtering*—A standard on 3D graphics cards that reads four texels; calculates the averages of their positions, colors, and other properties; and displays the result as a single-screen texel. This technique is used to reduce blockiness in the display.

- *Bump mapping*—A technique used in place of embossing to create the illusion of depth or height on a textured surface. This is the process used to create rough roads, bomb craters, and bullet holes on walls.

- *Filtering*—A process that smoothes the textures applied, to blend, or slightly blur, the colors of adjacent pixels to eliminate a blocky look.

- *Mip mapping*—A technique that improves the appearance of textures by grouping pixels into mip-maps that cluster four texels together to remove jagged edges between pixels and texels.

- *Shading*—A process that applies the right colors to each pixel to create visual effects. The simplest type of shading is flat shading, in which each polygon of pixels is just one color. A more complex shading technique, called Gouraud shading, blends the colors where two polygons join to create a smooth transition from one to the next.

- *Texture mapping*—A technique that applies a picture in 2D format over 3D objects to create levels of detail and texture, or to create a perspective change, such as an object moving closer or farther away.

- *Z-buffering*—An encoding protocol. As the pixels of a 3D image are rendered, the accelerator does not know which pixel is to be displayed first. Z-buffering encodes each pixel with a Z-value that is used to sequence the pixels.

3D Graphics Accelerators

The three-dimensional images displayed on computer monitors are actually surface modeling, or creating the illusion of 3D objects on a 2D surface. Surface modeling represents 3D objects using a mesh of polygons, typically triangles, to create images with their outside edges. If enough triangles can be used to create an image, even the curved surfaces can be made to look smooth on the PC display. A variety of geometric descriptions are used to define each triangle, including its vertices (corners), its vertex normals (which side is pointing out and which is inside to create shading), the reflection characteristics of its surface, the coordinates of the viewer's perspective, the location and intensity of a light source, the location and orientation of the display plane, and more.

With this information available, the GPU and graphics chipset render the 3D image onto the 2D screen. To create the 3D look, mathematical equations calculate the tracing through a scene, determine any light reflections and light sources, place some objects in view and obscure others, and make distant objects smaller and darker (called depth cueing). Obviously, the 3D rendering process is very complicated, and involves a tremendous number of calculations, regardless of the complexity of the scene displayed. If shading is added to the process, the number of computations required is doubled.

To speed up the process, all of the computations are made on the video card by the GPU and chipset, and the graphics program, the one running on the PC, is written in a standard 3D graphics language, such as Open GL. The graphics program may also use an API that provides a library of standard graphics commands that can be passed to the graphics processor. Graphics APIs allow the game or application to remain compatible to all versions of a 3D card.

Tools and Diagnostic Processes

For the most part, installing a video card involves little more than a screwdriver to remove and replace the screw that anchors the card into the motherboard and case slot.

As far as diagnostics go, the diskette or CD-ROM included with the graphics card, primarily to provide the device driver, may have a proprietary diagnostics utility on it as well. Otherwise, very little is available in the way of software that is designed to specifically troubleshoot or diagnose 3D video card problems.

Because most of the components on a video card are mounted directly to the board, perhaps with the exception of its RAM, if the card is not functioning properly (and it will usually be very apparent), it may just be time for a new card. Be sure to fill out the warranty cards and use care when installing or removing the video card, treating it very much like you would a motherboard.

Immediate Solutions

Finding the Problem When Nothing Is Displayed on the Monitor

First, check the obvious:

- Is the monitor plugged into a power source?
- Is the monitor switched on?
- Is the monitor connected to the proper connection on the back of the PC?

If you really want to eliminate the monitor as a suspect (or confirm that it is the problem), try connecting another monitor (one you know for sure works) to the PC. If it works, then the original monitor may be bad. If the second monitor also does not work, then the problem is likely not the original monitor.

If the above is as it should be, check the following:

1. When you boot the system, if you are getting three short beep tones, or something similar (depending on your BIOS; see Chapter 4), and nothing is displaying on the monitor, then your video card may be loose or defective.

2. Open up the system case and reseat the video card.

3. Reboot the system. If the problem persists, try the video card first in another slot on the same PC, and if that fails, try it in another PC. If the card fails in the new system, it's time to get a new video card. If the video card works in either the new slot or PC, you may have a bad expansion slot on the motherboard. Hopefully, it is not the AGP slot, because that means you either need to switch to a PCI video card or get a new motherboard.

Unscrambling the Display

If the display looks like the picture on a badly adjusted TV set, the problem is most likely that the refresh rate on the video card is set too high for your system. This is definitely the problem if the display is okay through the boot cycle and then dies out when Windows comes up.

1. Boot into Windows Safe Mode by pressing the **F8** key when Windows first starts up. In the Startup Menu that displays, select Safe Mode.

2. Windows will start up and load only the essential device drivers it needs to function. Once the Windows Desktop is displayed, right-click on an empty part of the display the Desktop shortcut menu (see Figure 11.5). Select Properties to open the Display Properties window. Select the Settings tab and click on the Advanced button at the bottom of the display.

3. Select the Adapter tab and, as shown in Figure 11.6, a Refresh Rate setting appears near the middle of the window. If it is not set to either Optimal or Adapter Default, you may want to check the documentation for the video card and monitor for the best rate. Typically, it will be around 70Hz or 72Hz. After clicking the OKs, restart the PC.

Figure 11.5   The Windows Desktop shortcut menu.

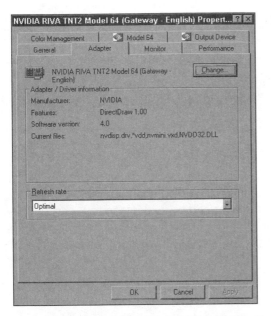

Figure 11.6 The Adapter tab on the Display Properties window.

Checking a Fuzzy or Blurry Display

A fuzzy or blurry display could be a problem with the refresh rate setting; see "Unscrambling the Display" earlier in this chapter. However, if the refresh rate is set as it should be and you have had your eyes checked recently:

1. The problem is not likely the video card and is probably in the settings on the monitor itself. Adjust the brightness and contrast settings on the monitor.

2. If the problem persists, the monitor may be defective.

Finding the Settings for the Video Card in the Windows Display Settings

If you have tried to change the Desktop settings in Windows to reflect a new video card, but only 640×480 and 16 colors are available, it is likely that the video card's software drivers are either not installed or need to be reinstalled.

1. To check on which video device drivers are installed, open the Device Manager and select the Display adapters group. To see which video driver you have currently installed, right-click on My Computer and select Properties. Then click on the Device Manager tab and find the video card entry. If the video card is a PCI card, you may need to drill down to it through the plug-and-play devices, and then the PCI bus entries. Once you have located it, if it is listed as "Standard VGA," you need to install the device drivers for the video card.

2. To install the device drivers, use the disk or CD-ROM that came with your video card. If it doesn't start by itself (if it is a diskette), use the Add Hardware icon on the Control Panel to install the video card and its drivers. Be sure you use the Have Disk button, when asked for the location of the drivers. If you can avoid it, never (repeat, *never*) use the driver from the Windows library when you have a disk.

Installing a Video Card

To install a new video card, follow the following process:

1. First, make sure you are following appropriate electrostatic discharge (ESD) safeguards to protect your video card, the PC, and yourself. Leave the card in its antistatic packaging until you are ready to install it.

2. Remove the old video card both physically and logically from the system. This means that before you open the system case, delete the card from the Windows Device Manager and track down and remove its device drivers.

3. Hopefully, before you bought the new video card, you determined the adapter interfaces available on your PC and made an appropriate choice. If you plan to use a PCI interface, be sure the card is a PCI card, or if you plan to use an AGP slot, you should have an AGP card. Now is a very good time to verify this.

   Motherboards with a Pentium II processor or higher usually have an AGP port that can be used for video cards only. You must also be running

Windows 95 OSR2 (the updated OEM version released in 1996), Windows 98, Windows NT, or Windows 2000. The fact that your PC has an AGP port most likely means you are able to install or upgrade to an AGP card.

4. When the case is open, remove the video card from its antistatic package. Holding it only by its ends, and avoiding contact with its components or edge connectors, align the card's edge connectors to the appropriate slot, with the metal mounting bracket fitting into the open slot in the case. With your fingers spaced evenly across the top of the card, press down firmly to seat the card in the slot. Align the mounting bracket with the screw hole in the case and attach it with a screw.

5. Some video cards, and especially AGP cards, have a power supply connector. Use an available connector to connect the card to the power supply. Check the card's documentation if you are unsure of which power supply connector, if any, to use.

6. The card is installed and ready to go as soon as the software is installed. If the PC's operating system, typically Windows, is installed, it is time to install the device drivers and utilities for the video card. Typically, the video card comes with a CD-ROM that will autostart when you close the CD tray and open an installation wizard of one kind or another that will guide you through the installation of the device drivers. See the previous section, "Finding the Settings for the Video Card in the Windows Display Settings," for instructions on installing software drivers.

7. After the video drivers and any other utility software for your video system are installed, restart the PC. If you have problems, see "Troubleshooting the Video Card," discussed next.

Troubleshooting the Video Card

If you are unsure of the problem on a video or graphics card, use the following general troubleshooting steps to determine the problem. Remember that when all else fails, most of the more popular video card manufacturers have technical support available or FAQs (frequently asked questions) on their Web sites. The documentation that came with the card may also contain a troubleshooting guide.

1. Make sure the video card is firmly seated in the appropriate bus slot. There is actually little worry that you have a PCI card in an AGP slot or vice versa—they shouldn't fit. If it was made to fit, the card is probably no longer good to use.

11. Video Cards

2. If the card requires it, verify that the card is properly connected to the power supply through one of the power supply's connectors. Most video cards that require power use the same type of power supply connector (Molex) used by a hard disk drive.

3. Verify that the video card has not been assigned system resources that had already been assigned to another conflicting device. Typically, video cards are not assigned IRQs, but check anyway; the card you are troubleshooting may just be one of the ones that do.

4. Verify that the device drivers are installed. You may want to reinstall the device drivers before taking any other more drastic measures.

5. Check the documentation of the video card. Many cards have specific requirements for the BIOS settings of the PC. If this is the case, reboot the PC and access the BIOS configuration data by pressing the key (typically **F1**, **F2**, or **DEL**) during the boot sequence to enter the CMOS (complementary metal-oxide semiconductor) setup. Verify that the BIOS settings are correct for the video card. In many cases, the Hidden Refresh, Byte Merge, Video BIOS shadow and cache RAM, VGA Palette Snoop, and DAC Snoop may need to be disabled. If you change any of the CMOS settings, be sure to save them before exiting.

6. If these steps do not solve or isolate the problem, it is time to call technical support at the video card manufacturer or check with the reseller.

Replacing Integrated Video Support

Review "Installing a Video Card" earlier in this chapter for some generic steps to use to replace an existing video or graphics card. This project adds to that one with steps on converting from an integrated video card to an expansion card.

1. Completely uninstall the previous video card's drivers and switch over to the Standard VGA Display Driver for Windows. The display may be bad until a few more adjustments are made.

2. Disconnect any cables attached to the video card and remove it by grasping it by the upper corners and pulling firmly upward.

3. Alternatively, if the PC has an integrated video card, which means that the graphics card is built into the motherboard, disable it before installing the new card. Check the documentation of the motherboard and chipset for instructions on how to disable this adapter. You may need to change a jumper or disable the port in the BIOS configuration data.

4. Follow the steps listed in "Installing a Video Card."

Determining the Type of Video Card in a PC

One way to find out the type of video card that is installed in a PC is to use the DOS Debug utility, which is included with virtually all versions of Windows.

1. Open an MS-DOS prompt or command line.

2. Type "DEBUG" and press **Enter**. A dash prompt will be displayed.

3. Enter "d c000:0010".

4. After the first block of data is displayed. Look at the text translation of binary data on the right side of the display. If the video card data is not shown, type a "d" and press **Enter** to display the next block of memory.

5. The video data should appear in either the first or second blocks.

Upgrading the RAM on a Video Card

The video RAM on many newer video cards can be upgraded to increase its speed, color palette, and the performance of its graphics.

1. Video RAM must be matched to the video card and to its bus structure (PCI, AGP, ISA). If you are unsure of the video card, see the previous section, "Determining the Type of Video Card in a PC."

2. Verify the amount of memory already installed on the card by the manufacturer and how much you can add. You should be able to get this from the card's documentation or from the manufacturer's Web site. You may need to call the technical support number of the manufacturer. If you want to upgrade the video RAM on the video card, you need to know these facts. Typically, you should add memory in 2MB increments, but follow the advice of the manufacturer.

3. You must remove the video card from the PC to add video RAM to it. Be sure you are working on a flat surface that is ESD-protected.

4. Follow the instructions in the video card's documentation or on the manufacturer's Web site on how new memory chips are installed on the card. However, if no instructions are available, use the following generic steps.

5. Locate the mounting on the card for the memory chip. The mounting should have four toothed edges that align with four dots on the corners of the memory chip. Align the edges and dots and push the memory chip into place, making sure the chip is firmly in place and will not fall off.

6. You can verify that the new video RAM is recognized by the system by checking the BIOS configuration data. Reboot the system—you need to anyway—and enter the BIOS setup utility. From the Startup menu, select Devices and I/O Ports, and from its menu choose Video Setup. The amount of video RAM recognized by the PC is listed. If the amount is not the new total, check the installation of the video RAM on the card and verify that the card is installed correctly.

Selecting Higher Resolutions

If there is not enough RAM on the video card to support a higher resolution or color depth, it is likely that they are disabled on the Windows Display Settings window. In order to provide access to capabilities that the video card has within its specifications, you may need to add more memory. Verify with the manufacturer how much additional video RAM can be added to the card, and then follow the steps in the previous section, "Upgrading the RAM on a Video Card."

To calculate the amount of RAM needed to support the resolution and color depth you desire, use the calculations shown in "How Much Video Memory Is Needed?" earlier in this chapter.

Chapter 12

Ports and Connectors

In Depth

Peripheral Overview

Because personal computers (PCs) do not all have exactly the same peripheral devices, they must provide for as many options as possible. A wide range of peripheral device choices are available for users to turn their standard computers into customized workstations, entertainment units, or publishing centers. To accommodate these choices, the PC must have input and output ports to accept the various connector types employed by the various peripheral devices.

To attach a device to the PC, two components—a port and a connector with complementary matching but opposite features (i.e., "male" versus "female")—must be connected. The port is the part that is attached to the PC itself, and the connector is on the end of the cable of the peripheral device. When the connector is plugged into the port, the peripheral device is available for use. The ports, which are also called connectors in some uses, are mounted either directly on the motherboard or on an expansion card installed in a motherboard slot. These ports extend through the back panel of the PC case. The motherboard also has ports, called connectors, on it, and these are used strictly for connections to internal devices.

The PC essentially comprises the processor, the motherboard, and the chipset. All other components and peripheral devices connect to these core components through a port or connector. This chapter focuses on the ports and connectors used to attach external as well as internal peripheral devices.

Motherboard Connectors

In the past, nearly all device connections were made through expansion cards. However, virtually all Pentium-class PCs have a standard set of internal and external ports and connectors integrated into the motherboard. Not all motherboards, including some newer ones, include all of the connectors discussed in this section, but most do.

Motherboard connectors are classified into three groups: back panel connectors, onboard (or mid-board) connectors, and front panel connectors (see Figure 12.1).

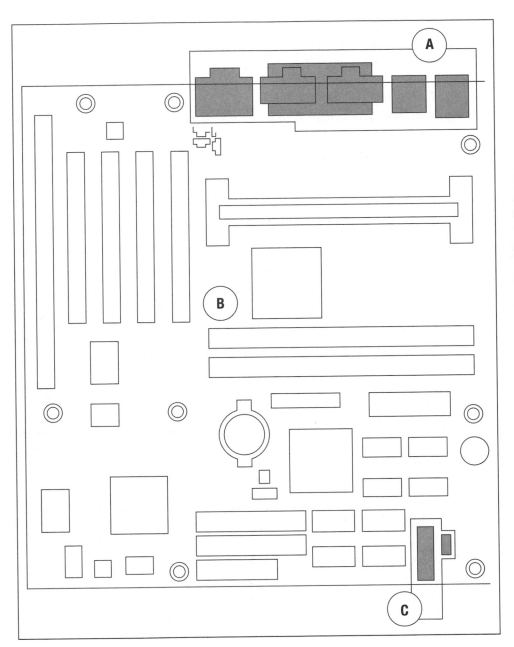

Figure 12.1   The general locations of the motherboard's connector groups.

These connectors are used to connect the motherboard to core internal devices (e.g., the power supply, system speaker, and the front panel switches and LEDs) as well as external peripheral devices (e.g., the printer, modem, keyboard, and mouse).

Back Panel Connectors

As illustrated in Figure 12.2, the motherboard's back panel typically includes several input/output (I/O) ports that support a standard set of peripheral devices. Other ports can be added with expansion cards. The standard ports usually found on most current PCs are shown in Figure 12.2. Each of these connectors is discussed in more detail later in this chapter.

Onboard Connectors

Several connectors are located on the central part of the motherboard to provide support for onboard device and bus services. The onboard, or mid-board, connectors are divided into the following five functional groups:

- *Audio/video*—Motherboards that have built-in support for sound, video, and CD-ROM include an auxiliary sound line in, a telephony connection, a legacy CD-ROM connector, and an ATAPI (AT attachment packet interface) CD-ROM connection. These connectors and their uses are explained in more detail in Chapter 20.

- *Peripheral device interfaces*—Virtually all new motherboards have a standard set of connectors located on the board to provide support for several internal devices. Typically, these connectors are integrated drive electroncs/advanced technology attachment (IDE/ATA) interface connectors, as illustrated in Figure 12.3, that support the hard disk, CD-ROM, and the floppy disk. These connectors are discussed in more detail in Chapter 8.

- *Hardware power and management*—These connectors attach the power supply to the motherboard, connect system and processor fans, and provide an interface for Wake on LAN (local area network) or Wake on Ring technologies.

- *Memory slots*—Every motherboard includes some form of connector, mounting, or slot for memory chips or modules. Newer boards include mounting slots (see Figure 12.4) for Rambus dynamic random access memory, or RDRAM, inline memory modules (RIMMs) and dual inline memory modules (DIMMs). Older motherboards may have slots for single inline memory modules (SIMMs) or even dual inline packaging (DIP) sockets. See Chapter 5 for more information on memory modules.

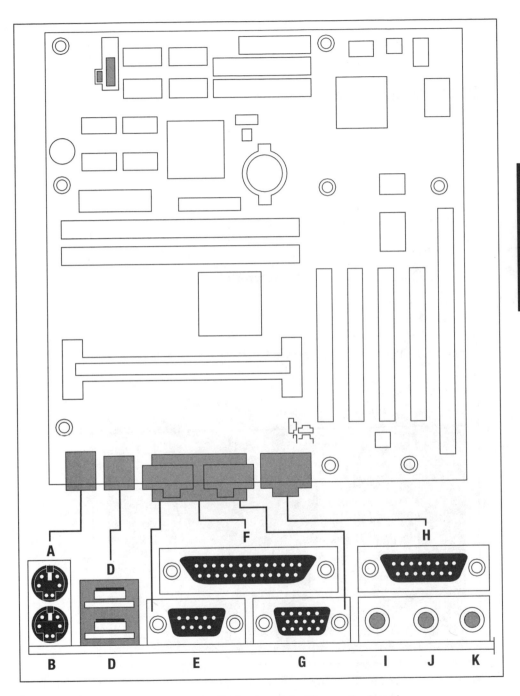

Figure 12.2   The common ports on the back panel of the motherboard.

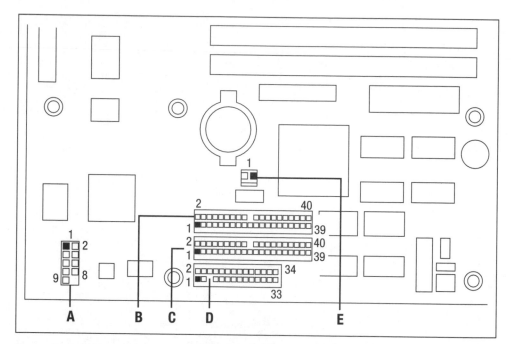

Figure 12.3   Peripheral device connectors located on a motherboard.

Photo courtesy of AOpen America, Inc.

Figure 12.4   The location of memory and expansion slots on a Slot A motherboard.

- *Expansion slots*—The expansion slots (see Figure 12.4) on the motherboard are used to add peripheral device adapters and interface cards to the PC. Motherboards support a variety of expansion slot types; the most common are Industry Standard Architecture/Enhanced ISA (ISA/EISA), peripheral components interconnect (PCI), and accelerated graphics port (AGP). See Chapter 10 for more information on expansion cards.

Front Panel Connectors

As described in Chapter 13, the front panel of the system case may have a variety of light-emitting diodes (LEDs) and switches that attach to the motherboard for power and activity signals. The front panel connector group typically includes a connection for hard disk LEDs (power and activity), the main power on/off button, a reset button, and a few power and grounding connections. Separately, the motherboard also has a connection for the system speaker that is also mounted either on or near the front panel. The motherboard may have an infrared (IR) serial port connector as well (IR connections are discussed later in this chapter under "Infrared Ports").

External Ports and Connectors

The external ports mounted on a motherboard's rear panel are set by its form factor. Most of the PCs in use today are built to the advanced technology extended (ATX) form factor, so they have a basic set of external ports. The ATX standard set includes, as shown in Figure 12.5, a serial port or two, a parallel port or two, USB ports or FireWire ports, a video port, a game device port, and speaker and microphone jacks. This set of ports is the focus of this chapter.

A Review of Interface Technologies

Before discussing each of the interfaces listed in the preceding section, it may be helpful to review some of the hows and whys of the operations of interfaces and the different types of data they support. Each of the specific interfaces is explained later in this chapter.

Character Data

Data is stored on a PC in the American Standard Code for Information Interchange (ASCII, pronounced "askee") format. ASCII defines the standard character set of PCs, including a number of special command, inquiry, and graphics characters, with upper- and lowercase alphabetic characters, special characters, and numbers of the American English language.

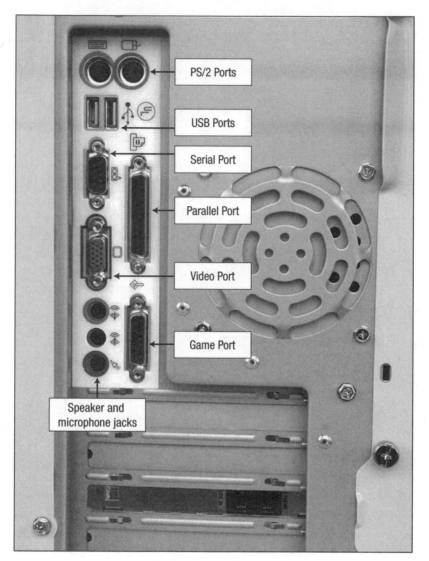

Figure 12.5   The standard interface ports on an ATX form factor PC.

Table 12.1 includes a sample of the ASCII character set, including the decimal and binary values for each character.

Serial and Parallel Data

Data is transmitted and moved in and out of the PC using either the parallel or serial format. A parallel transmission sends its data one character at a time with all the bits of each character being transmitted at the same time over parallel wires. In contrast, serial data is transmitted one bit at a time over a single wire. Figure 12.6 illustrates the difference between these two transmission formats.

Table 12.1   Sample ASCII characters.

Character	Decimal	Binary
Null	0	00000000
Backspace	8	00001000
Line feed	10	00001010
Form feed	12	00001100
Space	32	00100000
! (exclamation mark)	33	00100001
Dollar sign	36	00100100
0 (zero)	48	00110000
1	49	00110001
2	50	00110010
: (colon)	58	00111010
; (semicolon)	59	00111011
? (question mark)	63	00111111
A	65	01000001
B	66	01000010
C	67	01000011
X	88	01011000
Y	89	01011001
Z	90	01011010
a	97	01100001
b	98	01100010
c	99	01100011
x	120	01111000
y	121	01111001
z	122	01111010

Full, Half, and Single Modes

A communications connection can be restricted to only one way or be open for two-way simultaneous transmissions, depending on the transmission mode configuration established between two communicating devices.

A communications line can be configured with one of the following three transmission modes:

- *Simplex*—A simplex line communicates in only one direction. A speaker wire is an example of a simplex communications line.

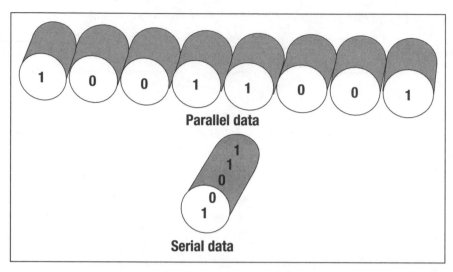

Figure 12.6   Character bits are sent at the same time in a parallel transmission and one bit at a time in a serial transmission.

- *Half-duplex*—A duplex line carries data in two directions. A half-duplex line carries data in two directions, but can transmit in only one direction at a time. A citizen's band (CB) radio is an example of a half-duplex line—one party must wait until the other party is finished before speaking.

- *Full-duplex*—A full-duplex line carries data in two directions simultaneously. An example of a full-duplex line is the telephone.

Serial Ports

Serial ports and connectors were used on the very first PCs to connect modems and early dot matrix printers. Serial ports transmit data one bit after the other in a series. All serial devices, cables, ports, and communications transmit their data this way. To transmit a single byte of data through a serial port, eight separate one-bit transmissions are sent. Serial transmissions can be viewed as sending data down a pipeline just big enough for a single bit.

Although an ASCII character can be defined with either seven or eight bits, more than this number are sent for each character, regardless of the transmission format. The extra bits are used for data integrity, data block identification, and data synchronization.

External serial devices connect to a PC through a serial, or COM (a legacy term for communications), port. The terms "serial" and "COM" are used interchangeably, and most operating systems refer to the serial ports as COM ports, with the first serial port being designated as COM1 and subsequent serial ports as COM2, COM3, and so forth. Serial ports are also called RS-232 ports, for reference standard 232, which is a standard created by the Institute of Electrical and Electronics Engineers (IEEE—referred to as "I-triple-E") for lines, ports, and connectors used to transmit standard serial data communications.

A typical PC has one serial port mounted on the motherboard. Serial ports are easily recognized because they use either 9-pin or 25-pin male D-type connectors, designated as DB-9 and DB-25 connectors, respectively. The serial port shown in Figure 12.5 is a single DB-9 serial port.

Because a serial transmission uses only 9 pins and wires, most PCs use the DB-9 port rather than the DB-25. The DB-9 connector is smaller and has fewer pins, reducing the potential for damaged or bent pins and taking up less space on the PC. Older PC models typically include a single DB-25 serial port on a multipurpose card that may also include a second serial port, typically a DB-9 port, a parallel port, or a game port. The DB-25 connector is also popular on external modems and serial printers.

Serial Connector Pinouts and Cable Connections

Table 12.2 shows the pinouts for DB-25 and DB-9 serial connections. Because the pin assignments differ between the two connectors, in a cable that has a DB-25 connector on one end and a DB-9 connector on the other end, the pins must be cross-matched to carry the signals to the appropriate pins on each end.

Table 12.2 DB-25 and DB-9 connector pinouts.

DB-25 Pin	DB-9 Pin	Use
1		Ground
2	3	Transmit
3	2	Receive
4	7	RTS (request to send)
5	8	CTS (clear to send)
6	6	DSR (data set ready)
7	5	Signal ground
8	1	Carrier detect
20	4	DTR (data terminal ready)
22	9	Ring indicator

A serial cable can have as few as 2 wires, but usually has not more than 20 wires; 8 wires is very common. The wires in the cable are color-coded to make it easier to find the same wire on each end of the cable when joining connectors to the cable. The connector is attached by soldering the wires to the back of a connector's pins. Plugging the connector onto a matching port completes the connection as the pins in the port make contact with the holes in the connector. With the serial connection established, the PC and peripheral device can send signals back and forth to communicate and control the transmission.

Asynchronous Communications

Asynchronous communications are used to connect to a printer, modem, fax, or other peripheral device. Asynchronous transmitters and receivers operate independently and are not synchronized to a common clock signal or to each other. Data blocks are separated by arbitrary idle periods on the line, as illustrated in Figure 12.7.

Asynchronous data blocks are fixed in size and format. To the 8-bit ASCII character is added a start bit before the character and one or two stop bits after the character. These bits indicate to the receiving device the beginning and ending of each character. Typically, the start bit is a 0 and the stop bit is a 1. If parity is in use, the parity bit is tacked onto the data block as well.

Parity Checking

The parity used with asynchronous communications is very much like that used with memory (see Chapter 5). The parity bit is used to force the count of "1" bits in the transmitted character to either an even or an odd number. For example, when an uppercase A is transmitted, actually it is its binary value (01000001) that is transmitted. If even parity is in use, the parity bit added to the end is set to 0 because there are an even number of 1s in the character. If odd parity is in use, the parity bit is set to 1 to force an odd number of 1s in the character. Should the receiving device detect an error in the number of 1s, it sends a request to resend the character.

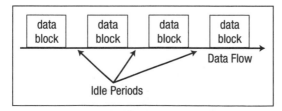

Figure 12.7 Asynchronous communications send data in 5-byte to 8-byte blocks that are separated by variously sized idle periods.

With everything added to the ASCII binary character (start bit, stop bit, and parity bit), the asynchronous data block is actually 11 bits long. For the transmitted character "A", the data block would have the following parts:

- Start bit: 0
- ASCII binary data pattern: 01000001
- Even-parity bit: 0
- Stop bit: 1
- Transmitted data block: 00100000101

UART

A specialized integrated circuit called a universal asynchronous receiver/transmitter (UART, pronounced "you-art") is used to control all serial ports and most serial device connections. A UART is located on a device adapter card, found directly on the motherboard, or is integrated onto a serial device's internal controller. A UART controls all the actions and functions of a serial port or device, including:

- Controlling all the connectors' pins and their associated signals
- Establishing the communications protocol
- Converting the parallel format bits of the PC's data bus into a serial bit stream for transmission
- Converting the received serial bit stream into parallel data for transmission over the PC's internal data bus

On the PC, a UART interprets and translates the data coming into and being sent out of a serial port by examining the incoming data, looking for the start and stop bits, and verifying the parity bit counts. The UART also inserts the start and stop bits and parity bit, if needed, into outgoing data. In addition, the UART controls the data speed of the serial port or device. Table 12.3 lists by identity number the UART chips that have been used in PCs, modems, and other serial devices over the years. Most modern PCs use the 16550 UART chip, which supports speeds up to 115.2 kilobits per second (Kbps).

Synchronous Communications

Synchronous communications have somewhat more overhead than asynchronous transmissions. Synchronous transmissions have a fixed interval length between data blocks. The data blocks and the intervals of a synchronous transmission are synchronized to a clock signal that is sent along with the data. The communicating devices also carry on a running dialog that confirms and acknowledges that each data block has been received. If the acknowledgment does not come back in

Table 12.3   UART chip characteristics.

Chip	Maximum Speed (Kbps)
8250	19.2
16450	38.4
16550	115.2
16650	430.8
16750	921.6
16850	1,500
16950	1,500

the proper time interval, the sending device automatically sends it again. Because synchronous devices must complete one operation before beginning the next, this communication mode is very accurate; however, most serial communications on PCs use asynchronous technology.

Serial Port Configuration

As mentioned previously, virtually all PCs have at least one serial port, designated as COM1. Additional serial ports, if any, are designated as COM2, COM3, and so forth. If you need to add more serial ports to a PC, you can add them one at a time or in sets of two or four. Individual serial ports require individual system resource assignments, and two such cards require two sets of system resources. However, a multiport serial card shares a single interrupt request (IRQ) among its ports, with an onboard processor handling the traffic management. If a PC requires multiple serial ports, it is likely more efficient to install a multiport card, or you may consider using a universal serial bus (USB), which is discussed in more detail later in this chapter under "The USB Interface."

Most PCs have default assignments for up to four serial ports. Table 12.4 lists the default system resource assignments for PC serial ports. COM1 shares an IRQ with COM3, and COM2 shares an IRQ with COM4, which means you must be

Table 12.4   Serial port system resource assignments.

Logical Device Name	IRQ	I/O Address
COM1	IRQ 4	3F8h
COM2	IRQ 3	2F8h
COM3	IRQ 4	3E8h
COM4	IRQ 3	2E8h

careful when assigning devices to COM ports to avoid competing devices. See Chapter 7 for more information on system resources. Typically, COM1 is a DB-9 male port and COM2, if present, is a DB-25 male port.

Parallel Ports

A parallel transmission sends the bits of a character at one time using parallel wires, which means a character is transmitted much faster than it would be over a serial connection. The internal bus structures inside the PC use parallel transmissions, which is why a serial port needs a UART to convert the internal parallel format into a serial format for transmission over a serial line.

Parallel Port Formats

Parallel ports are female DB-25 connectors into which a male DB-25 connector is plugged. Figure 12.8 shows both connector formats (on a networking device). Although originally used almost exclusively by printers, other devices have been adapted to the parallel port, including external CD-ROMs, external tape drives, scanners, and Zip drives. These devices take advantage of the bidirectional capabilities of the newer parallel port standards.

Parallel Port Standards

The IEEE has combined parallel port standards into a single standard called IEEE 1284. This standard incorporates two preexisting parallel port standards with a new protocol to create an all-encompassing parallel port model and protocol standard.

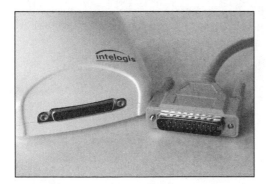

Figure 12.8   A LAN networking device that uses a parallel port and a cable with a DB-25 male connector.

The separate parallel port standards included in the IEEE 1284 standard are:

- *Standard parallel port (SPP)*—Defines a simplex parallel port that allows data to travel only from the computer to the printer.

- *Enhanced parallel port (EPP)*—Defines a half-duplex parallel port that allows the printer to signal out of paper, cover open, and other error conditions.

- *Enhanced capabilities port (ECP)*—Most PCs that list an IEEE 1284 port as a feature are indicating support for an ECP port. The ECP standard allows bidirectional, simultaneous communications between a parallel device, usually a printer, and a PC. The IEEE 1284 standard also defines an ECP standard cable. When shopping for a printer ECP cable, be sure it actually is an ECP cable; EPP cables will not work properly.

The USB Interface

The USB is a newer hardware interface standard that supports low-speed devices, such as keyboards, mice, and scanners, as well as such higher speed devices as digital cameras. The USB, which is a serial interface, provides data transfer speeds of up to 12 megabits per second (Mbps) for faster devices and a 1.5Mbps subchannel speed for lower-speed devices. A newer version of the USB standard, USB 2.0, supports up to 480Mbps for data transfer speeds.

A USB port offers the following features:

- The flexibility of plug-and-play (PnP) devices

- Standard connectors and cables with a wide variety of devices available, including keyboards, mice, floppy drives, hard disk drives, Zip and Jazz drives, inkjet printers, laser printers, scanners, digital cameras, modems, and hubs

- Automatic configuration of USB devices when they are connected

- Hot swapping—USB devices can be connected and disconnected while the PC is powered on

- The capability to support up to 127 devices on one channel

Connecting with the USB

The USB uses a unique pair of connectors and ports, as shown in Figure 12.9. Devices with permanently attached cables have USB Type A connectors. USB Type A connectors are used to connect devices directly to a PC or USB hub (see Figure 12.10). USB Type B connectors are found on devices that have a detachable cable. This cable uses a squarish Type B port on the device and connects to either a Type A or Type B socket (the cable usually has both on the other end) on the PC or hub.

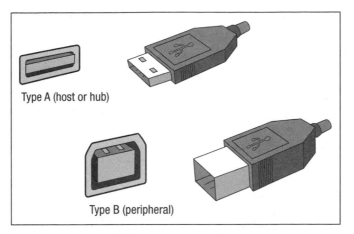

Type A (host or hub)

Type B (peripheral)

Figure 12.9   The two types of USB connectors and ports.

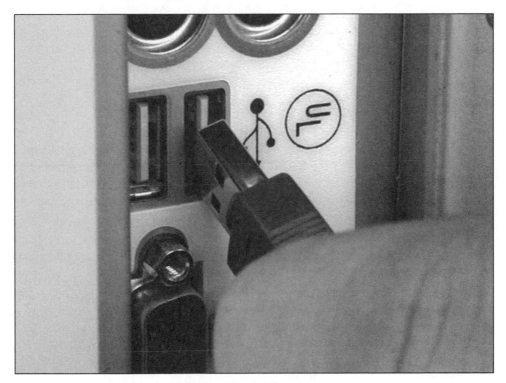

Figure 12.10   Connecting a USB device to a USB port on a PC.

12. Ports and Connectors

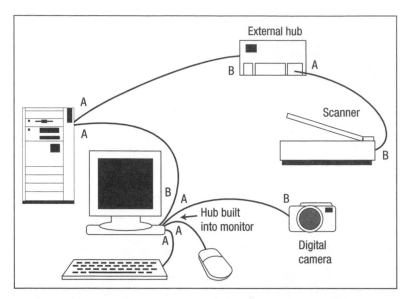

Figure 12.11   Multiple USB devices can be connected to a single PC.

A USB hub is used to add more than 127 devices to a USB channel. The hubs are daisy-chained to add more devices to the channel. Some newer devices, including monitors, as illustrated in Figure 12.11, also have USB channels. A USB port carries 0.5 amps of electrical power, which is usually enough for most low-power devices, such as a mouse or keyboard, so no additional power is required. This adds to the flexibility of the USB channel, because devices can be added without regard to location. Those USB devices that require more power than is carried on the channel have alternating current/direct current (AC/DC) adapters.

USB Interface Components

A USB interface has three essential components:

- *USB host*—The USB host device carries operating system, chipset, and basic input/output system (BIOS) support for the USB interface. Typically, the PC is the USB host.

- *USB hub*—A USB hub serves as a collector device to cluster USB devices onto a USB channel. USB devices can be added to the channel in a tiered fashion with one hub plugged into another and a connection to the USB host from the first hub.

- *USB devices*—Typically, a PC has only one or two USB devices plugged into its USB channels, but, as indicated previously, a USB channel can have up to 127 devices, counting USB hubs.

IEEE 1394 (FireWire)

The IEEE 1394 standard defines another high-speed serial bus that is officially known as the high-performance serial bus (HPSB), but more commonly called FireWire. This serial interface supports data speeds of 100Mbps to 400Mbps (which is the equivalent of 12 to 50 megabytes (MB) per second). Newer versions of the 1394 standard, which are being developed by the 1394 Trade Association (go to Web site **www.1394ta.org**), are promising data speeds of 800Mbps to 1.6 gigabits per second (Gbps).

An IEEE 1394 connector looks something like a USB connector, except that it is just a bit larger and somewhere between rectangular and square. Figure 12.12 illustrates the FireWire connection.

The IEEE 1394 bus is similar to the USB interface in many ways. Both are high-speed, PnP, hot-swappable interface buses. One major difference is that 1394 supports isochronous (or real-time) data transfers, by which data is transferred so that all of its parts arrive together, which can be very important for audio/video data, such as with multimedia data or images directly from a video camera. Other differences are that the 1394 standard is a peer-to-peer interface that, unlike the USB, does not require a host system, and an IEEE 1394 bus is able to support up to 63 external devices versus the USB's 127.

Wireless Ports

Wireless or cordless interfaces are becoming more popular for PCs. They can be used to connect peripheral devices to the PC or, as explained in Chapter 19, even to connect the PC to a LAN. Two types of wireless connection technologies are used on PCs: infrared (IR) and radio frequency (RF).

Infrared Ports

An IR port uses an invisible band of light to carry data between a peripheral device and a transceiver on the PC. IR light is just outside the red end of the light spectrum that humans are able to see. In contrast, ultraviolet (UV) is an invisible band of light at

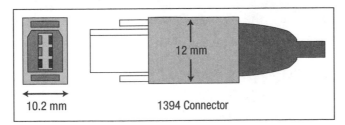

Figure 12.12   The IEEE 1394, or FireWire, connector.

the violet end of the light spectrum. IR devices are also called IrDA (Infrared Data Association) devices. IrDA is the trade organization for the infrared device industry that has established the standards that define the use of an IR connection. The IrDA port is the small, oval-shaped, dark red plastic window built into a PC case.

An IR device is a line-of-sight device, so it must have a clear, unobstructed path between its transmitter and receiver. With an IR connection, a portable PC or a personal digital assistant (PDA) can connect to another PC, a keyboard, a mouse, or a printer without using a physical cable connection. Built-in IR ports (receivers) are common on portable PCs, notebooks, and PDAs, but an external IR receiver also can be attached to a PC through a serial or USB port.

The following tips are important when working with IR devices:

- The two IR devices must have a clear, unobstructed line of sight between them.
- The devices you are trying to connect via IR must be at least 6 inches but not more than 3 feet apart.
- The transmission pattern of the IR signal is a cone about 30 degrees wide. Make sure the devices are oriented to one another inside the transmission cone.
- Make sure there are no competing IR devices, such as a TV remote control, in the vicinity, because they may interfere with the connection.

Radio Frequency Interfaces

Many cordless peripheral devices, especially those that are typically used in close proximity of the PC's system case, use RF transmitters, receivers, and transceivers (the combination of a receiver and transmitter) to send data to the PC. RF devices include mice, keyboards, modems, and even network adapters for desktop and portable PCs.

Cordless RF mice and keyboards, such as those shown in Figure 12.13, transmit data to a receiver attached to a PC through either a serial or PS/2 connection (discussed in the next section). The operating range of these devices is around 6 to 10 feet, despite claims of 50-foot ranges. In most cases, the performance of the cordless RF keyboard or mouse within its effective operating distance is as good as a wired device. RF networking devices, which are defined in the IEEE 802.11 wireless networking standard and the new Bluetooth technology, are discussed in more detail in Chapter 20.

DIN and PS/2 Connectors

The 5-pin DIN (Deutsche Industrie Norm) connector and the PS/2 (mini-DIN connector) are the two most popular connectors for keyboards, mice, and external IR and RF receivers. These connectors have become the standard for virtually all keyboards and mice on PCs. A brief description of these two connectors follows.

Photo courtesy of Logitech.

Figure 12.13 A cordless keyboard and mouse that connect to the PC through an RF transmitter and receiver.

- *5-pin DIN connector*—This connector, often called the AT style connector, has been in use since the very first PCs. The German standards organization Deutsche Industrie Norm, developed the round connector style used on this and the 6-pin version of this connector. Only four of the five pins are used to connect the clocking signal (pin 1), data signal (pin 2), a ground (pin 4), and +5 volts (V) of power (pin 5).

- *6-pin mini-DIN (PS/2) connector*—This DIN-style connector is a smaller version of the 5-pin DIN connector. Keyboard and mice connections use only four of the six available pins to connect the data signal (pin 1), ground (pin 3), +5V of power (pin 4), and a clocking signal (pin 5). This connector, which is now the *de facto* standard for all cabled keyboards and mice, was first introduced on the IBM PS/2, which is why it is commonly referred to as the PS/2 connector. Figure 12.14 illustrates the PS/2 connector.

Figure 12.14 The 6-pin mini-DIN (PS/2) connector is standard on most PC keyboards and mice.

Nearly all mice sold today use the PS/2 connector, but some serial mice that use a DB-9 serial connector are still around. However, the serial mouse has all but disappeared, except on some older systems, because newer PC systems rarely offer more than a single serial port and have specially designated PS/2 connectors for the keyboard and mouse.

Video Connectors

Regardless of the type of internal interface a video card uses (see Chapter 11 for more information on video adapters and the video interfaces), virtually all video ports use a female 15-pin DB port, such as the one shown in Figure 12.15. The standard port and connector used for video graphics array (VGA), super VGA (SVGA), and extended graphics array (XGA) monitor connections is the DB-15, which is also called a mini-sub D15 connector. Figure 12.16 shows the pin configuration of this connection, and Table 12.5 lists its pin assignments.

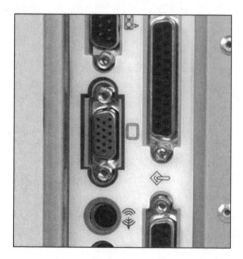

Figure 12.15   The standard DB-15 VGA video port.

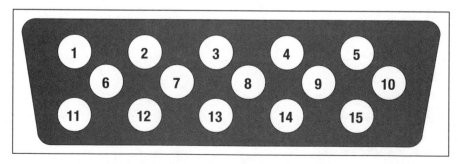

Figure 12.16   The standard VGA video connector has 15 pins arranged in three rows.

Table 12.5   Pin assignments in a video connector.

Pin	VGA/SVGA/XGA
1	Red video
2	Green video
3	Blue video
4	Monitor ID 2
5	Ground/not used
6	Red video return
7	Green video return
8	Blue video return
9	Not used
10	Ground
11	Monitor ID 0
12	Monitor ID 1
13	Horizontal sync
14	Vertical sync
15	Not used

SCSI Connectors

Small computer systems interface (SCSI, pronounced "skuzzy") controllers are built into SCSI devices, such as hard disk drives, tape drives, and CD-ROMs, among others. The SCSI bus is capable of connecting many devices, both internal and external, to a single SCSI controller on a common SCSI bus interface. Several different SCSI standards that use a variety of different connectors are available. Table 12.6 lists the connectors used externally and internally for each of the various SCSI standards in use. Figures 12.17 and 12.18 illustrate the connectors referenced in Table 12.6.

SCA Connectors

Single connector attachment (SCA) connectors are designed to simplify hard drive connections for hot-swappable hard disk drives, such as those used in a redundant array of independent disks (RAID) system (see Chapter 8 for more information on RAID). The SCA standard combines a Wide SCSI connector and a hard drive power connection into a single, compact 80-pin adapter, such as the one shown in Figure 12.19.

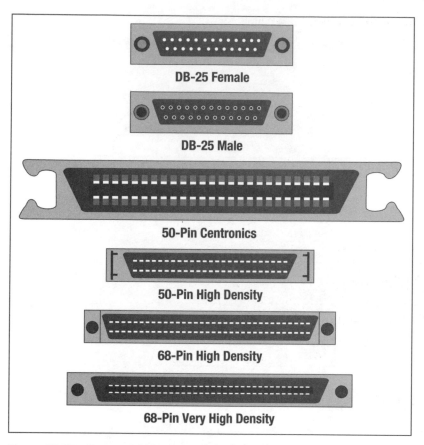

Figure 12.17   External SCSI connectors.

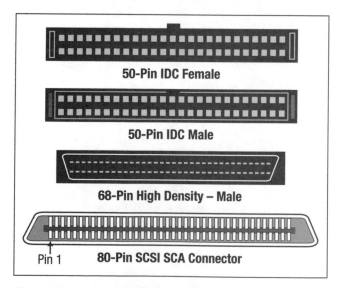

Figure 12.18   Internal SCSI connectors.

Table 12.6   SCSI standards and their connectors.

SCSI Standard	External Connector	Internal Connector
SCSI – 1	50-pin Centronics	50-pin IDC (insulation displacement connector)
SCSI – 2	50-pin high density	50-pin IDC
Ultra SCSI	50-pin high density	50-pin IDC
Fast SCSI	50-pin high density	50-pin IDC
Wide SCSI	68-pin high density	68-pin high density
Fast Wide SCSI	68-pin high density	68-pin high density
Ultra SCSI – 3	68-pin high density	68-pin high density
Ultra2 SCSI – 3	68-pin very high density	68-pin high density

Figure 12.19   An SCA adapter combines a SCSI connector with a power connection.

SCSI Voltage Differentials

SCSI connectors must support the voltage differential of the SCSI standard in use. When buying cables for a SCSI bus or a SCSI device, make sure you match the voltage differential of the standard in use. The voltage differential, which is also called the signaling type, affects the total length of the SCSI chain. The signaling types used on a SCSI bus are as follows:

- *Single-ended (SE)*—Supports a terminated SCSI bus chain not longer than 3 to 6 meters (m) or roughly 10 to 20 feet. SCSI measurements are usually in meters rather than feet.

- *High-voltage differential (HVD)*—Allows for a SCSI chain of up to 25 m.

- *Low-voltage differential (LVD)*—A less costly signaling method that supports an overall distance of only 12 m.

Immediate Solutions

Troubleshooting a Serial Port

A problem with a serial port is usually either a problem with the attached device or a system resource conflict. When troubleshooting a serial port problem, first try another device, if one is available. Next, check for system resource conflicts using either the System Information applet or the Device Manager on a Windows system.

If it begins to look like there might actually be a problem with the serial port, use the pinouts listed earlier in this chapter in the section, "Serial Connector Pinouts and Cable Connections," and use a multimeter to check the voltages of the serial port on the PC and the continuity of the cable.

System resource conflicts will cause a serial device to fail intermittently or perhaps cause it not to work at all. Other symptoms are that an existing serial device stops working when a new additional serial device is installed or the PC locks up during the boot sequence.

To troubleshoot a serial port problem, check the following:

- *Inspect the port for bent pins.* Certain pins absolutely must be straight for the device to work properly. If a pin is bent or broken, you should replace the connector (or cable) because the damage may be compromising the connection of other pins as well.

- *Check the connection and connectors.* Make sure that the cable wires are properly soldered to the pins in the connector and that the connector fits snuggly and correctly to the port. If any of the wires are touching each other (it takes only one strand to cause a problem), either replace the cable or repair the connector.

- *Test the port with another device.* A very good tool to have for testing serial ports is a serial mouse. If the port is the problem, and it is mounted on the motherboard, you will need to disable it and install an additional serial port with an expansion card, if you truly must use a serial port.

- *Test the serial device on a different serial port that is known to be good.* Test the serial device by connecting it to another PC on which you know the serial port is working. If the device works, you know that the problem is not the device, but you still have some troubleshooting to do on the original PC to isolate the problem.

- *Ensure the cable is appropriate for the device.* Some serial devices cannot use a straight-through or null modem cable. Check the pin and configuration requirements of the device and use the appropriate cable.

- *Check the length of the serial cable.* You may hear stories of successfully using longer cable lengths, but the nominal maximum length for a serial cable is 50 feet between two devices. Beyond 50 feet, you may suffer attenuation (the distance at which the signal begins losing its strength) and begin to see data errors.

- *Check the BIOS settings.* COM ports can be enabled and disabled in the BIOS Setup configuration data. Make sure that the port is enabled. A disabled port will not work.

- *Check the Windows Device Manager or System Information applet for system resource conflicts.* An IRQ conflict is the most common error with serial devices. Remember, only one active device at a time should be using an IRQ.

- *Check the software setup.* In most cases, application software is in use to manage or control the serial device, such as dial-up software for a modem. Check the configuration of the software and the settings it is using to configure the serial device.

Troubleshooting a Parallel Port

Because parallel ports are virtually featureless, and they either work or don't work, most of the time any problem you are having with a parallel port is caused by the physical part of the connector or port (bent pins or blocked holes), the cable (wrong type; SPP, EPP, or ECP), or the attached device.

Use the following steps to troubleshoot and isolate a parallel port problem:

- *Check for resource conflicts.* The problem rarely may be a system resource conflict, but it is usually caused by another device that was just added to the PC. See Table 12.7 for the default system resource assignments made to parallel (LPT) ports.

Table 12.7 Parallel port system resource assignments.

Port	IRQ	I/O Address	Direct Memory Access (DMA) Channel
LPT1	IRQ 7	378h	DMA 3 (ECP capabilities)
LPT2	IRQ 5	278h	not applicable

- *Check the cable and connectors for physical problems.* If a commercial printer cable is in use, make sure it fits tightly on both ends, to the port and to the printer. If a homegrown cable is in use, make sure that the cable wires are properly soldered to the pins in the connector and that the connector fits snugly and correctly to the port. If any of the wires are touching each other (it takes only one strand to cause a problem), either replace the cable or repair the connector.

- *Verify that the device is working properly.* To test the printer, try printing a plain text file to avoid issues on the printer itself. If the printer appears to be receiving data, but does not print, try the printer on another PC. If its still does not work, you know the problem is with the printer. Otherwise, check to make sure you have the proper device drivers and configuration for the printer or other device.

- *Verify system resource settings.* If the PC is equipped with more than one parallel (LPT) port, use the Windows Device Manager or System Information applet to verify that no system resource conflicts exist.

- *Check the BIOS Setup configuration.* You can set the IRQ assigned to the LPT ports in the BIOS Setup configuration data. Make sure that it is set to IRQ7 (default) for LPT1 and IRQ5 for LPT2. If the problem is with the port assigned to IRQ5, check for a conflict with the sound card.

- *Verify the communications mode of the parallel port.* Check the device's documentation to verify that the port is configured to the correct communications mode (SPP, EPP, ECP). Many printers require at least an EPP mode to be configured to the port in the BIOS Setup configuration data.

- *Check ECP settings.* If ECP mode is enabled on a parallel port, it can cause system resource conflicts that are avoided by other parallel modes. Although the LPT ports are assigned an IRQ, most parallel devices, such as printers, do not use it. However, a resource conflict can occur if ECP mode is enabled and the IRQ has been assigned to another device. ECP mode also requires a direct memory access (DMA) channel and could be in conflict with the sound card.

- *Verify the device drivers.* Check the device manufacturer's Web site for newer versions of the device driver. Make sure the device drivers in use are compatible with the operating system in use on the PC. Many Windows 9x drivers will not work on a Windows 2000 system.

Dealing with Serial Port System Resource Conflicts

The symptoms for a system resource conflict on one or more serial ports are fairly straightforward. The most common are the following:

- The modem on COM3 fails when the serial mouse on COM1 is used or vice versa.

- The system locks up when the serial devices on COM2 and COM4 are used at the same time.

Many variations of these two problems exist, but they almost all involve a system resource conflict, most likely an IRQ conflict. If the device on COM2 is having or causing the problem, that device should be reconfigured, either to a different COM port or a different IRQ. If the COM ports were installed on a multiport I/O controller card, you should change the configuration of the card through its jumpers, as specified in the card's documentation.

Dealing with Printing Problems

In most cases, if a printer is producing garbled or distorted print, or part of a page or image is missing, the problem lies with either the hardware or the software associated with the printer itself. However, if all appears to be right with the printer, the LPT port can cause one or two problems.

To diagnose this problem, check the following:

- *Check the print mechanism on the printer.* Although the focus is on the cable and the connector, the problem could very well be that the printer itself is not functioning. This is a good place to start when printing problems occur. The problem is rarely on the parallel port or the cable.

- *Verify that the most current printer driver is in use.* The printer driver must be compatible to the printer as well as the operating system on the PC or the network. A disk or CD-ROM comes with most printers, but you should visit the manufacturer's Web site to download the most current driver for the printer and operating system.

- *Try changing the parallel port mode.* Not all printers are compatible with the latest standards. Some printers can have problems with the ECP communication mode and work much better with EPP mode. Check the printer's documentation to verify its communications mode requirement and configure the port accordingly in the BIOS Setup configuration.

- *Verify that the cable is appropriate.* Check the cable for problems, sharp bends, cuts, any indications that it may have been crushed, or loose connector heads. Also check to see if the cable is the right one for the printer. If the printer requires an IEEE-1284 certified ECP printer cable, and the cable in use is only an EPP, a problem can occur.

Troubleshooting a USB Connection

If you are having problems with a USB port, you can check to make sure the USB ports are active on the system. The first place to look is in the Windows Device Manager to ensure that the USB ports are actually installed on the system. Figure 12.20 shows where the USB ports are listed in the Windows Device Manager.

If all appears to be normal in the Device Manager (no conflicts or missing drivers), then check the following:

- *Check the device connections.* Although it may seem obvious, this should always be the first troubleshooting step when dealing with device problems. Make sure the device is connected to the PC, and if it requires power, make sure it is plugged into a power source. Some USB devices, such as keyboards and mice, get their power from the USB channel, but others require additional power.

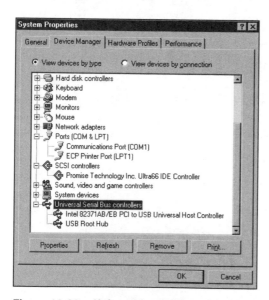

Figure 12.20   Universal serial bus controller information in the Windows Device Manager.

- *Enable the USB connection.* Make sure the USB ports are enabled in the BIOS Setup configuration data. Although the PC should be shipped from the factory with its USB ports enabled, you never know until you try to use one. It could be that the PC has USB ports, but the BIOS system does not support them. In this case, you may need to upgrade the BIOS (see Chapter 4) to support USB ports, if such an upgrade is available.

- *Verify the devices installed.* If both the host controller and the root hub are installed (and listed on the Device Manager), all is well. However, if one or the other is missing, the problem is in the .INF file used to install the device drivers. Try removing the device and then clicking the Refresh button to detect the devices. If this fails, find the USB.INF file in the Windows INF folder and install it.

- *Check for system resource conflicts.* The USB host controller shares its IRQ with other devices. This rarely causes a problem, but on occasion this can cause the USB device not to be recognized when attached to the USB port. If this happens, you should reassign the USB host controller to a different IRQ, provided one is available.

Assigning an IRQ to the USB Host Controller

Use these steps to force the USB host controller to a different IRQ setting:

1. With the Device Manager displayed, double-click the Computer item at the top of the device tree. This displays the Computer Properties window, shown in Figure 12.21.

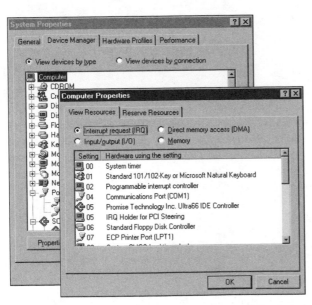

Figure 12.21   The Windows Computer Properties window.

2. On the Reserve Resource tab, click the Add button and enter the number of the IRQ currently in use by the USB host controller. Click OK to close the window.

3. On the Device Manager window, select the USB host device and click the Remove button.

4. Restart the system. The USB host controller will be detected and assigned to a different IRQ.

5. Return to the Device Manager's Computer Properties windows and remove the reservation of the IRQ entered earlier in step #2.

Enabling IRQ Steering

The USB host controller requires IRQ Steering to be enabled on the PCI bus in order to support multiple devices. To enable IRQ steering, perform the following steps:

1. From the Device Manager, choose the PCI Bus entry and click the Properties button.

2. Choose the IRQ Steering tab and select the checkbox for Use IRQ Steering, as illustrated in Figure 12.22.

3. The Use IRQ Steering checkbox lists four IRQ Steering options. The first two and the fourth settings should be checked.

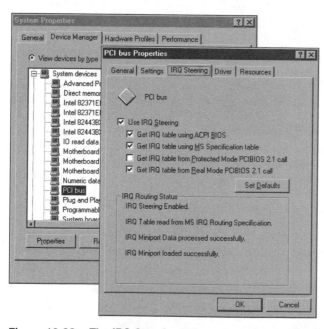

Figure 12.22   The IRQ Steering tab on the Windows PCI Bus Properties dialog box.

Part III

Power

Chapter 13

The System Case

In Depth

Overview

The PC's case is largely taken for granted. It is definitely not high on the list of components you commonly have to deal with. In spite of the fact that the system case has only one or two active components, namely the power supply and the front panel, it plays a major part in the overall operation of the PC.

The system case comprises six major components, as illustrated in Figure 13.1. Each of these components is discussed in the sections that follow. The major components of the case are:

- Chassis
- Cover
- Power supply
- Front panel
- Switches
- Drive bays

Although it is not actually a physical component in the hardware sense, the case's *form factor* is very important. It describes the shape and size of the case and the way the case components fit together. Form factors apply to the case as well as the power supply and motherboard that fit into it. These three components must fit together to provide protection, power, cooling, safety, and, of course, function. Therefore, these components must have the same or compatible form factors.

The Case of the Case

The PC case does much more than just sit on the desk or floor holding in the PC parts or holding up the monitor. It performs a number of very valuable functions that are, for the most part, taken for granted. The case provides the aesthetics of the system, it provides the physical structure of the PC, and it provides protection and cooling to the electronic components and other devices mounted inside its covers. The PC's case is not just another pretty face; it has a very important role to play in the overall function of the PC.

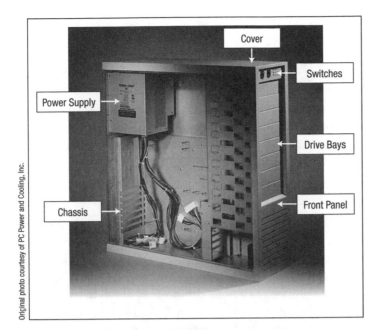

Original photo courtesy of PC Power and Cooling, Inc.

Figure 13.1   The major components of the system case.

Figure 13.2   An assortment of PC case sizes, shapes, and faces.

PC cases come in all sorts of sizes, shapes, colors, and even animals, as illustrated by those shown in Figure 13.2. The variances in size and shape are driven primarily by the form factor of the case, but increasingly, case designers are adding color, new plastic and metal materials, and even character faces to case designs in an attempt to make them less boring and more appealing to a wider audience. The cases shown in Figure 13.2 represent the wide variety of case types and form factors available from a number of different case manufacturers.

As shown in Figure 13.2, not all system cases are the same size or shape, but they all contain virtually the same components and parts. The most common system components found inside the PC's case are:

- *Chassis*—The chassis (pronounced "chass-ee") is the skeletal framework that provides the structure, rigidity, and strength of the case and plays a major role in the cooling system of the case.

- *Cover*—The cover, along with the chassis, plays an important role in the cooling, protection, and structure of the PC.

- *Power supply*—As you are undoubtedly aware, the power supply is a very important component of the PC in general. The power supply's primary job is to rectify (which means to convert) AC power into DC power for use by the PC's internal electronics. However, it also houses and powers the main system cooling fan. Power supplies are not discussed in detail in this chapter, other than to discuss how they fit in a case and their form factors. See Chapter 14 for more specific information on the power supply.

- *Front panel*—In addition to giving the PC its looks and providing placement of the power and reset switches, the front panel provides the user with information on the PC's status and a means of physically securing the PC. It can be the starting point for removing the case's cover.

- *Switches*—The two main switches on most newer systems, the power switch and the reset button, are on the front panel. If the power switch is not on the front panel, it is very likely either on the right-rear corner or near a corner on the back of the PC.

- *Drive bays*—Beginning with the PC XT, disk drives with removable media have been mounted in the case so that they can be accessed on the front panel. Typically, the drive bays house 5.25-inch and 3.5-inch disk drives, such as for floppy disks, CD-ROMs (compact disk-read only memory) and DVDs (digital versatile disks), and removable hard drives.

Chassis

Beneath the sheet metal or plastic exterior covers of a PC's case is the metal framework that provides the structure of the PC. Just like the interior of a building or the human skeleton—to stretch the point—the PC's chassis provides the frame on which all other parts of the PC mount, attach, or hang. As shown in Figure 13.3, the sheet metal of the chassis gives the PC its shape, size, rigidity, strength, and the location of its components.

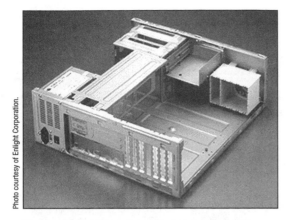

Figure 13.3   The chassis of a desktop PC.

Construction

The frame of the PC must be a rigid structure. Many of the components and devices in the PC cannot withstand being flexed, especially when they are operating. This is especially true of the motherboard. If the frame can twist and bend, the fragile electronic traces on the motherboard or other components could break, the motherboard's mountings could slip or break, or expansion cards could be partially ejected from their slots. Any of these situations could damage or destroy the motherboard or expansion cards. Therefore, the rigidity and strength of the case's chassis are among its key attributes. When evaluating a system case, assure yourself that the structural framework of the chassis is strong and able to protect the components mounted to it and within it.

The frame of the PC chassis should be constructed from a heavy-gauge steel that is at least 18-gauge steel (16-gauge steel is even better). Less expensive cases may use lighter gauge steel or aluminum. There is nothing wrong with a lighter metal or aluminum case, provided the case is reinforced in key supporting locations with heavier gauge steel. Be wary of bargain cases made of lightweight aluminum. These cases are much too pliable and can flex too much when being moved or lifted, causing the problems listed earlier. The few pounds of the PC's total weight you save by buying a lighter-weight case that is made of lighter-gauge metals are definitely not worth the potential for problems that a flexing or bending case can cause.

Internal Design and Layout

Something more to consider when choosing a case for a PC is its internal design and layout. The location of crossbeams in relation to the motherboard, power supply, disk drives, and other components can pose problems later when you are trying to repair or upgrade the PC.

Cover

The cover is attached to the chassis in various ways. The most common method is to use a few screws to attach the cover to the chassis, but there are also "screwless" or "toolless" systems in which the case covers literally hang on the chassis using keyholes or slide-and-lock features. Whatever method of attachment is used, it is extremely important that it has a snug and secure fit.

The case's cover is an important part of the engineering that went into the design of the case's airflow dynamics. It is also a key component of the RFI (radio frequency interference) and EMI (electromagnetic interference) protection designed into the system. If your PC is FCC (Federal Communications Commission) certified (and virtually all PCs are), the case was designed to be a major part of the radio frequency (RF) emissions control of the PC. One of the risks in having a cover that doesn't fit tightly and securely, without gaps or loose parts, is that it may emit RF signals that have an effect on other devices near it. The problem with loose or badly fitting case parts may simply be something as annoying as rattling in the breeze of the escaping airflow.

A wide variety of methods are used to attach the outer cover of the PC to the chassis. The most common is that the cover is attached with screws to the front, sides, and rear of the chassis. Rarely would you completely remove all sections of the PC's cover from the chassis. Normally, only the side (in a tower PC) or top (in a desktop PC) is removed to provide access inside the case. The following sections discuss the more common styles of covers and how they are attached and removed from the chassis.

Legacy Desktops

The desktop PC case, a sample of which is shown in Figure 13.4, is by far the most common of the case designs. There are desktop models for nearly every form factor (discussed in more detail later in this chapter), including the earliest PCs such as the PC XT and the PC AT systems, the more common PCs such as the Baby AT and ATX systems, and the newer LPX slimline systems. For the most part, older systems have a U-shaped piece that incorporates the covers for the top and sides of the PC. This piece is attached to the chassis with four or five screws on the rear panel. Unscrew this piece and remove it by sliding it all the way back or forward off the PC, or by sliding it back a bit and then lifting it straight up. The benefit of this cover design is its simplicity. Be careful when removing or replacing it that you don't snag power and data cables, expansion cards, or disk drives, and dislodge or damage them.

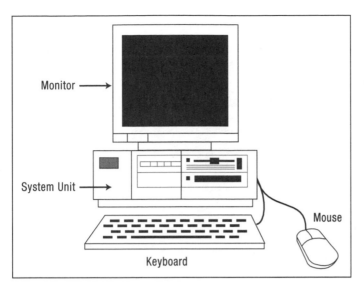

Figure 13.4   A desktop PC case style.

Legacy Towers

Among the many types of tower cases (see Figure 13.5), the most common designs are typically the full-size AT, Baby AT, or ATX cases. On these cases, the cover is a U-shaped piece with very long sides that fit down and over the frame of the tower's case. This cover is attached to the rear of the case with four to six screws. To remove this cover, remove the screws and lift the cover straight up and off, or slide it back a bit and then lift it up and off.

Toolless Cases

Many name-brand PCs feature a case that has one or two large knobby screws on the back panel of the case. This case design is called "toolless" because you should be able to remove and replace the screws with your fingers without the need for a screwdriver or other tools. The cover pieces are held firmly in place by spring clips that apply pressure to chassis points.

Screwless Cases

Screwless case covers have several individual cover pieces, generally one piece to a side. The key to removing this type of case cover is to remove the locking panel, which is usually the front panel, to unlock the remaining panels of the case. The front panel is attached by a spring clip. Pull up and lift off one or more of the hooklike tabs built into the chassis, as shown in Figure 13.6. After the front panel is removed, remove the top, typically by lifting it straight up, and then remove the sides, one at a time, if needed.

Photo courtesy of In-Win Development, Inc.

Figure 13.5   A PC in a midtower case design.

Figure 13.6   A toolless case design is secured with one or more large screws.

Some screwless cases have a cut-in indentation at the bottom of the front panel that can be used to grasp the edge of the panel to pull it up. On those with no such handhold, you may need to use a small screwdriver or pry tool to pull the front panel up enough to gain a grasp of its edge. One minor drawback to a screwless case is that you have several case parts to track instead of just the one-piece desktop case.

Release-Button Cases

On release-button cases, which are common on Compaq desktop models, the case is removed by pressing springed release buttons located on the front or rear of the PC. When you press the release buttons, the cover, which includes the front, rear, top, and sides, lifts straight off the case.

A case with a similar design is called the "flip-top" case. This case design also uses release buttons to unlock the cover, but instead of the entire top lifting off, the top cover lifts up like a top-loading washer. If, for some reason, you need to remove the entire case, strategically placed screws can be removed to release the entire cover.

Front-Screw Cases

On front-screw cases, the screws that hold the cover on the PC are located on the front panel, usually hidden behind sliding tabs or a snap-on panel. Remove the screws (and possibly some on the rear panel as well) and pull the case forward and off.

The Front Panel

The primary purpose of the *front panel*, or the *bezel*, as it is also called, is to cover up the front end of the chassis, but because it is the part that the user looks at most of the time, efforts have been made to make it useful and appealing, as illustrated in Figure 13.7.

Some PCs feature doors and snap-on panels to mask disk drives, the power and reset switches, and even the LEDs on the front of the PC. Typically, doors on the front panel are a characteristic of larger PCs and network servers. Figure 13.8 shows a server with two doors, one for the removable drives and the other to cover the normal parts of the front panel. This computer also features a key lock for the doors, to provide a small amount of security.

Photo courtesy of Rainer Company.

Figure 13.7   A unique front panel design by ColorCase that should appeal to cat lovers.

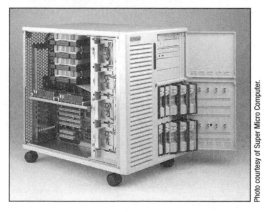

Photo courtesy of Super Micro Computer.

Figure 13.8   A WTX form factor computer with two front panel doors.

Status LEDs

Most PCs have LEDs (light-emitting diodes) on the front panel to show the status and activity of certain parts of the system. Typically, there are two LEDs: one that is lighted when the power is on and one that indicates when the hard disk is being accessed. The other LEDs visible on the front of the PC are generally part of the disk drive installed in a drive bay. Very old PCs also have a Turbo LED that indicates the system is in Turbo mode, which raises the processor speed of a PC. Turbo systems are generally obsolete now.

The following list provides a quick overview of the front panel's LEDs:

- *Power LED*—The power LED is typically green and is illuminated when the PC power is on.

- *Hard drive LED*—When the disk drive is seeking, reading, or writing data, this red, orange, or amber LED flashes. The speed with which the hard drive LED flashes is a good indicator of how busy the PC may be. Typically, this LED is wired to the motherboard or the disk controller or adapter, which means that it reflects the activity of all disk drives on the PC.

- *Turbo LED*—If present, this yellow LED indicates that the PC is in Turbo mode. The Turbo button was used on very early systems as a part of a backward compatibility strategy. But there wasn't a lot of software available to begin with, and when the 8MHz systems were released, many people had a fair investment in software that would run only in the older 4.77MHz, or PC XT mode. The normal mode on these systems, 286 and 386 processors, was Turbo mode. However, when the Turbo button was released, two things happened: The PC processor was slowed to 4.77MHz and the Turbo LED was turned off.

Switches

Nearly all PCs now have at least one main switch (usually the power switch) on the front panel of the PC. Some older designs have two switches: the power switch and a reset switch. Figure 13.9 shows a PC front panel with its power reset switch.

Power Switch

On older PCs, the power switch was a part of the power supply and extended through the case wall on the right-rear corner of the PC. On newer PCs, the power switch is on the front panel.

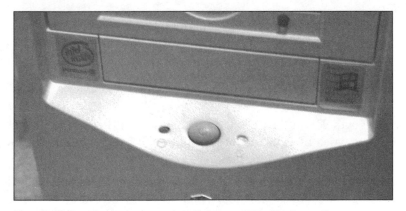

Figure 13.9   The power reset switch on a PC's front panel.

On Baby AT and earlier systems, the power switch located on the front panel is not a switch in the sense of a physical on/off switch. It is actually a proxy switch that transfers a press on the front panel switch to the actual power supply switch located on the back of the front panel and wired directly to the power supply.

Newer systems, such as the ATX, NLX, and LPX form factors, have an actual power switch on the front panel, but instead of being wired to the power supply, the switch is now electronic and is actually connected to the motherboard. On these systems, you don't turn the computer on or off with the power switch; rather, pushing the power button sends a request to the motherboard to power off the PC.

Reset Button

Although disappearing from the PC mainly to prevent accidental resets, the *reset switch*, also referred to as the *reset button*, performs a hardware reset when pressed. This provides the user with a means of restarting the PC should it halt and not respond to normal shutdown or restart commands. Using the reset button is better than powering the PC off and back on, which can sometimes result in power-on self-test (POST) or basic input/output system (BIOS) errors.

On some older PCs, the reset button was placed on the front panel and was easily accessed, which caused more than one unexpected system reset. Newer cases, if they feature a reset button, recess the button to prevent inadvertent resets. A few manufacturers have moved the reset button to the back of the PC, which is even safer.

Some manufacturers, such as Gateway, do not include a reset button on their systems. Resetting the PC must be done via the keyboard (**CTRL+ALT+DEL**) or by using the operating system's restart process.

Turbo Button

As explained earlier (see "Status LEDs" earlier in this chapter), the Turbo button and its functions are now obsolete except on 286 and early 386 computers. If your front panel has a Turbo button, chances are it is not connected to anything and, to avoid any possible problems, you should never press it.

Keylocks

Some cases have keylocks on their front panels, although these are not technically switches. Two types of keylocks are available on PC front panels: a keyboard lockout, and a front panel door lock.

- *Keyboard lockout*—When locked, this type of keylock sets a logical condition on the system that locks out the keyboard and prevents anyone from using the PC. When someone attempts to use the PC while this keylock is locked, an error message is displayed on the monitor, that stays in effect, that the system is not available for use. While this keylock is locked, the PC will not boot. The keyboard lockout keylock was intended to be a first level of security for PCs in large offices and work areas. The key for a PC keylock is usually a round key, and many manufacturers use the same key for all of their systems, so the security it provides is limited. Anyone with a screwdriver can open the case and disable the lock, and on some cases you don't even need the screwdriver.

- *Front panel door lock*—If the front panel of your PC has one or more doors, it may also have a door lock, either on the door or on the front panel. When the doors are closed and locked, curiosity seekers are prevented from accessing the drives behind the doors. However, because the doors are made of plastic and can easily be pried open, this feature should be used or thought of merely as a means to secure the system.

If your case has a keylock or a front panel door lock, be sure that it also has keylock keys. Typically, you will get two of each key. If you plan to use them, store one of the keys in a safe place, so that if you lose the other one, you will still be able to unlock your PC.

Drive Bays

Since the time of the PC AT, you have been able to decide how many and what type of disk drives you want in your computer. As long as the power supply and cooling system would support them, you could add floppy disk drives, hard disk drives, CD-ROM drives, tape drives, and more to your PC.

Generally, drives are installed in the drive bays provided on virtually all PC case designs and form factors. Figure 13.10 shows a desktop computer with its drive bays exposed. This system, an ATX case from Enlight Corporation, provides three 5.25-inch "half-height" drive bays, two 3.5-inch one-inch-high drive bays, and two 3.5-inch drive bays hidden inside the case.

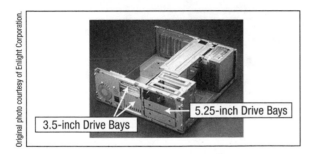

Original photo courtesy of Enlight Corporation.

3.5-inch Drive Bays

5.25-inch Drive Bays

Figure 13.10   The drive bays of an ATX desktop chassis.

Originally, disk drives required a drive bay that was 3.5-inches in height. As technology was able to reduce the size of the overall drive, this height was cut in half, and now most of the drive bays available for 5.25-inch devices are less than 2 inches in height, and are called *half-height* drive bays.

Internal versus External Bays

Two types of drive bays, external and internal, are available:

- *External drive bays*—These drive bays are actually internal to the case and chassis, but they can be accessed externally, which is why these physically internal drive bays are called "external." External drive bays are typically used for drives that have removable media, such as floppy disks, CD-ROMs, DVDs, tape drives, and the like.

- *Internal drive bays*—Internal bays are completely inside the system case and have no access from outside the chassis, as shown in Figure 13.11. These bays are designed for devices, primarily hard disk drives, with no need for external exposure. Simply put, internal drive bays are for hard disks.

Internal devices can be installed in external bays. Before internal bays were common, hard disk drives were installed in the external bays, the only kind available, and a solid face plate was put over the external opening of the bay to hide the drive.

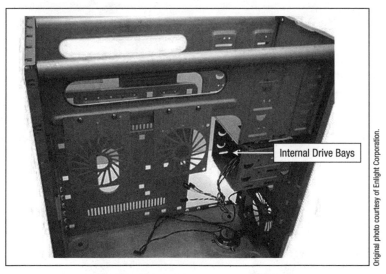

Figure 13.11   Internal drive bays inside a chassis.

Mounting Rails

A device can be mounted in a drive bay by either of two methods, whether that device is internal or external. One way is by using drive rails, and the other is by mounting the device directly to the walls of the drive bay (sidewall mounting).

- *Drive rails*—Drive rails are two strips of metal mounted to the sides of the disk drive. With the drive rails attached, a device is placed into the drive bay with the rails sliding into notches or facets on the sidewalls of the bay. The device is suspended from the rails, which are then secured to the walls of the bay.

- *Sidewall mounting*—Sidewall mounting is the method used in most newer cases. It involves attaching the disk drive to the sidewalls of the drive bay. Screws are placed through holes in the sidewall that match the standard placement and spacing of prethreaded holes on the sides of the disk drive. The drive is solidly attached to the chassis.

Drive Cages

A newer feature on system cases is the snap-in cage for internal drive bays, such as those shown in Figure 13.11. To install a hard disk in an internal cage, remove the cage, install the drive, and snap the cage and drive assembly back into place. If you use a cage to install an internal drive, think ahead to the cables and connectors that may be added later and the process that will be needed to remove the drive for servicing.

System Case Styles

The two basic styles of PC cases are the *desktop case* and the *tower case*. Figure 13.12 shows a family of PC cases from Enlight Corporation that includes both tower and desktop styles. The tall, thin one is the tower case style, and the flat,

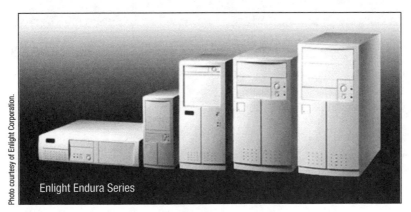

Photo courtesy of Enlight Corporation.

Enlight Endura Series

Figure 13.12   A family of PC cases.

boxy one is the desktop case style. At one time, these two case styles were actually very much alike and, in fact, the tower came about because people trying to save space turned their desktop PCs on their sides. Today, these case styles are very distinctive, with their internal designs, the way the case is attached, and the features each supports.

Desktop versus Tower

Which case style is right for a particular setting really depends on how it is to be used and, frankly, the setting itself. Tower cases are designed to sit on the floor or large shelves. Desktops are designed to sit on desks, which is how they got their name. A tower case does free up desktop space, but if the space on the floor is limited, this type of case can get in the way, get kicked, or be knocked over. The desktop cases of today are a lot smaller (shorter and narrower) than they were when the PC was first moved off the desktop.

The two case styles really aren't interchangeable, despite the claims of the vendors selling conversion kits. Turning a desktop PC on its side changes the orientation of the removable media drives, namely the CD-ROM, DVD, and other such drives. If you wish to move from a desktop to a tower, or vice versa, you should purchase the appropriate case and convert the PC into the new case.

Desktop Cases

Although the desktop case style has become less popular in recent years, it is still generally available from most PC manufacturers and resellers. Because it also doubles as the base for the PC's monitor, the desktop case is actually more space efficient than the mid-sized tower model. Some tower styles are small enough to sit on a desktop, but they cannot hold the monitor and therefore end up using more space than a desktop unit would. The desktop PC is better suited than a PC in a tower case primarily in situations for which floor space is limited.

Until about the last year or so, the desktop case style had been the unofficial standard for PC cases. The first PCs, the PC XT and PC AT, were desktop units. The desktop cases of today are smaller than those of the original PC AT and its clones. The common desktop form factor is the Baby AT and now the LPX low profile case, which is also known as the "pizza box" case. Newer slimline cases, such as the NLX, which was designed to replace the LPX, are becoming more popular.

Tower Cases

Today, the tower case style is far more popular than the desktop case style. This is largely because a tower case can sit under a desk to free up workspace on the desk, and it provides more space inside the case for upgrading the PC.

The three most popular tower case sizes are the mini-tower, the mid-tower, and full-tower. In addition, the midi-tower represents a size between the mid-tower and mini-tower.

- *Full-tower*—Full-tower cases are the largest standard PC cases available. They offer the most of any case style in the way of expandability, typically having three to five external drive bays as well as a few internal bays (see Figure 13.13). A full-tower case will normally have a high-end power supply, under the assumption that the case will be filled with devices. This style of case is popular among high-end users and for servers.

- *Mid-tower*—A mid-tower case is a slightly shorter version of the full-tower case. This particular size seems to vary the most among manufacturers, but within a single manufacturer's line, it represents a good compromise of size and price. For example, the mid-tower case shown in Figure 13.14, from In-Win Development (**www.inwin.com**), provides five external drive bays and can accommodate either ATX or full AT form factor system boards, which should provide room enough for most applications.

- *Midi-tower*—By definition, a midi-tower is smaller than a mid-tower and larger than a mini-tower. However, what you will typically find advertised as a midi-tower is either a small mid-tower or a large mini-tower or, as is available from one manufacturer, a mini-mid-tower. Regardless of the case's style name, if it fits your needs, than it is the right one.

Photo courtesy of PC Power and Cooling, Inc.

Figure 13.13 A full-tower case featuring 10 external drive bays.

Photo courtesy of In-Win Development, Inc.

Figure 13.14   A mid-tower case.

- *Mini-tower*—This case size is probably the most popular currently. It provides slightly more expansion capacity than desktop cases and is small enough to sit on a desktop next to the monitor. If you are considering converting a desktop case to a tower, this would be an excellent and economical choice (they run around $25 or less). Figure 13.15 shows a mini-tower case.

Variations on these sizes exist among manufacturers because there are no standard sizes associated with these case styles. Figure 13.16 shows a tower case family from one vendor, HungTech Industrial, and Figure 13.12 showed that of Enlight Corporation. What one vendor calls a mini-tower, another may call a mini-mid-tower.

Photo courtesy of AOpen, Inc.

Figure 13.15   A mini-tower case.

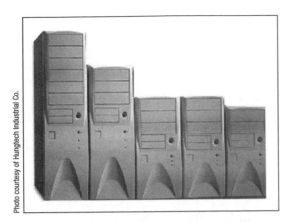

Figure 13.16   A family of computer cases showing a full AT tower on the left down to an ATX mini-tower on the right.

When buying a PC, first pick the brand you wish to buy, if you have a preference, and then look at the form factor, sizes, and styles of cases available. With a tower case, the primary difference among models is usually the number of external drive bays and the size of the power supply. As the number of external bays increases, the case gets taller and usually the power supply gets more powerful.

Rackmount Cases
Another type of case that has usage in special purpose or networking applications is the rackmount case. This case is designed to be attached to the rails of a rackmount cabinet or a rackmount stand. Figure 13.17 shows a rackmount PC with its cover opened.

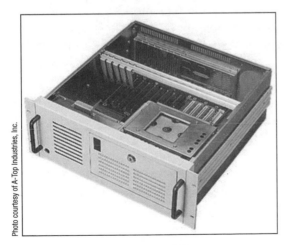

Figure 13.17   A rackmount PC case.

System Case Form Factors

As mentioned previously, the *form factor* of a PC case defines its style, size, shape, internal organization, and its compatible components. Computer form factors define a general standard for compatibility for the system case, the motherboard, the power supply, and the placement of I/O (input/output) ports and connectors, among other factors.

The three most popular types of case form factors are the Baby AT, ATX, and NLX.

- *Baby AT*—Although virtually obsolete by today's standards, the Baby AT form factor still has a very large installed base from its popularity in past years.

- *ATX*—The ATX form factor is the *de facto* standard for motherboards, power supplies, and system cases. Virtually all Pentium-based systems use the ATX form factor.

- *NLX*—The NLX form factor, which is also called the slimline form factor, is popular for mass-produced desktop systems.

Some of the other form factors that have been used or are still in use for system cases include:

- *PC XT*—This form factor was used on the original desktop PCs, the IBM PC and its successor, the PC XT. The case was made of heavy-gauge steel and was U-shaped. It was fastened on the rear of the PC and was removed over the front of the case. The power supply had 130 watts (only 63.5 watts on the PC) and was located at the rear of the case with a power switch that protruded through a cutout on the case.

- *AT*—The IBM PC AT, although not much different on the outside from its predecessors, was quite different on the inside. The motherboard and power supply, which were much larger, were repositioned inside the case. The AT quickly became the standard form factor among manufacturers, and all subsequent form factors—desktop or tower—are based in one way or another on the AT.

- *LPX*—Although never officially accepted as a standard form factor, the LPX is the oldest of the "low profile" form factors. Over the past 10 years, it has been one of the most popular slimline form factors sold. Slimline cases are a little shorter than Baby AT or ATX cases. This lower profile is achieved by moving expansion cards to a riser board that mounts horizontally instead of vertically in the case, thereby saving inches of height.

- *MicroATX* and *FlexATX*—These two ATX-based form factors define specifications for smaller versions of the ATX motherboard. MicroATX and FlexATX do not define case form factors, but manufacturers are designing cases to

Figure 13.18   In-Win's FlexATX case.

take advantage of their smaller footprint. These form factors are intended for PCs targeted to the mass market and home users. Figure 13.18 shows In-Win's FlexATX PC case, which is designed for mass-market appeal.

- *WTX*—The W stands for workstation. This is a form factor intended for high-performance workstations and servers. This form factor defines a modular case that features a motherboard twice the size of an ATX motherboard. A WTX case features space for high-capacity, redundant power supplies, removable panels for easy access to components, a large number of hard drive bays, and support for multiple cooling fans. Figure 13.8 shows a WTX form factor computer.

For more information on PC form factors as they relate to motherboards and power supplies, see Chapters 1 and 14, respectively.

System Case Features

When you buy a system case, such as the one shown in Figure 13.19 without its covers, it will include some preinstalled components and features, which are usually the optional pieces that conform a generic case to fit a particular form factor and your particular requirements. Because several of the form factors are very close in their size and component placement, manufacturers make cases that can be used with a number of form factors. By applying items such as an I/O template, the appropriate power supply, and motherboard mounts, the generic case can be turned into a custom case that is just right for your needs.

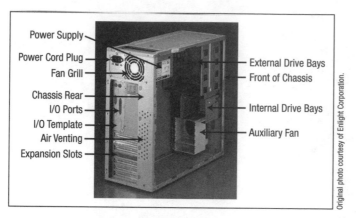

Figure 13.19   An ATX case and its components.

I/O Templates

Each motherboard form factor also defines the location and placement of the ports used for such input/output devices as the keyboard, mouse, printer, and others. For the most part, these ports are connected either directly or indirectly to the motherboard. Directly connected ports are physically mounted on the motherboard. The case must accommodate these ports with a hole in the right shape and place so the port can be accessed through the case. Indirectly connected ports mount to the case and are attached to the motherboard with a cable. Either way, the case has to either be manufactured with the portholes already in place or provide an adapter for this purpose.

Older form factor cases, such as the PC XT, AT, Baby AT, and the LPX, were manufactured with holes cut into the rear panel of the case to match a particular form factor. However, to make cases more flexible and allow them to service more than a single form factor, manufacturers devised I/O templates, which can be snapped into a case to provide the desired I/O port pattern. Figures 13.20 and 13.21 illustrate what the templates look like out of the box and where on the case an I/O template is located.

A current trend among case manufacturers is to leave a punch-out or knockout slug in the I/O ports on the I/O template, as shown in Figure 13.22, and in the expansion slots. If you are not using a port or slot, you can leave the slug in place. However, be sure you ask and understand how this affects the case cooling before assuming it is a part of the overall case design.

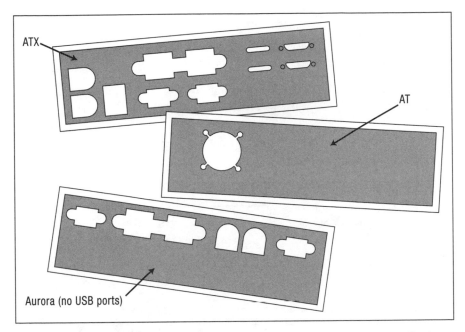

ATX

AT

Aurora (no USB ports)

Figure 13.20   I/O templates are used to custom fit a generic case to a particular form factor.

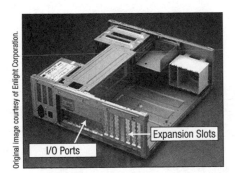

Original image courtesy of Enlight Corporation.

Expansion Slots

I/O Ports

Figure 13.21   The location of I/O ports and expansion slots on an ATX desktop chassis.

Power Supply

Most system cases come with a power supply (see Figure 13.23) matched to its form factor, but not all cases do. The power supply is not a part of the case, even though the two are generally sold together as one assembly. Be sure, when buying a PC case, that a power supply that is appropriate for your application is included, or that a power supply is not included, if you wish. Many case manufacturers sell

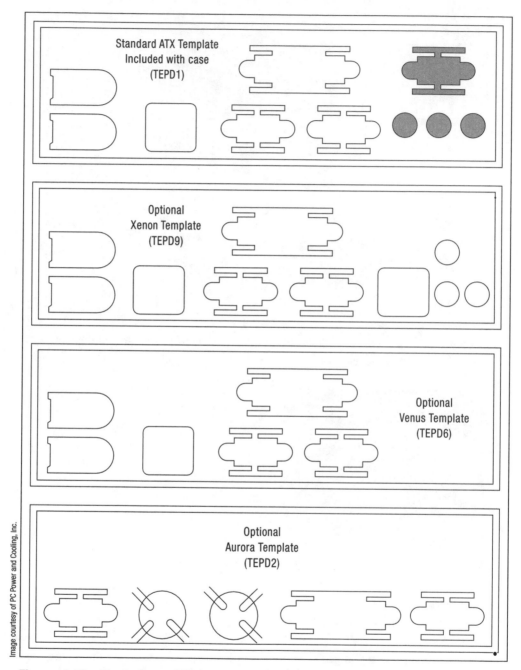

Standard ATX Template
Included with case
(TEPD1)

Optional
Xenon Template
(TEPD9)

Optional
Venus Template
(TEPD6)

Optional
Aurora Template
(TEPD2)

Image courtesy of PC Power and Cooling, Inc.

Figure 13.22   Illustrations of I/O templates showing the port slugs in place.

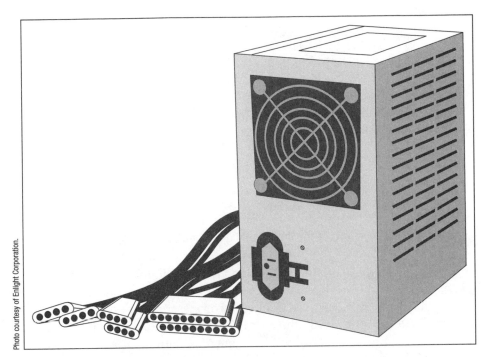

Photo courtesy of Enlight Corporation.

Figure 13.23   A power supply may be purchased separate from the system case.

their cases *a la carte*, and you can select the options and power supply to meet your needs. See Chapter 14 for more information on power supplies.

Auxiliary Fans

The main cooling fan in the PC is in the power supply, which is an important reason why you should match the power supply to the form factor of the motherboard and case, in that order. Many newer case form factors provide a location for an auxiliary or supplemental fan to help cool the inside of the PC. Typically, the location of the auxiliary fan, if available, will be on the front or back panel opposite from the main cooling fan, as shown in Figure 13.24.

LEDs, the Speaker, and Some Connecting Wires

The other components of a PC case are the LEDs, the system speaker, and the wiring that connects these two items, plus a few more, to the power supply and motherboard.

- *LEDs*—Most PC cases include at least two LEDs that are used as indicators for the power and hard disk. Some cases may have other LEDs, although fairly uncommon today, for Turbo mode and the CPU's activity level.

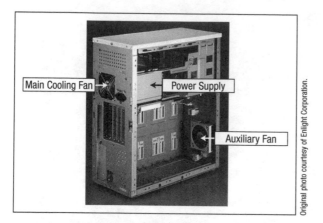

Figure 13.24   The locations of the main cooling fan and an auxiliary fan on an NLX case.

- *System speaker*—The system speaker is not intended for stereo sound or to play your audio CDs. It is meant only to be a basic means of communication between the motherboard, BIOS, chipset, processor, and other system components and the user. About the best it can do is sound beep codes during the boot and other monotone sounds by some application software. The system speaker is normally mounted inside the case near or on the front panel. On a new case, it may be included loose, allowing you to place it where you wish.

- *Front panel wiring*—On the back of the front panel, near the system speaker, the LEDs, and the keylock, should be a small bundle of multicolored wires that connect these items to the motherboard, and perhaps each other. The LEDs should have two wires: one that is either black or white (ground) and one that is some other color (positive).

Cooling Vents

Although it may seem obvious, air must have a means to get into or out of the system case. Usually, the case should have a grouping of small vent holes, cuts, louvers, or the like. A bigger case cools the internal components better than a smaller case because of its larger airflow, but both must still have a way to vent the case. You can assume that any case you buy from a reputable manufacturer, such as those that have been kind enough to supply figures for this chapter, have engineered their cases to properly cool them.

When assembling a system case and its components, be aware of where the vents are and take care not to block them.

Mounting Hardware

Any new case should come with mounting hardware. These pieces normally come with the case, and *not* the motherboard. Make sure you have the appropriate mounting hardware, or your PC building project will come to a halt. The exact hardware included varies greatly and depends on what the manufacturer decided to include in the case, but you will generally find some combination of the following:

- *Plastic standoffs*—These small plastic parts are also called spacers, risers, and sliders. The standoffs used inside the case to mount the motherboard are typically small plastic legs that snap into the mounting holes on the motherboard and then slide into the mounting slots on the case. In addition to anchoring the motherboard in place, the standoffs keep the motherboard from contacting the system case and grounding or shorting itself.

- *Metal standoffs*—Metal standoffs are rarely used for two reasons: They are a bother to work with and they cost more than the plastic type. However, if your case has threaded holes in place of mounting slots, these brass hexagon spacers need to be used. The standoff has screw threads on one end and a threaded screw hole on the other end. The screw end is screwed into the case; then the motherboard, along with some insulating Teflon, Delran, or paper washers, is attached to the other end with a screw. The washers are placed between the standoff and the motherboard and between the motherboard and the screw. This keeps the metal-edged mounting hole from contacting the screw and standoff and prevents it from shorting the board.

- *Fixed mounting hardware*—Some cases already have their mounting hardware fixed (meaning soldered or welded) in place to match the mounting holes of a motherboard of the same form factor as the case. This is intended to save you time, but if you ever want to move to another form factor motherboard, you'll need a new case.

Immediate Solutions

Preparing a New Case for the Installation of the Motherboard

If you are building a new PC from the ground (or from the case) up, you must first perform the following steps to prepare the case to accept the motherboard.

1. Open the case by removing the cover piece that exposes the inside of the case. The case should come with a manual that has instructions (and ideally, illustrations) on how to do this.

2. The case should have one or more plastic bags of parts you will need to assemble the case and to mount other system components in the case. At a minimum, you should have:

   - *Mounting hardware* for the motherboard, which are either plastic or metal standoffs or spacers.

   - *Metal slot inserts*, which are used to close any unused expansion slots in the back of the case. These may already be installed.

   - *Rubber feet* for the bottom of the case, which may already be attached.

   - *Drive cages* (if the case supports them) or drive rails.

   - *Power supply AC cord*, if a power supply is included with the case. If not, you will need to install one before installing any other components to the case.

3. Use compressed air to blow out any packing materials or dust in a new case.

4. Check the power supply for apparent damage. Check the cables, fan, and its casing. Make sure the voltage selector is set appropriately for your power source.

5. Install the feet if they are not already installed. Once the motherboard is installed, this may not be as easy as it is at this time.

6. Install the slot inserts into the expansion slots. This step can wait until after the expansion slots are installed, if you prefer.

7. Install any auxiliary fans you wish to use, if the case supports them.

8. If the case has a removable or swing-out motherboard panel, remove it (see the case's documentation) so you can install the motherboard to it outside of the case.

Lighting Up the Front-Panel LEDs

If the front-panel LEDs do not light up, the problem is most likely that the front-panel LEDs are not connected or have been connected incorrectly. The good news about connecting the front panel LEDs is that if you do it wrong, all that will happen is they won't light up.

The front-panel LEDs have a ground wire. The ground wire is either a black or white wire attached to a one-pin push-on connector that is connected to the motherboard's LED ground connector, which should be marked on the motherboard. The positive wire, of some other color, such as red, blue, or green, is connected to the motherboard's LED connector. It too is a one-pin push-on connector. These connectors are usually located along the front or side edge of the motherboard. Check the motherboard's documentation for the location of these connectors if you cannot find them.

Try reversing the wires of the bad LED or exchanging the wires of two or more of the LEDs. Chances are you will find a combination that works.

Producing Sound from the System Speaker

If no sound is coming from the system speaker, the problem is very likely that the speaker has not been connected to the motherboard or the connectors are plugged in incorrectly.

Like the LED wires covered in the preceding solution, the system speaker has two wires that connect to the motherboard with either a single four-pin connector or two one-pin connectors. If you get the connectors on backwards or off to one side or the other, the worst that can happen is that it just will not work. You won't damage the speaker by connecting it wrong.

Possibly the speaker is defective. If the wiring looks right and checks against the documentation, try using the speaker in a new PC or using a new speaker in this PC.

Restarting the PC with the Reset Button

If the PC has a reset button, it should restart the PC when pressed. If nothing happens when you press this button, the wires that connect the reset button to the motherboard probably were not installed, were not installed properly, have come loose, or there is a problem with the motherboard that you will just have to accept. Check the motherboard's documentation to verify the location of the connector for the reset button's wiring and verify that it is properly connected.

Making the Power On/Off Button Work

Before you do very much to troubleshoot the problem when the power on/off button does not work, make sure you know which case, motherboard, and power supply form factors you have. ATX form factor motherboards and power supplies pass live AC through to the on/off switches that are on the front panel, and getting these connections wrong can be dangerous to the motherboard and to you.

Follow the instructions in the motherboard's documentation for connecting these switches or the instructions in the case's documentation for the front panel switches. An ATX power supply does not have a front panel cable and may not have an on/off switch of its own. An ATX motherboard controls the power supply with a logic circuit that turns it on and off. The switch on the front panel sends a signal to the motherboard, which relays it the power supply. The ATX motherboard always has at least 5 volts of standby power on it, even when the power supply is off.

Figuring Out Why Putting the Monitor on the System Case Halts the PC

If the PC freezes, reboots, or powers off whenever you sit anything, especially the monitor, on top of the case, chances are that something is causing the motherboard to touch the case and short out, which should happen not very long after the system boots, if it will boot. The weight of the monitor or other object is apparently too much for the case's structure and is causing it to bend or flex.

Another possibility is that in some weird way the monitor or whatever else you are putting on the case is changing the airflow inside the system case and causing the processor or motherboard to overheat. The processor and chipset will shut down when they approach operating temperatures outside their normal ranges.

Check to see that the monitor is sitting evenly in the center of the case or over the main structural points of the case. Avoid sitting the monitor off to one side or on a corner of the case.

Try operating the system without the monitor on top of the case. If it works fine, then the case just isn't strong enough to hold the monitor, especially if it is a 17-inch monitor or larger. If workspace is an issue, several types of monitor stands are available that are similar to bridges placed over the PC's system unit to hold the monitor. You can also place the monitor on a swing arm mount that connects to the desk.

If the halting problem continues, investigate a cooling issue or perhaps a faulty power supply. You may try rearranging the cables inside the case to open up some airflow, or perhaps, if the case supports it, you may want to add an auxiliary fan.

Chapter 14

Power Supply and Electrical Issues

In Depth

PC Power Supply

Because a computer is an electrical device, and digital logic circuits require a nonfluctuating direct current (DC), a "switching" power supply is used to convert an alternating current (AC) power source to the DC power it needs. The electronic components of the PC, such as the processor and memory, require +3.3V (volts) DC or +5V DC; hard disk drives and other permanent storage devices need +12V DC.

Functions and Signals

The primary functions of a PC power supply are voltage conversion, rectification, filtering, regulation, isolation, cooling, and power management.

- *Voltage conversion*—This function involves changing the 110V AC primary power source into the +12V DC and +5V DC used by many older systems and the +3.3V DC used by most newer computers. During the reign of the 486, +3.3V DC processors were introduced; voltage regulators on the motherboard were used to reduce the DC current to this level. However, power supplies that now provide +3.3V DC are common.

- *Rectification*—This function is directly involved with converting the AC power of the power source to the DC power needed by the PC's components.

- *Filtering*—Rectification usually introduces a ripple in the DC voltage, which filtering smoothes out.

- *Regulation*—Along with filtering, voltage regulation removes any line or load variations in the DC voltage produced by the power supply.

- *Isolation*—Isolation refers to separating the AC power supply from the converted, rectified, filtered, and regulated DC power.

- *Cooling*—The system fan, which controls the airflow through the system case, is located inside the power supply.

- *Power management*—Most computers produced in the past few years have included energy-efficiency tools and power management functions that help reduce the amount of electrical power used by the PC. These power supplies also comply with the new so-called "green" standards that have established energy reduction and consumption goals for personal computers and monitors. The Energy Star program of the U. S. Environmental Protection Agency (EPA) is an example of these standards.

In those areas of the world where the power source is already a direct current, the power supply performs all of the same tasks, except rectification. Most power supplies have the ability to take either a 110V AC input or a 220V DC input, and have a slide switch on the outside by the fan grill to select the appropriate power source voltage. Choosing the wrong voltage setting can prove catastrophic to a power supply and very likely the PC's internal components as well.

Good Power

In addition to providing converted power to the motherboard and the other parts of the PC, the power supply sends a very important signal to the motherboard through its umbilical connection—the **Power_Good** (or **Pwr_OK** on an ATX form factor power supply) signal.

When the PC is powered on, the power supply performs a self test and checks to see if the required voltages (in and out) are correct. If so, the Power_Good signal line is set high (on) to indicate that the motherboard can rely on the power being supplied. If the signal is not set, the processor's timing chip (to which this signal line is attached) will send the processor a Reset command that starts the basic input/output (BIOS) initialization code. The effect of the Power_Good signal not being set is that the PC is trapped in a loop continuously calling the BIOS. In this situation, the power supply appears to be working, and some power is being supplied to the PC and its peripherals. The front panel lights may be on, the disk drives spinning, and the power supply fan running, but the BIOS will never reach the power-on self-test (POST) process and will appear to be hung up on something.

Power On and Off

On ATX, NLX, and most of the other later form factors, the motherboard can turn the power supply on or off. This is done through the **PS_ON** (power supply on) signal that passes between the motherboard and the power supply. If your PC powers off when Windows is finished shutting down, you have this feature.

Another indicator that your power supply supports **PS_ON** is the use of Momentary On or Always On power switches that are connected to the motherboard in place of an exterior switch connected to the power supply. When this signal line is pulled to a low voltage signal, the +12V DC, +5V DC, +3.3V DC, –5V DC, and –12V DC power lines (see Figures 14.1 and 14.2) are turned on. When it is pulled to a high-voltage signal, or open-circuited, the DC output lines should no longer have current. The +5V DC output is always on as long as the power supply is receiving AC power. Because the ATL, NLX, LTX, and other form factor motherboards have some power running to them at all times, you will always want to unplug the PC before working on it.

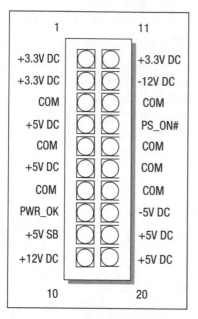

Figure 14.1   ATX/NLX power supply to motherboard connector and pin outs.

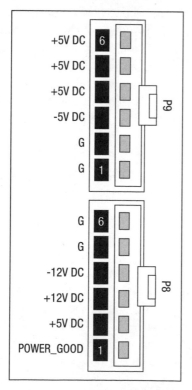

Figure 14.2   AT style power connectors and pin outs.

Figures 14.1 and 14.2 show the two most popular connector types used to supply power to the motherboard from the power supply. Figure 14.1 shows the connector used in the ATX and NLX form factors, and Figure 14.2 shows the two connectors used on the AT, Baby AT, and other AT-based forms. Notice on each diagram the separate wires used to deliver different voltages for different parts of the PC.

Power Supply Components

A PC power supply is technically a *switching power supply*. A switching power supply uses high-frequency switching devices such as bipolar junction transistors (BJT)—also known as "normal" transistors—metallic oxide semiconductor field effect transistors (MOSFET), insulated gate bipolar transistors, and silicon controlled rectifier (SCR) thyristors in combination to condition the converted power into pulsed waveform.

The following quick overview describes what these electronic switching devices are.

- *Bipolar transistor*—An active semiconductor device that amplifies an electrical current.
- *Metal oxide semiconductor field effect transistor*—A transistor type that uses a layer of oxide as insulation between its conducting channel and gate terminal.
- *Silicon controlled rectifier*—A thyristor type designed specifically for undirectional power switching and control.
- *Thyristor*—A semiconductor device that can be switched between off and on states. Thyristors are used for power switching applications.

Generally, you won't interact directly with these components, but you may come across these terms when reading up on PC power supplies.

After the AC signal is rectified (see Figure 14.3), the output is a 150V to 160V DC pulsed waveform current. At this point, a high-frequency transformer converts the pulsed waveform into the multiple output voltages needed by the PC, which are then rectified and filtered using a capacitor. A feedback signal controls the pulse frequency and width of the switching devices to maintain the proper voltage outputs.

Voltages

The PC power supply provides multiple voltage levels to the motherboard and to connected peripherals such as the disk drives. Each device and component in the PC is designed to operate on a certain DC voltage level, and the power supply rectifies the AC power input into these separate voltages. The various voltages typically provided by a power supply are:

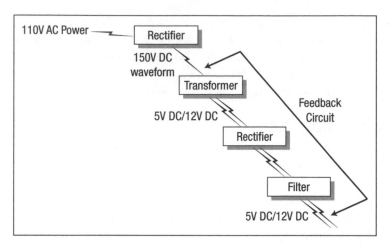

Figure 14.3   A simplified view of the power conversion process in a power supply.

- *±0V DC*—Circuits with zero volts DC provide the ground used to complete circuits with the other voltages on a PC. This is also referred to as the *common* or *earth ground*.

- *+3.3V DC*—This voltage is common on the ATX, NLX, and other newer form factors to provide power to Pentium central processing units (CPUs), memory, accelerated graphics ports (AGPs), and the other components on the motherboard. Before the ATX form factor, voltage regulators on the motherboard were used to reduce +5V DC to +3.3V DC.

- *+5V DC*—Prior to the second generation of Pentium processors, this was the primary voltage on the motherboard for the CPU and most of its attached components. This is the standard voltage on Baby AT power supplies and those preceding it. Most newer systems now use +3.3V DC.

- *–5V DC*—This voltage level is now essentially obsolete. It was used on some of the earliest PCs for floppy disk controllers and Industry Standard Architecture (ISA) bus cards. For backward compatibility purposes, most power supplies still generate this voltage, but it mostly goes unused.

- *+12V DC*—This voltage level is used to power devices directly connected to the power supply, such as disk drive motors, the main cooling fan, and other similar devices. It is in most cases not used by the motherboard in a modern PC but is passed on to the system bus slots for any cards that might need it. Of course, drives are connected directly to the power supply through their own connectors.

- *–12V DC*—Like –5V, this voltage is a holdover from earlier systems, where it was used for some serial ports. Most power supplies provide this voltage for backward compatibility with older hardware.

Form Factors

Power supplies, like motherboards (see Chapter 1), are available in a variety of different form factors, typically matching the form factor of the motherboard and system case. With the exception of the early IBM PCs, most AT-class power supplies, which include those for the AT, Baby AT, ATX, and others, are roughly the same, differing only in their size and mounting requirements.

The size and shape of the system case has a direct bearing on the capabilities demanded of its power supply. Tower cases (see Chapter 13 for more information on system cases) are usually larger and require more watts of power output to run their hard drives, cooling systems, and accessories. Desktop or mini-tower cases are smaller overall and usually have fewer internal devices needing power, which means that fewer watts of output are needed from the power supply.

In general, a power supply's *form factor* refers to its general physical shape, fit, and size. A power supply's form factor must be the same as the system case and, in most instances, the same as the motherboard. Because the power supply is typically purchased as a part of the system case, matching the two is rarely an issue. Only when a power supply must be replaced is its form factor, and that of the case and motherboard, a concern. However, newer designs of power supplies are compatible with more than one case form factor, and newer cases can take any one of many power supply form factors. Care must be taken, however, to match the power requirements of the motherboard to the power supply.

The following list overviews each of the form factors of the past and present:

- *PC XT*—The IBM PC and the IBM PC XT (extended technology) established the first form factor for power supplies, as well as for cases and motherboards. These desktop systems placed the power supply in the rear-right corner of the case, and an up-and-down toggle switch on the exterior of the power supply was used to power it on and off. The PC XT power supply (Figure 14.4) was used in many early clones as well.

- *PC AT*—The power supply of the IBM PC AT (advanced technology) (see Figure 14.5) was a little larger, had a slightly different shape, and had about three times the power wattage of the PC XT. The AT standard soon became the form factor of choice among clone manufacturers, who built a wide variety of AT-compatible systems. The AT form factor was the foundation of several form factors that followed.

- *Baby AT*—This form factor is a smaller version of the AT form factor. The Baby AT power supply (see Figure 14.6) is only 2 inches narrower than the AT, with the same height and depth. It is also compatible with the AT form factor, in either tower or desktop case styles. The Baby AT has the same motherboard and drive power connectors as the AT. The Baby AT was the most popular form factor for most of the late 1980s and early 1990s.

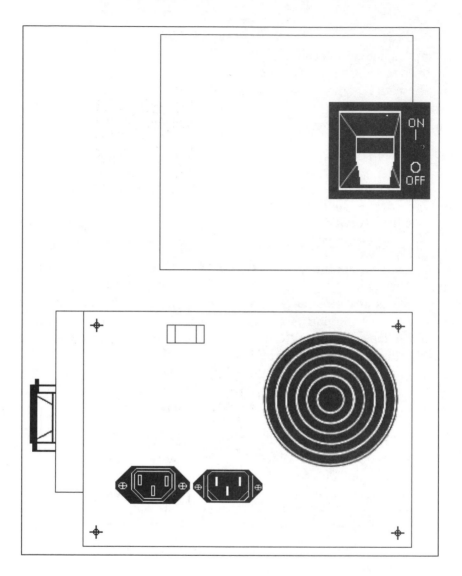

Figure 14.4   PC XT power supply.

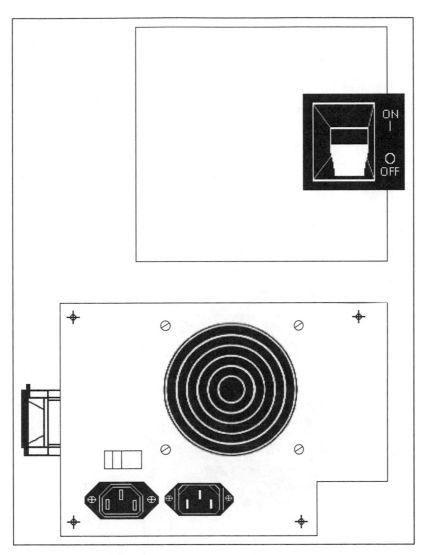

Figure 14.5   PC AT power supply.

14. Power Supply and Electrical Issues

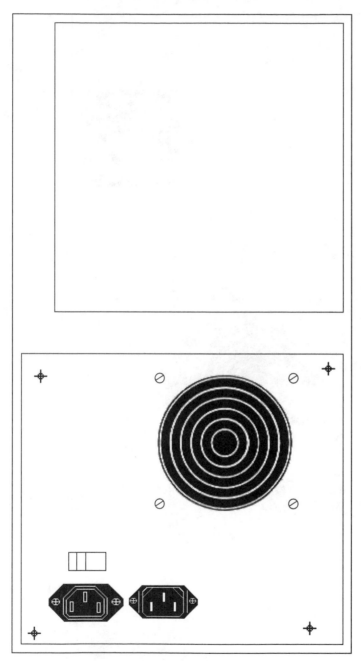

Figure 14.6   Baby AT power supply.

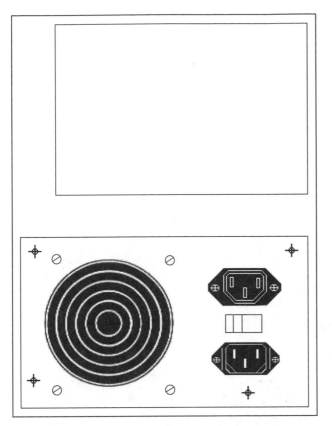

Figure 14.7   LPX (Slimline) power supply.

- *LPX*—Also known as the Slimline or PS/2 form factor, the LPX (low profile) power supply (Figure 14.7) has a reduced height and general dimension, while maintaining the same power production, cooling ability, and connectors as the Baby AT and AT. The LPX form factor has generally replaced the Baby AT.

- *ATX*—This form factor, introduced in 1995, was a major change over all previous form factors that were based on the PC XT and PC AT forms. The ATX form factor is generally considered the de facto standard for all PCs. On the outside, the ATX power supply (see Figure 14.8) is the same as the LPX power supply in size and the placement of its cables and other components. The most noticeable difference is the removal on the LPX of the AC power pass-through outlet used for PC monitors on early form factors.

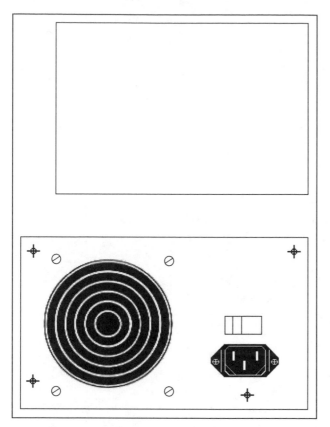

Figure 14.8   ATX/NLX power supply.

- *NLX*—The NLX form factor defines a motherboard and case design intended to replace the LPX form factor. It uses the same power supply as the ATX. Therefore, the ATX power supply form factor is also referred to as the ATX/NLX form factor.

- *SFX*—This form factor, which is one of the few power supply-only form factors, was developed by Intel for use in the microATX and FlexATX form factors. Its acronym refers to its "small form." Figure 14.9 is a diagram of the SFX power supply.

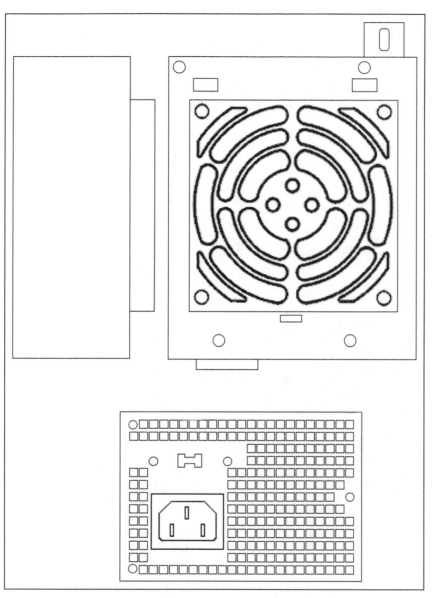

Figure 14.9   SFX power supply.

- *WTX*—The WTX form factor defines a form factor for motherboards, system cases, and power supplies for use in large workstations (which is where the W comes from) and servers. WTX is a modular design that locates parts of the PC into physical zones. The WTX power supply (see Figure 14.10) is larger and more powerful than most other power supplies. In addition to a range of power output options, it features two system cooling fans.

Figure 14.10   WTX power supply.

Table 14.1 summarizes and compares the differences of the power supply form factors just discussed. Table 14.2 lists the output voltages for each of the power supply form factors.

Table 14.1   Power supply form factor characteristics.

Form Factor	Dimensions (WxDxH) in Inches	Case Style	Form Factors	Motherboard Connection
PC XT	8.8×5.7×4.8	Desktop	PC XT	AT
AT	8.5×6×6	Desktop or Tower	AT	AT
Baby AT	6.6×6×6	Desktop or Tower	Baby AT & AT	AT
LPX	6×5.6×3.4	Desktop	LPX, Baby AT, AT, & ATX	AT
ATX/NLX	6×5.6×3.4	Desktop or Tower	ATX, NLX	ATX
SFX	4×5×2.5	Desktop or Tower	microATX, FlexATX, ATX, NLX	ATX
WTX	6×9.2×3.4 (single fan) 9×9.2×3.4 (double fan)	Tower	WTX	WTX

Table 14.2   Power supply form factor output voltages.

Form Factor	Output Voltage
PC XT	± 12V, ± 5V
AT	± 12V, ± 5V
Baby AT	± 12V, ± 5V
LPX	± 12V, ± 5V
ATX/NLX	± 12V, ± 5V, +3.3
VSFX	± 12V, +5V, +3.3V
WTX	+12V, +5V, +3.3V

Operational Ratings

On a manufacturer's specification list for a power supply, you are likely to find items such as operating range, frequency, efficiency, electromagnetic interference (EMI), output current, regulation, ripple percent, hold time, PG delay, agency approval, noise, and mean time before failure. At the very least, the operating range (or power range), outputs, and safety approval from agencies such as the Underwriters Laboratories (UL), C-UL (Canada UL), or Technischer Uberwachungs-Verein (TUV) should be listed. Some may also include their conformity with the FCC (Federal Communications Commission) radio standards or CE (European regulations) emissions standards.

The following definitions will help you with troubleshooting and help you understand the technical terms relating to power:

- *Operating range*—Operating range measures the minimum and maximum input voltages that the power supply can receive and still maintain an acceptable output voltage. A wide range denotes a power supply that can provide steady output even in areas with an unreliable or "dirty" power source.

- *Efficiency (percentage)*—Efficiency is the ratio of amount of output power that is produced to input power received.

- *Electromagnetic interference*—EMI lists the amount of electromagnetic noise generated by the power supply. The FCC puts limits on the amount of EMI a power supply can produce.

- *Output current*—The output current is the maximum current in volts that the power supply can consistently produce and supply to the motherboard (3.3V or 5V) and the hard drives (12V).

- *Line and load regulation*—Line regulation is the amount of change in the output voltage as it varies from the normal output voltage caused by fluctuations in the input voltage. Load regulation is a measure of the increase in output voltage load as a percentage of normal output voltage .

- *Ripple percent*—The amount of variance in the DC output levels due to incomplete rectification and filtering of the AC power input is called the ripple percent.

- *Hold-up time*—Hold-up time is the amount of time that output voltage continues to be provided following the loss of input voltage. This is an indication of the size of the power supply's capacitors and how much time you have until the uninterruptible power supply (UPS) takes over.

- *Power good (PG) delay*—The amount of time the power supply delays before sending the **Power_Good** signal to the motherboard is termed the PG delay. This time is necessary to allow the power supply to warm up and start producing good DC power.

- *Agency approvals*—There should be a list of test and certification agencies for the power supply. This is your assurance that the power supply meets the safety, environmental, and regulatory requirements of your country or location. Some of these agencies are the UL, CSA International, TUV, and FCC. These companies and agencies rate and certify power supply designs, radio frequency (RF) and EMI emissions, environmental issues, and product safety, among other tests.

- *Noise*—Noise is a rating in decibels (dB) of the actual noise the power supply produces. Most of the noise produced from the power supply comes from the fan. Each numerical increment denotes a doubling of the previous volume.

- *Mean time before failure*—Mean time before failure is generally an estimate based on the manufacturer's testing of how long the power supply will run before a failure. The larger this number is, the better.

Protecting the PC

The power supply accounts for nearly a third of the problems on a PC. This doesn't include the problems caused by the power supply that cannot be directly attributed to it, such as electronic components that are damaged over time by a faulty power supply. Generally, what causes the most problems with a power supply is the AC power source, which is usually an unreliable, noisy, and fluctuating electrical source.

A number of adverse events are associated with AC power. Your PC can be protected against most of them. You should be aware of these common electrical problems:

- *Spikes*—An electrical spike is an unexpected, short-duration (usually), high-voltage event on the AC power line. A spike can be caused by a variety of events, such as lightning strikes, generator switchovers, power pole incidents (a car hitting one, for example), or large electrical motors on the same power source. The safeguard against an electrical spike is a surge suppressor or a UPS that includes surge suppression.

- *Blackouts*—A blackout is a total loss of power. It can last anywhere from a split second to many days. If your power supply's hold-up time is greater than the amount of time you are without power, there is a good chance that all you will notice is a momentary flickering or dimming of your screen. The average hold-up time is around 1/20th of a second. Your PC will probably reboot itself for anything longer than that. The best defense against a blackout is a UPS.

- *Brownouts*—A brownout is the opposite of a spike, except that a brownout can last for a relatively long time. If the voltage lingers too long below the nominal point, the result can be the same as a blackout, or worse. Brownouts can destroy components by causing a power supply to draw too much current to make up for the low voltage. A UPS can protect against a brownout by making up the difference between the low-voltage level and what is the normal voltage level.

- *Power surge*—A power surge, or overvoltage, is a high-voltage situation that raises the voltage above normal levels, much like a spike, but for a longer period of time. Often, it is a spike followed by a slow tapering of the power level back to normal. A large nearby electrical user can cause the power level on the source lines to surge or drop should it suddenly cut its power consumption. Although not as instantly damaging as a spike, surges nonetheless can cause component failures. A surge suppressor or a UPS, which absorbs the increase in power, is good protection against a power surge.

- *Noise*—Electromagnetic interference and radio frequency interference (RFI) are the two primary causes of line noise on the AC power line. Power cables can act as antennas and pick up disruptive signals emitting from computer monitors, fluorescent lighting, electrical motors, radio transmitters, and natural phenomena such as lightning. Avoid placing any device that causes an interruption or static on an AM radio on the same electrical circuit as a PC. Some surge filters also include noise filters, but unless you are using a line conditioner, a UPS is your best bet to filter out line noise.

Surge Suppressors

Many of the power strips and plug strips on the market also contain surge suppressors, also known as surge protectors (see Figure 14.11). The active component in a surge suppressor is a metallic oxide varistor (MOV) that reacts to overvoltage situations and diverts (or shunts) the power to a grounding circuit.

Surge suppressors are rated by the amount of electrical power they can divert. The measurement unit is joules, which measures the amount of electricity the suppressor can absorb and not pass through. An MOV is essentially a one-shot device, much like a fuse. If an MOV is triggered by a power surge, it is simply not there anymore. In most cases there is no way to tell if it has been triggered. Some power strips include a fused light in series with the MOV that should also blow

Figure 14.11   A plug strip that includes a surge suppressor.

when a surge takes out the MOV. Sometimes the lighted fuse blows with a smaller surge, leaving the MOV to handle the next large surge or group of smaller surges. On the other hand, the fuse may be strong enough to withstand a small surge that itself may be strong enough to wear down the MOV. It may not take all that many small surges to knock out the MOV, while the fused light shines on.

Some surge suppressors have more advanced surge interception technology, such as gas discharge tubes and pellet arrestors, which are a little slower to react, but these types of suppression devices can be used more than once.

Overview of UPS Operation

A UPS is a large battery and battery charger that provides a PC or server protection against short-term power outages, surges, spikes, and brownouts. A UPS monitors its input voltage (AC power), and when the voltage level deviates more than a certain percentage from normal, it switches to provide electrical service from its battery. The DC battery power stored in the UPS is passed through an inverter to create an AC supply for the PC (which immediately converts it back to DC power). Figure 14.12 shows an example of the type of UPS commonly found in an office setting.

The best UPSs supply power to the PC when needed in a smooth wave more than likely better than the original AC source. Less expensive UPSs may provide the power in a square wave, which can contain potentially harmful frequencies that can damage sensitive equipment. A compromise between the expensive and the inexpensive units is a UPS unit that produces a wave made up of several small square wave steps. This type of UPS still has unfavorable frequency harmonics, but a lot fewer. When buying a UPS, be sure you are aware of the type of wave output it provides.

Figure 14.12   An uninterruptible power supply (UPS).

Types of UPS Devices

UPS units are available in two general categories, based on how they store and provide electrical power:

- *Standby UPS*—The standby UPS generally does nothing more than provide a battery backup to the PC connected to it as a safeguard against a power failure (blackout) or a low-voltage event (brownout). In standby mode, the UPS draws off a small amount of power to charge its battery and passes unfiltered AC power on to the PC. In the event of a blackout, the standby UPS provides the PC with an AC power source. The switchover does take some time, which increases the importance of the PC power supply's hold-out time. If it is of sufficient length to cover the switchover time, there shouldn't be any serious problems. One of the downsides to most standby units is that any large surges, spikes, or low-voltage events will most likely be passed through the UPS to the PC.

- *Online (or Inline) UPS*—An online (inline) UPS provides power to a PC through an AC power service provided from the UPS's battery and a power inverter that converts the battery's DC power to AC power. The UPS's battery is constantly being recharged from an AC power source through an input inverter. An online UPS requires no switchover because the UPS absorbs any events, such as spikes and blackouts, on the AC power line. An extended brownout would begin discharging the UPS's battery, which would eventually fail without the AC power being restored. Essentially the PC is running on AC produced by the battery, and the battery is being constantly kept charged while there is input power. Figure 14.13 shows a large inline UPS that would be used to protect one or more servers on a network.

UPS Characteristics

Characteristics you should keep in mind when choosing a UPS include:

- *Simple or interactive displays*—Even the least expensive UPS on the market tries to give a warning near the end of its charge. Low-end (meaning low-price) UPSs sound a beep at given battery charge levels, but it is up to you to guess how much of the battery's charge is remaining. A better UPS has

Figure 14.13   A rackmount UPS used for network servers.

light-emitting diode (LED) gauges to show the current level of charge, as well as how much is being demanded, to allow you to make an educated guess as to how much time you have to shut down your system before the battery is dead. The best UPSs display an estimate in minutes and seconds on their control panel based on the current battery level and draw rate.

- *Warning mechanisms*—A UPS designed to support a single computer will generally have a serial "heartbeat" cable that is attached to a serial (Com) port on the PC. The UPS generates a regular signal that is monitored by a background process running on the PC. If the UPS fails to signal (i.e., misses too many heartbeats), the monitoring software (typically supplied by the UPS's manufacturer or it could be a part of the PC's operating system) tries to gracefully shut down the PC.

  This is a very important feature for servers that cache a lot of data in memory instead of on a hard disk to speed data access times. In this case, should the power suddenly fail, all of the cached data would be lost if it could not be saved to disk before a shutdown or sync request. A newer UPS is as likely to use a universal serial bus (USB) cable as the serial cable. The heartbeat signal can also be broadcast over a network from a UPS that is supporting multiple servers. In this case, the UPS monitor checks incoming TCP/IP (Transmission Control Protocol/Internet Protocol) messages and sorts out the information coming from its UPS. The downside to this is if the server loses communication with the UPS (due to a pulled cable, bad hub, or the like), the server may shut down even though power is available.

- *Software interfaces*—The software monitor that interacts with the UPS in real time (see previous description of warning mechanisms) is typically supplied by the manufacturer of the UPS. At a minimum, these software programs monitor the heartbeat signal sent by the UPS to indicate that power is still available. Should the UPS stop sending the signal, the software begins the process of performing a system shutdown. Advanced systems are available that display console messages or send email or dial a pager to notify the system administrator. These systems also usually include support for remote status checking.

- *Line conditioners and alarm systems*—A true line conditioner (also known as a power conditioner) filters the incoming power to isolate line noise and keep voltage levels normal. It isolates the input power source from the output power in a transformer stage. A line conditioner cannot protect against a power outage, but it can smooth out any intermittent under- and overvoltage events (surges and spikes, respectively) that occur on the input source. When the input power becomes unreliable, a line conditioner (and most UPS units, for that matter) will send out an alarm should it detect that there are more problems on the line than it can handle.

Immediate Solutions

Determining What Tools Are Needed to Work on a Power Supply

The following tools are used when working with power supplies:

- Diagonal cutters
- Screwdrivers (including Torx bits)
- Needle-nose pliers
- Multimeter or digital voltage meter (DVM)
- An AC power monitor that plugs into a wall outlet
- Soldering iron
- Cable ties
- Continuity tester
- Variac (variable power supply)

WARNING! Notice that the electrostatic discharge (ESD) wrist strap is missing from this list. The reason is explained later in more detail, but essentially the power supply has a big capacitor in it that you really don't want to ground through your body. But then, you weren't planning to open up the power supply anyway, were you? If the power supply is bad, it is generally inexpensive enough to replace in total. Those big bright warning labels are not there for decoration. Read them and heed the warning.

Checking and Troubleshooting a Power Supply

The power supply is obviously a very important component of the PC, but it is also the one most likely to fail. Day in and day out it suffers the slings and arrows of electrical power, sacrificing itself for the good of your computer. On average, the common workstation or desktop PC suffers more than 120 power "events" every month. Not surprisingly, it can develop problems.

Three conditions require that you check out or troubleshoot the power supply:

- *Upgrading the system*—Suppose you are planning a big upgrade (new motherboard, new hard drive, digital versatile disk (DVD), and the works) and you are worried that your power supply may be too weak to handle the new load. When upgrading, remember that a power supply is rated by its power output in watts. You can get from 100- to 600-watt power supplies to fit the common form factors (ATX and LTX). A power supply rated between 230 to 350 watts works well for most average systems, unless you are planning to build a super server with quad Pentium III Xeons, a DVD, an internal tape drive, and four or five internal small computer system interface (SCSI) drives, in which case you'll need to look into the WTX form factor.

- *Intermittent problems*—If you have tried everything you can to track down an intermittent problem on the motherboard without isolating the problem, the power supply may be the real culprit if the problem is at all related to a power issue. But how can you tell whether the power supply is going bad? Some of the telltale signs that can tip you off that the power supply is on its way to failure are overheating, occasional boot failures or errors, frequent parity errors, noisy operation, or mild electrical shocks when you touch the case.

WARNING! If you ever receive a shock, other than ESD, when you touch the case, you have power supply problems of the first magnitude—replace the power supply immediately!

- *Catastrophic problems*—If smoke is coming out of the power supply or off the motherboard, it is very likely that the power supply has gone awry and needs to be replaced. If the system fan has stopped turning, then you absolutely need to replace the power supply. You should also test the motherboard with a new power supply, and be on watch for parity errors, system lockups that are becoming more frequent, and disk read and peripheral input/output (I/O) errors. These are signs of damaged motherboard components beginning to fail.

Steps you should use any time you suspect the power supply to be the source of a PC problem include:

1. First, determine that the problem is not something as trivial as a blown fuse caused by a legitimate overload. Be sure to remove the source of the overload before beginning work.

2. Try to classify the problem by when it is occurring and what it is affecting. The categories you might use are:

   - BIOS, boot, or startup problem
   - An input power-related problem

- An output power-related problem

- Excessive noise, ripple, or other power conversion errors

- Catastrophic failure that poses danger to the system or the operator (especially the technician)

3. Determine, based on the form factor, what the proper output voltages should be, and measure the output of the appropriate pins.

WARNING! Read the documentation for your power supply. Some power supplies cannot be removed from a load or connected to the motherboard or disk drives without damaging them. AT and earlier power supplies are generally safe to remove, but check the documentation anyway.

If these general steps do not solve or identify the problem with the power supply, or if they prove inconclusive, the problem may still be with the power supply, even though it may show up elsewhere. It is always a safe bet that when there is an electrical power problem on the PC, regardless of where it shows up, the power supply is involved in the cause in some way.

One of the quickest and easiest ways to troubleshoot a computer power supply is to put your hand in front of the cooling fan. If no air is passing into or out of the fan, chances are the power supply is bad. One exception to this test is that an ATX form factor motherboard may have a bad **PS_ON** switch.

The most effective way to absolutely tell if a power supply is the cause of a problem is to swap it out. If, after you install a replacement power supply, the problem is solved, there you are. However, if the new power supply does not solve the problem, then the problem is elsewhere. Don't jump to the conclusion that the old power supply is vindicated. Before you decide to put the old power supply back in its PC or put it on the shelf as a ready spare, try putting it in another system to see if it works there. Unfortunately, some problems that can be caused by a power supply with a low-level or intermittent problem may take days, weeks, or months to show up.

Remember that if the computer case is still under warranty, you don't have to send the entire computer case back—just to return a faulty power supply. The computer case has at least four or five major components, and the power supply is one of two electrical parts (the other is the front panel) that can be defective. Most manufacturers or resellers will likely want to replace the faulty part rather than the entire system case. Shipping back only the power supply will also save you money on the shipping charges.

Diagnosing POST Power Problems

You may run into situations that require you to know the symptoms that indicate a power supply problem. A few of the leading symptoms that indicate an ailing power supply are:

- The power light on the front panel is off.

- The power supply fan isn't operating.

- The computer sounds either a continuous beep or doesn't beep at all.

- The computer sounds a repeating short beep.

- The computer displays either a POST error in the 020 - 029 series (**Power_Good** signal error) or a parity error.

Determining Why Nothing Happens When the Power Switch Is Turned On

1. Check to see if the PC's power cord is plugged into an AC power outlet on a surge protector or a UPS and into the PC.

2. Check the surge suppressor switch to see if it is on and working properly. If it appears no AC power is being provided, move the plug to another outlet. If no power is available on more than one outlet, check the building's circuit breakers.

3. If power is available at the wall plug, then either the power supply's switch is bad or the power supply itself has completely failed. In either case, you should replace the power supply.

Checking a Fan That Is Not Spinning

The fan is a very important part of the cooling system designed into the case and motherboard form factor. If it is not spinning, there is something wrong, and if the fan is not replaced, serious damage to the PC could occur.

WARNING! Never insert anything like a screwdriver blade into the fan to turn the blades in an attempt to make it go. There is a serious shock hazard inside the power supply.

Use compressed air to clean around the spindle of the fan, blowing the air through the fan grill that is located on the outside of the case. Before you do this, remove the system case cover and perhaps even take the unit outside, depending on how dirty it is. If there is nothing obviously impeding the fan from spinning, immediately replace the power supply.

WARNING! *Do not open the power supply to replace the fan.*

Figuring Out Why the PC Does Not Boot and There Is No Sign of Power

If the PC does not boot and shows no sign of power, investigate the problem by the following steps:

1. Check whether the outlet into which the PC is plugged, such as the surge suppressor, UPS, or wall outlet, has power. If so, is the cord seated tightly and snuggly at the PC end and plugged in all of the way on the outlet end?

2. Disconnect everything except the power from the back of the computer. Boot the computer. If the PC boots, then add back one connector at a time, rebooting after each one is added, until the PC fails to boot.

3. If the PC fails to boot after a certain device is added, switch your focus to that device because the problem, this time, is not the power supply.

4. If you have reconnected all of the devices to the PC and the problem seems to have gone away, it is likely that the problem was a loose connection or a problem you should be looking for as an intermittent occurrence.

5. Obviously, if the computer will not boot or power up with just the power cord attached, you should replace the power supply. As you will find, the easiest way to solve power supply problems, especially pesky ones that are hard to pin down, is to replace the power supply and not waste your time trying to track down a problem that will cause you to replace the power supply anyway.

Determining Why an ATX System Does Not Work When the Power Is Turned On

An ATX power supply is soft-switched through the power supply switch on the motherboard and the functions in the system BIOS. An ATX power supply also requires a load to operate, and connecting it to the motherboard supplies a part of that load. So, if you install an ATX power supply in a system, don't expect it to work until you have connected it to a motherboard that also has a microprocessor, memory, and a video card installed on it.

If you install an ATX power supply and it fails to power up, the problem may very well lie in the motherboard, processor, memory, or video card—or it may not.

Related Solution:	*Found on Page:*
Making the Power On/Off Button Work	372

Setting the Input Voltage Selector Switch

If you are in North America (Canada, United States, and Mexico), your voltage selector, which is usually located on the back of the power supply near the fan grill, should be set to 110–115V. If you are located in Europe or another country outside of North America, more than likely the voltage selector switch should be set to 220–230V. If your computer is a laptop, notebook, or other portable manufactured in the past few years, it probably has a built-in voltage detector that automatically switches the voltage setting for you.

Because the vast majority of cases and power supplies are manufactured outside of North America, it is very likely that the power supply was tested using a 220V setting. If this setting is not reset for 110V for use in North America, when you first plug it in out of the box, it will appear to be dead because of a dead power supply. Before you use any PC, except notebook computers, right out of the box, first check the voltage selector switch to make sure it is set for the right voltage.

Testing Power Supply Peripheral Connectors with a DVM

If you keep a PC for any time at all, the chances are good that you will need to replace the power supply at some point. The following steps are used to test the power leads going to the peripheral devices:

1. Turn off the PC. If the PC is an AT or earlier form factor, it should remain connected to the wall outlet. However, if it is an ATX or later, unplug it from the wall outlet. ATX motherboards are "always on" and carry enough juice to power up the PC, so unplugging these systems is a good idea before placing metal objects, such as screwdrivers, inside the case.

2. Remove the system case covers, watching for any grounding wires attached to the case. If one of more of these wires are attached, leave them attached, if possible.

3. Set your DVM or multimeter to read DC volts in the range higher than 12V.

4. Locate a power supply connector (see Figure 14.14), either an unused one or by disconnecting one from the floppy disk or CD-ROM. This connector will be used to perform a test on the power supply. The pinning you will need for the test is listed in Table 14.3.

5. Power on the PC.

6. Insert the black probe of the DVM (it should have two probes: a black and a red) into the power connector on one of the two black wires in the center two holes. See Figures 14.14 and 14.15.

7. With the black probe in place, touch the red probe to the connector on the red wire of the power connector. You should get a reading of +5V DC.

8. Now touch the red probe to the connector on the yellow wire of the power connector. You should get a reading of +12V DC.

9. If either or both of the readings in Steps 7 and 8 are wrong, retest. However, if neither test gives a reading, replace the power supply.

Table 14.3   Power supply connector pin outs.

Pin	Signal	Color
4	+5V DC	Red
3	Ground	Black
2	Ground	Black
1	+12V DC	Yellow

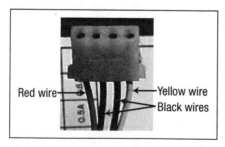

Figure 14.14   A peripheral power connector.

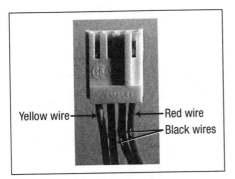

Yellow wire—— ——Red wire
——Black wires

Figure 14.15   The floppy drive power connector.

Sizing a UPS Correctly

A UPS is rated in volt-amps (VA) and may range from 200VA to greater than 5000VA. With a UPS, you definitely get what you pay for. The higher the volt-amps, the more powerful the UPS is and, in direct proportion, the higher the price tag will be.

The volt-amp rating of a UPS is the amount of VA the UPS can supply for a five-minute period. So, a UPS with a 500VA rating can deliver 500VA for five minutes. This assumes that the UPS will have a load equal to its rating. If the load on a 500VA UPS was only 250VA, the UPS would be able to supply power for 20 minutes.

Before picking the UPS for your PC, you should determine the amount of VA it needs to continue running for as long as you need it. Fifteen minutes is generally considered ample time to shut down a system properly without a loss of data. Remember, the more VA a UPS is rated for, the more it will cost. You can certainly find a UPS to power your PC for an hour, but the cost will be very high.

Use the following calculation to determine about how long you have before your UPS is exhausted:

```
(Max. amp drawx120) + (Power supply (in watts)x1.4) =
        Total volt amps required
```

- *Maximum amp draw×120*—This calculates the total amps of all of the devices in or attached to the PC to be powered by the UPS, including the internal devices, such as the hard disk, CD-ROM, and the like, and the external devices, such as the monitor or modem.

- *Power supply (in watts)×1.4*—This calculates the watts rating of your computer's power supply.

- *Full draw*—Drawing as many volt amps as the UPS's rating should provide you with about 5–7 minutes of power.

- *Half draw*—Placing a load on the UPS at about one-half its rating will provide about 20 minutes of power. For example, if the total volt amps required by a PC are 350VA and the UPS's rating is 700VA, the UPS should supply power for at least 15 minutes and perhaps as long as 20 minutes.

Table 14.4 lists the volt-amp draw for several common peripheral devices. The manufacturer or reseller of your PC should be able to tell you the VA requirements of your entire system. You may also try checking Web sites of the manufacturers of each of the major components of the PC.

Taking Preventive Measures

Things you can do to lengthen the life of a power supply include many environmental, hardware-related, and common-sense activities:

- The better the environment is for the PC, the better it will perform, just like for its human operator. Run the computer in a cool, moderately humid environment. The cooler the air entering the fan, the better. The power supply, like all other transformers, produces heat. Use an air-conditioned room, if possible.

- Either reduce the amount of dust and smoke in the air around the computer, or plan to clean the inside of the system case and fan often. Blow the dust bunnies off the fan and power supply grills frequently using compressed air. It can't hurt to do the same occasionally for the inside of the case.

- Use a surge protector, or better yet, a true line conditioner, and by all means, use a UPS.

Related Solution:	Found on Page:
Power Issues Involved with the Care and Maintenance of a PC	Chapter 20

Table 14.4   Common VA usage.

Device or Component	VA Usage
CD-ROM	20–25
Small expansion card	5
Large expansion card	10–15
3.5-inch floppy drive	5
Pentium II processor	38
Motherboard	20–35

Part IV

Peripherals

Chapter 15

Monitors and Displays

In Depth

The Importance of Video Display Devices

Without a video display device of some type, the personal computer (PC) would not be a very helpful tool. Monitors and displays provide the user with a view to the PC and its applications. A monitor is the source of information and entertainment for the PC user. Whether a cathode ray tube (CRT) or liquid crystal display (LCD) produces the picture, the purpose remains the same—to display the visual temporary output of the PC.

There would be no "What You See Is What You Get" (WYSIWYG) on a PC without some form of display to see what it is that you *do* get. PCs are limited to producing outputs that can be handled by human senses, and to this point, technology is limited to sight and sound. Given a choice, users still prefer sight over sound. Whereas much can still be accomplished on a PC without sound output, very little can be done without the ability to see the PC's output.

This chapter provides some basic background on CRTs and LCDs. There isn't much in the way of troubleshooting or problem-solving because the majority of problems that arise on a monitor are either handled through the monitor's adjustment controls or require the services of a monitor repair facility.

PC Monitors

In spite of the fact that PC technology is advancing as fast as it is, the monitor is about the only part of a PC that can be considered an investment because it holds its value over time and has a lasting durability. Good-quality monitors last for years and can be used with several generations of PC systems. A number of considerations should be taken into account when deciding about investing in a PC monitor, including:

- *Type*—Although features and costs vary between monitor types, the choice actually comes down to the traditional and conventional CRT display versus the state-of-the-art and expensive digital flat-panel LCD.

- *Size*—A monitor's size has a lot to do with its capability, but more important, it impacts your comfort in working with it. As is generally true—and especially with monitors—bigger is better. Many experts recommend that, given today's technology, the minimum monitor size that should be used is 17 inches, and the minimum resolution for an LCD monitor is 1,024×768.

- *Cost*—Cost can be a major consideration when selecting a new monitor. A monitor budget of less than $400 will not include an LCD display, at least until the prices come down a bit more. However, if cost is not a factor, the choices and comparisons are virtually unlimited.

The two general categories of PC visual display peripheral devices are the CRT and the LCD. A CRT looks and works very much like a standard, conventional television set (without the remote control, of course). On the other hand, LCDs are the flat-panel devices that are in standalone monitors, are attached to portable PCs, or can be hung on the wall. The CRT, shown in Figure 15.1, is largely a desktop or tabletop device, whereas an LCD, shown in Figure 15.2, not only can sit on a desk, it also can get up and move about, like the personal digital assistant (PDA) in Figure 15.3.

A display is really an adaptation of the display, but because it uses completely different technology, it is differentiated from the monitor. In this chapter, monitors and displays are discussed in some detail. The video card actually controls much of the capabilities of the PC's monitor. Chapter 11 provides more information on the features and functions of video cards.

Until recently, standard PC system packages featured only CRT displays. However, newer systems are being offered with flat-panel LCD displays. As prices for LCD displays continue to drop, experts believe that the CRT may soon be replaced by the LCD on standard PC packages, with a CRT display available only as an option. Recall, however, that the floppy disk was to have been obsolete more than five years ago.

Photo courtesy of ViewSonic Corporation.

Figure 15.1   A PC desktop monitor.

Photo courtesy of ViewSonic Corporation.

Figure 15.2   A flat-panel PC display.

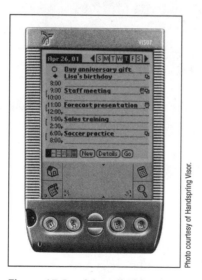

Photo courtesy of Handspring Visor.

Figure 15.3   A handheld personal digital assistant.

CRT Displays

CRT displays have some advantages over LCDs. A CRT is bright, well-lit, economical, and produces excellent color and graphics qualities. CRTs use the same common and well-developed technology found in conventional television sets (excluding high-definition TV, or HDTV). The manufacturing process is well-defined, and CRT costs are comparatively low. Larger screen sizes and higher visual standards continue to make the CRT the visual display of choice for many PC users.

The cathode ray tube is the biggest and most expensive part of a conventional PC monitor. It is a funnel-shaped glass tube that uses an electron gun to "excite" (light up) dots of phosphorous material on the back of the CRT's display glass (See Figure 15.4). Literally millions of phosphorous dots are on the CRT's display. The glowing phosphors combine into pixels that form images that show through the display glass for the user to see. The display glass is a pane of slightly curved glass, which is why the display is bright and easily viewed at an angle. Some detail on how the CRT creates its display is discussed in the following section.

Dots and Pixels

The images displayed on a PC's monitor are created by a pattern of phosphor dots arranged in much the same way as the halftone dots on a photograph in a newspaper. The dots on the newspaper are shaded lighter or darker, and the reader's eyes and brain form a visual image from them.

A monochrome (single-color) monitor has phosphor of only one color. Text characters are formed very much the same as characters on a dot-matrix printer, as illustrated in Figure 15.5. Although this illustration is exaggerated a bit, the concept is accurate. When the CRT's phosphor dots are illuminated, the text or graphic image appears as a single color on a contrasting background. Typically, the background is black and the display color is green, amber, or white.

Original photo courtesy of ViewSonic Corporation.

Figure 15.4   A CRT monitor is measured diagonally, case and all.

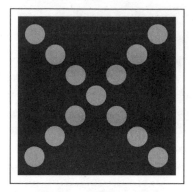

Figure 15.5   A text character formed on a monochrome CRT.

A color CRT has millions of phosphor dots on the display screen. One-third of the dots are red; one-third of the dots are green; and one-third of the dots are blue. Three phosphor dots are arranged so that dots of each color can be combined to create a triangular element called a triad, as shown in Figure 15.6. More commonly, the triad is called a picture element, or a pixel for short (See Figure 15.7). How much intensity is used to light each dot of the pixel determines the color your eye sees in the pixel. The blending of these three colors is the basis of what is called RGB (red/green/blue) color, which is the color display standard used in all monitors.

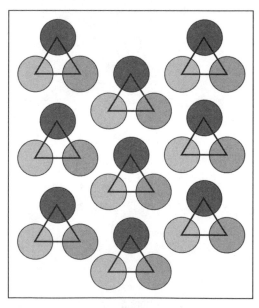

Figure 15.6   Pixels are formed from triangles of phosphor dots.

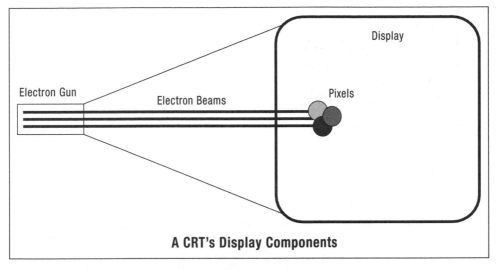

A CRT's Display Components

Figure 15.7   A pixel consists of three phosphor dots: one red, one green, and one blue.

On a color monitor, the electron beam is made up of three electron streams from three separate electron guns, one for each color in the pixel. The streams are arranged to match the standard arrangement of the dots in the pixels. By changing the intensity of the streams, the closely grouped dots will appear to the human eye to produce a certain color. Its color depth sets the number of colors the monitor can produce, but the video graphics array (VGA) standard is 256 colors. However, most of today's monitors are super VGA (SVGA) and are capable of displaying more than 16 million colors.

As the monitor receives an analog wave from the video card's digital-to-analog converter (DAC) with instructions for the image to be displayed, it is translated into the color and intensity of each dot in every pixel. As illustrated in Figure 15.8, the electron beam sweeps across and down the CRT's display area, illuminating the pixels to produce or refresh (redraw) the image. The electron beam moves left to right over the top row of pixels, and at the end of the row, it returns to the start of the

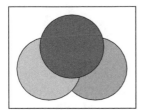

Figure 15.8   The pattern used by the electron beam to illuminate the CRT's
phosphorous material.

next row and scans it left to right, and so forth. At the bottom of the screen, the sweep moves back to the beginning of the top row and begins again. The intensity of the electron beam, which controls the color and brightness of each pixel on the screen, is adjusted as it moves across the screen to "paint" the display's image.

Flat Screen Vs. Flat Panel

Many people confuse the terms flat screen and flat panel. A *flat-screen* display is a type of CRT that has a flat glass screen, as opposed to the more standard curved glass screen found on the normal, everyday CRT. *Flat-panel* monitors use LCD displays to reproduce images on a screen, as discussed in the next section.

On conventional CRTs, the front glass panel is like a section cut out of a ball—curved both horizontally and vertically. Curving the face of the CRT places each phosphor dot the same distance from the electron beam. So-called flat screens have a flat glass front on the CRT in an effort to be easier on the viewer's eyes. However, because the electrons that are illuminating the phosphor must travel farther to reach the top, bottom, and side edges of the screen, the image along the edges of the screen can be fuzzy and distorted.

Some CRTs, such as Sony's Trinitron and Mitsubishi's Diamondtron tubes, offer a compromise to the flat screen with a screen that is more like a section out of a cylinder—curved horizontally but vertically flatter. Another alternative to the flat-screen monitor are CRTs with screens that are curved more like a section cut from a bigger ball with the center of this bigger piece used to make the CRT's screen appear to be flat to the viewer. The focus on the electron beam has also been improved, so the beam is able to travel longer distances accurately. Another attempt to solve the distortion problems of the flat-screen display involves placing a special glass plate over the CRT to optically remove the distortion near the screen's edges. The LCD display, which is naturally flat, avoids these problems by illuminating each pixel equally, without an electron gun, which eliminates the need for a curved screen or any optical effects.

LCDs

The major benefit, among others, of a flat-panel (LCD) monitor is its size, which really means its depth. A typical CRT display, especially the larger displays in use today, are 15 inches or more from front to back, which takes up a considerable amount of valuable real estate on a desktop. A flat-panel LCD display is typically only a few inches deep, including its foot. This makes it perfect for small desks, cubicles, or for places where a large CRT monitor could negatively impact the aesthetics or décor, such as on a reception desk. New style systems even integrate the PC and monitor into a single flat-panel package that is only a few inches thick from front to back.

LCDs are very common and are used in many products, including wristwatches, microwave ovens, CD players, and PC monitors. In fact, virtually all PC flat-panel monitors and portable computers sold today have an LCD screen. LCD is popular because it is thinner, lighter, and requires less power than other types of displays, especially the CRT.

Liquid crystal is a material that exists somewhere between a solid and a liquid. It is created by applying heat to a suitable substance to change it from a solid into a liquid crystal form. Because liquid crystals are formed from heat, they are sensitive to temperature changes. This makes them perfect for thermometers, mood rings, and PC monitors. This is also why the LCD display on a notebook computer may not work well immediately after being exposed to cold or heat for any length of time.

Three different types of LCDs can be used in various devices: common plane, passive matrix, and active matrix.

- *Common plane LCDs*—These LCDs are not used for PC displays, but are used on watches, handheld games, microwaves, and other devices in which the same numbers or objects are displayed repeatedly.

- *Passive matrix LCDs*—A passive matrix display has a layer of LCD elements on a grid (matrix) of wires. When current is applied to the wire intersections, the pixels block the light and the area appears dark. A passive matrix refreshes, or redraws, the display by applying current to the pixels at a fixed refresh rate.

- *Active matrix LCDs*—An *active matrix* display controls each LCD element individually with transistors that continually refresh each pixel.

Passive Matrix LCD

A passive matrix LCD has pixels, like a CRT, instead of electrodes. However, its operating principles are the same as those used in a common-plane LCD. A grid, organized in rows and columns, is used to energize the pixels, which are located at the intersections of the rows and columns. Integrated circuits control the rows and columns to ensure that a charge sent over the grid gets to the specific pixel it was intended to activate. The grid's rows and columns are on separate layers of a transparent conductive material that sandwich a layer of liquid crystal. A layer of polarizing film is added to the top and bottom substrates of this "sandwich."

A pixel is energized when an electrical charge is sent down the appropriate column on one substrate and a grounding charge is sent over the appropriate row on the other substrate. The two charges converge at the pixel located at the intersection of the row and column and cause the pixel's liquid crystal to untwist and block the light source and darken the pixel.

A passive matrix LCD has its disadvantages. Its refresh speed (called the response time) is slow, and the grid delivers electricity imprecisely to specific pixels. This latter problem can affect nearby pixels and create a fuzzy image or create contrast problems.

A passive matrix display uses one of two types of liquid crystal—twisted nematic (TN) or supertwisted nematic (STN).

Twisted Nematic Crystals

Computer displays are made from what are called twisted nematic crystals, which are rod-shaped crystals that have a 90-degree twist. When a current of electricity is applied to a TN crystal, it untwists in a predictable way. If enough electricity is applied, the TN crystal will completely untwist and become flat. The predictability of how the TN crystal reacts to the electricity and untwists is the property that most appeals to LCD display manufacturers. The TN liquid crystal is used in low-cost displays. Its display is black on a gray or silver background. TN liquid crystal is used primarily on consumer electronics and appliances.

In an LCD, TN crystals are placed on layers of polarized glass filters. Without any electricity applied to the liquid crystal, light passes through the first glass filter to the last one because the twisted crystal is narrow and does not block the light. When electricity is applied, the TN crystals untwist and block the path of the light, creating a darkened area on the display. Figure 15.9 illustrates the layers that make up what is called a common-lane LCD. The layers are (bottom to top):

- *Mirror*—The back of the LCD is a mirror for reflecting light.
- *Polarizing film*—A piece of polarizing glass.
- *Electrode*—The common transparent electrode plane for the assembly.
- *Liquid crystal*—TN liquid crystal is placed between the two electrodes.
- *Electrode*—A layer of glass with one or more smaller electrodes attached that define the static display.
- *Polarizing film*—This layer of polarized glass is placed with its polarization at right angles to that of the other polarized layer.

In a simple LCD, such as that on a wristwatch or handheld game, the top layer of electrodes provides the sections of the numerals or objects to be displayed. When these electrodes are energized in a pattern, the liquid crystal untwists to block the light source, the affected screen areas darken, and the viewer sees numbers or shapes. Figure 15.10 shows how seven electrodes are used to display numbers. When the electrode sections are energized, the corresponding portion of the display is darkened and numbers form, as illustrated in Figure 15.11.

15. Monitors and Displays

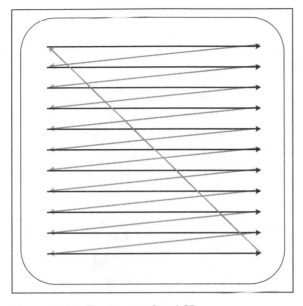

Figure 15.9   The layers of an LCD.

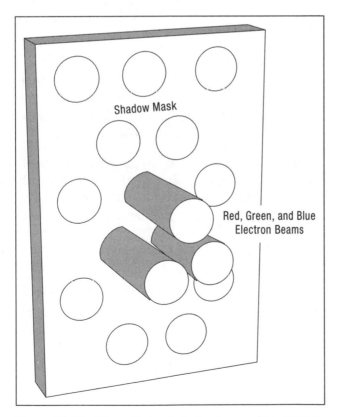

Shadow Mask

Red, Green, and Blue
Electron Beams

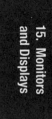

15. Monitors
and Displays

Figure 15.10   The pattern of electrodes used to produce a number on an LCD.

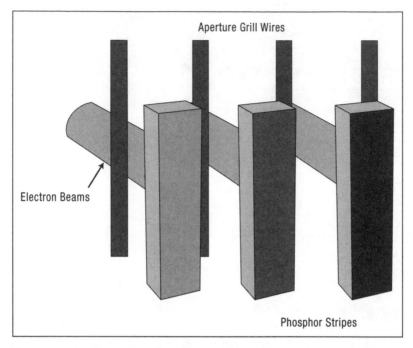

Figure 15.11   Examples of numbers displayed on an LCD.

Supertwisted Nematic Crystals

The STN is the type of liquid crystal made with either a 180-degree or a 270-degree twist, which gives it a much wider range of motion, which makes it more tolerant against any energy radiating from nearby pixels and allows it to provide more steps of color shadings. STN is used in both monochrome and color displays.

An application of passive matrix LCD technology is the portable pen-based computer, also known as the personal digital assistant or palmtop computer. Although it may also have a keyboard, commands and data are typically entered through the screen with a special nonwriting pen or stylus. The display is covered by a protective plastic covering, and beneath the display is a wire grid that recognizes the movements of the stylus. The wire grid records the movements of the pen over the grid's intersections, which is similar to the technology behind touch screens.

Although not a type of liquid crystal, dual-scan STN (DSTN) is a process used in some LCDs to double the number of lines refreshed and to cut the time to refresh the display in half. This is accomplished by dividing the LCD into two equal halves that are scanned simultaneously.

Active Matrix LCD

The pixels on an active matrix LCD use thin film transistors (TFTs), which is why this type of LCD is often called a TFT display. TFTs are switching transistors and capacitors that are etched in a matrix pattern on a glass substrate that forms one of the layers of the active matrix LCD. Each pixel consists of three TFTs, one for each of the RGB colors, which can add up to quite a few transistors in the display. For example, a VGA 640×480 color display uses 921,600 transistors, and a 1,024×768 ultra VGA (UVGA) color display uses 2,359,296 transistors, all of which are etched into the substrate glass. If a transistor is defective, it creates a bad pixel, and it is common for TFT displays to have at least a few bad pixels.

An active matrix LCD addresses its pixels somewhat like a passive matrix LCD. However, when one row is addressed on the active matrix display, all of the other rows are switched off, and the charge is sent down the appropriate column. Because only the addressed row is active, only the pixel at the intersection of the active row and column is affected. The TFT's capacitor holds the energy used to charge the pixel until the next refresh cycle.

The color of the pixel is provided by color filters that lay over the areas controlled by the pixel's three TFTs. Colors are created by the amount of light allowed to pass through the filters by each of the TFTs, which are controlled by the intensity of the charge sent to them by the image control circuits. As illustrated in Figure 15.12, the TFTs control how much the liquid crystal elements open (untwist) to block the light passing through the color filters. In the situation shown in Figure 15.12, a small amount of the light source is being allowed to pass through the red filter along with a wide-open blue filter, but no light is being passed through the green filter. Controlling the amount of electricity that flows to the pixel controls the action of the liquid crystal and the amount of light allowed to pass through the color filters. By controlling the light, active matrix screens are able to display 256 levels of color brightness per pixel.

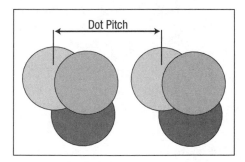

Figure 15.12   Controlling the color in an active matrix LCD.

LCD Lighting

An LCD uses one of two light source types: reflective and transmissive. A reflective LCD reflects only the light that enters through its polarized filters from its environment. In a well-lighted room or in sunlight, there is usually enough light to see the display. A transmissive LCD, which is the type used in portable computers and flat-panel monitors, incorporates lighting elements to backlight the display. Typically, built-in fluorescent tubes located around the edges of the display and sometimes behind the LCD provide the lighting.

Signals and Connectors

One of the major differences between CRT and LCD displays is that a CRT is an analog device and an LCD is a digital device. For a while, all monitors were digital devices, but when the demand grew for more than 64 colors, monitors became analog devices. Using an analog signal allows the CRT to develop more colors and shades from the three primary colors of red, green, and blue than did the digital signal.

Theoretically, an analog signal can represent an unlimited number of colors and shades. However, standard analog color is limited to 256 color variations for each of the 65,536 colors (16-bit color). This creates more than 16 million colors that can be encoded in an analog signal. Virtually all CRT monitors in use today are analog monitors.

CRTs, even those with a digital connection, use an electrical wave to create the display, which means the PC's digital signal must be converted into an analog signal. This is done either on the video card or in the monitor by a digital-to-analog converter. The *video card* sends the digital information generated by an application program to its DAC, which converts the signal into an analog wave and sends it over the connecting cable to the monitor. Even if the CRT has a digital interface, the signal must still be converted to analog. The video card also sends out the data needed by the monitor to refresh the image or renew it as it changes. For more information on video cards, see Chapter 11.

A flat-panel LCD monitor connected to a standard DAC video card must reprocess the analog signal through its analog-to-digital converter (ADC), which can lead to image degradation. Analog and digital flat-panel monitors are available. To use a digital flat-panel LCD monitor, the video card must be capable of producing digital output.

Video cards, graphics cards, and accelerator cards are all names for the adapter card inside the PC that is responsible for generating the signals that tell the monitor what to display. The relationship between the video card and the monitor should be carefully matched. These two devices must be compatible in terms of the signal used to communicate to the monitor, the type of connector used to connect them, the video display standards they support, and their speed.

Viewable Size

For some reason, which is probably related to marketing, the sizes stated for CRT monitors are anywhere from 1 to 2 inches overstated. On the other hand, an LCD display's size is actually the size of the display area. So, be careful when comparing the viewable area—the part of the screen where images are displayed—on these two types of monitors.

CRT Display Sizes

The most popular CRT monitor sizes on the market today are 15-inch, 17-inch, 19-inch, and 21-inch. These sizes are called the monitor's "nominal size," which is measured diagonally from the bottom-right corner to the top-left corner—case and all, as illustrated in Figure 15.13.

CRT monitor cases have a front bezel (the plastic around the edge of the display) that covers up a portion of the CRT's screen to hold it in place. The bezel cuts down the area of the CRT that can be viewed by as much as a full inch all of the way around the edge of the monitor. Most CRT monitor manufacturers now list the viewable size of the monitor along with the monitor's nominal size.

The viewable size of a 17-inch CRT display is actually a bit less than 16 inches. When comparing monitors, it is good idea to compare viewable areas rather than nominal screen sizes. Not all monitors have the same size bezels. Many smaller monitors can be better values when you compare the price-per-inch of the monitor's viewable area. Table 15.1 lists the average nominal and viewable screen sizes for CRT and LCD monitors.

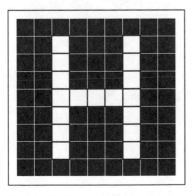

Figure 15.13   A CRT monitor is measured diagonally, case and all.

Table 15.1   Nominal display versus viewable screen sizes

Nominal Size (Inches)	CRT Viewable Size (Inches)	LCD Viewable Size (Inches)
14	13.2	13.5
15	13.8	14.5 or 15
17	15.9	17
19	18	19
21	19.8	21

LCD Display Sizes

As illustrated in Table 15.1, LCD flat-panel monitors can provide a better bargain on a per-viewable-inch basis. For the most part, the nominal size of an LCD display is the same as its viewable area, as opposed to the 1-inch or more margin of error used by CRT manufacturers. The display size for an LCD monitor is accurate, meaning that only the display area is measured diagonally. A 15-inch LCD display is usually 15 inches diagonally measured. And, as shown in Table 15.1, smaller LCD displays offer about the same display area as larger CRT monitors.

Resolution

The number of pixels on a display, whether CRT or LCD, determines the amount of detail that can be used to create an image. The more pixels in the display, the better the image quality a monitor is able to produce. The number of pixels in a display represents its *resolution*. A monitor's resolution is expressed as the number of pixels on each row and the number of pixel rows on the display. For example, a display with 640×480 resolution, which is read as "640 by 480," has 640 pixels on each horizontal row and 480 vertical rows of pixels of the display. This monitor uses 307,200 (640 times 480) pixels to create its displayed images. Table 15.2 shows the resolutions most commonly supported by today's monitors.

The *aspect ratio* of a monitor is the relationship of its height (in pixels) to its width (in pixels). On most of the commonly used CRT resolutions, the aspect ratio is 4:3,

Table 15.2   Monitor resolutions

Resolution	Total Pixels Used
640×480	307,200
800×600	480,000
1,024×768	786,432
1,280×1,024	1,310,720
1,600×1,200	1,920,000

which is by far the most common. The aspect ratio helps software determine how to place images on the screen in relationship to each other and to help circles look round and not elliptical, and squares look square and not like rectangles.

Monitor Size

The physical size of the monitor has a lot to do with the resolutions the monitor can support. Resolution is essentially a real-estate issue. As the space available to hold more pixels increases, so does the monitor's ability to handle higher resolutions. Another factor in this equation is the age of the monitor. Most newer monitors can display higher resolutions compared to many older and larger monitors.

Larger monitors, such as 19- or 21-inch monitors, natively support higher resolutions and have trouble displaying smaller resolutions. They can support lower resolutions by using fewer pixels or a smaller area of the screen to produce the display.

Most smaller monitors, such as 14- or 15-inch monitors, cannot produce higher resolutions with very good image quality. This is because higher resolutions require smaller pixels, and when applied on a smaller monitor, you may need a magnifying glass to read the screen. So, even though a 15-inch monitor may support 1,280×1,024 resolution, it may never actually be used. In fact, the highest resolution available on any monitor smaller than a 19-inch monitor may also never be used. Generally, LCD displays have fixed resolutions, and if you use a resolution that is higher or lower than its native resolution, the image quality will suffer. It is always best to match the monitor and its resolution to your needs.

Depending on the resolution in use, CRTs can enlarge or reduce images easily without too much image quality loss, but typically LCD panels have some trouble in doing so.

LCD Resolutions

Because of their construction, LCD displays have natural resolutions set by the number of pixels on each line of the display. Often, an LCD display must reduce the display area to reproduce images in lower resolutions. For example, a 12.1-inch LCD monitor (800×600 resolution) has 800 pixels on each row of its display. If the resolution is changed to 640×480, it is not possible to proportionately represent 640 pixels in the same area as 800 pixels and produce clear text or images. So, the display image area is reduced to 10.4 inches for the 640×480 image. However, as an LCD display's natural resolution and screen get larger, lower resolutions become much easier to reproduce in the standard display area. Table 15.3 shows how an LCD display adjusts for resolutions other than its natural resolution. In the table, "small" means the display is reduced, "full" means it is the natural resolution, and "linear" means that the user must scroll up and down and left and right to see all of the displayed image.

Table 15.3   LCD resolutions

Natural Resolution	640×480	800×600	1,024×768
640×480	Full	Linear	Linear
800×600	Small	Full	Linear
1,024×768	Small	Small	Full

Color Depth

A monitor's color depth is another very important characteristic. The color depth is the maximum number of colors a monitor can display. The color depth is represented as the number of bits required to hold the maximum number of colors in the color depth as a binary number. For example, an 8-bit color depth has a maximum of 256 colors, because that is the highest binary value that can be expressed in 8 bits. In binary numbers, the range of numbers available in 8 bits is 00000000 to 11111111, or the range in decimal numbers of 0 to 255, which represents 256 different colors. Table 15.4 lists the number of colors associated with each of the commonly used color depths.

Depending on the PC, video card, and monitor, either 24-bit or 32-bit color is typically designated as the true color setting. The number of colors that 32-bit color, which is popular with 3-dimensional (3D) video accelerator systems, can develop is perhaps overkill. The human eye cannot distinguish beyond 16 million or so colors. Above that, the eye has difficulty distinguishing the color differences of two adjacent pixels.

Refreshing the Display

Another key characteristic of a monitor is its *refresh rate*, which is the number of times per second that the screen can be entirely redrawn. The refresh rate is also a function of the video card and indicates how many times per second the data used to refresh the display is sent to the monitor.

Table 15.4   Color depths

Color Depth (Bits)	Colors Available	Common Name
1	2	Monochrome
4	16	VGA standard
8	256	256-color
16	65,536	High color
18	262,144	LCD color
24	16,777,216	True color (24-bit)
32	4,294,967,296	True color (32-bit)

One pass of the entire display by the electron beam requires only a small fraction of a second. However, the phosphor dots on the CRT's screen begin to fade almost immediately, so the electron beam must sweep back over each pixel multiple times per second to keep the display sharp and bright. A CRT's refresh rate is expressed in hertz (Hz, or cycles per second), and common refresh rates for CRT monitors (and video cards) are 60 to 85Hz, which translates to the screen being refreshed between 60 and 85 times per second. Most of the current monitors support refresh rates around 75Hz or faster. In the case of the refresh rate, 75Hz indicates that the screen will be completely refreshed 75 times per second. A low refresh rate can cause the CRT screen to flicker, resulting in eye fatigue and possibly headaches for the user. Due to how they work, LCD displays do not have refresh rate issues and can provide stable images at 60Hz, and sometimes less.

Interleaving

Interleaving divides the screen into two (or more) passes by refreshing every other row as it sweeps down the display. On one pass it refreshes the odd-numbered rows, and on its second pass, it refreshes the even-numbered rows. When you consider that most CRTs have at least 600 rows of pixels and 300 of the rows are refreshed in each pass, the screen has an even balance of refreshed pixels. Without interleaving, the top of the screen is fading when the bottom is being refreshed, which causes the image to appear to flicker.

Scan Rates

How fast a CRT is able to complete its sweep left to right and complete the refresh of the entire screen is an indicator of its brightness and image sharpness. The quicker the screen can be refreshed, the less likely it is that parts of the display will fade before they can be refreshed again. The horizontal and vertical *scan rates* of a CRT are used to indicate these speeds. The electron gun sweeps left to right to refresh the pixels on each row of the display hundreds of times per second. The number of times a horizontal row is refreshed in one second is expressed in kilohertz (kHz) or hundreds of cycles, as the horizontal refresh rate. The vertical scan rate indicates how fast the electron gun completes a scan of the entire display area. Table 15.5 lists the scan rates for the more commonly used CRT resolutions.

Table 15.5 Typical CRT scan rates

Resolution	Horizontal Scan Rate	Vertical Scan Rate
640×480	31.5–43kHz	60–85Hz
800×600	32–54kHz	50–85Hz
1,024×768	48–80kHz	60–100Hz
1,280×1,024	52–80kHz	50–75Hz

Masking the Display

Because the electron beam moves so fast, it is difficult for it to be very precise; therefore, a CRT will include one of two different types of guides—the shadow mask or the aperture grill—to prevent the beam from lighting up the wrong phosphor materials and producing the wrong colors.

Shadow Mask

The shadow mask is a very fine screen mounted between the electron gun and the pixels. The shadow mask, illustrated in Figure 15.14, has openings that permit each beam to hit only where it should. Any phosphor material in its shadow thus is masked and will not be illuminated. The holes in the mask are aligned to match perfectly with the pixels on the screen.

The distance in millimeters (mm) between two phosphor dots of the same color on the display is called the *dot pitch* (see Figure 15.15). This is an indication of the spacing of the pixels on the screen. A monitor with a low dot pitch produces better images than one with a higher dot pitch. Even the smallest difference in dot pitch shows up on the screen, especially on larger monitors. Current monitors offer dot pitch distances in the range of 0.24 mm to 0.31 mm, with the most common being 0.28 mm.

Aperture Grill

The alternative to the shadow mask method is the aperture grill, illustrated in Figure 15.16. On an aperture grill display, pixels are masked into vertical stripes between fine metal wires. The vertical wires perform the same function as the shadow mask—they keep the electron beam from illuminating the wrong parts of the phosphor. Two popular types of CRTs that use this method are the Sony Trinitron and the Mitsubishi Diamondtron, which are used in many of the popular monitor brands.

Figure 15.14   The shadow mask prevents the electron beam from straying off target.

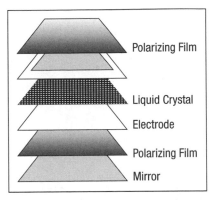

Figure 15.15 Dot pitch measures the distance between two dots of the same color.

Figure 15.16 The aperture grill divides the display into vertical stripes.

Aperture grill monitors have some advantages over those that use shadow mask CRTs. These advantages include a brighter picture, a sharper image, and, because the front of the tube is flat vertically, less glare and less distortion. However, because the vertical wires that are used to mask the phosphor tend to vibrate, especially in larger monitors, thin wires are placed horizontally across them to hold them in place and dampen the vibrations. This results in very faint lines across the screen where the horizontal wires run.

Stripe pitch is used on aperture grill monitors to indicate the distance between two stripes of the same color. Common stripe pitch distances are about the same as current dot pitch distances, from 0.24 mm to 0.32 mm.

Monitor Controls

Most CRT-style monitors have a control panel on the front or side so that their brightness, contrast, focus, and screen size or shape can be adjusted as needed. Some have separate knobs for each adjustable feature, and others have a single control knob or wheel. Virtually all new monitors, LCD and CRT, have an on-screen display (OSD) that allows the user to see on the screen the results of any adjustments.

Focus controls on a CRT adjust the convergence of the electron beams on pixels. The three beams can become misconverged or out of alignment. Misconverged beams cause a blurry or fuzzy image. The CRT's size and shape adjustments are used to fix barreling (when the sides of the display bow outward), pin-cushioning (when the sides bow inward), and rotation (when the top or bottom of the display is not level).

Although they do not have misconvergence problems, LCD monitors can have display and focus problems. A flat-panel monitor has adjustments to synchronize it to the video card. LCD monitors are set to standard VGA timings at the factory, and a particular PC and video card may use a slightly different timing, which can result in a distorted or blurry display. To correct this, LCD monitors have adjustments for their "Frequency/Clock" and "Focus/Phase" settings.

Video Display Standards

Video display standards are developed more to define the capabilities of video cards rather than monitors, but by listing the video standards to which the monitor is compatible, its capabilities in terms of color depth and resolution are automatically defined.

What differentiates one video display standard from another are the resolutions it supports, how it creates text characters, and whether it is color or monochrome, as well as its color depth, color palette, refresh rate, scan rates, and bandwidth. Table 15.6 lists the resolutions and color depths of the VGA and SVGA video standards, the two most commonly used today.

Over the years, several video display standards have been used. A few of the more popular ones are listed here:

- *Monochrome display adapter (MDA)*—MDA was the original text-only standard for monochrome monitors.

Table 15.6   Video standards

Standard	Name	Resolution(s)	Color depth
VGA	Video graphics array	640×480	16
		320×200	256
SVGA	Super VGA	800×600	16
		1,024×768	256
		1,280×1,024	256
		1,600×1,200	256

- *Monochrome graphics adapter (MGA)*—MGA, also called Hercules graphics, integrated graphics and text on a monochrome monitor.

- *Color graphics adapter (CGA)*—CGA was the first color graphics standard. It provided a 16-color palette on a 640×200 resolution.

- *Enhanced graphics adapter (EGA)*—EGA improved on the text and graphics capabilities of CGA and offered a 64-color palette.

- *Video graphics array (VGA)*—VGA is the *de facto* graphics standard for all monitors, video cards, and most software. As shown in Table 15.6, it supports a range of resolutions and color depths, but 640×480 is considered the VGA standard.

- *Super VGA (SVGA)*—SVGA is essentially all of the graphics standards above VGA, but it is typically associated with 800×600.

Of these video display standards, only VGA and SVGA are in common use today. The others were part of the video standard evolution, with each new standard improving on the last. Other video display standards in use are extended graphics array (XGA) and UVGA, which are loosely defined standards that vary from manufacturer to manufacturer.

The VGA display standard is considered the base standard for video display systems today. Virtually all current monitors and video cards support the VGA standard. It is the default standard for Windows and almost all other operating systems and device drivers that interact directly with the video system.

Most monitors on the market today claim to be at least SVGA-compatible. What this actually means is that they have some capabilities that are higher than the VGA standard, including resolution and color depth. The same holds true for UVGA and XGA, which are more marketing identities than they are video standards. The Video Electronics Standards Association (VESA) has recently defined the VESA SVGA standard in an attempt to standardize the definitions of the video interfaces above VGA.

Raster and Vector Graphics

An image drawn on the screen of a CRT can be produced using one of two different drawing techniques: raster or vector. Paint and imaging application software packages use raster graphics, and virtually all freehand drawing and animation software packages use vector graphics. Graphic output devices, including monitors and printers, are raster devices.

Raster Graphics

Raster graphics, also known as bit-mapped graphics, are a two-dimensional array of pixels that are drawn by assigning a value to each X (horizontal) and Y (vertical) pixel position on the screen. This is the most common technique used to create an image on the CRT display. Colors used in raster graphics are found in the monitor's Color Lookup table (CLUT), which contains the supported color subset of the full color palette of the video graphics standard in use.

Raster graphics are formed by patterns of pixels on the monitor's screen. A simple demonstration of raster graphics is text characters on a monochrome display. Characters are formed from a matrix of on and off pixels. For example, the letter "H" is created by illuminating certain pixels within the text character grid, as is illustrated in Figure 15.17. As shown, raster graphics are, by their nature, blocky images.

The blocky nature of raster graphics is even more apparent in images with curved or sloping edges, such as the diagonal line shown in Figure 15.18. The diagonal line has a jagged look, resembling a staircase. As the resolution increases, this effect is minimized because the jagged edge is more difficult to see. Some video systems apply a technique called *antialiasing*, which shades the pixels along the edge of a raster image to minimize the sharp contrast of the image to the background.

The advantage of a raster graphics CRT is that it provides fixed-rate refreshing and does not differentiate one graphic image type from another. However, as illustrated in Figure 15.18, its graphic images can have jagged edges, and every pixel must be redrawn in every refresh cycle. In spite of these relatively minor problems, raster graphics is the most popular type of CRT used with PCs.

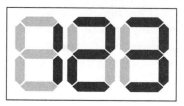

Figure 15.17   A text character created with raster graphics.

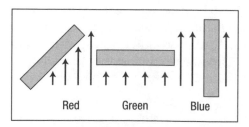

Figure 15.18   A diagonal line created with raster graphics.

Vector Graphics

Vector graphics, also called object-oriented graphics, are based on mathematical vectors that define how a graphic image is to be drawn. For example, a line created in vector graphics is defined in terms of its length, width, and the direction it is drawn from a source point. In contrast to the bit-mapped diagonal line in Figure 15.18, a line drawn in vector graphics is straight with smooth edges. The vector information to create a circle on the screen would contain the X (horizontal) and Y (vertical) pixel location of its center, and its radius, line thickness, color, fill texture, and other information. Vector graphics have smooth lines and edges and are easily resized, repositioned, or stretched without degrading the original image. Vector graphics also require less video memory than raster graphics.

Vector graphics monitors are very expensive and are typically reserved for use at engineering workstations and in special high-end applications such as GIS (geographic information systems).

Viewing Angles

A display's viewing angle measures how far above, below, and—more important—to the side of the display images on the screen can be accurately viewed. Table 15.7 compares the viewing angles of the two LCD displays to a CRT. Figure 15.19 illustrates the relative differences of the viewing angles of these displays.

The curvature of the screen has a lot to do with a display's viewing angle, but next on the list is the amount of contrast in the displayed image. An active matrix (TFT) display has deeper color, clarity, and contrast compared to a passive matrix display. LCD displays begin to lose their picture quality, in the eye of the viewer, as the viewing angle increases because less of the display's light (image) is able to reach the viewer. Obviously, the viewing angle champion is the conventional CRT. However, a flat-screen CRT may have a much lower viewing angle.

Integrated PC/Monitors

New systems that integrate the PC into the case of a flat-panel monitor are being introduced seemingly daily. These PCs integrate the motherboard, disk drive, CD-ROM, and sometimes a floppy disk drive into the housing of a flat-panel monitor.

Table 15.7   Display viewing angles

Display Type	Viewing Angle
Passive Matrix LCD	49–100 degrees
Active Matrix LCD	90–120 degrees
CRT	120–180 degrees

15. Monitors and Displays

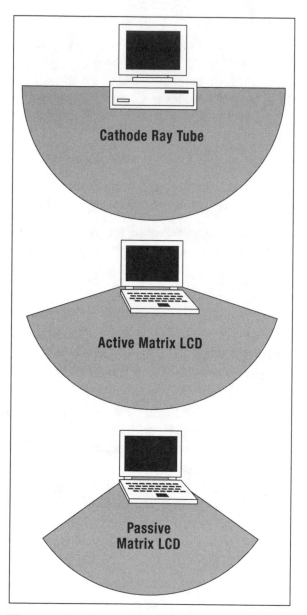

Figure 15.19   The relative viewing angles of LCD and CRT displays.

In effect, these devices are the equivalent of a notebook computer on a stand with a very large flat panel display. They are the ultimate in desktop space efficiency, with the keyboard having the largest footprint of the system. The PC's desktop footprint is literally its footprint—the space taken up by the foot on the monitor's stand.

These systems vary in features and price, and generally offer a fair to good configuration in terms of RAM and disk space. However, because of their tight packaging, there isn't much room for expansion cards, disk drives, or other internal devices. Any additional peripheral devices must be added through a universal serial bus (USB) or an IEEE 1394 (FireWire) connector.

Monitor Power

Monitors do not run off the PC's power supply. Even if the monitor is plugged into the back of the PC's power supply, it still gets its alternating current (AC) power from the wall outlet. The plug on the back of the power supply is an AC power pass-through plug. A PC's monitor uses more power than all of the other components of the PC added together, and, due to the way it works, several power issues exist on monitors that don't exist on a PC or its power supply.

Power Management

In an effort to reduce the tremendous amount of energy being consumed by monitors in active mode, governments and industry organizations have developed initiatives to reduce the amount of power consumed by PC monitors in general, but especially when they are idle. The U.S. Environmental Protection Agency (EPA) program named "Energy Star" certifies monitors and personal computers that meet guidelines for reduced energy consumption. These guidelines are that the monitors use less than 30 watts of power in all power modes and reduce their power consumption by 99 percent when in sleep or suspended mode. Most PCs sold today meet this standard, and the Energy Star logo is displayed on the monitor during the boot sequence on these PCs.

Virtually all monitors on the market today are also compliant with VESA's Display Power Management System (DPMS) protocol. DPMS is used to power down parts of the monitor and PC after they have been idle for a certain period of time. DPMS is a BIOS (basic input/output system)-supported protocol that can be enabled in the BIOS Setup configuration data) settings of the PC.

Degaussing

The internal components of a CRT can become magnetized over time. This magnetization can have a negative impact on the quality of the image produced by the monitor. Should the CRT become overly magnetized, color blotches may appear on the screen near the edges and in the corners. The CRT can be magnetized in many ways, including setting stereo speakers or other forms of magnets too close to the monitor (which can also distort the display), bumping the monitor very hard, or moving the monitor so that it is positioned over a PC's power supply.

15. Monitors and Displays

The cure for magnetization of the CRT is called *degaussing*. This term is derived from the word gauss, which is a measure of magnetic force. Most better monitors have built-in degaussing circuits that neutralize the CRT's magnetization through a coil of wire inside the monitor. The degaussing circuit is activated either by a manual switch or automatically through the monitor's controls.

On monitors with a manual degauss switch, pressing the switch activates a circuit that attempts to neutralize the CRT's magnetization. You can over-degauss a monitor and damage it. Therefore, you should not just keep pushing the degauss button to solve what may be display problems. The degauss process involves some clicking and buzzing and takes only a few minutes to complete its cycles.

Most newer monitors do an automatic degauss when they are powered up, which is the static buzz and click you hear when the monitor is powered up. If the built-in degaussing circuits of the CRT do not clear up the magnetization problem, the monitor should be taken to a repair shop for manual degaussing with a special degaussing tool.

Screen Savers

When monochrome monitors were the standard, screen-saver software was necessary to keep the electron beam from burning a static image into the phosphor and the CRT's glass. If a monochrome monitor became idle with an image on it, the CRT would continually refresh it to the point where the phosphor would eventually burn the image into the glass of the CRT screen. This is called "ghosting," and it is a threat to monochrome monitors that are idle for extended periods.

The solution was to install a screen-saver program. This software kept the screen changing and did not let the same image remain on the screen long enough to burn into the glass. Modern color monitors do not need screen savers because there is little chance of the pixels burning their image into the CRT display. Screen savers are primarily entertainment these days.

However, a screen saver can be a first-line security device to keep prying eyes from viewing your work. Most screen-saver systems can be assigned a password that controls who can deactivate the screen-saver and access the PC. On a Windows system, the screen-saver password is set on the Display Properties window, as shown in Figure 15.20.

Monitor Maintenance and Safety

The life span of a PC monitor, given fairly regular preventive maintenance and care, should be around five years. As mentioned earlier, the monitor is the one part of the PC that holds its value because the price of a monitor today is the same as what it was two to three years ago on a price per feature basis. As long as

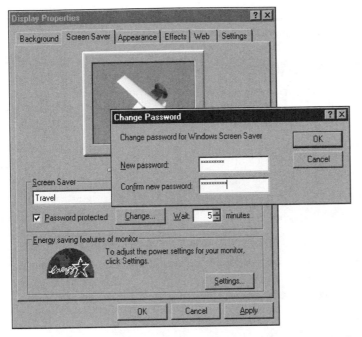

Figure 15.20   On Windows systems, a screen-saver password can be assigned.

the monitor is still doing its job, there is little need to replace it. The life of the monitor is essentially the same as the PC because it is typically purchased along with the PC and stays with it as long as both are working. However, if the processor should die, the monitor can be used with a different system.

The user—or most technicians, for that matter—should never attempt to repair a monitor for circuitry or electrical problems. Only the manufacturer or an authorized repair shop should repair a monitor, regardless of whether it is a CRT or an LCD. However, before any repairs are done, compare the cost estimate of the repair to the cost of a new monitor. In most situations, repair of a monitor is relatively inexpensive, but should the monitor need a new CRT or LCD, a new monitor may be a better investment.

WARNING! Rule number one—never—repeat, never—open the monitor's case. All repairs that require you to open or remove the monitor's case should be performed at a repair shop that is properly equipped to work on monitors.

Monitors are great to look at when all is working as it should, but should your monitor develop electrical or circuitry problems, you should never attempt to work inside the monitor's case. Even if it means you may need to buy a new monitor, you have to decide if your life is worth saving that $200 or $300, because you are actually risking your life if you attempt to work inside the monitor's case.

15. Monitors and Displays

Another issue, although somewhat controversial, is that of electromagnetic emissions from inside the case, discussed later in this chapter.

Avoiding Electrical Shock

The reason for the foregoing warnings, which cannot be emphasized enough, is that inside the monitor is a very large capacitor, which is an electronic device that holds power and uses it to regulate the power stream it receives. Remember that the monitor is not powered by the PC's power supply; it is plugged directly into an AC outlet. The monitor has a power supply much like the one in the PC itself. In this power supply is a large capacitor that stores enough electrical power to cause you very serious harm, even when the monitor is off and unplugged. The capacitor has a capacity of around 1,000 microfarads to absorb power spikes and fill in low-voltage events.

WARNING! Rule number two—Should you choose to risk your life by ignoring rule number one and open the monitor's case to work on it, absolutely do not wear an electrostatic discharge (ESD) wrist strap. If you do, you become the grounding circuit for all of the stored and static electricity in the monitor.

Electromagnetic Emissions

A CRT emits small amounts of very low frequency (VLF) and extremely low frequency (ELF) electromagnetic radiation. Whether this radiation is harmful to PC users is the subject of an ongoing debate. VLF and ELF are not lethal emissions, such as an X ray or gamma ray, but many experts believe they may be harmful after extended exposure periods.

Most of the CRT's radiation is emitted from its back and sides, with a very small amount emanating from the screen. The radiation does not carry far, and it is usually totally gone a few feet from the monitor. The general recommendation is for the user to sit at arm's length from the monitor screen. This will protect the user's eyes as well as put the user a relatively safe distance from the radiation emissions. Spacing monitors with a few feet of open space at the back and sides should keep everyone safe.

The debate on radiation emissions is that prolonged exposure may cause cancer, leukemia, and pregnancy complications, including miscarriage and birth defects. Nothing has yet been proven conclusively on whether this is fact or fear, but it is always better to err to the safe side. In fact, the Swedish government has created an organization to develop monitor standards that safeguard against monitor emissions. If you wish to purchase a monitor that conforms to these standards or check to see if your existing monitor conforms, look for a TCO certification. TCO is a Swedish abbreviation for the body of regulations governing monitor emissions. Four versions of these standards have been issued since their inception in 1991, with the latest being TCO '99.

Immediate Solutions

Performing Preventive Maintenance for a CRT Monitor

The life of a monitor can be extended with a regular program of preventive maintenance. Tips to prevent overheating and magnetization, as well as some cleaning tips are listed here. Most of these tips apply to CRT monitors, but can be applied to an LCD display as well. For an LCD monitor, check its documentation for cleaning and care tips. In these, and all other maintenance activities on PCs, let common sense be your guide.

- Keep a free space buffer of a few feet in each direction around a CRT monitor. This will help its cooling system to work efficiently as well as protect other users from radiation emissions.

- Never stack anything on top of the monitor or closely around it. Blocking the monitor's airflow will shorten the life of the CRT by causing it to overheat. The CRT is the most expensive part of the monitor to replace. Never place any form of magnetic media (diskettes, tapes, and the like) on top of the monitor because this may erase them. Remember that a very large magnet and lots of electromagnetic forces are housed inside the case.

- Never place heavy items on the monitor's top. This may cause the case to crack, or at least flex, and may cause something inside the case to short.

- Keep the monitor (and PC) at a distance from heat sources, damp environments, magnets (including those in standard PC or stereo speakers), motors, or areas in which static electricity is a problem. Magnets can affect the quality of the display.

- Use the power cord supplied with the monitor. Typically, this cord is specially designed to handle your monitor's voltage. If it is misplaced, obtain a replacement from the manufacturer or a dealer for that brand of monitor. Don't confuse the PC's power cord with the monitor's cord when moving the system.

- The monitor's case should be cleaned only with a damp lint-free cloth. Always unplug the monitor before cleaning it or before using any water-based cleaning solutions on it. The monitor's screen can be cleaned with the same cloth with a little diluted glass cleaner. Don't spray any liquids directly on the screen; spray the cleaner on the cloth and then wipe the screen clean. Always be sure to wipe the screen completely dry. Avoid strong degreasers or ammonia-based cleaners because they can impact the screen's glass and even affect the colors of the display.

15. Monitors and Displays

- The stand that shipped with the monitor is actually engineered as a part of the cooling system. If you remove it and sit the monitor on its case bottom, you run the risk of blocking the air vents on the bottom of the case. The monitor needs to be sitting up a bit to allow proper airflow for the cooling system.

- Avoid touching the screen with your hands. Oil and dirt from your hands are very difficult to remove from the screen.

Finding the Problem When the Monitor Is Blank or Has No Picture

A variety of problems can cause the monitor to be blank, dark, or appear to be dead. Use the following steps to debug this problem.

1. Verify that the monitor is connected to a power source and receiving power. Most newer monitors have a small light on the front that indicates the power is on.

2. Should the screen be white or gray (instead of black) and have a buzzing or high-pitched whine coming from the monitor, the monitor is probably not connected to the video card. Verify that the monitor is connected to the PC's video card and that the connection is snug. Also check the connection at the monitor end if the monitor uses a two-end video cable. Check the pins in the cable connectors for bent or broken pins before reconnecting them.

3. Check that the brightness and contrast controls have not been turned all the way up, which results in a dark screen. If these two controls are okay, check a few of the other controls because some combinations of settings will also darken the display. Use the monitor's documentation to locate and use the monitor's adjusting controls.

4. Reboot the PC. Listen for beep codes and watch for error messages from the power-on self-test (POST). If a single beep is sounded and the PC appears to be continuing with the boot, the problem is most likely in the monitor. Otherwise, the problem may be that the boot is hanging up before the video BIOS and device drivers are loaded. Verify with your BIOS or motherboard documentation what the beep code is for video adapter problems, and listen carefully for that or another beep code indicating a hardware problem.

5. Replace the monitor with a known good monitor. If the display appears, the original monitor is bad. Otherwise, replace the video card and continue troubleshooting.

Finding the Problem When the Monitor Has a Display, but Is Not Functioning Properly

If the monitor has a display but is not functioning properly, this is likely a device driver problem, a video card problem, or a failing monitor. Use the preceding project to troubleshoot the last two cases, but follow these steps to check the configuration of the monitor on the PC:

1. Verify the monitor's settings using the Windows Device Manager (right-click My Computer|Properties|Device Manager).

2. Drill down in the device tree to find the video card (graphics adapter). Highlight the video card's device entry and click the Properties button. On the device's Properties window, verify the driver and the system resources assigned to the video card. Resolve any resource conflicts.

3. You may want to check the video card's manufacturer for any updates or newer device drivers and install them.

4. If all is well, make sure the monitor is listed in the Windows system settings. Right-click the Desktop in an open space and choose Properties to open the Display Properties window. The Display icon on the Control Panel also opens this window. Select the Settings tab and click the Advanced button to open the video card's Properties window, as shown in Figure 15.21.

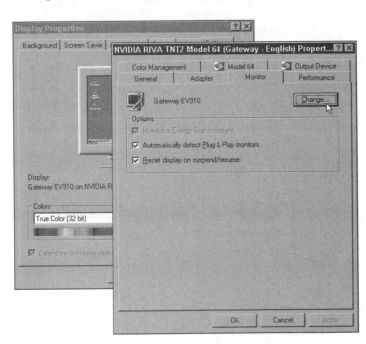

Figure 15.21   Check the monitor installed on the video card's Properties window.

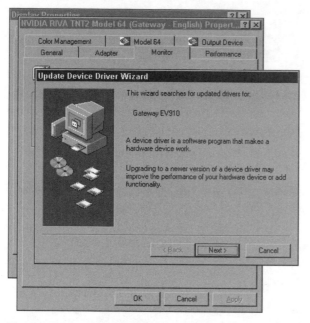

Figure 15.22   The Windows Update Device Driver Wizard.

5. Choose the Monitor tab, and if the monitor listed is not the type in use, click the Change button on the upper-right side of the window. This will open the Update Device Driver Wizard (shown in Figure 15.22), which will guide you through the installation of the proper device driver. If a disk came with the monitor, have it handy, and when asked to choose a driver, click the Have Disk button.

Finding the Problem When the Monitor Does Not Power On

If the monitor's power indicator light on its front bezel is lighted, the problem is likely not a power source problem. Use the prior "Finding the Problem When the Monitor Is Blank or Has No Picture" project to verify that the source of the problem is not elsewhere. If that does not find the problem, check the monitor on a different PC to verify that the video card is not the problem. Otherwise, the monitor may have internal power or circuitry issues, and this requires a trip to the repair shop.

To check the power, use the following steps:

1. Push the monitor's power button on and off a few times to make sure that the button isn't just stuck. If the monitor powers up, you will hear the static buzz and clicking associated with the automatic degauss and other startup steps performed by the monitor.

2. If the power button is not the problem, check that the power cord is snuggly seated in its connector. The power cord on many monitors is a specially designed cord. Check the documentation to see if the monitor uses a special power cord and how it is identified. Verify that the correct cable is in use.

3. Check the fuse on the back of the monitor. It probably looks like a small black knob with the word "Fuse" on the cap. If the fuse is bad, replace it. You can get replacement fuses at most computer or electronics shops. If the fuse needs to be replaced frequently, this indicates an internal electrical problem, and the monitor should go to the repair shop.

4. If the monitor is an enhanced graphics adapter (EGA) (or older) monitor, it may be plugged directly into the back of the power supply. If this is the case, the PC must be powered up before the monitor will have power. There is also the chance that the power supply pass-through plug is defective.

5. If the monitor is plugged into a power strip, make sure it is switched on and working. Plug the monitor into another AC source to check to verify the power source.

Changing the Color Depth and Resolution

To change the color depth (bit depth) or resolution settings for the monitor on a Windows PC or notebook computer, use the following steps.

1. At the Windows Desktop, right-click in an empty space to display the Desktop menu shown in Figure 15.23.

2. Choose Properties to open the Display Properties window shown in Figure 15.24.

3. Select the Settings tab.

4. Toward the bottom of the Settings tab are two side-by-side settings that control the color depth (Colors) and the screen resolution (Screen area), as shown in Figure 15.25.

5. Change the Screen area setting to its lowest value (the slide all the way to the left). It should be 640×480. Now change the color depth to 256 (8-bit)

15. Monitors and Displays

Figure 15.23   The Windows Desktop menu.

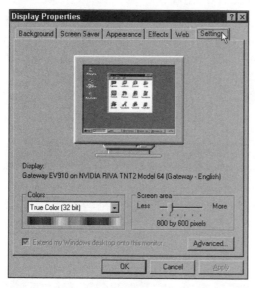

Figure 15.24   The Windows Display Properties window.

color. These settings are the VGA standard settings. Click Apply. Do not restart the system when asked, and apply the new settings without restarting the PC.

6. Unless these settings were what your monitor was set on to begin with, the displayed image should be constructed of much larger elements and may not all fit onto the display.

7. Reopen the Display Properties window and change the resolution (Screen area) and color depth (Colors) to the highest settings available. Once again, accept the settings without restarting your PC. The display should be much more detailed, and all of the elements should be much smaller than under VGA standard settings.

8. Reset the Display Properties to their original settings, unless you prefer their new values.

Figure 15.25   The Colors and Screen area settings on the Display Properties
Settings window.

Setting the Refresh Rate

To set the refresh rate on your monitor, or to check to see its setting:

1. Follow the steps used in the preceding project to display the Display
   Properties Settings window.

2. Click on the Advanced button to display the Properties window for the
   video adapter in your PC.

3. Select the Adapter tab. The refresh rate is selected from a list box that is
   located about in the middle of the window. On most Windows 9x or Windows 2000 PCs, the refresh rate is likely set to Optimal.

Recovering from an Incorrect Refresh Rate

If you change the refresh rate and the result is a distorted or blurry image, reboot
your PC into Windows Safe Mode and reset the refresh rate using the steps in the
preceding project.

15. Monitors
and Displays

Finding the Problem When the Monitor Goes Blank and Shuts Off after Being Idle

The monitor has its energy-saving settings activated. Use the following steps to adjust or turn off these features:

1. Open the Display Properties window by right-clicking the Desktop in an open area and choosing Properties.

2. Choose the Screen Saver tab. If your monitor contains energy-saving features, the lower quarter of the window will be an area with the Energy Star logo and a Settings button, as shown in Figure 15.26.

3. Click the Settings button to open the Power Management Properties window, shown in Figure 15.27. On this window, you can set the period of inactivity for each of the devices included in the energy-saving controls. The times available are in the list boxes for each device. If you would like to save a new custom energy configuration, use the Save As function. Selecting Never from the menu turns off the energy-savings feature for a device.

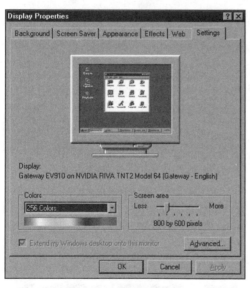

Figure 15.26   The Energy Star area on the Screen Saver window.

15. Monitors and Displays

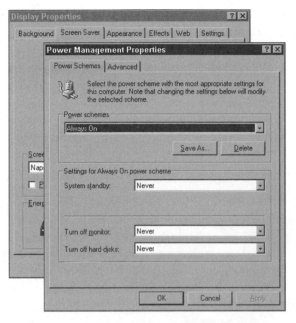

Figure 15.27   The Power Management Properties window is used to set the energy-
savings parameters of the monitor.

Disposing of a CRT Monitor

As much as 70 percent of a CRT's components contain lead, which is why CRTs
come under the Land Disposal Ban Program of the Resource Conservation and
Recovery Act (RCRA). This law requires CRTs to be disposed of using a very
prescriptive procedure. You cannot just throw them in the dumpster or the landfill. According to the RCRA regulations, a CRT must be dismantled, crushed, and
encapsulated in cement to be disposed of properly. Because this isn't something
that you should do yourself, even if you could, salvage companies exist that spe-
cialize in CRT and computer disposal, and they will do so for a small fee. By the
way, this law covers television sets as well.

Chapter 16

Printers

In Depth

Printer Characteristics

The general characteristics of a printer are essentially the same for all printer types. The following sections describe each of the major characteristics used to define the capabilities of a printer.

Type Quality

The type standard to which printers are compared is that of the typewriter and daisy wheel printer. These devices print whole characters by striking a solid raised form through a ribbon to impact the paper. *Type quality* is primarily used to describe the type capabilities of dot matrix printers, but can be applied to other printers as well.

The type qualities most commonly used to describe a printer's print are:

- *Draft quality*—Draft quality is a low-quality print in which the dots or print elements used to form the characters are individually visible on the page. Figure 16.1 illustrates a draft-quality character in comparison to other type qualities. Low-end ink jet and dot matrix printers produce draft-quality type.

- *Near letter quality (NLQ)*—This type quality is considered better than draft quality, but the dots or elements used to form the characters are partially visible, so it cannot be considered letter quality. An NLQ character is produced by printing the character twice, with the second pass slightly offset from the first. The results would look something like the example shown in Figure 16.1. Ink jet printers and dot matrix printers that print at 150 dots per inch (dpi, a print quality measurement used on ink jets and dot matrix printers) use NLQ as their type quality default.

- *Letter quality (LQ)*—This is the best type quality a printer can produce. A printer with a letter-quality rating is able to produce characters that appear to have been created by a typewriter or a solid character form. Daisy wheel, high-end ink jet and dot matrix, and laser printers produce letter quality type. Letter quality print requires a printer capable of producing 300 dpi. Letter quality characters appear to be solid without any gaps, as shown in the example in Figure 16.1.

Draft Quality   Near Letter Quality   Letter Quality

Figure 16.1   Examples of draft, near letter quality, and letter quality print types.

Print Speed

A printer's *speed* is measured in either the number of characters per second (cps) or the pages per minute (ppm) the printer can produce. However, these two measurements are rarely used together. Characters per second is used for printers that form characters one at a time, such as daisy wheel and dot matrix printers. Pages per minute is used for printers that produce documents without focusing on individual characters, such as ink jet and laser printers. Large printers that print an entire line at once (line printers), such as those used with mainframe computers, use lines per minute (lpm) as their print speed rating.

Daisy wheel printers are by far the slowest, with a top print speed around 30 cps. Line printers are the fastest at 3,000 lpm, or the equivalent of about 6,600 cps. Dot matrix printers print up to 500 cps, ink jet printers produce from 2 to 10 ppm, and laser printers range from 4 to 20 ppm. A laser printer with a print speed of 6 ppm has the equivalent speed of around 40 cps in letter quality. The quality of the print and whether it is color or black and white have a definite impact on a printer's speed.

Impact versus Nonimpact

Dot matrix, daisy wheel, and line printers are classified as *impact* printers because they make contact with the paper when they print. These printers use a striking mechanism to bang an inked ribbon into the paper to create a character or graphic. Impact printers are typically slower and noisier, but they are better for continuous and multipart forms. Ink jet, thermal, and laser printers are *nonimpact* printers. These printers do not make contact with the paper and use nonimpact methods to produce a document.

Text and Graphics

Those printers that have a locked-in character set, such as daisy wheel and line printers, are limited to a specific set of characters, which are usually only alphabetic characters, numbers, and some special characters. They are unable to produce graphics. Special printers, called plotters, use a combination of ink jet technology and the X and Y coordinates of the drawing elements to create drawings for use in engineering and other technical areas. Laser printers, ink jets, and many dot matrix printers are capable of merging text and graphics into a single document.

Fonts

A *font* or *typeface* is the style and design of the characters a printer prints, for example, Times New Roman, Courier, and Ariel. Figure 16.2 shows samples of some of the more common fonts. Word processing and graphics software now offer literally thousands of font styles and typefaces. However, not every printer is able to print every font. For example, a different wheel must be used in a daisy wheel printer for each font, and the wheel must be changed if the font changes. Most dot matrix printers offer 2 to 16 hard fonts (fonts that are built into the printer's firmware). However, soft fonts (fonts added from a disk or software) can be added and managed by the printer's device drivers. Laser and ink jet printers can produce just about any font the PC can generate because they treat the document as a graphic image. The issue concerning these printers is often printer memory and not fonts.

Print Styles

Fonts can be modified with print styles. A print style is applied to emphasize a character, word, title, or some other element. Figure 16.3 shows samples of the four standard print styles used with most fonts:

- *Normal*—This is the natural typeface of the font.
- *Boldface*—This print style darkens the type.
- *Italics*—This print style normally tilts the typeface slightly to the right.
- *Underline*—This print style places a horizontal line beneath the type.

In addition, the *strikethrough* is a print style that places a horizontal line through the center of the type. This is not a standard print style.

```
This is Times New Roman font
This is Courier font
This is Bookman font
This is Lucida font
This is Garamond font
This is Arial font
This is Script font
```

Figure 16.2   Samples of common fonts.

This is a natural typeface
This is a bold typeface
This is an italics typeface
This is an underline typeface
~~This is a strikethrough typeface~~

Figure 16.3   Common print styles used to modify text.

Print Sizes

Another feature of a font is its *scalability*, which is its ability to be printed in different character sizes. Font size is measured in *points* (pts). A point is $1/72$nd of an inch, or there are 72 points to an inch. Figure 16.4 shows a comparison of different point sizes for the Times New Roman font.

Font Classifications

Fonts fall into one of two classifications, bitmapped or scalable:

- *Bitmapped*—Bitmapped fonts form characters with patterns of dots. Each particular bitmapped font (e.g., Times Roman, Courier) specifies a dot pattern to be used for each letter, number, and special character, each print style (e.g., bold, italic), and each type size (e.g., 10 pts, 12 pts). Bitmapped fonts are stored in a font file that contains the predefined character patterns for each point size. If more point sizes are added to a bit-mapped font, the font file requires more disk space.

- *Scalable*—Scalable fonts are defined by a base font (a kind of starting point), which outlines the basic font typeface and design and contains a mathematical formula to generate the character in a requested point size or print style. Variations of a font are generated from the base whenever a point size other

This is 8 point font size
This is 10 point font size
This is 12 point font size
This is 18 point font size
This is 24 point font size
This is 36 point font size

Figure 16.4   A comparison of font point sizes.

16. Printers

than the base is needed. TrueType and PostScript fonts are examples of scalable fonts.

Printer Standards

Printers connect to PCs most commonly through a parallel port and use a standard protocol to communicate. A *protocol* defines the rules used by two devices when communicating. The IEEE (Institute of Electrical and Electronics Engineers) standardized parallel port protocols are known as the *IEEE 1284 standards*, which are:

- *Standard parallel port (SPP)*—A parallel port standard that allows data to travel only from the computer to the printer.

- *Enhanced parallel port (EPP)*—A parallel port standard that allows data to flow from the computer to the printer or from the printer to the computer, but only one way at a time (half-duplex). When not receiving a print file, the printer can send signals to the processor to indicate such conditions as out of paper or open cover.

- *Enhanced capabilities port (ECP)*—This parallel port protocol allows bidirectional simultaneous (full-duplex) communications between the printer and the PC over special IEEE 1284-compliant cables. EPP cables also are bidirectional, but they do not support ECP communications.

Printer Controls

Most PC printers have a set of buttons located on a front panel (see Figure 16.5) that are used to control the activities or change the configuration of the printer. Nearly all printers have buttons for at least online/offline, line feed (to advance the paper a single line), and form feed (to advance the paper one page). When a printer is online, it receives printing instructions from a computer that indicate the character to print and line and form feed commands. Other printers have buttons to cycle through a configuration menu or to select a font or point size. Many printers also include a small LCD screen, shown in Figure 16.5, on which the printer's status and activity are displayed, as well as menu and option choices during configuration.

Dot Matrix Printers

The daisy wheel printer is generally obsolete today, so our review of the various printer types begins with the dot matrix printer. The dot matrix printer uses a matrix of pins in its printhead to create text and graphics with a pattern of dots. The dot matrix printer is much faster and quieter than a daisy wheel printer, but it is still considered somewhat noisy. Dot matrix printers incorporate tractor-feed mechanisms to feed continuous-form paper and documents.

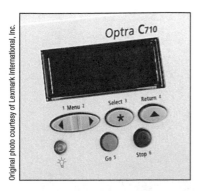

Figure 16.5   The control panel on a color laser printer.

The Centronics Corporation produced many of the first popular dot matrix printers for the early Apple computers. The cable connector Centronics chose for use on its printers was a distinctive 36-pin connector that featured pins arranged on a center bar (see Figure 16.6). The "Centronics" connector was actually developed by the Ampenol Corporation, but due to the early popularity of Centronics printers, it is commonly referred to as the "Centronics connector."

Dot matrix printers (see Figure 16.7) are impact printers, and have generally been replaced by ink jet and laser printers in the home and small office. However, the dot matrix printer continues to fill a market niche in the office and industrial applications because it accurately feeds multipart continuous forms. Dot matrix printers are common in pharmacies, receiving docks, and warehouses, and have many administrative purposes, including mailing labels, cash registers, and automatic teller machines (ATMs). Several manufacturers, including IBM, Epson, Oki Data, and Lexmark, still offer full lines of dot matrix printers.

Dot matrix printers are available in two standard physical widths: narrow and wide. A narrow-width dot matrix printer is usually limited to 80 columns. Narrow-width dot matrix printers are typically used only for correspondence and letter-size (8.5 × 11 inch) forms.

Figure 16.6   A standard printer cable has a 36-pin Centronics connector on the printer
end and a DB-25 connector on the computer end.

16. Printers

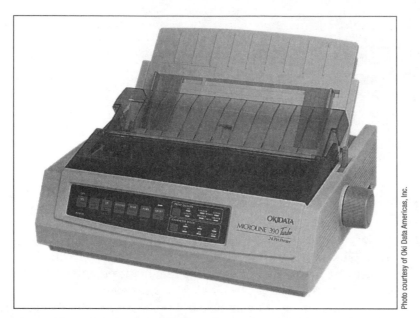

Photo courtesy of Oki Data Americas, Inc.

Figure 16.7   A dot matrix printer.

A wide-width dot matrix printer can print 132 columns or more. This type of dot matrix printer is typically used as a general printer. Wide-width dot matrix printers can be adjusted down to narrow widths to accommodate narrower paper sizes.

Dot Matrix Printing Operations

Compared to those of ink jet and laser printers (discussed later in this chapter), the operations of the dot matrix printer are fairly simple. However, printing data on a dot matrix printer does involve quite a few steps, many of which are also used with all other printer types.

The printing process for any type of printer always begins with the PC and its software. Typically, an application program, such as a word processor (e.g., Microsoft Word, Corel WordPerfect), a graphics package (e.g., Adobe Illustrator, Photoshop), or a desktop publishing package (e.g., Microsoft Publisher, Adobe PageMaker), generates a print-image file, which can be anything from a plain text document to a complex full-color photograph.

The following sections describe the processes used to print on a dot matrix printer.

Print Queue

After a user sends a document to the printer, the application in use communicates to the PC's operating system and the printer's device drivers to create a file that contains print commands and codes that are used by the printer to create the document. The commands included in this file are those needed to produce the letters, numbers, special characters, graphics, print styles, and other document effects, such as tabs, line feeds, and page feeds. This file is placed in the system's *print queue*, which is a buffer that holds print files waiting to be sent to a printer. When the printer is available, the file is sent to the printer. Otherwise, the print file is held until the printer is available and there are no other print files in the queue ahead of it.

Print Buffer

When a print file is transferred to a dot matrix printer, it is stored in the printer's *print buffer*. The print buffer is needed because the PC transfers data to the printer much faster than the printer is able to print it. The print buffer receives the print file and releases the PC to perform other tasks. Without a print buffer, the PC would have to wait while the printer processed each line of the print file and printed the data. Early PC printers either had no print buffer or had a very small one. This meant that the PC and the printer were both tied up until the print job completed.

Dot matrix print buffers typically hold 8 to 60 kilobytes (KB) of data, depending on the age, manufacturer, and model of the printer. Dot matrix printers with enhanced graphics or extended font capabilities tend to have larger print buffers. The size of a dot matrix printer's print buffer is commonly listed right along with its print speed as one of its major features, and more is always better.

Printer and PC Communications

Often the size of the print file exceeds the capacity of the print buffer. When the print buffer is full, it sends a command to the PC to stop sending data. Typically, this is a transmission off (XOFF) command. As the printer empties the print buffer and more space is available, the printer notifies the PC with a transmission on (XON) command that it can resume sending the file. This dialogue continues until the entire file is transferred. After the file is completely transferred to the printer, the computer disengages and moves on to other tasks while the printer finishes printing the file. These communications are not specific just to dot matrix printers.

Forming a Character

The printer's processor reads the instructions for one line of print from the print buffer and translates it into the dot patterns needed to print each character on the line. The printer's processor also decides the best travel direction for the printhead to print the line: whether to travel left to right or right to left. The processor also controls the movement of the paper, advancing it a single line, advancing it to the top of the next page, or feeding an entire page.

As was illustrated in Figure 16.1, a dot matrix printer forms its characters with a pattern of dots. Characters are formed in stages, depending on the number of pins in the printhead (see next section), which is commonly either 9 or 24. A 9-pin

16. Printers

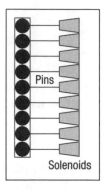

Figure 16.8   The arrangement of the pins in a 9-pin dot matrix printhead.

printhead, in which the pins are arranged in a single column (see Figure 16.8), forms characters by printing the appropriate dots in a series of connecting columns. Nine-pin dot matrix printers are capable of only draft quality print and are commonly used for forms, whereas 24-pin printers are used in high-end dot matrix applications.

The Printhead

The printhead is the most important part of the dot matrix printer. It forms the characters and prints them on the page. The major components in the printhead, as illustrated in Figure 16.8, are the solenoids and pins, along with a permanent magnet and the wire coils and springs of each pin.

Inside the printhead is a large permanent magnet that holds the pins away from the front of the printhead. On the shaft of each pin is a spring that pushes against the pull of the magnet and a wire coil. When the wire coil is charged, its electromagnetic force neutralizes the force of the magnet, and the spring pushes the pin forward to strike the ribbon and place a dot on the paper. When power is removed from the wire coil, the magnet counteracts the spring and retracts the pin.

The friction of the moving parts of the printhead and the constant energizing and de-energizing of the wire coils create heat. A dot matrix printhead gets very hot when it is printing, which is why most have a heat sink either attached to or designed into the housing. The tines of the heat sink provide multiple surfaces to cool the printhead.

Print Speeds and Resolutions

The speed of dot matrix printers has increased dramatically over the past few years. Dot matrix print speeds now range from as low as 200 cps to 1,200 and 1,400 cps. At the same time, the resolution of a dot matrix printer has also increased. Early dot matrix printers supported only 10 dpi, but now they offer resolutions of 360 dpi and higher. However, a typical dot matrix printer is more likely to support around 75 dpi printing for NLQ print.

16. Printers

Color Dot Matrix Printers

Some dot matrix printers require the addition of a color kit for color printing capability, but most color dot matrix printers have a built-in color capability. On the low end, the user must change the ribbon and choose a different print mode through the printer's control panel to change the printer from a monochrome printer to a color printer. High-end dot matrix color printers include color functions in their firmware, including the ability to produce thousands of colors using only the colors included in the ribbon. In addition to its firmware, the color functions of a dot matrix printer are controlled by the printer's device drivers, which handle the translation of a color image into the commands needed to produce it on paper. The ribbon of a color dot matrix is divided horizontally into two to four color stripes. The print mechanism shifts the ribbon up and down to place the correct color in front of the print head as needed.

Ink Jet Printers

Ink jet printers create printed images by spraying small droplets of very quick drying ink through tiny nozzles (jets) onto the paper (see Figure 16.9). The documents produced by an ink jet printer are typically of better quality than can be produced by a dot matrix printer. Ink jet printers are less expensive and usually physically smaller than most laser printers, which appeals to home and small office users. However, ink jet printers are slower than laser printers, have a reputation for occasionally smearing, bleeding, or running the ink on the page, and can have difficulties with page feeding. In spite of these problems, the ink jet printer has become very popular with home and small office users because it produces good quality printing at a reasonable price.

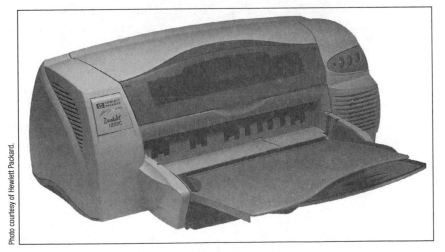

Photo courtesy of Hewlett Packard.

Figure 16.9   An ink jet printer.

Ink Jet Technologies

Ink jet printing uses small droplets of ink to print text and graphics on paper. An ink jet printhead has dozens of nozzles through which ink is jetted (fired) onto the paper. Two general types of ink jet technologies are used: continuous flow and drop-on-demand. Drop-on-demand ink jet printing has two forms: piezoelectric and thermal.

Continuous Flow

Continuous flow ink jet technology is not used in PC printers. In this ink jet technology, the ink flows continuously through the printhead, but not all of the ink is put on the paper. Ink droplets are passed through a variable charge chamber, where they are selectively given an electrical charge. Only the droplets selected by the timing mechanism for use in creating the printed image are charged. All of the droplets then flow over a deflector plate that fires the charged droplets onto the paper and deflects the uncharged droplets back into the ink supply to be reused. The printhead of a continuous flow ink jet printer is fixed in place, and the paper is moved back and forth under the print head. This prevents the ink from being splashed about, which would happen if the head were moved.

Drop-on-Demand

Piezoelectric, one of the two drop-on-demand ink jet approaches, operates as follows. As the printhead moves over the paper, a piezoelectric crystal in each nozzle is charged with electricity, which makes the crystal expand. As the crystal expands, it fires a droplet of ink, which is smaller than the width of a human hair, out of the nozzle with enough force to strike the paper. Piezoelectric ink jet printers can change the size of the droplet put on the paper by changing the amount of electricity applied to the crystal and altering the rate and amount of its expansion. A larger electrical charge causes more expansion in the crystal and forces more ink from the nozzle.

The other type of drop-on-demand ink jet printer is the thermal ink jet. The thermal process involves heating the ink in the ink channel between the ink reservoir and the printhead's nozzles. Heating the ink creates a bubble that forces the ink out of the nozzle similar to the piezoelectric crystal mechanism. Only about a third of the ink is actually heated, however, and at full speed, the ink increases in temperature only around 30°C (about 86F) over its normal temperature. Thermal ink jets are the most common type in use, with models produced by Hewlett-Packard, Lexmark, and Canon, the companies that also hold nearly all of the thermal ink jet patents.

Halftoning

The first step of the ink jet print process is called *halftoning*, which is the same technique used to print monochrome photographs in newspapers. If you look very closely at a newspaper picture, you will see thousands of small dots of various halftone shades of gray and black. Your eye and brain blend the dots to form an image.

To print an image in halftones, the page is first divided into an arrangement of cells. Each cell is a matrix of dots, as shown in Figure 16.10. A solid black cell has all of its dots printed, and a white cell has no printed dots. Printing only some of the dots in the cell will produce a shade of gray on the page. Lighter grays have fewer printed dots, and darker grays have more printed dots. For example, a 25 percent grayscale has one-fourth of a cell's dots printed black, and a 50 percent grayscale has half of its dots printed. The number of dots in a cell, which is set by the printer's resolution, determines the number of grayscale shades available. A cell that is 4 dots by 4 dots can produce 17 ($4 \times 4 + 1$) shades of gray. An 8×8 cell is capable of 65 shades of gray. The halftone cells are then applied across and down the page, just like tiles, to create an image.

The output from the halftoning process is a bitmapped version of the image to be printed. In addition to the bitmap image of the document, the file may also contain additional bits for color text or images. An additional bit is included for each of the four CMYK (cyan/magenta/yellow/black) colors, to indicate which color is

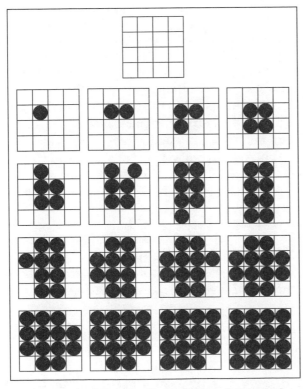

Figure 16.10   The 17 halftone dot possibilities using a 4 × 4 halftone cell.

on or off for each dot. The printer's device drivers compress the bitmap image file to minimize the amount of data transmitted to the printer.

An ink jet printer does not print an entire line of text in one pass; it can take many passes to complete one line of 12-point text. The controller interprets the data from the bitmap file for one pass of the printhead, and when a certain color is called for, a signal is sent to the printhead to fire the nozzles for that color when the printhead passes over the correct dots on the printed line. As the printhead passes over the exact spot on the print line that calls for a certain color, the nozzles for that color either heat up or the piezocrystals fire for precisely the right amount of time, and they place precisely the amount of ink called for in the image file sent from the application program. Remember that this process involves spraying drops of ink that are about one million times smaller than a small drop of water out of nozzles that are thinner than a strand of human hair.

Color Conversion

An image displayed on the monitor in an RGB (red/green/blue) color image must be converted to CMYK colors before it can be printed. The RGB color scheme, which uses up to 24 bits to specify each pixel of an image, depends on the radiance (wavelengths) of the RGB dots of each pixel to blend and create its colors. This additive approach to color creates a spectrum that ranges from black (the absence of color wavelengths) to white (the presence of all color wavelengths).

In contrast, paper is reflective and produces color through a subtractive process. A fresh sheet of paper appears white because it includes all color wavelengths. As color is printed on paper, the ink absorbs color wavelengths from the paper to create a color. Each of the CMYK colors absorbs different wavelengths, and when used in combination they absorb enough wavelengths to create a wide array of colors. For example, cyan (blue) ink absorbs red wavelengths and produces greenish-blue colors. Magenta (red) ink absorbs green wavelengths and creates reddish-blue colors. Yellow absorbs blue wavelengths to create yellowish-red colors. Black ink absorbs all color wavelengths.

Converting the colors from the RGB color scheme used inside the computer to the CMYK color scheme of the printer is the challenge of printing an application-generated or scanned color image on a color ink jet printer. The colors humans see are actually the combination of different light wavelengths. As color wavelengths are added or subtracted, different colors are created.

To convert from the RGB color scheme to the CMYK color scheme, a Color Lookup table (CLUT) is used. The binary RGB code for a color is looked up in the CLUT, and its corresponding CMYK binary code is used. Often the colors of an image are different on the monitor than on paper. This is because it is impossible to exactly match RGB colors with CMYK colors.

Color Halftoning

Whereas monochrome halftoning created the image to be printed using cells that produce shades of gray, color halftoning is able to produce a wide range of colors with only four ink colors. Color halftoning works very much like monochrome halftoning except that a separate halftone layer is created for each color. Four halftone layers are created, one for each color with a dot anywhere that color is used. When the layers are logically superimposed on the printed page, the actual colors of the image emerge.

The challenge of the halftone process is to hide the dots used to create an image and present a smooth blending of colors that create a realistic-looking image to the viewer. This requires very sophisticated software (which is why color qualities vary by manufacturer), and a process that allows the viewer's eye to smooth the dot patterns on the page. This is accomplished using one of two halftoning methods: ordered dithering or image diffusion. Most inkjet printers use image diffusion as their halftoning method because it creates more uniform dot patterns. However, some manufacturers, most notably Lexmark, offer both halftone methods and allow the user to choose which to use on a given project.

Ordered Dithering

Ordered dithering creates the transition from one color to another by evenly spacing pixels of each color along the common edge of the two colors (see the middle sample in Figure 16.11). This method, which is faster to create than image diffusion, is used on professional-level graphics that require more accurate color representations.

Like monochrome halftoning, ordered dithering divides each color plane into cells. Each cell uses a separate pattern of dots, depending on the size of the cell. The number of pixels in a cell is a function of the print resolution of the printer, but the more dots in the cells, the more shades of a color that can be represented.

A threshold matrix is applied that allows only the cells in certain locations to sbe printed and blocks other cells from being printed. This screening creates the

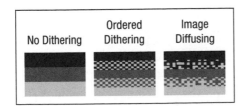

Figure 16.11   Samples of an image section showing no dithering, ordered dithering, and image diffusion.

dithering (or transition) for each color. A separate threshold matrix is used for each color layer. Remember that each layer of the color halftone represents only a single color, and the ordered dithering from one color to the next is handled partially on each color's layer. The threshold is actually a file with binary values that are used to determine whether a color is to print for a particular cell. Each cell has a binary value that indicates the dots that are to receive color. The threshold matrix has a corresponding binary value for each cell. The two binary values for each cell are compared, and if the value in the halftone cell is greater than that in the threshold matrix, the cell is printed. If the threshold's value is equal to or greater than that of the halftone cell, the cell is not printed.

Image Diffusion

Image diffusion, also called diffuse dithering and error diffusion, is the technique used by virtually all inkjet printers. This process treats each dot in the image as if it could be printed in one of 255 shades of a color or grayscale, despite the fact that an inkjet printer is capable of printing the dot in only one of its four colors. For discussion purposes, assume the color being printed is black, which has a value of 255 (in contrast, no dot, or white space, has a value of 0). The image diffusion process determines a grayscale color value for each dot in the image. It then calculates an "error" value that represents the difference of what will actually be printed at the dot's location (either a dot or no dot) and the grayscale value that was determined for that location.

For example, the printer driver determines that a dot should have a grayscale value of 128, but no dot is to be printed. The error for that dot would be 128 minus 0, or 128. If a dot *were* to be printed at that location, the error would be 128 minus 255, or an error of –127. The error values are used to diffuse the color of the adjacent dots. If the error is a negative number, then black dots are less likely to be printed in adjacent pixels. If the error is positive, black dots are more likely to be printed in the adjacent cells. The final determination depends on the error diffusion applied to the neighboring dots. The overall result is an averaging of the color in neighboring cells and a more subtle color change. See the example on the right in Figure 16.11.

Ink Jet Cartridges

Monochrome ink jet printers have only a single ink cartridge, and color ink jet printers typically have two cartridges, one black and one tri-color (CMY, or cyan/magenta/yellow). The reason the black cartridge is separate is that the vast majority of printing done on an ink jet is text or line drawings only in black. One of the downsides to having cyan, magenta, and yellow in the same cartridge is that when one color runs out, regardless of how much ink remains of the other colors, the cartridge needs to be replaced if you wish to use all the colors in the printer's palette. Newer color inkjet printers feature ink cartridges with a replaceable ink tank for each of the CMY colors, which solves this problem.

Virtually all ink jet cartridges have a built-in printhead, which guarantees a fresh printhead each time a new cartridge is installed. The printhead has either 64 to 128 micro jets through which the ink is fired to the paper. The printhead also contains built-in resistors on the flexible circuits located on the front on the cartridge. These resistors do wear out in time and can cause slanted or wavy print. When this happens, the cartridge should be replaced.

Printer Drivers

The workhorse of the ink jet printing process is the software device driver that converts RGB to CMYK, performs the calculations in halftoning operations, and manages the flow-of-print file from the PC to the printer. The printer driver controls the applications and hardware with which the printer will work and manages the communications between the printer and the computer to keep the printing process flowing smoothly.

A printer's device driver is usually included with the printer on a diskette or CD-ROM. Newer or updated versions of device drivers are constantly available, as well as updated BIOS (basic input/output system) and firmware for some printers. These updates are typically found on the manufacturer's Web site. Many manufacturers now have alert systems that notify you via email or fax when new drivers are available.

Laser Printers

A laser printer, such as the one shown in Figure 16.12, uses the same electrophotographic (EP) process used in a photocopier. A laser printer produces a printed document using a focused beam of laser light and a rotating mirror to reproduce the image of a document as an electrostatic charge on a photosensitive drum. Toner, the "ink" of the laser printer, is added, and the charge on the drum attracts and holds it in the image of the document. A sheet of paper is fed in from the paper supply and electrostatically charged. The paper is rolled over the drum and picks up the toner. Heat is then applied to the toner, the toner fuses with the paper, and the document is completed and placed on the output rack of the printer.

A laser printer is a page printer. It produces a finished page on each cycle. This is in contrast to the other types of printers that print single characters (daisy wheel, dot matrix) or all or part of a line of print (line printer, ink jet) on each cycle. A laser printer produces all the text and graphics of one full page at one time. It is a cut-sheet printer; its paper supply is a stack of individual sheets of paper. It cannot handle multipart forms or any type of continuous forms. The processes used

Photo courtesy of Lexmark International, Inc.

Figure 16.12   A laser printer.

to form the page to be printed are essentially the same as used for the ink jet printer, with some minor differences, which are explained earlier in this chapter in "Ink Jet Printers."

Laser Printer Technologies

Laser printers use three different printing processes to produce a printed page. Each of the technologies in use is directly attributable to one or more laser printer or photocopier manufacturer(s):

- *Electrophotographic process*—The EP process is the printing process used by virtually all laser printers. Its characteristics are the use of a laser beam to produce an electrostatic charge and a dry toner to create the printed image.

- *Light-emitting diode (LED) process*—An LED printer uses an array of around 2,500 light-emitting diodes (like very small light bulbs) in place of a laser as the light source used to condition the photosensitive drum.

- *Liquid crystal display (LCD) process*—An LCD printer uses light shone through an LCD panel in place of the laser to condition the photosensitive drum. See Chapter 15 for more information on how liquid crystal works.

Electrophotographic Process

The EP process used in the laser printer has its roots in the dry photocopy method called xerography. Closely aligned with the Xerox Corporation, xerography roughly translates to dry writing, and is the name for the photocopying process used in nearly all laser printers and all dry photocopiers. Xerography is ideal for the laser printer because it requires no liquid inks or special paper such as is used with a thermal copier. This process relies on the fact that some substances become electrically charged when exposed to a light source.

In the EP process, the printer's drum, which is made from selenium or another photosensitive (light-sensitive) material, is electrically charged. The print image file generated on the computer by an application is used to logically create an image of the document to be printed. This image is then used to guide the laser and mirrors that shine light on the drum where no text or graphic is to appear on the finished document. Where light strikes the drum, it loses its charge.

Next, negatively charged toner sprayed on the drum adheres to the parts of the drum that still have a charge. This creates the document in reverse image on the drum. A sheet of paper is fed from the paper supply and is positively charged. The paper is then fed closely past the drum and toner. The charge on the paper attracts the toner onto the paper and the paper and toner are fed through heated rollers that literally melt (fuse) the toner onto the paper. If multiple copies of the same document are being printed, more toner is added to the drum, and another sheet of paper is charged, passed by the drum, and fused. If only one copy of the page is being printed, any remaining toner is removed from the drum, the drum is recharged, and the process begins again.

The EP laser printing process can be organized into six separate phases, as follows:

1. *Conditioning*—The entire drum is uniformly charged to –600 volts (V) by the primary corona wire (also known as the main corona) located inside the toner cartridge.

2. *Writing*—The laser printer's controller uses a laser beam and one or more mirrors to create the image of the page on the drum. The laser beam is turned on and off to create a series of small dots on the drum to match the document to be printed. Where the light of the laser contacts the photosensitive drum, the charge at that spot is reduced to about –100V. After the entire image of the document has been transferred to the drum, the controller starts a sheet feeding through the printer, stopping it at the registration rollers.

3. *Developing*—Inside the developing roller, which is also located inside the toner cartridge, is a magnet that attracts the iron particles in the toner. As the developing roller rotates by the drum, the toner is attracted to the areas of the drum that have been exposed by the laser, creating a mirror image of the document on the drum.

4. *Transferring*—The back of the paper sheet is given a positive charge. As the paper passes the drum, the negatively charged toner is attracted from the drum onto the paper. The paper now has the image of the document on it, but the toner, held in place by simple magnetism, is not bonded to it.

5. *Fusing*—The fusing rollers apply heat and pressure to the toner, melting and pressing it into the paper to create a permanent bond. The fusing rollers are covered with Teflon and a light silicon oil to keep the paper and toner from sticking to them.

6. *Cleaning*—Before the next page is started, the drum is swept free of any lingering toner with a rubber blade, and a fluorescent lamp removes any electrical charge remaining on the drum. Any toner removed in this step is not reused but is put into a used-toner compartment on the cartridge.

LED Printing

An LED printer uses the same printing phases as a laser printer. However, an LED printer replaces the laser and mirrors of the laser printer with a bank of light-emitting diodes. The number of LEDs in the light source is directly related to the resolution of the printer. Because LEDs are tiny and very bright, one LED can be used for each dot in the printer's resolution. For example, a printer rated at 600 dpi has 600 LEDs in each inch of its light source. As the drum rotates past the light source, the LEDs are used to discharge the dots that form a single row of dots in the image.

LCD Printing

An LCD printer uses the same printing phases as the laser and LED printers. The difference is that an LCD printer uses light passing through an LCD panel to discharge the drum. These printers are also called LCD shutter printers due to the way liquid crystal elements work. (See Chapter 15 for more information on LCD technologies.)

A liquid crystal pixel is used for each dot on one pixel row of the drum. If a printer is rated for 1,200 dpi, then 1,200 liquid crystal pixels are used in each inch of the light source. As the drum rotates past the light source, the crystals are opened and closed to discharge the drum for each line of pixels in the document's image.

The Toner Cartridge

On most laser printers, a removable cartridge supplies the printer with several valuable parts of the printing process. Typically, this cartridge contains, as illustrated in Figure 16.13, the photosensitive drum, the primary corona wire (used to condition the drum), a developing roller (used to deposit toner on the drum), and toner. Including these components in the toner cartridge provides the printer with a fresh drum each time the toner cartridge is changed. Older laser printers and photocopiers have a fixed print drum and commonly experience scratches and grooves on the drum that are caused by paper bits, staples, or other foreign bodies that fall into the printer. The incidence of these problems is far less on printers with the print drum sealed inside a cartridge.

Figure 16.13   A laser printer toner cartridge.

Inside the Laser Printer

The primary components of a laser printer are used to drive the six printing phases described earlier. The primary components of a laser printer (see Figure 16.14) are:

- *Drum*—The photosensitive drum, which is made of selenium or another light-sensitive material, is located inside the toner cartridge on most laser printers. However, some larger systems have fixed drums.

- *High-voltage power supply*—The EP process uses very high voltage to charge the drum and to transfer and hold the toner on paper. The high-voltage power supply converts AC current into the higher voltages used in the printer.

- *DC power supply*—The laser printer's electronic components use direct current (DC) power. For example, the printer's logic circuits use ±5V DC (volts direct current), and the paper transport motors require +24V DC. The laser printer's DC power supply also houses the main cooling fan.

- *Paper transport*—A laser printer has at least four sets of rubberized rollers (each with its own motor) used to move paper through the printer: the feed roller (paper pickup) rollers, the registration rollers, the fuser rollers, and the exit rollers. The rollers are rubberized to grip the paper, and they grip with only the pressure needed to move paper through the process. Most printer problems occur in the paper transport system, particularly the paper feed rollers.

- *Primary corona*—Also called the main corona or the primary grid, this component forms an electrical field that uniformly charges the photosensitive drum to −600V during the conditioning phase.

- *Transfer corona*—This component supplies a charge to the back of the paper that pulls the toner from the drum onto the front of the paper. As the paper exits the transfer corona area, a static charge eliminator strip reduces the charge on the paper so that it won't stick to the drum. Not all printers use a transfer corona; some use a transfer roller instead.

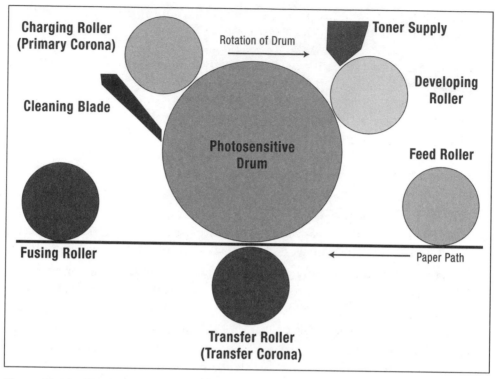

Figure 16.14 The internal components of the laser printing process.

- *Fusing rollers*—The toner is fused permanently to the page with pressure and heat by the fusing rollers. The temperature of the fusing rollers is between 165°C and 180°C (or 330°F to 355°F). The fuser, not the laser, is the reason why the pages coming out of a laser printer are hot.

- *Controller*—The controller is the laser printer's motherboard. It handles the communications with the PC, houses the memory in the printer, and controls the formation of the printed page. The printer's memory is located on the controller board. A laser printer's memory can be expanded; adding memory allows the printer to reproduce larger documents, higher resolution graphics, and additional soft fonts.

Color Laser Printers

Monochrome laser printers use the same halftoning techniques as the monochrome ink jet printer (see "Halftoning" earlier in this chapter). The difference is that a laser printer forms the document on the print drum all at once before it is printed, as opposed to a series of printhead passes.

The Raster Image Processor (RIP), which is part of the printer's internal control circuitry, translates the print commands sent from the PC into the cells that make up the image to be printed. The RIP computes the position of each cell and dot on the page and creates an image of the document in the printer's memory, where one bit of memory corresponds to each dot position of the image. The controller than directs the laser (or LED or LCD) to create the dot pattern on the drum. In a laser printer, the laser beam is focused on a multisided mirror that rotates to direct the beam onto the drum. Any place the beam touches the drum represents a dot in the image. LED and LCD printers turn their light sources on and off for each of the dot positions on the drum.

The number of dots in use to create printed pages varies with price and manufacturer. Laser printers commonly offer resolutions of 400 to 1,200 dpi, with 600 dpi being very common. Heavy-duty workgroup laser printers can offer up to 2,400 dpi, but these are normally outside the price range of most home or small office users. A 600 dpi laser printer offering standard paper widths (8.5 inches) uses more than 5,000 dots in each row on the drum.

A color laser printer has two page-per-minute ratings, one for monochrome and one for color. The difference arises because the laser printer forms the image for each of its colors separately. The color page-per-minute rating will always be the slower of the two. A laser printer may have a 16 ppm rating for monochrome, but only 3 ppm for printing color documents.

For each of the CMYK colors used in a document, a complete print cycle must be completed. This means that for each of the four colors, the drum is written, the correct color toner is applied, the partial image is transferred to the paper, the excess color toner is removed, and the process repeats for the next color. The paper may make as many as four passes around the drum—one trip for each color layer. The fusing process is performed only once on the page, however, after the toners for all of the colors have been transferred. A variation of this process is Hewlett-Packard's "one-pass" system, which applies each layer of toner to the drum before the full-color buildup is transferred to the paper. For each color in the image, the drum turns a complete cycle (except there is only one conditioning phase). After all of the colors are added to the drum, the paper passes the drum for a single transfer phase.

Building up the Image

The challenge of color laser printing is to create millions of colors and shades using only the four CMYK colors. To do this, two primary color printing methods are used in color laser printing: bilevel and multilevel.

16. Printers

- *Bilevel*—In this basic color printing method, no control is provided for the intensity of a color. Each color dot is either on or off with no in-between shading. Dithering, explained earlier in this chapter, is used to create transitions between colors.

- *Multilevel*—Multilevel color printers have the ability to adjust the intensity of each dot to produce 256 shades of each color (256 shades of cyan, 256 shades of magenta, and so on) and then mix the 256 shades of each color to produce a total of more than 16 million colors that can be printed. This ability eliminates the need for dithering to produce the transition from one solid color to the next.

Nearly all color laser printers use the fusing process to blend colors. One color dot is placed on top of another color dot and blended into the final color by the heat of the fusing phase. Some printers are able to control how much toner is placed on a dot by controlling how long the laser is allowed to strike the drum. The length of time the laser strikes the drum results in a larger or smaller dot. A bigger dot collects more toner during developing, and a smaller dot collects less toner.

Toner

Toner, the dry granulated "ink" used in laser printers, is made from the following ingredients:

- *Plastic*—Each toner particle is coated with an outer layer of styrene plastic or a blend of styrene and acrylic plastics. The plastic melts in the fusing phase to bond to the paper.

- *Iron*—Toner particles contain as much as 40 percent ferrous oxide, a magnetic iron material. During the print process, toner is negatively charged so that it will be attracted to the drum and paper to form a document image.

- *Silica*—Silica is a very fine sand-like material that prevents the toner from clumping.

- *Charge dye*—This special dye helps control the amount of electrostatic charge the toner can hold.

- *Wax*—When the wax melts during the fusing phase, it helps the toner flow and blend.

- *Carbon black*—Carbon black is added to black toner to deepen the color.

Line Printers

Larger systems, such as mainframes, that print thousands of pages of reports, checks, or billing statements daily are called *line printers*. The name indicates that an entire line of text is printed in one strike. These printers are usually capable of printing 132 to 168 characters per line. At each character position is a print chain that contains each of the characters in the printer's font set. As each line is formed, the chain at each character position is rotated to the proper character and the line is struck through the ribbon to the paper. The character positions are then reset and the next line is printed.

Thermal Printers

A thermal printer uses a heating element that writes by causing a chemical change on specially treated paper. Two types of thermal printers are available:

- *Direct thermal*—The direct thermal printer uses heat to change the chemical coating that has been directly applied to the thermal printer paper.

- *Thermal transfer*—The thermal transfer printer includes a ribbon or carrier that applies a thermally reactive chemical to the paper as it is fed to the printing mechanism.

The primary part of the print mechanism of a thermal printer is a stylus tip that heats up when electricity flows through it. This tip, called a *resistance*, is very small and heats up and cools down in a fraction of a second. A thermal printer moves the heated tip over the treated thermal paper to create text.

A real advantage to thermal printers is that they are virtually silent in operation. Thermal printers are typically used in specialized applications, such as server stations in restaurants, where their lack of noise is a plus. They are also used on a great many cash registers, and have been popular for portable printers for notebooks and other portable PCs.

Immediate Solutions

Diagnosing Common Printer Problems

Printer problems can originate from either the printer or the PC. Use the following steps to diagnose common printer problems on either the printer or the PC.

The Printer

1. *Verify that the printer is powered on.* There should be a power LED on the printer's front panel. If the power LED is not lighted, flip the printer's on/off (1/0) button to its on (1) position. If the power does not come on, verify that the printer is connected to a power source. If the power source is a plug strip or surge suppressor, verify that it has power or that its fuse is not blown.

2. *Verify that the printer is online.* There should also be an LED indicating whether the printer is online on the printer's front panel. If this LED is not lighted, press the Online button on the front panel to place the printer online with the PC. If the button does not light, either the printer is not powered up, the LED is burned out, or the printer is not connected to the PC.

3. *Verify that the printer is connected to the PC (or network).* A cable should connect the printer to the PC. This cable should be like the one shown earlier in Figure 16.6 with the Centronics connector on the printer end and the DB-25 end connected to a parallel port on the PC. If the printer is properly connected and the cable is not faulty, the printer's online indicator should light. You should also verify that the cable is the right one for the parallel port protocol in use. If an ECP protocol is in use, verify that the cable is IEEE-1284 ECP compatible.

4. *Look for error messages.* Are any error codes or messages displayed on the printer's LCD panel (if it has one)? Laser printers provide the most in diagnostic and error messages. Unfortunately, dot matrix and inkjet printers do not, but if these printers have a printing error, they are usually fairly obvious and easily isolated.

5. *Reset the printer.* The printer could have a print job stuck in its memory that, for some unknown reason, it is unable to process. Try powering off the printer, waiting a few seconds, and then powering it back up.

The PC

1. *Look for error boxes.* On a Windows PC, print errors are displayed in a dialog box, such as the one shown in Figure 16.15. Typically, if a printer error message is displayed, the problem is likely with the printer itself.

2. *Check the network printer.* If the printer is a network printer, a common error message is that the PC cannot find the network. The most common cure for this is to reboot the PC and resend the print file.

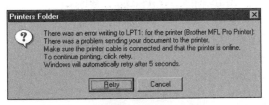

Printers Folder

There was an error writing to LPT1: for the printer (Brother MFL Pro Printer):
There was a problem sending your document to the printer.
Make sure the printer cable is connected and that the printer is online.
To continue printing, click retry.
Windows will automatically retry after 5 seconds.

[Retry]   [Cancel]

Figure 16.15   **The error message box displayed when a printer is unavailable to the Windows system.**

Connecting a Printer to a PC

Most PC printers connect through a parallel port, which is usually designated as LPT1 (line printer 1). A PC may have more than one parallel port, but most systems have only one. The connectors most commonly used to connect a printer directly to a PC are:

- *25-pin DB (data bus) female connector*—The LPT/parallel port on the back of a PC is usually a 25-pin female connector, as shown in Figure 16.16, into which a 25-pin male DB connector (see Figure 16.17) on the PC end of the printer cable is inserted. Most PCs have only a single LPT port, which is mounted on the motherboard or an expansion card.

- *36-pin Centronics connector*—The most common connector for the printer end of a printer cable is a 36-pin Centronics connector. This connector,

DB-25 Female

Figure 16.16   **DB-25 female connector.**

Figure 16.17   Centronics 36-pin connector and DB-25 male connector on a printer cable.

shown in Figure 16.17, is also the default for the HP-IB (Hewlett-Packard interface bus) used to connect Hewlett-Packard printers. The PC end of the cable is normally a 25-pin male connector.

- *USB*—Some of the latest printers offer a universal serial bus (USB) connection in addition to the standard parallel connector. If the parallel port is already in use by a scanner or Zip drive, the USB port allows the printer to be connected to the PC without using the parallel port or any additional system resources. Older printers can be connected via a USB connection, shown in Figure 16.18, by using a USB-to-parallel adapter cable, which has a Centronics connector on the printer end and a USB connector on the PC end.

- *IrDA*—Adapters are available that connect a parallel printer to a PC through its Infrared Data Association (IrDA) connection, which frees the parallel port on the PC for other uses. A number of small hand-held-size printers are available for use with notebooks and personal digital assistants (PDAs) with an IrDA connection.

Parallel cables have distance limitations. Older Centronics cables should not be more than 15 feet in length; between 9 feet and 12 feet is best. Newer IEEE-1284 cables can extend up to 30 feet in length, and some 50-foot high-end cables are available as well. Typically, if you need to be more than 10 feet away from a printer, you would connect into a network or move the printer or PC closer.

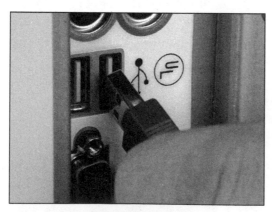

Figure 16.18   A USB connector.

Setting up a Printer in Windows

Setting up a printer on a Windows system is virtually the same for every type of printer. However, you should always follow the setup instructions and always use the device drivers that come with the printer. Windows 9x, Windows NT, and Windows 2000 each carry a remarkable number of printer drivers with them. However, to be absolutely certain that you have the very latest driver for the PC's operating system, visit the manufacturer's Web site. Some printers come with a separate printer driver included on a diskette or a CD-ROM.

To add a printer to a Windows PC, use the Printers function found on the Control Panel or on the Settings option of the Start menu. In either case, the Printers dialog box displays the Add Printer wizard icon (see Figure 16.19).

The following steps detail the process used to add a printer to a Windows computer.

1. *Printers icon*—From the Windows desktop, click the Start button to display the Start menu. Access the Settings menu and choose the Printers option. Another way to access the Printers window is to double-click the My Computer icon to display the My Computer folder. Open the Control Panel and choose the Printers icon.

2. *Add Printer wizard*—With the Printer folder open, choose the Add Printer icon (Figure 16.19) to start the Add Printer wizard, shown in Figure 16.20. If the printer being added is not listed in the supported printers list, use the diskette or CD-ROM that came with the printer to supply the device driver by clicking the "Have Disk" button when appropriate. In fact, even if the printer is listed and you have a disk, use the disk. After the printer driver loads, an

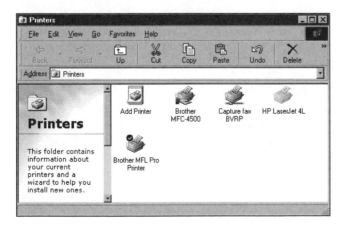

Figure 16.19   The Printer window showing the Add Printer icon.

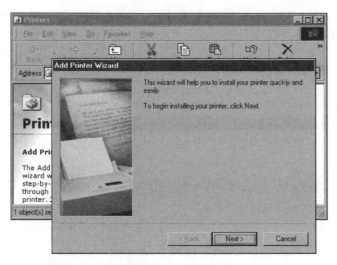

Figure 16.20   The Add Printer wizard.

icon for the new printer will display in the Printers folder. You many want to open the Properties windows for this printer and make any print control adjustments you desire or to set the new printer as the system default.

Using a Switchbox with a Printer

A switchbox, either manual or automatic, can be used to connect more than one nonlaser printer or any other parallel device or devices to a single parallel port. You can also use a switchbox to allow multiple PCs to share a single printer. A dial designates which PC or device is to be connected to the primary device of the switchbox. Switchboxes are also called A/B switches because the devices attached are labeled as A, B, C, and so on. An automatic switchbox senses activity on a line and automatically switches to that line.

In general, laser printers, especially the newer laser printers, should not be connected to a switchbox. Laser printers are highly interactive with the PC and have very high voltage requirements. There is also the issue of electrical noise. Taking the laser printer on- and offline by changing the active location, either manually or automatically, can interrupt device driver commands and create electrical noise spikes that could possibly damage the laser printer or the PC's parallel port.

Connecting to a Network

Due to the cost of a high-quality, high-volume laser printer, its best and most efficient use is likely as a workgroup printer attached to a network. It is wise to share such an expensive resource as a high-end color laser printer among several PCs by placing the printer on the local area network (LAN). Printers to be shared over a network can be purchased network-ready or can be easily adapted to connect to a network.

Network-ready printers have an internal network adapter into which an RJ-45 network connector can be inserted. A printer that is not network-ready can be attached to a network through a network printer interface such as Hewlett-Packard's JetDirect. These devices can be used to connect one or more printers to the network. A printer connects to a network interface device through its parallel port. The network interface device provides the network adapter that interfaces the printer to the network. Figure 16.21 illustrates a network-ready printer connected directly to the network as well as another printer that is not network ready connected with a network interface device.

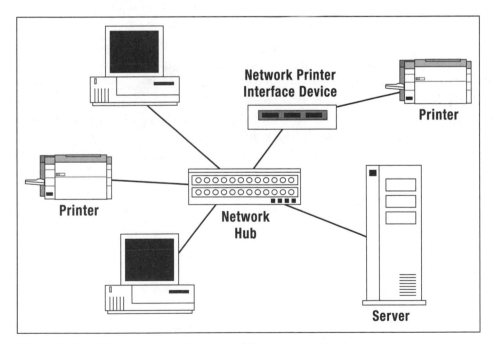

Figure 16.21 Many users can share a printer over a network.

Safeguarding a Printer

Some common-sense as well as technical procedures that you can use to keep a printer working and reliable are listed here:

- *Power protection*—Plug ink jet, dot matrix, and other non-laser printers into a surge protector or UPS (uninterruptible power supply). Never, however, plug a laser printer into a conventional UPS. Laser printers draw a tremendous amount of power at startup, and few UPS units have enough power to handle the demand. If you use a UPS for your laser printer, be sure the UPS can handle the peak loading (peak power requirements) of the laser printer.

- *Paper*—Always use the types and weights of paper recommended by the manufacturer for the printer, and never use paper heavier than the recommended maximum weight. This will help avoid print feed and paper path jams. Some manufacturers prefer laser printer paper that is finished on one side; check your printer's documentation.

- *Cleaning*—Clean dot matrix printers regularly with a vacuum or blow them out with compressed air. If you wish to vacuum out a laser printer, be sure you use a vacuum and dust bag specially made for that task. The toner can really gum up the works of a regular vacuum cleaner.

- *Conditioning*—Use a flexible wire brush or rubber-conditioning product to clean and maintain the paper transport of an inkjet or laser printer. Never put anything inside a laser printer while it is running to try to clear the paper path, and always wait until the fusing area has cooled down before working in that area of a laser printer. The fusing area uses high heat to melt the toner and stays hot for some time after the printer is turned off.

Caring for a Laser Printer

Laser printers have special needs when it comes to maintenance. The following sections contain tips to help you care for a laser printer.

Toner

A toner cartridge is typically a sealed unit that requires you to remove a strip, tape, or tab to install it in a laser printer. Toner incidents are rare, but should you ever spill toner either inside or outside the printer, don't use a standard vacuum cleaner to clean it up. Toner is actually very fine particles of iron and plastic, and it will seep through the walls of most vacuum bags and get into the vacuum cleaner motor, where it will melt and clog up the works. Special vacuums and vacuum bags are made for dealing with toner.

Never rinse toner off your skin with hot or even warm water. Hot water can cause toner to fuse to your skin. Wipe off as much toner as you can with a dry paper towel or soft cloth. Then rinse your skin with cold water and finish up by washing with soap and cold water.

Usually packed with a new toner cartridge is a cleaning brush or large plastic wand with a cotton pad that can be used to clean the transfer corona wire. You should clean the corona wires each time you change the cartridge, but only after the printer has cooled down. Be gentle when cleaning these wires because they are breakable.

Ozone

During the print process, a laser printer produces a gas called *ozone*. Most laser printers have an ozone filter that captures the ozone gas as well as toner dust and paper dust. This filter should be replaced or cleaned in accordance with the manufacturer's instructions in the printer's manual. Spare filters are usually shipped with the printer. If not, contact the manufacturer or vendor to get spare filters, if needed.

Mirrors

Inside the laser printer are two or more multisided mirrors that are used to reflect the laser onto the drum. Clean these mirrors periodically using a clean, lint-free cloth. Be sure the power is off and the unit is unplugged. Never—repeat, never—look directly at the laser and along this line, and never operate the printer with its covers off. Most printers will not power up with the cover open as a safety precaution.

Fuser Pads and Rollers

The fuser cleaning pad (which cleans the fusing roller after it presses the melted toner onto the paper) and the fusing roller can become dirty and begin to leave unwanted toner blobs on the paper. Check the fuser cleaning pad and the fuser rollers regularly and clean them as necessary.

Troubleshooting Dot Matrix Printers

Dot matrix printers, for all of their moving parts, really don't have a lot of problems. Some of the more common problems and some possible causes to investigate are listed here:

- *There is no power.* Check the obvious (power switch on, power cord connected, and so on). The problem could also be caused by the printer's power

16. Printer

supply, or a failure with the printhead motor. If the power light is on, but the printer will not work, check to see if the case may be open. If the printer is on and online, check out the printer cable connection or the printer cable itself.

- *The paper will not feed.* Most likely, there is an obstruction in the paper path, or the alignment guides are released. If the forms tractor or platen will not push or pull paper through the printer, there may be a broken or stretched belt, a bad platen motor, or perhaps the forms tractor itself is defective.

- *The ribbon will not feed.* If the ribbon is stuck in one place, any of the following could be the culprit: it may be time to replace the ribbon, the ribbon may be bad, the belt on the ribbon feed may be defective, or one of the ribbon gears may be broken.

- *The print is bad.* If the same part of each letter is missing, or if a line appears across an entire line of print, one of the following may be true: a pin has been bent, the print head is defective, or the cable that pulls the printhead across the platen has stretched or is about to break.

Troubleshooting Ink Jet Printers

Ink jet printers are relatively error-free, with the exception of a few ink smears and paper jams. In fact, most of the problems that the printer itself can have are nearly the same as those listed in the previous project for dot matrix printers. Instead of ribbon problems though, the ink jet can have cartridge problems. The more common cartridge problems are:

- *The printer goes through the motions without printing.* If the print cartridge moves from side to side as if it is printing, but the paper is blank, the problem is either a clogged or an empty ink cartridge. If the cartridge is not empty, the problem is most likely clogged nozzles on the ink jet. This is far more likely to happen on a monochrome ink jet printer. Gently wipe the cartridge's nozzles with a soft lint-free cloth (one you don't mind staining for life). Never use a facial tissue for this job.

- *One color does not print.* Either the color has run out, which means the cartridge must be replaced, or the nozzles for that color are clogged. As required, replace or clean the cartridge (see the preceding bullet item).

- *The printer cartridge light on the printer is flashing.* Something is wrong with the cartridge, and it should be reseated or, in the worst case, replaced. It could be that the resistors on the printhead are damaged.

- *The paper is feeding slightly askew.* The print feed rollers may be dirty, or part of the paper feed mechanism is broken. Clean the feed rollers with a cotton swab and denatured alcohol. If the feed mechanism is broken or defective, you have just discovered why ink jet printers are considered disposable technology.

- *Colors are misaligned and text is not aligned to graphics.* When you install a new ink cartridge, always take the time to align the printer's printheads. This process aligns the cartridge carriages and adjusts the positions of the nozzles so that ink that should be placed on top of other ink to create a color is exactly where it needs to be and not slightly off to the side.

Chapter 17

Keyboards, Mice, and Pointing Devices

In Depth

Keyboards

The keyboard, which is the most commonly used input device, allows users to communicate with a PC through keystrokes that represent data and commands. Every PC includes a keyboard in its standard package. Despite its many variations and styles, keyboards, such as the one shown in Figure 17.1, have been standardized to use the same basic keyboard layout, to attach to a PC with standard connectors, and to be interchangeable among manufacturers.

Keyboard Layouts

The layout of a PC keyboard—the alphabetic, numeric, and special character keys—can vary by continent, country, or language. However, with a few minor exceptions, virtually all English-language keyboards are the same. The keys on a typical keyboard can be grouped into functional groups, as illustrated in Figure 17.2:

- *Alphabetic keys*—The term "alphabetic keys" here refers to those that form the main body of the keyboard including the numbers and special characters above them, punctuation, and action keys. These keys typically have the same layout as on a typewriter.

- *Cursor keys*—Cursor keys are found only on keyboards with more than 100 keys. This group of keys, which is located to the right of the alphabetic keys,

Figure 17.1   A typical PC keyboard.

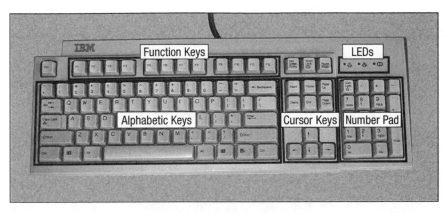

Figure 17.2   The major key groupings on a keyboard.

comprises two smaller groups: the cursor control keys and the cursor command keys.

- *Function keys*—A keyboard with fewer than 100 keys usually has only 8 function keys, which are located in two rows on the left-hand side of the keyboard. Newer keyboards typically have a single row of 12 function keys placed across the top of a keyboard.

- *Number pad keys*—All PC keyboards have a number pad in one form or another. On older 83- and 84-key keyboards, the number pad is placed alongside the alphabetic keys. Newer keyboards, with 101, 104, and 105 keys, place the number pad on the extreme right-hand side of the keyboard. The standard number pad has ten number keys and keys for the four arithmetic functions (add, subtract, multiply, and divide) as well as a key for "equals." By toggling off the **Num Lock** key, the number pad can also be used as a cursor control pad.

Alphabetic Keys

As mentioned previously, alphabetic keys make up the main area of the keyboard. They are the keys used for most keyboard input by the user. This group of keys includes:

- *Alphabetic keys*—Each of the 26 English-language alphabet characters A through Z has a separate key. The default is for a lowercase character, but an uppercase letter can be generated with either the **Shift** key or the **Caps Lock** key, used in conjunction with one of the alphabetic keys.

- *Special characters and punctuation*—These keys, which are located on the main area of the keyboard along the right side of the alphabetic keys (**A–Z**), are: \ (backslash), | (vertical bar); / (forward slash), **?** (question mark); . (period/dot), **>** (greater than); **,** (comma), **<** (less than); **;** (semicolon), **:** (colon); ' (open single quote), ' (close single quote/apostrophe); " (open double quote), " (close double quote); [(open/left bracket), { (open/left brace); and] (close/right bracket), } (close/right brace). These symbols are paired on keys as lowercase keys and uppercase keys that are selected through the **Shift** key, respectively.

- *Action keys*—This group of keys contains the primary action key of the keyboard—the **Enter** key—and two key subgroups: the character selection keys and the command action keys.

  - ***Enter** key*—This may be the most-used key on the keyboard, and it is generally the largest. The **Enter** key (sometimes called the **Return** key) is used to end a command, text line, or an entry in an application, as well as serving as a trigger or other action button in a game.

  - *Character selection keys*—The character selection keys are the two (right and left) **Shift** keys, the **Caps Lock** key, and the **Backspace** (or **Delete**) key. The **Shift** keys toggle the alphabetic, numeric, punctuation, or special character keys between lowercase and uppercase choices. The **Caps Lock** key locks the alphabetic keys into their uppercase characters. The **Backspace** key erases a character by replacing it with the character or white space that follows it.

  - *Command action keys*—These keys include the two (right and left) **Control** (or **Cntrl**) keys, the **Escape** (or **Esc**) key, and the two (right and left) **Alt** (alternate control) keys. The **Control** and **Alt** keys are used mostly to create key combinations with alphabetic, numeric, and function keys for actions or commands to software programs.

- *White space keys*—White space is any empty space on a page between characters, words, lines, or paragraphs. The keys that create white space are the spacebar and **Tab** key. The spacebar produces one character of white space per keystroke, and the **Tab** key defaults to a half inch of white space. The value of the **Tab** key, or the length of space it creates, can be adjusted in most word processing applications.

- *Number/special character keys*—The 13 or 12 keys in the row across the top of the alphabetic keys contain 26 (or 24) different numbers and special characters. The unshifted number keys (**1**, **2**, **3**, **4**, **5**, **6**, **7**, **8**, **9**, and **0**) are standard on all keyboards, but the special characters located on these keys vary by region. The special characters accessed with the **Shift** key are, respectively: **!** (exclamation point), **@** (at sign), **#** (pound or number sign), **$** (dollar sign), **%** (percent sign), **^** (caret), **&** (ampersand), ***** (asterisk), **(** (opening/left parenthesis), and **)** (closing/right parenthesis). The remaining special character pairs are: **~** (tilde), **`** (accent grave); **-** (hyphen), **_** (underscore); and **=** (equal sign), **+** (plus sign).

Toggle Keys and Locks

The **Shift**, **Control**, and **Alt** keys are *toggle keys*, which are keys that are used to toggle another key between two or more values. On most keys, the two values a key represents are a default value (the value of the key when no toggle key is used to modify its value) and an alternate value (selected when a toggle key is pressed). For example, pressing the **A** key without pressing the **Shift** key produces the character "a" (assuming the **Caps Lock** key is not locked), which is the key's default value. Pressing and holding the **Shift** key and then the **A** key produces the character "A," or the key's alternate value. Pressing and holding the **Shift** key toggles any alphabetic key to its uppercase or alternate value. The toggle value is in effect only while a toggle key is being pressed. When the key is released, the value reverts to its default.

Locking keys, which are the **Caps Lock**, **Num Lock** (numeric lock), and **Scroll Lock** keys, also toggle between two actions or values, but, unlike the **Shift**, **Control**, and **Alt** keys, they must be pressed a second time to release the toggle. A locking key works similar to an on/off button on a monitor—when the on/off button is pressed, the monitor is powered on and stays on until the button is pressed again to power the monitor off. When the **Caps Lock** key is pressed, it has the same effect as pressing the **Shift** key permanently. The **Caps Lock** key affects only the alphabetic characters, which are then shifted to uppercase as their default values. In fact, if you use the **Shift** key after the **Caps Lock** is pressed, the shifted value will be a lowercase character. The **Num Lock** key toggles on and off the number pad, alternating it into a cursor control pad. The **Scroll Lock** key enables and disables software control for the scrolling of the display.

Repeating Keystrokes

Many keyboards and operating systems allow you to repeat a key (virtually forever) by merely holding it down. This is called a *typematic* key function. You can set the typematic settings for a keyboard through the Windows Control Panel's Keyboard icon, which opens the Keyboard Properties window shown in Figure 17.3.

Cursor Keys

Keyboards with 101 or more keys include a group of cursor control keys separate from those on the alternate positions of the number pad keys. The **Num Lock** key can be used to toggle the number pad into a cursor control pad. On the 101-key design and the keyboard designs that followed it, two small sets of keys are included to provide for cursor movement and control. One is a set of four dedicated cursor (arrow) keys and the other is a six-key set of cursor command (or navigation) keys located between the alphabetic keys and the number pad.

17. Keyboards, Mice, and Pointing Devices

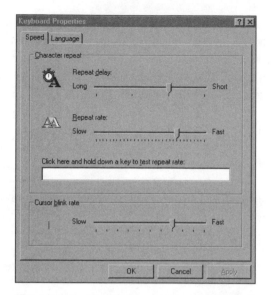

Figure 17.3   The Keyboard Properties window is used to control repeating keys.

The group of cursor keys includes:

- *Cursor control (arrow) keys*—These four directional keys, which are supported by virtually all software, are used to move the cursor left, up, down, and right on the screen. A large percentage of PC game software uses these keys to move characters through scenes by assigning each key to a point of the compass (up is north, down is south, left is east, and right is west). Some higher-end keyboards add four more keys, which are used to move the cursor diagonally between the directions of the four standard keys.

- *Cursor command keys*—This group of six keys is located right above the cursor control keys and just to the right of the alphabetic keys. These keys duplicate the six cursor commands and control functions of keys located in the number pad. These keys allow the number pad to remain in use while the cursor is being manipulated. The keys included in this group are the **Insert** key, **Delete** key, **Home** key, **End** key, and the **Page Up** (**PgUp**) and **Page Down** (**PgDn**) keys.

  - *Insert*—The **Insert** key is a locking key that toggles software between insert and replace modes. *Insert mode*, which is the default mode for most word processing systems, inserts characters at the point indicated by the cursor. *Replace mode*, which is also called type-over mode, replaces any existing characters with the characters being entered.

  - *Delete*—The function of the **Delete** key is typically controlled by software. It is generally used to erase a single character to the right of the cursor, or to delete a selected object.

- *Home and End*—In most applications, the **Home** key is used to position the cursor at the beginning of a text line; its opposite, the **End** key, moves the cursor to the end of a text line. When used with the **Control** key, the **Home** key moves the cursor to the beginning of a document and the **End** key moves the cursor to the end of a document.

- *Page Up and Page Down*—These two keys are used to scroll the screen up or down to the previous or next page, respectively. "One page" in this context is the amount of a document that the screen can display.

The Number Pad

Even though every one of the number pad's keys is duplicated somewhere on a keyboard, these keys were added as a standard feature of PC keyboards to aid the entry of numeric data. The layout of the number pad, shown in Figure 17.4, duplicates the keys on a ten-key calculator, adding machine, or keypunch machine. For the many users who must enter large volumes of numeric data, the numeric keypad is an absolute necessity.

The keys on the number pad are:

- *Num Lock*—This locking key toggles and locks the number pad between its number pad function and its cursor control function. The state (on or off) of the **Num Lock** is assigned during the boot sequence and can be set in the PC's BIOS settings. Virtually all PCs lock the **Num Lock** key on during the boot.

- *Arithmetic operators*—The keys for the four standard arithmetic operators, **/** (divide), ***** (multiply), **-** (subtract), and **+** (add), are included around the upper edge and right side of the number pad.

Figure 17.4   The number pad on a standard keyboard.

- *Number/cursor keys*—When the **Num Lock** key is toggled on (and the Num Lock LED is lighted), the 10 number keys type the digits 0 to 9. When the **Num Lock** key is toggled off (the LED is off), these keys are now cursor control keys, including keys for diagonal movement.

- *Insert* and *Delete*—These two keys are the zero and decimal point of the number pad when it is in number mode, but in cursor control mode, they duplicate the actions of the **Insert** key and the **Delete** key, respectively.

- *Enter*—The number pad includes an **Enter** key so the end of a number or entry can be marked without leaving the number pad.

Function Keys

The top row of all newer keyboards contains 12 function keys that are controlled strictly by software and do not have any default functions of their own. Some software applications, such as Corel's WordPerfect, and the MS-DOS operating system, make extensive use of the function keys. For example, on the MS-DOS (and Windows) command line, the **F3** key is used to repeat the last line entered. In WordPerfect, the **F7** key exits the program and the **Shift** and **F7** keys together print a document. In virtually all Windows applications, the **F1** key is used to open the Help system.

The earliest PCs had 10 function keys on the left side of the keyboard arranged in two columns of five keys each. When the enhanced (101-key) keyboards were introduced, the function keys expanded to 12 keys and were placed on the top edge of the keyboard, partly to make room for the cursor keys.

Special-Purpose Keys

The standard keyboard has a few special-purpose keys. For the most part, users rarely or never use these keys because they are not supported by all software, and even when they are, the need for their functions is not frequently required. These keys are:

- *Esc*—The **Escape** key is typically enabled as either an exit or cancellation key by most software. It is used to either cancel a command or to exit an application, such as its use in Windows to close a context menu. It can also be used in combination with another key to create a special key value, such as with the **Control** key to access the BIOS settings of a PC.

- *Print Screen* and *System Request*—The **Print Screen** (or **PrtScrn**) key is used on an MS-DOS system to send the contents of the display to the printer. On a Windows PC, the **Print Screen** key sends the contents of the display to the Windows Clipboard. Figure 17.5 shows a screen capture generated by the **Print Screen** key in the Windows Clipboard Viewer. The **System Request** (or **SysRq**) mode of this key has no real function on most PCs, unless the PC

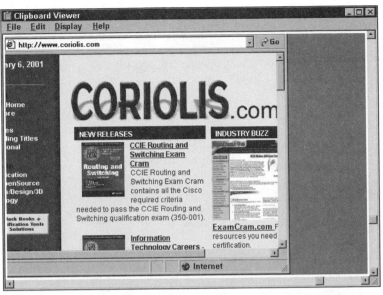

Figure 17.5 The Windows Clipboard Viewer showing a screen captured by the **Print Screen** key.

is emulating an IBM terminal connected to a mainframe computer, and then only if the terminal emulation software supports it.

- ***Pause*** *or* ***Break***—If this key has been enabled by software, its default (**Pause**) mode freezes the display or pauses the action of an application program. The **Control** key toggles this key in the same manner that the **Shift** key is used with other keys. When used with the **Control** key, it becomes a **Break** key, which interrupts or halts some software programs, primarily MS-DOS commands and applications.

Windows Menu Keys

The difference between a 101-key keyboard and a 104-key keyboard are the three Windows-specific keys that provide shortcuts to Windows menus. Figure 17.6 shows the two keys to the right of the spacebar.

- ***Windows*** *keys*—These keys, which are marked with a flying Windows symbol, pop up the Windows Start menu when pressed. However, when used in combination with other keys, they perform the equivalent of several keystrokes to display menus, start applets, or open windows.

- ***Context Menu*** *key*—This key is located on the right side of the spacebar between the **Windows** key and the **Control** key. Pressing the **Context Menu** key performs the same action as right-clicking on the display to pop up a context menu for the current application.

17. Keyboards, Mice, and Pointing Devices

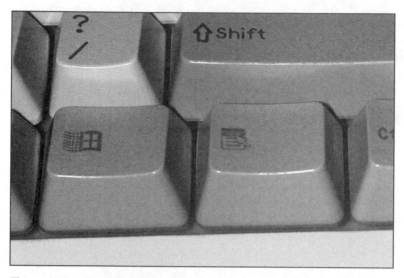

Figure 17.6   The two **Windows** keys to the right of the spacebar are used to display the Windows Start menu and the current context menu.

Keyboard Forms

The PC keyboard has evolved from its beginning on the first PCs, where it was not much more than a typewriter keyboard attached to a PC, to the sophisticated multifunction input device of today.

Early Keyboards

The very first PC keyboards, those of the IBM PC and PC XT, had 83 keys or more than 20 keys fewer than most current keyboards. The IBM PC keyboard, which established the design basis for all future PC keyboards, introduced some enduring characteristics: It was a separate device from the PC, it had 10 software-controlled function keys, and it included a 10-key number/cursor control pad. The PC AT keyboard had 84 keys (it added a **System Request** key), but it improved on the spacing of the keys, enlarged the **Shift** and **Enter** keys, and added the three LED indicators for the **Caps Lock**, **Num Lock**, and **Scroll Lock** keys.

Enhanced Keyboards

In 1986, IBM released its last PC AT model (Model 339) that included what IBM called an "enhanced" keyboard. This 101-key keyboard continues to be the *de facto* standard for all newer systems. The 17 keys that were added to the 84-key keyboard that preceded it are dedicated cursor control keys, multiply and divide keys on the number pad, **Control** and **Alt** keys on the right side of the spacebar, and two more function keys.

The 101-key keyboard has variations in virtually all non-English speaking regions of the world. The variations of the keyboard from one region to the next are primarily that the keys on the keyboard are moved or replaced. For example, the top row of keys on an English-language keyboard begins with the QWERTY keys (**Q**, **W**, **E**, **R**, **T**, and **Y**). In France and some other countries, the corresponding keys are **A**, **Z**, **E**, **R**, **T**, and **Y**, with other characters also rearranged.

Windows Keyboards

The current standard for keyboard layout is the Windows keyboard that features 104 keys. The three keys added to the 101-key design are the **Windows** and **Context Menu** keys discussed previously under "Windows Menu Keys."

Natural Keyboards

In an attempt to relieve such repetitive stress injuries as carpal tunnel syndrome, which can be caused by the position a user's hands and wrists must be in to use the standard keyboard, manufacturers have developed keyboard designs that reshape the keyboard so the user's hands and wrists are in a more natural position. These popular keyboards, such as the one shown in Figure 17.7, are called *natural* or *ergonomic* keyboards.

Portable PC Keyboards

The keyboard of a notebook computer with the same number of keys must be smaller than a normal keyboard just to fit inside the portable PC's case. To accomplish this feat, the arrangement, layout, and even function of the keys must be altered slightly, resulting in a keyboard that is smaller, with the keys more closely placed and a nonstandard layout that locates the cursor control and number pad keys either into the alphabetic keyboard or as alternate values on other

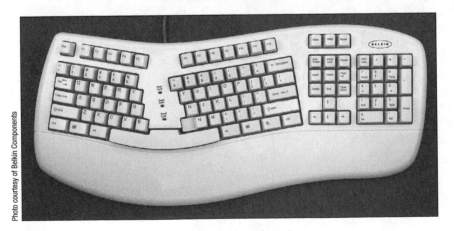

Photo courtesy of Belkin Components

Figure 17.7　A natural, ergonomic style keyboard.

17. Keyboards, Mice, and Pointing Devices

keys. Many notebook PCs include a special function (**Fn**) key that is used like a **Shift** or **Control** key to modify function keys to control display, sound, and other input/output (I/O) actions of the PC.

Figure 17.8 shows a sample keyboard of a notebook PC. A notebook PC with a 12-inch display has a fairly limited space for a keyboard, dictated by the PC's overall size. However, a notebook with a 15-inch display has more overall size to accommodate the keyboard and provide for a better arrangement of the keys. Notice the glidepoint mouse in the center of the keyboard in Figure 17.8; this type of mouse is discussed later in this chapter, under "Glidepoint Mouse."

Notebook PCs also provide PS/2 and USB ports, which can be used for an external standard keyboard and mouse. An external number pad can also be added to compensate for the lack of a dedicated number pad on virtually all portable PCs.

Miscellaneous Keyboard Styles

Several "Internet" keyboards are available that include buttons preprogrammed to connect to the Internet, open a browser, or check email. "Multimedia" keyboards include audio controls, such as sound volume and CD controls (play, stop, pause, previous, next, and others), as illustrated in Figure 17.9. Several new keyboard designs have buttons to perform the same actions as the buttons on a mouse, and some have a mouse, trackball, or touchpad built right into the keyboard on the style of a portable PC.

Figure 17.8   The keyboard on a notebook PC.

Photo courtesy of Belkin Components

Figure 17.9   A multimedia keyboard.

Keyboard Technology

Each key on the keyboard is a combination of a *keycap*, which provides a surface for fingers, and a *keyswitch*, which registers the keystroke. Beneath each key on the keyboard is the keyswitch, which closes a circuit or creates a change in an electrical field when its keycap is pressed. A simplification of the events that occur when a key is pressed on a keyboard follows:

1. All of the keys of the keyboard are either attached to or are a part of a grid or matrix that is constantly being scanned by the keyboard's built-in processor. When a key is pressed, the keyswitch contacts the grid and is detected by the keyboard processor, which then assigns a scan code to the keystroke data, based on its grid position. The keys, as indicated by the keycaps, remain in the same positions at all times. The **A** key is always the **A** key, which allows the processor to remember the scan code, which represents only a key's grid position and not the character printed on its keycap.

2. The keyboard processor clocks the scan code to the PC's keyboard interface. What this means is that the keyboard processor sends the scan code data over a serial line in the keyboard's interface cable along with clock signals that are sent over the clocking line of the cable. The clocking data helps the PC know when keystroke data begins and ends.

3. After the keyboard interface receives the keystroke data, it starts the keyboard service routine that converts the scan code data and the keyboard status byte (which indicates whether the **Shift**, **Control**, or **Alt** keys are in use) into the two-byte key code that is put into the keyboard buffer.

4. The key code indicates the ASCII (American Standard Code for Information Interchange) code of the character. The keystroke's ASCII code is passed to the application.

Make and Break Codes

There are actually two different codes used to indicate the beginning and ending of a keystroke. When the keyboard processor detects a key has been pressed, a "make" code is sent to the PC, and when the key is released, a "break" code is sent. Each key location on the grid has a unique pair of make and break codes, which are used by the PC to determine the character or value associated with the keystroke and whether the keystroke is beginning or ending. If a key is held down, the keyboard controller sends a scan code for each scan of the keyboard until the key is released. This is how you are able to repeat a key simply by holding it down. Table 17.1 lists a few of the scan codes of most 101-key and 104-key keyboards.

Table 17.1   Sample make and break codes.

Key	Make Code	Break Code
1	16	F0 16
0	45	F0 45
Backspace	66	F0 66
Q	15	F0 15
A	1C	F0 1C
Enter	5A	F0 5A
Right Shift	59	F0 59
Left Control	14	F0 14
Space	29	F0 29
Escape	76	F0 76
F1	05	F0 05
Num Lock	77	F0 77
Insert	E0 70	E0 F0 70
Page Up	E0 7D	E0 F0 7D
Delete	E0 71	E0 F0 71
Up Arrow	E0 75	E0 F0 75
Print Screen	E0 12 E0 7C	E0 F0 7C E0 F0 12

To type an uppercase "A," the following actions would take place:

1. The **Right Shift** key is pressed, which causes the make code for the **Right Shift** key (59) to be sent to the keyboard interface.

2. The **A** key is pressed, and the **A** key's make code (1C) is sent.

3. The **A** key is released and the **A** key's break code (F0 1C) is sent.

4. The **Right Shift** key is released, which causes the **Right Shift** key's break code (F0 59) to be sent to the keyboard interface.

When the keyboard interface receives the break code, it translates the make code into its ASCII equivalent and stores it in the keyboard buffer in random access memory (RAM). Scan codes and ASCII codes are represented as hexadecimal values. For more information on hexadecimal values, see Chapter 2. A few of the ASCII values used with PC keyboards are listed in Table 17.2.

Table 17.2   PC ASCII codes.

Character	Hexadecimal
Space	20
!	21
"	22
0	30
1	31
2	32
=	3D
>	3E
?	3F
A	41
B	42
C	43
H	48
I	49
J	4A
a	61
b	62
c	63

Keyswitches

The keyswitches used in a PC keyboard are typically one of two general types: contact keyswitches and capacitive keyswitches. Most users cannot tell the difference between these two switch types or their variations, but differences do exist among the various types.

Contact Keyswitches

For a contact keyswitch to complete a circuit, two parts of the switch must make contact. The types of contact keyswitches commonly used in PC keyboards are:

- *Foam and foil keyswitch*—The core of this keyswitch is a foam pad that has a piece of foil on its underside. When the key is pressed, a plunger presses the foam pad and its foil into contact with a pair of copper contacts on the keyboard's circuit board.

- *Rubber dome keyswitch*—The core of this keyswitch is a small rounded dome of rubber that has a pad of carbon material on its underside. When the key is pressed, a plunger presses down on the rubber, which collapses under the pressure, and the carbon contacts the circuit board to complete the circuit. This type of keyswitch is the most common type used in current keyboards.

Capacitive Keyswitches

Capacitive keyswitches operate on the general principles of a capacitor. A capacitor stores an electrical charge between two metal plates. The energy in the charge is its *capacitance*. As the plates move closer together or farther apart, the capacitance changes. The change in the capacitance signals that a keystroke has occurred.

A capacitive keyswitch has a plunger at the bottom of which a metal plate is attached. At the bottom of the switch and beneath the plunger is another metal plate. When the plunger is pressed, the space between the plates is reduced (or increased in some designs) to create a change in the capacitance of the switch. The keyboard controller's circuitry detects the change in capacitance, and a keystroke is generated.

Keyboard Controller

The keyboard controller consists of a microprocessor and a ROM (read-only memory) chip that holds the keyboard processor's instructions. The keyboard controller constantly scans the keyboard grid, which is typically a circuit board beneath the keys. Any keystrokes detected are translated into scan codes and transmitted to the PC.

Keyboard Cable

The keyboard's interface cable is a four-wire (data, clocking, ground, and power) cable that carries the signals sent between the PC and the keyboard. The cable has four plastic-coated copper wires around which a metal grounding sheath is placed. The wire bundle is covered with a thick plastic or rubber outer sheath. The cable is usually 4 to 6 feet in length and is typically a straight cable, although coiled cables are also common. Should you require additional cable length, a keyboard cable extension can be used to extend it.

Keyboard Connectors

Keyboards attach to a PC through one of five connector types:

- *5-pin DIN connector*—Also known as the AT connector, the 5-pin DIN connector has been used since the very first PC. Deutsche Industrie Norm (DIN) is a German standards organization that developed the round connector style used on the 5-pin connector and its 6-pin version. Only four of the five pins in this connector are used: clocking (pin 1), data (pin 2), ground (pin 4), and +5V of power (pin 5).

- *6-pin mini-DIN (PS/2) connector*—This DIN connector is smaller than the 5-pin AT connector and uses four of its six pins for: data (pin 1), ground (pin 3), +5V of power (pin 4), and clocking (pin 5). This connector, now the standard for virtually all cabled keyboards, is also called the PS/2 connector because it was first introduced with the IBM PS/2 computers. Figure 17.10 shows this connector.

- *Universal serial bus connector*—The USB connector, shown in Figure 17.11, is becoming a common connector for keyboards (as well as mice). This connector is useful when a notebook computer has only one PS/2 port and both external keyboard and mouse are to be connected.

Figure 17.10   A 6-pin mini-DIN (PS/2) connector is standard on most PC keyboards.

Figure 17.11   A USB connector and port.

- *IrDA connector*—Several keyboard styles are available with an infrared (IR) cordless interface for use with desktop and notebook PCs that support the Infrared Data Association (IrDA) standard interface, which is that small red plastic window on the front, side, or back of the PC. IR devices require a direct, unobstructed, line of sight between the transmitter and receiver to work properly.

- *Radio frequency connection*—Radio frequency (RF) is the most common method used for cordless connection between a keyboard (or mouse) and a PC. Unlike IR devices, an RF device does not need a line of sight to work. An RF keyboard communicates to the PC through a transceiver, which attaches through either a PS/2 or USB port.

The Mouse

The PC mouse, shown in Figure 17.12, is a natural, intuitive, inexpensive pointing device that has become a standard part of the PC's hardware. Introduced by Microsoft, but popularized by the Apple Macintosh, the PC mouse really gained popularity after Windows and its graphical user interface (GUI) were released. Virtually every PC sold today includes a mouse as standard equipment.

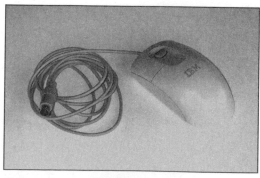

Figure 17.12   A PC mouse.

Three types of mouse units are used with PCs:

- *Mechanical mouse*—This type of mouse was used with early Macintosh and PC GUI systems. In a mechanical mouse, moving a rubber ball causes a pair of wheels to spin. Sensors detect the movement of the wheels, and signals are sent to the PC.

- *Optomechanical mouse*—This type of mouse uses light-emitting diodes (LEDs) to sense mouse movements. This is the most commonly used type of mouse.

- *Optical mouse*—This type of mouse has no moving parts. The mechanical devices (balls, rollers, and wheels) are replaced with an optical scanning system that detects the movement of the mouse over virtually any surface.

Inside the Mouse

This discussion of how the mouse works focuses on the optomechanical mouse because it is the most popular design in use. A mouse translates the motion of the user's hand into electrical signals that the PC uses to track a pointer across the monitor's display. To capture the motion of the user's hand, an optomechanical mouse uses seven primary components:

- *Ball*—The rubber ball is the largest and certainly most important part of the mouse. When the user grasps the mouse and moves it over a mousepad, the ball rolls inside the mouse, which is key to detecting the motion.

- *Rollers*—There are two rollers in contact with the ball. As the ball rolls inside the mouse, the two rollers track its rotation side to side and up and back.

- *Roller shafts*—The two rollers are each connected to optical encoding disks by roller shafts.

- *Optical encoding disks*—The movement of the ball causes the rollers to spin, which in turn spins the shafts and the optical encoding disks attached to them. Each disk has 36 holes along its edge, as illustrated in Figure 17.13.

- *Infrared LED and sensor*—On one side of each optical encoding disk is an LED that shines an IR light beam on the part of the disk where the holes are located. On the opposite side of the disk is an IR sensor. As the disk turns, the solid areas between the holes break up the IR beam so that the IR sensor sees pulses of light. The rate and duration of the light pulses translate to the speed and distance, respectively, of the mouse's travel. Figure 17.13 illustrates the placement of the infrared LED and sensor to the optical encoding disk.

- *Processor*—Inside the mouse is a processor that converts the light pulses into binary data that represents the motion of the mouse, which is sent to the PC's interface.

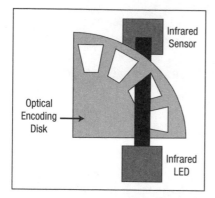

Figure 17.13   As the mouse moves, the holes and solids of the optical encoding disk create light pulses that translate into cursor movement on the screen.

- *Buttons*—The mouse also has one, two, or three (or more) buttons that the user can use to indicate actions to the PC. As the user clicks the buttons, which are connected to small switches, to select an object or start a program, the processor converts the clicks into binary data that is sent to the PC. Windows systems most commonly use two-button mice, whereas Macintosh systems have gotten by very nicely with a single mouse button. Many Unix and Linux applications make use of a third (middle) mouse button.

As an example of how all this works together, assume a mouse has a ball that is 21 millimeters (mm) in diameter and optical encoding disks with 36 holes. When the user moves the mouse 1 inch (25.4 mm), the ball rotates slightly more than once, and the rollers cause the disks to spin a little more than one complete revolution, matching the movement of the ball. This results in the sensor detecting about 40 light pulses, and the PC is sent 40 bits of data to indicate the mouse's movement.

Actually, each optical encoding disk has two sets of LEDs and sensors, one on the left side of the disk, and one on the right. Having two sets of LEDs and sensors enables the processor to detect the direction of the disk's rotation. Although not shown in Figure 17.13, a small plastic window is placed between each LED and disk to aim the LED's IR light beam. The plastic windows on each side of a disk are set at slightly different heights, which forces the sensors to see the light pulses at different times. Figure 17.14 illustrates how the sensors see the light beams. As the disk rotates, the IR beams are in view through the disk's holes at slightly different times. The processor is able to determine the mouse's direction by the beam that is detected first.

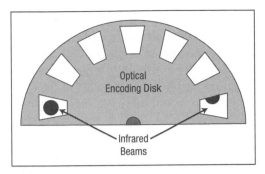

Figure 17.14   One of the mouse's LED beams is set slightly higher than the other to help detect the mouse's travel direction.

Mouse Connectors

The most common connector for PC mice is the 6-pin mini-DIN (PS/2) connector, shown earlier in Figure 17.10. Early mouse units used a DB-9 serial connector, which is still available, to connect a mouse to a serial port. Newer PC systems typically include PS/2 connectors for the keyboard and mouse, which has led to the serial mouse all but disappearing.

The mouse connects and communicates to the PC through the PS/2 connector with four pins. The communications technique used by the mouse is the same as that used by the keyboard. Data is sent along with clocking signals that tell the PC when each piece of data begins and ends. The four pins of the connector carry +5V of power (pin 2), clocking signals (pin 4), a grounding circuit (pin 5), and data signals (pin 6). A mouse uses the +5V of power for its processor and IR LEDs.

USB Mouse

Other popular connectors for a mouse are USB, IrDA, and RF connections. The USB connector is hot-swappable, which means that it can be plugged in while the PC is running and it does not require the system to be reset. The USB gives the user an additional option, especially on portable PCs that have only one PS/2 connector. PS/2 and serial devices should not be connected while the system is running.

Cordless Mouse

Cordless mice use either an IR light beam or an RF receiver to connect and communicate with a PC. Many newer PCs include an IrDA or RF receiver, but both can be added as external devices through a PS/2 or USB port. A corded mouse gets its power over its cable, but a cordless mouse, which has no power connection, runs on a pair of AAA batteries.

Because IR connections are line of sight, they must have a clear, unobstructed view between the transmitter (in this case, the mouse) and the receiver. They do not operate well beyond a few feet of the receiver. In contrast, RF connections don't require a line of sight, so they can be used within any proximity of the receiver. However, the RF device also must be within a few feet of the receiver.

Data Interface

Whenever the user moves the mouse or clicks a mouse button, the mouse sends a three-byte data packet to the PC. The first byte of the mouse's data packet contains:

1. One bit for each of the right and left mouse buttons to indicate if a button was clicked (0 = not clicked, 1 = clicked)

2. A 2-bit packet ID (01)

3. One bit for each of the X and Y axis to indicate the direction of the mouse's movement (0 = negative [backward/left], 1 = positive [forward/right])

4. One bit for each of the X and Y axis to indicate that the speed of the mouse was faster than 255 pulses in 0.025 seconds

The second and third bytes contain the number of pulses detected by the X axis (side-to-side) and Y axis (up and back) sensors, respectively, since the last packet was sent. These counts indicate the speed of the mouse in either or both directions.

The packet is sent to the PC over the data line of the connector as a serial data transmission with clocking signals used to indicate when each bit begins and ends. For each byte sent by the mouse to the PC, 11 bits, which includes 1 start bit, the 8 data bits, a parity bit, and 1 stop bit, are sent. The standard PS/2 mouse sends data at a rate of 1,200 bits per second, which translates to about 40 packets each second sent to the PC to report the mouse's status. Although this is fast enough for most situations and applications, extremely fast movement of the mouse can overwhelm the mouse's ability to report it accurately.

Wheel Mouse

The wheel mouse, shown in Figure 17.15, gets its name from a finger wheel that is usually placed between its buttons and can be used to scroll the display. The wheel allows the user to scroll forward and backward through a document in place of clicking on a window's scroll bar or using the **Page Up** and **Page Down** keys or buttons or the cursor control arrow keys.

Optical Mouse

The optical mouse replaces the mouse ball with optical sensors that track the movement of the mouse over a surface. Older optical mice required a highly reflective mousepad with a printed grid that was used to detect movement. Although this

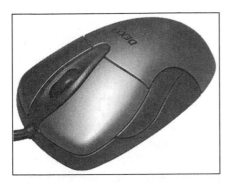

Figure 17.15   An example of a wheel mouse.

mouse did eliminate the mouse ball and its inherent problems, it had its own set of problems. It was slow, and if the mousepad were lost, the mouse could not work.

The newer optical mouse captures images of the surface under the mouse at more than 1,500 images per second. Figure 17.16 shows the underside of an optical mouse and its sensors. A DSP (digital signal processor) inside the mouse analyzes and compares the images to detect even the slightest movement of the mouse. This optical mouse design works on virtually any flat surface and does not need a mousepad, although one can be used. However, some surfaces, such as glass, mirrors, or smooth shiny, solid-color surfaces without detail, do not work well with an optical mouse.

The fact that it does not need to be cleaned internally is the biggest advantage an optical mouse has over a conventional mouse. An optical mouse has no moving parts, and thus it does not pick up the dust and dirt that plague a mouse with a ball. Manufacturers also claim that optical mice are 33 percent faster and more accurate than optomechanical mice.

Other Pointing Devices

Many other types of pointing devices exist, but the four that have some popularity beyond the mouse are the touchpad, the track ball, the glidepoint, and the joystick.

17. Keyboards, Mice, and Pointing Devices

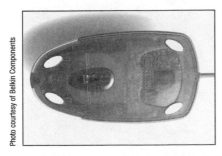

Photo courtesy of Belkin Components

Figure 17.16   The bottom of an optical mouse.

Touchpads

Touchpads are becoming very common on notebook computers. A touchpad, such as the one shown in Figure 17.17, is a fixed-place, small, flat, square, or rectangular surface on which the user touches, slides, or taps a finger to guide the cursor on the display, to select objects, and to run programs. A touchpad is able to duplicate all of the actions of a mouse.

A touchpad uses a two-layer grid of electrodes to apply the principle of coupling capacitance. This grid includes an upper layer of vertically placed electrodes and a lower layer of horizontally placed electrodes. When the user's finger passes over a pair (one horizontal and one vertical) of electrodes, an integrated circuit (IC) attached to the grid detects the changes in the grid's capacitance, and data is sent to the PC using essentially the same technique used by a mouse and keyboard. Like an optical mouse, the touchpad has no moving parts and does not require cleaning other than that given to the keyboard to which it is attached. Touchpads are most common on notebook PCs, but are also being integrated into desktop keyboards as well. An external touchpad can be added to a PC via its PS/2 port.

A digitizing tablet, such as the one shown in Figure 17.18, works on the same principle as a touchpad, but is typically used with a drawing stylus to create vector art or engineering objects.

Figure 17.17   A touchpad integrated into a notebook PC.

Figure 17.18   A digitizing tablet.

Trackballs

As shown in Figure 17.19, a trackball, which is essentially an upside-down mouse, has two or more buttons, like a mouse, but its ball is on top. The ball is manipulated with either a thumb or finger to move the cursor on the screen. Because only the ball moves, a trackball device requires less space on the desktop. A trackball is typically attached to a PC with a cord and uses the same technology as an optomechanical mouse to communicate movement to the PC over a PS/2 or USB connection.

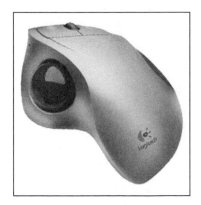

Figure 17.19   A trackball.

Glidepoint Mouse

A glidepoint mouse, which is common to notebook PCs, is the pivoting rubber-tipped device located between the **G** and **H** keys that looks like an eraser tip. A glidepoint mouse, such as the one shown in Figure 17.20, works like a very small joystick, but acts like a mouse on the screen. The benefit of the glidepoint technology is that the user's hands remain on the keyboard for mousing actions.

Joysticks

Joysticks are used primarily with game software on a PC. The joystick device consists of a handle connected to a pivoting mechanism that allows it to move in any direction around a center point. Sensors inside the device detect the movement of the handle on an X or Y axis and send data signals to an adapter card. A software device driver interprets the data and translates it to actions on the screen. Most joysticks attach to a game port on a game, video, or sound card installed in an expansion slot on the motherboard, but newer models support a USB connection as well.

Figure 17.20   A glidepoint mouse in a notebook computer keyboard.

Immediate Solutions

Troubleshooting the Keyboard

Keyboards are considered throwaway technology. They can be repaired, but the time, expense, and risk of introducing other problems are such that it is often better just to replace a problem keyboard. However, before the keyboard is isolated for a problem that may actually be on the motherboard, the following steps should be performed:

1. Power off the computer.
2. Unplug the keyboard connector from the motherboard.
3. Power on the computer.
4. Use a digital multimeter to check the voltages of the connector pins. If all of the connector's voltages are in range, which is normally in the range of +2V to +5.5V, depending on the pin, the problem may likely be in the motherboard's keyboard interface circuits. The keyboard's documentation should list the specific voltage for each pin in the connector.
5. If the voltages in the connector check out, connect a known good keyboard and reboot the system. You should never install a PS/2 connector in a port while the PC is powered up because it could damage the bus circuitry on the motherboard. If the new keyboard works, then the original keyboard is bad. If the new keyboard also fails to work, the problem is likely on the motherboard or its connector. Before replacing the motherboard because of a bad keyboard port, you may want to consider a USB keyboard if a USB port is available.

Solving Keyboard Boot Sequence Problems

Keyboard-related problems, which are extremely rare, are usually detected during the power-on self-test (POST) process. If the POST should detect a keyboard problem, a beep code is sounded. Remember that the beep codes are unique to the BIOS on a PC, so check the documentation of the motherboard or BIOS, or visit the BIOS manufacturer's Web site for the beep code set in use. If the keyboard error is detected after the POST completes, a boot error message with an error code in the 300 to 399 number range is displayed.

17. Keyboards, Mice, and Pointing Devices

The most common keyboard boot error is a keystroke detected during the POST. This could be the result of a stuck key, an accidentally pressed key, or even someone leaning on the keyboard or a book lying on the keyboard. The remedy is simple: Clear the problem and reboot the computer.

Setting Keyboard Controls on a Windows PC

On a Windows 9x or Windows Me PC, the Keyboard icon on the Control Panel includes some settings that can be used to adjust and set the language set of the keyboard as well as a few performance levels. The Keyboard icon opens the Keyboard Properties window, which has two tabs:

- *Speed tab*—This tab contains the typematic settings for the keyboard, which includes the amount of time between repeated characters, how quickly a character repeats when you hold down a key on the keyboard, and how fast the cursor blinks on the display. These speed settings are each controlled by a slide that sets the rate between long and short or slow and fast, as applicable. For most folks, the default settings are usually okay.

- *Language*—This tab is used to set the language of the keyboard. To see the list of available languages (including the eight versions of English) that Windows supports by default, click the Add button. If you wish to add a different language, you will need the Windows CD or a disk with the appropriate keyboard device driver. If you wish to have multiple languages available on a system, you can enable them here and assign shortcut keys so you can easily switch between them. The option for an indicator in the system tray is also available.

Setting the Accessibility Options on a Windows PC

Windows includes the Accessibility Options on the Control Panel to help make a PC easier to use for people with physical handicaps. As shown in Figure 17.21, the options indicated by the tabs on the Accessibility Properties window allow the keyboard, display, sound system, and mouse to have customized settings to meet the special needs of handicapped users.

The Keyboard tab contains the following options:

- *StickyKeys*—This feature converts the **Shift**, **Control**, and **Alt** keys into locking keys that stay toggled until they are pressed again. This allows

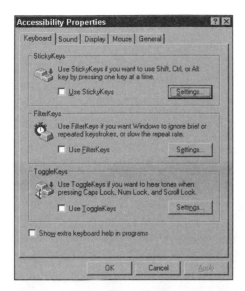

Figure 17.21   The Accessibility Properties Options window.

someone able to press only a single key at a time to enter key combinations such as **Control+Alt+Delete** or **Ctrl+Shift+F7**.

- *FilterKeys*—Recognizing that someone may not be able to release a key as quickly as would normally be required without repeating the key, this option works like the opposite of the typematic features discussed under "Speed tab" in the preceding solution.

- *ToggleKeys*—This feature enables or disables an audible tone that is sounded when any locking key is pressed. This option is the sound equivalent of the LEDs on the keyboard.

Configuring the BIOS Settings of a Keyboard

The BIOS contains a number of settings that can affect the operation of the keyboard. The most important ones to check are:

- *Halt On Errors*—This option tells the BIOS that it should or should not stop and display error messages when a certain error is detected during the POST or boot. This is important for systems, such as servers, that may not have a keyboard attached when booted. The "all errors but keyboard" setting instructs the BIOS to continue to boot if the only error is a bad or missing keyboard.

- *Keyboard Present*—This BIOS configuration setting is a very specific indication as to whether a keyboard is ("Yes") or is not ("No") attached to the system.

- *Typematic Delay*—This value can be set in Windows or in the BIOS data (in milliseconds).

- *Typematic Rate*—This option can be set in the Keyboard Properties of the Windows system or in the BIOS (in characters per second).

- *USB Legacy Support*—This option allows a USB keyboard to be used. It is not on every BIOS.

Performing Preventive Maintenance on a Keyboard

Keyboards should be cleaned regularly, even if it involves only shaking them out. A keyboard can be cleaned, provided it is detached from the PC, by using the following steps:

1. Turn the keyboard upside down and shake out any paper, potato chips, cookie crumbs, paper clips, or the like.

2. Use an aerosol can of compressed air to dislodge any dust or stubborn bits of debris.

3. Use an all-purpose, nonsudsing cleaner and a soft cloth to clean the key tops.

4. Use a lint-free swab with the cleaner to clean between the keys. Of course, the less water or liquid you get down into the keyboard the better.

If soda pop or something very sticky spills on and into the keyboard, the keyboard can be rinsed with water, soaked in a sink or tub, or even put through a dishwasher's rinse cycle without soap if the stickiness is very stubborn. If the problem is so bad that the dishwasher is the only option, perhaps a new keyboard may be a better choice. If you do rinse or wash the keyboard, be absolutely sure it is completely dry before reconnecting it to the computer and turning the PC's power on. Any water left on the keyboard can at best cause phantom key connections, or, at worst, short out the keyboard membrane or switches.

Cleaning a Dirty Mouse

Most mouse problems are related to cleaning problems and can be resolved with a cotton swab, some denatured alcohol, and perhaps a soft-bristle toothbrush.

Optomechanical Mouse

The mouse's ball can pick up lint, dust, and other debris from the mousepad, especially one that is heavily textured or painted. Because of this, the mouse should be cleaned regularly by the following steps:

1. Power off the PC and disconnect the mouse (disconnecting the mouse is not required, but it can make the job much easier).

2. Turn the mouse over to expose the bottom and find the ring that holds the ball inside the mouse. Turn the ring counterclockwise and remove the ball from the mouse.

3. Don't try to dig the ball out; just turn the mouse over and let the ball fall out into your hand. Avoid squeezing or compressing the ball while holding it. Don't use solvents or harsh cleaners on a mouse ball because they can leave the mouse ball out-of-round or flat-spotted on one or more sides.

4. Dampen a lint-free cloth with water or the alcohol and gently rub the ball. When the ball has been completely wiped, let it air-dry.

5. Use the swab and alcohol to clean the rollers or contacts inside the ball cage. Use compressed air to blow any dust out of the ball cage and the interior of the mouse. If the rollers have a dark buildup, gently scrape away the dirt with a small blade, being careful not to cut or score the roller. Replace the ball and cover, then try moving the mouse again.

6. Replace the ball in the mouse and replace and turn the retaining ring clockwise to lock the ball in place.

Optical Mouse

Because the optical mouse has no moving parts (other than the user's hand), there is very little involved in cleaning it. On the bottom of the optical mouse is a set of pads (feet) that are used to raise the mouse above the mousing surface and for the mouse to glide on. If the pads aren't cleaned regularly, the user may need to use more effort to move the mouse around. Use a toothbrush to clean the pads and a soft cloth to wipe the underside of the mouse.

Installing a Mouse

The steps used to install each type of mouse vary in their degree of difficulty. The following projects describe the processes used to install a serial mouse, a PS/2 mouse, and a USB mouse.

17. Keyboards, Mice, and Pointing Devices

Serial Mouse

A serial mouse connects to the PC with a female DB-9 (9-pin) connector. Nearly all newer PCs, and many older ones, have a 9-pin serial port available. Some PCs have only a 25-pin serial connection; if a serial mouse is the only option and this is the only type of serial port available, a 25-pin to 9-pin adapter can be used to connect the mouse to the 25-pin port.

When installing a serial mouse, first check to see that a COM (serial) port is available. On systems with both a 25-pin and a 9-pin serial port, the smaller port is often COM2 or COM3, depending on whether an internal modem is installed. Any operating problems that may happen after the mouse is installed could very well be an interrupt request (IRQ) or I/O address conflict.

A primary difference between a PS/2 mouse and a serial mouse is that a PS/2 mouse gets its power from a wire in the connector, whereas a serial mouse can be connected and removed while the PC is on. Never connect a PS/2 mouse to a running system.

A serial mouse can also be installed into a PS/2 port with a special serial-to-mini-DIN adapter. Adapters that allow a PS/2 mouse to be installed on a serial port also exist. However, you need to understand that because of the electrical differences between the serial and the PS/2 devices, these adapters do not always work as well as they should. Many newer mouse units are actually combination mice that come with both connectors or the adapter to convert its default plug for the other connection.

Fortunately, connecting the mouse to the port is the most difficult part of this process. All Windows versions have built-in mouse device drivers for virtually every type of mouse, and most mouse units are plug and play (PnP). After you install the new mouse and reboot the system, Windows should recognize it and complete its installation by loading the appropriate device driver.

If Windows does not recognize the serial mouse, use the following steps to install it:

1. Before you start the system, examine the serial port on the PC for bent or broken pins. A female connector such as the one on the mouse, if not pushed straight on, can bend or break pins in the serial port.

2. When you reboot the system, enter the BIOS configuration data to verify that the COM port you are trying to use is disabled. If it is, enable it, save the configuration data, and continue with the boot sequence. The system may not see the mouse. If this is so, continue with the following steps.

3. Because you don't have a mouse, you must use keyboard commands to recover:

- Press a Windows key to display the Start menu and use the up arrow key to choose Run. In the Open box of the Run window enter **CONTROL.EXE** or use the Browse button (tab to it) to find this program in your Windows folder. **CONTROL.EXE** is the Control Panel.

- Tab over to the Add New Hardware icon and press the **Enter** key.

- Choose the options (typically the **Next** button three times) that allow Windows to search for new hardware.

4. Windows should respond that it found the serial mouse and chose the options that allow Windows to complete the installation. Restart the PC, and the mouse should be working.

PS/2 Mouse

The PS/2 mouse is the *de facto* standard for all PC systems. The PS/2 mouse is installed identically to a serial mouse with two exceptions. A PS/2 mouse typically uses IRQ12 instead of a COM port IRQ, which reduces the potential for resource conflicts. The PS/2 interface is powered and should not be connected to a running system because it may damage the mouse and the motherboard.

A PS/2 mouse is a PnP device for which Windows should load a device driver. If there are any problems, make sure they are not with the mouse itself before you start tearing into the system. Use a spare mouse (one that you know works) to verify the problem. If there are resource conflicts, see the preceding project or see Chapter 7 for more information.

USB Mouse

Here is the entire installation instruction for a USB mouse: Plug it in. USB devices are hot-swappable and thus they are instantly recognized by the system and all necessary drivers are automatically installed.

17. Keyboards, Mice, and Pointing Devices

Troubleshooting an Optomechanical Mouse

Only a few things can go wrong with a mouse. If you are having problems with the mouse, check the following:

1. If the mouse rolls over the mousepad smoothly, but the movement of the cursor on the screen is erratic or jerky, the problem is likely that the mouse is dirty and needs to be cleaned. When dirt accumulates on the ball or the

interior rollers, they slip when rotated against one another, forcing the other components out of sync and showing up as a jerky cursor motion.

2. If a clean mouse is still exhibiting erratic motion, it is likely that either the mouse or its cable is damaged, or that the ball is damaged or is not gripping the underlying surface. This latter problem may simply be that the mousepad is too hard or smooth for the mouse to gain a grip. Softer material works better for optomechanical mice.

3. If the mouse is a serial mouse and works okay, but the PC freezes when you try to use the modem, the problem is a classic IRQ resource conflict. Both devices—the mouse on COM1 and the modem on COM3—are trying to use IRQ4 at the same time. The modem will work fine as long as you don't use the mouse and vice versa. The solution is to change the mouse to IRQ12 or another available IRQ.

4. If the mouse is a PS/2 mouse that is not working at all, check to see if its connector is installed in the keyboard socket, which is directly connected to the keyboard interface circuitry on many motherboards and will not support the mouse.

Configuring a Mouse on a Windows PC

The Mouse Properties window that is accessed from the Mouse icon on the Control Panel allows the user to set performance settings for the mouse. The Mouse Properties window, shown in Figure 17.22, has three tabs:

- *Buttons*—This tab contains options to set the mouse to either a right-handed (default) or left-handed device as well as to specify the actions associated with each button on a two-button mouse. Also on this tab is a slide control that sets the speed of the double-click action (how fast you must click and then click again for the PC to recognize the action as a double-click).

- *Pointers*—This tab lets you choose from a variety of pointer schemes that specify the type of pointer you wish to associate with a number of system activities. You can use a custom scheme if you have the appropriate file.

- *Motion*—This tab has two settings that are very important for how the mouse moves around the screen. The Speed setting sets the ratio of how far the mouse must move to move the pointer on the screen. If this setting is set to "fast", then small movements by the mouse result in large movements of the pointer on the screen. If the setting is set to "slow", a long movement by the mouse moves the cursor only slightly. Most users use the default setting, which is about in the middle. The other setting in this tab adds a trailing

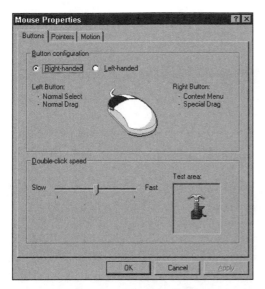

Figure 17.22   The Windows Mouse Properties window.

image tail on the mouse pointer on the screen. This trail helps some people keep the mouse pointer in view when moving over some backgrounds.

Installing a Joystick

A joystick connects to a game port, which is also called a MIDI (musical instrument digital interface). Virtually every PC has a game port included on either its video adapter or its sound card. For most users, a PC's standard game port works well enough, but for power gamers, it may be better to install a speed-adjustable game card with a dedicated game port.

1. A joystick must be recognized by the system before it can be configured. If, after connecting the joystick, the system does not detect it, use the Add New Hardware icon on the Control Panel to add it or to add the game adapter card.

2. Only one active game port is allowed on a PC. If you need to disable the existing game port, check the documentation of the card on which it is mounted or use the Game Controllers icon on the Control Panel to access the Game Controllers window, shown in Figure 17.23. This window is used to add and remove game controllers to the system. Windows 9x systems include most of the software device drivers needed for basic joysticks. Advanced or 3D joysticks may require a proprietary driver, which should come with the device.

Figure 17.23   As the mouse moves, the holes and solids of the optical encoding disk create light pulses that translate into cursor movement on the screen.

3. The next step is to calibrate the joystick. Calibration adjusts the mechanical and electrical alignments of the joystick. Open the Game Controller window from the Control Panel and choose the Advanced tab. Find the joystick in the list and double-click it. The display should show you that the joystick has an "OK" status. Choose the Properties button.

4. On the Properties window, click the Calibrate button and perform the steps as instructed to calibrate the joystick. After you have completed all of the calibration steps, click the Test button to check the joystick's calibration. If it is not properly set, redo the calibration steps.

5. If, during the calibration process, a message displays indicating that the joystick is not properly connected, you may have selected the wrong device driver from the Advanced tab list. Typically, this means that the joystick you have selected has more axes than the driver or Windows is able to detect. First, check out the physical connection of the joystick on the game port, and if it is good, retest the joystick with another driver. To test the connection, select a 2-axis, 2-button joystick, which is a default option (much like setting the monitor to VGA to troubleshoot it).

6. The problem could be a system resource conflict or that the joystick driver is defaulting to an incorrect I/O address value. A game port does not use an IRQ, but uses a default I/O address of 0201 (or 0200 to 0207 for a PnP device). Use the device manager to check these settings. See Chapter 7 for more information on checking system resources.

Chapter 18

Networks and Communications

In-Depth

Network Basics

Personal computers (PCs)—whether they are in a home, office, or large corporation—are all attached to a network in one form or another. PCs in corporate settings are typically attached to a local area network (LAN) and possibly a wide area network (WAN). PCs in a small office may be interconnected on a peer-to-peer network; and a PC in a home connects to the Internet with a dial-up connection over the public switched telephone network (PSTN). Because almost all PCs are connected in some way to a network, this chapter focuses on computer networking and its place in the world of communications.

A network is defined as two or more computers connected by a communications line for sharing resources. Figure 18.1 illustrates a basic network used to connect two PCs so they can share a printer and a modem. The sharable resources on a network are files and data as well as such hardware as printers, modems, CD-ROM drives, and other peripherals. The communications line can be a cable that directly connects PCs through their parallel or serial ports to their network interface cards (NICs). Two computers that are connected to each other by a cable between their NICs, and thus are able to share their attached hardware as well as their data, form a very basic and small network, but a network nonetheless. Most networks are more complicated than this, but regardless of how sophisticated the network becomes, its purpose is only to allow networked devices to share or be shared.

Network Types

The levels and types of networks are classified by their size and the scope of the area they encompass. The most common classifications for networks are:

- *Local area network (LAN)*—A LAN is typically an arrangement of PCs in a relatively small area, such as a single office or building.

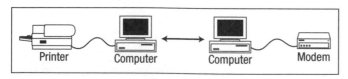

Figure 18.1   A basic and simple network structure.

- *Campus area network (CAN)*—CANs are a type of LAN that extends to include PCs and other devices in buildings within an office park or campus setting. The buildings in a CAN are connected by cables or perhaps by a wireless network.

- *Wide area network (WAN)*—A WAN is a network that interconnects two or more LANs over a large geographical area. The Internet, which gets its name from the concept of internetworking, or the interconnection of networks, is actually a very large WAN. A more typical WAN, however, is a network that connects a company's Dallas office LAN to the LAN at its headquarters in Seattle.

- *Metropolitan area network (MAN)*—A MAN is a variation of a WAN that interconnects LANs and PCs within a specific geographical area, such as a city or a cluster of campuses or office parks. Several cities, including Cleveland, Chicago, and Spokane, have established MANs to provide connectivity to the Internet for their downtown businesses and citizens.

Network Structures

A network can be as simple as two PCs or as complex as a thousand PCs connected throughout the world. The needs of the users should be what drives the structure of any network, and, depending on those needs, the network can be very simple or quite complex. The two basic structures are peer-based and server-based networks:

- *Peer-based (peer-to-peer) networks*—This network involves two or more computers directly connected to one another for the sole purpose of sharing data and hardware resources. The very simple network shown in Figure 18.1 is a peer-to-peer network. A cable directly connects these two PCs, and their users are able to grant permission to one another to access files on their hard disks or CD-ROM drives, as well as printers and other hardware. On a peer-based network, the user is responsible for setting permissions to allow other network users access to his or her PC. A peer-based network does not have a central administrator. A peer-to-peer network is limited to a maximum of 10 PCs for practicality. For more than 10 PCs, the administration of the permissions becomes so complex that a central administrator is required, and the network activity that must be passed from one PC to the next becomes so heavy that a central server is more efficient.

- *Server-based (client/server) networks*—This network involves computers and peripherals connected to at least one centralized computer. The central computer is called a server because it services requests for data, software, and hardware resources from the network users. The PCs attached to the network are called clients in this network model. Servers process requests from network clients for network resources and services. A client/server network typically has a central administrator that manages the permissions and access to the resources of the network. This structure is used for the majority of LANs and virtually all WANs as well as other network types that connect over a WAN.

Actually, any PC on the network can be a server in much the same way as any PC can be a client. In fact, on a peer-based network, the PCs alternate between being clients and servers. They are clients when they request a file or a service from another PC, and they are servers when they provide a file or service to another PC.

For example, suppose that Joe has a new laser printer attached to his PC and he has granted permission to Rose to use it. When Rose sends print files to Joe's printer, Rose's PC is the client and Joe's PC is the server (a print service, actually). In contrast, on server-based networks, the centralized server processes a variety of service requests from the client PCs on the network, as illustrated in Figure 18.2. Typically, on a larger network, clients are strictly clients and servers are strictly servers.

Network Components

Server-based networks, the most common implementation of a LAN, are constructed from servers, workstations (clients) and nodes (printers, modems, and so forth), a network operating system (NOS), connectivity devices, and the cabling or media used to interconnect it all. A network may actually have many of these components, but as already mentioned, it must have at least one server and two workstations (one of the workstations, or PCs, may be the server).

The purpose of a server and the role played by the workstations has been defined, but other components are also essential to the network's efficient operation. The roles played by each of the major network components are:

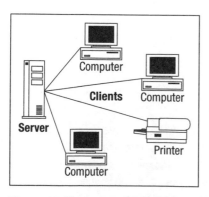

Figure 18.2   A server processes the requests for network services from network clients.

- *Server*—A server is a network computer from which clients (workstations and nodes) request files, printing, communications, and other services. Servers can perform a single service, such as being a file server, print server, application server, Web server, and so forth. A server can also become a client that must request services it does not itself provide.

- *Workstation*—A workstation is a PC connected to a network; it is also called a client or node.

- *Node*—A network node is any addressable networked device, including workstations, peripheral devices, and network connectivity devices. A workstation is a node, but not all nodes are workstations. Examples of nodes are printers, routers, modems, and so forth.

- *Cable or media*—The most common form of network is one that connects its nodes using a cable. The most commonly used cable types are coaxial, copper twisted-pair, and fiber-optic. However, a network can be created without a physical cable, and wireless network technology can be used to connect network elements.

Servers

A server is a networked computer set up to service the resource needs of the network's workstations (clients). A network may actually have a number of different servers that each performs a single function on behalf of the network. A majority of networks have only one server, which performs a variety of services for the network. However, a server is not specifically a piece of hardware; it can be the software used to provide a specific service to network clients. A single hardware server can support many different software servers.

Table 18.1 lists the most common types of servers implemented on a network.

Table 18.1 Network servers.

Server	Function
File server	Stores common network files and users' data files.
Print server	Manages network printers, print queues, and the printing of user documents.
Communications server	Handles such common communications functions as email, fax, dial-up modem, or Internet services.
Application server	Shares common application software, eliminating the need for the software to be installed on each workstation.
Database server	Manages the common database by handling all data storage, database management, and requests for data.

18. Networks and Communications

Cabling

If the network is a wired network, copper or glass cabling is used to carry data signals. Copper and glass are both relatively inexpensive and abundant, but—more importantly—they are excellent conductors of electricity and light, respectively. A conductor is a material through which energy, either electricity or light, can pass easily.

Cable Types

Three standard cable types are commonly used on wired networks: coaxial, twisted-pair, and fiber-optic. Twisted-pair cable is the most commonly used network medium, but for some situations, fiber-optic or coaxial cable is better suited.

Coaxial Cable

The type of coaxial (coax) cable used for networking is similar to the coax cable used to connect a television set to a cable outlet. Actually, two coax cable types are used in networks: thick coaxial cable and thin coaxial cable. Thin coax (also called thinnet and thin wire) is still commonly used in many networking environments, such as those in which a cable run must be longer than twisted-pair cable can support without additional equipment (see "Cable Characteristics" later in this chapter). Thick coax (also called thicknet, thick wire, and yellow wire) is rarely used today in LAN situations.

As shown in Figure 18.3, coaxial cable is constructed with a single solid copper wire core surrounded by an insulator made of plastic or Teflon material. A braided metal shielding layer (and in some cables, another metal foil layer) covers the insulator, and a plastic sheath wrapper covers the cable. The metal shielding layers act to increase the cable's resistance to electromagnetic interference (EMI) and radio frequency interference (RFI) signals. The connector shown in Figure 18.4 is a BNC (Bayonet Neil-Concelman) connector, which is a common connector for coaxial cable.

Copper Twisted-Pair Cable

Twisted-pair cable is available in two types: unshielded twisted-pair (UTP) and shielded twisted-pair (STP). UTP is less resistant to EMI and RFI noise than STP, but it is also less expensive and easier to work with, which makes it popular. UTP is very similar to the wiring used to connect a telephone. STP is the cable medium of choice for certain situations in which EMI and RFI are a problem or the wire must be installed near other electrical components.

As shown in Figure 18.5, in an STP cable, each wire pair is wrapped with a grounded copper or foil wrapper that shields each wire pair from electrical noise and other interference. However, STP supports higher transmission speeds and can carry signals over longer distances. See "Twisted-Pair Wire" later in this chapter for more information on UTP and STP cables.

Figure 18.3   A thin coaxial cable showing its components and a BNC-style connector.

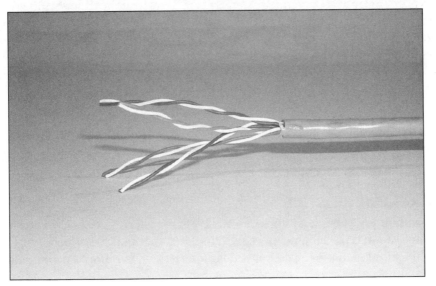

Figure 18.4   Unshielded twisted-pair network cable.

18. Networks and
Communications

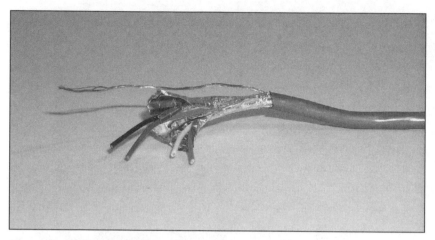

Figure 18.5   Shielded twisted-pair network cable.

Fiber-optic Cable

Glass fibers carry modulated pulses of light to represent digital data signals. Light travels through a fiber-optic cable much faster than electrical impulses travel through a copper cable, which is why fiber-optic cable is used for the long-line portion of WANs and to carry signals between cities.

A fiber-optic cable carries data in the form of modulated pulses of light. To simulate how data travels through a fiber-optic cable, you would need to turn a flashlight on and off around two million times a second. The core of fiber-optic cable consists of two (or more) extremely thin strands of glass. Glass cladding covers each strand, helping to keep the light in the strand. Light is carried one way only on each strand because light cannot travel in two directions simultaneously on a single strand. The two core strands carry light either up or down the cable run. A plastic outer jacket covers the cable. Figure 18.6 shows the makeup of a fiber-optic cable.

Because it uses light and not electrical signals, fiber-optic cable is not susceptible to EMI or RFI, which gives it incredibly long attenuation and maximum segment lengths. Network backbones commonly use fiber-optic cable.

Cable Characteristics

The most commonly used network cable is UTP. However, UTP is not always the best choice. Each type of cable has characteristics that make it appropriate for a given networking situation. The cable characteristics that should be considered when making a cable choice are the following:

- *Bandwidth*—The bandwidth is the amount of data that a cable can transmit in a second, measured in kilobits per second (Kbps) or megabits per second (Mbps). Most copper cabling is nominally rated at 10Mbps.

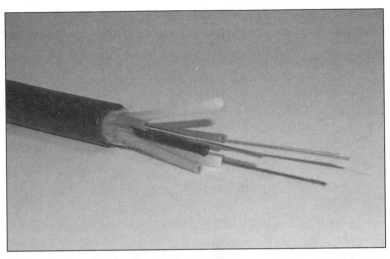

Figure 18.6   A section of a fiber-optic cable showing the individual glass strands of the cable.

- *Maximum segment length*—Each type of cable has a distance at which a transmitted signal begins to weaken and must be reenergized to prevent data loss. This natural tendency of transmitted signals to weaken over a physical medium is called attenuation. The maximum segment length, expressed in meters (m), represents the distance at which attenuation begins to impact the quality of the data signal. In other words, this is the maximum distance between two network nodes for a particular type of cable.

- *Maximum number of nodes per segment*—When a node is added to a network cable, its attenuation distance is reduced. This works somewhat the same as what happens when you punch holes in a water hose—each hole reduces the water pressure in the hose, and eventually no water reaches the end of the hose. To guard against a reduction in its bandwidth and data loss, each type of cable limits the number of nodes that can be supported on its maximum segment length.

- *Resistance to interference*—Each type of cable resists EMI and RFI in varying degrees. EMI and RFI are caused by electric motors, fluorescent light fixtures, and other electrically noisy devices located near the network cable. Just as the construction of the cable and its covering varies, so does the cable's resistance to EMI and RFI signals.

Table 18.2 lists the characteristics of thin and thick coaxial cable, unshielded twisted-pair cable, and fiber-optic cable.

18. Networks and Communications

Table 18.2   Common network cable characteristics.

Cable Type	Bandwidth	Maximum Segment Length	Maximum Nodes per Segment	Resistance to Interference
Thin coaxial	10Mbps	185 m	30	Good
Thick coaxial	10Mbps	500 m	100	Better
UTP	10–100Mbps	100 m	1,024	Poor
STP	16–1,000Mbps	100 m	1,024	Fair to good
Fiber-optic	100–10,000Mbps	2,000 m	No limit	Best

Twisted-Pair Wire

Because it provides the most installation flexibility and ease of maintenance of the cable options, UTP cabling is by far the cable type most commonly used on LANs. The Electronics Industries Association (EIA) and the Telecommunications Industries Association (TIA) divide UTP cable into five cable categories, each of which is referred to as a "Cat" (short for category):

- *Cat 3*—4-pair (8-wire) cable that supports bandwidths up to 10Mbps, the minimum standard for 10BaseT networks (see the next section, "Ethernet Network Cable Designations," for a definition of this term).

- *Cat 4*—4-pair cable commonly used in 16Mbps token ring networks.

- *Cat 5*—4-pair cable that supports 100Mbps and higher bandwidths. Cat 5 cable is commonly used for 100BaseT networks. This category is what is being referenced by the term "UTP cable" for most networks.

- *Cat 6*—4-pair cable that supports 1000BaseT and other high-speed networking applications.

- *Cat 7*—4-pair cable that supports Gigabit Ethernet and ATM. Cat 7 cable transmits data at speeds of at least 1Gbps (a billion bits per second) and support multiple applications at different frequencies over the same cable.

TIP: *A specification called NEXT (near end cross talk) is a higher performance level for Cat 5 cabling that allows a Cat 5 cable to be used as a replacement for 25-pair communications cable.*

UTP cable uses an RJ-45 connector, shown in Figure 18.7, which is very much like the RJ-11 connector used on your telephone.

Ethernet Network Cable Designations

Ethernet networking standards (the Institute of Electrical and Electronics Engineers [IEEE] 802.3 standards) define cable media with a code that describes the cable's performance characteristics. The most common designation is for 10BaseT cable, which is essentially Cat 3 UTP wire.

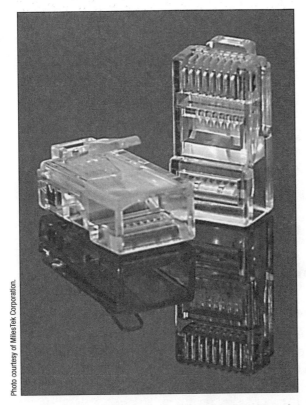

Photo courtesy of MilesTek Corporation.

Figure 18.7   An RJ-45 connector is used with twisted-pair cabling.

The common designations for Ethernet cable are:

- *10Base2*—10Mbps Ethernet implemented on thin coaxial cable
- *10Base5*—10Mbps Ethernet implemented on thick coaxial cable
- *10BaseT*—10Mbps Ethernet implemented on UTP cable
- *10BaseF*—10Mbps Ethernet implemented on fiber-optic cable
- *100BaseT*—Along with 100BascX, the generic term for Fast Ethernet
- *100BaseTX*—A two-pair wire version of 100BaseT
- *100BaseT4*—A four-pair wire version of Fast Ethernet
- *100BaseFX*—Fast Ethernet using two-strand fiber-optic cable
- *100BaseVG*—A 100 Mbps standard over Cat 3 cable
- *1000BaseTX*—Gigabit Ethernet networking implemented on Cat 6 cabling
- *1000BaseF*—Gigabit Ethernet networking implemented on a fiber-optic backbone

The 10Base or 100Base part of this code indicates that the cable is capable of supporting 10Mbps or 100Mbps bandwidth on a baseband (digital) signal. On the coax cable, the 5 and 2 indicate maximum segment lengths of 500 m and 200 m, respectively. The T in 10BaseT refers to twisted-pair cable. Fiber-optic cable is designated with an F.

Baseband versus Broadband Networks

Baseband networks use only one channel to support digital transmissions. This type of network signaling uses twisted-pair cabling. Most LANs are baseband networks.

Broadband networks use analog signaling over a wide range of frequencies. This type of network is unusual, but many cable companies now offer high-speed Internet network access over broadband systems.

Additional Network Terminology

Networking virtually has a language all of its own. When troubleshooting common network problems, you may encounter one or more of the following terms:

- *Bridge*—A bridge is a device used to connect two different LANs or network segments to create what appears to be one network. A bridge intelligently sends network messages to the network segment using information it gathers about the addresses of the nodes sending messages through it.

- *Gateway*—A gateway is a combination of hardware and software that enables two networks using different transmission protocols to communicate with one another. Gateways are implemented in three primary forms:

  - *Address gateway*—An address gateway connects networks that use different addressing schemes, such as connecting a Microsoft Windows network to a Novell NetWare network.

  - *Protocol gateway*—A protocol gateway connects networks using different communications protocols, such as a router connecting a LAN to the Internet (WAN). This is the most common type of gateway.

  - *Format gateway*—The format gateway is used to connect networks that use different data format schemes, such as a network using the American Standard Code for Information Interchange (ASCII) and another using Extended Binary-Coded Decimal Interchange Code (EBCDIC). This type of gateway is used to connect a PC to a mainframe computer.

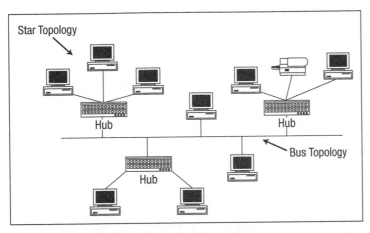

Figure 18.8   A hub is used to distribute network signals to nodes and to connect the nodes to the network backbone.

- *Hub*—As illustrated in Figure 18.8, a hub connects PCs, workstations, and peripheral devices to a network. Network devices are connected directly to the hub, which is, in turn, connected to the network backbone. Hubs are commonly used on Ethernet twisted-pair networks, especially 10BaseT and 100BaseT configurations. A typical hub is configured with 8, 16, or 24 ports.

- *Repeater*—A repeater is used to extend the maximum segment length of network cabling and to eliminate attenuation. A repeater is used to regenerate a cable's signal, thus allowing the signal to reach its destination.

- *Router*—A router is used to send network messages across the network using the most efficient path available, which it determines from the destination of the network message. When a network node does not know the address of a particular workstation or node, it broadcasts a message to the entire network. When too many workstations are sending broadcast messages, a broadcast storm results. A router can also be used to control broadcast storms on a network.

- *Segments*—A segment is a discrete portion of a network, usually represented by a single run of cable, a group of workstations, or even a LAN in a WAN. A cable segment is a single run of cable with terminators at each end. Typically, a network segment is located on one side of a bridge or router.

- *Switch*—A switch is used to connect network segments to form a single network or a larger network segment.

18. Networks and Communications

Network Interface Cards

The device used to connect a PC to a network is typically an NIC. The NIC is installed in an expansion slot inside the PC (and some peripheral devices) and attaches the PC to the network cabling. The NIC also contains a transceiver (transmitter/receiver) that serves as the intermediary between the PC and the network media and operating system.

The major characteristics of an NIC are:

- *Data bus compatibility*—Most newer NICs are designed for the PCI (peripheral component interconnect) bus. However, many ISA (Industry Standard Architecture) NICs are still in use.

- *Media access control (MAC) address*—Every NIC is assigned a universally unique identification number that is also used as its unique identifying address on a network. This MAC address is used to identify the PC housing the NIC to the network. The MAC address is explained in more detail in the following section.

- *System resources assignments*—An NIC requires an interrupt request (IRQ), an input/output (I/O) address, and a direct memory access (DMA) channel. The commonly used resources assignments for an NIC are IRQ3, IRQ5, or IRQ10; I/O address 300h; and an available DMA channel.

- *Transceiver type*—Special NICs are available that have different ports for two or more cable types. For example, an NIC may have separate ports and transceivers for UTP and thin coax. This provides flexibility to environments transitioning from one media to another.

Network Addressing

Two levels of addressing are used on networks: physical and logical. The physical address of an NIC is its MAC address, which is supplied by the manufacturer. The logical address of a workstation or node includes its network name and, if Transmission Control Protocol/Internet Protocol (TCP/IP) is in use, its IP address.

MAC Addressing

The MAC address assigned to every NIC or network adapter is universally unique. A MAC address is a 48-bit address, expressed as 12 hexadecimal digits. The MAC address is burned into the NIC's firmware during manufacture and cannot be altered. An NIC's MAC address is used for physical-level LAN addressing of the workstation, and all of the other LAN addressing schemes are cross-referenced to it.

The WINIPCFG command (shorthand for Windows IP configuration) can be used on a Windows 98 PC to display its MAC access. Figure 18.9 shows a sample of the

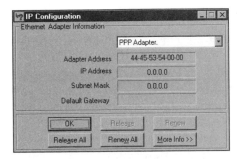

Figure 18.9   The WINIPCFG command displays the MAC (adapter) address of a PC's NIC.

WINIPCFG display. The first three segments of the MAC address, 44-45-53-54-00-00, identify the manufacturer, and the remainder is the unique number assigned to the NIC.

IP Address

If a network is running over the TCP/IP protocol (and most do), each workstation is also assigned an IP address. This address is a logical address in that software is used to interpret and direct messages to and from IP addresses.

An IP address is a 32-bit address expressed in four 8-bit octets, or four sets of eight. The IP address for a PC, as well as other IP addressing information, can be displayed using the IPCONFIG command. As shown in Figure 18.10, the information displayed by IPCONFIG includes the IP address (192.168.1.100), a subnet mask (used to determine how much of the address is used to designate the network), and the IP address of the default gateway of the network.

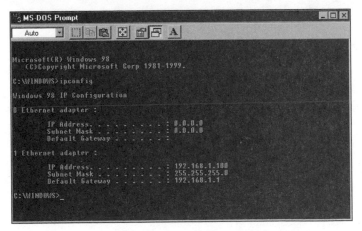

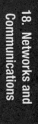

Figure 18.10   The IPCONFIG command is used to display the IP address configuration of a PC.

Network Names

On a Windows network, a PC is assigned a network basic input/output system (NetBIOS) name, which is also called a network name, by the network administrator. Users can also create network names by assigning share names to workstations and other networked devices. The Windows name conversion protocol WINS (Windows Internet Name Service) correlates the IP and NetBIOS names of each network node, so that messages can be directed to the correct workstation.

The NetBIOS name is a unique 15-character name that is periodically broadcast over the network to be cataloged by the Network Neighborhood function. The NetBIOS name is the one that shows up on the Windows Network Neighborhood, as shown in Figure 18.11.

Modems

A modem (modulator/demodulator) converts (modulates) the digital data of a PC into analog data to be sent over the plain old telephone system (POTS). A modem is connected to a PC internally through an expansion slot on the motherboard or externally through a serial or USB port.

Most newer internal modems do not require physical configuration, but some older modems use a dual inline packaging (DIP) switch or jumper to select the configuration, including transmission speed, or to designate the COM port to be used. Most modems today, however, are configured through the operating system. On a Windows system the modem is configured through the Modem Wizard. An external modem is attached to a PC through a serial port and is configured with DIP switches on the modem itself or through a proprietary installation and configuration disk packed with the modem. Typically, the only configuration

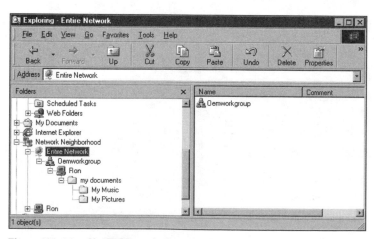

Figure 18.11   NetBIOS and share names displayed in the Windows Explorer.

issues you may have with an external modem are possible system resource conflicts, and usually only conflicts with the IRQ, if any. The cable used to connect an external modem to a PC is called a null modem cable. If not included with the modem, this cable can be purchased at most computer supply stores.

Device Drivers

Virtually all modems perform the same tasks. Modems can differ, however, in their device drivers. The two general types of modems are:

- *Standard modem*—A standard modem can be an internal or external device. It can also be plug and play (PnP) or legacy. Standard modems are operating system neutral and use generic device drivers.

- *Windows modem*—A Windows modem is an internal PnP device that requires a device driver provided by the Windows operating system to function properly.

As long as you have the proper device driver for your system's modem, it will work fine. If you are not sure about what type of modem you have, consult the documentation that came with the PC or the modem, or visit the manufacturers' Web sites.

AT Commands

Virtually all PC-compatible modems use the Hayes Standard AT command set. The AT command set gives you the ability to control the modem's functions and settings directly through a modem interface on the PC or by creating a script command that is sent to the modem each time the PC is booted.

The abbreviation "AT" refers to "attention," and precedes each of the modem action commands in the AT command set. Table 18.3 includes a few of the more commonly used AT commands. For example, if you must dial 9 to get an outside line and you wish the dial program to pause a bit to wait for the second (outside) dial tone, the AT command string used to dial a phone number using touch tone dialing is:

```
AT DT 9,555-1212
```

Table 18.3   A sampling of Hayes AT commands.

Commands	Action
A0	Answer incoming call
A/	Repeat last command
DT XXX-XXXX	Dial the telephone number using touch-tone dialing

(continued)

Table 18.3   A sampling of Hayes AT commands. *(continued)*

Commands	Action
H	On hook (hang up)
L	Speaker loudness (volume)
M	Mute (speaker off)
Z	Reset the modem to default settings
&X	Advanced configuration commands, where X is a command letter

Establishing a Dial-Up Connection

The most common use of a modem today is to connect to the Internet. The modem is connected to a telephone line with an RJ-11 connection on the modem. Figure 18.12 shows an RJ-11 connector, which is just like the connector used on nearly all phones.

Making the Call

On a Windows PC, the modem is controlled through the Dial-Up Networking (DUN) applet. DUN includes a built-in dialer that is automatically activated each time an application is opened that requires a connection through the modem, such as a browser, email client, or file transfer agent. The dialer sends the appropriate AT command string to the modem to dial the target phone number and make the connection.

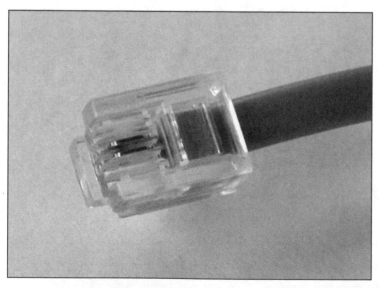

Figure 18.12   An RJ-11 connector is used to connect a modem to a telephone line.

The telephone portion of the dial-up action is the same as is used to place a call to anyone. The number is dialed, the phone company does its part, and the remote number rings. At this point, the modem at the other end, if properly configured, takes over and answers the call. Before data can be exchanged between the two modems (and the PCs to which they are attached), the local and remote modems must establish the connection using a process called a handshake. The hand-shake process involves the exchange of a series of signals between the two mo-dems. In effect, it establishes the communications session that remains open until one of the modems disconnects. See Chapter 12 for more information on the handshaking process.

Dial-up networking uses the Point-to-Point Protocol (PPP) to send packets over the PSTN. PPP inserts the data to be sent into a PPP packet and carries it over the transmission line to the remote modem. At the receiving end, the original data is removed from the PPP packet and passed to the remote computer for processing.

Digital Subscriber Lines

A digital subscriber line (DSL) transmits high-speed data over a standard tele-phone line, usually to the Internet. Data transmission speeds vary with the type of DSL service installed; they can range from 128Kbps for IDSL (integrated services digital network) (ISDN over DSL; for a discussion of ISDN, see the section "ISDN Terminal Adapters" later in this chapter) to 1.1 Mbps for SDSL (symmetrical DSL). Some services have higher speeds, and some have unpredictable speeds. The most common type of DSL service is ADSL (asymmetrical DSL), which is the common service for home users. ADSL transmits and receives asymmetrically, or at differ-ent speeds. SDSL, which transmits and receives symmetrically, or at the same speed, is typically used for business and high-end users that require larger amounts of bandwidth.

The equipment used at the customer's location, called the customer premise equip-ment (CPE), is typically an external DSL modem, or bridge, for ADSL. The DSL modem is attached to a PC much like a network connection would be made, through a twisted-pair cable and an RJ-45 connector to an NIC installed in the PC. The DSL modem, which can also be an internal device, bridges the incoming data from the phone line into a format usable by the NIC and PC and vice versa. SDSL lines use either a bridge or a router for the CPE. A router allows several PCs to share the DSL bandwidth.

NOTE: *A typical ADSL installation requires installation of an additional telephone line. The DSL companies and the telephone companies have worked out "line-sharing," which uses a splitter to allow a home to use a single telephone line for both voice and data transmissions. At the time this chapter was written, line-sharing was not widely implemented.*

Cable Modems

Another alternative to a dial-up modem for accessing the Internet is a cable modem connected to the cable TV system. Nearly all homes have cable TV lines already in place, so this service, where its available, is easy to obtain. The Internet service provided over the cable system is similar to ADSL service, with faster downloads and slower uploads. The CPE for cable Internet access is a modem that is usually an external device.

A cable modem allows you to get high-speed Internet access without impacting your phone line. You can even watch television while surfing the Internet. A signal splitter is used to separate the data and television signals.

ISDN Terminal Adapters

The Integrated Services Digital Network (ISDN) is another Internet service that can be purchased from either an Internet service provider (ISP) or the telephone company. Two types of ISDN services are available: BRI (basic rate interface) and PRI (primary rate interface). BRI is used for home or small office Internet connections, and PRI is most commonly used to provide high-bandwidth connections for voice and data to larger companies and telecommunications providers. The focus here is on the BRI service.

BRI ISDN is single-line service or single-user ISDN. BRI connects to your PC through a device called a terminal adapter. The terminal adapter feeds digital data from the PC directly to the ISDN line with no DAC (digital-to-analog converter) required. BRI service carries data over two bearer channels (called B channels), and it carries control signals over a single digital channel (called a D channel). Each B channel carries 64Kbps, and the two B channels combine to carry 128Kbps. The D channel has a bandwidth of 16Kbps, so altogether the ISDN line has a capacity of 144Kbps.

Wireless Networks

A wireless network does not use a physical cable to interconnect workstations and nodes to the network. Instead, a wireless network uses radio frequency (RF) devices to transmit and receive data. A wireless RF connection can be used to connect one or more workstations to a conventional wired network, or it can be used as the backbone of an entire network, forming what is called a wireless local area network, or a WLAN (pronounced as "w-lan"). A WLAN is very flexible and can overcome building or area problems that make installing a cable impractical.

802.11 Networks

The IEEE 802.11 standard, commonly called the WI-FI (wireless fidelity) standard, defines wireless networking. Wireless network adapters used to connect a PC or portable computer to a WLAN are called 802.11 cards (see Figure 18.13). Devices manufactured to this standard are interoperable with devices from other manufacturers.

A wireless network is formed in clusters around a device called an access point (AP), much like a 10BaseT network is formed around a hub. A wireless AP, such

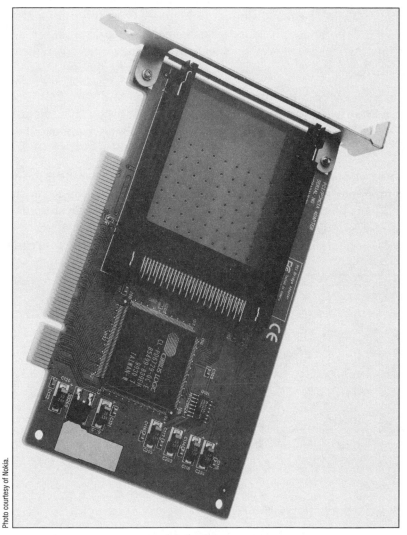

Photo courtesy of Nokia.

Figure 18.13   An 802.11 (WLAN) network bridge adapter card.

Figure 18.14   An 802.11 (WLAN) network access point.

as the one shown in Figure 18.14, serves as a master station for any wireless adapters within its broadcast area. It transmits and receives data to and from the 802.11 PCI and PCMCIA (Personal Computer Memory Card International Association) cards either permanently in its area, or just passing through. An access point can be mounted on a tabletop, on a wall, in a cabinet, or even on a ceiling. The AP is normally connected to a conventional network backbone.

Wireless network adapter cards, such as the one shown in Figure 18.13, are installed inside a PC in a PCI slot on the motherboard. In addition, 802.11 cards for notebook PCs (see Figure 18.15) allow the notebook PC to move about inside the WLAN's coverage area.

A wireless bridge can be used to connect two or more wired or wireless networks as much as a mile apart. Each network has a wireless bridge that is connected to an external antenna that has a clear and direct line of sight to the antenna connected to a wireless bridge on the other network. A wireless bridge can be used to create a CAN by interconnecting the buildings on a business or school campus.

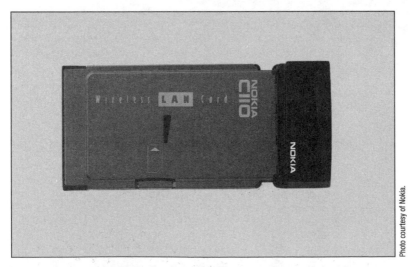

Figure 18.15   An 802.11 (WLAN) PCMCIA Type II network adapter card.

Bluetooth

Bluetooth is another emerging wireless technology (Bluetooth was the name of an ancient Swedish king). Bluetooth technology is used to connect PCs with external peripheral devices, such as modems and printers, to create what is called a wireless personal area network (WPAN, pronounced "w-pan"). Bluetooth wireless devices must be within 10 m of a PC or other host device to work effectively. Bluetooth technology transmits encrypted data at 721Kbps by using frequency-hopping, which helps to secure the data from other Bluetooth devices that may be nearby. Bluetooth has become very popular for use with personal digital assistants (PDAs), such as the Palm Pilot and Visor, and is being built into or can be added to several models. Like other RF devices, a Bluetooth transceiver can be connected to a PC through a USB or serial port, but many newer PCs, keyboards, mice, and other peripherals are available with built-in Bluetooth capability.

Immediate Solutions

Displaying the MAC Address of a Windows PC

To display the MAC address on a Windows $9x$ PC:

1. From the Windows desktop, open the Start Run dialog box.

2. Enter WINIPCFG in the Open box to display the WINIPCFG information, as shown in Figure 18.16.

WINIPCFG shows more information than just the MAC address. This command can also be used to troubleshoot Dynamic Host Configuration Protocol (DHCP) conflicts.

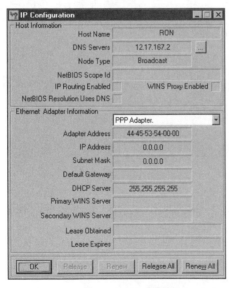

Figure 18.16   The WINIPCFG command can be used to display the MAC address of a Windows PC.

Displaying the IP Address of a PC

Many LANS and virtually all WANs use IP addresses to identify their nodes. An IP address for a networked workstation combines the addresses of the network and the node into a 32-bit address that is expressed in four 8-bit octets, or four sets of eight.

To check the IP address assignment on your networked PC:

1. Open an MS-DOS command prompt.

2. Enter IPCONFIG on the command line and press the Enter key. Information such as that shown earlier in the chapter in Figure 18.10 will be displayed.

3. Enter EXIT to close the MS-DOS window.

Figure 18.10 shows the display of an IPCONFIG command. The display includes the IP addressing information for a networked PC, in this case a PC with two NICs, one of which is disabled. IPCONFIG displays the IP address assigned to the workstation (in this case, 192.168.1.100), its subnet mask (which is used to determine how much of the address is used to designate the network or the node), and the default gateway of the node.

Troubleshooting a Modem That Fails to Establish a Connection

To troubleshoot a modem that is failing to connect to a remote modem or establish a connection, check the following:

- *Dial tone*—The sound produced by the modem allows you to track the progress of the connection during the handshake process. The first sound is normally the dial tone on the phone line. If you do not hear a dial tone, the problem is probably with the wall jack connection, the connection between the phone line and the modem, or the phone line itself. Most dialer software displays an error message when no dial tone is detected.

- *Modem*—If the remote modem answers and the handshake process begins but fails to establish a connection, most likely one of the modems is not configured properly. In most cases, the modems will adjust themselves for speed, but the character length, start and stop bits, and possibly speed configurations need to be checked.

- *Protocols*—If the connection is established by the modems, but no data is being transmitted and the connection is broken off after a few seconds, the

18. Networks and Communications

problem is most likely the protocols. This problem is common with newly installed modems. The TCP/IP or PPP protocols have not been properly configured. Verify that the protocols are enabled and that the proper bindings are set for the protocols.

- *Remote response*—It could be that the remote NAS (network access services) or modem is down or having problems. Call the ISP to check.

- *Telephone company*—The telephone companies have not always been able to keep up with the expansion of suburbs around large cities, and on occasion the lines have enough static or crosstalk to cause the modem to disconnect. If the modem disconnects soon after completing the connection and transferring data, or if the line is exceptionally slow, the problem is likely line noise on the phone line.

Configuring a Modem Connection

Virtually all PCs come with an internal modem installed as part of the standard equipment. However, you may need to upgrade a PC by installing an internal modem or to replace a faulty or out-of-date modem. After the modem is physically installed, use the following steps to configure the modem on a Windows PC:

1. Open the My Computer window to determine if Dial-Up Networking is installed. If not, add this service from the Windows distribution CD using the Add/Remove Program applet from the Control Panel.

2. Double-click the Dial-Up Networking icon and choose Make New Connection to start the Make New Connection Wizard. Should the Wizard indicate that the modem is not detected, let Windows try again to detect the modem.

3. Set up the dialing (and connection) information asked for by the Wizard, including the phone number to be dialed by the modem, and click Finish to close the Wizard.

4. From the Control Panel, open the Network icon and choose the Identification tab. Give the computer a name, a workgroup, and a description. Entering this information updates the device information database and requires a system restart.

5. From the Control Panel, open the Network icon, choose the Configuration tab (see Figure 18.17), and click the Add button.

6. From the Select Network Component Type window (see Figure 18.18), which displays next, highlight the Protocol selection and click the Add button to display the Select Network Protocol window (see Figure 18.19).

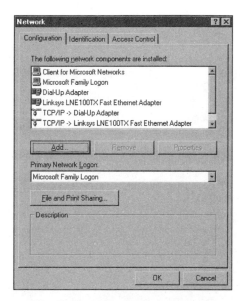

Figure 18.17   The Network window is used to configure a Windows PC to a network.

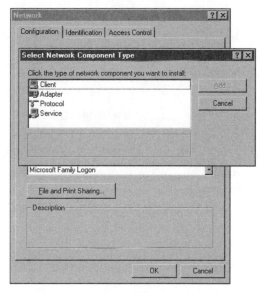

Figure 18.18   The Select Network Component Type dialog box is used to choose the network component to be configured.

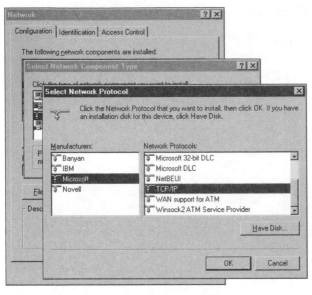

Figure 18.19   The Select Network Protocol window is used to add new dial-up or network protocols to a Windows PC.

7. Highlight Microsoft and find TCP/IP in the right pane. Click OK to return to the Network window and OK to exit the window.

8. From the My Computer window, double-click the Dial-Up Networking folder.

9. Right-click the icon of the new connection and choose Properties.

10. Select the Server Types tab (see Figure 18.20). Click the TCP/IP Settings button to open the TCP/IP Settings dialog box (see Figure 18.21). The settings on this box should be verified with the ISP or the network administrator, depending on the use of the modem and the network to which the PC is connecting. Except for the IP addresses, which are unique to each ISP or network, however, the settings shown in Figure 18.21 are fairly typical.

11. Use the OK button to apply the settings. The PC will need to be restarted.

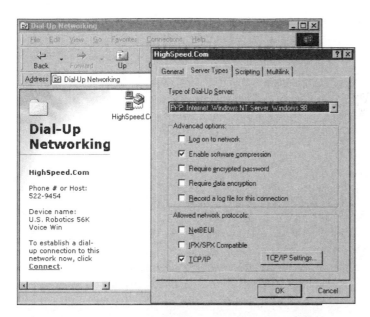

Figure 18.20   The Server Types tab on the Dial-up Networking dialog box.

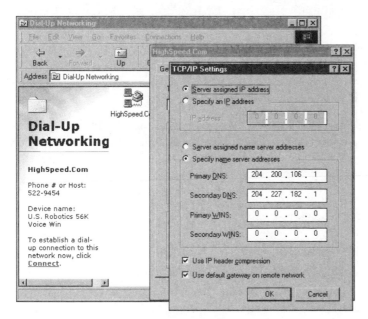

Figure 18.21   The TCP/IP Settings window is used to configure the network settings of a dial-up or LAN connection.

Installing and Configuring an NIC

An NIC is installed in a PC to connect the PC to the network or to replace a failed NIC. To install an NIC in a PC, follow these steps:

1. If you are replacing an existing NIC, before physically removing it, even if it is the very same manufacturer and model, uninstall it from the operating system. To do this, open the Network applet from the Control Panel, highlight the adapter to be removed, and click Remove.

2. Before you insert the NIC in an expansion slot, check the documentation to determine if any physical configuration steps are necessary. Most PCI cards are plug and play, but may still require a DIP switch or a jumper to be set. You absolutely want to do this before inserting the card in a slot. Be sure to handle the card only by its non-connecting edges.

3. Install the NIC card in the appropriate expansion slot. NICs are usually PCI cards, but some ISA or EISA (Extended ISA) cards are still around.

4. From the Windows Control Panel, open the Network icon to display the Network window, as shown in Figure 18.17.

5. Click the Add button to display the network component type list, as shown in Figure 18.18. Four network components can be configured from the Network window:

   - *Adapters*—This choice identifies and loads the device drivers for an NIC. To configure a PC to a network, an NIC must already be installed. An NIC installed in a PCI slot should already be listed.

   - *Protocol*—A protocol is a set of rules that communicating devices must follow when transmitting data, controls, and commands to one another. To communicate with a network, the PC must be using the same protocols as the network.

   - *Client*—Network clients allow a PC to communicate with specific network operating systems, such as Windows NT, Windows 2000, or Novell NetWare. To communicate with the network, a PC must have at least one client configured.

   - *Service*—Network services include specialized drivers that facilitate specialized capabilities, such as File and Print Sharing, and support for file systems on non-Windows systems.

6. On the Configuration tab of the Network window, click the NIC card in the list and click the Properties button to open the Properties window for the NIC (see Figure 18.22).

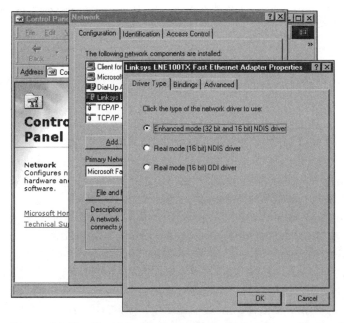

Figure 18.22   The Adapter Properties window is used to configure an NIC.

7. The Driver Type tab should indicate an Enhanced mode (32-bit and 16-bit) Network Device Interface Specification (NDIS) driver for the NIC. The other choices are for cards without 32-bit NDIS support or NICs requiring an open data-link interface (ODI).

8. The Bindings tab shows the protocols that have a binding to the NIC. In most cases these are preconfigured, but they can be modified. A binding is a network term for two protocols that perform different networking functions but have an active connection. If you are on an Ethernet network that has access to the Internet, your bindings will reflect your NIC card with a binding to TCP/IP protocols.

9. The contents of the Advanced tab vary by NIC and the characteristics of the network. The properties list may reflect the media and connector in use or it may be used to turn on a log file.

10. From this point, click any Apply or OK buttons that appear. You will be asked for other network information, IP address, gateway, and Domain Name System (DNS). The user or the network administrator should provide this information. The system will update its information database, and you may be asked to restart the system.

18. Networks and Communications

Related solutions:	Found on page:
BIOS Not Detecting the Hard Disk During the POST	112
Resolving Resource Conflicts	175
Installing an Expansion Card	271

Troubleshooting an NIC Connection

If a newly installed NIC is having problems connecting to or communicating with a network, check the following items:

1. Nearly all NICs come with an NIC diagnostics disk or utility, which is usually included on the disk with the device drivers. If so, run the diagnostic program to determine if the problem is on the NIC, PC, or network.

2. Assuming the NIC is connected to the network—meaning that the cable is connected to the NIC and the device drivers are installed—check the light-emitting diodes (LEDs) mounted on the exterior of the NIC. The LEDs actually have a purpose beyond indicating a connection. Table 18.4 lists the LED descriptions for a 3Com dual-speed NIC. Because the meanings of the LEDs vary by manufacturer, check the NIC's documentation for the meanings for your particular NIC.

3. If the LNK LED does not light, check the following:

    • Make sure the correct device drivers are loaded.

    • Check the cable and connections to the NIC and hub.

    • Change the hub port.

    • Check the duplex mode settings on the NIC and hub for compatibility.

4. If the ACT LED does not light, check the following:

    • Make sure the correct device drivers are loaded.

    • Make sure there is network activity; the network may just be down or idle.

Table 18.4   NIC LED display definitions.

LED	Color	Purpose	Flashing	On	Off
LNK	Green	Link integrity	Reversed polarity	Good connection	No connection
ACT	Yellow	Port traffic	Traffic present	Heavy traffic	No traffic

- Replace the NIC.
- Check the connection of the RJ-45 to the cable.

5. Check the physical installation of the NIC, making sure it is properly seated in the expansion slot. If the NIC is an ISA or EISA card, verify that jumper or DIP switch settings, if required, are correct. If all looks good, you may want to try a second identical card to eliminate the possibility of a bad card. Check the expansion slot for broken contacts or move the card to another slot.

6. Check the Windows Device Manager to see if it indicates a problem. If either the yellow and black exclamation point or the red and white x are showing on the NIC, look at the NIC's properties for an indication of the problem.

7. Check the cables and connectors. In addition to problems within the connector or the cable, the cable may be too long. Verify that the workstation is not beyond the maximum segment length or that there aren't more nodes than the cable medium can effectively support. If the problem is on a peer-to-peer network in which two PCs are directly connected without a hub or switch, make sure a crossover cable is being used.

8. The problem could very well be the PC's basic input/output system (BIOS). Verify that you are running the latest version of the BIOS and, if not, check with the motherboard or BIOS manufacturer to see if upgrades that affect PCI ports or NICs have been made.

9. Verify that the correct device driver is installed. Using the driver that came with the NIC or one downloaded from the manufacturer's Web site, reinstall the driver using the Windows Device Manager. You may want to check the compatibilities of the driver as well. Not all drivers work with every operating system.

Resolving Computer Hang-Ups When the NIC's Device Drivers Are Loaded

More than likely this problem is caused by the NIC's PCI interrupt settings in the BIOS. Check the NIC and BIOS documentation for the correct settings.

Another cause may be the high-memory device driver. If the PC is running EMM386.EXE, many PCI NIC device drivers require version 4.49 or later.

18. Networks and Communications

Restoring the Wake on LAN Feature Supported by the NIC

Wake on LAN (WOL) is a feature, supported by many NICs, that allows a PC to be powered up by the network server or from a remote location on the network. If WOL is not working, check these items:

1. Check the BIOS to ensure that it supports WOL. If it does, enable it. If it does not, check with the BIOS or motherboard manufacturer for a BIOS upgrade that includes this support.

2. For WOL to be functional, a WOL cable must be connected between the NIC and the motherboard. Check the documentation of the NIC and the motherboard to determine where this connection should be made. Without this cable, the WOL signal cannot be passed to the motherboard.

3. Check the network cable connection on the NIC.

Chapter 19

Audio/Visual Devices

In Depth

Audio

Not long ago, the only sounds coming from a PC, aside from a noisy fan or hard drive, were from a tiny, tinny speaker mounted somewhere inside the case. This PC speaker was useful primarily as a way to hear diagnostic power-on self-test (POST) messages (beeps) or operating system alerts. In recent years, sound systems have become standard equipment for most new PCs. They range in complexity from simple playback devices for games and system sounds all the way to full-fledged digital audio workstations (DAW) used in professional audio and video production and postproduction.

Components of a PC Sound System

The components common to most PC sound systems are the sound card, amplifier, speakers, and software.

Sound Card

The sound card combines into a single unit all of the inputs, outputs, and signal processors (digital-to-analog converters, or DACs, and analog-to-digital converters, or ADCs) required to convert audio information to and from digital form. These cards were traditionally packaged as an ISA (Industry Standard Architecture) or PCI (peripheral component interconnect) adapter card. Recently, the trend has been toward mounting an integrated audio chip directly on the motherboard, eliminating the need for a separate device to handle audio.

Amplifier

Once digital audio has been converted into an audible signal, it has to be amplified before it can be played back on speakers. Most sound cards include a weak amplifier capable of driving a set of headphones or small passive PC speakers. Many PC speaker systems integrate an amplifier into one or both of the speaker enclosures, taking the burden of amplification off the sound card.

With the correct cabling, the signal from a sound card can be routed to any stereo or home theater system, creating the possibility of true audiophile-quality sound from a PC. In a digital audio workstation configuration, the signal is often routed through a mixing console before it is amplified.

Speakers

PC speakers come in a wide range of configurations, from small passive systems powered by the sound card's headphone output, to active (amplified) three-way and surround systems that would rival many home theaters. Some computer monitors have integrated speakers either incorporated into the bezel or designed to snap on and off the sides of the monitor.

A recent development in PC audio is the universal serial bus (USB) speaker system. USB speaker systems do not require a separate sound card. Digital audio is sent directly to the speakers via the USB cable, and all signal processing is done within the speaker enclosure itself, external to the PC. This has a few advantages, including reducing the potential for audible interference (hum or static) from other PC components. One disadvantage of USB speakers is that they do not provide a way to connect to the analog output of a compact disk-read only memory (CD-ROM) or digital versatile disk (DVD) player (See "CD-ROM and DVD Interfaces" later in this chapter).

Magnetic Shielding

Dedicated PC speaker systems differ from conventional home stereo speakers in an important way: Because they are typically placed fairly close to the computer monitor, PC speakers must be magnetically shielded to avoid distorting the image on the screen and ultimately damaging the monitor. Therefore, use caution when configuring a PC audio system with components not specifically designed for PC audio.

Software

With the exception of the basic playback controls on the front of some CD-ROM drives, most PC audio operations are controlled by software. All of the Microsoft Windows family of operating systems, as well as many distributions of Linux, include basic tools for recording, playing, and mixing audio from different sources. Advanced tools for recording and manipulating digital audio are available from a variety of vendors.

The Web sites for some of the better-known audio software publishers are:

- Sonic Foundry, Inc. (**www.sonicfoundry.com**)
- Steinberg Media Technologies AG (**www.steinberg.net**)
- Twelve Tone Systems, Inc. (**www.cakewalk.com**)
- Real Networks, Inc. (**www.real.com**)
- Waves LTD (**www.waves.com**)
- Nullsoft, Inc. (**www.winamp.com**)
- Microsoft, Inc. (**www.microsoft.com/windows/windowsmedia**)

Sound Cards

The sound card combines the components required to transfer sound into and out of a PC, including:

- *Digital-to-analog converter*—The DAC converts audio data stored on a hard drive or other medium into audible information that can be played back on speakers or headphones.

- *Analog-to-digital converter*—The ADC converts analog audio information, such as a voice or a musical instrument, into digital data that can be stored and edited on a PC.

- *Analog inputs*—Most sound cards have separate line-level and microphone-level (mic-level) inputs. Line-level inputs are designed to accept a signal from an electronic source such as a compact disk (CD) player or tape deck, or direct input from a musical instrument such as a synthesizer. Mic-level inputs are designed to accept the much lower voltage signal generated by a microphone or an unamplified electric guitar. Professional sound cards for DAW applications often have one or more stereo pairs of analog inputs for recording multiple channels simultaneously. The most common type of connector for analog input is a standard $\frac{1}{8}$-inch phone jack identical to those found on a portable stereo. More specialized sound cards may include left and right stereo RCA jacks or $\frac{1}{4}$-inch phone jacks to be more compatible with professional studio gear.

- *Analog outputs*—A sound card frequently has two analog outputs. One, often identified as Phones Out or Speaker Out, is powered by a small amplifier capable of driving a pair of headphones or passive speakers. Another, usually called "Line Out," is designed to send a line-level signal to an input such as that found on a home stereo receiver. Professional sound cards for DAW applications commonly have one or more stereo pairs of analog outputs for playing back multiple channels simultaneously. As with the inputs, $\frac{1}{8}$-inch phone jacks are most common, but some cards use RCA or $\frac{1}{4}$-inch phone jacks.

- *Digital input/output (I/O) interfaces*—Once found only on high-end professional sound cards, digital interfaces are beginning to show up on consumer sound cards as well. Digital I/O makes it possible to transfer data to and from digital devices such as minidiscs and digital audio tape (DAT) machines without ever leaving the digital domain. This eliminates the potential for signal degradation that accompanies the use of a DAC or ADC. The most common types of digital interfaces found on sound cards are the S/P-DIF (Sony/Philips Digital Interface) and the AES/EBU (Audio Engineering Society/European Broadcasting Union) interface.

- *Game/MIDI port*—This versatile connector, found on many sound cards, is most often used for game controllers such as joysticks or gamepads. With a special cable, this port can be connected to any external musical instrument digital interface (MIDI) device to send and receive MIDI data. Most sound card MIDI interfaces are designed to emulate the MPU-401 interface developed by Roland Sound.

- *Digital signal processor*—Another feature formerly found only on high-end sound cards, digital signal processors (DSPs) are finding their way to less expensive cards as well. DSPs can serve a variety of functions, but the goal is always the same—to reduce the burden on the computer's central processing unit (CPU) when processing audio. Among the tasks performed by DSP chips are resampling (changing the bit depth and sample rate of audio data) and digital effects such as reverberation and echo.

- *Synthesizer*—Some of the sounds produced by a sound card are generated by the card itself using a synthesizer chip. Unlike digital audio, which resides on a hard drive or other storage medium until it is sent through the DAC, the sound card's synthesizer responds to MIDI messages, which tell it what sounds to play, at what frequency, and for what duration. The synthesizer can be controlled by an external MIDI device as well as the PC. Synthesizer chips vary widely in capability and sound quality. Many newer sound cards incorporate a process called wavetable synthesis to produce a higher-quality sound. Wavetable synthesis uses digital samples of actual instruments in place of synthesized sounds.

Installing a Sound Card

Sound card installation is subject to the same safety considerations as expansion cards, discussed in detail in Chapter 10. These considerations are reviewed in brief here.

ISA Sound Cards

Like other ISA expansion cards, ISA sound cards usually require manual configuration of resources such as port address, direct memory access (DMA), and interrupt request (IRQ). These values are typically set with a series of jumpers on the card. Some cards require a combination of jumper settings and lines in the **AUTOEXEC.BAT** and/or **CONFIG.SYS** files.

ISA sound cards can be especially complicated to configure because they often use a separate set of values for different functions. For example, some sound cards require a separate port address, DMA, and IRQ for general use; another set of values for Sound Blaster emulation; and a third set of values for MPU-401 emulation. That's nine resources to configure for a single expansion card!

As you can see, no universal set of steps exists for configuring an ISA sound card. The only way to know exactly what values need to be assigned and how to assign them is to refer to the manufacturer's documentation. If the manual for the card is unavailable, many sound card manufacturers publish installation guides on their Web sites (see "Tools and Diagnostic Processes" later in this chapter for a list of sound card manufacturers' Web sites).

SET BLASTER

Creative Labs' Sound Blaster (along with its many variations) was one of the first sound cards to gain widespread use among PC gamers and multimedia enthusiasts. As a result, many game and multimedia publishers began developing titles with audio content specifically designed to work with Sound Blaster. A number of these titles rely upon the SET BLASTER environment variable in **AUTOEXEC.BAT** to determine how to route sound data. Unfortunately, manufacturers of sound cards with Sound Blaster emulation often omitted the SET BLASTER variable from their installation routines. In many cases, this meant that there would be no sound, even if Sound Blaster emulation had been implemented correctly.

A typical SET BLASTER line looks like this:

```
SET BLASTER=A220 I5 D1 T6 P330
```

where A is the port address, I is the IRQ, D is the DMA channel, T identifies the type of Sound Blaster being emulated, and P is the MIDI port address.

PCI Sound Cards

Many of the difficulties associated with configuring an ISA sound card are eliminated with PCI sound cards. Although a number of resources still need to be assigned, this is typically accomplished by the plug-and-play basic input/output system (BIOS) in conjunction with a plug-and-play operating system such as Windows 95, 98, or 2000. In most cases, resources such as IRQ and DMA cannot be assigned manually.

A few conditions must be met before a PCI card can be installed:

- First, and most obviously, there must be an available PCI slot.

- Many early motherboards use an earlier revision of the PCI BIOS that may not be compatible with newer sound cards. Check with the motherboard manufacturer if you have an older PCI motherboard and are not certain that the PCI BIOS revision may be less than version 2.1.

- Motherboard manufacturers commonly develop system BIOS updates after the motherboard is released. Sometimes these updates are designed to address issues such as plug-and-play device enumeration that can affect whether or not a card is successfully installed.

Chapter 4 presents details about BIOS upgrades.

A PCI sound card is typically installed as follows:

1. Insert the card into an available PCI slot, observing the precautions listed earlier in this section and in Chapter 10.

2. Power on the system.

3. When the operating system prompts you for an installation disk, insert the manufacturer's driver disk and point to the directory specified in the manufacturer's documentation.

Although Windows 98 and Windows 2000 include drivers for a handful of PCI sound cards, in most cases you will need the manufacturer's drivers to set up the card correctly. If a driver disk is unavailable, drivers can often be found on the manufacturer's Web site (see "Tools and Diagnostic Processes" later in this chapter for a list of sound card manufacturers' Web sites). Manufacturers frequently release updated drivers that include features or bug fixes not found on the original installation disk, so it is always good practice to check the Web site for updates.

Sound Capture and Playback

Once the card is installed and speakers are attached, the system is ready to record and play back sounds.

Capture

The sound card input used to capture audio depends upon the source. If the source is an electronic device such as a CD player, stereo receiver, or synthesizer, a line-level input is used. Although most sound cards use $\frac{1}{8}$-inch phone jacks for their inputs, very few other devices use these jacks, so a special cable or adapter is usually required (readily available at any electronics supply store). In most cases, the appropriate cable for recording from home stereo sources is one with left and right male RCA plugs on one end and a single stereo male $\frac{1}{8}$-inch phone plug on the other end. Many synthesizers use $\frac{1}{4}$-inch phone jacks, so the appropriate cable would have left and right male $\frac{1}{4}$-inch phone plugs on one end and a single stereo male $\frac{1}{8}$-inch phone plug on the other end.

If the source is a live sound such as a voice or an acoustic musical instrument, a microphone needs to be connected to a mic-level input on the sound card. Inexpensive PC microphones are designed with $\frac{1}{8}$-inch phone plugs to connect directly to the mic input of most sound cards. Higher-end microphones typically have $\frac{1}{4}$-inch phone plugs or XLR connectors, so they would require an adapter or specialized cable to connect to a $\frac{1}{8}$-inch phone jack. By the way, XLR doesn't stand for anything; it was the original part number assigned to it by Canon.

If the source is a device with digital I/O such as a minidisc or DAT machine, and the sound card also has digital I/O, the proper cabling depends upon what type of ports are available. When cabling between digital devices, it is especially important to use cables specifically designed for digital data. S/P-DIF cables, for example, look almost identical to standard RCA audio cables, but their construction is quite different. The same is true for AES/EBU cables, which look like standard XLR microphone cables, but in fact are very different underneath the wrapper.

Once the connections are made, the rest of the operation takes place within the software. Audio software has a wide variation of capabilities and controls. At the most basic level, to record a sound, just click **RECORD** and start making noise. When capturing audio to a PC, however, a number of considerations must be addressed:

- *File type*—Although a bewildering array of audio file types are available, the most common audio capture format in Windows systems is the WAV file. Even if the ultimate format for the file will be something other than WAV, the WAV format provides the most flexibility in terms of editing and conversion to other file types. Many audio capture applications will capture only to WAV files.

- *File size*—One of the first things many people notice when they start capturing audio is how quickly their hard drive fills up. Audio files can be enormous, particularly if the sound is captured at a CD-quality sample rate and resolution. For instance, just 10 seconds of stereo sound recorded at 44.1kHz (kilohertz) and 16 bits (or what is referred to as "CD-quality") will use approximately 2MB (megabytes) of disk space. If disk space is an issue, consider whether the material being recorded actually needs to be reproduced at such high quality. Also consider whether it can be stored as a mono rather than a stereo file, which would cut the file size in half.

- *Input level*—If a sound is recorded at too quiet a level, playing it back at an adequate volume may produce a noisy result. Recording a sound at too high a level can result in clipping—literally cutting off the peaks of the digital audio waveform—producing distortion. Most audio capture programs provide visual cues to let you know how loud the input is and whether it is close to clipping.

- *Sample rate*—The sample rate (in kilohertz) refers to the number of samples taken from the audio input per second. The sample rate used by a CD, 44.1kHz, will produce good results for most applications. Audio recorded for professional applications may be sampled at a higher rate to increase fidelity and provide more headroom for audio editing. Lower sample rates will use less disk space, but at the cost of audio quality. The maximum and minimum sample rates available are subject to the limitations of both the sound card and the software being used.

- *Sample resolution*—Expressed in bits, sample resolution refers to the size of the samples taken. CD audio is stored at a resolution of 16 bits. Sample resolution involves the same trade-offs with regard to file size and sound quality that apply to sample rate.

Digital Audio Extraction

Digital audio extraction (DAE) is a method of capturing data from an audio CD without leaving the digital domain. DAE differs from other audio capture methods in that it does not require the use of a sound card. DAE makes it possible to make an exact copy of an audio CD without introducing any of the signal loss inherent in digital-to-analog conversion. Most new CD-ROM drives support DAE (check with the manufacturer). In addition to a CD-ROM drive that supports DAE, special software is also required. DAE tools are frequently bundled with CD writing software and with MP3 creation suites. DAE output is typically stored in the form of a WAV file.

Playback

A Windows system (any version) may be configured by default to play back sounds that correspond with certain system events such as error messages, running an application, or minimizing a window. These system sounds can be configured using the "Sounds" applet in the Windows 98 Control Panel or the "Sounds and Multimedia" applet in the Windows 2000 Control Panel.

Other playback events involve more active participation from the user. A Web site or a multimedia title such as an encyclopedia may include icons that the user will click to hear an audio file. Audio capture programs usually include tools for playing back various types of sound files.

Windows includes a basic mixer for adjusting the volume level of various sound events. Some games, for instance, will send different audio events to separate channels on the sound card: speech and digital audio to the Wave channel, CD music to the CD Audio channel, and synthesizer output to the MIDI channel. The relative volume of these different sound sources can be balanced using the Windows mixer, accessed via the yellow speaker icon in the Taskbar notification tray. Many sound cards are bundled with an enhanced mixer application that duplicates the functions of the Windows mixer and adds features specific to that card's capabilities.

Sound Files

A number of audio file types can be played on a PC. Audio file types are typically expressed using their extension. The most common of these are discussed in the following sections.

WAV

WAV is the Windows audio standard. Recording and playback support is built into the operating system. Double-clicking on a WAV file will launch a Windows applet by default, unless a third-party program has been associated with WAV files.

MP3

Short for MPEG-1 Layer 3, MP3 is an audio compression standard developed by the Moving Pictures Experts Group (MPEG). Audio compression is a means of reducing the size of WAV files to make them more portable and to take up less storage space. MP3 compression has become popular in recent years because file sizes can be reduced dramatically while retaining most of the original WAV file's audio quality. For example, a 50MB WAV file stored at 44.1kHz and 16 bits can be reduced to around 5MB and still maintain a sound quality comparable to that of a CD. Less compression results in larger file sizes but also higher sound quality. The portability of MP3 has led to an explosion of music trading on the Internet, as well as considerable controversy surrounding the potential for copyright infringement.

MP3 files require specialized software for playback, and a number of free MP3 applications are available on the Internet. Nullsoft's Winamp is one of the most popular of these applications. Microsoft has included MP3 support in newer versions of its Windows Media Player, available on its Web site (see "Components of a PC Sound System" earlier in this chapter for a list of audio software publishers' Web sites). MP3 files are also sometimes available as streaming content on Internet sites, meaning that the file need not be copied to the local system before it can be played. Streaming audio is commonly handled by Web browser plug-ins.

MP2

MP2 (MPEG-1 Layer 2) is an earlier MPEG compression format that produces lower-quality results than MP3. It can be played back with any MP3 player.

AAC

The MPEG compression standard expected to succeed MP3, AAC (advanced audio coding) is another name for MPEG-2, not to be confused with MP2.

AU

AU (short for "audio"), is the audio file standard on Unix systems. PC users may encounter AU files on Internet sites. Most Web browsers have built-in AU support, and newer versions of the Windows Media Player will also play back AU files.

AIFF

AIFF (audio interchange file format) is the Macintosh equivalent of the Windows WAV format, and can be played back on newer versions of the Windows Media Player.

RA or RAM

RA and RAM both refer to Real Audio files, a streaming audio format developed by Real Networks. The quality of Real Audio files varies with the speed of the Internet connection. Real Audio files targeted for high-bandwidth connections such as DSL (Digital Subscriber Line) or T1 can approach CD quality, whereas files designed for modem downloads are similar to the quality of an AM radio signal. Real Audio files require a dedicated Real Audio player or browser plug-in for playback.

WMF

Windows Media File (WMF) is Microsoft's answer to Real Audio. Like Real Audio, WMF sound quality is bandwidth-dependent. WMF files can be played back on Windows Media Player.

MID

Files with the .MID extension are not digital audio files at all but instead contain MIDI data. MIDI can be thought of as a language, a standard for sharing information about musical events such as the pitch and duration of a note, between multiple devices. How a PC handles MID files depends upon the system's configuration. Often MID files are routed to the sound card's onboard synthesizer, which in turn generates the corresponding sounds. MID files can also be played back on an external device attached to the sound card's game/MIDI port. Windows Media Player will launch MID files, but dedicated MIDI sequencing software is required to create and edit MIDI music.

CD-ROM and DVD Interfaces

CD audio is unique among PC audio formats in that the computer does not process the output from an audio CD. Instead, both CD-ROM and DVD drives send CD audio directly to the sound card via a specialized cable. Although it may appear that the computer is processing CD audio, because volume levels can be adjusted with a software mixer, in fact, all that is being controlled is the sound card's output level. In most cases digital audio from a CD is converted to analog by a DAC on the CD-ROM or DVD drive itself. Less commonly, a digital output on the CD-ROM or DVD drive is cabled to a digital input on the sound card to allow the card's DAC to handle the conversion. Whereas digital outputs on CD-ROM and DVD drives are fairly common, digital CD audio inputs on sound cards are still somewhat rare.

Cabling between a CD-ROM or DVD drive and a sound card can be fairly straightforward, especially if the drive is shipped with its own audio cable (most are). The analog output is always located at the rear of the drive, often to the left of the integrated drive electronics (IDE) or small computer system interface (SCSI) connector, and is usually well marked. Working with older drives and those that ship without an audio cable can be a bit more complicated because there is no single standard for cabling between a CD-ROM or DVD drive and a sound card. Sound card and drive manufacturers often use proprietary connector types, creating a situation in which a "Panasonic to Sound Blaster" or "Sony to Pro Audio Spectrum" cable might be required. Fortunately, inexpensive (less than $10.00) universal cables are now available with multiple connectors for almost any combination. These can be found at many computer superstores and online PC hardware vendors.

Image Capture

The objectives of image capture are not unlike those of audio capture. In both cases the purpose is to convert analog information such as a photograph or a human voice into digital data that can be stored and edited on a computer. Although they are not yet as universal as PC sound systems, image capture devices have increased in popularity with the rise of the Internet, and have quickly become essential tools for developing visual content for Web pages.

Scanners

Scanners are devices for capturing still images using a light source that reflects off of the image being captured. Information about the reflected image is digitized and sent to software, where it can be stored, edited, and printed. Scanners are available in a wide variety of configurations, which can be categorized according to imaging method, how the scanner interfaces with the PC, and how the original image is delivered to the scanner.

Imaging Method

The imaging methods available with scanners are:

- *Photomultiplier Tube*—Photomultiplier tube (PMT) scanners use a vacuum tube to convert light reflected from an image into an electrical signal that is amplified before ultimately being sent to the PC. PMT scanners are typically more expensive and more difficult to use than their CCD counterparts (discussed next) and are reserved for high-end applications that can take advantage of their wider dynamic range.

- *Charge-Coupled Device*—Charge-coupled device (CCD) scanners make up the vast majority of general-purpose scanners found in homes and offices. A CCD is a small solid-state sensor that converts light into an electric charge, which in turn is converted into data that can be stored on a computer. Thousands of CCDs are arranged into an array that scans the entire surface of the image. A larger number of CCDs in the array translates into a higher maximum resolution for scanned images.

- *Multipass versus Single Pass*—Multipass scanners collect color data by using three passes of the light source and CCD array over the surface of the image. A single scan requires one pass each for red, green, and blue information, at the end of which the three passes are combined to make a full-color image. The drawbacks of this method are fairly obvious. In addition to the time it takes to make three passes, image quality can suffer from tiny inaccuracies in the alignment of the three sets of data used to create a composite image. These problems are eliminated with the advent of single-pass scanners, which collect all color data at one time. The result is usually a faster scan with less potential for image distortion than with a multipass scan.

Interface

The interfaces available with scanners are:

- *SCSI*—SCSI scanners are either designed to work with standard SCSI interfaces from such manufacturers as Adaptec, or they ship with their own, sometimes proprietary, adapter cards. SCSI scanners are often faster than their parallel counterparts, but overall cost can be higher, especially when the price of the SCSI adapter is figured in. Because a SCSI adapter is required, installing a SCSI scanner can be more difficult than installing a parallel scanner.

- *Parallel*—Parallel scanners connect to the PC's parallel port over a standard DB-25 cable. Most parallel scanners include a pass-through connector to allow a printer to share the same port. An advantage of parallel scanners is that they do not involve the additional expense and trouble of a SCSI adapter, but there is usually a trade-off in speed. In addition, some printers and other parallel devices such as Zip drives can have problems with a scanner's pass-through port.

- *USB*—USB scanners eliminate most of the problems of SCSI and parallel scanners. Speeds are comparable to many SCSI scanners, typically with a lower price and simpler installation. Obviously, USB scanners are appropriate only for operating systems that support USB. All versions of Windows 98 and Windows 2000 support USB out of the box. Patches are available that will allow Windows 95 to work with many USB devices. Some USB devices, including some scanners, will not work in Windows 95, even if the patches for USB support have been applied.

Delivery Method

The delivery methods available with scanners are:

- *Drum*—Drum scanners are PMT scanners, which require the original to be mounted to a transparent cylindrical spinning drum in order to capture an image.

- *Handheld*—Handheld scanners must be moved across the surface of the original by hand. Because they are often narrower than a typical page, more than one scan may be necessary to capture a full-page image. When this is the case the multiple scans must be "stitched" together in software before the image is complete.

- *Sheet-fed*—Sheet-fed scanners use rollers to move an image past the light source and CCD array. Some sheet feeders can automatically feed one page after another, making it possible to scan multiple images in a single event. The obvious disadvantage of sheet-fed scanners is that they can accept only loose pages and are not useful for scanning books, magazines, or rigid objects.

- *Flatbed*—Flatbed scanners have become the most popular type of scanner because of their flexibility and ease of use. The material to be scanned is placed on a flat glass surface, and the light source and CCD array pass underneath it. The dimensions of scanner beds vary significantly. For example, many flatbed scanners are unable to scan an entire legal-sized page in a single pass. Therefore, a scanner should be chosen with some consideration of the size of the material likely to be scanned.

Like digitized sound, a visual image must be sent to software before it can be manipulated and stored. Scanners come bundled with software for controlling the scanning process, and typically include some basic tools for image editing. Advanced tools for image editing are available from a number of publishers, including:

- Adobe: **www.adobe.com**
- Corel: **www.corel.com**
- Jasc: **www.jasc.com**
- Ulead: **www.ulead.com**
- Xara: **www.xara.com**

Video Capture Devices

The term "video capture" can be somewhat misleading because it suggests that what is captured is always a moving image. Many video capture devices do capture full-motion video, but many others, such as the popular Snappy from Play Inc., capture only still images, just like a scanner. Video capture devices, then, are devices that use video cameras or videocassette recorders (VCRs) as a source for still or moving images. Video capture devices can be categorized according to whether moving images can be captured, as well as how they attach to the PC, whether they accept a digital signal, and the type of compression used.

Internal Vs. External

Video capture devices typically connect to the PC in one of three ways: An adapter card (usually PCI), an external parallel interface, or an external USB interface.

The distinction between internal and external video capture devices may be blurred by the fact that many capture cards use a *breakout box*, a separate piece of hardware that attaches to the rear of the card and contains all of the connectors for interfacing with the input device (video camera, VCR). Some video cards also double as video capture devices, with varying capabilities.

Digital Vs. Analog

Some video capture devices will accept only an analog signal, such as that from a traditional camcorder or VCR, using Composite or S-Video inputs. Digital video capture devices use high-speed IEEE 1394 (also known as FireWire) interfaces to transfer data directly from digital video cameras. Some capture devices include a combination of digital and analog inputs.

CODEC

Digital video, like digital audio, takes up a huge amount of storage space. One second of uncompressed, full-motion video and audio captured at 24-bit, 640×480 resolution will take up approximately 30MB of disk space. Because of this, all video capture devices use one or more methods of compression, or CODECs (COmpression/DECompression), to reduce the amount of storage space required. The compression method has a direct bearing upon the applications for which the captured video will be appropriate, so it should be chosen carefully. The most common CODECs used by video capture devices are:

- *MJPEG*—MJPEG is a motion video CODEC based on a still image CODEC developed by the Joint Photographic Experts Group (JPEG). MJPEG is optimized for transfer to and from videotape, but is less appropriate for multimedia and Internet applications because it requires specialized hardware for playback. Image quality is high, but varies with the amount of compression.

- *MPEG-1*—MPEG-1 is one of two common video CODECs developed by the Moving Pictures Experts Group (MPEG). MPEG-1 is ideal for multimedia and Internet video because playback is software-based, and file sizes can be reduced dramatically while maintaining a good image quality.

- *DV*—DV is the CODEC used by digital video cameras, which perform their own compression during recording. DV capture cards connect to digital cameras over an IEEE 1394 interface, which transfers digital video at very high speeds with no signal loss. DV is not scalable, meaning that screen size and data rate (the number of megabytes per second of playback) cannot be adjusted.

- *MPEG-2*—MPEG-2 is the newest CODEC video capture device. MPEG-2 improves upon MPEG-1 in a number of ways, including supporting resolutions up to four times higher. MPEG-2 compression is scalable, so it can be used for multimedia or Web-based applications all the way up to broadcast-quality video at higher data rates (which, of course, translates to larger file sizes).

Digitizers

All of the sound and image capture methods discussed so far are designed to reproduce an original as faithfully as possible. If captured correctly, a digitized sound is virtually identical to the original. Similarly, a printed copy of a scanned page and the original, sitting side by side, may be impossible to distinguish from each other. Digitizers are unique in that their function is to create something that did not exist before. There is no "original" in the sense that these other technologies duplicate an existing sound or image.

Digitizers (also called *digitizing tablets*, *drawing tablets*, or just *tablets*) are drawing tools designed to capture the movements of the operator's hand. Their operation is similar to that of a mouse, but there is a significant difference between the type of information a mouse generates and the data sent to the computer by a digitizer. Mouse input is always relative to the position of the cursor on the screen. If you draw a line with a mouse, then pick up the mouse and move it to a different position on the desk, the input will continue from the last position of the cursor. With a digitizer, however, each position on the tablet corresponds to a specific position on the screen. This makes it possible to accurately trace an existing drawing, or to create original drawings, such as architectural designs, that must correspond to very precise dimensions.

A digitizer accomplishes this with two main components: an electronic tablet, and one of two types of drawing devices. A *pen* (also called a *stylus*) is held like an ordinary pen and is used to "draw" directly on the tablet, creating a corresponding drawing on the PC. A *puck* (also called a *cursor*) more closely resembles a mouse and is used in much the same way. A small window with crosshairs makes the puck ideal for very precise tracing of existing drawings. In both cases the tablet detects the exact position of the drawing device and sends x and y coordinates to the PC. Both pens and pucks are available in either corded or cordless configurations. Many digitizers include software that allows the pen or puck to duplicate the functions of an ordinary mouse.

Like scanners, digitizers connect to the PC in a variety of ways. Many digitizers use a proprietary controller card, either ISA or PCI, which must be installed before the tablet can be operated. There is no standardization among the types of cables used between these proprietary interfaces and the tablet, so the manufacturer must be contacted for any replacements. Another common interface for digitizers is the serial port. Although one end of the connecting cable uses a standard DB-9 or DB-25 connector, the other end is designed specifically to connect to the tablet. Again, the manufacturer can provide information about replacement cables. Some newer digitizers connect to the PC through the system's USB port using a standard cable.

Tools and Diagnostic Processes

The first step in troubleshooting any audio/visual device is to make sure the most recent drivers are installed on the system. Fierce competition among hardware developers has created a situation in which devices are released to the public as quickly as possible, often before all of the bugs have been worked out of the drivers. Even if a device is fresh off the shelf, it is likely that a newer driver than the one in the box is already available. The Internet has become an indispensable tool for PC technicians looking for the latest drivers for the equipment they are troubleshooting. The following list of URLs for major audio/visual hardware manufacturers points directly to the driver download area wherever possible.

Sound Cards

- Aztech Systems: **www.aztech.com.sg/support/drivers_sound.htm**
- Creative Labs: **www.creative.com/support/files/download.asp**
- SONICblue: **www.diamondmm.com**
- ESS (ESS supplies audio chips to motherboard and sound card manufacturers. It provides generic drivers that work with many, but not all, of the third-party products that use its chips): **www.esstech.com/Technical/drivers/downloadable/drivers/driver.htm**
- SIIG: **www.siig.com/drivers/**
- Voyetra/Turtle Beach: **www.voyetra-turtle-beach.com/site/sales_support/ftp.asp**

Scanners

- Afga: **support.agfa.com/swPubDTP/**
- Canon: **www.usa.canon.com/support/files/scanners.html**
- Epson: **support.epson.com/filelibrary.html**
- Fujitsu: **www.fcpa.com/cgi-bin/goFrames.cgi/support/su_driver_scan.html**
- Hewlett-Packard: **www.hp.com/cposupport/software.html**
- Mustek: **www.mustek.com/Imaging/drivers/driverindex.htm**
- Microtek: **204.31.16.250/~admin/scannerframe_windows.html**
- Plustek: **www.plustekusa.com/technicalsupport/drivers.html**
- Ricoh: **www.ricoh-usa.com/softcen/scanners.htm**
- Umax: **www.umax.com/scanners/standard/support/download.cfm**
- Visioneer: **support.visioneer.com/customer/updatesoft/#Drivers**

Digitizers

- www.acecad.com/support.html
- Altek: **www.altek.com/drivers.htm**
- Calcomp and Summagraphics: **www.gtcocalcomp.com/support.htm**
- Numonics: **www.interactivewhiteboards.com/drivers.htm**
- www.wacom.com/productsupport/index.html

Video Capture

- www.adstech.com/support.html
- ATI: **support.atitech.ca/drivers/index.html**
- Dazzle: **www.dazzle.com/support/updates.html**
- Iomega: **www.iomega.com/software/**
- Play: **cf.play.com/play/support/**
- Matrox: **www.matrox.com/mga/drivers/home.htm**
- Pinnacle: **www.pinnaclesys.com/support/**
- Sigma: **www.sigmadesigns.com/support.htm**

Immediate Solutions

Fixing Common Sound Card Problems

The following list provides solutions to common sound card problems:

- *No Sound*—If you know you have a working sound card but there is no sound, check every point along the signal path starting with the master volume control in Windows. Make sure that the mixer channel for the sound source (CD Audio, WAV, MIDI) is turned up. If the volume is set correctly, check the connection between the sound card and the speakers, making sure that the correct output is used. If the speakers are passive, make certain they are plugged into an amplified output, usually Phones Out or Speaker Out. If the speakers are active, make sure they are switched on, and that the volume control on the speakers themselves is set correctly. If there is still no sound, try attaching another set of speakers or headphones. Many PC speakers are cheaply made, and frequently they are the first part of a sound system to fail.

- *Stuttering Playback*—If a brief segment of sound stutters or repeats over and over again, there is probably an interrupt conflict with another device. Use the Windows Device Manager to determine what devices are conflicting. If the sound card allows you to set the IRQ manually, try a different setting. Many PCI sound cards do not allow you to manually set resources, but you may be able to change the IRQ assigned to a PCI device within the system BIOS (consult the motherboard documentation). You may also be able to change the interrupt assigned to the sound card by putting it into another slot. If necessary, try changing the IRQ for the device with which the sound card is conflicting.

- *Skipping Playback*—If digital audio within a game or multimedia title skips or sounds choppy, particularly when accompanied by full-motion video, the system may simply not be powerful enough to keep up. If the software allows it, try reducing the resolution of the video. If the sound improves when video is played at a lower resolution, a CPU upgrade and/or a faster video card would probably improve performance at higher resolutions.

- *Distorted Recordings*—If recordings made with the sound card sound fuzzy or distorted, the input volume was probably set too high. Most audio capture programs use input meters to give the user a graphical depiction of the input level. Typically, these meters will turn red if input levels are too high. Many of these applications include an "audition" mode, which makes it possible to set input levels without actually recording. Distortion can also occur when recording with a microphone if the source is either too close to the microphone or too loud.

- *No MIDI Music*—Assuming the MIDI channel on the mixer is turned up, it is possible that MIDI data is being routed to the wrong destination. The Multimedia applet in the Windows Control Panel makes it possible to route MIDI data to either the sound card's internal synthesizer or to the game/MIDI port to control an external device. Obviously, if there is no external device and MIDI data is sent to the game/MIDI port, there will be no sound.

- *No CD Audio*—Assuming the CD audio channel on the mixer is turned up, the most likely reason for no CD audio is that the drive and the sound card are improperly cabled.

Connecting a CD-ROM or DVD to a Sound Card

Connecting the cable between a CD-ROM or DVD drive and a sound card involves working inside the PC case, so the usual precautions should be observed. A sound card typically has a number of connectors on its surface, each serving a different function. There may even be more than one CD-audio connector to increase compatibility with different drives and cables, but you need to use only one. Other connectors include modem, auxiliary, and PC speaker interfaces, any one of which can easily be mistaken for the CD-audio connector. If the card is not clearly labeled, consult the manufacturer's documentation. The drive may have a digital output next to the analog output on the back of the drive, but these are usually well marked. The connector for the drive's digital output is usually very different from the analog connector, so it is unlikely that the cable can be attached to the wrong output.

Many CD-audio cables are keyed to prevent inserting them incorrectly. If the cable is not keyed, often it is marked to correspond with markings on the drive and sound card, indicating the pin outs for left and right audio channels. An unkeyed cable inserted with the right and left channels swapped will not damage the drive or sound card, but CD audio channels will be reversed so that the left channel is heard from the right speaker and vice versa.

If the drive manufacturer's audio cable is unavailable, the easiest solution is to obtain a universal audio cable with multiple connectors for most types of drives and sound cards, unless a specific part number for the cable can be found.

Resolving System Resource Conflicts

System resource conflicts, discussed in detail in Chapter 7, are a common source of problems with audio and visual hardware. Plug-and-play, PCI, and USB devices are much less susceptible to resource conflicts than their ISA counterparts. When a conflict does appear on one of these newer devices, however, there is often no simple solution because resources usually cannot be assigned manually. A well-behaved plug-and-play device will not claim a resource that is already in use elsewhere in the system. An exception to this is found in the case of PCI chipsets that support IRQ steering, a process that allows multiple PCI devices to share a single interupt.

Because of IRQ steering, seeing two devices in the Windows Device Manager using the same interrupt does not necessarily indicate a problem. In rare instances, however, two PCI devices assigned the same interrupt will conflict with each other, causing system lockups when an audio or video file is played back. In many cases the IRQ for a PCI device can be changed in the system BIOS, by assigning a fixed interrupt to a given slot. Sometimes simply moving a PCI device to another slot will force the system to assign a different, possibly less problematic, IRQ. In other cases it may be necessary to disable IRQ steering altogether. Typically, this is accomplished in the BIOS, Device Manager, or both. Consult the motherboard manufacturer's documentation for information about BIOS settings. To disable IRQ steering in the Device Manager, open the System Devices branch and double-click PCI Bus. On the IRQ Steering tab, click the Use IRQ Steering check box to clear it. Note that disabling IRQ steering means that there must be an available interupt for every device on the system because interrupts will no longer be shared.

Connecting a Scanner to a PC

Most SCSI and USB scanner connections are trouble-free, assuming the SCSI card or USB interface has been correctly installed and recognized by the operating system. However, a few potential problems may be associated with parallel scanners, many of them related to the passthrough parallel port. Some parallel devices perform erratically or not at all when connected to a passthrough port.

Two hardware solutions are available. A *switch box* allows two devices to attach to a single parallel port without the use of a passthrough. Note, however, that only one device has use of the port at a time. This can create problems for devices that must be initialized when the system boots, including some scanners. Another solution is to add a second parallel port to the system. Adding a parallel port is subject to all of the considerations discussed at length in Chapter 10. Traditional ISA parallel cards use the standard resources for parallel ports, so that a port set for lpt2 would use an address of 278 and IRQ 5. Therefore, those resources must be available if an ISA parallel card is to be installed. Newer PCI parallel cards often can overcome those restrictions, and may even share an interrupt on a system with IRQ steering.

Many scanner manufacturers either recommend or require a bidirectional parallel port for use with their parallel scanners. Most parallel ports found on Pentium-class and newer motherboards are bidirectional, but it may be necessary to enable bidirectional communication in the system BIOS. Consult the motherboard manufacturer's documentation for specific settings. Windows will usually detect bidirectional ports automatically, and this can be confirmed by checking the Device Manager to see if the port is listed as bidirectional, EPP (enhanced parallel port), ECP (enhanced capabilities port), or EPP/ECP, all of which are bidirectional modes. In addition, scanners that require a bidirectional port will often require an IEEE 1284 cable to take full advantage of the port's capabilities. Parallel port issues are discussed in depth in Chapter 12.

Downloading Images from a Digital Camera

Digital cameras differ from the other audio/visual devices discussed in this chapter in that they do most of their work without the aid of a computer. Like traditional cameras, digital cameras are portable devices used to capture images in the field. Unlike traditional cameras, however, "developing" a picture involves dumping the camera's memory into a computer, where images may then be stored and edited.

Digital cameras come bundled with software for transferring data from the camera to the PC. Physical connections between the camera and the PC are usually straightforward. A cable provided with the camera is run from the camera either to a serial port or USB port on the PC. Assuming the ports are correctly recognized by the operating system, all that is required is to configure the software for the specific port being used. In the case of a camera attached to the serial port, the software typically defaults to COM1, which is fine unless another device, such as a mouse or a PDA, is already using that port. If the camera is attached to COM2, the software must be configured to download from that port. If problems persist, make certain that COM2 has been enabled in the BIOS and correctly detected in the Device Manager. It is not uncommon for an unused COM2 to be disabled in the BIOS in order to free up resources for other devices.

Part V

Preventive Care

Chapter 20

Maintaining the PC

In Depth

PC Preventive Maintenance

When viewed objectively, the PC is simply a machine or an appliance that has moving parts, electronics, and glass and plastic surfaces that need to be maintained. Dirt, dust, and other debris can get in and on the components of the PC. In the best case, they just make the PC dirty and dusty, but in the worst case, they can damage or destroy components inside the system case. Just as you schedule maintenance on your car, you should perform preventive maintenance (PM) on a PC to avoid failures and repairs and to extend the PC's life.

In a perfect situation, a PC should be in an environment that is relatively dust-, moisture-, and smoke-free. Nothing would ever be spilled into or onto its components, it would never be bumped or dropped, and the electrical power source would always run at 110 volts. Unfortunately, though, PC's don't operate in perfect worlds. They are used in homes, offices, factories, and just about anywhere else a computer is needed. These environments have dust, smoke, and other airborne debris that can get inside the unit and clog up the works. In addition, the electrical power fluctuates, due to the multiple users on the supply system, and on occasion it suffers blackouts and brownouts. The world of the PC is not perfect, which is why you must develop a PM program that provides corrective action for the hazards of the PC's environment.

Scheduled Maintenance

To be effective, a PM program must be applied on a regular basis. At the back of your car's owner's manual is a schedule for its required maintenance. Many PCs are now including a similar maintenance schedule in their owner's manual, which details the maintenance, adjustments, and cleaning that should be done and a suggested schedule for when these tasks should be done. Table 20.1 presents a sample version of a PC maintenance schedule.

Table 20.1 A sample PC maintenance schedule.

Frequency	Component	Activity
Daily	PC	Perform a virus scan of memory and hard disk.
	Windows	Restart or shutdown Windows.
	Hard disk	Create a differential/incremental backup.
Weekly	Hard disk	Remove all .tmp files and clear C:\TEMP and C:\WINDOWS\TEMP.
	Hard disk	Create a full/archive backup.
	Web browser	Clear browser cache, history, and temporary Internet files.
	Antivirus software	Update antivirus data files.
	Windows desktop	Empty the Windows Recycle Bin.
	Inkjet printer	Run printhead nozzle cleaning utility.
Monthly	Hard disk	Defragment the drive and recover lost clusters.
	Hard disk	Uninstall all unnecessary applications.
	Keyboard	Clean the keyboard with compressed air and check for and repair stuck keys.
	Mouse	Clean ball and rollers and check for wear.
	Monitor	Turn off and clean screen with soft cloth or antistatic wipe.
	Dot matrix printer	Clean with compressed air to remove dust and bits of paper.
	Laser printer	Use cleaning kit to clean interior rollers.
On failure	Floppy disk drive	Clean floppy drive head.
	System	Troubleshoot and replace failed component, if necessary.
Yearly	Case	Clean with compressed air to remove dust and other debris.
	Motherboard	Check chips for chip creep and reseat if needed.
	Adapter cards	Clean contacts with contact cleaner and reseat.
As required	CMOS	Record and back up CMOS setup configuration.
	PC	Keep written record of hardware and software configuration of system.
	Printer	Check ink and toner cartridges or ribbons and replace, if necessary.
	Hardware	Clean the keyboard, mouse, monitor, and case.

Commonsense Preventive Maintenance

A very good start to protecting your PC is to apply some commonsense guidelines that can protect the PC and extend its service life. A few general tips for keeping your PC in working order follow.

- A PC should be located in a room that is as cool and dry as possible. Two major hazards to the PC's electronics are heat and humidity.

- The PC should have an airflow buffer space all around it. The buffer doesn't need to be more than a few inches wide, but make sure there is ample air space around the PC, and avoid drafty and dusty areas.

- The PC's cords and cables can be a hazard to you and other people, so keep them together and tucked away to protect the cords, the PC, yourself, and others.

- When a PC is powered up and down frequently, the heating and cooling can stress the motherboard and other electronics, leading to intermittent problems from degradation and eventual catastrophic failures. Avoid powering the system on and off frequently.

- Most newer PCs have many energy-saving features built into the basic input/output system (BIOS), chipset, and operating system, such as suspending the hard disk and monitor. Not only do these features save electricity, they also extend the life of the PC and its components.

- Always connect the PC to the alternating current (AC) power source through a surge suppressor or an uninterruptible power supply (UPS). This protects the PC from possible damage caused by electrical spikes, blackouts, and brownouts.

- Always wear an antistatic wrist or ankle strap when working inside the PC's case to avoid possible damage from electrostatic discharge (ESD). However, never wear an antistatic device when working on the monitor or inside the power supply. In fact, you should never work on a monitor or inside a power supply because the combination of the resistor in the wrist strap and the capacitor in the monitor or power supply can create enough of an electrical charge to potentially kill you.

- Always close any open applications, shut down the operating system, and power off and unplug the PC from its power source before beginning work on the PC or its peripherals.

- Never place a PC—especially its monitor or stereo speakers—near any strongly magnetized objects, which can distort the image and sound produced by the monitor or speakers, and could eventually damage disk storage devices as well.

- Always power down the PC before connecting or disconnecting a serial, parallel, or video device. Universal serial bus (USB) and FireWire devices can be hot-plugged and are a better choice for devices that need to be removed and replaced often.

- Always shut down the operating system before powering down the PC. On a Windows system, use the Shutdown option on the Start Menu.

PM Tools and Cleaning Supplies

To properly care for your PC, you need a few simple tools, cleaning supplies, a boot disk, an emergency repair disk (ERD), and a PC maintenance schedule. The tools and supplies you need can be obtained from computer and hardware stores—and even grocery stores for some items. The maintenance schedule for your PC is likely included in the documentation for your PC. Table 20.1 presents a sample schedule.

The tools and supplies you should have on hand to care for and maintain your PC include:

- A quart bottle of 70% isopropyl alcohol, which is used to clean the plastic, case, many of the smaller parts of the PC, keyboard, printer, connectors, and mouse. Unless you use more than you should, a quart should last you at least a few months.

- A can or two of compressed air. This is a very versatile tool to have in your cleaning kit. Compressed air is very useful for blowing dust and small bits of paper and other debris out of hard-to-reach places. It is also very good for cleaning those areas of the PC and its components that should not get wet.

- Every PC cleaning instruction calls for you to use a "clean, lint-free cloth." A section of an old T-shirt works very nicely, but you can also use non-shredding cleaning tissues. A recently introduced product that is excellent for use on a PC is the Scotch-Brite™ HPCC cloth made by the 3M Corporation.

- A package of cotton swabs of high quality, which means the cotton tips stay on the swab. These are used for cleaning just about any small object inside or outside of the PC with alcohol and other liquid cleaners.

- A #8 Chinese bristle artist's brush or any other soft-bristle brush that has bristles about 2 inches long. You can typically find these at craft stores that sell tole painting supplies.

- An inexpensive pair of pointed-tip tweezers, which are useful for removing bits of debris from between the keys on the keyboard, inside the mouse ball chamber, or inside the computer case.

- A small brush-head vacuum cleaner. This is an excellent investment if you care for two or more computers on a regular basis. Several models are available with a gooseneck brush head that allows you to clean the keyboards and inside the system case easily. The danger of using a standard type of vacuum inside the PC is that some vacuum cleaners generate a lot of static electricity, and their cleaning nozzles are large and can easily damage the electronics on the motherboard and expansion cards.

- A medium-size Phillips screwdriver for case, keyboard, and adapter board screws.

- A bottle of non-ammonia window cleaner to clean the glass on the monitor. Although a bit more expensive, special cleaning solutions are made just for monitors. The Scotch-Brite HPCC cloth is also excellent for cleaning a monitor without water.

- An ESD grounding strap. You can use either a wrist strap, such as the one in Figure 20.1, or a heel strap. If you have a permanent workstation where you work on PCs, equip it with an ESD mat.

Data Backups

Creating a copy of the data on the hard disk on a removable storage media that can be stored not only outside the PC but also outside the building is definitely a preventive maintenance step. Data backups protect you from the loss of the data

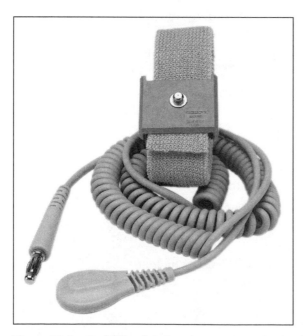

Figure 20.1   An ESD wrist strap is necessary for any PC preventive and repair kit.

in the event of a hard disk failure, other PC problems, or other forms of disaster. Should some catastrophic mishap, such as a fire, earthquake, or tornado, destroy the building, in most cases the hardware can be replaced, but too often the data cannot be. Creating a backup copy of your data files is a safety precaution that ensures the data can outlive its internal storage device.

Backup Media

Any removable storage medium, such as a floppy disk, tape cartridge, recordable compact disk (CD-R), optical disk, or even another PC's hard disk, can be used to hold a backup copy of your hard disk's data. The medium to use depends on the amount of data to be backed up. If you are backing up a 40GB hard disk, you probably should consider a tape drive, but if you are creating a backup of only a 100MB hard disk, a Zip disk is probably adequate.

Backup Software

The popular operating systems in use today all include a utility for creating a backup. Windows has its Backup utility (see Figure 20.2), Unix and Linux have the **tar** (tape archive) command, and Novell has a NetWare Backup Service utility. A backup utility is typically included with most tape, CD-R, and other writable media drives. Also available for purchase are software packages specifically designed to perform backups, such as Computer Associates' ARCServe, Dantz's Retrospect Backup, and Veritas's Backup Exec.

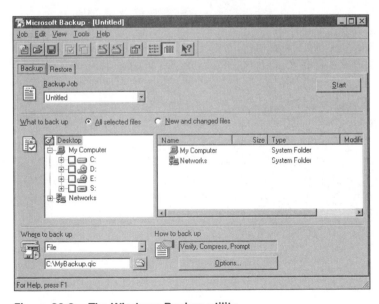

Figure 20.2   The Windows Backup utility.

Backup software offers some advantages over just copying a file to a removable medium, including data compression techniques that reduce the number of tapes or disks needed to hold the backed-up data. Most backup software also provides cataloging routines and single directory or file restore capabilities.

Backup Types

The type of backup you use depends on the volatility of your data. If a high percentage of all of your data is added or modified each day, then you may want to consider taking a full data backup each day. However, if only a small percentage of your total data store is new or modified, a backup scheme that uses an incremental or differential backup daily and a full weekly backup may serve your needs.

When a directory or file on the hard disk is added or modified, it is flagged as such with its archive bit. The archive bit, which is one of the four attributes assigned to each directory and file, is used by backup utilities to determine which files should be included in the backup. The other attributes are read-only, hidden, and system.

The four types of data backups you can use in your backup scheme are the following:

- *Full backup*—Also called an archive backup, this backup includes every directory, folder, file, and program from the hard disk. A full backup copies every file to the backup medium regardless of the archive bit's status. However, all archive bits are reset.

- *Incremental backup*—This backup includes only those files that have been modified or added since the last full or incremental backup. An incremental backup clears the archive bit on the files it copies to the backup medium.

- *Differential backup*—This backup includes the files created or modified since the last full or incremental backup. A differential backup does not clear the archive bit. This backup type, if used daily, accumulates the files that are new or changed since the last backup that cleared the archive bit.

- *Copy backup*—This backup includes the files and directories that you specify and copies them to a particular location or drive. When you copy a file from the hard disk to a diskette to safeguard it, you are creating a copy backup. The DOS command **XCOPY** is commonly used to create copy backups because it will copy a directory along with its files and subdirectories.

A common backup scheme is to take a full backup once a week and then create a differential or incremental backup each day. The choice between a differential and an incremental backup depends on the amount of data affected each day. If the daily backups are large, an incremental may be the better choice to avoid a huge differential backup by the end of the week. If the amount of data to be backed up is small each day, however, the differential has its advantages. The idea behind using a combination of full and partial backups is that in the event of a hardware failure, you need only load the last full backup and the last differential or each of the incremental backups made since the full backup to recover your data.

Virus Detection and Protection

A computer virus is software that attacks a PC with the intent of disrupting its operations, destroying its data, or erasing part or all of its disk drives. A computer virus attaches itself to another file or piece of code on a floppy disk, downloaded file, or email attachment. It can also take the form of an executable file that runs when opened on the target system. A computer virus typically has a built-in propagation scheme that allows it to replicate itself and infect other systems, duplicating itself from one computer to another on a removable media or by email.

A computer virus can show up on a PC in a variety of ways, including (but not limited to):

- Spontaneous system reboots
- System crashes
- Application crashes
- Sound card or speaker problems
- Distorted, misshapen, or missing video on the monitor
- Corrupted or missing data from disk files
- Disappearing disk partitions
- Boot disks that won't boot
- All of your email address book contacts receiving copies of the virus via email

The best defense against a virus on your PC is antivirus software. Several antivirus offerings, such as Norton Antivirus, McAfee VShield, and Trend Micro's PC-cillan, are available on the market. These companies provide you with the ability to update the virus database about as often as new viruses show up, which is almost daily.

Protecting the PC from Electricity Problems

Several levels of protection are available to protect a single PC or an entire network. How much protection you need is based on the amount of equipment you are trying to protect against electrical over-voltage and under-voltage conditions.

The first line of defense is a surge suppressor, such as the one shown in Figure 20.3. The entry-level surge suppressor is a plug strip that includes a varistor designed to

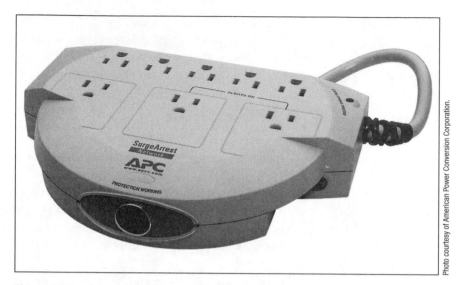

Photo courtesy of American Power Conversion Corporation.

Figure 20.3   A surge suppressor can help protect a PC from electrical surges and spikes.

absorb spikes and surges on the electrical supply line and not pass them on to any devices plugged into it. Even higher-end models are available that will protect your phone lines, modems, and network connections. The best protection from electrical problems is one that also provides backup power should the power fail or run below normal voltage levels. This device is a UPS. See Chapter 14 for a more detailed discussion of surge suppressors and UPS units.

Disposing of Hazardous Materials

A PC has several components, including batteries, mercury switches, the power supply, and the cathode ray tube (CRT) in the monitor, that by law or environmental common sense require special handling or disposal procedures.

Batteries

It may be difficult to believe that PC batteries, which are usually very small lithium batteries used to power complementary metal oxide semiconductor (CMOS) memory, need care in handling or disposal, but these batteries, like all batteries, should not be disposed of in either fire or water. In fact, all batteries should not be casually discarded. They should be disposed of according to whatever local restrictions and regulations are in effect regarding the disposal or recycling of batteries. Leaking batteries should be handled very carefully, and if you must handle a leaking battery, be very sure you do not get any of the electrolyte (the stuff oozing out from the inside of the battery) into your eyes or mouth.

Monitors

A CRT in a monitor (just like the picture tube in your television set) contains the following contaminants: solvents and solvent vapors, metals (including a very high level of lead), photoresistant materials, deionized water, acids, oxidizers, phosphor, ammonia, aluminum, carbon slurry, and a long list of other chemicals and caustic materials. This is why a monitor should not just be thrown in the dumpster, trashcan, or landfill. It should be disposed of carefully and properly. The best and most environmentally conscious way to dispose of a monitor is through a disposal service that handles computer equipment.

Nearly 70 percent of a CRT contains lead, which is why it comes under the Land Disposal Ban Program of the Resource Conservation and Recovery Act (RCRA) administered by the U.S. Environmental Protection Agency (EPA). This is the same act that created all of the Superfund toxic waste dump site cleanups. This law requires that old CRTs (and old television sets as well) be dismantled, crushed, and encapsulated in cement. This is something that everyone with an old monitor is able to do because many salvage and recycling companies now exist that are equipped to properly dispose of CRTs—for a fee, of course.

Chemicals

The liquid cleaning compounds you use to clean the PC (or your home or car) can pose a safety or environmental problem or may require special handling. Many of these solutions can be poisonous or hazardous. If you are unsure of the safety, handling, storage, or use of a cleaning product, the best reference available for information on any particular chemical solution or cleaner, including household cleaners, is its Material Safety Data Sheet (MSDS). Every chemical product that has any possible hazard has an MSDS prepared and readily available. Typically, information on how to obtain an MSDS for a product is included on the product's label.

A standard MSDS includes the following sections:

- *Section 1*—Chemical Product Section
- *Section 2*—Composition/Information on Ingredients
- *Section 3*—Hazard Identification
- *Section 4*—First Aid Measures
- *Section 5*—Firefighting Measures
- *Section 6*—Accidental Release Measures
- *Section 7*—Handling and Storage
- *Section 8*—Exposure Control/Personal Protection
- *Section 9*—Physical and Chemical Properties

- *Section 10*—Stability and Reactivity
- *Section 11*—Toxicological Information
- *Section 12*—Ecological Information
- *Section 13*—Disposal Considerations
- *Section 14*—Transportation Information
- *Section 15*—Regulatory Information
- *Section 16*—Other Information

You can also obtain a copy of a product MSDS through the Internet. Two Web sites, among others, list many of the products you might use and need information about:

- The Northwest Fisheries Science Center of the National Oceanic and Atmospheric Administration (NOAA): **http://research.nwfsc.noaa.gov/msds.html**

- The Vermont Safety Information Resources, Inc. (SIRI): **http://siri.org/msds/index.html**

Of course, the best place to look for product safety information is the product's label or any documentation included inside its packaging. Hazardous products from reputable manufacturers will always list the hazards and handling requirements for their products on the product's label. If a cleaning solution or solvent does not list hazards or other product safety information, do not assume it to be safe. The cleaning supplies you should be concerned about include the solutions used to clean the contacts and connections of adapter cards, glass cleaners, and plastic- or metal-case cleaning products.

Other PC and peripheral components for which you should use special disposal procedures are laser printer toner cartridges and refill kits and the used or empty containers of chemical solvents and cleaners. The best place to find information on the proper way to dispose of an item is in its documentation, such as the information that comes with a printer cartridge, or the MSDS or WHMIS (Workplace Hazardous Materials Information System) information on a chemical product.

Immediate Solutions

Performing Preventive Maintenance for a Keyboard

The standard keyboard, such as the one shown in Figure 20.4, is an open-faced device that collects whatever falls or spills on it. A keyboard can develop a number of problems when dirt, food, or liquid gets between and under its keys, including stuck keys, keys that stutter, or keys that just stop working. A stuttering key does not stick down permanently, but sticks for a few keystrokes and thus repeats its character a few times. A stuck key is actually stuck down and does not issue its character.

The best way to care for a keyboard is to keep food and beverages completely away from it, but that is probably not likely; therefore, the keyboard needs regular cleaning. Along with the PC's monitor, the keyboard should be cleaned more frequently than the PC's other components.

Use the following steps to clean a keyboard and to perform its preventive maintenance:

1. The easiest way to clean a keyboard is to simply turn it upside-down and shake it. Make sure you are not over your PC when you do this. Just about anything that has fallen under the keycaps should fall out, unless it is a larger item that is stuck behind the keys, such as a paperclip.

Photo courtesy of Belkin Components.

Figure 20.4   A standard 104-key keyboard.

2. If you wish to open a "cleaning hole" to let larger debris fall out, you can remove the keycaps of the last three keys on the right-hand end of the keyboard. These are the – (minus/dash), + (plus), and Enter keys on the numeric keypad. To remove the keycaps, use a flat blade screwdriver and gently pry the keycap up and off the key switch. Be sure to disconnect the keyboard from the PC before removing these keycaps. Keyboards get their power from the PC over the connection cable.

3. Use compressed air to blow out the keyboard using the air stream to sweep the debris toward the removed keys or toward one end of the keyboard.

WARNING! Always wear safety glasses or other eye protection when working with compressed air.

4. Use a nonstatic blower brush, brush vacuum, or a probe to lightly loosen any large or stubborn debris and then shake the keyboard or use compressed air to blow it out.

5. If one key is sticking or has stopped working, disconnect the keyboard from the PC and pry off the affected keycap. Clean under and around the keyswitch using a cotton swab and a small amount of isopropyl alcohol to remove whatever is jamming the key. Use compressed air to blow it dry and then replace the keycap. Repeat for other stuck keys. If any key still does not work after cleaning, you can replace the keyswitch, but it is far easier—and in most cases less expensive—to just replace the keyboard.

6. Any time liquid spills on a keyboard, immediately disconnect it from the PC (it gets its power from the PC cable) and turn it upside down to allow the liquid to drain.

    If the keyboard had soda pop, fruit juice, or any other sugary drink spilled on it, there is a chance that the keys may stick or stutter. Your choices to clean the keyboard are to replace the keyboard or wash it. Putting water on any electronic device is always risky, but with care, you can wash a keyboard. As explained in Chapter 17, newer keyboards are sealed under the key switches to protect the keyboard grid. Anything that spills in the keyboard will therefore either settle on the keyboard membrane as sticky residue or simply run off.

    To clean any sticky residue resulting from a spill, use warm, clean water to rinse it out of the keyboard. By continually testing the keys, you can tell when you have rinsed the keyboard long enough. In an extreme case, you can wash the keyboard in the upper tray of a dishwasher with no soap. Even after the dishwasher's dry cycle, let the keyboard sit facedown for a few hours and then blow it out with compressed air. Before connecting it to the PC, be absolutely sure the keyboard is completely dry.

7. After you have cleaned the keyboard, replace any keycaps you have removed or replace the keyboard's cover.

8. If you want to get the keyboard really clean or want to also do a close visual inspection of it, you can remove the keyboard cover. Between 4 and 16 screws hold the keyboard's cover in place. Unless you have a very serious cleaning problem on the keyboard, though, avoid doing this, especially on older PCs with mechanical switch keys (see Chapter 17). If the problem on the keyboard is serious enough for major intervention, you may want to consider just replacing it.

9. Use a soft, lint-free cloth and a little isopropyl alcohol or a non-sudsing general-purpose cleaner to wipe away any body oils, ink, or dirt on the keys or keyboard case. Alcohol works best because it evaporates without leaving moisture behind to seep inside the keyboard. Never pour the alcohol directly on the keys or case. Pour a small amount on the cloth and then wipe the keys and case. The same goes for the cleaner, if you choose to use one. A cotton swab dipped in cleaner or alcohol will get to the tight spots. Again, be absolutely sure that the keyboard is dry before connecting it to the PC and powering it up.

10. After cleaning and absolutely drying the keyboard, reconnect it to the PC and reboot the system. Watch the power-on self-test (POST) process carefully for keyboard errors. After the PC is running, test the keyboard by pressing each key and verifying its action.

Cleaning a Mouse

When the ball or insides of a conventional mouse (see Figure 20.5) get dirty, the mouse may begin working erratically or not at all. Dirt from the mouse pad or work surface gets on the ball and is transferred to the sensors and rollers inside the mouse. The sensors are used to detect the movement of the mouse and translate it to movement of the pointer on the screen. If the sensors are dirty, they are unable to translate any movement precisely.

To care for and clean the mouse, use this procedure:

1. The first thing to check is the mousepad. If the mouse ball is dirty, it is likely that the mousepad is also dirty and needs to be either cleaned or replaced. The mousepad sits in the open where it gets dusty, dirty, and wet, and it suffers any accidents that happen on the desktop. If the mousepad is not cleaned or replaced regularly, the mouse picks up the dirt and transfers it inside to the rollers and sensors. To clean the mousepad, just wipe it with a damp cloth, but make sure it is dry before using it again with the mouse.

Figure 20.5   A conventional ball mouse.

2. Check the mousepad for wear, both to its fabric or plastic surface and for places where a track, dent, or dip may have been worn into it. A worn-out mousepad can cause lint, bits of rubber, or threads to get pulled up inside the mouse.

3. It is a good idea to shut down the PC when cleaning the mouse. In most cases, the mouse has either a serial or PS/2 connector, neither of which should be removed or inserted while the PC is running. If you have a USB mouse, such as the one shown in Figure 20.6, you can disconnect the mouse from the PC while the PC is running to clean it and then reconnect it when you are finished. However, open applications, including Windows, can do some strange things if you clean the mouse while it is connected and the PC is running.

4. Place the mouse on its back and remove the ball access slide cover. As illustrated in Figure 20.7, the mouse ball is held in place by a locking cap that rotates to its locking or release positions. Turn the cap in the direction of the arrows printed or molded on it.

5. Wash your hands thoroughly before touching the mouse ball. Tip the mouse up to drop the ball into your palm, cupping your hand so the ball doesn't fall on the floor or table. Examine it for pits, cracks, or flat spots, and make sure the ball is not lopsided or oval-shaped. If the ball has any of these problems, it needs to be replaced, but because spare mouse balls are not always easy to get, you should just replace the mouse.

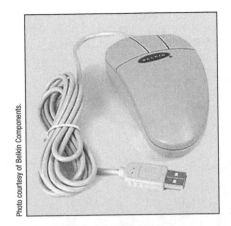

Figure 20.6   A USB mouse.

Figure 20.7   A mouse ball is held inside the mouse by a rotating locking cap.

6. Inspect the mouse ball chamber (see Figure 20.8) for lint, dirt, and even threads. Carefully remove debris you find with tweezers or a cotton swab with just a drop of alcohol on it.

7. Inspect the rollers inside the ball chamber for dirt or lint and, if needed, use tweezers or a swab with a small drop of alcohol to remove any debris.

20. Maintaining the PC

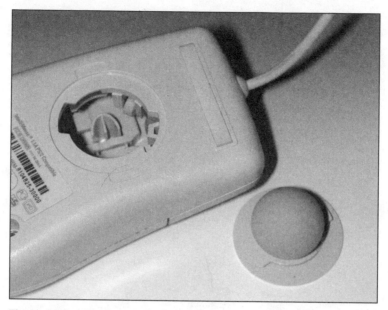

Figure 20.8   The mouse ball chamber.

8. Use compressed air to blow out the mouse ball chamber, directing the air stream to one side. Try not to blast the rollers to avoid causing damage to the small electronic parts inside the mouse. You should not blow out the mouse ball chamber with your mouth for two reasons: saliva and you can get dust in your eyes.

9. Use a slightly damp, lint-free cloth or a Scotch-Brite HPCC cloth to clean the mouse ball. If you use a damp cloth, use only water. Do not use cleaners or alcohol on the mouse ball because they can shrink or distort the ball. Also, do not soak it or scrub it. Just wipe the ball clean, let it dry, and then reinsert it in the chamber and replace the locking cap.

10. If needed, use isopropyl alcohol or a general-purpose, no-rinse cleaner to clean the exterior of the mouse.

11. Reconnect the mouse and restart the PC. Watch for any POST problems with the mouse or connector. Give the mouse a complete test, including its buttons.

TIP: *An alternative to a conventional mouse is an optical mouse. An optical mouse eliminates most of the cleaning and care required of the conventional mouse. See Chapter 17 for more information on the optical mouse.*

Caring for Other Input Devices

A PC can have other types of input and data capture devices, which—mainly because they are input devices—should also be cleaned regularly. How frequently these are cleaned depends on the device and how often it is used. Cleaning hints for several of the more common input devices include the following:

- *Scanner*—The biggest issue with a flat-bed scanner is its inside glass surface. Use either a non-ammonia glass cleaner and a lint-free cloth or the Scotch-Brite HPCC for Electronics cloth.

- *Digitizing tablet*—Follow the cleaning instructions included in the device's documentation. Some of the rubber-like materials used for the touchpad can be cleaned with a general-purpose cleaner and a damp lint-free cloth. Take care not to get the unit too wet and to dry it completely.

- *Digital camera*—Clean the camera lens with a lens cleaner solution, such as you would use for eyeglasses, and a soft lint-free cloth or the Scotch-Brite HPCC for Electronics cloth. Use either isopropyl alcohol or a general-purpose cleaner to clean the exterior of the camera. Avoid getting the unit very wet.

- *Microphone*—Use the same steps as used for the digitizing tablet. Be very careful not to get water or alcohol in the openings and down inside the microphone.

Cleaning and Caring for a Monitor

The monitor's glass screen (see Figure 20.9) requires cleaning more often than any other component on a PC. Because the monitor's screen produces a lot of static electricity, it attracts and holds dust and flying lint. A dirty screen can put a strain on your eyes if you view it for extended periods.

Most PC users take a safety risk when cleaning a monitor's screen. Because the screen holds a large amount of static electricity, if you should place your hand flat on the screen with a wet cloth, you invite the monitor to ground itself through you. The following steps detail the process you can use to safely keep the monitor screen clean and clear.

1. Turn the monitor's power off and unplug it from its power source before beginning to clean it. There is no need to disconnect it from the PC. After turning the monitor off, wait a few minutes before beginning to clean it to allow the built-up static charges to dissipate a bit.

WARNING! Do not wear an ESD ground strap when working with a monitor, even to clean it.

Photo courtesy of ViewSonic Corporation.

Figure 20.9   The monitor screen collects dust and should be cleaned regularly.

2. Use compressed air to clean any dust on the top of the monitor's case. Blow the air stream across the top of the monitor and not directly down to prevent any dust from blowing into the monitor's vents.

WARNING! Never open and remove the cover of a monitor! An extreme high voltage hazard exists inside every monitor, regardless of its size.

3. Use a soft cloth and either isopropyl alcohol or a general-purpose, no-rinse cleaner to clean the outside of the monitor case. Alcohol is the better choice because it will not create a safety hazard if it drips inside the case.

4. Use an antistatic cleaner or a Scotch-Brite HPCC for Electronics cloth to clean the monitor's glass screen. Never use an ammonia-based glass cleaner on the monitor glass. The monitor screen is coated with filtering chemicals to help improve the image and reduce eyestrain. By using a harsh cleaner, you can remove these coatings and thus harm the monitor and potentially harm your eyes.

WARNING! *Never use water or a liquid cleaner to wash the monitor's glass with the power on. Water is an excellent conductor of electricity, and should your hand make sufficient contact with the screen, you could be the ground for the electricity in the monitor.*

5. Reconnect the monitor and test the video. If nothing displays, check the power switch, the power cord, the video connection, and the brightness and contrast settings, any of which could have been accidentally dislodged, moved, or turned while you were cleaning the case.

Cleaning and Maintaining a Printer

The cleaning procedures and the supplies used to clean and maintain a printer vary, depending on the type of printer in use. Laser printers have completely different cleaning and maintenance requirements than do inkjet and dot matrix printers. This section gives a general overview of the cleaning and preventive maintenance steps you can use for each type of printer. However, you should follow the specific instructions provided by the manufacturer of your printer in the owner's manual or from the manufacturer's Web site.

Caring for a Laser Printer

The following procedure is a general process for cleaning a laser printer such as the one shown in Figure 20.10. Due to the many different designs for how the laser toner and drum cartridge fit into a laser printer, the process used for any specific printer is likely to differ slightly. Check your printer's documentation for specific cleaning instructions.

1. To clean a laser printer thoroughly, you need a laser cleaning kit for your printer's make and model and a small vacuum cleaner specifically designed to handle laser printer toner. If the cleaning kit does not include cleaning paper, you should purchase a package from your local computer supply store or online.

   Laser printer toner consists of minute particles of ferrous oxide (iron) coated with a plastic resin material. During the printer's fusing process, the plastic resin is melted to bond the toner to the paper. A standard vacuum cleaner passes whatever it picks up near or through a very hot motor, where these particles can melt and clog the system; therefore, special vacuum cleaners are available just for cleaning up toner. You can also contract an office supply company to have the laser printer professionally cleaned.

Figure 20.10   A laser printer.

Cleaning kits typically contain cartridge cleaning sheets, cleaning solution, lint-free swabs, an antistatic cloth, plastic gloves, and a few ink- and toner-remover hand wipes.

2. If the printer has been in use very recently, let it sit idle for at least 15 minutes to allow the fusing assembly to cool before removing or opening the covers.

3. Switch off the power on the laser printer and unplug it to prevent the power from being accidentally switched back on. Remove any paper or paper cartridges from the printer.

4. Open or remove the part of the printer's case that exposes the fusing assembly. Follow the printer manufacturer's instructions for cleaning the fusing rollers. Typically, this is done with a lint-free cloth and either the cleaning solution that came in the cleaning kit or some denatured alcohol (which is not the same as isopropyl alcohol). Wipe the rollers lightly and do not rub. Do not touch any of the gears inside the printer.

5. Using an appropriate vacuum with a soft brush attachment, clean the fusing area of any debris or at least use compressed air to blow out any debris in this area. In either case, you should wear eye protection. Be very careful not to snag or pull any wires in the fusing area.

6. Clean the transfer roller area (see the printer's documentation for specific instructions on how to clean the transfer rollers). The transfer rollers are typically located under the toner cartridge, so you must remove the toner cartridge and set it on some newspaper or other large sheets of paper. The paper is easily disposed of should any of the toner spill.

7. Laser printer cleaning kits contain a soft brush that is used to clean the transfer rollers. After brushing the rollers, use a vacuum or compressed air to clean away any debris in this area of the printer.

8. Check the paper path and use a soft brush to clean the feed rollers if needed. Replace the toner cartridge (with a new one, if needed) and any of the printer's cover parts that were removed in earlier steps.

9. Before reconnecting the printer to its AC power source, clean its exterior. The best cleaner is a mild liquid detergent, such as that used for dishes. Mix a solution of the detergent with water and wipe the printer clean with a cloth dampened with the solution. Never pour or spray water or cleaners directly on the printer. If you are using a prepared cleaner, spray or pour a small amount on the cloth and wipe the printer with the cloth.

10. If you cleaned the printer's exterior, wait a few minutes to make sure the printer is dry before replacing the paper supply and reconnecting the printer to its power source.

11. If you have laser printer cleaning sheets, run one or two through the printer, following the instructions on the sheet pack to clean the components inside the cartridge. You should run a cleaning sheet each time you change the toner cartridge. In normal operations, if the printer is smearing or smudging the print, use a cleaning sheet to clean the toner cartridge, transfer rollers, and fusing rollers. You also want to be sure you are using laser printer paper.

Cleaning and Caring for an Inkjet Printer

Chapter 16 explains the inkjet printing process in detail, especially how the inkjet cartridge works to print a page. The most common problem with an inkjet printer is a clogged print head on the inkjet cartridge. Other than that, inkjet printers, such as the one shown in Figure 20.11, are fairly simple printers that are largely considered to be disposable technology. Several inkjet models are now on the market that cost between $40 and $100, which is not all that much more than the ink cartridge itself. Should anything major happen to an inkjet printer, such as

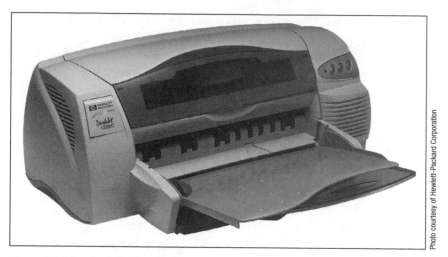

Photo courtesy of Hewlett-Packard Corporation

Figure 20.11   An inkjet printer.

misaligned feed rollers or the cartridge gearing that moves the print cartridge side-to-side failing to operate, it is usually less expensive just to get a new printer.

Some cleaning and maintenance tips that can help you to extend the life of your inkjet printer include the following:

- Clean the print nozzles on the cartridge regularly. Most inkjet printers have a built-in utility to clean or unclog the print head nozzles, and you should use it regularly as a part of your preventive maintenance program and whenever the printer has sat idle for a couple of weeks or longer. If the cleaning utility is unable to unclog the nozzles, remove the ink cartridge and use a swab or lint-free cloth (one you don't mind staining permanently with the ink) dampened with a small amount of isopropyl alcohol, and wipe the print head lightly. Don't rub back and forth across the nozzles, but wipe lightly across the nozzles in one direction. Reinstall the print cartridge and redo the printhead cleaning utility. If the cartridge is still clogged, replace it.

- Never turn the printer off at a plug strip, surge suppressor, or other power source. Always use the printer's power switch to turn it off. The printer has some built-in functions, such as parking the printhead, that are tied to the power-off function of the printer's on/off switch.

- Use inkjet-quality paper. Standard bond paper, which is not treated for inkjet inks, absorbs too much ink. On black-and-white printing, the result may be a fuzzy or blurry print image. On color prints, the result may be light or blurred images. Inkjet paper is treated to provide the best possible image. The printer's owner's manual most likely has a recommendation for the paper that should be used.

- Dust and paper scraps and bits can collect in the bottom of the paper path in an inkjet printer. On a fairly regular basis, you should check the inside of the printer and remove the paper scraps and blow out any dust or paper bits that have accumulated. Always wear eye protection when using compressed air, especially when blowing about bits of paper.

Cleaning a Dot Matrix Printer

After the noise and the slow speed, the problem with a dot matrix printer is its ribbon. The ribbon is messy to install and replace, and it is messy to operate. An operational problem is that dot matrix ribbons are not evenly coated with ink, and they drop bits of dried ink down inside the printer's case.

Dot matrix printers typically use a forms tractor to pull tractor-feed paper through the printer using the pinholes along the sides of the paper (see Figure 20.12). Unfortunately, as the paper is pulled through the printer, bits of paper from the holes and the perforations along the edges of the paper fall down inside the printer.

The paper and dried ink bits should be cleaned out of the printer regularly with either a vacuum or compressed air (definitely wear eye protection). Follow the manufacturer's documentation on how to remove the cover and the ribbon to get down into the printer. Typically, a ribbon release lever unlocks the ribbon cartridge so it can be lifted up and out of the printer. However, because dot matrix printers and their setups vary greatly by manufacturer, check the documentation before cleaning the printer, especially the printhead.

Figure 20.12   A dot matrix printer with a forms tractor.

Some controversy exists over whether a dot matrix printhead should be cleaned. The printhead can get very hot and should not be touched while in operation. Because it prints by pushing pins that are mounted on very thin wires into the ribbon, you could possibly bend a wire when cleaning the printhead and render the pin useless. You should never lubricate the printhead, because the oil or lubricant could stain your paper during printing. However, by using a cotton swab to remove bits of ink and paper fuzz from the printhead, if done very gently, you probably won't damage the head and will likely improve the function of the printer.

Performing Preventive Maintenance Inside the System Case

Because the system case is rarely—and in many cases never—opened, the inside of the system case is not cleaned regularly, if at all. If the PC is located in a dusty environment or one with airborne particles, such as oil mist or metal particles, that could be sucked inside the PC's case, the system case should definitely be cleaned regularly. In fact, in any environment, regular cleaning of the system case is good practice.

The power supply's cooling fan either pulls air into or pushes air out of the system case, depending on the age of the system. Because air passes into or out of the air vents on the case, the system case should be on your list of regularly cleaned items. For example, a mid-tower PC case that sits on the floor in an office, bedroom, or family room accumulates dust either around its air vents, on the grill or blades of the fan, or both. If not cleaned, the dust could eventually clog the cooling system, accumulate on the processor's heatsink and fan or on the motherboard, and cause the processor and memory to overheat and malfunction.

At a minimum, you should clean inside the PC's case at least once every 6 months. Use a soft brush vacuum cleaner (the standard type is okay here) or compressed air to blow the dust out of the case (be sure to wear eye protection).

Use the following steps to perform preventive maintenance inside the system case:

1. Power off the PC, after properly shutting down the operating system, and remove the power cord from the AC power source.

2. Carefully remove the case cover, watching for cables and cords inside the PC that may get snagged on the case cover. Examine the inside of the case cover for dirt streaks that indicate an air leak caused by a badly fitting case, which can be the cause of an overheating processor.

3. Perform a visual inspection of the inside of the case to determine how much cleaning is needed. On virtually every PC, the inside and outside vents should have some dust accumulation. If dust is collecting where it shouldn't, the cooling system may not be working as well as it could. The case may be cracked or a part (perhaps an expansion slot filler) may be missing.

   Examine the interior of the case thoroughly for dust, corrosion, leaking battery acid, or other problems. If the case has only a light accumulation of dust, use compressed air to clean it. Use a vacuum with a brush head to clean away any larger accumulations of dust.

4. Check the data and power cables on the motherboard, power supply, disk drives, and so on, for loose connections. Check the adapter cards to make sure they are properly seated. Also check for any signs of corrosion on the edge connectors of the memory modules and expansion cards. If you find any corrosion, use contact cleaner to clean them.

5. Use compressed air to blow off the outside vents of the power supply and then the inside vents. Use compressed air to also clean the drive bays, adapter cards, and finally the outside vents of the case.

TIP: Always wear ESD wrist or ankle straps when working inside the PC case. It is always a good idea to ground yourself with one of the metal chassis parts even when wearing ESD gear.

6. Replace the case cover, taking care not to snag any cables when placing or sliding the cover into place.

7. Use a general-purpose cleaner to clean the outside of the case, and be careful not to get any moisture inside the case.

8. Power on the PC and monitor the POST process for errors. If any errors occur, they will most likely be adapter data cable, power connector, or expansion card errors. Open the case and check these connections for a snug fit.

Housekeeping on a Hard Disk Drive

Other than checking its connectors and removing any dust that may have accumulated on the hard disk assembly (HDA), there isn't very much you can do physically for a hard disk drive in terms of preventive maintenance. Hard disk drive HDAs are sealed units, so no physical cleaning needs to be done, and the preventive maintenance actually centers around the optimization of the drive's storage space.

To perform housekeeping and optimization on a hard disk drive, you need to include the following activities in your preventive maintenance program:

- Create full and partial backups of the data on the hard disk. Always create a full backup of the hard disk drive before doing any work on it, and create backups according to your needs or those of the organization.
- Run ScanDisk regularly to check the hard disk for media and file errors.
- Run the Disk Defragmenter disk optimization program.
- Empty the Recycle Bin on the Windows Desktop at least monthly.
- Run the Disk Cleanup applet weekly to remove unneeded files from the hard disk.

The utilities listed in the preceding list are on the System Tools menu (see Figure 20.13), which is accessed from Start|Programs|Accessories|System Tools on a Windows system.

Running ScanDisk

The ScanDisk utility is used to scan the disk surface for media errors, to scan files and folders for data problems, or both. The ScanDisk utility runs automatically

Figure 20.13   The Windows Accessories System Tools menu.

each time Windows is not shut down properly to ensure that no disk and data problems were created when the system was powered off. Windows assumes the only reason that the system would not have been shut down properly is a power failure, and so it runs ScanDisk to check for disk problems that may have been caused by the sudden loss of power.

You should run ScanDisk at least once a week to search for and repair small errors on the disk before they become big problems. Figure 20.14 shows the startup window for the ScanDisk utility on a Windows 98 system.

Defragmenting the Hard Disk

The Disk Defragmenter utility is used to rearrange your disk files and combine and organize unused disk space to help applications run faster. During the course of working with the operating system and your applications, files are opened, modified, and removed from the hard disk, which causes the files on the disk to become fragmented. See Chapter 8 for more information about how data is stored on the hard disk drive.

The Defragmenter reorganizes the data files and eliminates the fragmentation so that a file is readily available to programs asking for it. Figure 20.15 shows the startup windows of the Disk Defragmenter.

Removing Unused Files on a Disk Drive

Another Windows System Tool applet that can be used to remove unnecessary files from your hard disk and free up valuable hard disk space is the Disk Cleanup utility. This tool scans the disk you designate (it works on every type of disk

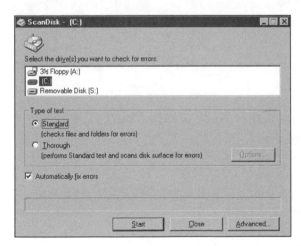

Figure 20.14   The Windows ScanDisk applet scans the disk for surface or data errors.

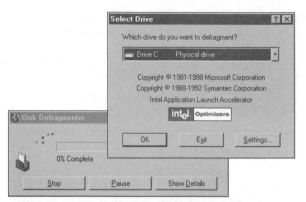

Figure 20.15   The Windows Disk Defragmenter organizes data and free space on the disk.

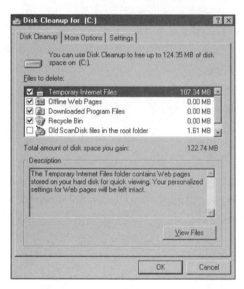

Figure 20.16   The Windows Disk Cleanup utility is used to remove unnecessary files from a disk.

drive, including diskettes and Zip disks) to find files that can be removed without seriously impacting the operation of the PC and Windows operating system. Figure 20.16 shows the dialog box of the Disk Cleanup applet.

Caring for a Floppy Disk Drive

About the only preventive maintenance you can perform on a floppy disk drive is to clean its read/write head, and you really shouldn't do that until the drive begins to have read/write errors. A floppy disk drive's read/write head can be overcleaned and worn out in the process. So, other than blowing out the drive to remove dust or bits of media, there is not much to be done on a floppy disk drive.

When the drive begins to exhibit signs of reading or writing problems, use the cleaning kit to clean the read/write heads by following the directions on the kit. You can buy a drive cleaning kit at virtually all computer supply stores for less than $10. Like the one shown in Figure 20.17, the cleaning kit typically has a special diskette and a small vial of a cleaning solution.

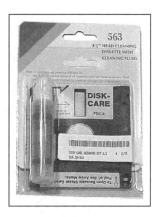

Figure 20.17   A 3.5-inch floppy disk drive cleaning kit.

Caring for CD-ROM and DVD Drives

Two things should be regularly cleaned on a CD-ROM (compact disk–read-only memory) or DVD (digital versatile disk): the disk tray and the CD-ROM's read/write lens. The tray is cleaned with some general-purpose cleaner or isopropyl alcohol by applying the solution to a soft, lint-free cloth or cotton swab and gently wiping down the tray. Avoid pressing down on the tray. A swab is good for getting down into the creases of the disk tray without pressing down on it. Allow the tray to completely dry before closing it.

To clean the lens, you need to purchase a CD drive cleaning kit that is designed for tray-based CD players. Many versions of CD cleaning kits are available, including some for caddy drives, automobile drives, and others. The cleaning kit typically contains a CD disk that has a set of very small brushes built into it and perhaps some CD disk-cleaning wipes. The brushes on the cleaning CD sweep across the lens and clean it as the disk spins in the drive. Follow the directions on the package exactly to avoid damaging your CD drive.

To clean a CD-ROM disk, remember to wipe the silver side (gold side on a DVD) with a soft, lint-free cloth or a Scotch-Brite HPCC cloth. Don't use paper towels

20. Maintaining the PC

or other textured paper that may leave streaks or scratch the disk. To wipe the disk, start from the center and move outward from the inside edge to the outside edge and don't use a circular motion.

Cleaning Expansion Slot Connectors

The connectors in an expansion slot should be cleaned at least twice a year by using the following steps:

1. Typically, all that is needed is to wipe the contacts with a soft cloth, such as the Scotch-Brite HPCC cloth.

2. Remove the expansion card from its slot without touching its contacts. Wipe each contact gently from top to bottom. Do not wipe from the top of the contact down or across all of the contacts to avoid dislodging the contacts from the card. Blow out the expansion slot using compressed air.

3. If signs of corrosion or oxidation appear on the contacts, use a contact cleaner, which is a solution made especially for cleaning metallic electronic connectors.

4. Also check the contacts in the expansion slots, which are called gold fingers, for discoloration and oxidation. Figure 20.18 shows the gold fingers, or contacts, in the expansion slots on a motherboard. Use a cotton swab and the contact cleaner to clean the gold fingers, but avoid rubbing them with a cloth because they are easily bent or broken.

Figure 20.18   The contacts in the expansion slots on a motherboard should be cleaned regularly.

Cleaning External Ports

About all you can do for the external ports that extend through the case's rear panel is to keep them from getting too dusty when not in use. A very dusty port may make a poor connection when you need it.

Use compressed air to blow the dust from any unused external ports, especially the USB ports. Do not use water or alcohol on female ports because it can get down inside the pinholes and possibly corrode the connection.

Caring for a Portable PC

Portable PCs, including laptops, notebooks, and palmtops, have many of the same preventive maintenance requirements as full-sized desktop PCs. The peripheral devices on a notebook PC, such as the hard disk, floppy disk, CD-ROM, keyboard, mouse, and ports, use the same cleaning and maintenance procedures as non-portable PCs. On a notebook or portable PC, however, some components—the batteries, video display, and case—have special care requirements.

Dealing with Portable PC Batteries

It may come as a surprise to many users that the battery in a portable PC will probably not last the life of the PC. These batteries are expendable and they all lose their ability to be recharged. Although the life of the battery, in terms of the number of times it can be recharged, ranges from 600 to more than a thousand, eventually the battery will not be able to be recharged and must be replaced.

The most popular battery type used on portable PCs is the nickel metal-hydride (NiMH) battery. This very heavy battery can be recharged around 600 times, or for about one year of use, before it will begin to have recharge problems.

TIP: *The best way to get the most out of a battery is to discharge it completely before you recharge it.*

The newest form of portable PC batteries is the Lithium-Ion (Li-Ion) battery, which has a rechargeable life of about 1,200 charges. This battery type is used primarily on more expensive systems because of its cost, which is higher than the NiMH battery.

When a battery begins to have recharge problems, the best thing to do is replace it. However, the following tips will help you to get the most out of your portable PC battery:

• Use a port replicator or the AC power adapter whenever possible.
• Because disk drives are the biggest drains on a battery, avoid disk access when you can.

- Enable and use the built-in power-saving features or software on the portable PC. These power-saving features typically include slowing the processor speed, suspending the hard disk, display, and on many systems, the entire PC, when idle for a specified period. If you don't need the speed, save the power by turning on these features.

- If the portable PC is designed for the Green Star energy standard, it reduces its power consumption as much as 99 percent when it goes into "sleep" or "suspend" modes, which simulate a shutdown of the PC. The downside to suspending the PC is the time it takes the PC to reawaken when you are ready to work again.

Caring for an LCD Display

To clean a liquid crystal display (LCD) on a portable PC, you should not use harsh cleaners because an LCD display is easily scratched. You should not use anything more harsh than a general window cleaner (without ammonia) on a soft, lint-free cloth (such as an old tee-shirt) or a Scotch-Brite HPCC cloth.

Cleaning the Portable PC's Case

Portable PC cases, except those on ruggedized portables, are fragile and are designed for lightness rather than strength. Dropping a portable PC can very well damage just about all of its components.

To clean the portable PC's case, avoid using any liquid in or around the keyboard. Use a soft, damp, lint-free cloth to wipe over the keyboard and the exterior of the case. Use compressed air to clean the keyboard. Clean the floppy disk and CD-ROM drives by using cleaning kits, just like on a desktop PC.

Part VI

General Troubleshooting and Repair

Chapter 21

Troubleshooting the PC

In Depth

Basic Troubleshooting

This chapter, like the other chapters of this book, provides some in-depth background information and suggestions for troubleshooting, diagnosing, and resolving common PC problems. However, the focus of this chapter is on generic approaches you can use to troubleshoot and repair a PC, including a generic troubleshooting process and some suggestions on how to make troubleshooting easier and involve less guesswork. Also included are some additional troubleshooting guides for many of the PC's hardware components.

The Need for a Troubleshooting Plan

When a problem occurs on your PC, chances are you remember whether it had happened before. However, unless the last time the problem happened was in the past few minutes, there is also a chance that you won't remember exactly what was going on with your PC when the problem occurred.

One of the true frustrations about problems on a PC is that in most cases they are not what they seem. The cause behind a frequent lockup of a PC could be any one of six or more easily solved problems or a dozen or more not so easily identified problems. The problem could be software-related—but which software? The problem could be hardware-related—but which hardware? What exactly was going on when the problem first occurred? Are you sure?

Even with years of experience and training, PC technicians can apply solutions that do not solve the real problem. As an example, on a Pentium III notebook PC running Windows 2000 Professional, input/output (I/O) operations to any external device, such as the PCMCIA NIC (Personal Computer Memory Card International Association network interface card) or Zip disk drive attached through the parallel port, would freeze the screen, mouse, and keyboard and take as long as 3 minutes before responding. After adding more memory, installing new parallel port and NIC device drivers, and spending literally hours of diagnostics, defragmenting the disk, and head scratching, the technician finally checked the system logs to find that a vital operating system library was corrupted and needed to be reinstalled, which solved the problem. The point is that had the technician used a systematic approach to troubleshooting, the problem would likely have been solved much sooner and a lot less expensively.

Elements of a Troubleshooting Plan

A troubleshooting plan can be a written checklist that you use for any problem, or just a routine procedure that you follow each time a problem occurs, with adjustments for the situation. Whatever form your plan takes, as long as it works and is used, it will be the right plan.

The elements that should be included in any troubleshooting plan are:

- Maintenance journal
- Diagnostic checklist or questions
- Identification of possible causes
- Identification of possible solutions
- Application and testing of solution
- Follow-up

The Maintenance Journal

You may be surprised to learn that perhaps the most important troubleshooting tool you can use to solve problems on a PC is created the day the PC is installed. This tool is a maintenance journal for the PC. In this journal, you record the hardware installed in the PC when it is installed, all preventive maintenance activities, all software updates or additions, and all hardware installations and upgrades. In addition, any problems that occur and the actions you take to resolve them should be recorded in the journal. When it comes to troubleshooting a PC, having a record of the hardware and software life of the PC can be very helpful in trying to pin down a problem and devise a solution.

A PC maintenance journal does not need to be elaborate. A simple notebook, such as a school theme book, works very well. It is typically better to keep a handwritten journal outside the PC than to create one on a word processor, especially on the PC itself, for what should be obvious reasons. If you support several PCs, then you may develop a library of maintenance journals, so you also want to identify each journal clearly with a model, serial, or property identification number.

The first entry in the maintenance journal should be a profile of the PC, which includes its configuration, operating system, and the date each component was installed. This can look something like Table 21.1.

Table 21.1   Sample maintenance journal.

Component	Configuration	Date in Service	Notes
CPU	PIII 667MHz	2/1/00	Fan and heatsink factory installed
System RAM	256MB (2–128MB DIMM)	2/1/00, 3/1/00	Second DIMM added 3/1/00
Hard disk	20GB IDE	2/1/00	Interface on motherboard
Chipset	810EX	2/1/00	
Op Sys	Windows 2000 Pro	2/1/01	Windows 98 replaced on 2/1/01

Table 21.1 gives an idea of the type of information you should include in the system configuration, as summarized here:

- The processor's make, model, and speed
- The total amount of random access memory (RAM) and the module type, size, and configuration of the memory
- The interface type and size of the hard disk(s)
- The make, model, and speed of the floppy disk drive
- The make, model, and speed of the compact disk (CD) or digital versatile disk (DVD) drive
- The make, model, and memory size of the video or graphics adapter
- The make, model, type, and size of the monitor and the resolutions it supports
- The make, model, and speed of the internal modem
- The make, model, and sampling information of the sound card
- The version number of the operating system
- A list of the software applications installed on the PC
- A list of the peripheral equipment attached to the PC, indicating the port to which each attaches

When the PC is first installed—that is, when it is first put into service either out of the box or in a new location—the owner's manual, packing slip, and your own observations will provide the information you need to complete the initial system configuration. Create the maintenance journal at that time by filling in the configuration data, including the serial numbers of those components that carry one, such as processors, NICs, expansion cards, disk drives, and so on.

Should you have any problems with the PC right out of the box, be sure to record the configuration data before documenting the problem in the maintenance journal and contacting the manufacturer. On new equipment, even if you can easily fix the problem, you may want to notify the manufacturer's technical support if the problem is caused by something the manufacturer did.

Recording Maintenance Activity

The maintenance journal should be updated each time you take any maintenance actions on the PC. The maintenance journal should be something like a diary, with dated entries for each activity performed on the PC.

Make an entry into the journal each time you perform your regular preventive maintenance. Record everything, even things as minor as cleaning the monitor's screen, and include a list of the materials and solutions used to clean the PC.

Any time new or replacement hardware is installed, record the activity and update the system configuration. The activity entries in the journal should include:

- The date of the activity or change.
- The make, model, and serial number of any hardware removed or added to the PC.
- The name, version, and publisher of any software added to the PC.
- Detailed information on any configuration changes you had to make to the basic input/output system (BIOS) or other configuration for the new device or software.
- Notes on any installation problems or changes you had to make that deviate from the device or software's documentation to get it to work properly. You may also want to notify the manufacturer of this situation.
- Although not completely necessary, you may want to note the date you completed the product registration either online or via the mail.

A General Troubleshooting Process

When a problem does happen on a PC, the information you have collected in the maintenance journal and a systematic problem-solving approach for isolating the problem are your best bets for finding and fixing the problem quickly.

Using a Systematic Problem-Solving Approach

By using a systematic approach to identifying a problem, you reduce the chance of leaving out anything you should have considered. The standard problem-solving process has six steps:

1. *Identify the problem.* This part of the process is typically the most difficult. The problem may not actually be what it seems. You need to gather all of the data you can about the problem.
2. *Identify possible causes.* Any problem, such as the system locking up after running a few minutes, can have several causes, all of which need to be identified and considered. You can then rank the possible causes by the most likely to the least likely.

3. *Identify possible solutions.* You should identify a solution for each of the possible causes you have identified. A possible cause could have more than one possible solution, in which case you need to rank the solutions by which will yield the most positive results.

4. *Analyze the possible solutions.* If two solutions will produce the same result, other considerations may be involved. Perhaps, one is less expensive or adds value to the PC.

5. *Apply a solution.* From your analysis of the possible solutions, you should pick the one that looks most promising and implement it.

6. *Test the solution.* If it solves the problem and provides the desired result, be sure you update the maintenance journal and all other pertinent documentation. If it doesn't solve the problem, you may need to repeat as much of the problem-solving process as necessary to find a better fix.

Not every problem requires that you formally and methodically work through these steps individually. Some problems are very apparent, and the fix is obvious, but you should practice applying this technique on every problem for a while. You will find that even on the simplest of problems, you still run through these steps in your mind.

Working through the Problem

Even when you use a systematic approach to isolate a problem and you find a solution, you should do some things to ensure that you have the best possible information available for your decisions. In most cases, this involves making sure you ask the right questions, either of a user or of yourself. The following are the types of questions to ask:

- Did the problem first happen immediately after a change was made to the PC?

- How did the problem manifest itself?

- Was a beep code sounded or an error message displayed to indicate or describe the problem?

- Has the problem component ever worked correctly?

- When did you first notice the problem?

- What software applications or operating server services were active when the problem happened?

- Has the same problem occurred in the past?

- If the problem has occurred in the past, how recently and how often?

- What activity was the user doing at the time the problem appeared?

- Were any configuration changes made during the current session that required a restart that was not performed?

You may also want to ask about environmental conditions:

- Have unusual electricity events occurred recently?
- Have any uncommon heating or cooling changes or problems been experienced in the room?
- Is the user new to the PC?
- Has the PC been moved recently?

As you gain experience with a particular PC or with a certain device, you will add more specific questions. If you are new to PC maintenance, the above list is a good starting point for gathering the data you need.

Reproducing the Problem

Another very important step in identifying the problem is the ability to reproduce it. You can do little more than document a problem that simply goes away when you attempt to reproduce it. Document in detail what you think may be an incidental problem that you cannot reproduce. Chances are that you are unable to reproduce the problem because you are unable for some reason to create the same set of conditions that caused it in the first place. That doesn't mean it will never happen again, and when it does, you need to be able to look back and compare the conditions that caused it in each instance. If you are dealing with an intermittent problem, you should document the answers to the questions in the preceding section and any other facts you have gathered.

Treat all problems as failure mode problems and never assume a problem to be intermittent when it first appears. As soon as you have a problem you believe is a system error (as opposed to an operator error), you should begin the documentation and problem-solving processes. Determining whether a problem is intermittent or a full-failure condition is difficult until you attempt to re-create it. Should the problem go away when you attempt to reproduce it, any data you may need for your journal may also be gone. If you are on a Windows 2000 system, the system logs will provide information as well.

When attempting to reproduce an error, reconstruct the PC's operating environment as best you can. If the problem is a boot failure, the reconstruction should not be difficult because you need only to reboot the system. However, if the problem occurs while a certain application is running or when a certain task is attempted, you need to be sure the conditions are the same for each attempt. Load all of the software that was running when the problem occurred. If possible, reconstruct the problem in the same sequence of events that led to the problem in the first place. One way to note the sequence of events, at least for the application software, is to note the sequence of the entries on the taskbar, reading left to right.

Eliminating Possible Causes

If you are able to reproduce a problem, your next challenge is to begin identifying possible causes. Too many technicians have solutions for which they are looking for problems. You should reserve judgment on any possible solutions until after you have had the chance to identify as many of the possible causes of the problem as you can.

Perhaps the best way to eliminate a possible cause is to remove it from the system and retest. This is true of hardware and software elements that you believe may be causing a problem. For example, if you think a conflict exists between two pieces of application software, you should stop one of the software programs to see if the problem clears up. This same principle applies to hardware problems. If you think a problem is being caused by conflicts between devices or expansion cards, you should open the case, remove the suspected component, and restart the system. If the problem disappears, you have found the cause; otherwise, keep eliminating devices until the problem goes away. If you must remove all of the expansion cards before a problem clears up, you may also need to begin reinserting the cards in the reverse order to which you took them out to see when the problem reappears.

Another excellent way to isolate a hardware problem on a PC is to use the *known-good method*. The known-good method involves replacing the suspected hardware with another of the same make, model, and type that you absolutely know to be good. If the problem goes away, you have a bad part; otherwise, keep testing.

If the problem appeared immediately after a change was made to the system, it is safe to say that you should remove or uninstall the changes. The most recent systems rarely have an unexpected hardware failure. Typically, hardware problems are caused by changes made to the system, outside forces (environmental and physical), or the failure of another component, such as the power supply (a very common occurrence). Electrical problems probably account for as much as 90 percent of PC hardware problems, even if the problem doesn't show up in the power supply itself.

Applying a Solution

In most situations, the fix to a problem is obvious, especially with software issues. If two applications have conflicts, not running them together, upgrading one or both, or reinstalling one or both will usually fix the problem. Always check the software manufacturer's Web site for information relating to a problem. You may also want to check the operating system manufacturer's Web site for information on this and similar problems with the software in question. If no information on your problem is available from either the application or operating system manufacturer, report the software conflict and problem to them, if for no other reason than to put it on the record.

If the problem is a hardware issue, check to see if the hardware is under warranty and, if so, what restrictions the warranty imposes before you begin making too many changes. Never make changes that would void a device's warranty. Contact the manufacturer with all of your information and work with its technical support people to devise a solution to the problem.

If the hardware is not under warranty, and you are sure that a particular device is the problem, use the known-good test to verify your conclusions and replace the device.

Writing It Down

This discussion began with advice to document the system before problems began, which is very good advice. However, if you do not also document every incident that requires you to perform problem identification and resolution on the PC, your records will be incomplete and eventually useless.

Document everything you do to your PC and you will have all the information you need to implement good, effective, and economical problem solutions when they are required.

Troubleshooting Tools

A variety of hardware, software, and information resources are available for use during troubleshooting procedures.

Hardware and Software Tools

The tools that you should have available to troubleshoot a PC include the following:

- A good set of screwdrivers, including a Phillips screwdriver
- Antistatic wrist strap, antistatic mat, and antistatic bags (for removing and storing components)
- Software system testing utilities, such as AMIDiag software from American Megatrends, Inc., Symantec's Norton Utilities, and Eurosoft's PC check, among others
- A digital multimeter for checking power supply voltages
- A supply of spare known-good components for replacement testing

Your senses are probably the most important "tools" when troubleshooting a PC. For example, your eyes or nose will find a burned out component faster than any other tool.

Information Resources

The Internet and Web are full of information resources you can use to gain information about a particular device or application, or to learn how others have dealt with a problem you are having. Chances are pretty good that you are not the first to have whatever problem you are having.

The first place to look for information is the manufacturer's Web site. It doesn't matter whether you need help on a disk drive problem or system memory, the manufacturer most likely has the information you need available on the Web. Many PC manufacturers, such as Compaq (**www.compaq.com**), Dell (**www.dell.com**), Gateway (**www.gateway2000.com**), and IBM (**www.ibm.com**), among others, have extensive troubleshooting and self-help information for your use on their Web sites.

Other, more generic, troubleshooting sites are:

- The PC Guide (**www.pcguide.com**)
- Everything Computers.Com (**www.everythingcomputers.com**)
- Troubleshooters.com (**www.troubleshooters.com**)
- Troubleshooting Resources and References (**www.pcsupport.about.com/ compute/pcsupport/cs/troubleshooting/**)

Optimizing the PC

If your PC is not running as sprightly as it once did, or if it is unable to keep pace with the demands of newer software, you may want to consider updating or optimizing your PC to enhance its performance. Some optimization steps cost money, but many involve software you already own or software readily available on the Web.

Optimizing the BIOS and Boot Process

Dozens of settings in the BIOS Setup configuration data are stored in the BIOS complementary metal-oxide semiconductor (CMOS). Whether these settings reflect the actual hardware environment of your PC can make a difference in how quickly the system boots and performs. Chances are that there is little you can or should change, but a valuable feature that you do have, such as system caching or using the Quick POST (power-on self-test) process, could be disabled and should be enabled for optimum performance.

For more detailed information on the features you may want to check, visit the BIOS Optimization Guide at **www.adriansrojakpot.com/Speed_Demonz/ BIOS_Guide**.

Optimizing the Hard Disk

The best tools available for optimizing the hard disk in terms of usage and access speeds are the Windows ScanDisk and Disk Defragmenter utilities found on the System Tools menu in the Accessories menu of the Windows Desktop. ScanDisk, shown in Figure 21.1, is used to check a disk for errors and repair them or remove unrecoverable areas of the disk from the usage tables to prevent future errors.

The Disk Defragmenter utility (see Figure 21.2) organizes data file fragments into a more optimized and logical format that provides for faster access times and less head movement. As files are written and rewritten to the disk, data file fragments can become scattered about the disk. The Disk Defragmenter utility should be run about once a month or more, depending on how frequently the disk files are modified.

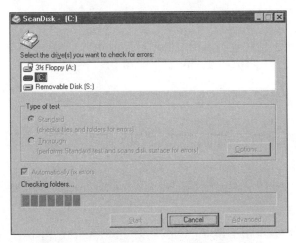

Figure 21.1   The Windows ScanDisk utility.

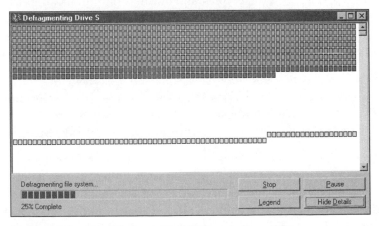

Figure 21.2   The Windows Disk Defragmenter utility.

Optimizing Expansion Cards

The best way to optimize I/O controllers and other expansion cards is to install them in the correct order. No harm is done to the PC if expansion cards are installed out of order, but there is some benefit to be gained from putting them in the proper sequence.

On a Pentium system, try to use peripheral component interconnect (PCI) cards, and avoid Industry Standard Architecture (ISA) cards, if possible. Just about all I/O adapters, including video cards, sound cards, NICs, modems, and small computer system interface (SCSI) adapters, are available for the PCI expansion bus.

When installing the cards in a PC, put the video card in the first slot, followed by the NIC, modem, and sound card, in that order. If you are unsure of which PCI slot is the first PCI slot, you should consult your motherboard's documentation or download a PCI numbering utility from the motherboard manufacturer. PCI 0, the first slot, is not necessarily the first one on the left or right on the motherboard, but it is the first one detected by the BIOS during the boot process.

Optimizing the Processor

You can speed up the processor in three ways:

- Replace it with a faster speed or higher-level processor.
- Use a utility from the processor manufacturer to apply patches or fixes to the processor's logic.
- Overclock the processor.

The requirement for replacing your processor with a higher-level or faster processor is that your motherboard and chipset will support the new processor both logically and physically. Logically, the chipset and motherboard must support the bus speed of the processor and have the supporting circuits it requires. You can check with the processor manufacturer or the motherboard manufacturer to verify these compatibilities. It is often much better to replace the motherboard as well.

The manufacturer of your processor may have some utilities available that will improve some aspect of the processor's capabilities, such as video processing, buffer handling, caching, and other processor-based functions. You can also find them on the Web at such sites as **www.motherboard.com** and **www.tomshardware.com**.

Overclocking a processor means running a processor at speeds faster than it was released to support. Most processors are capable of running at speeds higher than their nominal speeds. The nominal speed of a processor is the speed at which it has been tuned to run with a certain chipset, motherboard, cooling system, and other component of the PC.

Raising the speed of the processor can create heating problems on the processor and lead to frequent system lockups, memory problems, and other issues. Overclocking the processor can also harm the processor itself.

The speed of the processor is controlled by the internal clock, which is controlled by a feature called the internal clock multiplier. To change the internal clock multiplier, you need to locate the CPU to BUS Frequency Ratio Selection jumper on the motherboard. Consult your motherboard's documentation or refer to an overclocking guide on the Web (such as Tom's Hardware Overclocking Guide at **http://www6.tomshardware.com/guides/overclocking**) for more detailed instructions on overclocking a processor. Most likely, you will also need to change the bus speed of the motherboard and perhaps the processor voltage level as well.

21. Troubleshooting the PC

Immediate Solutions

Troubleshooting Sources of Non-Software Problems

Any time your PC fails for no apparent software reason, check out these 10 possible causes:

1. Ensure that the power cord is plugged into an AC (alternating current) outlet and that the outlet is active.

2. Scan the PC for a computer virus.

3. Verify that the fan is spinning, the case is clean, and no case parts are missing.

4. Snug up any loose external I/O connectors.

5. Reseat the expansion cards and check the power and data cables of internal devices.

6. Troubleshoot the power supply.

7. Nearly all boot problems are the result of a recent change, so check out the BIOS Setup configuration data to ensure that the new device is enabled.

8. If the operating system provides a hardware compatibility list (HCL), verify that any new hardware is included on the list. Windows 2000, Linux, and other operating systems provide an HCL.

9. Visit the manufacturer's Web site to check for any known conflicts or incompatibilities for any new hardware or software you wish to install.

10. If new hardware or software has just been installed, or existing hardware or software has been reconfigured, check for resource conflicts or other incompatibilities.

Related solutions:	Found on page:
BIOS Not Detecting the Hard Disk During the POST	112
Installing an Expansion Card	271
Checking and Troubleshooting a Power Supply	396

Troubleshooting a Dead PC or One That Locks Up During the Boot Process

The troubleshooting sequence for a PC that is either dead to begin with or dies during the boot process follows the same sequence of events performed in the boot process.

If the PC is dead and will not start up:

1. Make sure the PC and the monitor are both plugged into an active AC outlet.

2. If the outlet is a surge suppressor or plug strip, be sure that the strip itself is switched on.

3. Check the outlet by plugging in a lamp or another device.

4. Move the plug to a new outlet.

5. Replace the power cable.

WARNING! *Never cut the grounding prong off a PC power cable to insert it in a two-prong outlet. You are absolutely asking for serious power supply problems, not to mention creating a potentially dangerous situation.*

The power supply is commonly the problem when the PC will not start up. Some things to check on the power supply are the following:

1. Check the line voltage switch on the power supply. It may have been inadvertently switched to 220V (volts) or 110V, whatever is different from your normal power source's voltage.

2. Use a multimeter to check the continuity of the wires going from the power supply or motherboard to the power switch. Be sure the power supply is unplugged from its AC power source.

3. Do not check the power supply's fuses that are located inside the case. A blown fuse is very rare and it is extremely dangerous for you to be poking around inside the power supply.

4. The problem could be a shorted out component that draws power from the power supply. Remove the power connectors from everything except the motherboard and retest. Then begin replacing the power connectors on the internal devices until the boot fails and you have found the problem device.

If the PC has power, but locks up during or after the boot process, check the following:

1. Listen very carefully during the boot for the beep codes that signal the source of the problem. You may need to reboot a number of times before

you are able to clearly decipher these codes. Write them down and use the system documentation or the BIOS manufacturer's Web site to determine the meaning of the beep code sounded.

2. Check the connections of the internal storage devices, such as the hard disk drive, CD-ROM drive, floppy disk, or any other device that is listed in the BIOS as being a boot disk drive. If the data cable is not installed correctly on the boot device, it can cause the system to halt without a message or display that the boot device is missing.

3. If the PC does boot up completely, but locks up after a few minutes of operation, the cause could be a virus or that the processor is overheating and shutting down. Scan the hard disk drive for a virus.

4. Check the case for missing parts, including expansion slot fillers, and make sure the processor's fan and heat sink are installed correctly.

If the PC hangs up during startup or after Windows loads, this problem is typically the result of recent changes to the PC that are causing resource conflicts or conflicting software. Remove or uninstall any recent changes and restart the PC. If the problems are gone, check the compatibility of the new hardware or software before reinstalling it.

Related solutions:	*Found on page:*
Troubleshooting Guide for the Motherboard	15
Troubleshooting a Hard Disk Drive	217
Troubleshooting a Floppy Disk Drive	219
Checking and Troubleshooting a Power Supply	396

Troubleshooting the Monitor

1. Ensure that the monitor is connected to the video adapter installed in the PC's system unit.

2. Check both ends of the video cable for a snug connection. Many newer monitors have a video graphics array (VGA) connection at the monitor end of the cable as well.

3. Check the monitor's power cable for fit at the monitor end and verify that the power cord is plugged into a good power source.

4. Replace the monitor with a known-good monitor. If the replacement monitor works, then there is something wrong with the existing monitor, and you should take it to a repair facility or replace it.

5. If the replacement monitor does not work, the problem is likely with the video adapter card. Reseat the card and retest. If the problem persists, replace the video adapter card.

6. If the video card is installed in the accelerated graphics port (AGP) slot, try testing with a known-good video card. If the video still does not display, the problem is likely in the AGP slot or on the motherboard itself.

7. If the problem is not hardware, boot the system with the startup disk provided with the PC or that you created when you installed the operating system.

8. The startup disk provides you with a list of options for recovery, diagnostics, and, on Windows systems, the ability to boot into Safe Mode, which you should do.

9. Use the Device Manager to verify the video settings, including the device driver. If the device driver is not loading or cannot be found, locate it or download it from the manufacturer's Web site and reinstall it.

Related solution:	Found on page:
Finding the Problem When the Monitor Is Blank or Has No Picture	438

Troubleshooting When the PC Locks Up Before the Operating System Loads

1. Watch the boot sequence messages very carefully for boot error messages. Often these messages flash on and off the display so quickly that they go unnoticed. Use the Pause/Break key to freeze the screen when the message displays.

2. The problem could be that a device driver is failing to initialize because of a bad connection to an expansion card. Reseat the expansion cards; check the contacts for corrosion or the need to be cleaned.

3. Boot Windows into Safe Mode, if you can, and use the Device Manager to check for any device and system resource conflicts.

Troubleshooting When the PC Fails or Crashes During Severe Weather

If the weather is extremely cold, hot, or stormy, the chances are good for numerous overvoltage (surges, spikes, and line noise) and undervoltage (sags, brownouts, and blackouts) events on the AC power supply. If the PC is not connected to a surge suppressor, a line conditioner, or an uninterruptible power supply (UPS), get one immediately to protect the PC from the problems on the AC power supply.

Troubleshooting the Power Supply

The power supply is always a good place to begin looking for power-related problems. If a disk drive is failing, the system is frequently locking up, or the system will not boot, you should probably check out the power supply as a part of your troubleshooting process.

1. Remove the power supply connector of the failing device and use a multimeter to verify the +5V DC (direct current), +12V DC, and ground on the appropriate pins (see Chapter 12 for the pin values of the power supply connectors). Check the documentation of the power supply for pinouts and voltages for your power supply, or visit the manufacturer's Web site.

2. Check the voltage on all of the power supply connectors, including the motherboard connectors. In fact, checking the voltage of these connectors should be a part of your regular preventive maintenance program.

3. Verify that the fan is spinning without any high-pitched sounds. Should the fan be making a high-pitched sound, the bearings in the fan are likely wearing out.

4. If the power supply is not producing the correct voltages or the fan is having problems, the power supply should be replaced. The power supply accounts for the majority of component failures in the PC, so do not hesitate to replace even a suspected bad power supply.

Related solution:	*Found on page:*
Checking and Troubleshooting a Power Supply	396

Troubleshooting Suspected Hard Disk Drive Problems

Hard disk drives are not infallible; the bearings on the spindle, the actuator motor, or the spindle motor can fail, although this is relatively rare. If you are getting intermittent read errors or there is a high-pitched whine coming from the disk, chances are good that the hard disk is developing a problem. You are always better off to replace a very noisy hard disk drive.

When hard disk drive problems first appear:

1. Check the disk for a computer virus.

2. Run the ScanDisk utility.

3. Run the Disk Defragmenter.

4. Use a PC diagnostic utility, such as AMIDiag, Norton Utilities, or PC check, to verify the disk's function.

Related solution:	*Found on page:*
Troubleshooting a Hard Disk Drive	217

Troubleshooting Floppy Disk Drive Problems

Floppy disk drives are essentially disposable technology. If a floppy disk drive stops working, before you simply replace it, check out the following:

1. If you have recently installed new hardware inside the system unit, check the power and data connectors on the floppy disk to ensure they were not dislodged inadvertently.

2. Use the Windows Device Manager to check for any system resource conflicts. However, resource conflicts are unlikely because the floppy disk uses system resources that the manufacturers of other PC hardware avoid.

3. If the floppy disk is having read errors, use a cleaning kit to clean the read/write heads.

4. If the floppy disk connects into an adapter card in an expansion port, reseat the adapter card or replace the adapter.

21. Troubleshooting the PC

Related solution:	Found on page:
Troubleshooting a Floppy Disk Drive	219

Troubleshooting a Problem Mouse

Most mouse problems, at least on an optomechanical mouse (the kind that has a ball), are the result of the mouse being dirty. However, a mouse can wear out as well. If the mouse is clean and all else is well, check out these issues:

1. On occasion, the device driver for the mouse may just stop running for some reason and you must shut down the PC and restart it. Use the keyboard commands to close any open work and shut down the PC.

2. Check the mouse connection on the back of the PC. The mouse connection commonly becomes dislodged from the constant tugging and pulling on its cable. The cable can also become damaged, in which case the mouse should be replaced.

3. If new hardware has been recently installed, use the Device Manager to check for system resource conflicts, especially if the mouse is a serial mouse.

4. If the mouse is a universal serial bus (USB) device, check its connection and verify that the USB device driver is running.

Related solutions:	Found on page:
Troubleshooting a USB Connection	338
Configuring a Mouse on a Windows PC	516

Troubleshooting the Sound Card

If the sound card on a PC stops working, check out the following:

1. Make sure the sound is turned up on the speaker and in the Windows Volume Control panel.

2. Check the speaker cables to make sure they are connected to both the speakers and the sound card.

21. Troubleshooting the PC

3. Verify that the connectors are installed in the correct jacks.

4. If other hardware has been recently installed, check for resource conflicts, which are relatively common with sound cards.

5. Make sure the sound card's device driver is loaded, that you are using the latest version, and that the driver is appropriate for the operating system.

6. If no sound is coming from the CD-ROM drive, make sure that the CD-ROM drive is connected to the sound card with the appropriate cable.

Related solutions:	Found on page:
Troubleshooting CD-ROM Sound Problems	247
Correcting a CD-ROM or DVD to a Sound Card	572

Troubleshooting a Modem

An internal modem is typically a plug-and-play device that is configured automatically when the system boots. However, conflicts with other devices can occur. An external modem, which connects through a serial port, can have setup problems. Check the following:

1. If the modem is an internal device, verify that no resource conflicts exist and that it has been properly configured using the Modem icon on the Control Panel and the Dialup Networking icon in the My Computer folder.

2. If the modem cannot be detected by the PC, open the system case and reseat the card.

3. For an external modem, check for resource conflicts on the COM (serial) port to which it is attached and verify the settings in the Modem icon and Dialup Networking.

4. If the modem is used for an Internet connection, which is very common, contact the Internet service provider (ISP) for the correct settings.

Related solution:	Found on page:
Configuring a Modem Connection	544

Troubleshooting a Printer

Printer problems are typically on the printer itself, but check the following:

1. Verify that the printer is plugged into an AC power source. Laser printers should not be connected to a UPS.

2. Verify that the printer is online.

3. Check the parallel cable connections and verify that the cable in use is the proper cable for the parallel protocol (enhanced capabilities port, enhanced parallel port) in use.

4. If new hardware has been recently installed, check for resource conflicts.

5. Verify that the printer is properly installed using the Printers icon on the Control Panel.

Related solution:	*Found on page:*
Diagnosing Common Printer Problems	422

Glossary

10BaseT—The generic designation of a 10Mbps Ethernet implementation on twisted pair cabling. See *Twisted pair wire*.

100BaseT—The generic term for a 100Mbps Fast Ethernet implementation on twisted pair cabling.

286—This processor was first used in the IBM PC AT and formed the baseline for virtually all PCs that followed. Officially known as the 80286, this 16-bit processor ran at speeds of 6 to 20 MHz.

386—The 386 processor was one of the first of the Intel x86 processors to offer 32-bit processing in both 16-bit and 32-bit modes. After the introduction of the 386SX, which featured a disabled coprocessor, the original 386 was designated the 386DX.

386DX—See *386*.

386SX—An Intel 386 processor with a disabled math coprocessor. By disabling the math coprocessor, manufacturers could offer this chip at a lower price, and thus compete with lower-end chips from other manufacturers.

486DX—An improved version of the Intel 386DX that supported 32-bit processing and processor speeds of 25 and 33MHz.

486DX2—A 486DX processor that was overclocked to provide twice the processor speed of a 486DX. Two versions of the 486DX2 had 50 and 66MHz processor speeds, respectively.

486DX4—A 486DX processor that was overclocked to provide three times the processor speeds of a 486DX processor. Two versions of the 486DX4 that offered 75 and 100MHz.

486SX—An Intel 486 processor with a disabled math coprocessor.

586—See *Pentium*.

8088—The first of the 8-bit Intel microprocessors.

80286—See *286*.

80386—See *386*.

80486—See *486DX*.

For more information on:	See:
Microprocessors	Chapter 2
Network cabling	Chapter 18

Access time—The measurement of the time required to position a disk's read/write heads over a particular track and sector on the disk. Access time adds latency, or rotational delay, to the seek time to calculate the total time required for the disk to position the read/write head over a specific data location.

Active backplane—Also called the intelligent backplane, this motherboard design style moves the CPU or some device and interface controllers to a daughterboard.

Active matrix LCD—The type of liquid crystal display (LCD) that uses thin film transistors (TFT), which are switching transistors and capacitors, etched into a matrix pattern on a glass substrate. The glass substrate forms one of the layers of the active matrix LCD.

Address bus—The bus structure that carries the address in the part of memory containing data that has been requested or is to be stored.

Advanced Audio Coding (AAC)—This MPEG compression standard, which is also known as MPEG-2 (not to be confused with MP2), is expected to succeed MP3 audio.

Advanced Configuration and Power Interface (ACPI)—A power management specification used on desktop and portable PCs, it enables a PC to power on and off its peripheral devices to conserve power. A PC supporting AICP can also be powered on or off remotely.

AGP (Accelerated Graphics Port)—An expansion bus designed solely for video cards, AGP improves video performance and eliminates the need for memory storage on video cards. There are different AGP speed ratings: 264 MBps or 1xAGP, 528 MBps or 2xAGP, and 1GBps or 4xAGP. The AGP slot is a brown slot typically located near the PCI slots on a motherboard.

Analog to Digital Converter (ADC)—An ADC converts analog audio information, such as a voice or a musical instrument, into digital data for storage and editing on a PC.

Anti-aliasing—A process used to smooth the jagged edge appearance of a bitmapped image's diagonal lines. Shades of gray or the background color are used to blend the edge of the image into the background.

Antistatic mat—A mat on which a PC is placed during troubleshooting and repair that absorbs static electricity and reduces the chance for the system to be damaged by ESD. See *ESD* and *Antistatic wrist strap*.

Antistatic wrist strap—Typically an elastic band, attached to a grounding cable that can be connected to an antistatic mat or to the metal chassis of the PC to provide protection from ESD damage. See *ESD* and *Antistatic mat*.

Antivirus software—Software used to detect and remove computer viruses on a PC. Common antivirus software inlcudes Norton Antivirus, McAfee VShield, and Trend Micro's PC-cillan.

Aperture Grill—One of two methods used to guide the electron beams that light the screen display of a monitor. (The other method is the shadow mask.) An aperture grill masks the display's pixels into vertical stripes using thin metal wires and focuses the electron beam on the parts of the display's phosphor to be lighted.

Application server—A server that shares common application software with clients (workstations) on a network. Common applications shared on an application server are database management systems, groupware applications such as Lotus Notes, and corporate accounting and management systems. On occasion, even common desktop applications, such as word processing and spreadsheet software, can be shared from an application server.

Application-Specific Integration Circuit (ASIC)—An integrated circuit made for a specific application, such as a PC chipset.

Arbitration—The method used by a chipset to interface between different bus speeds and interfaces.

Arithmetic and Logic Unit (ALU)—The ALU performs the calculations and comparative logic functions for the processor, including add, subtract, divide, multiply, equal to, greater than, less than, and other arithmetic and logic operations.

Areal density—An indicator of a hard disk's storage capacity in bits per square inch. Areal density is calculated by multiplying the disk's bits per inch (BPI) by its total number of tracks. An area density of around 1.5Gb per square inch is common on newer disk drives.

ASCII (American Standard Code for Information Interchange)—ASCII defines the standard character set used on PCs that includes special command, inquiry, and graphics characters along with the upper and lower case alphabetic characters, special characters, and numbers of American English language.

Aspect ratio—The ratio of a display's horizontal pixels to vertical pixels that is used to define the height to width ratio of shapes and graphics on the display. The standard aspect ratio is 4:3.

Glossary

Asynchronous cache—The type of cache memory that transfers data without regard to the system clock cycles.

Asynchronous SRAM (ASRAM)—This type of static RAM (SRAM) transfers data in and out of memory without using the system clock to control its actions. ASRAM is slower but less expensive than synchronous SRAM. See *RAM*.

Asynchronous communications—Data transmissions from the processor to a printer, modem, fax, or other peripheral devices that use asynchronous transmitters and receivers that operate independently and are not synchronized to a common clock signal, or to each other.

AT (Advanced Technology)—Derived from the name of an early IBM PC model, the PC AT, this term in most usages refers to adaptations of the bus structure and form factor of the PC AT. See *AT form factor*, *AT bus*, and *AT Attachment*.

ATAPI—An interface standard that provides commands used to provide access for a CD-ROM, DVD, or tape drive to standard AT attachment (ATA) interfaces. The ANSI standard for EIDE drives. See *ANSI*, *AT Attachment*, and *EIDE*.

AT Attachment (ATA)—See *Integrated Drive Electronics (IDE)*.

AT bus—See *Industry Standard Architecture (ISA)*.

AT command set—A standard command set used to control and configure Hayes-compatible modems. AT means "attention," which precedes each of the action commands of the command set.

AT form facto—The motherboard and power supply of the IBM PC AT established the baseline in design, shape, and size for the system case, motherboard, and power supply. All PC form factors that followed the PC AT, whether desktop or tower, are based on the AT form factor in one way or another.

Athlon processor—This powerful 1GHz processor is manufactured by Advanced Micro Devices (AMD) and includes 22 million transistors. The Athlon is plug compatible with the Slot 1 connector, but it is designed for the Slot A bus.

ATX form facto—The current de facto standard for Pentium-class motherboards, power supplies, and system cases.

Audio Interchange File Format (AIFF)—This file format is the Macintosh equivalent of Windows' WAV format.

Audio Unix (AU)—The audio file format standard on most UNIX systems.

Auxiliary fan—An additional cooling fan added to the system case to provide for supplemental airflow and cooling. Typically, an auxiliary fan is placed opposite from the main cooling fan located inside the power supply.

For more information on:	See:
Bus structures	Chapter 10
Cache memory	Chapter 6
Chipsets	Chapter 3
Displays and monitors	Chapter 15
Hard disks	Chapter 8
Motherboards	Chapter 1
Networks and communications	Chapter 18
Preventive maintenance	Chapter 20
Processors	Chapter 2
Sound cards	Chapter 19
System case	Chapter 13
Video cards	Chapter 11

Baby AT form factor—A slightly smaller version of the AT form factor that was very popular before Pentium PCs popularized the ATX form factor. Baby AT motherboards and cases are still available from several manufacturers.

Backplane—A motherboard or mainboard style that mounts add-in cards, called daughterboards, to add a processor, memory, or other motherboard features.

Baseband—A data communications mode that uses a single channel to support digital transmissions, typically over twisted-pair cabling. Most LANs are baseband networks. See *Local area network* and *Twisted pair wire*.

BEDO (Burst Extended Data Out) DRAM—EDO memory with pipelining technology added, BEDO memory can transfer data from memory access while accepting the next request. It bursts data over successive clock cycles and is common on PCs with clock speeds up to 66 MHz. See *EDO DRAM*.

Beep codes—Any hardware issues detected before the video is available during the POST process of the boot sequence are signaled with one or more beep tones from the system speaker. The major BIOS manufacturers each use a different number and pattern for the beep codes to indicate hardware problems.

Bi-linear filtering—A standard on 3D graphic cards that reads four texels (texture elements), Bi-linear filtering calculates the averages of the texel positions, colors, and other properties, and displays the result as a single-screen texel. This technique is used to reduce blockiness in the display.

BIOS (Basic Input/Output System)—The BIOS performs a number of functions on a PC, including booting the PC, verifying the CMOS configuration, and providing an interface between the hardware and the software.

Glossary

BIOS POST Card—A special purpose ISA bus card that can be used to trouble-shoot BIOS POST errors. The POST card captures and displays error codes written to memory address 80h by the BIOS POST process.

Bipolar transistor—An active semiconductor device that amplifies an electrical current.

Bit—Short for binary digit. A bit, which is a single transistor or capacitor, holds a single binary value, either 0 or 1.

Bitmapped font—A font that forms characters with patterns of dots. Each particular bitmapped font (Times New Roman, Courier, etc.) specifies a dot pattern to be used for each letter, number, and special character, print style (bold, italic, etc.), and type size (10 pts, 12 pts, etc.).

Blackout—A blackout is a total loss of electrical power that lasts anywhere from a split second to several hours or more. The best defense against a blackout is a UPS. See *UPS*.

Bluetooth—A close proximity wireless device interconnect system that is used to connect PCs with external peripheral devices, such as modems and printers, to create what is called a wireless personal area network (WPAN).

Boldface font—This is a print style that darkens the typeface to emphasize a word or phrase.

Boolean algebra—The binary mathematic laws used by the processor to perform logical and data shift operations. The Boolean functions are: AND, OR, and EXCLUSIVE OR.

Boot—The process used to startup a PC. This term originates from the phrase "pulling yourself up by your own bootstraps," meaning the ability to self-start.

Boot block—A 4K program included as part of the BIOS that allows the PC to recover from an incorrect or corrupted BIOS by restoring the BIOS from a special floppy disk or CD-ROM.

Bridge—A network connectivity device used to connect two different LANs or network segments to create what appears to be one network. A bridge intelligently sends network messages to the proper network segment using information it gathers about the addresses of the nodes sending messages through it.

Broadband networks—A data communications mode that uses analog signaling over a wide range of frequencies. Wireless, cable, and DSL (digital subscriber line) high-speed Internet services are broadband systems.

Brownout—A brownout occurs when the voltage of the electrical supply dips below its normal voltage for an extended period.

Bump mapping—This 3D graphics technique is used in place of embossing to create the illusion of depth or height on a textured surface. This is the process used to create rough roads, bomb craters, and bullet holes on walls in 3D graphic images.

Burst mode access—Memory accesses that are done in bursts of four data segments, which are read in a series from a starting memory address.

Bus—The pathways on the motherboard and processor that carry signals, addresses, and data between the PC's components.

Bus mastering—The process used by a DMA (direct memory access) device to take over the bus and transfer data to and from memory without assistance from either the processor or the DMA controller. See *DMA*.

Byte—Stands for binary digit eight. A byte is a logical grouping of 8 bits and is the smallest addressable unit of storage in the PC. A byte is normally associated with a single ASCII character.

For more information on:	See:
Audio/visual systems	Chapter 11
BIOS	Chapter 4
Electricity and power	Chapter 14
Memory	Chapter 5
Motherboards	Chapter 1
Networks	Chapter 18
Processors	Chapter 2
System resources	Chapter 7

Cache—Any buffer storage that is used to improve a computer's performance by reducing its access times. A cache holds instructions and data that are likely to be needed for the CPU's next operation. Caching copies frequently accessed data and instructions from either primary memory or disk (secondary) storage.

Cache controller—A special circuit that controls the interface between the CPU, cache, and the main memory controller.

Cache hit—The caching system anticipates the data the processor should logically request next. Each time the caching system is correct, it is called a cache hit.

Cache memory—Smaller, faster memory that is placed between primary memory (RAM) and the processor to hold instructions and data from the primary memory for high-speed access by the processor.

Cache miss—The functional opposite of a cache hit. When the data or instruction requested by the processor is not located in cache, a cache miss is recorded. See *cache hit*.

Campus area network (CAN)—A CAN is a type of LAN that includes PCs and devices in several buildings of an office park or campus setting.

Capacitive keyswitch—This type of keyboard keyswitch stores an electrical charge between two metal plates. As the plates move closer together (when a key is pressed) or further apart (when a key is released), the capacitance changes, which signals that a keystroke has occurred.

Capacitor—An electronic component that stores an electric charge, which on a PC is either a positive or negative voltage value, indicating a 1 or 0 binary value.

Case cover—The plastic outer covering of a PC that protects the contents inside the system unit and plays an important role in the cooling and structure of a PC.

Cat 3 cable—A 4-pair (8-wire) cable used on networks with bandwidth up to 10 Mbps.

Cat 5 cable—A 4-pair (8-wire) cable used on networks with 100 Mbps and higher bandwidth. Cat 5 cable is commonly referred to as UTP cable. See *UTP cable*.

CD caddy—A plastic-hinged case in which a CD-ROM disk is placed for use in some CD-ROM drives.

CD-Digital Audio (CD-DA)—The first standard CD format, CD-DA was developed to hold recorded music and other sounds. The CD-DA standard is also known as the Red Book standard and CD-DA is known as Red Book audio. CD-DA is equivalent to 1X speed for PC CD-ROM drives.

CD-ROM (Compact Disk–Read-Only Memory)—Originally developed as an alternative to the cassette tape for analog audio content, CD-ROM drives are now standard on PCs. A CD-ROM holds around 650MB of data.

Celeron microprocessor—The low-cost model of the Pentium II processor series that features clock speeds of 333MHz to 500MHz. Newer models, built on the Pentium III core, offer clock speeds of 566MHz or faster.

CGA (Color Graphics Adapter)—An early PC graphics standard, it was the first to include a range of colors. CGA could display 16 colors at its lowest resolution, but only 2 colors at its highest resolution of 640×200.

***Charge-coupled device* (CCD)**—This is technology used in most general-purpose document and image scanners. A CCD is a small solid-state sensor that converts light into an electric charge, which in turn is converted into data that can be stored on a computer. Thousands of CCDs are arranged into an array that scans the entire surface of the image.

Glossary

Chassis—The skeletal metal framework that provides the structure, rigidity, and strength of a PC's case.

CHS (cylinder-head-sector) addressing—This is the addressing scheme used by IDE/ATA drives to place and locate data on a hard disk drive using its cylinder, head, and sector references.

Chip creep—A condition where socket mounted ICs and expansion cards become unseated or are pushed out of their sockets by the heating and cooling cycles of the PC and its components.

Chipset—A group of standard PC functions combined onto one, two, or more related integrated circuits. The chipset provides the software and protocols necessary for the microprocessor and other components of the PC to communicate with and control all of the devices plugged into the motherboard.

Choke point—When too much data must pass through too small a pathway. For example, an ISA video card used on a Pentium PC can cause a choke point when the monitor's graphics attempt to run over the low-speed ISA bus.

CELP (card edge low profile) socket—The type of socket used to mount a COAST cache module on the motherboard.

Client/server network—A network of computers and peripherals connected to at least one centralized computer that services requests for data, software, and hardware resources from network clients.

Clock speed—The operating speed of the processor in megahertz (MHz), which sets up the number of cycles per second on the PC. A computer rated at 5MHz has 5 million processing cycles per second. The more cycles per second a computer supports, the more instructions it can execute.

Cluster—A logical grouping of disk sectors that is used by an operating system to track and transfer data to and from the disk. Typically, there are around 64 sectors in a cluster. However, the hard disk's capacity and the operating system determine the size of a cluster.

CMOS (Complementary Metal Oxide Semiconductor)—The technology used to manufacture nearly all integrated circuits built into digital processors and memories. CMOS also is used to refer to the memory used to store the BIOS Setup configuration. CMOS is also called NVRAM (nonvolatile RAM).

CMOS battery—A barrel or flat battery that provides the power sufficient for the CMOS memory to retain the BIOS Setup configuration data.

COAST (cache on a stick)—The popular design for socket-mounted cache modules that are similar in style and design to a SIMM memory module. See *SIMM*.

Coaxial (coax) cable—A networking cable that is very similar to the cable used to connect a TV set to a cable TV outlet. Two coax cable types are used in networks: thick coaxial cable and thin coaxial cable.

Codec (Compression/Decompression)—The hardware or software mechanism used to convert sound and video data into a digital format and to reduce the size of captured audio or video data for storage or transmission.

Color depth—The number of individual colors that each pixel of a monitor's screen is capable of displaying. The color depth is expressed as the number of bits used to describe each color in the color set, which is commonly 8-bits, 16-bits, 24-bits, or 32-bits.

COM port—A legacy term for communications port. This is the logical name identifier assigned to a PC's serial ports, with the first serial port being COM1 and subsequent serial ports designated as COM2, COM3, etc.

Communications server—This type of server provides common communications functions, such as email, fax, dialup modem, or Internet services to network clients.

Conductor—Any material that allows electrical current to pass through it. Copper, aluminum, and gold are good conductors of electricity.

Constant angular velocity (CAV)—The speed of CD-ROM and hard disk drives that use a constant spin speed, meaning that every spin of the disk media takes the same amount of time.

Constant linear velocity (CLV)—A CD-ROM drive adjusts the speed of the spindle motor to keep the linear velocity of the disk constant, which means that the spindle turns slower when the read/write head is nearer the outer edge of the CD and turns faster as the head moves toward the hub ring.

Contact keyswitch—An electromechanical device used on keyboards for each key. When pressed, the contact keyswitch completes a circuit when its parts make contact.

Control bus—The bus structure that carries signals between the processor and other PC components to control and request actions.

Control Unit (CU)—The control unit controls and coordinates the actions and interactions between the different elements of the processor, including what to do, what data to use, and where to put the results.

Conventional memory—The first 640K of system memory that is for standard DOS programs, device drivers, TSRs (terminate-and-stay-resident programs), and anything that runs on standard DOS.

Copper wire—See *Twisted pair wire*.

Glossary

Coprocessor—A secondary processor that is used to offload a specific activity or group of actions from the system processor. Common coprocessors on a system are math and graphics coprocessors. Virtually every processor since the 386DX, with the exception of the 386SX and 486 SX models, has had an FPU (floating point unit) coprocessor integrated into the CPU chip. Graphics coprocessors are typically located on video cards.

Copy backup—A type of data backup that is created using the File Manager, Windows Explorer, or the DOS commands **COPY** or **XCOPY**.

Cordless devices—Devices that use radio frequency (RF) and infrared (IR) transmitters, receivers, and transceivers (the combination of a receiver and transmitter) to send data to the PC. Cordless devices include mice, keyboards, modems, and even network adapters for desktop and portable PCs. See *RF* and *IR*.

CPS (characters per second)—A common measurement of the speed of character printers, such as daisy wheel and dot matrix printers.

CPU (central processing unit)—Also known as *the processor*. The CPU is the primary computing device of a computer. See *Microprocessor* and *Processor*.

CRT (cathode ray tube)—The device in a PC monitor that produces a video display on its screen. A CRT looks and works very much like a standard, conventional television set.

Cylinders—All of the tracks with the same number on all of the platters of a hard disk drive form a logical cylinder.

For more information on:	See:
BIOS	Chapter 4
Cache	Chapter 6
CD-ROM drives	Chapter 9
Chipsets	Chapter 3
Hard disk drives	Chapter 8
Keyboards and mice	Chapter 17
Networks	Chapter 18
Ports and connectors	Chapter 12
Processors	Chapter 2
Scanners	Chapter 19
System case	Chapter 13

D connector—Cable connectors that have a D-shaped plug head shell. A D connector is designated with two letters: D plus a letter that designates the size of the connector. Common D connectors are the DA-9 (serial), DB-25 (serial), and DE-15 (VGA connector).

DA-9 connector—A D-type connector, commonly and erroneously referred to as a DB-9 connector, used as an alternate to the larger DB-25 connector.

Database server—A server that manages a common database, handling all data storage, database management, and requests for data on a network.

Data bus—A bus structure that carries data between the processor, main memory, and the I/O bus.

Data RAM—A division of cache memory that stores data or instructions.

Data store—The area in Level 2 cache where the data is stored. The size of a cache's data store determines the amount of data the cache can actually hold.

Data transfer rate—The amount of data in megabytes that can be moved between a storage device and the PC's main memory (RAM) in one second. Current hard disks support transfer rates from 5 to 70 MBps.

Daughterboard—A computer circuit board that plugs into a motherboard or backplane board to add additional capabilities to the system.

DB-9 connector—See *DA-9 connector.*

Degaussing—The process used to neutralize a CRT's magnetization. Most monitors have a built-in degaussing circuit that uses a coil of wire inside the monitor. The degaussing circuit is activated by either a manual switch or automatically through the monitor's controls.

Dental mirror—This tool is used to see around corners inside the system unit.

Dielectric gel—A special material, also called *thermal grease,* used to insulate a processor from a fan or heat sink attached to it. A dielectric material is an insulator that can hold an electrostatic charge, but does not allow a current to pass through it. See *Thermal grease.*

Differential backup—A type of data backup that includes files created or modified since the last full or incremental backup. A differential backup does not clear the archive bit. This backup type, if used daily, accumulates the files that are new or changed since the last backup that clears the archive bit. See *full backup* and *incremental backup.*

Diffusion—See *Image diffusion.*

Glossary

Digital Audio Extraction (DAE)—A method of capturing and playing back data from an audio CD without the use of a sound card.

Digital data—Data encoded in a binary format for transmission or storage.

Digital multimeter—An electrical measurement instrument that has the built-in ability to measure volts, amps, and ohms and display the results on an LCD screen.

Digital Signal Processor (DSP)—A special-purpose CPU that supports the fast instruction processing needed for math-intensive signal processing applications, such as sound cards, fax machines, modems, cellular phones, and high-capacity hard disks.

Digital to Analog Converter (DAC)—The DAC converts audio data stored on a hard drive or other medium into audible information that can be played back on speakers or headphones.

Digitizing tablet—A drawing tool that works on the same principle as a touchpad and is used with a drawing stylus to create vector art or engineering objects.

DIMM (Dual Inline Memory Module)—A 168-pin memory module that is the current memory standard on 64-bit PCs.

DIN (Deutsche Industrie Norm)—A German standards organization.

DIP (dual inline packaging)—This is a common packaging for memory and integrated circuit chips. DIP chips, are mounted onto individual sockets directly on the motherboard.

Direct-mapped cache—The type of cache that assigns only one possible location to each cached data entry.

Direct Rambus DRAM (DRDRAM)—A proprietary DRAM technology that features RAM speeds up to 800MHz.

Disk cache—An area in main memory or memory on the disk controller used to provide caching between the disk and the processor.

Disk spindle—Inside the HDA, the disk platters are mounted to the disk spindle.

Disk spindle motor—The disk spindle motor rotates the disk spindle at speeds between 3,600 and 10,000 RPM (revolutions per minute) or faster. The spindle motor is a direct-drive motor mounted to the bottom on the spindle assembly.

Display Power Management System (DPMS)—DPMS is a protocol used to power down parts of a monitor and PC when they are idle for a certain period. DPMS is a BIOS-supported protocol that can be enabled in the CMOS settings of the PC.

Dithering—See *Ordered dithering*.

DMA (direct memory access)—An input/output technique that allows a peripheral device to access memory directly without the assistance of the CPU.

DMA controller—The controller that manages the seven DMA channels used by ISA/ATA devices on a PC.

Dot matrix printer—This printer uses a matrix of pins in its printhead to create text and graphics with a pattern of dots. Dot matrix printers incorporate tractor-feed mechanisms to feed continuous-form paper and documents.

Dot pitch—The distance in millimeters (mm) between two phosphor dots of the same color on a display. A monitor with a low dot pitch produces better images than one with a higher dot pitch. Even the smallest difference in dot pitch shows up on the screen, especially on larger monitors. Current monitors offer dot pitch distances in the range of .24 mm to .31 mm, with .28 mm the most common.

Double Data Rate (DDR) SDRAM—An SDRAM type that operates on bus speeds of at least 200MHz (or double a 100MHz data rate).

Draft quality—A low quality print style in which the dots or print elements used to form the characters are individually visible on the page. Low-end inkjet and dot matrix printers produce draft quality type.

DRAM (dynamic random access memory)—This is the type of memory most commonly used for a PC's main memory.

Drive bays—Disk drives that support removable media, such as a floppy disk or a CD-ROM, are mounted so that they can be accessed from the front panel in a drive bay built into a PC's case.

Drive rails—Mounting rails that are attached to the sides of a disk drive in the drive bays of some case designs to enable installation of the drive. The drive rails allow the drive to be placed in the drive bay by sliding the rails on notches or facets of the drive bay's sidewalls.

DSL (Digital Subscriber Line)—A high-speed broadband Internet access service that transmits over a standard telephone line. Data transmission speeds vary with the type of DSL service installed, but data speeds can range from 128 Kbps (for IDSL – ISDN over DSL) to 1.1 Mbps (for SDSL, Symmetrical DSL). The most common type of DSL service is ADSL (Asymmetrical DSL), the common service for home users. ADSL transmits and receives asymmetrically or at different speeds. SDSL, which transmits and receives symmetrically, or at the same speed, is typically used more for business and high-end users who require larger amounts of bandwidth.

Dual-porting—A video RAM technique that allows data to be written to memory at the same time it is being read by the video controller.

Duron processor—The AMD Duron processor is designed for general computing, including business, home user, and portable applications. The Duron processor is available at clock speeds of 600MHz, 650MHz, and 700MHz.

DVD (Digital Versatile Disk)—A storage medium capable of storing the equivalent of 17GB of data or about 25 times more than a CD-ROM.

DVD-RAM—A special rewritable type of DVD that looks more like a big diskette than a CD-ROM. A DVD-RAM stores 4.7GB per side and is available in both single-sided and double-sided versions.

DWS (depth, width, and speed)—The memory size of a SIMM or DIMM is specified as *DWS*, which is something like "16×64-60" to indicate a DIMM module with 16 million bits available for each of its 64-bits of width with a speed of 60 ms.

For more information on:	See:
Audio/video systems	Chapter 19
BIOS	Chapter 4
Bus structures	Chapter 10
Cache	Chapter 6
Connectors and ports	Chapter 12
DVD	Chapter 9
Hard disk drives	Chapter 8
Input devices	Chapter 17
Memory	Chapter 5
Monitors	Chapter 15
Networks	Chapter 18
Printers	Chapter 16
Processors	Chapter 2
System case	Chapter 13

ECP (Enhanced Capabilities Port)—An IEEE 1284 parallel port standard that defines bi-directional, simultaneous communications. ECP systems require a specific IEEE 1284-compatible cable.

EDO (Extended Data Out) DRAM—The most commonly used form of DRAM. EDO is slightly faster than FPM (fast page mode) memory and is common in most Pentium class and later PCs with bus speeds of 75MHz or lower. See *DRAM* and *FPM*.

EEPROM (Electronically Erasable Programmable Read-Only Memory)—An EEPROM chip is commonly used as the BIOS chip on newer PC systems. EEPROMs can be updated with a process called flashing through specialized software.

Glossary

EGA (Enhanced Graphics Adapter)—A legacy video adapter standard that improved the CGA standard by increasing on screen resolution to 640 × 350 with 64 colors.

EIDE (Extended IDE) controller—Most mid- to upper-range motherboards include an EIDE connector to support multiple hard disks, CD-ROMs, DVDs, or other types of internal storage drives. The EIDE controller supports up to 4 devices with an ISA, ATA, and perhaps an ATA-33 or ultra-DMA (UDMA) interface. See *IDE*.

EISA (Extended ISA)—EISA extends the 16-bit ISA bus to 32 bits and adds bus-mastering capabilities to the expansion bus. An EISA expansion slot is backward compatible for ISA cards and will run at 8MHz for compatibility.

Emergency Repair Disk (ERD)—A floppy disk or CD-ROM used to boot and repair a PC that will not boot because of an operating system or hardware problem or driver conflict.

EMI (electromagnetic interference)—Electrical noise on a circuit caused by natural causes, such as an electrical storm; other electromechanical devices; or RFI (radio frequency interference) from other equipment nearby. See *RFI*.

Endec (encoder/decoder)—The part of a disk drive's read/write head that converts voltage pulse signals into binary data and binary data into flux transitions for recording on the media.

Enhanced DRAM (EDRAM)—EDRAM is a combination of faster SRAM (static RAM) and slower DRAM that is used for Level 2 (L2) cache. See *DRAM, Level 2 cache,* and *SRAM*.

Enhanced keyboard—A 101-key or 102-key keyboard that continues to be a standard for many new systems. The basic difference between this keyboard and the 104-key extended keyboard is the Windows functions keys added to the 104-key keyboards.

Enhanced SDRAM (ESDRAM)—ESDRAM is SDRAM with a small additional SRAM cache that lowers memory latency times and supports bus speeds up to 200MHz.

EP (Electrophotographic) process—The printing process used by virtually all laser printers. Its characteristics are the use of a laser beam to produce an electro-static charge and a dry toner to create the printed image.

EPROM (Erasable Programmable Read-Only Memory)—An EPROM can be erased and reprogrammed, which means the EPROM can be reused instead of being discarded when its contents are no longer valid. An EPROM chip has a quartz crystal window on the top of the chip that is used to erase the chip's contents using ultraviolet (UV) rays.

EPP (Enhanced Parallel Port)—A half-duplex parallel port standard that allows the printer to signal out of paper, cover open, and other error conditions. See *Half-duplex*.

Glossary

Error Correction Code (ECC)—An error detection and correction procedure built into a memory controller. ECC is able to detect up to 4-bit errors and correct 1-bit errors in data transferred to or from memory.

Error diffusion—See *Image diffusion.*

ESCD (extended system configuration data)—The part of the CMOS Setup data that holds the system resource assignments of plug-and-play devices. The ESCD also serves as a communications link between the BIOS and the operating system.

ESD (electrostatic discharge)—When a static electricity charge builds up on an object, such as your body, it will jump to any object with a reverse polarity, such as your PC. The voltage of this discharge can damage or destroy the components of the PC. You should wear an antistatic wrist strap when working inside the system case. See *Antistatic wrist strap.*

ESDI (Enhanced Small Disk Interface)—An early hard disk drive standard that was used on high-end systems from brand-name manufacturers in the late 1980s. This interface is now largely obsolete, but remains on a few high-end proprietary systems.

Expansion bus—An input/output bus architecture that interfaces adapter and controller cards inserted in the expansion slots on a motherboard. Examples of expansion buses are ISA, EISA, PCI, or VL-bus. See *Expansion slot, ISA, EISA, PCI,* and *VL-bus.*

Expansion slot—A slot on a motherboard into which an adapter or controller card is inserted. An expansion slot is unique to one or more of the expansion buses supported by the motherboard and chipset.

Extended memory—In the DOS memory management scheme, which is also used by Windows 9*x* systems, extended memory is all memory above 1MB and after the high memory area. Extended memory is used for programs and data. See *High memory area.*

External cache—Also called *secondary cache* or *Level 2 (L2) cache,* external cache is normally placed on the motherboard but can also be located inside the processor's packaging. External cache ranges from 64K to 1MB, but 256K and 512K are common cache sizes.

Exabyte (EB)—One quintillion bytes.

Extended partitions—A disk partition that can be logically divided into as many as 23 logical sub-partitions, each of which can be assigned its own drive identity, such as D:, E:, F:, etc., and used for any purpose.

Glossary

651

External drive bays—Disk drive bays that are accessible from outside the system case. See *Drive bays*.

For more information on:	See:
Audio/video systems	Chapter 19
BIOS	Chapter 4
Bus structures	Chapter 10
Cache	Chapter 6
Hard disk drives	Chapter 8
Keyboards	Chapter 17
Memory	Chapter 5
Ports and connectors	Chapter 12
Power issues	Chapter 14
Printers	Chapter 16

Fake parity—This technique is applied by some systems to avoid memory parity errors. The memory controller forces every bit count to come out correctly even or odd. Fake parity has the effect of turning off the parity checking.

Fault tolerant—Also called high-availability, fault tolerant systems include built-in mechanisms and protocols to overcome the impact of a device failure. Typically, fault tolerant systems are created to guard against the loss of a server, hard disk, power supply, network adapter, and other mission-critical components.

FDISK—A DOS command line utility that is the most commonly used utility for partitioning a hard disk drive.

Fiber Channel-Arbitrated Loop (FC-AL)—A storage device interface standard that is used primarily in large network disk arrays. The FC-AL interface has built-in data recovery and fault tolerant components. Also called the fiber channel interface.

Fiber Channel Interface—See *Fiber Channel-Arbitrated Loop*.

Fiber optic cables—Glass or plastic fibers that carry modulated pulses of light to represent digital data signals.

File server—A network server that stores and shares common network files and users' data files.

FireWire—See *IEEE 1394*.

Flash memory—Flash memory cards are credit card sized memory modules that incorporate flash memory (SRAM). A flash memory PC card is added to a portable PC to extend its working storage. PC Card flash memories are available with from 8MB to 512MB of flash memory.

Flash ROM—Another name for a BIOS chip (EEPROM) that can be upgraded with flashing. See *EEPROM* and *Flashing*.

Flashing—The process used to update an EEPROM chip through specialized software supplied by the BIOS or chip manufacturer.

Flat-panel monitor—This is a type of PC monitor that uses a flat-panel LCD display in place of a CRT (cathode ray tube). Flat-panel monitors are perfect for smaller desks, cubicles, or in places where a CRT monitor is too large.

Flat-screen monitor—A type of CRT that has a flat glass screen as opposed to the more standard curved glass screen found on the normal, everyday CRT.

FlexATX—See *MicroATX*

Floating Point Unit (FPU)—The FPU, which is also known as the math coprocessor, the numerical processing unit (NPU), or the numerical data processor (NDP), handles floating point operations for the arithmetic and logic unit (ALU) and control unit of the processor. Floating point operations involve arithmetic on numbers with decimal places, and high math operations like trigonometry and logarithms.

Flux reversal—The process used by a hard disk's read/write head to reverse its polarity back and forth to change the particle alignment of the media on a disk. See *Magnetic flux*.

FM (frequency modulation) encoding—A data encoding method used on disk storage devices that simply records binary values as different polarities. FM was popular through the late 1970s, but it is not used on newer disk drives.

Font—The style and design of the characters a printer prints, such as Times New Roman, Courier, and Ariel.

Form factor—Computer form factors define a general standard for compatibility for the system case, the motherboard, the power supply, and the placement of I/O (input/output) ports and connectors, and other factors.

FORMAT—A DOS command used to format hard disk partitions and floppy disk media for use by the operating system.

FPM (Fast Page Mode) DRAM—Also known as non-EDO DRAM, FPM memory is compatible with motherboards with bus speeds over 66MHz.

FRAM (ferroelectric RAM)—A RAM technology with the features of both DRAM and SRAM, which gives it the ability to save stored data when its power source is removed.

Front panel—In addition to providing the PC with its looks and placement of the power and reset switches, the front panel provides the user with information on the

PC's status, a means of physically securing the PC, and can be the starting point for removing the case's cover.

Full-associative cache—A caching technique that allows a memory location to be referenced from any cache line.

Full backup—Also called an archive backup, this type of data backup copies every directory, folder, file, and program from a hard disk to the backup medium and resets all archive bits.

Full duplex—A full duplex line carries data in two directions simultaneously. An example of a full-duplex line is your telephone.

Full tower— Full tower cases are the largest standard PC cases available. They offer the most expandability with three to five external drive bays, a few internal drive bays, and a high-end power supply. This style of case is popular among high-end users and for servers.

Function keys—The top row of the keyboard contains 12 function keys that can be assigned operating system and application software task to control. Some software applications makes extensive use of the function keys, such as Corel's WordPerfect, and the MS-DOS operating system.

Fusing rollers—During the laser printing process, toner is fused permanently to the page with pressure and heat by the fusing rollers. The temperature of the fusing rollers is between 165 and 180 degrees Celsius (or 330 to 350 degrees Fahrenheit). It is the fuser and not the laser that is the reason why the pages coming out of a laser printer are hot.

For more information on:	See:
BIOS	Chapter 4
Cache	Chapter 6
Connectors and ports	Chapter 12
Hard disk drives	Chapter 8
Keyboards	Chapter 17
Memory	Chapter 5
Monitors	Chapter 15
Motherboards	Chapter 1
Networks	Chapter 18
Printers	Chapter 16
Processors	Chapter 2
System case	Chapter 13

Game port—A versatile connector found on many sound, video, and multifunction cards. It is most often used for game controllers such as joysticks or game pads. This port can also be used as a MIDI interface. See *MIDI*.

Gateway—A combination of hardware and software that enables two networks using different transmission protocols to communicate and work together as a single network.

Gigabyte (GB)—A memory and storage size unit that is the equivalent of 1,073,741,824 or approximately one billion bytes.

Glidepoint mouse—A pointing device common to notebook PCs. A glidepoint mouse is a pivoting rubber-tipped device located between the G and the H keys that looks like an eraser tip. A glidepoint mouse works like a very small joystick, but acts like a mouse on the screen.

Graphics coprocessor—A supplementary and specialized processor located on the video or graphics adapter card that offloads graphic image processing from the system processor.

Gunning Transceiver Logic (GTL)—A processor standard that provides higher data speeds on lower voltages.

For more information on:	See:
Connectors and ports	Chapter 12
Hard disk drives	Chapter 8
Memory	Chapter 5
Mice	Chapter 17
Networks	Chapter 18
Processors	Chapter 2
Video cards	Chapter 11

Half-duplex—A half-duplex line carries data in two directions, but only transmits in one direction at a time. A CB (citizen's band) radio is an example of a half-duplex line —one party must wait until the other party is finished speaking.

Half-toning—Virtually the same technique used to print photographs in newspapers, where thousands of small dots of various halftone shades of gray and black are used to create the shading and solid forms of the image.

Head actuator—A component of a hard disk drive that positions the hard disk's read/write heads by extending and retracting the heads over the platters. See *Stepper motor actuator* and *Voice coil actuator*.

Glossary

Head crash—When a hard disk read/write head strikes the disk's media. A head crash can damage the media and make it unusable. Head crashes are caused by sudden power failures, something striking the PC very hard, or the PC falling.

Head disk assembly (HDA)—The HDA is the sealed unit that encloses the primary components of a hard disk drive, including the disk platters, disk spindle, and read/write heads.

Heat sink—A coated aluminum device that is attached to another device to absorb heat as a part of a cooling system. A heat sink is commonly added to Pentium processors, along with a fan.

Hertz (Hz)—A measurement that represents the number of clock or process cycles in one second. More commonly, process speeds are stated as kilohertz (KHz) or thousands of cycles per second and megahertz (MHz) or millions of cycles per second.

Hexadecimal numbers—A base sixteen number system that expresses its values with the decimal numbers 0 through 9 and the six letters A through F to represent the decimal values of 0 through 15. Hexadecimal is commonly used to express addresses in memory.

High-availability system—Systems that have been designed or engineered to be fault-tolerant and continue to operate even after device or software failures. Examples of high-availability applications are hot-swappable components and RAID implementations. See *Hot-swappable device* and *RAID*.

High-level formatting—The process used to prepare a disk media for use by the system. High-level formatting adds the logical structures, including the file allocation table (FAT) and the root directory to the disk media. See *Low-level formatting*.

High memory area—The first 64K (less 16 bytes) after the first megabyte of memory. Used to store the startup (boot) utilities. The 16 bytes that are set aside are used to hold the boot address for the processor.

High Performance Serial Bus (HPSB)—See *IEEE 1394*.

High-voltage Differential (HVD)—A SCSI signaling standard that supports a SCSI chain of up to 25 meters.

Hit ratio—The effectiveness of cache memory is expressed as a ratio of the number of cache hits to cache misses. See *Cache hit* and *Cache miss*.

Hot swappable device—A device that can be removed or inserted while the PC is running. PC Cards and USB devices are hot swappable devices. On high availability network servers, the power supplies and hard disks can be hot swappable.

Hub—A hub connects PCs, workstations, and peripheral devices to a network. A hub is commonly used on Ethernet twisted-pair networks.

For more information on:	See:
Cache	Chapter 6
Connectors and ports	Chapter 12
Expansion cards	Chapter 10
Hard disk drives	Chapter 8
Memory	Chapter 5
Networks	Chapter 18
Printers	Chapter 16
Processors	Chapter 2

IDE (Integrated Drive Electronics)—IDE devices incorporate the disk drive controller into the drive itself. IDE drives connect either directly to the motherboard or through a pass-through adapter card using the ATA (AT Attachment) interface.

IDE/ATA (Integrated Drive Electronics/AT Attachment) interface—The most popular hard disk interface on PC systems. IDE and ATA are used interchangeably for hard disk and other storage drives. The IDE/ATA interface supports up to two devices on a single channel, one of which must be configured as the master and the other the slave.

IEEE (Institute of Electrical and Electronics Engineers)—A membership organization of professional engineers that meets to establish standards for various engineering related activities, including networking, I/O interfaces, and cabling.

IEEE 1284—The standard that incorporates legacy parallel port communications standards with newer standards for bi-directional communications over a parallel port.

IEEE 1394—The standard that defines the High Performance Serial Bus (HPSB) also known as FireWire.

Image diffusion—A process used by virtually all inkjet printers to create graphic images on paper, using the difference or "error" of the actual color and what is actually printed to place the dots that form an image.

Impact printer—A printer that produces a printed image without making physical contact with the paper.

Incremental backup—A data backup that includes only those files that have been modified or added since the last full or incremental backup. An incremental backup clears the archive bit on the files copied to the backup medium.

Infrared (IR) port—A connection type that uses an invisible band of light to carry data between a peripheral device and a transceiver on the PC. IR light is just outside the light spectrum visible to humans.

Glossary

Inkjet printer—This type of printer creates text and images by spraying small droplets of very quick-drying ink through tiny nozzles (jets) on the paper. Inkjet printers, are also less expensive and usually physically smaller than most laser printers, which appeal to home and small office users.

Inline UPS—See *Online UPS*.

Insulator—A material that does not allow an electrical current to pass through it, such as rubber, wood, or glass.

Integrated circuit (IC)—A combination of electronic components, such as transistors, capacitors, and resistors, designed to fulfill some logical function. An IC can be used as a timer, counter, computer memory, or a microprocessor.

Internal cache—Also called primary cache or Level 1 (L1) cache. Internal cache is located on the CPU chip and ranges from 1K to 32K in size.

Internal drive bays—Drive bays located inside the system case that have no access from outside the chassis. These bays are designed for devices, primarily hard disk drives that have no need for an external exposure.

I/O (input/output)—Devices and services that control or manage data, the flow of data, and instructions between the PC's components are I/O devices. The primary software for I/O functions is the BIOS (Basic Input/Output System).

I/O (input/output) address—Also called an I/O port or I/O base address, an I/O address is a primary system resource assigned to all I/O devices and used by the processor to pass information, such as memory addresses, to a device, component, or service. Every device attached to a PC is assigned an I/O address.

I/O templates—Interchangeable templates that can be snapped into a PC case to provide a desired I/O port pattern.

IP (Internet Protocol) address—This is a 32-bit address that is expressed in four 8-bit octets. IP addresses are the primary addressing scheme used on networks based on the TCP/IP protocol suite, such as the Internet.

IrDA (Infrared Data Association)—An association formed by infrared device manufacturers and software developers to establish interface and operating standards.

IrDA device—Another name for an infrared device.

IrDA port—The small oval-shaped dark red plastic window built into a PC's case. IrDA ports are more common on notebook and other portable PCs.

IRQ (Interrupt Request)—An IRQ is one of the primary system resources assigned to an I/O device and is used by the device to request services from the central processing unit (CPU).

IRQ steering—The process used to map the four interrupts (PIRQs or PCI interrupt requests) assigned to each PCI (peripheral components interface) slot to a single system IRQ.

ISA (Industry Standard Architecture)—An expansion bus structure that was first used on the IBM PC AT (also referred to as the AT bus), and is still included on some newer motherboards for backward compatibility purposes. The ISA bus runs at 8 MHz on a 16-bit bus that can also support 8-bit cards.

ISDN (Integrated Services Digital Network—A broadband communications service that is implemented over standard telephone lines. There are two types of ISDN service available: BRI (Basic Rate Interface) and PRI (Primary Rate Interface). BRI is used for home or small office Internet connections and PRI is most commonly used to provide high bandwidth connections for voice and data to larger companies and telecommunications providers.

Italics—A print style that slants the typeface slightly to the right.

For more information on:	See:
Cache	Chapter 6
Connectors and ports	Chapter 12
Hard disk drives	Chapter 8
Networks	Chapter 18
Preventive maintenance	Chapter 20
Printers	Chapter 16
Processors	Chapter 2
System case	Chapter 13

Jaz drive—A proprietary high-capacity removable hard disk and disk drive manufactured by Iomega Corporation. A Jaz disk holds up to 2GB of data on a removable disk.

Joules—The measurement of how much electricity a surge suppressor can absorb before it fails and passes power through to the devices connected to it.

Joystick—A type of pointing device that is used primarily with game software on a PC. The joystick device consists of a handle connected to a pivoting mechanism that allows it to move in any direction around a center point.

Jumper—An electronic device that is used to select and set one of a range of values by placing a plug over one, two, or three pins attached to a circuit. Jumpers are commonly used to select options on motherboards, adapter cards, and some peripheral devices.

For more information on:	See:
Hard disk drives	Chapter 8
Joysticks	Chapter 17
Motherboards	Chapter 1
Power systems	Chapter 14

Keyboard—The primary input device on a PC. Alphabetic, numeric, and special characters are entered into the PC through keyboard.

Keyboard controller—The component on the motherboard (and often as a part of the chipset) that interacts with the controller located inside the keyboard, using the serial link built into the connecting cable and connector to transfer data to memory.

Kilobyte (KB)—The equivalent of 1,024 bytes, a common measurement for data transfer speeds and memory sizes on pre-Pentium PCs.

Kilohertz (KHz)—The equivalent of one thousand clock or processor cycles in one second.

For more information on:	See:
Keyboards	Chapter 17
Memories	Chapter 5
Networks	Chapter 14

Laser printer—A printer that prints a document by creating the document's image on a photosensitive drum with a focused laser beam, using what is called an electro-photographic process.

Latency—A wait time or a delay. On a hard disk, latency is a measurement in milliseconds of the time required for the disk to rotate the desired sector under the read/write heads. In memory, it is the extra time required to locate an address in memory. See *Memory latency*.

LBA (logical block address)—LBA addressing assigns each sector on the disk a logical block address. SCSI and EIDE disk drives use LBA addressing.

LCD (liquid crystal display)—A very common display type that is used in wristwatches, microwave ovens, CD players, and PC monitors. Most PC flat-panel monitors and virtually all portable computers have an LCD screen.

LCD printer—LCD printers use light shining through an LCD panel in place of the laser to condition the photosensitive drum.

Glossary

LED (light emitting diode)—An LED is an electronic component that produces light when power is applied. LEDs are used on PC cases to indicate power and hard disk status.

LED printer—A printer that uses an array of around 2,500 light-emitting diodes in place of a laser as the light source used to condition the photosensitive drum.

Letter quality (LQ) print—The highest quality a printer can produce. Letter quality characters appear to be solid without any gaps showing.

Level one (L1) cache—Cache located closest to the processor. L1 cache, which is also called primary cache and internal cache, is typically located on the processor chip.

Level two (L2) cache—Typically, L2 cache is located outside the processor on the system board, but some newer forms include it inside the processor's packaging. L2 cache is also known as secondary cache.

Line Printer—A high capacity printer used with larger systems, such as a mainframe. A line printer produces an entire line of text in one strike, is capable of printing 132 to 168 characters per line, and can print up to 1,100 lines per minute, or the equivalent of 50 pages per minute on a laser printer.

Lines per minute (lpm)—The speed rating for a line printer.

Local area network (LAN)—A LAN is two or more computers typically located in a relatively small area that are connected using a communications link for the purposes of sharing resources.

Local bus—Local bus devices are connected to a bus structure that is local to the processor through a dedicated controller that bypasses the standard bus controller. PCI and VESA (Video Electronics Standards Association) local bus, or VL-bus, are the most common of the local bus structures.

Locality of reference—This is the rule applied to caching that presumes the next data to be processed, or the next instruction to be fetched by the CPU, is the one immediately after the last data or instruction passed to the CPU.

Low-level formatting—Creates the organization structures on the disk, including the tracks and reference points for the sectors on each track. As a rule, low-level formatting should not be done outside of the factory.

Low-voltage differential (LVD)—A popular SCSI signaling method that is limited to an overall distance of only 12 meters for the entire SCSI chain.

Glossary

For more information on:	See:
Cache	Chapter 6
Hard disk drives	Chapter 8
Monitors and displays	Chapter 15
Motherboards	Chapter 1
Networks	Chapter 18
Printers	Chapter 16

MAC (media access code) address—Each network interface card (NIC) is assigned a universally unique ID code, its MAC address, when it is manufactured. A MAC address is a 48-bit address, expressed as 12 hexadecimal digits that is used for the physical address of each network node. A MAC address is usually something like 01 40 00 0A 23 4D.

Mainboard—See *Motherboard.*

Master disk drive—IDE/ATA disk drives must be configured as either a master or a slave on an ATA channel. Master refers to disk drive 0 and slave refers to disk drive 1. A master disk drive is not a supervisory device.

Megabyte (MB)—The equivalent of 1,048,576 bytes, megabytes are used as a measurement of memory and storage capacities on a PC.

Megahertz (MHz)—The equivalent of one million processor or clock cycles in one second.

Magnetic flux—The process used to record data on a disk's media. Flux refers to the process used to align the particles in a single magnetic field to a single direction. The read/write head uses a series of flux reversals to alter the particles in a bit cell, or a cluster of magnetic particles that represents a single binary digit (bit). See *Flux reversal.*

Magneto-Optical (MO) disks—More commonly known as CD-RW (read/write) disks, a MO disk can be written to, read, modified, and written to again.

Magneto-Resistive (MR) head—This type of hard disk head is used in most 3.5-inch disk drives with capacity over 1GB for the read head. Hard disks with MR read heads typically have a thin film head for writing data. See *Thin film head.*

Material Safety Data Sheet (MSDS)—Every chemical product that has any possible hazard has an MSDS prepared and readily available. Typically, information on how to obtain an MSDS for a product is included on the product's label.

Memory—There are two types of memory used in a PC: read-only memory (ROM) and random access memory (RAM), each with its own characteristics. See *ROM* and *RAM.*

Glossary

Memory bank—On a PC motherboard, memory is installed in groupings that match the data bus in width. Each of these groupings is a memory bank. In order for the PC to use the memory in a memory bank, it must be completely filled.

Memory cache—This memory bank serves as a holding area between main memory and the processor. It is slower than the processor, but much faster than main memory. Memory cache consists of two parts: A Level 1 (L1) cache, which is located on the CPU chip, and a Level 2 cache (L2) that serves as a staging area to L1 cache. Memory cache is typically SRAM. See *Level 1 cache*, *Level 2 cache*, and *SRAM*.

Memory controller—The logic circuit that controls the movement and storage of data to and from system memory (RAM). Requests from other devices for access to memory are processed by the memory controller, which also includes the routines for parity checking and ECC (error correcting code). See *Parity* and *ECC*.

Memory Expansion Card (MEC)—A daughter board that can hold up to 16GB of additional RAM (usually SDRAM) and mount in a standard DIMM slot.

Memory latency—The time required to find the row, column, and starting cell of data in memory. Because it takes longer for the first cell than the next one, two, or three cells, the additional time is measured as latency.

Memory-mapped I/O—Each I/O device is assigned an I/O address system resource to which it is mapped in memory. Because of the mapping, when a device contacts the processor with an IRQ, the processor knows where in memory the device's I/O buffer is located.

Memory parity—See *Parity*.

Metal-In-Gap (MIG) head—This type of hard disk read/write head adds metal to the leading and trailing edges of the head gap. This allows the head to ignore nearby fields and focus only on the fields beneath the head.

Metallic oxide varistor (MOV)—A circuit included in a surge suppressor that reacts to over-voltage situations and diverts the power to a grounding circuit.

Metropolitan area network (MAN)—A variation of a WAN that interconnects LANs and PCs within a specific geographical area, such as a city or a cluster of campuses or office parks.

MFM (modified frequency modulation)—The encoding method used on floppy disks. MFM stores twice as much data in the same number of flux transitions as the FM encoding method. See *FM encoding*.

Micro-AT form factor—A variation of the AT and Baby AT form factor. Micro-AT motherboards fit into the mounting hardware of an AT or Baby AT case but are nearly half the size of the Baby AT motherboard.

Glossary

MicroATX—The MicroATX and its virtual twin, the FlexATX, form factor defines a smaller version of the ATX motherboard but does not define a case form factor. Both form factors are intended for mass market and home PCs.

Microprocessor—A multi-function integrated circuit that is also called the central processing unit (CPU) or system processor.

Mid tower case—A mid tower case is a slightly shorter version of the full tower case.

MIDI (Musical Instrument Digital Interface) port—Using a special cable, a MIDI port is connected to an external MIDI device to send and receive MIDI data. This port is typically located on the sound card or is an alternative configuration for the game port. See *Game port*.

Midi tower case—A midi tower case is smaller than a mid tower and larger than a mini tower.

Mini DIN connector—See *PS/2 connector*.

Mini tower case—This is currently the most popular case. It provides slightly more expansion capacity than desktop cases, will work for small servers, and is small enough to sit on a desktop next to the monitor.

Mip mapping—This graphics technique improves the appearance of textures by grouping pixels into mip-maps that cluster four texels (texture elements) together to remove jagged edges between pixels (picture elements) and texels.

MMX (multimedia extensions)—The additional instructions added to a processor to handle the generation of multimedia audio/visual objects and graphic image reproduction. The Pentium MMX processor included a set of 57 such instructions.

Modem (modulator/demodulator)—This device allows you to connect to and communicate with other computers over the public telephone network. A modem can be installed inside the PC in an expansion slot or connected externally through a serial or USB port.

Monochrome Display Adapter (MDA)—MDA is a legacy video adapter standard that displays only text on a monochrome (one color) monitor.

Monochrome Graphics Adapter (MGA)—MGA combined graphics and text on a monochrome monitor.

MOSFET (Metal Oxide Semiconductor Field Effect Transistor)—A transistor that uses a layer of oxide as insulation between its conducting channel and gate terminal.

Motherboard—A large printed circuit board that is home to many of the essential parts of the computer, including the microprocessor, chipset, system memory (RAM), cache memory, bus structures, and I/O ports.

Mouse—The standard pointing device on virtually all PCs (including the Apple Macintosh and other brands as well). The mouse translates the movement of the user's hand to move a screen point around the display to highlight, select, open, and execute objects on the PC.

MP2—MPEG-1 Layer 2 or MP2 is an earlier MPEG compression format that produces lower quality results than MP3. MP2 files can be played back with an MP3 player.

MP3—MPEG-1 Layer 3 or MP3 is an audio compression standard that reduces the size of WAV (Windows Audio/Video) files for portability and storage.

MPEG (Moving Picture Experts Group)—A standard for multimedia data compression and decompression.

MTBF (Mean Time Before Failure)—An estimate of how long a component will operate before it fails, based on the manufacturer's testing. A larger MTBF is better.

For more information on:	See:
Audio/visual systems	Chapter 19
Cache	Chapter 6
CD-ROM and DVD	Chapter 9
Connectors and ports	Chapter 12
Hard disk drives	Chapter 8
Memory	Chapter 5
Mice	Chapter 17
Motherboards	Chapter 1
Networks	Chapter 18
Preventive maintenance	Chapter 20
Processors	Chapter 2
System case	Chapter 13
Video cards	Chapter 11

N-way set associative cache—A caching approach that divides the memory cache into sets with N (a number of) cache lines each, typically 2, 4, 8, or more.

Natural keyboard—A keyboard designed to relieve repetitive stress injuries to users' hands and wrists These popular keyboards are also called ergonomic keyboards.

Near letter quality (NLQ)—NLQ is somewhere between letter quality and draft quality print. Inkjets and dot matrix printers that print at 150 DPI (dots per inch) use NLQ as their default type quality.

NIC (network interface card)—The PC connects to a network through a NIC. The NIC is installed in an expansion slot inside the PC and attaches the PC to the network cabling. A NIC contains a transceiver (transmitter/receiver) that serves as the intermediary between the PC and the network media and operating system.

NLX—The NLX form factor, which is also called Slimline form factor, is a popular device for mass-produced desktop systems. The NLX motherboard is distinctive because of its use of a daughterboard for the expansion bus.

Node—A node is any addressable device on a network, including workstations, peripheral devices, and network connectivity devices. A workstation is a node, but not all nodes are workstations. Some nodes are printers, routers, modems, etc.

Non-blocking cache—This caching technique, which is commonly used for L2 cache on several Pentium processors, sets aside requests for data not in cache to service other data requests while the missing data is transferred from memory.

Non-impact printers—Printers that do not make contact with the paper and use non-impact methods to produce a document. Laser printers, thermal printers, and inkjet printers are non-impact printers. See *Impact printers*.

North Bridge—A two-chip chipset consists of North Bridge and a South Bridge chips. The North Bridge chip, which is the larger of the two chips, contains the major bus circuits that support and control main memory, cache memory, and the PCI bus.

NVRAM (nonvolatile RAM)—See *CMOS*.

Nybble—A 4-bit binary word that can hold one hexadecimal digit, which is the binary equivalent of the decimal values 0 thorugh 15.

For more information on:	See:
Cache	Chapter 6
Chipsets	Chapter 3
Connectors and ports	Chapter 12
Keyboards	Chapter 17
Motherboards	Chapter 1
Networks	Chapter 18

Octet—An 8-bit segment of an IP (Internet Protocol) address.

Online UPS (uninterruptible power supply)—Also called an inline UPS. An online UPS provides a PC with its AC power from its battery, which is constantly being recharged by the AC power coming into the UPS. Should the power fail, an online UPS requires no switchover and continues to supply power from its battery until the power is restored or the battery is drained.

Optical mouse—An optical mouse has no moving parts. The mechanical devices (balls, rollers, and wheels) of the optomechanical mouse are replaced with an optical scanning system that detects the movement of the mouse over virtually any surface.

Optomechanical mouse—The type of mouse that uses light-emitting diodes (LEDs) to sense mouse movement. This is the most commonly used mouse.

Ordered dithering—This is a graphic image technique that creates a smooth transition from one color to another by evenly spacing pixels of each color along the common edge of the two colors. This method, which is faster to create than image diffusion, is used on professional-level graphics that require more accurate color representations.

Overclocking—Running a processor at a speed higher than that recommended by the manufacturer. This can be done by changing a jumper on the motherboard or by changing the clock crystal.

Oxide media—The media used on older hard disk drives. The oxide medium is a relatively soft material that is easily damaged by a head crash. The primary ingredient in oxide media is ferrous oxide (iron rust).

For more information on:	See:
Hard disks	Chapter 8
Mice	Chapter 17
Monitors	Chapter 15
Printers	Chapter 16
Power systems	Chapter 14

Pages per minute (PPM)—A measurement used to rate the speed for laser, inkjet, and other printers that print an entire page in one pass through the printer.

Palmtop computer—A small computer that literally fits on the palm of your hand . Typically, a palmtop runs a specialized operating system, such as Windows CE, has a small standard keyboard, or uses a pen-based screen for input, and a LCD screen.

Parallel data—Parallel data is transmitted with multiple bits being sent over a cable or set of wires at the same time (in parallel). In general, parallel data transmits one character at a time with the character's 8 bits being sent together. See *Serial data*.

Parallel port—A connection, typically a DB-25 female connector, that is used to connect a printer or other parallel device to a PC. See *IEEE 1284*.

Parameter RAM (PRAM)—This is the Macintosh computer equivalent of CMOS memory on a PC. PRAM is used to store the internal configuration information, the date and time, and other system-wide parameters that need to be saved between system restarts.

Glossary

Parity—An error-checking technique applied to data transmission that uses an extra bit on each character to setup either an even (even parity) or odd (odd parity) number of 1 bits. Odd-parity validates that the number of 1 bits in the byte is an odd-number and even-parity validates that the number of 1 bits is an even number.

Parity bit—The extra bit added by parity checking systems to force the count of 1 bits to an even or odd number.

Parity error—The error that results when the parity bits of a character do not have the appropriate number of bits.

Partition—A logical division of a hard disk created to reduce the effective size of the hard disk, to hold one or more operating systems, or to segregate one type of data from another. Two types of partitions can be created: a primary partition and an extended partition. A hard disk is typically partitioned with the DOS FDISK command. Before a partition can be used it must be formatted. See *FDISK* and *FORMAT*.

Passive backplane—This style of motherboard is strictly a receiver card. It has open slots into which a processor card that contains a CPU and its support chips, and I/O cards that provide bus and device interfaces are inserted.

Passive matrix LCD—This type of LCD screen uses pixels, like a CRT, instead of the electrodes used in other types of LCDs.

PC Card—See *PCMCIA*.

PCI (Peripheral Component Interconnect)—The PCI bus first appeared with the Pentium processor. It is now the standard for motherboard expansion buses; most motherboards include three or four white PCI slots. PCI supports full Plug-And-Play capability.

PCI bridge—This chipset-based device logically connects the PCI expansion bus on the motherboard to the processor and other non-PCI devices.

PCMCIA (Personal Computer Memory Card International Association)—An interface developed by the standards organization with the same name. PCMCIA cards (PC Cards) use a 68-pin socket that connects directly to the computer's expansion bus.

PCMCIA Type 1 slot—This slot and card is 3.3 millimeters (mm) thick (top to bottom) and is used to add additional RAM and flash memory. Type 1 slots are most common on very small computers, such as palmtops.

PCMCIA Type 2 slot—This slot and card is 5mm thick and its cards are typically able to perform I/O functions, such as modems and network adapter cards.

PCMCIA Type 3 slot—This slot is 10.5mm thick and used mainly for add-in hard drives and wireless network devices.

PC XT form factor—The form factor used on IBM's original PCs (IBM PC and PC XT) that included a heavy-gauge steel, U-shaped case and a power supply with 130 watts located at the rear of the case.

Peer-based network—See *Peer-to-peer network*.

Peer-to-peer network—Two or more computers connected directly to one another for the sole purpose of directly sharing data and hardware resources. The user of each computer controls security and sharing.

Pen-based system—A device or computer that accepts input entered with a stylus or pen on a flexible screen. See *Personal digital assistant*.

Personal digital assistant (PDA)—A small handheld computer that is typically pen-based and can be used as a personal organizer that includes name and addresses, appointments, task lists, email, and similar functions.

Petabyte (PB)—The equivalent of one quadrillion bytes.

Photomultiplier Tube (PMT) scanner—This type of scanner uses a vacuum tube to convert light reflected from an image into an amplified electrical signal. PMT scanners are typically more expensive and more difficult to use than CCD scanners, which are more common. See *charge-coupled device (CCD) scanner*.

Piezoelectric—An inkjet process that uses piezoelectric crystals to control the flow of ink from the printhead nozzles.

Pin grid array (PGA)—A standard processor packaging style.

Pipelined burst (PLB)—A synchronous memory transfer technique used in caching that transfers the blocks of a memory burst in an overlapping way so they are partially transferred at the same time.

Platter—One of the primary components of a hard disk drive on which data is recorded. Hard disk platters are made from primary two materials: aluminum alloy and a glass-ceramic composite and coated with magnetic media.

Plug and Play (PnP)—PnP automatically detects and configures system resource assignments for new PC hardware. To work effectively, it must be supported by the PC's operating system, the chipset, and the BIOS.

POST (Power On Self Test)—This BIOS-based utility is run each time a PC is started from a powered off state. The primary function of the POST is to check that the essential components of the PC are in place and working and to verify the configuration stored in the CMOS data. The POST signals any error found with beep codes and error codes. See *Beep codes* and *POST error codes*.

POST error codes—Should an essential component of the PC not be functioning properly during the POST process, the POST routine displays an error code to identify the source of the problem. POST error codes are segmented to assign a block of one hundred codes to particular devices, for example: the floppy disk is assigned the 600 series. Table G.1 lists a few of the common POST error codes.

Table G.1   Common POST Error Codes

Error Code Series	Component Group
100	Motherboard
200	Memory
300	Keyboard
400	Parallel ports (LPT)
600	Floppy disk controller
700	Math coprocessor/FPU
1100	Serial ports (COM)
1200	Serial ports (COM)
1700	Hard disk drive and controller
2400	Video adapter
8600	Mouse/Pointing Device

POTS—The Plain Old Telephone System. See *PSTN*.

POWER_GOOD (Pwr_OK) signal—The signal sent to the motherboard after the power supply performs its power up testing when a PC is started from a powered off state. This signal indicates to the motherboard that it can startup the PC.

Power supply—The power supply rectifies (converts) AC power into DC power for use by the PC's internal electronics. It also houses and powers the main system cooling fan.

Power surge—The voltage of the electrical supply is raised above normal levels for an extended period in this overvoltage situation.

Primary cache—See *Internal cache*.

Primary corona—This laser printer component, which is also called the main corona or the primary grid, forms an electrical field that uniformly charges the photosensitive drum to a -600V during the conditioning phase.

Primary partition—A primary partition is created to hold an operating system and is typically the partition used to boot the PC. A hard disk can be divided into as many as 4 primary partitions, but only one primary partition can be active (set as the boot partition) at a time.

Primary storage—The PC's main memory, or RAM, that temporarily stores data and programs while being used by the system.

Print server—A network server that manages network printers, print queues, and the printing of user documents.

Pentium processor—A 32-bit multitasking microprocessor housed in a PGA (pin grid array) package that mounts with 273 to 321 pins, depending on its version. The Pentium processor includes two internal 8K caches and superscalar pipelining, which can execute two instructions in the same clock cycle. This processor uses a 64-bit internal bus, a variety of high-speed bus, and cache controllers that enhance its performance. The Pentium models run at clock speeds of 50 to 200 MHz.

Pentium MMX processor—A Pentium MMX processor has 57 additional instructions added to its instruction set to provide improved multimedia performance. See *MMX*.

Pentium Pro processor—The Pentium Pro, which was developed for use in servers and high-end workstations, was released with models running 150MHz to 200MHz. The Pentium Pro, which also supports SMP multiprocessing, is better at running 32-bit operating systems than a Pentium and is able to address 64GB of memory. The Pentium Pro does not include MMX instructions. See *SMP*.

Pentium II processor—The Pentium II, is essentially a Pentium Pro with MMX instructions added. It supports clock speeds of 233 MHz to 400 MHz, uses a 66MHz system bus, and is packaged in SECC.

Pentium III processor—The Pentium III processor adds SSE multimedia instructions to the Pentium II and runs at clock speeds over 1GHz. The Pentium III architecture is also used on the Xeon processors. See *SSE* and *Xeon*.

Pentium 4 processor—The Pentium 4 processor is the latest processor from Intel. It was introduced in late 2000 with clock speeds of 1.4 and 1.5 GHz and a 400MHz system bus, as well as many new and faster technologies.

Programmable interrupt controller (PIC)—Circuits integrated into the PC's chipset that control the IRQ (interrupt request) lines on the expansion bus.

PROM (Programmable Read-Only Memory)—A PROM is a ROM chip that can be programmed with data or instructions using a ROM burner or ROM programmer. PROM chips are used for ROM BIOS on older PCs.

Programmed I/O (PIO)—This is the data transfer protocol used by nearly all older disk drives that relied on the PC's processor to execute the instructions needed to move data from the disk to the PC's memory.

Glossary

PS/2 connector—A 6-pin mini DIN connector used to connect keyboards and mice to a PC. First introduced on the IBM PS/2 PCs, it is now the standard connector for mice and keyboards on virtually all PCs.

PSTN (Public Switched Telephone Network)—The public telephone network that connects your home or office to the switching system used to connect telephone calls anywhere in the world.

For more information on:	See:
Audio/visual systems	Chapter 19
BIOS and CMOS	Chapter 4
Cache	Chapter 6
Connectors and ports	Chapter 12
Hard disk drives	Chapter 8
Memory	Chapter 5
Monitors and displays	Chapter 15
Motherboards	Chapter 1
Networks	Chapter 18
Power supply and power issues	Chapter 14
Printers	Chapter 16
Processors	Chapter 2

Queue—A sequence of events or files waiting for services. For example, print files waiting to be sent to the printer wait in the print queue.

RA (Real Audio) files—Files with an RA or RAM (Real Audio Media) file extension contain streaming audio or media data stored in a proprietary format developed by Real Networks. Real Audio files require a dedicated Real Audio player or browser plug-in for playback.

Rackmount case—A case design used for special purpose or networking applications. Rackmount cases are attached to the rails of a rackmount cabinet or a rackmount stand or rack.

Radio frequency interference—See *RFI*.

RAID—A high-availability technique used to create a fault-tolerant environment that protects the data stored on disk from the failure of a disk drive. RAID systems store mirrored copies of data files on separate disks or spread data over several disk drives in "stripes." RAID technology is not frequently implemented on standalone PCs or small networks. RAID, usually because of its cost and overhead, is reserved for larger enterprise level networks.

RAID 0 (data striping)—Data is divided into stripes and distributed across the RAID disk drives. Data striping does not provide redundancy, but it does spread the risk of losing data due to a disk drive failure. If a disk drive fails, the data stripes written to it are lost.

RAID 0+1 (data striping and mirroring)—also known as RAID 01, this RAID implementation doubles the number of disk drives required, but adds redundancy to data striping.

RAID 1 (data mirroring)—Data mirroring creates a duplicate and redundant copy of a disk drive and the files stored on it. Although it doubles the amount of disk space needed to store the same data, RAID 1 is very popular because it provides complete data redundancy.

RAID 1+0 (data mirroring plus striping)—also known as RAID 10, this RAID implementation adds fault tolerance to mirroring by striping the mirrored data across additional hard disk drives.

RAID 3 (data striping with fault tolerance)—RAID 3 adds parity and error correction code (ECC) to RAID 0 to provide some fault tolerance. The parity information is maintained on a separate disk and can be used to reconstruct the data should a hard disk drive fail. RAID 3 uses at least three hard disk drives—two for the data stripes and one for the parity information.

RAID 5 (data striping with fault tolerance)—RAID 5 uses at least three hard disks to store data stripes on all disk drives along with data stripes of parity information. This adds fault tolerance to all aspects of the RAID configuration.

RAM (random access memory)—This is the type of memory used for system and video memory. RAM is volatile memory, which means that it requires a constant power source to retain its contents. Should the power source be lost, so is anything stored in RAM. See also *DRAM*.

RAMDAC (RAM digital-to-analog converter)—This device converts digital video instructions into analog signals that are used by a CRT (cathode ray tube) to generate the monitor's display. The RAMDAC, which is typically located on the video adapter, reads data from the video memory, converts it to an analog signal wave, and then sends it the monitor.

Random access memory—See *RAM*.

Raster graphics—also known as bit-mapped graphics, a raster graphic is a two-dimensional array of pixels drawn by assigning a value to each X (horizontal) and Y (vertical) pixel position on the screen. This is the most common technique used to create the images on PC monitors.

Glossary

Raster Image Processor (RIP)—A component in a printer's internal control circuitry that translates print commands into the cells to create an image. The RIP computes the position of each cell and dot on the page, creates an image of the document in the printer's memory, and directs the laser to create the dot pattern on the print drum.

Read-only memory (ROM)—ROM cannot be modified, which is why it is called read-only memory. ROM is nonvolatile, which means that its contents are safely held even after a power source is removed. The BIOS is stored on a ROM chip.

Read/write heads—A hard disk has a read/write head for each side of a platter. The hard disk's read/write heads are constructed with a magnetic core wrapped by one or more electrical wires through which an electrical current is passed in one direction or the other to change the polarity of the magnetic field emanating from the core. As the read/write head passes over the magnetic media, the polarity of the core is changed as needed to change the value stored in a certain location on the platter's magnetic media.

Real Audio—See *RA files*.

Real-time clock (RTC)—The RTC holds the date and time on the PC, which is displayed on the monitor and is used to date-stamp file activities. This should not be confused with the system clock, which provides the timing signal for the processor and other devices.

Repeater—A networking device used to extend the maximum segment length of network cabling and to eliminate attenuation (the loss of signal strength in the cable). A repeater regenerates the signal to facilitate the signal reaching its destination.

Rectification—The process of converting AC power to DC power. Rectification is the primary task of the PC's power supply.

Red Book standard—This is the common name for the standard that defines CD-DA (compact disk–digital audio), including the number and spacing of tracks on the disk, the number of minutes of contents, the data transfer (playback) rate, the error correction methods used to correct for minor sound errors, the format of the digital audio, and the media's size. The Red Book standard is still used for audio CDs.

Redundant Array of Independent (or Inexpensive) Disks—See *RAID*.

Refresh rate—The number of times per second a monitor's screen is entirely redrawn. The refresh rate of a video adapter indicates the number of times per second the data used to refresh the display is sent to the monitor.

Register—The processor includes a number of holding areas and buffers, called registers, which are used to temporarily hold data, addresses, and instructions being passed in and out of the CPU.

Release-button case—A case design, common on Compaq desktop models, which is removed by pressing springed release buttons located on the front or rear of the PC. After pressing the release buttons, the cover, which includes the front, rear, top, and sides of the cover, lifts straight off the case.

Rendering—The process used by the graphics card to generate the instructions that will be used by the monitor to draw the screen, creating the triangles and filling in those triangles with appropriate textures.

Resolution—The number of pixels used to generate a visual image on a display or printer. A monitor using 640×480 resolution uses 307,200 pixels to create the image it displays. The same monitor set to display with a resolution of 1,280×960 would use 1,228,800 pixels and in the same display space.

RFI (radio frequency interference)—High-frequency electromagnetic waves that are generated from virtually every form of electronic device.

RIP—See *Raster Image Processor*.

RLL (run length limited)—The most commonly used encoding method on hard disk drives, RLL achieves higher data density than MFM. RLL also supports data compression techniques, and virtually all current disk drives (IDE/ATA, SCSI, and so on) use some form of RLL encoding.

ROM—See *Read-only memory*.

ROM BIOS—The chip on which the system BIOS is stored. On older systems, the ROM BIOS cannot be upgraded without replacing the entire ROM chip, but on newer systems, the ROM is actually an EEPROM that can be upgraded through flashing.

ROM shadowing—A process that copies the contents of the ROM BIOS into memory, which allows the computer to ignore the ROM and work directly with the much faster RAM.

Router—A networking device used to send network messages across the network using the most efficient path available based on the destination of the message.

RS-232—RS-232 means "reference standard 232," which is a standard created by the IEEE for communications lines, ports, and connectors used to transmit standard serial data communications.

RTC—See *Real-time clock*.

Run length limited—See *RLL*.

For more information on:	See:
Audio/visual systems	Chapter 19
BIOS	Chapter 4
CD-ROM and DVD	Chapter 9
Chipset	Chapter 3
Connectors and ports	Chapter 12
Hard disk drives	Chapter 8
Memory	Chapter 5
Monitors	Chapter 15
Networks	Chapter 18
Power supply	Chapter 14
Printers	Chapter 16
Processors	Chapter 2
System case	Chapter 13

Sampling—The process used to convert analog sound into a digital format. Sampling takes a snapshot (sample) of the sound at different points along a sound wave, and creates a binary description. The sampling rate indicates how many samples are taken in a second of sound. The standard digital audio sampling rate is 44.1KHz, or 44,100 samples per second. A 16-bit sample size indicates that 16-bits are used to describe the sound in a digital format.

SCA—See *Single connector attachment.*

Scalable fonts—Fonts that can be adjusted to different point sizes or print styles. Scalable fonts are defined in a base font that outlines the standard font typeface and design. A mathematical formula is used to generate the character to other point sizes or print styles. TrueType and PostScript fonts are examples of scalable fonts.

Scan line interleaving (SLI)—This interface enables two 3D graphics acceleration cards to share the load of generating the displayed image by dividing the screen between the two cards.

Screen saver—Software that keeps the monitor display changing. On older systems, a screen saver was needed to prevent the image from burning into the phosphor of the CRT. Modern color monitors do not require screen savers, and screen savers are primarily for entertainment on these systems.

Screwless cases—The case cover of a screwless case is locked into place typically with a single locking panel (usually the front panel). Removing the locking panel unlocks the remaining panels of the case, which can then be removed without removing screws or having to use of tools.

SCSI (small computer systems interface)—An interface standard that connects a wide range of peripheral devices, including hard disks, tape drives, optical drives, CD-ROMs, and disk arrays, on a common interface bus. The common interface is called a SCSI bus or SCSI chain.

SCSI bus—The SCSI bus attaches peripheral devices to a PC through a dedicated host adapter card that supports a chain of devices on a dedicated interface structure. A SCSI bus can be either or both internal and external on a PC. A SCSI host adapter is added to the PC through an expansion slot, typically a PCI slot. See also *SCSI*.

SCSI host adapter—An expansion card, typically added to a PCI slot, that serves as the device controller for the SCSI devices attached to the internal and external SCSI bus.

SCSI ID—Each device on a SCSI bus is assigned a unique SCSI device ID number. Typically, the host adapter is device 7 and a bootable SCSI hard disk is device 0.

SDRAM—See *Synchronous DRAM*.

SECC (single edge contact cartridge)—also known as a single edge connect, this is the packaging type used to combine the CPU and external cache into a single package. This type of packaging has been used for all Intel processors beginning with the Pentium II. SECC modules plug into a slot-style socket (see Slot 1 and Slot 2) on the motherboard.

Secondary storage—The hard disk and floppy disk are secondary storage devices on a PC. Primary storage is main memory. Secondary storage is permanent storage that holds data, programs, and other objects even after the power goes off.

Sectors—The tracks on hard disks and floppy disks are divided into addressable pieces, called sectors. A sector is 512 bytes in length. A hard disk has from 100 to 300 sectors per track, and a floppy disk has from 9 to 18 sectors per track.

Seek Time—The time in milliseconds (ms) required for the head actuator to move the read/write heads from one track to the next. Hard disk drives have an average seek time between 8 and 14 ms.

Semiconductor—Material that is neither a conductor nor an insulator, but can be chemically altered to be either one.

SEPP (single edge processor package)—The packaging used on the Celeron processor.

Serial data—Serial data is transmitted one bit at a time, typically in an asynchronous mode. In contrast, see *Parallel data*.

Glossary

Serial port—A port located on the motherboard or added via an expansion card that supports serial data transmissions. See *Serial data*.

Server—A network computer that services requests from network clients (workstations and nodes) for data files, printing, communications, and other services. A server can perform a single service, as in the case of a file server, print server, application server, Web server, and so on, or a server can become a client that must request services it does not provide itself.

Server-based network—See *Client/server network*.

Servo systems—Special data, called gray code, is stored on a disk during manufacturing that helps position the read/write heads precisely over a specific location on the disk. The gray code, which comprises the servo system on the disk, identifies each track and each sector on the disk.

SGRAM—See *Synchronous graphics RAM*.

Shadow mask—A very fine screen mounted between the electron gun and the phosphor pixels on a monitor's screen. The shadow mask has openings that permit each electron beam to hit only where it should. Any phosphor material in its shadow is masked and will not be illuminated. The holes in the mask are aligned to match perfectly with the pixels on the screen.

Shadow RAM—RAM used to hold 32-bit drivers that are loaded during system startup to bypass the 16-bit ROM drivers of the BIOS.

Shielded twisted-pair (STP) wire—Networking cable consisting of one or more pairs of copper wiring that is wrapped in a metal sheathing to help eliminate problems from external interference. Each pair is twisted one wire around the other to help cut down problems from interference as well.

SIMD (single instruction stream–multiple data stream)—A multiprocessing architecture that can perform a single operation on multiple sets of data. One of the processors is used as a master to perform control logic and the other processors are slaves that execute the same instruction, but each on a different data set.

SIMM (single inline memory module)—A memory module that consists of DRAM chips in special packaging (small outline J-lead [SOJ] or thin, small outline package [TSOP]) soldered on a small circuit board with either a 30- or 72-pin edge connector. The capacity of a SIMM can range from 1 to 128MB, and chips are mounted on either one or both sides of the board.

Simplex—A simplex line can communicate in only one-direction. A speaker wire is an example of a simplex communications line.

Single connector attachment (SCA)—A connector used with SCSI systems that simplifies hard drive connections for hot-swappable hard disk drives. SCA connectors include both data and power connections.

Single-ended (SE) voltage differential—A SCSI signaling standard that supports a terminated SCSI bus chain not longer than 3 to 6 meters.

Single inline memory module—See *SIMM*.

Single SIMD Extension—See *SSE*.

Single edge contact cartridge—See *SECC*.

Single edge processor package—See *SEPP*.

Slave disk drive—On an IDE/ATA interface, disk drives must be designated as either a master or a slave. The slave drive is not subordinate to the master, but is designated as disk drive 1, and the master disk drive is designated as disk drive 0.

SLI—See *Scan line interleaving*.

Slot 1 (SC-242 connector)—The Slot 1 processor socket is a proprietary Intel 242-pin processor mounting slot that supports Celeron SEPP, Pentium II SECC, and Pentium II and III SECC2 packages.

Slot 2 (SC-330 connector)—An Intel processor slot for Pentium II Xeon and Pentium III Xeon processors that enhances SMP support.

Slot A—The Slot A processor socket is used by AMD Athlon processors. It is physically the same as a Slot 1 connector but has incompatible pinouts.

Small computer system interface—See *SCSI*.

Small outline DIMM (SODIMM)—A special type of DIMM for use in portable devices. This module is thinner and smaller overall than a standard DIMM and has only 144 pins. See *DIMM*.

Small outline J-lead (SOJ)—A smaller and lower profile form of DRAM that is used to add memory chips to a SIMM or DIMM. See *SIMM*, *DIMM*, and *DRAM*.

SMM—See *System management mode*.

SMP (Symmetric Multiprocessing)—Multiprocessing environments in which multiple processors share the same memory. SMP systems can support from 2 to 32 processors, but if one processor fails, the entire SMP system fails.

Socket 0—A 168-pin in-line-layout processor connector for 5V 486DX processors.

Socket 1—A 169-pin in-line-layout processor connector for 5V 486DX and 486SX processors.

Glossary

Socket 2—A 238-pin in-line-layout processor connector for 5V 486DX, 486SX, and 486DX2 processors.

Socket 3—A 237-pin in-line-layout processor connector supporting 3V and 5V 486DX, 486SX, 486DX2, and 486DX4 processors.

Socket 4—A 273-pin in-line-layout processor connector supporting 5V Pentium 60 and Pentium 66 processors

Socket 5—A 320-pin staggered-layout connector supporting early 3V Pentium processors

Socket 6—A 235-pin in-line-layout processor connector for 3V 486DX4 processors.

Socket 7—A 321-pin staggered-format socket created to support later Pentium processors.

Super 7 Socket—An extension of the Socket 7 design to support 100MHz bus speeds on AMD K6-2 and K6-3.

Socket 8—A 386-pin staggered ZIF-socket format for the Pentium Pro processor.

Socket 370—The original Celeron main board connection. This supported the early Celerons in the plastic pin grid assembly (PPGA) format.

SODIMM—See *Small outline DIMM*.

Socket 423—Like its name implies, this socket is used as the mounting for the 423-pin Pentium 4 PGA form.

Sound Blaster—One of the first sound cards to gain widespread use in PCs was the Sound Blaster from Creative Labs. It established the standard for sound cards and sound reproduction from PC manufacturers and multimedia publishers.

South Bridge—The South Bridge chip in a chipset includes controllers for peripheral devices and those controllers that are not one of the PC's basic functions, such as the EIDE controller and serial port controllers.

Spike—An electrical spike is an unexpected, short-duration, high-voltage event on an AC power line. A spike can be caused by a variety of events, such as lightning strikes, generator switchovers, power pole incidents (a car hitting one, for example), or large electrical motors on the same power source.

SPP—See *Standard parallel port*.

SRAM (Static RAM)—Dynamic RAM requires constant refreshing to retain its contents, but static RAM does not need to be refreshed. SRAM is also faster than DRAM, but it is more expensive and requires more space to store the same data as DRAM. The primary use for SRAM is for cache memory.

SSE (Single SIMD Extension)—SSE is a group of 70 new instructions that are added to the Pentium III to improve 3D graphics, including floating point instructions for 3D geometry calculations. SSE is the second set of multimedia instructions added to the Pentium processors. The first was the MMX set. See also *MMX*.

SSE2—A set of 144 new multimedia instructions added to the Pentium 4 processor.

ST506/412 interface—This was the first widely adopted disk interface standard. It was used for Seagate Technologies' 5MB (ST506) and 10MB (ST412) disk drives, and was universally adopted because it used standard cables to connect any compatible drive to a ST506/412 adapter. This interface is now obsolete, except in older systems still in use.

Standard parallel port (SPP)—A standard that defines a simplex parallel port that allows data to travel only from the computer to the printer.

Standby UPS—This type of UPS generally does nothing more than provide a battery backup to the PC connected to it as a safeguard against a power failure (blackout) or a low-voltage event (brownout).

Standoffs—Standoffs are used inside the system case to mount the motherboard. Two types of standoffs in use are plastic and metal standoffs, which are also called spacers, risers, and sliders.

Stepper motor—An electrical motor that moves in a series of steps. Hard disk drives use a stepper motor to move the read/write head actuator.

STP—See *Shielded twisted pair wire*.

Stripe pitch—This measurement, which compares to dot pitch on shadow mask monitors, is used on aperture grill monitors to indicate the distance between two stripes of the same color. Common stripe pitch distances are about the same as current dot pitch distances, from .24 mm to .32 mm. See *Dot pitch* and *Shadow mask*.

Super I/O controller chip—This chip, which is included in the chipset on some systems, incorporates many of the controller functions previously performed by separate chips. Combining these functions onto a single super chip not only provides an economy of scale for similar activities, it also minimizes the space required on the motherboard.

Superscalar—A processor architecture that supports more than one instruction being executed in a single clock cycle.

Super video graphics array—See *SVGA*.

Surge suppressor—otherwise known as a surge protector, a surge suppressor protects devices plugged into it by absorbing electrical surges, spikes, and other over voltage events. See *Metallic oxide varistor*.

Glossary

SVGA (super video graphics array)—A video graphics standard developed by VESA (Video Electronics Standards Association) that defines the video graphics standards with better resolution or more colors than VGA.

Switch—A networking device used to interconnect network segments to form a single network or a larger network segment.

Switching power supply—A switching power supply uses high frequency switching devices to condition the converted power into a pulsed waveform.

Synchronous burst—The type of memory and cache memory transfers that are tied directly to system clock cycles.

Synchronous communications—The data blocks and the intervals of a synchronous transmission are synchronized to a clock signal that is sent right along with the data. Synchronous transmissions have a fixed interval length between data blocks. The communicating devices also carry on a running dialog that confirms and acknowledges that each data block has been received. If the acknowledgment does not come back in the proper time interval, the sending device automatically sends it again.

Synchronous DRAM (SDRAM)—SDRAM is synchronized to the system clock and reads or writes memory in burst mode. SDRAM is becoming more common for higher bus speeds.

Synchronous graphics RAM (SGRAM)—A single-ported DRAM technology that runs as much as four times faster than conventional DRAM memories.

Symmetric Multiprocessing—See *SMP*.

System board—See *Motherboard*.

System speaker—The system speaker is used by the motherboard, BIOS, chipset, processor, and other system components to signal the user of error conditions. The system speaker is normally mounted inside the case near or on the front panel.

System management mode (SMM)—An energy-saving system built into the Intel Pentium processors. When the system is idle, SMM puts the peripherals or the entire PC into sleep mode, which reduces power consumption by 90 percent. Power continues to be supplied to RAM, where the PC's status is held in a protected area.

Synthesizer—Many of the sounds produced by a sound card are generated by a synthesizer chip on the card. The sound card's synthesizer responds to MIDI messages that tell it what sounds to play, at what frequency, and for what duration. The synthesizer can be controlled by an external MIDI device as well as the PC.

For more information on:	See:
Audio/visual systems	Chapter 19
Chipset	Chapter 3
Connectors and ports	Chapter 12
Hard disk drives	Chapter 8
Memory	Chapter 5
Monitors	Chapter 15
Networks	Chapter 18
Power supply	Chapter 14
Printers	Chapter 16
Processors	Chapter 2
System case	Chapter 13
Video cards	Chapter 11

Tag RAM—The value stored in tag RAM is used to determine whether a cache search will result in a hit or a miss.

Terabyte (TB)—The equivalent of 1,099,511,627,776 bytes or approximately one trillion bytes.

Texture mapping—A graphic image rendering step that applies a 2-dimensional picture over 3-dimensional objects to create levels of detail and texture, or to create a perspective change, such as an object moving closer or farther away.

TF—See *Thin-film heads*.

Thermal grease—A conductive substance used to transfer heat from one device to another. When a heat sink is attached to a processor, thermal grease (also known as dielectric material) is used to fill in the gaps between the two devices and bond them together.

Thermal inkjet—This type of inkjet process involves heating the ink to create a bubble that forces the ink out of the nozzle. Thermal inkjets are the most common type in use, with models manufactured by Hewlett Packard, Lexmark, and Canon.

Thermal printer—A printer that uses a heating element to cause a chemical change on specially treated paper to create printed text and images.

Thick coaxial cable—also known as thicknet, thick wire, and yellow wire, thick coaxial cable is a heavy and stiff cable that is rarely used in LAN situations today.

Thin coaxial cable—also known as thinnet and thin wire. This cable type is similar to that used to connect a television to a cable television system. It is commonly used in many networking environments that require a longer cable run than can be supported by twisted-pair wire.

Glossary

Thin, small outline package (TSOP)—A low-profile memory packaging used on SIMM and DIMM memories.

Thin-film (TF) heads—A type of read/write head manufactured from semiconductor material. It is used in small form factor, high-capacity hard disk drives because thin-film heads are light and much more accurate than ferrite heads and can operate much closer to the disk's surface.

Thin-film media—The media used on virtually all hard disk drives manufactured today. Thin-film media is an extremely thin layer of metals plated on disk platters in the same way used to plate the chrome on your car. Thin film media is harder, thinner, and allows stronger magnetic fields to be stored in smaller areas.

Thyristor—A semiconductor device that can be switched between off and on states. Thyristors are used for power switching applications.

Thin film transistor (TFT) display—See *Active matrix LCD*.

Toggle keys—Keyboard keys, such as the Caps Lock and Insert keys, that are used to switch and lock a key between two values.

Toner—The dry granulated "ink" used in a laser printer.

Toner cartridge—A removable cartridge that supplies a laser printer with toner and several valuable parts of the printing process, including the photosensitive drum, the primary corona wire, and the developing rollers.

Tool-less case—A case design that uses one or two large knobby screws on the back panel to secure the case covers. Removing the case screws does not require the use of a tool other than your hands. The cover pieces are held firm by spring clips that apply pressure to chassis points to hold the cover pieces in place.

Torx—A special screwdriver that has a multipoint star shaped head. Some PC cases use Torx screws in place of the Phillips head screws.

Touch pad—A fixed, small, flat, square or rectangular surface on which the user touches, slides, or taps a finger or stylus to duplicate the actions of a mouse to guide the cursor on the display, select objects, run programs, or create images.

Track—Data disks are organized into tracks on which data is written. A floppy disk has around 80 tracks and a hard disk may have a thousand tracks or more. Hard disk and floppy disk tracks are concentric bands that complete one circumference of the disk. The tracks on a CD-ROM are placed on a spiral that runs the length of the media. The first track on a disk is track 0, which is located on the outside edge of the disk.

Trackball—A device much like an upside-down mouse with its ball on top that has two or more buttons. The ball is manipulated with either a thumb or finger to move the cursor on the screen. Because only the ball moves, a trackball device requires less space on the desktop.

Transactional cache—See *Non-blocking cache.*

Transistor—An electronic circuit that basically stores the electrical voltage representing one bit. A transistor is the primary electronic circuit in a microprocessor.

Transfer corona—The laser printer component that places on the paper the static electric charge that pulls the toner from the drum onto the paper. Not all laser printers use a transfer corona; some use a transfer roller instead.

Twisted copper pair—Twisted-pair cable is made up of one or more pairs of copper wire. The twists in the wire help reduce the impact of EMI and RFI. Twisted-pair wire is available as unshielded twisted-pair (UTP) and shielded twisted-pair (STP).

For more information on:	See:
Audio/visual systems	Chapter 19
Chipset	Chapter 3
Connectors and ports	Chapter 12
Hard disk drives	Chapter 8
Memory	Chapter 5
Monitors	Chapter 15
Networks	Chapter 18
Power supply	Chapter 14
Printers	Chapter 16
Processors	Chapter 2
System case	Chapter 13
Video cards	Chapter 11

UART (universal asynchronous receiver/transmitter)—Used to control all serial ports and most serial device connections, a UART is located on a device adapter card, directly on the motherboard, or integrated onto a serial device's internal controller.

Uninterruptible power supply—See *UPS.*

Universal asynchronous receiver/transmitter—See *UART.*

Universal serial bus—See *USB.*

Upper memory area—also known as expanded memory or reserved memory, this is the upper 384KB of the first megabyte of main memory. The upper memory area is located immediately above conventional memory and is used for system device drivers and special uses such as BIOS ROM shadowing.

Glossary

UPS (Uninterruptible power supply)—A device used to provide backup power and surge suppression to PCs and other devices. A UPS typically has a large battery to provide a PC or server with protection against short-term power outages, surges, spikes, and brownouts. See also *Online UPS* and *Standby UPS*.

USB (Universal Serial Bus)—A hardware interface standard that supports low-speed devices, such as keyboards, mice, and scanners, as well as higher-speed devices, such as digital cameras. USB, which is a serial interface, provides data transfer speeds of up to 12Mbps for faster devices and a 1.5Mbps subchannel speed for lower speed devices. A newer version of the USB standard, USB 2.0, supports up to 480 Mbps for data transfer speeds.

Unshielded twisted pair—A copper wire cable commonly used for local area networks. The cable is called unshielded because no additional shielding is added to the cable to protect it from EMI and RFI. See also *Twisted copper pair*.

For more information on:	See:
Connectors and ports	Chapter 12
Memory	Chapter 5
Power supply	Chapter 14

Vector graphics—also known as object-oriented graphics, vector graphics are based on mathematical vectors that define how they are to be drawn. A line created in vector graphics is defined in terms of its length, width, and the direction it is drawn from a source point. The vector graphic line is straight with smooth edges, as opposed to the jagged edges of a bit-mapped graphic.

Very large scale integration—See *VLSI*.

VESA (Video Electronics Standards Association)—An industry association that creates PC interface standards, including the VL-bus (VESA local bus), EISA (Extended ISA), and others.

VESA local bus (VL-bus)—VL-bus is a 32-bit local bus architecture developed by VESA for use with the 486 processor that supports bus mastering and runs at up to 40MHz.

VGA (video graphics array)—A video graphics standard that supports 256 colors on a resolution of 640×480. The VGA standard remains the default standard for many operating systems, including Windows.

Video graphics array—See *VGA*.

Video memory—Memory placed on the video adapter card to store the incoming graphics instructions from the PC and the instructions going to the monitor to generate the display. See *Video RAM.*

Video RAM (VRAM)—Dual-ported DRAM placed on a video adapter card that needs to be refreshed less often than ordinary DRAM.

Video Electronics Standards Association—See *VESA.*

Virtual memory—Space set aside on a hard disk drive that provides an extension of system RAM that is used by the operating system to expand the effective amount of memory available on a PC.

Virus—Software written purposely to attack a PC with the intent of disrupting its operations, destroying its data, or erasing part or all of its disk drives. A computer virus attaches itself to another file or piece of code on a floppy disk, downloaded file, or email attachment. It can also take the form of an executable file that runs when opened on the target system. A computer virus typically has a built-in propagation scheme that allows it to replicate itself and infect other systems, duplicating itself from one computer to another on a removable media or by email.

VLSI (very large scale integration)—This level of integration means that between 100,000 and one million transistors are included on a processor or integrated circuit (IC).

Voice coil actuator—A servo-based system used to position hard disk read/write heads over a particular location on the disk. A voice coil actuator receives feedback signals from the servo to guide it exactly to the correct location.

Volatile—Memory that must have a constant power source to retain its contents is volatile memory.

Voltage conversion—Also called rectification, this process involves converting 110-volt (V) AC input power into +12V, +5V, or +3.3V DC power used by the internal components of a PC.

For more information on:	See:
Audio/visual systems	Chapter 19
Memory	Chapter 5
Power supply	Chapter 14
Processors	Chapter 2
Video cards	Chapter 11

WAN—See *Wide area network.*

WAV (Windows audio/visual)—The Windows audio standard for recording and playback that is built into the Windows operating system. WAV files can hold either 8-bit or 16-bit audio samples created with sampling rates of 11,025Hz, 22,050Hz, or 44,100Hz. A WAV file recorded at its highest quality, which is 16-bit samples sampled at 44,100Hz, requires 88KB of disk space per second recorded.

Wide area network (WAN)—A network that interconnects two or more LANs over a large geographical area. The Internet is actually a very large WAN. However, a more typical WAN is a network that connects a company's Dallas office LAN to the LAN at its headquarters in Seattle.

Windows audio/visual—See *WAV*.

Windows keyboard—also known as the 104-key enhanced keyboard. This is a keyboard with three keys added to the 101-key enhanced keyboard design. The three additional keys are the Windows and Context Menu keys, located on either side of the Space bar.

Windows RAM (WRAM)—A video memory type that is dual-ported like VRAM, but because its contents can be accessed in blocks, it is faster than VRAM. See *Video RAM*.

Wireless network—A network that does not use a physical cable to interconnect its workstations and nodes to the network. A wireless network uses radio frequency (RF) devices to transmit and receive data. A network with a wireless backbone is called a wireless local area network (WLAN).

Word—A data unit, 16 to 64 bits in length, used to transfer and store numeric values, including addresses in memory and on the secondary storage devices.

Workstation—A workstation can be a very large PC used for a specific purpose, such as an engineering workstation or a graphics workstation, or it can be any PC connected to a network.

WORM (write once/read many)—A CD-R disk to which data or music can be stored, but only once. Data written to a WORM disk is permanently recorded and cannot be erased or modified.

WRAM—See *Windows RAM*.

Write-back cache—This type of caching reduces the number of write cycles to memory, which speeds up the caching process. When data in the cache is updated, it is not written back to memory until it is cleared from the cache.

Write once/read many—See *WORM*.

Write-through cache—Updates to data currently held in cache are written to both cache and main memory at the same time. This caching policy is simpler to implement

Glossary

and ensures that the cache is never out of sync with main memory. However, it does not perform as well as a write-back caching policy.

WTX form factor—This form factor defines a workstation version of the ATX form factor that is intended for high-performance workstations and servers. WTX defines a modular case with a motherboard about twice the size of an ATX motherboard. A WTX case features space for high-capacity, redundant power supplies, removable panels for easy access to components, a large number of hard drive bays, and support for multiple cooling fans.

WYSIWYG—A monitor and software acronym that stands for What You See Is What You Get.

For more information on:	See:
Audio/visual systems	Chapter 19
Cache memory	Chapter 6
CD-ROM and DVD	Chapter 9
Memory	Chapter 5
Monitors	Chapter 15
Networks	Chapter 18
Power supply	Chapter 14
Printers	Chapter 16
Processors	Chapter 2
System case	Chapter 13
Video cards	Chapter 11

Glossary

Xeon—A Pentium CPU chip designed for server and high-end workstation use. Xeon chips mount into a Slot 2 socket. The difference of a Xeon processor and the standard version of the Pentium processor is that the L2 secondary cache runs at processor speeds. A Pentium II Xeon and a Pentium III Xeon are available.

Yellow Book—This CD standard divides the disk into two content sectors and uses two recording modes to record a CD-ROM. Computer data is stored using Mode 1, and compressed audio, video, graphic, or multimedia data is recorded using Mode 2.

Z-buffering—As the pixels of a 3D image are rendered, the graphics adapter does not know which pixel is to be displayed first. Z-buffering encodes each pixel with a Z-value that is used to sequence the pixels.

Zero insertion force—See *ZIF*.

ZIF (zero insertion force)—A type of processor mounting that uses a locking arm to secure a processor in a socket mounting.

ZIP disk and drive—A 3.5-inch removable disk and either internal or external drive manufactured by Iomega. Two models, a 100MB and a 250MB, are available.

For more information on:	See:
Audio/visual systems	Chapter 19
CD-ROM and DVD	Chapter 9
Hard disk and floppy disk drives	Chapter 8
Monitors	Chapter 15
Processors	Chapter 2
Video cards	Chapter 11

Glossary

Index

A

AAC file, 562
Accumulator, 42
Action keys, 486
Active backplane mainboard, 6
Active matrix LCD, 419
Address gateway, 530
AGP, 255–256, 296
AGP Aperture Size, 103
AIFF file, 562
Air filters, 200
Alphabetic keys, 485–486
Alt key, 486
AMI beep codes, 96
Amplifier, 233, 554
Analog inputs, 556
Analog outputs, 556
Analog-to-digital converter, 556
AND operation, 29–30
Antialiasing, 298
Aperture grill, 426–427
Areal density, 210
Arithmetic logic unit (ALU), 42
Arithmetic operators, 489
Aspect ratio, 291
Asynchronous cache, 147
Asynchronous communications, 320–321
Asynchronous SRAM, 155
AT bus, 68
AT commands, 535–536
AT form factor
motherboard, 7–8
system case, 362
ATX form factor
motherboard, 10–12
power supply, 385
system case, 361
AU file, 562

Audio
amplifier, 554
CD-ROMs, 563–564
components of PC sound system, 554–555
described, 554
digital audio extraction (DAE), 561
DVDs, 563–564
playback, audio, 561
software, 555
sound capture, 559–561
sound cards, 554, 556–559
sound files, 561–563
speakers, 555
system resource conflicts, 573
Audio playback controls, 232–233
Audiovisual outputs, 266
Auto Configuration, 102
Auxiliary fans, 364–365
Award beep codes, 96

B

Baby AT form factor
motherboard, 7–8
power supply, 381
system case, 361
Backspace key, 486
Backup media, 583
Backup software, 583–584
Bandwidth, 526
Baseband networks, 530
Basic input/output system, *See* BIOS
Batteries, disposal of, 586
BEDO DRAM, 128
"Beep, boot, bam" problem (motherboard), 21–22
"Beep, no boot" problem (motherboard), 18–21
Beep codes, 95–97
Bilinear filtering, 298

C

R

W

X

Z

What's on the CD-ROM

The *PC Technician Black Book*'s companion CD-ROM contains demonstration and shareware copies of popular personal computer diagnostic and analysis software specifically selected to enhance the usefulness of this book, including:

- *#1-TuffTEST-Lite*—A "Standalone" diagnostic program from #1-PC Diagnostics Company (**www.tufftest.com**) that has its own proprietary self-booting operating system. For more information, visit the Tuff Test Web site.

- *Diskkeeper 6.0*—This is a very fast disk defragmenter program from Executive Software (**www.executive.com**) that can be scheduled in a "Set it and Forget it" manner to have defragmentation run on a PC daily, weekly, or on whatever schedule you desire. For more information, visit the Executive Software Web site.

- *Doc Memory*—This is an excellent memory test, diagnostics, and analysis program from CST, Inc. (**www.simmtester.com**) that creates a boot disk that allows the product to be operating system independent. For more information, visit the **www.simmtester.com** or **www.dimmtester.com** Web sites.

- *ExpertCheck*—ExpertCheck is an easy-to-use computer software package from TriniTech, Inc (**www.pcdiagnostics.net/expertcheck.htm**) that quickly tests and certifies your PC for proper operation. For more information about this and other TriniTech products, visit its Web site.

- *PC-Check*—An excellent general diagnostics program for PC hardware from Eurosoft USA (**www.eurosoft-usa.com**) that creates a bootable disk. For more information on PC-Check and other Eurosoft products, visit its Web site.

System Requirements

To run the trialware, demo, and sample programs included on the CD, you need the following system specifications:

Software:

- **Operating system:** PC systems (non-Macintosh) running Windows 95, Windows 98, or Windows Me. Two of the products (#1-TuffTEST-Lite and PC-Check) create a boot diskette that boots to their own proprietary operating systems. Two versions of Diskkeeper 6.0 have been included: one for Windows 9x and Me versions and another for Windows NT and Windows 2000. Make sure you use the one matching your PC's operating system.

Hardware:

- **Processor:** Pentium processor 75 MHz or higher.
- **RAM:** 32 MB
- **Disk space:** Diskkeeper requires just under 5 MB of disk space. Each of the other programs requires a floppy disk on which the executable software is created.